THE TECH SET

Series Editor
ELLYSSA KROSKI

Wikis for Libraries

LAUREN PRESSLEY

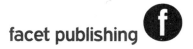

facet publishing **f**

© Neal-Schuman Publishers, Inc. 2010

Published by Facet Publishing,
7 Ridgmount Street, London WC1E 7AE
www.facetpublishing.co.uk

Facet Publishing is wholly owned by CILIP: the Chartered Institute of
Library and Information Professionals.

First published in the USA by Neal-Schuman Publishers, Inc., 2010.
This UK edition 2010.

British Library Cataloguing in Publication Data
A catalogue record for this book is available from the British Library.

ISBN 978-1-85604-725-8

Printed and bound in the United States of America.

To my husband, John Borwick,
who first introduced me to wikis way back in 2002
and has continued making my world
a bigger and more interesting place every day since then.
Thank you for being such an amazingly supportive partner in all things.

CONTENTS

Don't miss this book's companion wiki and podcast!

Turn the page for details.

THE TECH SET is more than the book you're holding!

All 10 titles in THE TECH SET series feature three components:

1. the book you're now holding;
2. companion wikis to provide even more details on the topic and keep our coverage of this topic up-to-date; and
3. author podcasts that will extend your knowledge and let you get to know the author even better.

The companion wikis and podcasts can be found at:

techset.wetpaint.com

At **techset.wetpaint.com** you'll be able to go far beyond the printed pages you're now holding and:

- ▶ access regular updates from each author that are packed with new advice and recommended resources;
- ▶ use the wiki's forum to interact, ask questions, and share advice with the authors and your LIS peers; and
- ▶ hear these gurus' own words when you listen to THE TECH SET podcasts.

To receive regular updates about TECH SET technologies and authors, sign up for THE TECH SET Facebook page (**facebook.com/ nealschumanpub**) and Twitter (**twitter.com/nealschumanpub**).

For more information on THE TECH SET series and the individual titles, visit **www.neal-schuman.com/techset**.

FOREWORD

Welcome to volume 5 of The Tech Set.

Wikis for Libraries is a comprehensive guide to harnessing the power of the wiki as a collaboration tool, content management solution, and reference resource. Readers will learn how to leverage the potential of wikis to create internal knowledge bases and intranets within their organizations, facilitate collaboration among diverse team members, design library instruction tools, support special events, and create valuable online resources. Author Lauren Pressley deftly conveys the process of how to create a wiki and transform it into a "living" resource that will continue to evolve with your organization. Everything from planning and choosing a software product to extending your wiki through widgets can be found in this all-in-one manual.

The idea for The Tech Set book series developed because I perceived a need for a set of practical guidebooks for using today's cutting-edge technologies specifically within libraries. When I give talks and teach courses, what I hear most from librarians who are interested in implementing these new tools in their organizations are questions on how exactly to go about doing it. A lot has been written about the benefits of these new 2.0 social media tools, and at this point librarians are intrigued but they oftentimes don't know where to start.

I envisioned a series of books that would offer accessible, practical information and would encapsulate the spirit of a 23 Things program but go a step further—to teach librarians not only how to use these programs as individual users but also how to plan and implement particular types of library services using them. I thought it was important to discuss the entire life cycle of these initiatives, including everything from what it takes to plan, strategize, and gain buy-in, to how to develop and implement, to how to market and measure the success of these projects. I also wanted them to incorporate a broad range of project ideas and instructions.

Each of the ten books in The Tech Set series was written with this format in mind. Throughout the series, the "Implementation" chapters, chock-full of detailed project instructions, will be of major interest to all readers. These chapters start off with a basic "recipe" for how to effectively use the technology in a library, and then build on that foundation to offer more and more advanced project ideas. I believe that readers of all levels of expertise will find something useful here as the proposed projects and initiatives run the gamut from the basic to the cutting-edge.

There's a reason Lauren Pressley was named a Library Journal Mover and Shaker in 2009—she's a creative innovator who "walks the walk." And her knowledge and experience shine through in *Wikis for Libraries*, which leads readers through the entire process of creating and using one of these social media tools. Library wiki enthusiasts will want to keep this volume at hand for both ideas and techniques.

Ellyssa Kroski
Information Services Technologist
Barnard College Library
www.ellyssakroski.com
http://oedb.org/blogs/ilibrarian
ellyssakroski@yahoo.com

Ellyssa Kroski is an Information Services Technologist at Barnard College as well as a writer, educator, and international conference speaker. She is an adjunct faculty member at Long Island University, Pratt Institute, and San Jose State University where she teaches LIS students about emerging technologies. Her book *Web 2.0 for Librarians and Information Professionals* was published in February 2008, and she is the creator and Series Editor for The Tech Set 10-volume book series. She blogs at iLibrarian and writes a column called "Stacking the Tech" for *Library Journal's* Academic Newswire.

PREFACE

In an age when libraries must provide users with up-to-the-minute information, wikis are a powerful tool for collaboration and communication. If you're stuck wondering "What is a wiki?", then you are already behind in providing the latest in Web 2.0 customer service. Wikis are at the forefront of ways in which libraries are communicating with staff, patrons, and other libraries.

Wikis are nothing more than really easy-to-edit Web sites. In fact, many Web sites run on wiki software, though the average user would not identify them as a wiki because using the software doesn't mean they have to look like Wikipedia. The wiki's strength is that a user can change the content displayed on the page just by clicking an "edit" button on that page. Even those who tend to resist technology can learn to edit a wiki page. This is a radical shift from the early days of the Internet, when only coders and computer experts had the ability to alter content on the Web. Today anyone can do it. Wiki Web sites make use of various levels of access and privacy, allowing one person, a select group of people, or everyone to contribute to or edit an organization's Web site without needing to know HTML or how to FTP to the Web site server. Wikis using a WYSIWYG editor are so easy to use that everyone in your organization can participate, and the simplicity of the technology means staff can use their time for more creative purposes.

Wikis for Libraries walks you through the step-by-step process of implementing library wikis, from the initial stages of planning through to marketing, and then measuring their overall effectiveness. Every library operates under a different set of circumstances with varying financial and technical resources, and this book discusses the various options, from free and simple-to-use solutions to solutions that require extra financial and technical resources, so that all librarians can take advantage of this versatile and valuable tool.

▶ ORGANIZATION AND AUDIENCE

This book can be read from start to finish or used as a reference to quickly find solutions to specific problems, depending on your background and experience with wikis. If you are just getting started, you will probably want to turn to Chapter 1 to get background information about wikis. If you are already using a wiki in your workplace, you may want to turn to the sections on marketing, best practices, and assessment.

Chapter 1 introduces wikis, highlights their benefits for library service, and provides screenshots to demonstrate features all wikis have in common. Chapter 2 explains the different types of wikis that libraries implement, steps for planning a wiki, and types of software needed to run a wiki. Chapter 3 unveils a step-by-step process you can use to quickly launch a basic wiki. It also covers locally hosted versus vendor hosted wikis, as well as internal versus external use of wikis in libraries. Chapter 4 discusses how to market your wiki, from programming to social media. Chapter 5 showcases best library practices, and Chapter 6 details the metrics of how to assess the usefulness of your wiki in meeting your community's information needs.

As you may have deduced by its name, Wikipedia is a wiki. However, Wikipedia is just one example of an active wiki. Because most people will be familiar with Wikipedia, I use this site for illustrative purposes throughout this book. Please realize that other wikis exist, and there is a good chance that you regularly visit wiki-based Web sites without even realizing it.

Wikis for Libraries is designed for all information professionals. Whether you work in an academic library, a school media center, a public library, or a special library, the pages that follow are aimed at you and your services. Library staff in public services and youth services and those in behind-the-scenes technical support roles can all find ways to use wikis for better communication, awareness, and information service.

I hope after reading this book you will use wikis for content management, reference information, and collaboration. With a little creativity, and following the steps in this book, you can establish a wiki that will help you bring your library to the forefront of Web communication.

ACKNOWLEDGMENTS

Part of what makes this field so remarkable is the extended library community of people interested in exploring new Web 2.0 tools and technologies. I am grateful to be part of a community of library bloggers and Twitterers who come together to discuss emerging technology and its potential impact on our field.

Writing this book has been a commitment in both time and energy. In particular I would like to thank John, Mom, Dad, Katherine, and my family for their support along the way.

I would also like to thank my library's visionary dean, Lynn Sutton, who embraced wikis early on, and my innovative supervisors, Susan Smith and Erik Mitchell, who are always willing to give something new a try. Thank you to Kaeley McMahan, Kevin Gilbertson, and Elizabeth Novicki, who are constantly ready for a discussion on the future of the field. I would also like to thank Giz Womack, Roz Tedford, and Tim Mitchell, who are always willing to chat about technology. Thank you to Mary Scanlon, Sarah Jeong, Mary Lib Slate, Ellen Daugman, Bobbie Collins, and my colleagues at the Z. Smith Reynolds Library for their continued support.

I would like to especially thank Ellyssa Kroski for the opportunity to participate in this project and for her insightful comments and conversation along the way.

▶1

INTRODUCTION: WIKI BASICS

- ▶ **Definition and Evolution**
- ▶ **Benefits of Wikis**
- ▶ **Elements of a Wiki**
- ▶ **Wiki Culture**

▶ DEFINITION AND EVOLUTION

Wikis are essentially Web sites that are really easy to manipulate. You have used a wiki if you have visited Wikipedia. There is also a good chance that you have used other wikis and not known it. Many Web sites use a wiki to put Web content online but don't explicitly market their site as a wiki. This is part of what makes wikis a useful tool: they can be used for anything from a site created to publish information for others to a collaborative and interactive Web site designed with user participation in mind.

The word "wiki" comes from the name of the first wiki Web site. It was named the "WikiWikiWeb" after the Hawaiian term "wikiwiki," which means "very quick" (*Oxford English Dictionary,* 2007, http:// dictionary.oed.com). This nomenclature is appropriate because the nature of wikis is not only that they are easy to create, but they are quick to contribute to and edit, as well. In fact, for most wikis editing is as easy as clicking an edit button, modifying the existing information, and clicking "Save."

Today, wikis are used in a number of ways: as stand-alone Web sites, as "live" reference resources, as supplemental information (like for this book), or as community collaboration spaces.

The first Web site to refer to itself as a wiki was the WikiWikiWeb. This site was released in 1995. Soon after this there were other wiki Web sites. These sites were primarily used by programmers but grew in scope and topic. Wikis became known to a larger world of users with the introduction of Wikipedia in 2001. According to Alexa (www.alexa.com/topsites), a Web information company, the interactive encyclopedia's growth has steadily increased. Today, Wikipedia ranks in the top ten most visited Web sites. Wikipedia serves as an excellent example of a wiki. As with any wiki, Wikipedia is a Web site composed of linked pages. Its content is a collaborative effort, which anyone can edit. There is little organization, and most content is found through searching the entire Web site.

Librarians have had a contentious relationship with Wikipedia for some time. The very nature of the site—unclear authority, fluidity in content, no prepublication vetting—means the source lacks key features librarians look for in quality information. However, countless articles have been written about Wikipedia's credibility, and some librarians are beginning to embrace Wikipedia, if not for the content, then for the fact that it provides solid bibliographies on a number of topics and good outlines to help broaden and narrow a topic. The very characteristics that have caused librarians to avoid Wikipedia can be useful when teaching library instruction sessions. Pointing out issues such as lack of authority, official editing processes, and possible biases in Wikipedia can lead to dynamic class discussions about the importance of these characteristics in any resource.

It is possible that library staff might be hesitant to incorporate wikis into their technology toolkit if they have been wary of Wikipedia. If your library staff is predisposed to avoid Wikipedia and make a case against it, it might be necessary to focus on education and thoroughly plan your implementation before discussing the use of a wiki for your community.

Although librarians might not have always liked Wikipedia, some librarians have appreciated a use for wikis from their earliest days. Librarians have used wikis to create handbooks, research guides, training modules, and Web sites. These librarians do not necessarily know computer languages or have time for tedious

Web site editing, but they have made use of the benefits of this type of tool from its earliest days. Sometimes wikis are used for Web sites created for external audiences. Other times, wikis are used to create intranets for internal use only.

As wikis become increasingly part of the mainstream Internet, many librarians are becoming more comfortable with them, Wikipedia included. Although there are no concrete numbers, it is clear that wikis are becoming part of the common toolkit that libraries use to better serve their users. The Library 2.0 movement encouraged this adoption, and certain providers, such as PBworks, have specifically designed their wikis to meet the library demand driven by this trend. The American Library Association offers wikis for committees, divisions, and other ALA groups. A number of individuals and other library groups have created wikis to help library staff share tips and tricks from their organization with the larger library community. Increasingly the question is not if a library uses a wiki, but how it got started using them and what the library uses a wiki to accomplish. This book is designed to help people starting at this point. But first, let us take a look at the elements of a wiki.

▶ BENEFITS OF WIKIS

Wikis have a number of potential benefits, which is why so many libraries and other organizations have adopted them. Here are some of the primary reasons people choose to implement wikis:

- ▶ Ease of Web site creation
- ▶ Ease of adding and editing content on the Web
- ▶ Capability of adding information to the Internet without knowing HTML
- ▶ Ability to see the revisions of a document over time
- ▶ Distinct space for the content as well as a space for discussion about the content
- ▶ Ease of sharing files with a number of people

One question that people frequently face is when to use a wiki versus another type of technology, such as a blog. In order to make a decision, first you need a clear understanding of what your goal is for your project. Once you understand your needs, you'll know what features you need, and once you have this list you will be in a good position to select a tool.

For example, if you want a way to share news and recent events with your community, you might select a blog. If you need a way to make short announcements quickly, you might select a micro-blogging service like Twitter. However, if you're looking for a way to easily make a Web site, and you want the Web site to function as a portal, a reference resource, or a collaborative workspace, a wiki will meet your needs best.

▶ ELEMENTS OF A WIKI

Although wikis vary depending on the software that runs them, there are a number of features that you can expect to find in nearly any wiki-based Web site. Figure 1.1 shows a screenshot of a hand-book created for student assistants at the Z. Smith Reynolds Library of Wake Forest University. The screenshot is of a MediaWiki Web site and contains features specific to wikis running that software platform as an example of the typical layout and navigation of a specific type of wiki. Although not every type of wiki shares the same layout or organization, there are trends among wiki plat-forms. For example, the "Article," "Discussion," "Edit," and "History" tabs you see across the top of the page in this example could be included as a sidebar in another type of wiki. The links in the sidebar of this wiki could be located elsewhere on the page. This Student Assistants wiki migrated across several different wiki Web sites and had a different layout and design on each platform, before finding its permanent home as a MediaWiki Web site stored on a library server. Although the site changed each time it migrated to another platform, some features were present in every version of the wiki: an overall wiki title, editing and other site page tabs, and a sidebar (see Figure 1.1).

▶ Figure 1.1: Structural Elements of a Wiki

Every wiki will have a **title**. This is the name of the wiki site. Although the portion of the wiki shown in Figure 1.1 is about microforms work, the content is part of the broader Student Assistants wiki. The wiki title refers to that broad topic.

As wikis are editable Web sites, most will provide **tabs** or links that will let users edit the wiki and give them a place to discuss the wiki content before editing and to see previous revisions of the wiki content. These features give wikis their core strengths: the ability to edit, negotiate content, and see how the information on the Web site evolves. The History feature also allows editors to revert to a previous version of the wiki if something accidentally happened to the content or if it has been vandalized.

Finally, there are a number of useful links that are located in the **sidebar** of a wiki. Users can search the wiki for specific information, log in to edit the content, and use a variety of wiki tools, depending on the wiki software's options.

In addition to this basic structure of a wiki, a number of other features are also consistently part of specific pages within a wiki. The pages within a wiki contain the content of the wiki. This is where wiki editors add content for others to read or where they go to collaborate on projects. Library employees collaborated on creating the Student Assistants content (see Figure 1.2), and student assistants read the content and use the wiki as a reference source.

Each page within a wiki has its own **page title**. This is different from the wiki title as it describes the specific content on a given page. The majority of the information on a wiki page is the **content**. This is where editors add the information they wish to include in the wiki and is what people visit the wiki to see. Wiki editors may choose to include text, charts, or multimedia on their wiki pages.

Some wikis allow users to upload **images** and **videos** to the wiki, where they can be saved and viewed. Other times, wikis allow users to embed images and videos from other sites, using the "embed" code that can be found on YouTube and Flickr pages. Wikis that allow you to embed images and videos often also allow you to embed other Web site widgets, extending the functionality of your wiki. Other wikis have built-in modules to ease the process of adding other types of content. These modules allow you to click a box to select the pieces of information you would like to include in your wiki.

▶ Figure 1.2: Content Elements of Wiki

Figure 1.3 shows a screenshot from a collaborative wiki created by library workers from a number of organizations. These librarians use their Library Day in the Life wiki to link to blog posts describing the daily work they do. This resource was created to share information with other library staff members as well as potential library workers. The wiki is hosted by PBworks, a Web-based wiki provider. This type of wiki provides a WYSIWYG, or "What You See Is What You Get," editor. This means that as you edit the wiki, the text displays as it will when you publish the page. Instead of learning a special syntax to write for the wiki, you can use the buttons at the top of the page as you might in a word processing program.

The edit **tab** allows you to change the **content** on the page. The editing interface for any wiki page will display the current page content as well as allow editors to make changes and additions to the existing information. The editing side of the wiki parallels the read-only side. The key features that exist in most wiki editing platforms include buttons to **format** and **save** the content and a text box for the wiki content. Editors can save and see previews of the content before publishing. Wikis also provide a way to format text,

▶ Figure 1.3: Editing Wiki Content

either through the use of wiki markup syntax or through a formatting toolbar that is familiar to users who have used word processing programs. Some wikis give editors the ability to provide a summary of their changes for the benefit of other users who may want more information about the changes.

These are the basic features of wikis, their content, and the editing side, no matter if the site is a MediaWiki installation on a local server or if it is a freely hosted PBworks wiki on the Internet. The exact layout and descriptors might be different, but the basic idea remains true across most wikis. You should be able to click an "Edit" link to edit a page, make changes, and save them. In many of these cases you should be able to see the history of the page as well.

▶ WIKI CULTURE

Now that you have a background in the evolution of wiki use and the basic ways that editors can interact with a wiki site, let's take a look at the controversy that has surrounded Wikipedia. As a popular and controversial Web site, Wikipedia provides us with a familiar example of some of the objections people might raise to a wiki-based site. Wikipedia also is an excellent example of how some of the features that could concern some users can also be the strengths that make the Web site a productive and useful one.

One of the key criticisms of Wikipedia is that there is a lack of authority in each article. It is rarely clear exactly who edits what page, and, in most cases, the pages have several authors. This lack of authority increases the difficulty in judging the quality of the content on any given page. In addition, as multiple people edit every page, the pages are fairly fluid. Someone adds content to a page, and a few minutes later someone else could edit his or her additions. Citations typically point to a fixed work so that researchers can follow up on the original research. Wiki pages are never fixed, so the only way to cite a specific work is to include the exact moment in time in which you accessed the page. Finally, there is no governing body checking the accuracy of any of the content in Wikipedia. There are general rules for contribution, but they rely on the volunteer community of editors to enforce it. Occasionally, when there is sufficient controversy, specific pages will be locked down to minimize vandalism. But there is no final editor checking content for accuracy and style.

For obvious reasons you can see why librarians and educators have been hesitant to encourage the use of Wikipedia and why some teachers do not allow students to use it in their homework. However, even with all these flaws, Wikipedia ends up being a fairly reliable resource. In 2005, Giles reported in *Nature* (available at www.nature.com/nature/journal/v438/n7070/full/438900a.html) that Wikipedia was approximately as accurate as *Encyclopedia Britannica.*

Today many Wikipedia articles are very good. In fact, savvy users can identify the editors with a strong reputation to help identify which articles to trust. Users can look for locked articles to see where a controversy might surround a topic. They can check the "Discussion" tab to see what people have argued about in the content of the article and what is generally agreed upon. Regardless of the quality of the article, the references that follow can lead users to more reliable articles elsewhere on the Internet. The table of contents for Wikipedia articles can help students broaden or narrow a research topic. The links within articles can help users find related keywords for library database or catalog searches.

Librarians can help their users by teaching them to acknowledge Wikipedia as a first step in research. Helping students and community members learn that Wikipedia can give them a general understanding of a topic, which will help them as they progress through the research process, is a way of acknowledging that the source is a useful one. It also points out that the library has additional information that will make their research stronger.

In other words, the key is to realize that Wikipedia is a fundamentally different type of reference source. You cannot trust that the content is reliable because of the credibility of the author or publisher or that an editor oversaw the resource. You have to use a few more information literacy skills, new strategies, and a critical eye when deciding if the material is relevant for your work. These approaches are growing in importance with Web 2.0 sources of information and the emergence of online self-publishing, so they are useful skills to develop.

In realizing that wikis are a different type of resource, and being aware of some of the concerns people raise, you have a good perspective from which to think about how you will use a wiki in your own work. If you want your wiki to be authoritative, you might choose to have only a few specific people edit it. For example, if you want your wiki to explain how the library works, you can limit the editors to the library staff only. If you want to make sure that the content is consistent, you can have guidelines for contribution so that the wiki does not change that often or so that when it does you note recent changes or have a "Last Updated" link to let users know what changes have occurred. However, if you want the site to be a collaborative one that is open to everyone, you can plan to put strategies in place first. You can create policies that people must follow to participate in the wiki, you can monitor changes to make sure nothing is vandalized, or you could simply put a disclaimer on the front page letting people know that the site is open and regularly changes. Thinking through the concerns people might have with a wiki site, and how you will respond to them, before you begin will help you avoid controversial issues or problems in your own wiki Web site.

If you are using a wiki as a workspace, or if you are creating a community-created Web site, you might want to start your wiki using more traditional rules and norms, such as open access to content, limited rules about content and editing, and inclusion of community-driven content. Creating strict guidelines for contribution will increase the challenge in encouraging a wide use of the tool. You will need to give up some control if you want the community to contribute and feel ownership.

Wikis, as prime examples of Web 2.0 participatory culture, tend toward more flexible rules for participation. This flexibility is what gives them strength. This is a shift in thinking that has challenged some traditional approaches in the way we work and have inspired countless blog posts, articles, and, recently, several books.

If this topic is interesting to you, please see the Recommended Reading list at the end of this book for more information.

Giving your community an opportunity to contribute offers them more ownership of the organization, promotes an interest in what your organization is doing, and creates an atmosphere in which they are *part* of the library rather than just *users* of the library. To get started, let's take a look at the different types of wikis you will consider when starting a wiki Web site.

►2

PLANNING

- ► **Determine the Purpose of Your Wiki**
- ► **Choose Your Wiki Software**
- ► **Assess Staff and User Skills**
- ► **Get Staff Buy-In**

► DETERMINE THE PURPOSE OF YOUR WIKI

A successful wiki requires a strong plan for implementation. Determining the purpose of your wiki, the strengths and weaknesses of different software options, and the skills and financial situation of your library will help you identify the variables that will affect your decisions about the type of wiki you choose to implement.

Content Management

One of the most basic ways you can choose to make a Web site is by using a wiki. Once you install a wiki and have added the appropriate logos and style to it, you can enable other people within your organization to add content to the pages. The library staff will know the Web site is a wiki, but your users will just see it as a Web site.

Libraries that choose a wiki platform for their Web site do so because it allows multiple content creators to have access to the Web site so that they can add their own information without having to go through a gatekeeper. It is an efficient way for a reference librarian and a children's librarian both to manage their appropriate sections of the library Web site without having to depend on a

Examples of Wiki Use in Libraries

Content Management	University of Minnesota Libraries Staff Wiki	https://wiki.lib.umn.edu
	University of South Carolina Aiken's Gregg Graniteville Library	http://library.usca.edu/
Collaborative Workspace	Durham County Library Strategic Plan	http://dclstrategicplan .pbworks.com
	Library Information and Technology Association's BIGWIG	http://wikis.ala.org/lita/ index.php/BIGWIG
Reference Resource	Albany County Public Library Staff Wiki	http://albystaff.pbworks .com
Training Guide	Z. Smith Reynolds Library	http://wiki.zsr.wfu.edu/ studentassistants/

Webmaster. This gives library staff more authority over their work while freeing up Webmasters to spend their time on other responsibilities.

Collaborative Workspace

Wikis can also provide a collaborative workspace. In this sense the look of the wiki does not really matter, The important aspect is that the wiki is located in a place where everyone can access, contribute, and edit content. These collaborative workspaces can be for a library staff, for an association committee, or for a community of librarians spanning the country. A wiki can be project based, or it can be a community-driven reference resource. A wiki can also provide space for collaboratively writing an article or planning a presentation.

Those who use wikis as collaborative workspaces use the sites as a space for a number of people to add and edit content as well as multimedia. This allows the group to collaborate without sending numerous e-mails back and forth, and it saves the group from having to keep multiple files organized and up-to-date. When thinking about using a wiki as a collaborative workspace, keep in mind that you can easily set privacy and control settings to allow only specified people to see and edit the content.

Reference Resource

Wikis excel as a reference source. Wikipedia is a good example of this. Library wikis can be used in the same way: as a reference source for patrons on local history, detailing library policy, or any other topic that the library staff can authoritatively address. Some use wikis to create research guides on subjects of interest for their community. Wikis can also be created specifically for library staff, students, and volunteers as an internal resource to help them to know what they need to know for their job.

As many people are already used to using Wikipedia as a reference source, it is not a stretch to teach them to use another wiki as another type of reference source. Building on the strength of the software and users' expectations, reference wikis are easy to explain to patrons and easy for them to use.

Training Guide

Along the same lines, wikis can be used to create training guides for staff, students, and adult learners. Using the internally linking pages, a wiki can contain a linear path that users must take to get the information they need in the order in which they need it. The benefit of using a wiki to do this is that it can both be a handbook and a reference source for staff. Within the reference Web site you can add modules for staff and students to work through in order to come away with the required skill set.

▶ CHOOSE YOUR WIKI SOFTWARE

Once you have decided to use a wiki for your library, you will need to decide which wiki software to use. Your decision will be based on all the same factors you considered when you were thinking about using a wiki: the skill set that you or your library staff has, the amount of time you want to invest in setting up the wiki, the amount of customization you want to be able to do, as well as the financial resources you would like to devote to the project. Knowing as much as you can about your library's technical capabilities, financial abilities, workload, and desired wiki features will give you a strong background from which to consider different wiki software packages. Involving your technology staff in this process from the very beginning is a good idea as well. They know the most about your library's technology infrastructure and can help you understand what the options are earlier in the decision-making process. Knowing as much as possible about your own position will situate you to make the best decision for your library.

Locally Hosted vs. Vendor Hosted

The first decision you need to make is if you want someone else to host your wiki for you or if you want to host the wiki yourself. This means that you have to decide if you want to go to a wiki Web site and create your own account and wiki there or if you want to install it on your own server space.

Hosting a wiki on another Web site has some clear benefits. The barrier to entry is lower. You do not have to know the technical side of things—you just need to know how to set up an account and click "Save." Because the process is simple and does not require technical staff, it can be easier and faster to get the wiki started. Most hosting sites will back up your content for you, giving you one less thing to worry about. Many vendor hosted wikis also are set up to be especially easy to use. Editing windows will likely use a WYSIWYG editor, making editing more like contributing to a Word document than something technical. Many make the process of hosting files easy by allowing you to put a document in one place for several people to access. Vendor hosted options can be particularly useful for a proof-of-concept example or a pilot program.

However, there are drawbacks to vendor hosted options. It can be difficult in the future to migrate content between a vendor hosted option and an installed, or locally hosted, option if you do not plan ahead. When you host a wiki yourself, you do have to have a skilled staff and sufficient time, as well as your own server space to host the wiki. If you have all of these and choose to host your own wiki, you will be able to have a much higher level of customiz-

Pros and Cons of Locally vs. Vendor Hosted Wikis

Locally hosted wiki:

PROS

- ▶ Wiki can be customized as much as your technical staff is able
- ▶ Your organization has access to the content and can archive as you wish
- ▶ The ability to host means you have access to any wiki platforms and can make your decision based on your specific needs
- ▶ Access may be limited using more sophisticated tools such as LDAP

CONS

- ▶ Requires more staff time and technical skills
- ▶ Requires server space
- ▶ Must create plans for archiving and backing up content
- ▶ May require more support and training as people learn to edit the wiki

Vendor hosted wiki:

PROS

- ▶ Can create a pilot wiki without requiring support from technical staff
- ▶ Can go live quickly and easily
- ▶ No technical knowledge required
- ▶ Vendor takes care of backing up content
- ▶ Editing interface tends to be fairly simple
- ▶ Training is simple

CONS

- ▶ Fees may be associated with a vendor hosted wiki
- ▶ Advertisements might display on your wiki
- ▶ Aesthetic customization may be limited
- ▶ If the vendor goes out of business, you may find yourself manually converting content for your next wiki platform

ation. You can put the wiki at the URL of your choosing, you can change the look of the wiki as much as you would like, and you can control the data. One library issue of particular relevance today is ownership and preservation of digital content. When you host a wiki yourself, you can back up, preserve, archive, and ensure the content will continue to be available into the future.

Some libraries might not be able to use vendor hosted wikis. Some school libraries have blocks and filters that limit Internet access, and wiki sites sometimes fall into the category of Web sites that are blocked. If this is the case, your only option might be a locally hosted wiki. In this case, you would need to pay careful attention to privacy settings to ensure an environment appropriate to your institution. If you do not have the technical skill or access to servers, you will need to see if someone in IT can install and set up the wiki for you. In some cases, the IT department or school administration might decide that a wiki is not appropriate for the institution. If your library has a filtered Internet connection, it would be wise to talk with the administration to determine if a wiki is worth pursuing before investing time in planning and the creation of content.

Vendor Hosted Solutions

If you are looking for a vendor hosted wiki that is easy to use and is frequently used among libraries, consider PBworks (http:// pbworks.com). PBworks was designed with ease in mind. PBworks sites are quick to set up and easy to work with. One of their target audiences is the education market, and many libraries make use of their product. Figure 2.1 shows the start screen for a new PBworks wiki. Note the clearly marked links in the sidebar for creating new pages, uploading files, sharing specific wiki pages, and organizing the wiki content. PBworks pages also allow for community comments, a feature that is particularly useful if the wiki is designed to be a collaborative and interactive Web site.

Another easy-to-use wiki platform is Wetpaint (www.wetpaint .com). This prevalent wiki service makes it easy to create a Web site for free using a wiki format. Although Wetpaint's emphasis is on creating a Web site, their wikis can still function as a collaborative space for a committee or group to work together. Figure 2.2 shows

▶ Figure 2.1: PBworks Wiki Start Page

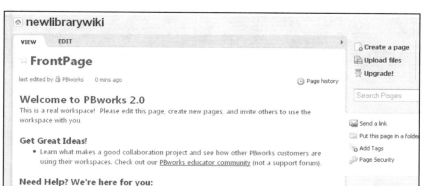

▶ Figure 2.2: Wetpaint Wiki Start Page

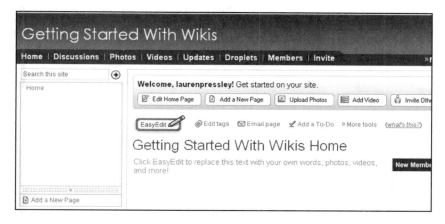

a new Wetpaint wiki start page. The buttons across the top of the wiki page make it quick and easy to add new pages, photos, and videos, which help make these sites dynamic and engaging.

Wikispaces (www.wikispaces.com), like PBworks, targets the education market as one of their core audiences. They emphasize that their editing interface is particularly intuitive. Figure 2.3 shows the first page of a new Wikispaces wiki. You can see that the

▶ Figure 2.3: Wikispaces Start Page

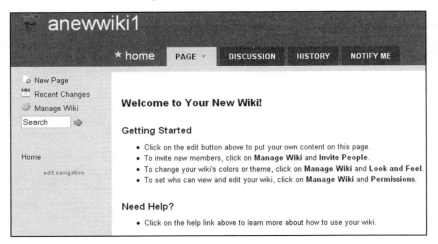

clean design is easy to navigate and that the "Discussion" and "History" tabs are easy to locate. If you are using a wiki for an information literacy class, Wikispaces has the added benefit of emphasizing the process of knowledge creation. The use of the "Discussion" and "History" tabs can be part of the course work and can help students reflect on the process of creating knowledge and publishing.

There are other vendor hosted wikis, for example Wikia (www.wikia.com), from which to choose. With any hosted option, you will have a free (or trial) version that you can use to get started. You can choose to start with the upgrade version if you think the service is worth it or if you need additional space or features. If you are not sure which vendor to commit to in the beginning, you can create accounts with several and use them for personal projects for a while to get a sense of the strengths and weaknesses of each one.

Locally Hosted Solutions

If you choose to host your own wiki, you will have many options available to you. Fortunately, many wiki platforms are open source. Open source programs are written by people with the intention that the programs be available for others to use and modify. You should be able to find a wiki platform that is free and part of the open source community. When choosing, it is wise to base your decision on:

▶ how commonly the software is used,
▶ how active the developer community is, and
▶ the strengths the software offers.

When considering an open source option, make sure you investigate the developer community. An active developer community indicates that the platform will continue to improve and that it is likely that you will be able to get software upgrades as needed. An inactive developer community means that you or your technical staff will probably need to create any new customizations or developments you may want.

Finally, you should note that, although open source software has an appealing price tag, you are not really getting the software for free. While you save money in purchasing costs, you will spend more in staff time on the back end. Once you understand all the benefits and drawbacks of open source software and if you are still considering using one, here are a few of the open source options available to you.

If you are specifically interested in documentation of processes or policies, you might want to consider a wiki designed to do exactly that. DokuWiki (www.dokuwiki.org) is an example of a wiki designed specifically for documentation. Figure 2.4 shows a page on the DokuWiki site. Users can easily see older versions and recent changes from buttons at the top of the page, making the site a particularly useful one if you are using it to keep track of library policy or processes.

MediaWiki (www.mediawiki.org) is the most familiar wiki platform (see Figure 2.5), as MediaWiki is the software that powers Wikipedia. MediaWiki's added benefit is that when users edit MediaWiki, they are also learning how to edit Wikipedia, and vice versa. The size of Wikipedia is evidence that MediaWiki is scalable to a size larger than most libraries would require.

If you are particularly interested in getting started with a basic wiki, adding features as you need them, you might be interested in PmWiki (www.pmwiki.org). This wiki platform was designed to be

▶ Figure 2.4: DokuWiki Web Page

▶ Figure 2.5: MediaWiki Web Page

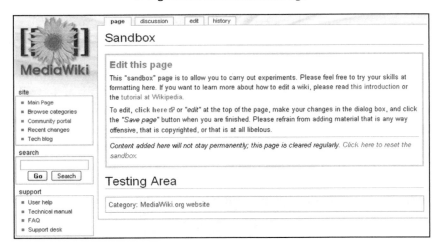

simple to use with minimal features. However, it's also easy to customize and offers a number of add-ons, making it more useful based on what you choose to add. Figure 2.6 shows the clean design of a PmWiki page that still allows for easy access to all the basic wiki features: editing, reading about its history, and attaching files.

TikiWiki (http://info.tikiwiki.org) is a wiki that considers itself more of a content management system. This platform integrates forums, chat rooms, polls, blogs, file and image galleries, a FAQ, and calendaring into the wiki platform. Notice in Figure 2.7 that the homepages of TikiWiki wikis include a Twitter stream and links

The Wiki Sandbox

Most wikis include a "sandbox." This space is designed for users to experiment with editing a wiki. It is a designated space within a wiki that is safe for people to test out the software, allowing users to make changes without worrying about disrupting the wiki or altering important content. The sandbox can be used to experiment with editing pages, formatting text or layout, or incorporating more advanced features such as widgets or extensions.

▶ Figure 2.6: PmWiki Web Page

to recent blog posts. TikiWiki is particularly well suited to be the foundation for collaborative and interactive Web sites.

Choosing any of the locally hosted wikis discussed here requires that someone from your library have the capabilities and permissions to install the wiki on your own server space. If you do not have someone on staff who can do this, you could consider hiring a consultant for the initial setup as well as for follow-up support if your wiki needs upgrading or if your library decides that it needs further customization.

Understanding some of the basic features you can expect in a wiki, vendor or locally hosted, gives you enough background to begin thinking about how a wiki might meet your users' needs. Understanding some of the differences between vendor and locally hosted wikis helps you understand what you might need to ask of your technical staff and what your options might be. You will also

▶ Figure 2.7: TikiWiki Wiki Homepage

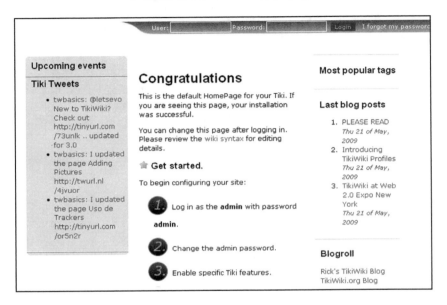

want to think about the skill level of your users, the culture of the community, and how you will get buy-in as you plan your wiki.

▶ ASSESS STAFF AND USER SKILLS

It is now time to consider the human side of wiki implementation. The skills and comfort levels of the staff will have an important impact on their support of and interest in using a wiki. The organizational culture will influence the adoption and use of one. Getting good buy-in from all the staff, whether it was the administration or the front-line workers who initiated the idea, will be important as well. This section will discuss the human side.

Staff Skills

There are a number of skills you will want to consider when thinking about the people who will make the wiki a success. This will help you refine your expectations about the wiki as well as know what it is that you are asking your colleagues to do.

The level of staff skills will impact the costs, in both money and time, associated with creating and maintaining a wiki. If you are planning to host the wiki yourself, and you use an open source option, the expense of the wiki is primarily the cost of the server space and the time the staff spend on creating and maintaining the wiki. Consider both the implementation costs and the recurring maintenance costs of running the wiki. If you do not have a person on staff who knows how to work with open source software, the costs may include consultants to set up the initial site and to do upgrades as they are needed. These costs are minimal if the library already has server space and staff who spend time on projects like this, but it is still worth noting when starting up a project. If you choose, instead, to go with off-site hosting, you might have a solution that is nearly free. Many vendor hosted wikis offer free service in exchange for viewing ads when visiting their site. In addition, wiki setup is often extremely easy, taking no more than 15 minutes. In these cases staff time is negligible, too. Often these free sites have a paid version if you are looking for more space, more features, or fewer advertisements, but this is not often something you need when starting a first wiki.

Another thing to consider is the skill required to create the wiki. As we have discussed, vendor hosted sites do not require specialized skills, but hosting a wiki on your own server does. You will need to either learn these skills yourself or find someone on the staff who has them and is able to help with the project. A larger library, where there is already technical staff, might not have a problem with this. Smaller libraries might be limited in the staff available to help with this type of project and may not even have a position on staff with the skills necessary to create the wiki. In this case, you have to decide if you are able or willing to learn the necessary skills to create the wiki yourself or if you should instead go with a vendor hosted option on the Web.

Once you have created and set up the wiki, time must be available to maintain the wiki. Someone needs to be the primary person responsible for maintaining it. This person does not need to add all the content and read everything everyone writes. He or she should check the wiki for spam and pay attention to the general use of the wiki. If a designated position is accountable for the wiki, the staff member is more likely to feel responsible for the project and will be in a good position to know when the wiki needs more marketing or when users need more training.

If some library staff members are unfamiliar with wikis, but are expected to participate, you will want to conduct training for them. This training should address both the mechanics of how to edit your specific wiki as well as the organization's expectations for content and participation. Finally, if everyone is expected to participate on some level, you will want to think about how this impacts the staff's ability to do their daily work. If wiki participation is mandated and includes documenting work for the sake of documenting it, this participation just adds to the staff's workload. However, if participation is documenting work so others can perform the work or so the department can continue running when a staff member is out sick or on vacation, participation might actually save staff time in the long run.

Finally, you will want to explore the privacy settings available on your wiki and adjust your wiki in light of the library's expectations. When you are training staff you should clearly state what types of information should be behind the password and what types of information can be public. It is useful to have staff discussions about the purpose of the wiki and the audience when talking about privacy settings.

User Skills

Wiki users are both its readers and its editors. The power of a wiki is in blurring this line between readers and editors. For some library wikis, the wiki user is a library patron. For others, the wiki users are library staff or student employees. No matter who your target audience is, you should think about them when making decisions about your wiki.

One of the first things you will want to think about is the level of computer or technology literacy that you believe your users to have. Will they know that the wiki is a wiki, or will they think that it is a regular Web site? This is important if you expect your audience to contribute to the wiki. If you plan to create a wiki for your audience to use as a Web site, it is less important. If you plan on your audience making edits, you might want to think about their wiki experience. If you know that you have an audience composed of many people who have edited Wikipedia, you have a strong argument for using MediaWiki. If you know some of your audience has used PBworks for a class or committee, closely consider PBworks.

You will also want to consider the user interface. If the wiki looks fundamentally different from your library's Web site, will your audience be confused? How do you navigate the wiki? Is it easy to find all the information your audience will need? Perhaps you would want to make a page for people who are just getting started that explains how to use the wiki. For librarians, most of whom expect good metadata and organization of information, the search box might not be a preferable way to navigate the wiki. If your primary audience is other library staff, you would want to create a table of contents for the wiki to provide some hierarchy and a map of the information available. You might also want to explore the use of tags or categories to further organize the wiki's information.

Finally, you will also want to think about how to integrate your wiki with library resources. If the wiki is a reference source for your patrons, you will probably want to include links to books and databases on relevant topics. If the wiki provides detailed information about services, you might want to link to specific pages from the library's Web site.

Fitting into an Organizational Culture

In addition to identifying the technical skills that you will want when implementing a wiki, you should also consider the organizational culture. Some institutions have been playing with Web 2.0 technologies for years, and in these libraries it will most likely be easy to pitch a wiki. These communities already have a background where everyone is familiar with the concept of a wiki. There are other libraries that have never considered implementing Web 2.0 technologies for any part of their services. If you are in a library in this position, you might need to educate the library staff as to what a wiki is before suggesting that they use one.

The first cultural point to consider is the staff's experience with Web 2.0 technologies. A staff member who is familiar with Web 2.0 tools and has had positive experiences will likely understand the point of a wiki and in the appropriate situation will support its use.

However, a staff member who has had less positive experiences with a wiki might resist introducing or even using the tool, even if they are already familiar with it. It will probably take a stronger case and implementation plan to convince a staff member in this position that a wiki might be useful.

If you are planning a wiki to support the work that takes place in the library, either as a tool for letting patrons know or as a channel for staff communication, a wise first step is to examine how information is currently being shared within the organization. Is the library fairly transparent in its decision-making and administrative information? If so, a wiki will not challenge the way the library communicates. However, if many decisions are made behind closed doors, or people prefer to keep information quiet within specific levels of the organization, it could be difficult to convince them to move to an open wiki model.

Larger libraries might have to deal with changing communication patterns within the building. If there are silos within the library, where information is not shared easily between teams or departments, it could be a challenge to get everyone on board to participate in the wiki. However, in these settings, it is important to find ways to share information across silos, so there is value in exploring how to implement a wiki as a tool to encourage this type of communication.

Finally, consider the likelihood that staff will contribute. Even if everyone agrees the wiki is a good idea, and fellow staff members are supportive of the wiki's creation, it will not be successful unless you can get a pool of people to contribute. As with any new project, it might be a challenge for your colleagues to find time to contribute. You have to make sure that people feel that contributing to the wiki is valuable if you want them to be successful.

▶ GET STAFF BUY-IN

Luckily, there are many methods you can use to get staff buy-in for a wiki project. If people are behind the project, they will be more likely to contribute, and you will be more likely to have a successful wiki.

The best way to get people on board is to demonstrate a need. You can do this in a number of ways. If patrons are looking for specific information and they are unable to find it, the patrons' needs establish that there is a clear need for a new resource. If the library Webmaster is having difficulty finding enough time to update all the library content in addition to his or her other duties, a wiki will provide a way for staff members to take care of the content while the Webmaster takes care of coding issues. If reference staff find themselves answering the same questions over and over, a wiki site will allow them to create their own information bank where they can collaboratively contribute to answering reference questions. Find a need and show how the wiki will solve it.

Another way of getting people interested in using wikis is to create a pilot project. Using a vendor hosted wiki, you can create a prototype to demonstrate how a wiki would be useful for a specific service or type of information. Once you have worked on the pilot, you will have an idea of the strengths and drawbacks of your approach and can make a good case, supported by evidence, for the use of wikis in a given situation.

Once you know that you will be creating a wiki, you will want to seed the wiki with useful information. People visit wikis only when there is useful information contained in them. To get people interested in and visiting the wiki—even staff for internal wikis—some useful information needs to be there. If you have enough information to get an audience coming, then you have a pool of people who are familiar with the wiki and who can contribute to it. A good source of seeding information is existing documentation. Internal wikis can start with information from staff handouts, meeting minutes, and handbooks. These documents contain information that is relevant to your workplace and have increased value when contained within one searchable Web site.

When starting your wiki, you will want to create training opportunities for the people who you think will want to edit it. These training sessions can address both technical and cultural issues and provide as much support as your users need. In some cases you might want to consider one-on-one training for those who are most unsure about getting started with the wiki.

Finally, a good way of getting people involved with wiki editing is to create a fun wiki for people to practice on. Some groups create "sandbox" wikis, wikis where anything goes. This is a good way for people to feel safe experimenting with all aspects of wiki editing. Because sandbox users know no one will use the sandbox wiki's content in any way, their edits won't misinform anyone. Another technique is to create a non-work-related wiki. This takes some of the pressure off potential users, as those editing the wiki will not hurt anything work related but will still have the opportunity to edit in a real-world setting. If you are interested in this style of a wiki, you could consider creating a staff cookbook, a guide to restaurants in town, or a directory that can include photos, personal statements, and other personal features.

►3

IMPLEMENTATION

- ► **Discover Your Wiki Options**
- ► **Start Your Wiki**
- ► **Develop Internal Wikis**
- ► **Develop External Wikis**
- ► **Explore Other Wiki Uses**

Once you have decided to use a wiki, the next step is to think about which type of wiki you would like and how you plan to host it. Think about who will be using the wiki you create and who will set it up. This section of the book includes very basic explanations of how to set up two types of wikis: one that is hosted on a local server and one hosted by a third-party vendor. This background should be enough of a foundation so that you understand the general process of setting up a wiki. Of course, every wiki is slightly different, so if you select a wiki other than one of the two listed here, your process will be slightly different. After explaining how to set up a local or a vendor hosted wiki, the rest of this chapter focuses on different types of implementation you might find useful for your institution.

► DISCOVER YOUR WIKI OPTIONS

MediaWiki: A Locally Hosted Option

Many libraries choose to have local installations of a wiki. There are many options for locally hosted wikis. WikiMatrix (www

.wikimatrix.org) may prove most useful to you. The site includes a feature that allows you to specify the requirements you have for your wiki and will respond with a list of wikis that meet those requirements.

For the purposes of an overview, we will discuss MediaWiki. This is the software that runs Wikipedia, which is evidence of its stability, scalability, and community of support. Because this is the software that runs Wikipedia, you might find that a number of your potential wiki editors are already familiar with how to edit your wiki.

Manual Installation

The first decision you will make when installing a wiki is where you will install it. If you have a person on your staff in charge of the Web site, this might be a good person to approach. If you will be tackling the project, you will want to look at the software's Web site and see if there is a page for system administrators or installation. For example, when using MediaWiki, you will begin with the page shown in Figure 3.1.

▶ Figure 3.1: MediaWiki's Download Page

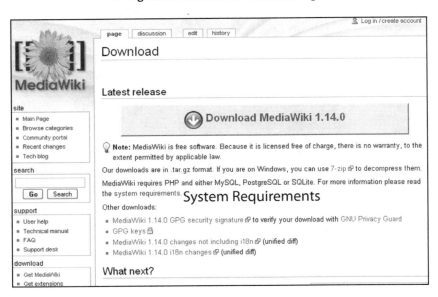

The page in Figure 3.1 shows both the link to download the MediaWiki software and a link to MediaWiki's specific system requirements. MediaWiki requires access to a specific type of Web server that would allow you to install the software. The page explains that the Web server needs to support the use of PHP, a programming language primarily for the Web that MediaWiki uses. This Web server will also need to be able to communicate with a MySQL database, which is where the wiki content will be stored. Your technology staff will know if you have these capabilities. Discuss the list of system requirements with your technology staff or service provider to get an accurate understanding of whether you have the system to support the wiki.

Once you know where you will put the wiki, the next step in creating a MediaWiki site is to create a database. In the case of MediaWiki, you would need to create a MySQL database and a user. Once you have set up this foundation, you can download the software you plan to use and upload it to your account using FTP. You create a folder to extract these files to, and, once extracted, this will be the wiki location. MediaWiki will then prompt you to set up your wiki. To do so, you will follow a link to the installation page, and configure your wiki, including the name for your site, contact e-mail, language, and license. You will be asked to configure your database as well. Once you have been through all of the steps, you will be presented with an "Install" link, and clicking that link will complete the process.

Automated Installation

Depending on your system, you might have the option for a simpler installation of your wiki. Some Web hosting services, such as DreamHost (www.dreamhost.com), offer a "one click install" that allows users to click a button to automatically install MediaWiki, as well as other Web applications. This method is nearly as simple as it sounds. You click an install button, and the software walks you through the installation process. You will need to answer a few questions as you go through the process regarding specific wiki settings.

Configuration

Once you have MediaWiki on your server, you can configure it to fit your needs. Following the directions on the Web site, you point your browser to a specific URL, and then you are given a list of configuration options. This is the point where you choose privacy options, the wiki styles, and other basic setup details. On one hand, it is useful that MediaWiki guides you through the process, but it is also worth noting that, if you run into trouble, there is much more information on the MediaWiki Web site (see Figure 3.2). Again, if you choose a wiki with an active developer community, you will likely find a similar resource for any installed options.

If you selected a locally hosted wiki so that you could have more control over its aesthetic design or privacy settings, this is when you would begin work in those areas. If you are technically inclined and comfortable experimenting with the site, this may be a simple process. If you are less technically inclined, you may want to contact your technical staff to see if this is something they can do for you. You might also want to consider a vendor hosted option to avoid these steps altogether.

▶ Figure 3.2: MediaWiki Help Page

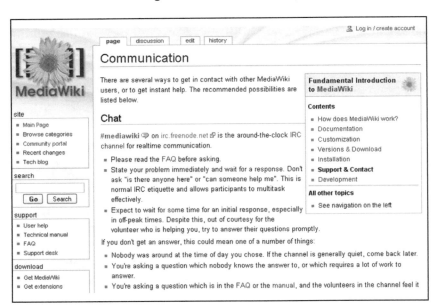

Customization

You can customize a number of things within your wiki. You might want to change the look of the wiki or some part of the layout. You can do some basic customization within the wiki, and you can make other changes by modifying the wiki's theme or style sheet. The style sheet allows the Webmaster to make changes to one file that impact the look of every page on the wiki.

You can also make personal customizations. This is where you modify the look of the wiki that you see when you log in to the wiki. If you just want to make a basic change, you can click on "My Preferences" once you have installed and logged into the wiki. From there you can change the theme settings.

Preparing to Go Live

Before releasing your wiki to the staff or to the public, you will want to do some work behind the scenes. The rest of this chapter will address specifics for setting up different versions of a wiki for your library. But regardless, you will want to set up the basic framework and seed the wiki with some basic information to get people started. You will want to set up privacy and permissions appropriate to the use of the wiki. For example, perhaps you want everyone in the world to be able to see a page for the community book club. You might want everyone to see the library mission page but only the director to edit it. You might want the library staff meeting minutes to be available only to staff. You can set up these permissions in most wikis as you create the site.

PBworks: A Vendor Hosted Option

If you need a wiki quickly, are planning to use it for a small project, and you are not planning on putting any sensitive data on it, you have some good reasons to select a vendor hosted option. These hosted options can help people become familiar with wikis without too much technical overhead. Many people who start with a vendor hosted wiki end up hosting their own later on. If you suspect this might be the case for you, consider how you will move the data from the vendor hosted wiki to the local one if that time comes. There are many options for vendor hosted wikis just as there are for locally hosted ones. Again, you can find a list of wikis with a simple Google search, or use a site like WikiMatrix to find one that meets your requirements.

For the purposes of this overview, we will discuss PBworks. This provider has become very popular with libraries and has an emphasis on supporting educational uses. PBworks has recently redefined itself to focus on easy collaboration, so you might find it more functional than some of the other providers available on the Web.

PBworks, as with many vendor hosted options, has several account levels. There is a basic free account, but there are also paid accounts with more features and options. It is always a good idea to pilot a free account to make sure the wiki meets your needs before committing to a larger, more costly account. You will often get better customer support and more customizations with paid accounts.

Creating an Account

When starting your PBworks wiki, you will need to create an account with some basic information. Once you have submitted this, you will be able to create your wiki. PBworks prides itself on the ease of setting up its wikis, and it should be a fairly quick and familiar process for anyone who has registered with a social Web site in the past. Notice in Figure 3.3 that PBworks simply asks for the URL, why you are using it, and what type of organization and workplace purpose you have for creating the site.

Editing a Vendor Hosted Wiki

When you log into PBworks for the first time, you will see a page with basic information about your wiki. When you click on the "Edit" tab you will see the screen shown in Figure 3.4. This page displays the content as well as a bar of buttons similar to what you would see in Word or Google Docs.

PBworks uses a "What You See Is What You Get" (WYSIWYG) editor. This means that you do not have to know any code to format the text the way you want it to look. Just click on the buttons to make bold text, links, or bulleted lists. Once you have made the changes you want to keep, click "Save," and the page is created, just like that.

▶ Figure 3.3: PBworks Sign-Up Page

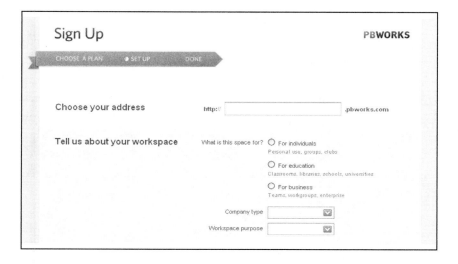

▶ Figure 3.4: PBworks Editing Page

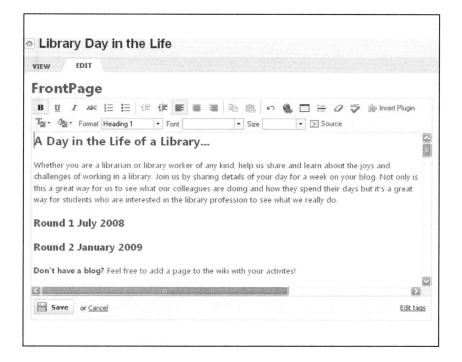

Personalizing a Vendor Hosted Wiki

There are a number of things that you can customize within your hosted wiki. You might want to change the colors of the wiki or some of the privacy settings. How much customization, and how to make these changes, varies from wiki to wiki. In PBworks, you will want to explore the "Settings" tab. This tab has options for changing the colors, logos, user access, and more advanced alterations. Figure 3.5 shows PBworks' "Settings" tab. On the settings page you can adjust the colors of your site and add your organization's logo to the wiki. You can also use Access Controls to add specific users to the wiki, adjust security, and set up notifications for when the wiki is modified.

► START YOUR WIKI

Just as in the MediaWiki example, before releasing your wiki to the staff or the public you will want to do some work behind the scenes. Providing a basic framework and basic information and set-

► Figure 3.5: PBworks Settings Page

ting appropriate privacy controls and permissions will help your audience understand the way to use the wiki for your project and how they can participate.

Extending Your Wiki

In the past several years, there has been a large growth in a type of Internet tool referred to as a "widget." Widgets are small parts of Web sites that you can include on other Web sites with minimal technology skills. For example, if you keep a Google Calendar, you can use a Google Calendar widget to pull a small version of the calendar into your wiki. If you use chat reference, there are widgets to embed a chat box on another Web page. If you use Twitter, you can pull that over, too. Widgets are a way to give your wiki additional functionality while also making the site more engaging for the user. An added benefit is that anytime you update information on these other sites, the information is automatically updated in your wiki. You do not have to remember to update things in more than one place.

If you are hosting your own wiki, you will want to consider extensions, features beyond the ones that come with the basic wiki software, that you can add to your wiki. Look for extensions, add-ons, or plug-ins that allow your wiki to do more, such as change the way the text displays on a page, the way you can edit content, the type of media that you can include, or statistics you are able to keep. This work would likely be done by the person who was involved with the technical side of installing the wiki. So, if you are hiring a consultant to install your wiki, you will want to think about extensions while the consultant is working on your project.

PBworks and other vendor hosted wikis often integrate widgets into their wikis. Look for links to "Insert Plug-In" or "Add Multimedia" to add this type of functionality to your vendor hosted wiki. It is worth noting that not all wikis will offer all the same plug-ins, so if you are thinking about this and have decided that you know of something that you will need to add, this might be a factor to use in selecting your wiki provider.

Wiki Extensions

The available options for extending your wiki will vary depending on the software that runs the site. If you are using MediaWiki, you will have a number of options:

▶ **GISWiki kwBreadCrumbs**: This "bread crumbs" extension (www.mediawiki.org/wiki/Extension:GISWiki_kwBread Crumbs) enables links to appear at the top of the wiki page, showing users their path to their present location within the wiki, and allowing them to click back to the page they are most interested in.

▶ **Bibwiki**: This useful extension (www.mediawiki.org/wiki/Extension:Bibwiki) was written to make it easier to create and manage scientific bibliographies and is especially helpful in libraries.

▶ **YouTube Tag**: You might be interested in incorporating multimedia into your wiki. This extension (www.mediawiki.org/wiki/Extension:YouTubeTag) allows you to pull in a video from YouTube.

▶ **FireStats**: If you are interested in collecting statistics for the use of your wiki, you might want to consider this extension (www.mediawiki.org/wiki/Extension:FireStats) to help collect that data.

Once you are comfortable with MediaWiki, and have an idea of something you would like to be able to do within your site, you should search the Internet to see if someone has created the extension that will meet your needs. MediaWiki has a large and active developer community, and due to this you can find many interesting extensions. You can find more information about MediaWiki extensions at www.mediawiki.org/wiki/Category:Extensions.

PBworks also offers this type of increased functionality; however, the PBworks community refers to them as plug-ins. These plug-ins are built into every PBworks wiki. PBworks organizes their plug-ins by categories, such as office applications, HTML, gadgets, page information, video, photos, and interactive media. Some of these plug-ins pull in content from other sites, such as Google or YouTube. Others make use of services like Skype. Yet, you still have tremendous flexibility with the HTML plug-in option, as long as you are comfortable with HTML.

Early Wiki Questions

While you are early in the process of creating your wiki, you will need to consider several issues. Thinking about these topics early in your implementation will guide you through the process and help you have a more successful wiki.

1. What is the mission statement of your wiki? How does it relate to the mission of your library?
2. Who should be able to read the wiki content?
3. Who should have the ability to edit the wiki content?
4. Where will you host the wiki?
5. Who will add seed content? Where will they get this content?
6. How will you market your wiki?

▶ DEVELOP INTERNAL WIKIS

How to Create a Wiki Intranet

A wiki can be useful as an intranet for your library. It is easy to set up, and all that the library employees need to know is the URL to access it. Employees can get to the information online from the library, away at conferences, and at home. Figure 3.6 shows an ex-

▶ Figure 3.6: Wiki as an Intranet

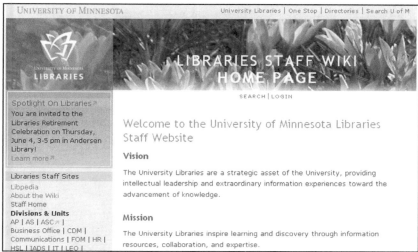

ample of the University of Minnesota Libraries' wiki intranet. As you can see, the wiki contains vision and mission statements as well as announcements and links to library staff sites. The site also contains other relevant information, including the library organizational chart and information on budgets and planning.

An intranet is a portal for internal use by an organization. This portal can contain reference information about the business, files such as images or documents that employees might need to use on a regular basis, and information about upcoming events and scheduling, as the University of Minnesota wiki does. For example, you might find the following in an intranet site:

- ▶ Announcements
- ▶ The library's schedule of events
- ▶ Reminders about upcoming deadlines
- ▶ Current room availability
- ▶ Meeting minutes
- ▶ Forms such as timesheets and vacation requests

Intranets are often protected with passwords so that information can be included that would typically go in a handbook behind a desk.

Knowing that you can embed other content and use widgets to extend your wiki, you may choose a wiki designed to simplify the process of adding calendar entries, embedding useful widgets, or adding other multimedia content. Think about the gadgets that will make the wiki more valuable and engaging and where you will put them in the wiki. When thinking about widgets, it is worth considering which ones will streamline your input process rather than duplicate it. If you are already updating a 30 box calendar, look for a widget to import that content into the wiki automatically rather than creating a second calendar within the wiki.

When starting an intranet, you will want to think about how to set it up before you start putting work into adding content. What information will people expect to find? What information is important enough to include on the front page? Should you use a hierarchical organization or something more flexible such as tagging or search? It is worth talking to other staff members about their expectations and interests so that you can best design the intranet to fit their needs. You will also want to talk to colleagues to get a broad sense of the overall information issues of the organization. Once you have some basic ideas, it would be a good idea to begin developing a FAQ page to let people know what to contribute and how. Taking a little time to do this in the beginning will save you a lot of time in answering e-mails and fielding questions in the long run.

Once you have figured out the basic information that people will be interested in knowing, you will need to get the content. In some cases, you will be able to start up sections by yourself. Other topics will require content from others who have subject expertise. For example, if you work in archives, you might want to talk with someone from reference to see if he or she can write up some information to start off the reference section of the wiki. If you want to make it really easy to contribute, you could just ask for the content in Word format and enter it into the wiki yourself. Incorporating this basic information at an early stage ensures that the other library staff members will find the wiki useful enough to return and hopefully to contribute themselves.

Once you have set up the basic wiki outline, you will want to make sure that someone from each department will keep an eye on the wiki for content related to their department. To make the wiki a valuable intranet, information will need to be current and accurate. Designating a person from each unit means that someone is responsible and will be more likely to check in every once in a while. This could be a permanent function for some positions, or it could be a committee with rotating membership.

Once you have a wiki, a basic outline, seeded content, and designated wiki editors, all that is left to do is to roll the wiki out to the rest of the staff. This approach will vary depending on the culture of your library. If people are fairly comfortable with new technologies, you may choose to mention the wiki in a staff meeting, send the link out, and offer to be available if there are questions. If people are very hesitant about new tools, you might need to offer a series of staff development sessions, teaching people about how wikis work, how to edit them, and how to use your wiki to find and share information. In any case, your coworkers will appreciate having someone they can call if they have a question. You might be the point person, but the designated editors in each department will also be good resources for the rest of the staff. It is best if you can get a broad group to participate in this work so that people do not think of it as your wiki. You really do want the wiki to be a community project!

Incorporating the wiki into the workflow of your place of employment will largely depend on the vision of your library administration. If they see the wiki as a supplemental tool, you might continue using traditional patterns of communication within the library but also include links to the pages in the wiki that have the same content. If they see the wiki as a way to decrease e-mail, meeting time, and communication gaps, they might have a stronger investment in supporting the use of a wiki. If the administration is solidly behind the wiki, you will need to help people remember to use the wiki and where to look for information.

How to Create a Wiki Knowledge Base

Wikis also make strong knowledge bases. Knowledge bases are resources that provide access to information. They commonly exist at help desks or to share information about the different work within the organization. A knowledge base could be helpful at the reference desk for questions that are very specific but common enough to be predictable, at the circulation desk to keep staff abreast of the most recent policies, or even for student workers, a group with a very high turnover yet who still need a lot of needed knowledge for their work.

Knowledge bases often make great first wikis for an organization. You can pick a specific department and create a small wiki for its use. As it becomes more successful, and people get used to it, the idea will spread throughout the organization. You can get a sense of what works for your organization and how people use it, which, in turn, can inform your future wiki work.

When setting up a knowledge base, you will need to decide if it will be a searchable FAQ or if you are going to have a hierarchical reference source. This, of course, depends on the context your wiki will be used in. If you are creating a resource for student employees, you might design the wiki content to read like a handbook so that they can read it in their first week on the job. The wiki will still need to function as a knowledge base, though, so students will need to be able to search the wiki as well in order to get to information at the point in time when they need it. This is a great system because so many students work when full-time staff members are not in the building. This is a resource they can consult in the early hours of the morning—getting the information a patron needs at that moment—instead of leaving a note for a staff member to deal with first thing in the morning. If, instead, the wiki will be primarily for full-time staff who are already acclimated to the environment, you might not need as much narrative structure. A simple list of questions could suffice.

To start a knowledge base wiki, you can include a list of common departmental questions. Then, you can brainstorm additional questions with your department. Besides generating more questions, brainstorming will help participants buy into the project as they are being included in the creation of the resource.

Whereas with the intranet you would want to seed the wiki with enough information to be useful enough to draw staff members in, this might not be necessary for a knowledge base wiki. If staff have really bought into the concept of a knowledge base and can see how it could save them time or help patrons get better service even when the staff are not around, you may be able to start with just a list of questions. Or, you might even be able to start with a few open-ended questions about whether people can figure out how to fit the new knowledge base into their workflow.

If the knowledge base wiki is not accepted by its audience, you can begin targeting a smaller audience focusing on those who would benefit the most from it. For example, a busy reference desk with a lot of complex business questions could benefit from having the answers to complex business questions and steps for finding the relevant information. This will help everyone at the desk find the answers quickly and will help the business librarian regain some uninterrupted time in the office.

When deciding how to set up the wiki, you will also need to consider how to convey the information most effectively. For example, if the questions are about a physical task—labeling books, loading microfilm, or fixing paper jams—you may consider including embedded videos demonstrating how to accomplish these tasks. However, if these videos are likely to be watched at a public desk, you would want to make silent videos, with text overlaid on the images, so as not to disturb patrons.

Again, you will want to think about colleagues who could support the wiki as well. Getting a few people on board will make the whole process easier and will mean that you are not doing all of the work yourself. It also will make the project be more of a grassroots effort and more likely to spread through the entire staff.

Once you have some content in your knowledge base and you have trained people to use the site or offered to help, you are ready to put the wiki in production. Posting the link near departmental computers, making the wiki the homepage for the browser, or stopping by people's offices to show them the wiki and walk them through using it are all methods of helping colleagues get on board with the new wiki.

If the wiki acts as a handbook, you can ask the people who have read the content what is still unclear and incorporate that content into the wiki for the next user. The whole point of using the wiki is that it is easy to update content in this way. If the site is a FAQ wiki, you can point out to desk workers that they can check it as they get questions. If the answer is there, the wiki will be helpful; if the answer is not, they can contribute it.

Figure 3.7 shows the Wake Forest (NC) University Z. Smith Reynolds Library knowledge base wiki. This wiki is organized by department and includes a few library-wide project categories as well. Each department page contains links to other pages within the wiki that explain processes or make meeting minutes available.

How to Use Wikis for Facilitated Collaboration within a Library

Wikis also help facilitate collaboration within a library. Small committees, task forces, and groups working on a common project can use a wiki to facilitate this work. The wiki can be a home base for the work of the group. It can include the objectives and specifications of the project, meeting minutes, discussions about the group's tasks, and even allow space for drafting out written work.

▶ Figure 3.7: Wiki as a Knowledge Base

Sometimes you can look for things that are fun to communicate about to get people interested in using a wiki. My library, for example, shares recipes after potluck lunches or other special occasions. These recipes were listed in a "cookbook" on the library's Web site. But to get the recipe listed, an individual had to rely on the Webmaster to add the content to the site. One of the first sections of the library wiki was our cookbook. The idea was to take something we already enjoyed doing and use the wiki to facilitate that behavior.

Once people are comfortable with using a wiki collaboratively, you can use the wiki to facilitate work within the library. Durham County (NC) Library used a wiki for their strategic planning process, as shown in Figure 3.8. This wiki includes goals, documents

▶ Figure 3.8: Wiki for Internal Collaboration

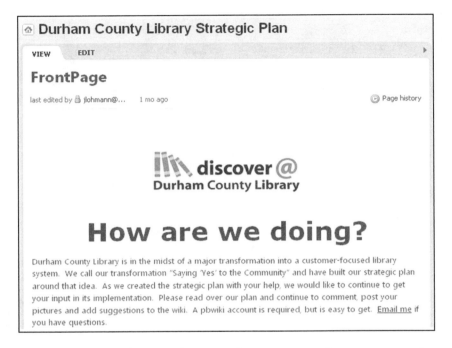

from brainstorming sessions, and comments from community members on the future of the library.

When working with a small group to set up a wiki to facilitate collaboration, you have the luxury of coming to consensus. You will want to discuss what channels you will be using and how much information goes on the wiki. Will you avoid e-mail altogether and rely on everyone to check into the wiki once a day? Maybe you will put all the information in the wiki and send a message to the group reminding them to check in when you update it? Or, maybe you will e-mail and meet as always but add the information to the wiki, too, so it is all in one place.

Once everyone is in agreement, you should be able to create a framework that fits with the expectations of the group members. With a small group, you can rely on the different members to contribute as is relevant to their position within the group. You might want to designate a note-taker to ensure meeting minutes are all in one place. Perhaps committee homework assignments include updating different sections with content.

You might want to think about vendor and locally hosted options specifically designed for internal work. If any information is sensitive, you will probably prefer to investigate local options. If information is not sensitive, and you want to trade files, you might choose to go with a third-party vendor that makes it easy to share files through the wiki.

How to Use Wikis for Facilitated Collaboration with People at Other Locations

Wikis can facilitate collaboration whether participants are geographically nearby or across the country. Many professional committees use wikis to collaborate across long distances. Particularly if a committee is national in scope, and members see each other only twice a year, it is helpful to have a virtual workspace in the interim. A wiki can be an ideal solution in a situation like this.

When setting up a wiki for this type of work, you will want to identify the types of wikis that everyone is comfortable using. If people already edit Wikipedia, for example, it is worth asking if any of the committee members can host a MediaWiki option on their server. Or, if everyone already has a PBworks log in, the group might choose to host their wiki there to streamline their wiki work. It is likely that everyone will have a different background; in this case the group might need to discuss what options everyone is comfortable with using.

In the course of that discussion, you will also want to address how you will be using the wiki. Is it mostly for conversation? Brainstorming? Holding final drafts of committee work for review? These decisions will likely influence what wiki you choose and how you set it up. BIGWIG, an interest group of the Library Information Technology Association (LITA), uses wiki space within the larger LITA wiki, as shown in Figure 3.9. In this case, you can see that the wiki contains meeting minutes, information about three upcoming projects, and a link to information for their conference. Each project includes some basic background, a space for people to sign up to volunteer, as well as next steps for the group to accomplish. This is a collaborative space that also produces final products for others to view. These documents are sometimes hosted on

▶ Figure 3.9: Wiki for Collaboration with Other Libraries

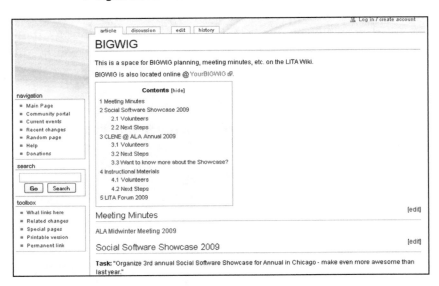

the wiki for others to see and other times are migrated to other publication platforms.

If you set up a wiki to use with people in other locations, you will want to think about the site's organization and discuss your plans with the other committee members. You might choose to designate one area for notes, one for discussion, one for brainstorming and preliminary work, and one for work that is approaching the final version of the committee's product. If the committee belongs to a larger organization, you might also want to include some information for visitors who are not part of your wiki. Again, a relevant wiki takes some planning and scaffolding. You will want to include some places where people can add content as it comes up, and you will want to work with others to make sure they feel comfortable contributing.

How to Use Wikis for Project Management

Wikis can also be useful tools for project management. When working on a project, you will need to record many pieces of information: the desired outcomes, requirements to meet the goals, deadlines, meeting minutes, tasks to be done, and responsible individuals. Keeping all of this information in one central place allows project team members to know where to find authoritative information and how to record the work that they have done. This has the added benefit of making it easy to share progress with supervisors and other stakeholders so that everyone is clear on what the project's aims are and if the project is meeting its timeline.

Figure 3.10 shows the Lupton Library's Building Project from the University of Tennessee–Chattanooga. This wiki contains the official announcement, the program statement, and suggested visit information for those involved. The wiki brings transparency to the Library Building Project and allows interested people to follow along with the progress of the group.

One way to help a new project succeed is to build in early wins. You can do this when you are planning how you will use the wiki as a project management tool. In the very first meeting, for example, you can have the wiki open and projecting on a screen. You can take minutes directly in the wiki, add dates and deadlines, and then e-mail links out to committee members while they are all present. Everyone will see that the wiki saves time because you won't need to go back to your desk to type up formal notes, send e-mails back and forth, and negotiate out information through other channels. Members will also see the information going into

▶ Figure 3.10: Wiki for Project Management

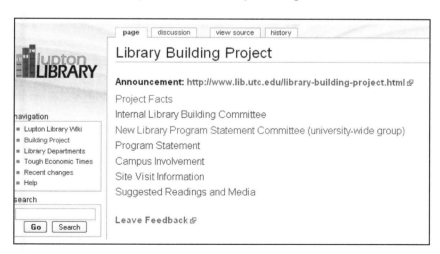

the wiki and know that they can turn to it for answers to those questions. Hopefully, in seeing how easy it is to edit, they will also know that they can go in and make updates as they accomplish tasks. In this case there would be two wins: demonstrating an immediate and obvious connection between saving time and using the wiki and providing an informal example of how easy it is to edit a wiki.

When in that first meeting, you will want to discuss the types of information you would like to include and how authoritative the resource will need to be. You will want to organize the information in a way that will be easy for participating committee members to understand, but if you are planning to share the content with other stakeholders, you will want to organize the wiki so that it will be intuitive to navigate for their purposes as well. You might include a link on the front page for committee members and a link for stakeholders. Then, you can have an index designed for each group individually. For example, you would probably choose to include a link in both indexes to the timeline but a link to discussion for committee members only. Some wikis will also let you share pages with different configurations of people, so you might make use of this feature as well.

You will again want to designate who is responsible for what. The person ultimately responsible for the project may choose to monitor the use of the wiki. In checking in regularly, the wiki monitor will see what has not happened and what the group's next actions should be. This will help the monitor follow up with individuals as they work, too.

If there is buy-in early in the process, you will not need to push too much to market the wiki. However, if there is not an early win, you will want to help people get comfortable with using the wiki as the group progresses through its goals. You might do this by meeting one-on-one with each participant to walk him or her through the process or, if people want to add information, volunteer to do it with them.

If everyone understands that the project wiki is the source of information about the project's status, it should be easy to incorporate it into workflow. This also means that once the project is complete, there will be documentation for people if others have to repeat the project later or if someone needs to modify some aspect of the work after someone has left the organization.

These internal uses of wikis are designed to make work easier and communication simpler. Internal wikis also allow members of the organization to access information at the point in time when they need it.

▶ DEVELOP EXTERNAL WIKIS

So far we have focused on ways to use a wiki internally. Internal wikis are often good places to start. The staff is generally a smaller audience than the library's community would be, so your risk is smaller. You tend to know the people you work with, so you can ask for opinions more easily than you can with the entire library community. If the wiki doesn't work with the staff, you can step back, reevaluate, and try another one with a different implementation. This can be harder to do with a larger, more general audience. Starting internally will help you understand how your colleagues feel about using a wiki, how they will incorporate it into their workflow, and how it will impact how the library works.

Once you suspect a wiki will be useful for your library, you might start to consider how a wiki could be a solution for external communication and collaboration as well. Or, perhaps you have the perfect situation for using a wiki, and now you will be working on your colleagues to help them understand how a wiki will help the community. You might consider using a wiki to create a Web site for the library, to create a site for a special event, to be a collaborative resource or a subject guide, or to be part of your instructional toolkit. This section will address these external uses of wikis.

How to Create a Wiki Web Site

Some organizations use wikis to run their Web site. This is true for organizations of all different types and sizes, and it can be true for libraries, too.

For example, Figure 3.11 shows the University of South Carolina Aiken Gregg Graniteville Library Web site. This Web site was built using a wiki, but it still retains features common to library

▶ Figure 3.11: Wiki Web Site

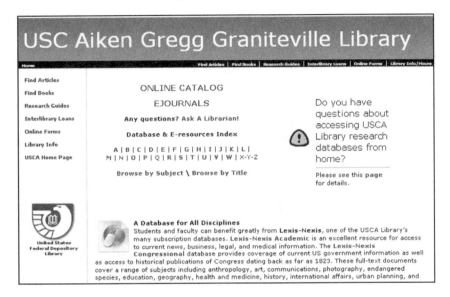

Web sites, including "Ask A Librarian," links to resources, and database information.

If you choose to use a wiki to host your library Web site, you may want to look into ways to make the site look less like a wiki. If you have a Webmaster on staff who is familiar with CSS (cascading style sheets), he or she can adjust the style to look less like a wiki. The Webmaster can remove the "Edit" tabs from pages, and give the site the colors and logos that are familiar to your users. If you are hosting it yourself, you can locate the site at your current URL so that patrons can continue using their own bookmarks. If you were to use a vendor hosted option, you would probably need to look into redirecting the URL to your current library address so that a strange domain doesn't confuse your users. A vendor hosted site will give you less control of the look of your wiki, but again this depends on the provider you are using and the level of membership you have.

When setting up a wiki Web site, you will want to take the same approaches that you would take when creating your own Web site. Initially, you might want to make the wiki Web site look and act as much like your regular Web site as possible so that your users will not be too confused by the new site and its organization. Of course, some libraries redesign their Web sites from scratch and release the new version with an education campaign, so you might choose this path and redesign your Web site from scratch with the new wiki site. If you do redesign your Web site you might want to hold focus groups with various constituencies—library board, users, students, faculty, parents, staff members—to see what expectations people have of the Web site, what they really like and would not want to lose, and what is missing from the current design. You can use this information to create a Web site that better fits the needs of your users based on what they actually request.

When doing this, you will already have most of the information you will want to include—it is already on your Web site! To save time, you can copy this information into the new Web site. Assuming your current Web site is up-to-date, you will know the information is accurate and timely.

Now, the people who were responsible for contributing to the Web site are probably likely candidates for contributing to this new Web site. However, if the contributors had been limited to folks who understood HTML, you now can consider a broader pool of candidates. The Web site could even be opened up to everyone, if administration felt comfortable with that.

Because the Web site is typically an important source of information about your library, and with the wiki structure anyone can save changes, you might consider how to get the appropriate signoff on changes to the Web site. You might have people add suggested changes to the discussion section of a page, or even submit it to a specific page of the wiki designated for changes. Then, once a week or once a month, appropriately ranked staff members could make the changes or let people know that changes have been approved and can be made.

You will probably also want to establish a workflow for this new initiative. This workflow gives you a process that you can train people to follow and makes it clear to everyone how changes will work and who can make them. If everyone can learn the process and how to make the changes, it will inevitably save you and the technology-savvy staff members the time and burden of making all of the changes to the wiki.

You might, at this point, worry about what happens if someone makes a malicious change without approval. This tends to happen far less frequently than we worry about in work and classroom settings. People know they will be held accountable if they make a change and will not risk damage to their position or their grade. However, you might have someone who has nothing to lose make a change. Because most wikis make reverting to a previous version of any given page very easy, you can quickly get back the content as it was before it was damaged.

Library patrons do not need to know that the library Web site is a wiki, although they might need to be notified that they have a new library Web site. You will probably want to do standard user education to let them know what to expect out of the site and its organization. Library staff members who do not edit the wiki will need the same training. Those staff who will be editing will need an introduction to the new site, instructions on how to edit and where to put information, and training on what expectations are for editing the site.

How to Create a Special Event Wiki

A wiki can be a good solution if you are creating a Web site for a special event but do not want to bother your Webmaster with the regular updates you are planning to make. A wiki may require only an initial setup, which may impact your technology staff if it is locally hosted and would impact event organizers only if it is hosted by a third-party provider.

If you choose to host the wiki yourself, you will need to work with a Webmaster when setting up the wiki. This initial work will ensure that the site is up and running and has the basic theme that you want it to have. If you have the logo and color scheme at this early stage, you can work with the Webmaster to ensure that the site has an appropriate appearance. Once the Webmaster has set up the back end, or you have set up a third-party site to meet your requirements, you are ready to start adding content.

LITA used a third-party site to host a wiki for their recent camp. Notice, in Figure 3.12, that the page was not open for editing by participants. This wiki included content relevant to the event, including sponsors, a link to related social software, registration, the

▶ Figure 3.12: Special Events Wiki

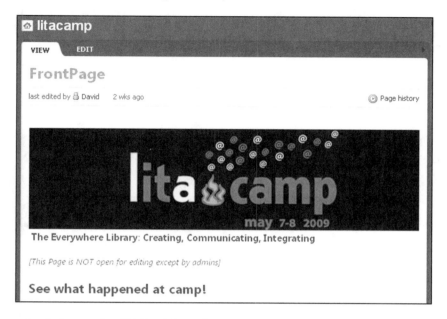

schedule, and a FAQ. After the camp was completed the site included information about what happened at the event. The wiki transitioned from an active site promoting the event before it happened to one archiving and preserving the event once it was over.

Like any upcoming event site, you will want to design your wiki to include relevant information for the participants you are targeting. If you are planning a lecture series, you will want to include when, where, and who will be speaking. Your audience will find it useful to include an image of the speaker and a biography. You may consider embedding video footage of the speaker at another event. If you are planning a workshop or conference, you might start the wiki with just an announcement. As you figure out more about what is going to happen at the conference, what hotel will offer a discount, who the keynote speaker will be, and all the other conference details, you will want to add this information to the Web site.

If you are starting the wiki site early on, before many decisions are made, you might not need to organize much information. A site early in the planning cycle could consist of just a front page with a list of all the current information. However, as you get closer and closer to the event, you will have more to share. Think about having a section on the front page for news, and as you develop other wiki content you can create entire wiki pages devoted to it.

If the library is small and only one person is organizing the event, that person would also be in charge of the wiki. Many libraries planning events might have a staff member or committee focused on marketing. In this case, the marketer may be in charge of the wiki. Large events, with subcommittees focused on different aspects of the project, might benefit from assigning a person on each subcommittee with updating their group's portion of the wiki.

If you are using a wiki to market an event, it makes sense to use the wiki to hold the planning documents as well. This will keep all your project information in one place. However, it is understandable that you may not want your event participants to have access to the documents you were using to plan the event. In this case, you can make these pages private for the event staff. They will be hidden from the participants but still be available for the people who will need them.

You will want to market the wiki to your users the same way that you would market any event Web site to the public. You might create flyers with the URL, make bookmarks that are distributed at circulation, or add a line about it to e-mail signatures from the reference desk. Essentially, though, a special events wiki is a marketing piece for an event, so you will just want to include the URL anywhere you are mentioning the event—your Web site, newspaper and radio advertisements, evening news stories—anywhere people will learn about the event. If your event is targeting a broad audience, for example, a statewide book or something new to your community, you might consider buying Google AdWords as part of your marketing strategy. This will help people searching for similar information find your wiki, even if they are not your library's typical audience.

How to Create a Wiki Online Resource

As you probably understand by now, wikis are highly flexible. You can use them to meet a variety of needs and interests. Some libraries might want to create their own resource. For example, in Figure 3.13 you can see a wiki that the Guilford County, North Carolina, librarians created to provide information about their community for their community. This wiki contains information about the site for potential users, explaining the Librarian's Guide to Guilford County. It contains basic information about the community on the front page, and links in the sidebar point to areas of specific interest, such as "Books and Reading," "Education," and "Events."

Similarly, you might want to create a local history Web site or a site about your special collections. Maybe you want to create a Web site for people interested in your larger organization, school, or university. A wiki can make it easy to do so.

Presumably, you are coming to the project with a specific information need in your community. You have likely gained an understanding of community needs and interests from your work in the library. This background will help you know if a resource is needed and if the library has people in a position to create one.

You will want to decide who will be involved in this project and what their roles will be. Will participants want to find information and give it to you to enter in the wiki? Will they be comfortable

▶ Figure 3.13: Online Resource Wiki

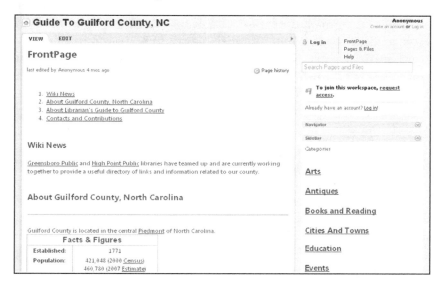

with all stages of the project and be able to handle everything from finding the information to editing the information to entering content into the site?

If you are getting others involved before making the site public, you can use the wiki much as you would an internal project wiki as you are working. Then, before releasing the wiki, participants will want to clean up the wiki content and remove or password protect pages that are not relevant to users interested in the topic. This will streamline the workflow process for you and your colleagues and remove any information your users would find confusing.

When marketing an online resource wiki, you will want to use the techniques that you have developed for marketing other online resources: digital collections, electronic databases, or virtual reference. You will want to market it within your library building, in local media outlets, as well as to people interested in the specific issue your site is dealing with. You can do this by e-mailing groups, writing up articles for relevant publications, or, again, by buying Google AdWords. The main goal is to get the wiki in the public where people can find it.

How to Create a Wiki Subject Guide

Libraries often have a number of subject guides. These handouts and Web sites help users find authoritative and relevant content on a specific topic. For example, an academic library might have a subject guide for freshman English classes to help students find literary criticism articles, relevant reference resources, citation guidelines, and how to contact a librarian. A public library might have a subject guide on gardening, with links to library resources as well as to local information created by the community.

Wikis have made a relatively significant impact in these areas. Because contributing to a wiki requires little technical knowledge, all librarians using wikis are in a position to edit and create their own subject guides without the aid of technology staff.

Chad Boeninger created the first business reference wiki, the Biz Wiki (see Figure 3.14). His Web site goes far beyond a typical subject guide. He includes a video introducing himself, a chat widget that allows users to talk with him in real time, and typical pages devoted to finding specific types of information. This wiki also in-

▶ Figure 3.14: Subject Guide Wiki

cludes a feed from the business blog that he also maintains. An added benefit of including all the different subject guides in the one wiki is that any business students can search across the wiki to find more information relevant to their area of study, even if their professor has not requested something specific for their class.

St. Joseph County Public Library, Indiana, has a collection of subject guides in one wiki (see Figure 3.15), as well. These subject guides deal with the local community and with ways the library can help its users.

The culture of your library will impact the openness of your wiki. You may choose to have a wiki that only a few specified people on staff can edit, or you may choose one that is open to any interested people in the community. If an open wiki makes library staff nervous, but the library staff appreciate that there is value in creating a community Web site, a possible solution is to create a club or volunteer task force that receives special training before they can update the site.

When creating a subject guide wiki, take a look at the subject guides you already produce. What information do you typically include? If you are already using video, for example, you will want to

▶ Figure 3.15: Subject Guide Wiki

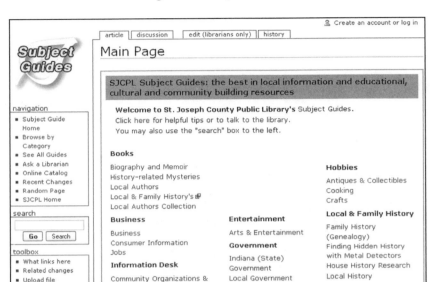

select a wiki option that will allow you to embed video. If your current guides are only text and links, any wiki will do.

As always, you will start out wanting to theme your wiki to look like your library Web site. Once your wiki is appropriately themed, you can pull content into the wiki from a few existing subject guides as a proof of concept. This is an excellent way of helping others understand your vision of the wiki as a subject guide and can be a good way to create a pilot study. If people think the idea is interesting but are not sure how your users will respond, you can do a study with users comparing and contrasting the original and wiki-based subject guides. This will help you know if a wiki is a good solution for subject guide creation in your community.

If you decide a wiki will meet your subject guide needs, you will probably want to pull over all your existing subject guides into the wiki. Patrons can become confused if there is similar information in two different places. Pulling over content will be relatively simple and most likely will require only copying and pasting content from existing documents. You might even be able to enlist student employees or volunteers to help so that library staff members do not have to spend a lot of time doing this routine work.

Once existing content has been moved to the wiki, you might want to set up a redirect so that anyone who visits the old pages is redirected to the new wiki. This will keep your patrons' bookmarks up-to-date and will minimize the advertising you will have to do to notify people of the change. You might, however, notice an increase in reference questions if people find the new format confusing. Note any increase in these questions as this will help you determine if the transition requires user education or a redesign of how the content is organized within the wiki.

Finally, you will want to work with those who create subject guides to make sure they are comfortable creating and editing them. You might want to offer classes or to sit with people who are starting out so that they see that editing the wiki is not too difficult.

How to Use Wikis for Instruction

Wikis can be used for instruction as well. Credit-bearing courses can use a wiki as a learning management system, and one-shot library instruction sessions can use a wiki to supplement classroom teaching. In either of these cases, a class wiki would include information about what you are planning to teach, information about the content, and information for students to help them with their work. Wikis are also a convenient way to provide learners with hyperlinks in lieu of a handout that would require students to type in the URLs.

Figure 3.16 shows a class wiki for an information literacy course at Wake Forest University. The wiki includes course content, information about group work, and class readings. Note that the wiki includes information to help the students use it effectively.

A course wiki could include the syllabus, lecture notes, information about projects, and collaborative spaces for students to work in. You might even create a final project that students can include in the wiki. You would want to create a framework for the class wiki before the first day so that when students come in at the beginning you can walk them through the wiki and explain how you plan to use it. You do not necessarily have to fill in all the sections, though. You can do that as the class progresses. Your students will dictate how much time you have to spend teaching the technology in the classroom. If you know your students will not be familiar with edit-

▶ Figure 3.16: Wiki for Instruction

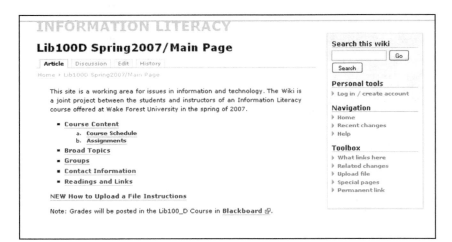

ing wikis, you might choose to use a vendor hosted option with a WYSIWYG editor so that you can spend your class time on content rather than on teaching the technology. If you suspect your students are already familiar with creating online content, or one of the outcomes of the class is for them to be comfortable participating in today's information environment, you might sacrifice some class time to teach them how to edit a MediaWiki site, giving them additional skills in case they want to edit Wikipedia as they participate in class.

In the case of a one-shot session, you will probably choose to include some of the standard information that you include in subject guides. But you might also choose to incorporate instruction. If you use the wiki to teach skills such as how to perform an advanced search in the catalog or how to choose a database, you do not have to focus as much on this in class, freeing up time for critical thinking and evaluative skills training.

No matter how you incorporate a wiki into your classes, you will want to make sure students know that it is available to them. Be sure to tell them the URL and e-mail it to them. It is not worth creating the content for a wiki if your audience will never see it. Letting the reference staff know the URL for the wiki could help students who have misplaced it the night before the project is due.

Wikis are ideal solutions for many Web sites that library staff need to create in the course of library work. Because these projects are more about communicating with the users rather than about the tool that you use to create them, you will want to approach these projects the same way you would if you were using a traditional Web site. Do a needs assessment, use focus groups to find out what users want, and design the site with your users in mind. Then, behind the scenes, you can consider how to use a wiki when meeting these goals.

▶ EXPLORE OTHER WIKI USES

Conference Wikis

The American Library Association conferences have used wikis since 2005, and a growing number of conferences choose to have a wiki as their conference site or as a supplemental site for participants. These wikis often include information about travel and transportation, places to stay and roommate arrangements, information about dining and entertainment in the area, and other relevant information. Some include pages for participants to list their blog URL or Twitter username so other people can follow along with the conference activities. Some are very casual, created for and by attendees. Others are more formal, created by the conference organizers and containing official conference information (see Figure 3.17).

If you are setting up a conference wiki, begin by thinking about the purpose of the site. Is it the official Web page for the conference, or is it supplemental? Are you creating a conference site where only planners will edit the content, or is it going to be a collaborative site in which participants will be able to contribute? Does the wiki need to have a formal and official voice, or is the wiki creating a venue for the participants to share information for their own planning? Knowing how you and the conference committee feel about these questions, and what your participant's expectations are, will help you know how to design the wiki for your conference.

▶ Figure 3.17: Conference Wiki

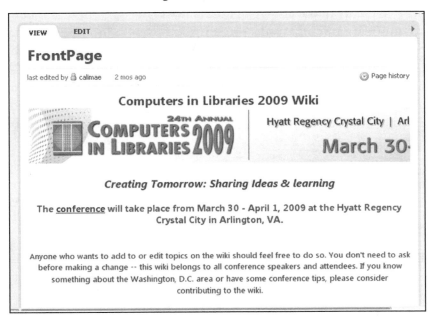

Once you have made your decisions and set up a basic framework, you will want to let participants know about the site, what they can expect to find there, and how they can participate if this is an option. You might want to seed a few sections to make the wiki worth visiting, for example, with information on local restaurants or transportation, and send out periodic e-mails pointing to the pages with the most relevant information for users at that point in time.

As is often the case, you might find that people visit the site more than they contribute, and this can be okay. It all depends on the goals and purposes of your wiki. If the purpose of the wiki is primarily to distribute information to make the conference a better experience, and secondarily about creating a community of conference goers, it is more important that people visit the site than it is for them to contribute to it, so your wiki is still a success.

Professional Resources

There are already many professional wikis for library staff and their work. These wikis can help you learn about best practices and techniques for your work, but they can also be a place for you to share what you are doing as well. These wikis can help you find the best practices for any given issue in the field as well as provide a way to connect with others who are doing work you are interested in.

Library Success Wiki

www.libsuccess.org

Library Success Wiki is designed for libraries to share what they are doing with others in the field. This list will help you find who is offering text messaging reference, new marketing ideas, and new programming ideas. The Library Success Wiki is run using MediaWiki and is primarily a best practices wiki.

Lyrasis Library Leadership Network

http://pln.palinet.org/wiki

Another professional MediaWiki site is hosted by Lyrasis, a library consortium. This wiki is the Library Leadership Network. It contains articles from people in the field dealing with leadership issues or current library news impacting the field. The site is a wiki that anyone can contribute to, but it also includes signed articles. People may modify these articles, but one of the community rules is that people will not change the meaning or message of another person's signed article.

ALA Read Write Connect

http://wikis.ala.org/readwriteconnect

ALA has a number of wikis, for everything from conferences to division wikis to wikis for specific projects. These wikis provide members with information about the organization and a place for collaborative work. These professional wikis exist both to help people with their association responsibilities and to let the library community learn about the association's work.

Contributing Original Content

In addition to professional wikis, you might consider contributing to Wikipedia on behalf of your organization. If your users turn to Wikipedia first, after all, why not put your content there? If you consider this, it would be wise to read about the culture of Wikipedia. Wikipedia has fundamental principles (see Pressley and McCallum, 2008, at www.infotoday.com/online/sep08/Pressley_McCallum.shtml) that guide people's contributions to the wiki:

- ► Nonmarketing
- ► Neutral point of view
- ► Verifiability
- ► No original research

When you set up an account on Wikipedia, you will need to register as an individual. Accounts that are known to belong to an organization can be deleted from the system without any warning. Once you have set up the account, you will want to follow best practices for editing Wikipedia. Of particular importance, Wikipedia does not allow individuals or groups to use the site for marketing. This includes not-for-profit organizations and libraries. Because of this, rather than adding an entry in the encyclopedia for your special collection, you might choose to add a link to your collection on a page already dealing with the topic of your collection. This way you are not using Wikipedia to pitch your library but instead including your library in the references as a place people can go to for more information.

Wikipedia does not allow original research, and you can include only information that has been documented and is verifiable. If you add a statement to an entry based on information in your collection, include a citation to the specific work. This can drive traffic to your special collections page. The citations are important. Not only do they prove you are not contributing original ideas, but they also provide verifiability to your additions. You will want to make sure you are writing with a neutral point of view. Wikipedia requires authors remove bias from their writing.

Once you have made changes to Wikipedia, you might find that they have been altered or removed after the fact. If this is the case, examine the discussion tab of your entry, the rules for editors, and the founding principles for the encyclopedia. There is a good chance that the reason your information is no longer there is because it violated Wikipedia's standards.

Making Wikipedia Better

If you have committed to editing Wikipedia to push people to your library's Web site, it is not a far stretch to approach Wikipedia editing as a professional responsibility. When you edit Wikipedia you are helping to improve one of the primary resources people turn to today. If you are interested in this work, you might want to start small with editing punctuation and formatting or contributing in spaces in which you are really comfortable. You may choose to participate in the discussion tabs to negotiate what is appropriate and relevant for a given entry.

Another way to improve Wikipedia for your users is to incorporate Context Objects in Spans, or COinS. COinS is a specific way of citing a source on a Web site, and it is integrated into Wikipedia. With a browser plug-in, and a click of a button, users can see links to full-text options for works cited with COinS. Figure 3.18 shows how the COinS displays in the browser. Users can click on the "Full Text Options" link to be redirected to a library site with the full text of the articles.

▶ Figure 3.18: COinS

▶4

MARKETING

- ▶ Get the Word Out
- ▶ Market to the Intended Audience
- ▶ Advertise via Social Media
- ▶ Create a Marketing Plan

A Web site is only useful if it is relevant and used by its intended audience. A wiki is no different. You can spend hours planning and setting up a wiki, but if no one visits your site or it does not include information users find valuable, then all your wiki efforts will be in vain.

This chapter addresses ways that you can market your wiki and help create an audience base to sustain it over time. Your strategy will depend on whether the wiki is designed for internal or external use. The initiator of the wiki will also impact your marketing strategy. If the administration initiates the wiki, your marketing strategy will be very different from marketing a wiki that was initiated by the larger community. This section will provide you with the tools necessary to plan a marketing strategy for your new wiki.

▶ GET THE WORD OUT

When you start thinking about marketing your wiki, you will want to consider who it is for. This information can help you craft a marketing plan for your specific audience. For example, if administration would like the staff to use a wiki, but the staff had not indicated an interest in the site, you might need to call on the administration to offer rewards for participation or some other incentive. However, if your patrons have requested a community wiki, you can begin your marketing plan with your patron's word-of-mouth advertising. Incentives and word-of-mouth advertising won't be your entire marketing plan, but they can be a component of your plan. You should consider using a number of approaches, including prominent location on your Web site, special meetings or programming, publications or flyers, and one-on-one sessions with interested users. This section will address these methods in more detail.

Location on the Library Web Site

As part of your marketing plan, you will want to consider what role you wiki has on the main library's Web site. Is the wiki easy to find? You will want to consider how prominently you would like the wiki to be displayed on your Web site, and the location will probably change over time. For example, when the wiki is new, you might want to make sure it is more visible as part of the kick-off campaign. Once the wiki is more established you might choose to reserve the most prominent space for new programs.

You will want to link the wiki in the appropriate place on the Web site. If you are using the wiki to provide subject guides, you will want to put it in the research section. If you want the wiki to provide answers to frequently asked questions, you might want the wiki to replace that section of the Web site.

If the wiki is for library staff only, you may choose to keep the wiki in a less prominent area of the site, or you may choose not to link to the wiki at all. In this case you would want to make sure to market the wiki's address prominently to staff through e-mail and maybe even on paper so that they will be able to find it despite the lack of a link on the library's homepage.

Programming

Another effective marketing technique is to offer programming related to the wiki for its intended audience. This programming can focus on what the purpose of the wiki is and on how one can use it to make life easier. You can also offer an instructional program on how to edit and participate in the wiki.

When planning your program, be guided by the reason the wiki exists and by who the primary users are. Perhaps for a group of teens you could create a game in which, over the course of a month, the teen who contributes the most content gets a prize or recognition on the front page of the wiki. For an adult book club you might consider having a meeting to which everyone brings their favorite book and walks through the steps of adding an entry on their favorite book to the wiki.

The programming, of course, will be structured differently depending on if your audience is your community or your library staff. Wiki programs could be offered along the same lines as other community programs. A program could be part of your regular schedule for any user interested in the topic or the technology. If you are working on a wiki for library staff, the training could be rolled into staff meetings or integrated into the library staff training program.

Flyers/Publications

In all likelihood, your library already has a system for communicating with your users. You can make use of this system to market your wiki as well. If you distribute a newsletter, it makes sense to highlight what the wiki offers in an article introducing the new site. If you send out regular e-mails whenever there is something newsworthy, you may choose to send an e-mail announcing your new wiki. If you are already using blogs, you might even offer a series of posts on what the wiki is and how to use it.

It does not hurt to market your wiki in public places as well. You can post flyers around your building letting people know specific features that might make their lives easier. You might choose to post flyers in more public spaces reminding people of the library and highlighting the wiki as a new service that you are offering the community.

If you have a person, or committee, on staff that is responsible for this type of marketing, it certainly makes sense to see what recommendations they have and to empower them to market the wiki as well.

One-on-One Sessions

You might also find yourself in settings where you can introduce individuals to your wiki one-on-one. These are excellent opportunities to teach a user how to interact with the wiki and also to get a sense of where the wiki could be clearer, easier to use, or reorganized. Once you have successfully worked with a user, that individual might even develop enough interest to talk about the wiki with other library users, encouraging others through word-of-mouth advertising.

▶ MARKET TO THE INTENDED AUDIENCE

The question of your audience is an important one. Your approach will vary depending on if your audience is your users or your fellow library staff members. If your wiki is designed for public use, you are marketing to a broad base of people with a broad level of technology skills. Some of your users might be familiar with wikis and edit Wikipedia. Others will not be able to distinguish your wiki site from any other type of Web site. You may choose to create marketing plans for people at different comfort

Technology Skill Levels and Wiki Use

Novice:
- ▶ Use the search box
- ▶ Cut and paste
- ▶ Embed links
- ▶ Know terms such as "wiki"

Intermediate:
- ▶ Embed media
- ▶ Plug in widgets
- ▶ Create new pages
- ▶ Know terms such as "history" or "discussion tabs"

Advanced:
- ▶ Use extensions
- ▶ Add CoinS
- ▶ Know terms such as "hosting" and "extensions"

levels with the technology. For those who are really technologically advanced, you might create programming focused on how to enhance the wiki to make it more useful. For those with less experience, you might choose to emphasize that the Web site exists and teach users how to find information on it.

These approaches might work well for staff as well, but you can also make different assumptions about a wiki created for library staff. For example, if administration requires that all library staff use the wiki as a centralized repository for information about the running of the library, everyone will need to be able to use and edit the wiki. You might still have to plan programming and documentation for people across the spectrum, but you can assume everyone will need to gain the same level of competency.

External Strategies

We have talked a little about how marketing and training might vary based on audience, so let us go into strategy a little bit deeper for both internal and external marketing. Marketing a wiki to an external audience is similar to anything you might market to your users. You might choose to post flyers and signs around your library or distribute bookmarks with the wiki's URL. You may set the screen on the library computers to the wiki as a way to make sure all computer users see the wiki at least once. Your marketing strategy for the community should be focused on how the wiki could help them out.

Although the wiki is on the computer, you can use the launch as an excuse to get out into the community. You can have a launch party at the mall for teens or partner with local businesses. You could set up a table in a grocery store to show people how to add cooking tips or information about local foods. This might increase interest in the community and give people a reason to come back and visit other sections of the wiki.

Internal Strategies

Your biggest influence on strategy for an internal wiki is the initiator of the wiki. If management requires the wiki, you can count on people learning what they need to know to participate in the use of the wiki as part of their jobs, but there might be more initial resistance to a new wiki as well. You might need to get a statement from administration requiring that everyone contribute one piece of information or offering incentives for those who make a contribution.

Marketing the Idea Behind the Wiki

Many people today recognize the importance of an organization's Web presence. Some even understand how to make use of social software and Web sites like blogs, Facebook, or Twitter. Though Wikis are part of this type of technology, they are not understood by as many people. When speaking with stakeholders and staff members, it will be important for you to explain the purpose of your Web site and to define "wiki" in a way that is meaningful to them. You will also want to describe how a wiki will enable you to better meet users' needs and to accomplish your goals.

If the wiki is a grassroots product, you will not need as many incentives, but you may have to spend more time making sure everyone is on board— not just the subset of people who requested it. In this case you might have to convince the administrators to support the project and teach them exactly what a wiki is and how it can be helpful. When getting people on board early, you should talk with your technology staff from the very beginning! These staff members know your technical system best and will help you avoid software that's not compatible with your current system or choosing an outdated product. If you can get their buy-in at an early phase, they will be more invested in your project and have their own incentive to work on it.

As discussed in Chapter 3, initiating a wiki requires seeding the wiki with relevant information. You will want to have enough information to make it worth your colleagues' time to visit it. If there is not enough information in the wiki, your colleagues will not use the site. If they do not use the wiki, they will not add content. If you seed the wiki with information, and people find it useful, they will begin marketing the wiki for you by letting others know about the information available. As they become more familiar with the wiki they will also be more comfortable contributing their own content.

Perhaps the most effective strategy for working with staff is to let people know how to get help. This help could be programming, handouts, one-on-one training, or even a buddy system whereby staff members pair up to make changes. If people know they can get the help they need—easily and quickly—they will be more willing to take a chance contributing.

▶ ADVERTISE VIA SOCIAL MEDIA

Today we also have new media options for marketing products, including other wikis. The users who are on Facebook and Twitter and who blog are also probably going to be your primary candidates for early wiki adoption. If you are marketing the wiki to an external audience it makes sense to look into marketing in these places. You can buy advertisements fairly cheaply through Facebook and target them to specific demographics such as your students or people who live in your ZIP code. You can write about your wiki in blogs, and you can leave comments about your wiki on others' blogs. Please note that some bloggers might perceive self-promotional comments as spam, so it is important to consider if your comment is appropriate.

You can also make media for people to add to their own sites to market your wiki. You can make a small badge or logo to link to

Google AdWords

Google AdWords is a way of marketing your public wiki through Google. The text ads you see at the top or the right of a search are generated using the AdWords system. To participate, you begin by selecting relevant keywords. When users search Google with these keywords, your site comes up in the search as an advertisement. Costs vary; http://adwords.google.com can provide you with an estimate of how much a particular string of keywords would cost based on keyword traffic. You set a daily amount that you are willing to spend, and how much you are willing to spend per click, and you will not be charged beyond that.

your wiki that fans can put on their own Web sites. You can make short videos or screencasts of your wiki and share them on media Web sites like YouTube and Vimeo. There are a number of relevant social media sites with users who are good candidates for working with wikis. Use this to your advantage and market with them!

▶ CREATE A MARKETING PLAN

Your total marketing strategy will be based on the purpose of the wiki, the group or people who requested it, and the state of the wiki at the point when you begin marketing it. Once you have a clear understanding of your wiki, its audience, and its context, you can create an effective plan. You will want to consider its placement on the Web site, the training and programming you will offer, advertisements in publications and other media, and what forms of help you will provide to those who need it. A holistic approach to marketing will allow you to share your wiki with a wide audience of people who will benefit from its creation.

▶5

BEST PRACTICES

- ▶ **Know How to Plan**
- ▶ **Outline the Implementation Steps**
- ▶ **Strategize Marketing**
- ▶ **Maintain Your Wiki**
- ▶ **Keep Your Software Current and Have a Preservation Plan**

No matter the type of wiki you are using, or the way you intend to use it, there are a number of concepts that are useful across the board. When implementing a wiki you will want to have strong plans in place for a number of areas:

- ▶ An assessment to understand the context of the wiki and its audience
- ▶ A rollout plan for introducing the wiki to its audience
- ▶ A training plan for those who will use and edit the wiki
- ▶ A marketing plan for advertising the wiki
- ▶ A maintenance plan for keeping the wiki current and up-to-date
- ▶ A migration plan in case you choose to move the wiki at a later date
- ▶ A preservation plan in case your vendor stops offering the wiki service or if you plan to take down the wiki at a later point

This chapter will discuss some of the essential practices for using wikis in libraries.

▶ KNOW HOW TO PLAN

When designing your wiki, you will want to spend some time in the planning stages, making sure that you have thought through the objectives of the wiki, how you will use it, as well as how you will get others on board and establish its place within your library. The planning stage is behind the scenes but extremely important. This is the phase during which you will lay the groundwork for what you are trying to do. The work in this phase can be really exciting, as you are experimenting with new ideas and ways of doing things, but it may also be less engaging because you will not immediately see the outcome of the work that you are doing. Keep these questions in mind during the planning phase:

1. What are the goals and expected outcomes of your wiki?
2. How will this wiki make your library's work easier or of a better quality?
3. What tools and widgets make the most sense given the goals, functional expectations, and technological expectations of your place of work?
4. Who will be responsible for the wiki?
5. What is your plan for seeding the wiki?
6. How do you plan to train others to participate?
7. How will you determine if the use of the wiki was a success?

Spending time thinking through and answering these questions will help you formulate your plan for the use of the wiki and will help ensure that the wiki is a success. If you are planning a very small pilot project to get a feel for how a wiki might work for you in your workplace, you may want to read through these questions a number of times as you experiment to remind yourself of what to look for. There are times for pure experimentation and times for clear and thorough planning, and the amount of preplanning you do depends on where you are in this process.

▶ OUTLINE THE IMPLEMENTATION STEPS

A strong rollout of your wiki is the foundation for a good implementation process. Good wiki implementation includes creating an outline of the information you anticipate adding to the wiki, what information you will seed it with, details of your training program, and details of your marketing plan.

When creating the basic outline of the wiki, you are creating the container in which people will add information. You will want to think through how people would want information organized. You will probably need to have conversations with various stakeholders to ensure that you are making something that will be useful to everyone.

There are, of course, a few basic ways people can think about this. If you are creating a library wiki, you might want to create a page for each department and let the department staff figure out how to organize the information in a structure relevant to them. If your wiki is for an event, you will want a page for the who, what, where, when, and why of the event. If you are not sure about how to get started organizing your wiki, you can take a look at any number of library wikis out there to see how others have organized theirs.

At this point, you might guess that another very important part of implementation is seeding the wiki with relevant information. This comes up again and again because it is so important to the

Seeding Your Wiki

Seeding the wiki depends on the use you envision for your wiki. If it is going to be a reference source for how the library works, you might create a section for each department. For example, you might choose to have sections of the wiki devoted to reference, circulation, children's services, technical services, technology, and administration. If you are planning to use a wiki to collaborate on a specific project, you might create sections to deal with an overview of your goals and deadlines, background information, task lists, and contact information for all involved parties. Based on the intended use for your wiki, you can create the basic outline for the information that will be contained and begin the overview text for each section. Over time, as the project or resource develops, the community can refine the organizational structure and information contained within the site.

success of your wiki. If you do not have good information in the wiki to start with, people will not have any reason to visit it. You should plan to add as much information as you possibly can during the implementation phase. Do you have manuals stored digitally that you can copy and paste into the wiki? Do you have e-mails that contain instructions for how to perform specific tasks? Any existing documentation is a good candidate for copying and pasting into the wiki. If you do not have access to existing files, or if you do not know enough to populate the wiki yourself, it is time to enlist the help of others who might be able to contribute. You might choose to turn to a representative from each department if you are in a larger library. Getting participation from a wide variety of people in your library will help you once you are marketing the wiki and trying to encourage its use.

While in the implementation phase, you will want to decide how to approach training. As we have discussed, you should include a variety of approaches to training. Consider choosing a hybrid approach of at least some of the following:

- ▶ Face-to-face classes
- ▶ One-on-one training
- ▶ Online tutorials
- ▶ "Cheat sheet" worksheets
- ▶ An "on call" system with someone who is willing to help

Once you've figured out the structure of the wiki, included some introductory information, and decided how you will approach training, you will be ready to roll out the wiki. And when you do this, it is time to increase your marketing activities.

▶ STRATEGIZE MARKETING

As discussed in Chapter 5, marketing is a core part of getting your wiki out there and in use by its audience. We discussed several ways of marketing in Chapter 5:

- ▶ Post flyers and signage.
- ▶ Create bookmarks and takeaways.

▶ Place the wiki prominently on your Web site.

▶ Offer a training program.

▶ Run related programs.

▶ Use the wiki as the homepage on library computers.

▶ Use social networking and Web 2.0 sites.

▶ Target a few key players who can influence others.

When thinking about marketing it is always important to think about who your audience is and what they can get from the wiki. Will it be just another source of information for them, or will it be a social networking opportunity? How would this wiki fit into their day-to-day lives? Is there any aspect of it that will make their lives easier? Understanding your users, and how the wiki will be useful for them, is an excellent starting place for developing your marketing plan. That marketing plan will guide the advertising you do for the wiki and ultimately the use and success of the project. Start with where your users are, and you will be able to make good inroads.

▶ MAINTAIN YOUR WIKI

After you have planned the wiki, implemented it, and marketed it to others, the wiki becomes a living Web site. Others are editing and contributing, and you are stepping away from individual ownership. At this point, it is worth thinking about maintenance.

It is easy for people to add information to a wiki, once they know how. It is generally easy for users to remember to add information when something new happens, a policy is changed, or there is a new frequently asked question. However, some information in the wiki might become outdated because no one thinks about checking up on it. In a large organization, this could be less of an issue. A larger audience has more potential for catching errors in the wiki. However, mistakes might slip through the cracks even in a large organization. It is a good idea to have a few designated people check designated sections of the wiki on a regular basis. Your organization might do this when it checks the library Web site for out-of-date information or dead links.

Your staff might include one or two people who really enjoy working with the wiki, who would not mind going through and tagging pages that seem to be out of date or incomplete. These editors could follow up by sending an e-mail to the people who have the newer information and can update the pages. This is the perfect task to fill those last few hours before a conference or a slow shift at the reference desk. The goal at this point is to make sure that the old and out-of-date information is removed from the wiki so that people can rely on the wiki to be accurate and up-to-date.

► KEEP YOUR SOFTWARE CURRENT AND HAVE A PRESERVATION PLAN

Finally, you will want a plan for the life span of your wiki. This is less of an issue for vendor hosted wikis. However, you will have to check for software updates periodically for those on your own server and then update the wiki when a new version is released. This could become difficult if you are hosting a large number of wikis or if your technology staff is already pressed for time.

If you know that a wiki will be relevant only for a given amount of time, you will want to plan an archival method so that the information is not lost. This way you will not need to keep updating the wiki software, but you will be able to continue providing the information to those who were interested in the topic.

If you plan to keep the wiki for a long period of time, you will want to pay attention to the software and the hosting company to ensure that the software is still current and good. If you can tell that the company is about to go out of business, or if you would like to switch to a locally hosted option, you will want to make sure that you can easily convert the information between the two wiki platforms.

This will vary depending on the wiki platform that you are leaving and the one you are beginning to use. If there is not an easy way to export and import your wiki's data, you will need to pull the content out of your first wiki and enter it into the second one manually. A volunteer or student, depending on the sensitivity of the information and responsibility of the individual, can do this work.

Tips for Converting Your Wiki

1. Learn the syntax for the new wiki. How do internal and external links work? How does this compare to the first wiki?
2. Copy the basic organizational structure from the first wiki and paste it into the new wiki. Edit the syntax so internal pages are created.
3. One page at a time, copy content from the original wiki, and put the content in the new one, editing syntax as you go. As you do this, you can delete the pages from the original wiki.
4. Once you have made significant progress, you can access the list of pages for the original wiki to make sure you are not missing any in the conversion process.

▶6

MEASURES OF SUCCESS

- ▶ People Use the Wiki to Look for Information
- ▶ People Add Information to the Wiki
- ▶ People Are Aware of the Wiki
- ▶ People Initiate Other Wikis
- ▶ The Wiki Is Part of Library Culture

Wiki adoption can be slow. Although wikis can help organizations in a number of ways, sometimes people are hesitant to integrate them into their daily work. People may be reluctant for a number of reasons. Perhaps people prefer to avoid new technologies. It might be difficult to change a workflow pattern after a tradition of accomplishing tasks a specific way. Perhaps people do not understand why the wiki has been introduced to the organization. It is worth monitoring the use of your new wiki with any of its intended audiences to get a sense of how people are feeling about the site and if they have any hesitations. If they do, you can create training and target marketing to alleviate them. If users have a discomfort with the tool, you might want to offer more training or one-on-one help. If the problem is workflow, you could work with administration to see if there is a way to relieve staff of some duties while they develop their new workflow processes.

It is worth noting that, although wiki adoption can be slow, as long as you see the adoption moving in a positive direction, then it is likely that the adoption is progressing well. The dynamics of wiki adoption change over time, often starting with acceptance and use by a small group and then moving toward a general adoption. One person can begin to build the interest and use of a wiki and then

Survey Questions to Consider

Question	Rationale
What led you to this Web site?	This will let you know if people are coming to the Web site because they know about it or if they are coming to it through an Internet search.
What information were you seeking?	With this information, you can learn what information people need, and what sections of the wiki you might enhance.
Did you find the answers you needed?	This will let you know if the information was in-depth enough or if you need to add more content.
Would you recommend this Web site to others in the future?	You will learn if you need to make large changes to meet users' needs and if you can count on word-of-mouth marketing.
Would you be willing to participate in a focus group on our Web site? If so, please leave your contact information.	The best feedback you can get on the usefulness of your wiki comes from your users. Focus groups allow you to have conversations about your wiki, its organization, the content, and other variables that might impact the usefulness of the wiki.

win over others one by one. If you don't want to wait for a slow adoption, there are some techniques you can consider to get people on board more quickly:

▶ Be sure your new wiki starts out with enough information to be useful.

▶ Monitor the information in your wiki to ensure it is accurate, and check up on it periodically.

▶ Enlist a few people to be early adopters, and reward your first editors for their participation.

▶ Monitor e-mail discussion lists. When questions arise, post the answer in the wiki and reply with a link to the page with the answer.

▶ PEOPLE USE THE WIKI TO LOOK FOR INFORMATION

For the wiki to be useful for the community, the community needs to know they can look there for information. To educate them, you have to do a few things: make sure there is enough useful information in the wiki for your community to find it relevant, market the wiki well so that people know how to find it, and make it easy to use so that your users will find the information that they look for.

We have talked about these issues in previous chapters, but if you find yourself wondering why people are not looking in the wiki and are turning to other sources, these could be issues. Consider the usefulness of your wiki. Does the wiki have information in it that you would look for yourself? Is the site organized in a way in which you can find what you need? Ask others if they find the wiki useful and what improvements they might suggest. If people agree that the wiki is generally useful, perhaps you should look into how you marketed the wiki. If your users visit the library Web site, can they easily find the wiki? Do you mention it in other online places where people regularly visit? Have you sent out e-mail reminders when people ask about information that you know to be in the wiki? You need to explore a variety of different factors when trying to determine where the marketing is not working.

▶ PEOPLE ADD INFORMATION TO THE WIKI

A sign that your wiki is working is the growth of the site. If people find the wiki valuable they will participate, and the wiki will continue to grow and become more valuable over time. If you find that the wiki is not growing, or that you are the only one contributing, it is worth exploring how to make the wiki a friendlier site to use. Perhaps you find that people do access the wiki but are not adding information as regularly or consistently as you had hoped. In this case, perhaps the interface is not as intuitive as you had thought or perhaps the staff need a second round of training.

If you want to get people to add more content, you might find value in revisiting Chapter 3 on implementation for specific suggestions. In general, however, make sure that it is easy for people to add content, and provide plenty of educational opportunities. You can offer one-on-one training, workshops, or online instructional videos to help. If you are looking to create a feeling of ownership in the wiki's audience, you could agree to add others' information for them for a specified period of time.

Helpful Online Instructional Videos

To get a sense of the tone, styles, and type of information people convey in online instructional videos, take a look at the following. You might even find that some already answer the questions you know your community members have, and you can send the link to them as a response.

> ► Getting Started with PBWiki (now PBworks):
> www.youtube.com/watch?v=A2O4JcGQiYO
> ► WetPaint in Plain English:
> www.youtube.com/watch?v=F7BAU2XX5Ws
> ► Wiki Basic Editing Tips:
> www.youtube.com/watch?v=xvLIR1FbC2Y
> ► Editing a Wiki:
> www.youtube.com/watch?v=bH15MEfOJRY
> ► Creating and Editing a Wiki Page:
> www.youtube.com/watch?v=0S9KQS-twFU
> ► Add and Edit a Page in MediaWiki:
> www.youtube.com/watch?v=6gbMNhnl1SU
> ► Introduction to a Class Wiki:
> www.youtube.com/watch?v=6NRbbskf3cA

► PEOPLE ARE AWARE OF THE WIKI

Another way that you can know that the wiki is going well is if people seem more aware of what is going on or at least more aware of how to find out what is going on. When there is a general sense that the information is findable, especially since the launch of the wiki, you can assume that it is playing a role in the community. You will know this for certain if you see others responding to questions by pointing to the wiki.

Again, by monitoring library discussion lists, you will get an idea of how people are responding to the wiki. Are there more, the same, or fewer requests for information? When people send information to the discussion list, do they also post it to the wiki? How active is your listserv? If you are not sure, you can look through the archives, comparing the same month or even week over a couple years.

If you have not noticed a change in people's awareness, revisit the marketing and training chapters of this book. You might also want to contribute more information to the wiki so that people know to look there first. Perhaps enlist a few others to add content as well. This will create a core group of people to recommend the wiki when people ask questions. Hopefully these additional voices will also help your audience learn where the wiki is, why it is useful, and how to participate.

▶ PEOPLE INITIATE OTHER WIKIS

You will know that the wiki is a success if you find that people are creating new sections in the wiki for their own committee or departmental use or if they are creating their own wikis for specific projects or events. This is a sign that others see the value of the tool and have learned ways that a wiki can improve their own work.

This adoption might take a while, and it could benefit from reminders along the way. People may not think of their own use for a wiki, but, after learning how one works and hearing other ideas, they might become interested in trying to establish one on their own. If you would like to support this type of adaptation, be willing to share some of the ideas mentioned in this book and other tips that you learn along the way. Truly, wikis are helpful in many contexts; it is just a matter of thinking through what would be most helpful in a given area.

▶ THE WIKI IS PART OF LIBRARY CULTURE

The clearest indicator that the wiki is successful is when it is no longer your own project. At some point, a successful wiki will become part of the library's culture. Others might even tend to the project more than you do. The introduction of wikis has been successful when you are no longer the primary source of information on the topic and the general institutional culture expects people to be comfortable with the tool.

This transition may feel strange at first—losing authority over a tool that you introduced to the culture. However, it is good for the organization. It is an indication that the wiki is now a core part of the library culture and is a foundation for the work the library does. If you can get your organization to this point, your wiki is a success.

RECOMMENDED READING

▶ BOOKS

Klobas, Jane E. and Angela Beesley. 2006. *Wikis: Tools for Information Work and Collaboration.* Oxford: Chandos.

Shirky, Clay. 2008. *Here Comes Everybody: The Power of Organizing Without Organizations.* New York: Penguin Press.

Tapscott, Don and Anthony D. Williams. 2006. *Wikinomics: How Mass Collaboration Changes Everything.* New York: Portfolio.

▶ CHAPTERS

Casey, Michael. 2007. "The Wonderful World of Wikis: Applications for Libraries." In *Library 2.0 and Beyond: Innovative Technologies and Tomorrow's User,* edited by Nancy Courtney. Westport, CT: Libraries Unlimited.

Farkas, Meredith G. 2007. "Wikis." In *Social Software in Libraries: Building Collaboration, Communication, and Community Online.* Medford, NJ: Information Today.

Kroski, Ellyssa. 2008. "Wikis." In *Web 2.0 for Librarians and Information Professionals.* New York: Neal-Schuman.

Russell, John. 2008. "Wikis and Collaborative Reference Services." In *The Desk and Beyond: Next Generation Reference Services,* edited by Sarah K. Steiner and M. Leslie Madden. Chicago: Association of College and Research Libraries.

► WEB SITES

ALA Read Write Connect. Available: http://wikis.ala.org/read writeconnect/index.php/Main_Page (accessed December 14, 2009).

Library Success: A Best Practices Wiki. Available: www.libsuccess .org/index.php?title=Main_Page (accessed December 14, 2009).

Lyrasis Library Leadership Network. Available: http://pln.palinet .org/wiki/index.php/LLN_Home (accessed December 14, 2009).

MediaWiki Handbook. Available: http://meta.wikimedia.org/ wiki/Help:Contents (accessed December 14, 2009).

WikiMatrix: Compare Them All. Available: www.wikimatrix.org (accessed December 14, 2009).

► CITED ARTICLES

Giles, Jim. 2005. "Special Report: Internet Encyclopedias Go Head to Head." *Nature* 438 (December). Available: www.nature.com/ nature/journal/v438/n7070/full/438900a.html (accessed December 14, 2009).

Pressley, Lauren and Carolyn McCallum. 2008. "Putting the Library in Wikipedia." *Online* 32, no. 5 (September/October). Available: www.infotoday.com/online/sep08/Pressley_McCallum .shtml (accessed December 14, 2009).

INDEX

Page numbers followed by the letter "f" indicate figures.

ABOUT THE AUTHOR

Lauren Pressley is the Instructional Design Librarian at Wake Forest University. She holds a BA degree in Philosophy and Communication from North Carolina State University and an MLIS from the University of North Carolina–Greensboro. She is active in the American Library Association, Library and Information Technology Association, and the Association of College and Research Libraries, and she regularly presents and writes on issues relating to education and technology in libraries. She was a member of the 2008 ALA Emerging Leaders class. In 2009, she was named a *Library Journal* Mover & Shaker. Lauren's first book, *So You Want to Be a Librarian*, was published in 2009 by Library Juice Press. More information can be found on her Web site at www.laurenpressley.com.

Southwest USA

THE ROUGH GUIDE

There are more than one hundred Rough Guide titles
covering destinations from Amsterdam to Zimbabwe

Forthcoming titles include
Bangkok • Barbados • Edinburgh
Japan • Jordan • Syria

Rough Guide Reference Series
Classical Music • The Internet • Jazz • Opera • Reggae
Rock Music • World Music

Rough Guide Phrasebooks
Czech • French • German • Greek • Hindi & Urdu • Indonesian • Italian
Mandarin Chinese • Mexican Spanish • Polish • Portuguese • Russian
Spanish • Thai • Turkish • Vietnamese

Rough Guides on the Internet
http://www.roughguides.com
http://www.hotwired.com/rough

Rough Guide Credits

Text Editor:	Ann-Marie Shaw
Series Editor:	Mark Ellingham
Editorial:	Martin Dunford, Jonathan Buckley, Samantha Cook, Jo Mead, Kate Berens, Amanda Tomlin, Paul Gray, Vivienne Heller, Sarah Dallas, Chris Schüler, Helena Smith, Julia Kelly, Caroline Osborne, Kieran Falconer (UK); Andrew Rosenberg (US)
Online Editors:	Alan Spicer (UK); Geronimo Madrid (US)
Production:	Susanne Hillen, Andy Hilliard, Judy Pang, Link Hall, Nicola Williamson, Helen Ostick
Cartography:	Melissa Flack, David Callier, Maxine Burke
Finance:	John Fisher, Celia Crowley, Catherine Gillespie
Marketing & Publicity:	Richard Trillo, Simon Carloss, Niki Smith (UK); Jean-Marie Kelly, SoRelle Braun (US)
Administration:	Tania Hummel, Alexander Mark Rogers

Acknowledgements

Thanks above all to Samantha Cook for her tolerance, encouragement and all the good times; my parents for their unflagging support; Annie Shaw for her adept ways as editor, neighbour and friend; Edie Jarolim for sharing her expertise so entertainingly; the much-missed Alison Cowan, who emigrated to Australia to help with the research; Robert Jones for collaborations and lunchtimes; Jules Brown for being in the same boat; Dave Reed for an evening in Basalt; Jamie Jensen; and Rona Gindin. Those who worked on the production of this book also have my gratitude, among them the inimitable Judy Pang for faultless typesetting; Maxine Burke and Stratographics for painstaking cartography; Elaine Pollard for sharp proofreading; and Nicola Williamson for inspired picture research.

Thanks also to everyone who helped while I was on the road, including Mike Pitel and Sharon Maloof in New Mexico, Jennifer Franklin in Arizona, Jean McKnight in Tucson, Steve Lewis in Santa Fe, Patty Taylor in Taos, Julie Vermontez in Monument Valley, Mary Rittman in Moab, James McKnight in Mesa, Jeri Cartwright in Salt Lake City, Jeremy Jordan in Lincoln, Mary Kay Cline and Tom Garrity in Albuquerque, and Jane Gillespie at the Grand Canyon.

The publishers and authors have done their best to ensure the accuracy and currency of all information in The Rough Guide to Southwest USA; however, they can accept no responsibility for any loss, injury, or inconvenience sustained by any traveller as a result of information or advice contained in the guide.

This edition published October 1997 by Rough Guides Ltd, 1 Mercer Street, London WC2H 9QJ.
Distributed by the Penguin Group:
Penguin Books Ltd, 27 Wrights Lane, London W8 5TZ.
Penguin Books USA Inc, 375 Hudson Street, New York 10014, USA.
Penguin Books Australia Ltd, 487 Maroondah Highway, PO Box 257, Ringwood, Victoria 3134, Australia.
Penguin Books Canada Ltd, 10 Alcorn Avenue, Toronto, Ontario, Canada M4V 1E4.
Penguin Books (NZ) Ltd, 182–190 Wairau Road, Auckland 10, New Zealand.

Printed in England by Clays Ltd, St Ives PLC
Typography and **original design** by Jonathan Dear and The Crowd Roars.
Illustrations throughout by Edward Briant.
Design and **layout** of photo inserts by Jerry Williams

A catalogue record for this book is available from the British Library.

ISBN 1-85828-239-X

Southwest USA

THE ROUGH GUIDE

Written and researched by
Greg Ward

THE ROUGH GUIDES

Help us update

We've gone to a lot of trouble to ensure that this first edition of the *Rough Guide to Southwest USA* is as accurate as possible. However, if you do spot any detail which may have changed since publication – roads get paved, trails get washed away, restaurants and hotels come and go, opening hours change, and so on – or find something that you feel should be included, we would be extremely glad to hear from you.

All future contributions will also be credited in print, and a copy of the next edition (or any other *Rough Guide* if you prefer) is the reward for the best letters.

Please mark all letters "Rough Guide to Southwest USA update" and send to:
Rough Guides, 1 Mercer St, London WC2H 9QJ or
Rough Guides, 375 Hudson St, 9th floor, New York, NY 10014.

Email should be sent to:
mail@roughguides.co.uk

Online updates about Rough Guide titles can be found on our website at http://www.roughguides.com

Rough Guides

Travel Guides • Phrasebooks • Music and Reference Guides

We set out to do something different when the first Rough Guide was published in 1982. Mark Ellingham, just out of University, was travelling in Greece. He brought along the popular guides of the day, but found they were all lacking in some way. They were either strong on ruins and museums but went on for pages without mentioning a beach or taverna. Or they were so conscious of the need to save money that they lost sight of Greece's cultural and historical significance. Also, none of the books told him anything about Greece's contemporary life – its politics, its culture, its people, and how they lived.

So with no job in prospect, Mark decided to write his own guidebook, one which aimed to provide practical information that was second to none, detailing the best beaches and the hottest clubs and restaurants, while also giving hard hitting accounts of every sight, both famous and obscure, and providing up-to-the-minute information on contemporary culture. It was a guide that encouraged independent travellers to find the best of Greece, and was a great success, getting shortlisted for the Thomas Cook travel guide award, and encouraging Mark, along with three friends, to expand the series.

The Rough Guide list grew rapidly and the letters flooded in, indicating a much broader readership than had been anticipated, but one which uniformly appreciated the Rough Guides' mix of practical detail and humour, irreverence and enthusiasm. Things haven't changed. The same four friends who began the series are still the caretakers of the Rough Guide mission today: to provide the most reliable, up-to-date and entertaining information to independent-minded travellers of all ages, on all budgets.

We now publish 100 titles and have offices in London and New York. The travel guides are written and researched by a dedicated team of more than 100 authors, based in Britain, Europe, the USA and Australia. We have also created a unique series of phrasebooks to accompany the travel series, along with the acclaimed series of music guides, and a best-selling pocket guide to the Internet and World Wide Web. We also publish comprehensive travel information on our two websites: http://www.hotwired.com/rough and http://www.roughguides.com

The Author

Greg Ward has worked for *Rough Guides* since 1985, in which time he has written *Rough Guides* to Hawaii, the Big Island, and Brittany and Normandy, edited and co-written the *Rough Guide* to the USA, edited the India guide, contributed to books on China, Mexico, France, Spain and Portugal, and helped to set up the company's desk-top publishing system.

Contents

Chapter 6 The Grand Canyon

List of Maps

MAP SYMBOLS

⊢⊣—⊢⊣	Railway	⚱	Butt
⟨15⟩	Interstate	⌓	Cave
⟨89⟩	U.S. Highway	♠	Museum
⟨21⟩	State Highway	⅃⅃	Waterfall
- - - - -	Footpath/Track	ⓘ	Tourist Office
— —	Ferry Route	⊠	Post Office
————	Waterways	ⓒ	Telephone
– – – –	Chapter Division Boundary	▣	Restaurant
■-■-■	International Borders	◎	Hotel
—··—··—	State Borders	▮	Building
✈	Airport	✛	Church
〰〰	Mountains	▦	National Park
▲	Peak	▨	Park
⋀	Arch	▨	Indian Reservation
⟁	Campsite		

Introduction

The Southwest is the most extraordinary and spectacular region of the United States. The splendour and scale of its scenery consistently defies belief – a glorious panoply of cliffs and canyons, buttes and mesas, carved from rocks of every imaginable colour, and enriched here by groves of shimmering cottonwoods and aspens, there by cactuses and agaves. In addition, the Southwest is unique in being the only part of the United States whose original inhabitants remain in residence. Though century after century has brought fresh waves of intruders, somehow none has managed entirely to displace its predecessors, leaving all to co-exist in an intriguing blend of cultures and traditions.

The area covered by this book roughly corresponds to the former Spanish colony of **New Mexico**, which has belonged to the US for a mere 150 years and is now divided between the modern states of New Mexico, Arizona, Utah, Colorado and Nevada. Though rainfall is scarce everywhere, not all the region is **desert**; indeed, the popular image of the Southwest as consisting of scrubby hillsides studded with many-armed saguaro cactuses is true only of the Sonoran Desert of southern Arizona. Towering snow-capped **mountains** rise not only in southern Colorado and northern New Mexico, at the tailend of the Rockies, but scattered across Utah and Arizona as well, while dense **pine forests** cloak much of northern Arizona.

The most dramatic landscapes are to be found on the **Colorado Plateau**, an arid mile-high tableland, roughly the size of California, that extends across the **Four Corners** region of Arizona, Utah, Colorado and New Mexico. Atop the main body of the plateau, further layers of rock are piled level upon level, creating a "**Grand Staircase**" of successive cliffs and plateaus. During the last dozen or so million years, the entire complex has been pushed steadily upwards by subterranean forces. As it's risen, the earth has cracked, warped, buckled and split, and endless quantities of crumbling sandstone have been washed away by the Colorado River and its tributaries. The **Grand Canyon** is simply the most famous of hundreds of dramatic **canyons**, and can seem too huge for the human mind to

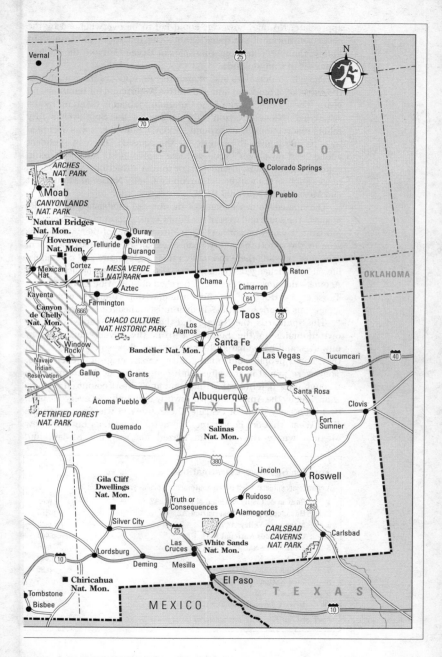

appreciate. No one, however, could fail to be overwhelmed by the sheer weirdness of **southern Utah** – the red rocks of **Monument Valley**, the fiery sandstone pinnacles of **Bryce Canyon**, the endless expanses of **Canyonlands**.

Though to outsiders such harsh terrain appears inhospitable in the extreme, it has been home to **Native Americans** for ten thousand years. These days, much of the Colorado Plateau is taken up by the self-styled "**Navajo Nation**", the largest of the Southwest's fifty Indian reservations. Until around 1300 AD, however, it was occupied by a people known to posterity as the **Anasazi**. Their magnificent adobe "cliff dwellings", squeezed like eagles' nests into crevices in soaring canyon walls, are now major tourist attractions, preserved in places such as the gorgeous **Canyon de Chelly National Monument** and **Mesa Verde National Park**.

The immediate descendants of the Anasazi established new settlements to the south and west of the Four Corners, most notably along the Rio Grande valley of northern New Mexico. Many of their villages, as seen by the sixteenth-century Spanish explorers who first called them "**pueblos**", are still there today, with their architecture and ceremonial life all but unchanged. Visiting a modern Pueblo community such as **Ácoma** – the amazing "Sky City", perched on a glowing golden mesa – **Taos**, or the **Hopi mesas** offers a unique opportunity to experience indigenous American cultures in their most authentic surviving form.

The **Spaniards**, the **Navajo** and the **Apache** all carved out their own domains in the Southwest from the seventeenth century onwards, and have shared the region – not always peacefully – with the Pueblo peoples and other Native American groups ever since. They were joined in the nineteenth century by the **Mormons**, who through utter determination and communal effort colonized modern Utah, and by the **Americans**, who swiftly outnumbered everyone else.

In the early years of US rule, the Southwest was very much the **Wild West**; that era is now recalled in towns such as **Lincoln**, New Mexico, where Billy the Kid blazed his way out of jail, and

---

Top Ten Southwest Destinations

A completely subjective list of ten Southwestern places you *must* see:

1	**Canyon de Chelly National Monument**, AZ	p.48
2	**Havasupai Indian Reservation**, AZ	p.313
3	**Monument Valley**, AZ/UT	p.43
4	**Canyonlands National Park**, UT	p.403
5	**Mesa Verde National Park**, CO	p.65
6	**Las Vegas**, NV	p.443
7	**Ácoma Pueblo**, NM	p.86
8	**Zion National Park**, UT	p.345
9	**Santa Fe**, NM	p.92
10	**Bryce Canyon National Park**, UT	p.365

Further "Top Ten" lists are scattered through the Index, beginning on p.498.

Tombstone, Arizona, where the Earps and the Clantons fought it out at the OK Corral. The century since Utah, Arizona and New Mexico achieved statehood has been characterized by attempts to transform the landscape on an unprecedented – not to say unnatural, let alone unsustainable – scale. A series of monumental **water** projects – including the construction of the **Hoover Dam**, the damming of Utah's Glen Canyon to form **Lake Powell**, and the creation of a network of canals across hundreds of miles of the Arizona desert – has brought the region prosperity as the **Sunbelt**.

While the proximity of the wilderness remains the supreme attraction for most visitors, some Southwestern **cities** make worthwhile destinations in their own right. **Santa Fe** is the best example, with its 400-year history, top-quality museums and galleries, and superb array of hotels and restaurants; **Tucson** holds an enjoyable combination of desert parks, Hispanic history, restaurants and ranch resorts; and **Las Vegas**, entirely and quintessentially a product of the twentieth century, is far too amazing to miss. **Phoenix**, on the other hand, is one to avoid; it's possible to have a good time there, but you'd have to have a *very* long vacation before there'd be much point bothering.

Though most of the region's **smaller towns** are best treated as overnight pit-stops, some have blossomed into appealing bases for a few days' stay. **Moab** is a welcome exception to the typical monotony of southern Utah farming communities; the college town of **Flagstaff** is a lively enclave within easy reach of the Grand Canyon; and **Taos** still has the feel of the artists' colony that attracted Georgia O'Keeffe and D H Lawrence.

Planning your itinerary

The only way to explore the Southwest in any detail is to **drive** yourself around; the very limited public transport options are outlined on p.20. However long your vacation may be, aim to spend most of your time on the Colorado Plateau, seeing as much as possible of the Four Corners region and southern Utah.

Your exact itinerary will depend largely on which city serves as your starting point. In **one week**, you could fly into **Las Vegas**, and loop around the Colorado River to Grand Canyon, Zion and possibly Bryce Canyon national parks; into **Phoenix**, to reach Canyon de Chelly, Monument Valley, and the Grand Canyon; into **Albuquerque**, and see Santa Fe, Taos, and Ácoma Pueblo; or to **Salt Lake City**, and make a lightning tour of all southern Utah's national parks.

With **two weeks**, you can extend any of the above itineraries to cover most of the Colorado Plateau, making sure you get to Canyon de Chelly, Monument Valley and Mesa Verde. Only if you have three weeks or more are you likely to manage any large-scale hiking – for example into the stunning Havasupai Indian Reservation, or down to Phantom Ranch in the Grand Canyon – or to detour south into southern New Mexico or southern Arizona.

When to go

Summer is the peak tourist season for most of the Southwest, though temperatures in excess of 100°F render cities such as Phoenix and Tucson all but unbearable, and make it an ordeal even to get out of your car in many of the national parks. Hikers, bikers and rafters do better to come either between mid-September and mid-October, when the crowds are gone and dazzling fall colours brighten the canyons, or in April and May, when wildflowers bloom in the desert.

If your timings aren't flexible, however, don't worry. It's always possible to escape the heat – the thermometer drops by 3°F for every thousand feet above sea level, so Santa Fe, for example, is always relatively cool – and the summer is also peak period for the region's festivals, as detailed on p.28.

Winters can be seriously cold, and snowfalls close down certain areas altogether – don't reckon on seeing Mesa Verde, or the North Rim of the Grand Canyon, between October and April. Those parks that remain open are often at their most beautiful when frosted with snow, however, while ski resorts like Telluride and Taos are in full swing, and Tucson and Phoenix fill up with sun-seeking "snowbirds" from colder states.

Average Temperature and Rainfall

	Jan	Feb	March	April	May	June	July	Aug	Sept	Oct	Nov	Dec
Grand Canyon (South Rim)												
Av High °F	41	45	51	60	70	81	84	82	76	65	52	43
Av Low °F	18	21	25	32	39	47	54	53	47	36	27	20
Rainfall (in)	*1.3*	*1.5*	*1.4*	*0.9*	*0.7*	*0.4*	*1.8*	*2.3*	*1.6*	*1.1*	*0.9*	*1.6*
Las Vegas, NV												
Av High °F	56	67	68	77	87	98	104	101	94	81	66	57
Av Low °F	33	37	42	49	59	68	75	73	65	53	41	33
Rainfall (in)	*0.5*	*0.5*	*0.4*	*0.2*	*0.2*	*0.1*	*0.5*	*0.5*	*0.3*	*0.3*	*0.4*	*0.3*
Phoenix, AZ												
Av High °F	65	69	75	84	93	102	105	102	98	88	75	66
Av Low °F	38	41	45	52	60	68	78	76	69	57	45	39
Rainfall (in)	*0.8*	*0.8*	*0.8*	*0.5*	*0.3*	*0.3*	*0.7*	*0.9*	*0.6*	*0.6*	*0.6*	*0.8*
Salt Lake City, UT												
Av High °F	37	43	51	61	72	83	93	90	80	66	50	38
Av Low °F	20	27	30	37	45	53	62	60	50	39	29	22
Rainfall (in)	*1.4*	*1.3*	*1.7*	*2.2*	*1.5*	*1.0*	*0.7*	*0.9*	*0.9*	*1.1*	*1.2*	*1.4*
Santa Fe, NM												
Av High °F	40	44	51	60	69	79	82	80	74	63	50	41
Av Low °F	19	22	28	35	43	52	57	56	49	38	27	20
Rainfall (in)	*0.6*	*0.8*	*0.8*	*0.9*	*1.2*	*1.1*	*2.4*	*2.3*	*1.7*	*1.1*	*0.7*	*0.7*
Tucson, AZ												
Av High °F	64	67	71	80	89	99	99	96	94	84	72	65
Av Low °F	38	40	44	50	58	67	74	72	67	57	45	39
Rainfall (in)	*0.8*	*0.6*	*0.7*	*0.3*	*0.1*	*0.2*	*2.4*	*2.1*	*1.3*	*0.9*	*0.6*	*0.9*
Zion National Park												
Av High °F	52	57	63	73	83	93	100	97	91	78	63	53
Av Low °F	29	31	36	43	52	60	68	66	60	49	37	30
Rainfall (in)	*1.6*	*1.6*	*1.7*	*1.3*	*0.7*	*0.6*	*0.8*	*1.6*	*0.8*	*1.0*	*1.2*	*1.5*

The Basics

Getting There from the US and Canada

For US and Canadian travellers who live too far from the Southwest USA simply to drive to the region, the most cost-effective way to visit is to **fly** to one of the four major cities described in this book, rent a car, make a loop tour, and fly back from the same airport. **Las Vegas**, Nevada, is probably the best bet, as it offers low air fares and rental-car rates, and makes an exhilarating starting point for tours to the Grand Canyon and the national parks of southern Utah. Sky Harbor International Airport in **Phoenix**, Arizona, is equally well served by the major carriers, and although Phoenix itself is a less appealing destination it's convenient for both the Grand Canyon and the deserts of southern Arizona. New Mexico's prin-

Airlines Serving the Southwest

Air Canada BC ☎ 1-800/663-3721	
www.aircanada.ca	
Eastern Canada ☎ 1-800/268-7240	
Alberta, Saskatchewan	
& Manitoba ☎ 1-800/542-8940	
US ☎ 1-800/776-3000	
Air Nevada ☎ 1-800/634-6377	
Alaska Airlines ☎ 1-800/426-0333	
www.alaska-air.com	
Alpine Air ☎ 801/575-2839	
America West ☎ 1-800/235-9292	
www.americawest.com	
American Airlines ☎ 1-800/433-7300	
www.americanair.com	
American Trans Air ☎ 1-800/435-9282	
www.ata.com	
Arizona Airways ☎ 1-800/274-0662	
Continental Airlines ☎ 1-800/525-0280	
www.flycontinental.com	
Delta Airlines ☎ 1-800/221-1212	
www.delta-air.com	
Frontier Airlines ☎ 1-800/432-1359	

Great Lakes ☎ 1-800/274-0662	
www.greatlakesav.com	
Hawaiian Airlines ☎ 1-800/367-5320	
www.hawaiianair.com	
Mesa Airlines ☎ 1-800/637-2247	
Northwest Airlines ☎ 1-800/225-2525	
www.nwa.com	
Reno Air ☎ 1-800/736-6247	
www.renoair.com	
Scenic Airlines ☎ 1-800/645-2494	
Skywest ☎ 1-800/453-9417	
www.delta-air.com	
Southwest ☎ 1-800/435-9792	
www.iflyswa.com	
TWA ☎ 1-800/221-2000	
www.twa.com	
United Airlines ☎ 1-800/241-6522	
www.ual.com	
US Airways ☎ 1-800/428-4322	
www.usairways.com	
Western Pacific ☎ 1-800/930-3030	
www.westpac.com	

Discount Travel Companies in the US and Canada

Airtech, 588 Broadway, Suite 204, New York, NY 10012; ☎212/219-7000 or 1-800/575-TECH. *Confirmed and stand-by seats.*

Council Travel, 205 E 42nd St, New York, NY 10017-5706; ☎212/822-2791 or 1-800/226-8624; www.ciee.org.
Student/budget travel agency with branches in many US cities.

Educational Travel Center, 438 N Frances St, Madison, WI 53703; ☎608/256-5551 or 1-800/747-5551; www.edtrav.com.
Student/youth and consolidator fares.

STA Travel, 10 Downing St, New York, NY 10014; ☎212/627-3111 or 1-800/777-0112; www.sta-travel.com.
Discount travel firm specializing in student/youth fares and related services, with branches in many US cities.

Travel Avenue, 10 S Riverside, Suite 1404, Chicago, IL 60606; ☎1-800/333-3335; www.travelavenue.com.
Full-service travel agent offering 7–12 percent rebates off airfares, car rentals and hotels.

Travel CUTS, 187 College St, Toronto, ON MFT 1P7; ☎416/979-2406 or 1-800/667-2887 (Canada only).
Student fares, IDs and other travel services.

Travelers Advantage, 3033 S Parker Rd, Suite 900, Aurora, CO 80014; ☎1-800/548-1116; www.TravelerAdvantage.com.
Full-service travel club.

Worldtek Travel, 111 Water St, New Haven, CT 06511; ☎203/772-0470 or 1-800/243-1723.
Discount travel agency.

Southwest Tour Operators

Actyve Ski Vacations
☎1-800/345-5021
Seven-night, first-class ski packages to Taos, NM, including air, hotel, transportation and lift passes; $1000 per person.

American Adventures
☎1-800/864-0335
Active camping tours and hosteling treks for 18- to 35-year-olds. Tours cost $39 per day and include transportation by small van, campground accommodations, guide services and park and attraction entrance fees.

Backroads, Inc
☎1-800/462-2848
Luxury hotel and camping tours covering New Mexico, Arizona and Southern Utah.

Holidaze Ski Tours
☎1-800/526-2827
Four- to seven-night moderate to upscale ski packages to Taos, NM.

Kemwel's Premier Selection
☎1-800/234-4000
Eight-night vintage train tour taking in Santa Fe and Grand Canyon, Zion and Bryce national parks, plus Salt Lake City and Denver, with historians aboard; $4000–5000.

Mountain Travel-Sobek
☎1-800/227-2384
Six-day hiking tours of Zion and Bryce national parks; $1735.

Nature Expeditions International
☎1-800/869-0639
Eight- and 16-day tours of ancient and modern native American sites in New Mexico, Arizona and Colorado; $1490–2690.

Smithsonian Odyssey Tours
☎1-800/258-5885
14-night guided tours focusing on geological wonders, including stops in Santa Fe, Durango, the Grand Canyon and Zion National Park.

Suntrek
☎1-800/292-9696
Three-week camping adventure tour of the Southwest; $882–1038.

cipal airport, in **Albuquerque**, receives fewer long-distance flights, but it's the obvious point of arrival if you want to see Santa Fe and Taos, and it's also closer than the rest to the Four Corners region. Finally, **Salt Lake City** may be in Utah's mountainous northwest corner, but it's only half a day's drive from fashionable Moab and national parks such as Canyonlands and Arches.

Fares

Flights are at their most expensive in summer, which despite soaring temperatures is the **peak season** for travel to the Southwest. Prices drop during the "shoulder" seasons – September to December, and March through May – and are lowest during January and February (excluding Christmas and New Year). Fares also vary widely according to how far in advance you make a reservation. Finding the best price of course involves shopping around; any travel agent should be prepared to check with several different airlines, and it's increasingly easy to do it yourself on the Internet.

A good first call is to contact *Southwest Airlines*, which in recent years has set out to establish itself as the lowest-price carrier to the region, travelling to Phoenix, Las Vegas, Tucson, Salt Lake City and Albuquerque from about 45 other US cities. While regular fares are competitive, travellers who plan in advance can take advantage of special promotions, such as sixty percent off published fares, with no fare higher than $99 one way. Check your local paper for promotions if *Southwest* flies from your home town.

More generally, a round-trip from New York to **Phoenix** can cost from $318; equivalent figures for Chicago might be $258, and for Los Angeles, $78. Sample fares from Montréal to Phoenix start from CAN$592, and from Vancouver CAN$282.

Fares to **Albuquerque** are similar, with a round-trip from New York costing $258, and from Chicago $496, while a round-trip between New York and **Salt Lake City** starts at $407. In general, the best bargains tend to be on routes to **Las Vegas**, although the only airline that has a regular nonstop service from New York to here is *America West*. By checking advertisements in your local newspaper, it's possible to find fares to Las Vegas for as little as $158 from Seattle, and even a two-week **fly-drive** trip from New York to Las Vegas can cost just $407 per person.

Regional and commuter airlines

Commuter airlines connect each of the Southwest's major airports with lesser communities in the region. Thus several airlines link **Phoenix** with towns such as Tucson, Flagstaff, Sedona, Yuma and Page – *America West* has the most extensive service – while **Salt Lake City** is connected with various regional airports in southern Utah. **Albuquerque** is the hub for *Mesa Airlines*, which flies to destinations including Carlsbad, Farmington, Santa Fe, Silver City and Taos. **Las Vegas** has the best connections of all, including direct flights to (and over) the Grand Canyon; operators are detailed on p.297.

Few of these flights are particularly suited to the needs of tourists, however. The cheapest fares tend to be on the scale of $50–100 for a one-way trip, and it's far easier to drive from place to place than to have to rent another car every few days.

Much the best plan if you need to get somewhere that only has a minor airport is to fly to the Southwest with a specialist **regional carrier** that will also be able to fly you to your ultimate destination for a small additional cost. For example, *Skywest*, *Delta*'s commuter airline, which serves all four principal regional airports, can fly you on to Tucson, Yuma, Page, St George and Cedar City, while if you fly into Phoenix with *America West*, it can cost just $30 extra to continue to Tucson, whereas an ordinary round-trip flight between Phoenix and Tucson can cost a ludicrous $540.

By rail

Amtrak **rail service** to and within the Southwest is restricted to three completely separate east–west routes, two of which pass through Arizona and New Mexico on the way to and from Los Angeles, while the other crosses northern Utah.

The daily *Southwest Chief* originates in Chicago and crosses from Colorado into northern New Mexico near Raton, passing close to Santa Fe (connected by a bus service from tiny Lamy) and through **Albuquerque** before heading due west via Gallup and **Flagstaff**, where connecting buses run north to the Grand Canyon. Between Albuquerque and Gallup, an onboard Native American interpretive guide talks about natural and Native American sites.

The thrice-weekly *Sunset Limited* from New Orleans reaches southern New Mexico via El

Paso, Texas, then calls at **Tucson** and Yuma as it heads across Arizona. There is no longer any rail service to **Phoenix**, though *Amtrak* run connecting buses from both Flagstaff and Tucson, or to **Las Vegas**, which is linked by bus with Barstow, California. It is however possible to reach **Salt Lake City** and **Green River** in Utah by rail, on the daily *California Zephyr* between Chicago, Denver, and San Francisco.

For fares and schedules, call ☎ 1-800/USA-RAIL or visit *www.amtrak.com*; do not contact individual stations.

By bus

If you're happy to sit on a bus for days on end, in most cases *Greyhound* offers the cheapest possible way to get to the Southwest. A one-way trip to Albuquerque from Los Angeles costs $66 and takes a day and a half; the ride from Milwaukee also takes a day and a half, and costs $131; and the two-day cross-country trek from New York costs $159.

For full details of routes and fares, and to make reservations, call *Greyhound* toll-free on ☎ 1-800/231-2222.

Insurance

Before buying an **insurance policy**, check that you're not already covered – some homeowners' or renters' policies are valid on vacation, and credit cards such as *American Express* often include some medical or other insurance, while most Canadians are covered for medical mishaps overseas by their provincial health plans. If you only need trip cancellation/interruption coverage (to supplement your existing plan), this is generally available at around $6 per $100. If you aren't already covered, however, you should consider taking out specialist **travel insurance**. The best premiums are usually to be had through student/youth travel agencies – *ISIS* (☎ 212/627-3111 or 1-800/777-0112) policies, for example, cost from $48 for fifteen days, $80 for a month. If you're planning to do any "dangerous sports" (skiing, mountaineering, etc), be sure to ask whether these activities are covered: some companies levy a surcharge. Other reliable agents include *Access America* (☎ 1-800/284-8300), *Travel Guard* (☎ 1-800/826-1300) and, in Canada, *Desjardins Travel Insurance* (☎ 1-800/463-7830).

Getting There from Britain and Ireland

Only one airline currently flies nonstop from Britain or Ireland to any of the cities covered in this book: *British Airways*, which has a daily service from London Gatwick to **Phoenix**, Arizona. Most other transatlantic carriers can get you to Phoenix, Las Vegas, Salt Lake City or Albuquerque, but all require at least one stop en route.

From **Britain**, you can either fly nonstop to the West Coast and then double back towards the Southwest, or touch down on the East Coast and then fly west; time-wise, it makes little difference. For the cheapest possible deal, and the shortest flight, it makes sense to fly nonstop to **Los Angeles** – *British Airways* and *Virgin* fly twice daily from London, while *American* and *United* fly

Airlines, Flight Agents and Tour Operators in Britain and Ireland

AIRLINES	BRITAIN	IRELAND
Aer Lingus		☎01/844 4777
Air New Zealand	☎0181/741 2299	
American Airlines	☎0345/789789	
British Airways	☎0345/222111	☎1-800/626747
Continental	☎0800/776464	
Delta	☎0800/414767	☎01/676 8080
Northwest	☎01293/561000	
TWA	☎0171/439 0707	
United	☎0181/990 9900	
Virgin Atlantic	☎01293/747747	☎01/873 3388

FLIGHT AGENTS

Campus Travel
London	☎0171/730 2101	Cambridge	☎01223/366966
Birmingham	☎0121/414 1848	Manchester	☎0161/834 0668
Brighton	☎01273/570226	Leeds	☎0113/244 9212
Bristol	☎0117/929 2494	Oxford	☎01865/792800
Cambridge	☎01223/324283		
Edinburgh	☎0131/668 3303	**Trailfinders**	
Manchester	☎0161/833 2046	London	☎0171/938 3366
Oxford	☎01865/242067	Birmingham	☎0121/236 123
		Bristol	☎0117/929 9000
Council Travel		Glasgow	☎0141/353 2224
London	☎0171/437 7767	Manchester	☎0161/839 6969

Joe Walsh Tours

Travel Bug
Dublin	☎01/676 3053	Manchester	☎0161/721 4000

STA Travel — **USIT**
		Belfast	☎01232/324073
London	☎0171/ 361 6262	Cork	☎021/270900
Bristol	☎0117/929 4399	Dublin	☎01/679 8833

TOUR OPERATORS

AmeriCan Adventures		**Greyhound International**	
Tunbridge Wells	☎01892/512700	East Grinstead	☎01342/317317
American Holidays		**North America Travel Service**	
Belfast	☎01232/238762	Leeds	☎0113/246 1466
Dublin	☎01/679 8800	**Trans Atlantic Vacations**	
Bon Voyage		Horley	☎01293/774441
Southampton	☎01703/330332	**TrekAmerica**	
British Airways Holidays		Banbury	☎01295/256777
Crawley	☎01293/722727	**Unijet**	
Destination USA		Haywards Heath	☎01444/255670
London	☎0171/253 2000	**United Vacations**	
Explore Worldwide		Heathrow Airport	☎0181/750 9648
Aldershot	☎01252/319448	**Virgin Holidays**	
		Crawley	☎01293/617181

once daily, and *Air New Zealand* five times weekly – and **drive** to the Southwest from there, taking advantage of California's low rental-car rates.
San Francisco is another possibility, though the
drive is a little longer; *British Airways* and *United*
fly there twice daily, *American* and *Virgin* fly once
daily. If you'd rather not spend time in California,
then **Las Vegas** is an inexpensive alternative;
fares tend to be relatively low, as do car-rental
rates once again.

From **Ireland**, you can either fly to New York,
Boston or Atlanta, with *Delta* or *Aer Lingus*, or fly
to London and take your pick of transatlantic
routes.

Fares and airlines

Britain remains one of the best places in Europe
to obtain flight bargains, though fares vary widely according to season, availability and the current level of inter-airline competition. Shop
around carefully for the best offers by checking
the travel ads in the weekend papers, on the holiday pages of *Teletext* or *Ceefax*, and, in London,
scouring *Time Out* and the *Evening Standard*.
Giveaway magazines aimed at young travellers,
like *TNT*, are also useful resources.

Generally, the most expensive time to fly –
high season – is from mid-June to the end of
September, and around Easter and Christmas.
March to mid-June and October, **shoulder season**, are slightly less pricey, and the rest of the
year is considered **low season** and cheaper still.
Check the exact dates of the seasons with your
operator or airline; you might be able to make
major savings by shifting your departure date by
a week – or even a day. **Weekend rates** for all
return flights tend to be around £30 more expensive than those in the week.

For an overview of the various offers, and
unofficially discounted tickets, go straight to an
agent specializing in low-cost flights. Especially if
you're under 26 or a student, they may be able
to knock up to thirty percent off the regular fares.
In low or shoulder season, you should be able to
find a return flight to California, Las Vegas or
Phoenix for around **£300** – students may get
closer to £250 – while high-season rates are
more likely to be between £400 and **£450**.

With an **open-jaw** ticket you can fly into one
city and out of another; fares are calculated by
halving the return fares to each destination and
adding the two figures together. Remember,

however, the high **drop-off fee** for returning a
rental car in a different state to the one where
you picked it up (see p.18).

Packages

Packages can work out cheaper than arranging
the same trip yourself, especially for a short-term
stay. **Fly-drive** deals, which give cut-rate (sometimes free) car rental when buying a transatlantic
ticket from an airline or tour operator, are always
cheaper than renting on the spot and give great
value if you intend to do a lot of driving. On the
other hand, you'll probably have to pay more for
the flight than if you booked it through a discount agent.

Several of the operators listed below go one
stage further and book accommodation for **self-
drive tours**. *Bon Voyage*, for example, arranges
tailor-made packages in the Southwest; the cost
of two weeks in Arizona, including the flight to
Phoenix and standard hotels, ranges from £1000
per person in low season up to £1200 in high
season. Having your itinerary planned and
booked by experts can be a real boon. Schemes
under which you buy **pre-paid hotel vouchers** in
advance, and then have to seek out hotels that
will accept them, tend to be more bother than
they're worth, and seldom save any money.

Companies such as *TrekAmerica* and
AmeriCan Adventures organize **camping tours** of
the Southwest, usually starting in California or Las
Vegas, and circling through Utah's national parks
and the Grand Canyon. Typical rates for a two-
week trip – excluding flights – range from £550
in low season up to £650 in mid-summer.

Entry requirements

Citizens of **Britain**, **Ireland** and most European
countries in possession of full passports do not
require **visas** for trips to the United States of less
than ninety days. Instead you are simply asked to
fill in the **visa waiver form** handed out on incoming planes. Immigration control takes place at
your initial point of arrival on US soil. Visitors on
the visa waiver scheme are entitled to cross the
land border into Mexico and return to the US. For
further details, contact the **American embassies**
in Britain (24/31 Grosvenor Square, London W1A
1AE; ☎0171/499 9000) or Ireland (42 Elgin Rd,
Ballsbridge, Dublin; ☎01/668 7122).

There is no British or Irish **consulate** in the
Southwest.

Insurance

Though not compulsory, **travel insurance** including medical cover is essential in view of the high costs of health care in the US. Credit cards (particularly *American Express*) often have certain levels of medical or other insurance included, especially if you use them to pay for your trip; in addition, if you have a good "all risks" home insurance policy it may well cover your possessions against loss or theft even when overseas, and many private medical schemes also cover you while abroad. If you plan to participate in potentially dangerous activities such as watersports or skiing, you'll almost certainly have to pay an extra premium; check carefully that your policy will cover you in case of an accident.

Most travel agents and tour operators sell travel insurance – policies offered by *Campus Travel* or *STA* in the UK and *USIT* in Ireland are usually reasonable value. If you feel the cover is inadequate, or you want to compare prices, any insurance broker, bank or specialist travel insurance company should be able to help: call *Columbus Travel Insurance* (☎0171/375 0011), *Endsleigh Insurance* (☎0171/436 4451), or *Frizzell Insurance* (☎01202/292 333). Two weeks' cover for a trip to the US should cost around £40, a month more like £60.

Getting There from Australia and New Zealand

There are no direct flights from Australia or New Zealand to any of the Southwestern cities, so you'll have to fly to one of the main US gateway airports and pick up onward connections – or a rental car – from there.

The cheapest route, and the one with the most frequent services from Australasia, is to **Los Angeles**, which also has plenty of onward flights to Phoenix, Las Vegas, Salt Lake City and Albuquerque. *Air New Zealand* and *Qantas* fly to LA twice daily, while *United* fly once a day; other airlines that serve LA include *America West*, *Garuda* and *Japan Airlines*.

Fares and tickets

Whatever kind of ticket you're after, start by calling one of the travel agents listed on p.11 for the latest fares and special offers. If you're a student or under 26, you may be able to undercut some of the prices given here; *STA* is a good place to start.

The most expensive time to fly, **peak season**, is during the northern summer (mid-May to end Aug) and over the Christmas period (Dec to mid-Jan); **shoulder seasons** cover March to mid-May and September, while the rest of the year is **low season**. Exact dates vary slightly between the airlines, so it's worth shopping around, especially if you have the flexibility to change your departure date by a day or two.

Airlines

	SYDNEY	AUCKLAND
Air New Zealand	☎ 13 2476	☎ 09/357 3000
America West Airlines	☎ 02/9290 2232	
American Airlines	☎ 1-800/227 101	
British Airways	☎ 02/9258 3300	☎ 09/356 8690
Garuda	☎ 1-800/800 873	☎ 09/366 1855
Japan Airlines	☎ 02/9272 1111	☎ 09/379 9906
Qantas	☎ 13 1211	☎ 0800/808 767
United Airlines	☎ 13 1777	☎ 09/379 3800

Los Angeles is the main US gateway airport for flights from Australia; when they have surplus capacity, airlines frequently offer special fares to LA, which can be as low as A$1499 from the eastern states. Otherwise, the best you're likely to find are the regular *Air New Zealand, Qantas* and *United* flights: low-season return fares to LA cost around A$1599 from the eastern states, rising to A$1629 from Western Australia; flying during peak season will add at least another A$500. Fares from New Zealand start at NZ$1799.

If you want to cover a lot of ground in a short time, US **air passes** can be a worthwhile add-on. *America West's Tri-State Pass,* available in conjunction with any international ticket, is valid for travel within California, Nevada and Arizona only; two coupons (the minimum purchase) cost approximately A$225 (prices fluctuate with the exchange rate), and additional coupons (up to a maximum of nine) cost A$75.

Packages and tours

Package deals available to Australasian travellers range from fly-drive deals to fully escorted bus tours and camping treks, and can work out significantly cheaper than making the same arrangements yourself; some of the no-frills flight and car-rental packages, for example, can cost less than a flight alone. *Insight's* West Coast fly-drive, for example, is between A$1650 and 2250, depending on the season, including return flights to LA, 14 days' car rental, and accommodation on your first night. *Creative Tours* and *Qantas Holidays* offer similar deals,

with prices starting at A$1649 for seven days, including all your accommodation.

Adventure travel companies operate hotel and camping tours, such as *Explore Worldwide's* twenty-day jaunt around Yosemite, Death Valley, Las Vegas and the Grand Canyon (A$2045–2120, airfares extra). *TrekAmerica* offers several itineraries ranging from 7 to 21 days, taking in all the main sights and national parks; their 14-day "Indian Trail" focuses on Anasazi and Navajo sites, with time for some R&R at Las Vegas (A$1305–1448, not including flights).

Entry requirements

Australian and New Zealand citizens who have full passports do not require **visas** for trips to the United States of less than ninety days; simply fill in the **visa waiver form** handed out on incoming planes. Immigration control takes place at your initial point of arrival on US soil. Visitors on the visa waiver scheme are also entitled to cross the land border into Mexico and return to the US. For further details, contact the **American embassies** in Australia (21 Moonah Place, Canberra; ☎ 02/6270 5000; premium-rated visa information service; ☎ 1902/262 682) or New Zealand (29 Fitzherbert Terrace, Thorndon, Wellington; ☎ 04/472 2068).

Neither Australia nor New Zealand has a **consulate** in the Southwest.

Travel insurance

Travel insurance, for periods ranging from a few days to a year or even longer, is available from most travel agents (see opposite) or direct from

Travel Agents And Tour Operators In Australia And New Zealand

Anywhere Travel
Sydney ☎ 02/9663 0411

Brisbane Discount Travel
Brisbane ☎ 07/3229 9211

Budget Travel
Auckland ☎ 09/366 0061 or 0800/808 040

Destinations Unlimited
Auckland ☎ 09/373 4033

Flight Centres
Sydney ☎ 13 1600
Auckland ☎ 09/309 6171

Northern Gateway
Darwin ☎ 08/8941 1394

STA Travel
Australia nearest branch ☎ 13 1776
fastfare telesales ☎ 1300/360 960
New Zealand Auckland ☎ 09/309 0458
fastfare telesales ☎ 09/366 6673

Thomas Cook
Australia local branch ☎ 13 1771
direct telesales ☎ 1800/063 913
New Zealand Auckland ☎ 09/379 3920

Specialist Agents

American Town and Country Holidays
Melbourne ☎ 03/9877 3322

American Travel Centre
Brisbane ☎ 07/3221 4788

Sydney International Travel
Sydney ☎ 02/9299 8000

Wiltrans
Sydney ☎ 02/9255 0899

Tour Operators

Creative Tours
Sydney ☎ 02/9386 2111

Explore Worldwide
Sydney ☎ 02/9956 7766
Auckland ☎ 09/524 5118

Insight
Sydney ☎ 02/9901 0444

Qantas Holidays
book through travel agents (see above)

TrekAmerica
book through STA (see above)

---

insurance companies such as *Cover More* (☎ 02/9202 8000 or 1-800/251 881) and *Ready Plan* (☎ 03/9791 5077 or 1-800/337 462). Most policies are similar in premium and coverage – but if you plan to indulge in high-risk activities such as mountaineering or bungee jumping, check the policy carefully to make sure you'll be covered.

A typical policy for travel in the United States costs A$130/NZ$145 for two weeks ,A$190/NZ$210 for a month, and A$280/NZ$310 for two months.

Information and Maps

Phoenix and Santa Fe, also have **free newspapers** carrying dining and entertainment listings. In addition, you're likely to come across the useful **Welcome Centers**, along the interstates close to the state borders, which dispense maps and information on the entire state.

The **USTTA** – United States Travel and Tourism Administration – has offices all over the world, usually in US embassies and consulates. These serve mainly as clearing houses, stocking vast quantities of printed material, but are unable to help with queries on specific states or cities. In Britain, you can only contact them by telephone, on ☎0171/495 4466 (Mon–Fri 10am–4pm).

Each state in this book has its own **tourist office**, which can provide prospective visitors with a colossal range of free maps, leaflets and brochures. Contact them in advance of your departure, and be as specific as possible about your interests.

Visitor centers in most towns – often known as the "Convention and Visitors Bureau", or CVB, and listed throughout this book – provide details on the area. Larger towns such as Las Vegas,

Maps

By far the best general-purpose **map** for the principal areas covered by this book is the *Guide to Indian Country*, available free to members of the *American Automobile Association* (see p.19), and sold throughout the Southwest at $3.95. It focuses on the Four Corners region, however, and does not extend into southern Arizona, southern New Mexico, or Nevada. Each individual state also issues a free **highway map**, which is fine for general driving and route planning, and can be obtained either direct from the tourist office or

---

State Tourist Offices

Arizona Office of Tourism
2702 N Third St, Suite 4015 , Phoenix, AZ 85004
☎602/230-7733 or ☎1-888/520-3434,
fax 602/542-4068
www.arizonaguide.com

Colorado Tourism Board
1625 Broadway, Suite 1700, Denver CO 80202
☎303/592-5510 or ☎1-800/433-2656
www.colorado.com

Nevada Commission on Tourism
Capitol Complex. Carson City NV 89710
☎702/687-4322 or ☎1-800/638-2328,
fax 702/687-6779
www.travelnevada.com

New Mexico State Tourism
491 Old Santa Fe Trail
Santa Fe NM 87503-2003
☎505/827-0291 or ☎1-800/733-6390
www.newmexico.org

Utah Travel Council
Council Hall, Capitol Hill
Salt Lake City UT 84114
☎801/538-1030 or ☎1-800/200-1160,
fax 801/538-1399
www.netpub.com/utah!

---

from local visitor centers. Free **town maps** are generally available at local visitor centers.

All **national parks**, and most state parks, national forests and the like – as detailed on p.21 – provide reasonable maps to visitors. Both these, and the maps throughout this book, are adequate for day-hikes on the most popular trails. Serious hikers and backpackers, however, should equip themselves with detailed **topographical maps**. Among the best are the waterproof and tearproof maps of individual national parks published by *Trails Illustrated* (PO Box

3610, Evergreen CO 80439; ☎1-800/962-1643), who also produce state maps of Colorado, Utah and New Mexico.

Rand McNally produce good **commercial maps**, bound together in their *Rand McNally Road Atlas*, or printed separately for each state. They also run 24 stores across the US; call ☎1-800/333-0136 (ext 2111) for their locations, or for direct mail maps. Britain's best source of maps is *Stanfords*, at 12–14 Long Acre, London WC2E 9LP (☎0171/836 1321), who have a mail-order service.

Costs and Money

This book contains detailed price information for lodging and eating throughout the Southwest. Accommodation rates are coded according to the system explained on p.15, which excludes any local taxes that may apply, while restaurant prices include food only and not drinks or tip. For museums and similar attractions, the entrance fees quoted are for adults; unless specified otherwise, assume that children get in half-price. Naturally, costs will increase slightly overall during the life of this edition.

Costs

North American travellers find **prices** in the Southwest broadly similar to the rest of the US, with food and lodging generally cheaper than in major US cities and tourist regions, and gas and groceries,

especially in out-of-the-way places, a little more expensive. Most visitors from Europe and Australasia feel that their money goes further in the US than it does at home. However, if you're used to travelling in the less expensive countries of Europe, let alone in the rest of the world, you can't expect to scrape by on the same minuscule budget in the US.

As explained on p.18, the only way to reach most of the places described in this book is to drive. If you can't bring your own vehicle, your least avoidable major expense will be **car rental**, at around $150 per week. What you spend on **accommodation** is more flexible. For most of the year, in most places, you should have no problem getting a motel room for under $40, though even the cheapest peak-season rates in or near certain national parks, or in downtown Santa Fe, are more like $70. Although hostels offering dorm beds – usually for $12 to $15 – are reasonably common, they're by no means everywhere, and in any case they save little money for two or more people travelling together. **Camping** is not only cheap, with federal and state park campgrounds ranging from free to perhaps $10 per night, but for many wilderness areas it's the only option.

As for **food**, $15 per day is enough to get an adequate life-support diet, consisting of perhaps one full-scale meal in a local diner supplemented by a stash of groceries, while for a daily total of around $30 you can eat pretty well. If you're visiting a significant number of **national parks** and monuments, buy a *Golden Eagle* pass (see p.21); the $25 fee covers all passengers in your vehicle. You'll probably also average another $5 or $10 a day on admissions to state parks, museums and the like.

The most economical possible vacation, therefore, with two people sharing a rental car, camping in state and federal parks most nights, and eating one restaurant meal per day, will work out at something over $200 per person per week.

For advice on **tipping** and **taxes**, see p.26 and p.32.

Taking, changing and accessing money

Expect to pay most of your major expenses by **credit card**; hotels and car rental agencies usually demand a credit card imprint as security, even if you intend to settle the bill in cash, and you'll be at a serious disadvantage if you don't have one. *Visa, Mastercard, Diners Club, American Express* and *Discover* are the most widely used.

You'll also need to carry a certain amount of **cash**. If you have a *Mastercard* or *Visa*, or a cash-dispensing card linked to an international network such as *Cirrus* or *Plus* – check with your home bank before you set off – you can withdraw cash from appropriate automatic teller machines (**ATMs**). For both American and foreign visitors, **US dollar travellers' cheques** are a better way to carry money than ordinary bills; they offer the great security of knowing that lost or stolen cheques will be replaced. Cheques such

as *American Express, Visa* and *Thomas Cook* are universally accepted as cash in shops, restaurants and gas stations, and change from your transactions will be rendered in hard currency. Be sure to have plenty of $10 and $20 denominations, and don't be put off by "no checks" signs, which only refer to personal cheques. Foreign travellers should *not* bring travellers' cheques issued in their own currencies; it can be hard to find a bank prepared to change them, and no other business is likely to accept them.

Emergencies

Assuming you know someone who is prepared to send you money in a crisis, the quickest way is to have them take the cash to the nearest *American Express Moneygram* (☎1-800/543-4080) office and have it instantaneously **wired** to the office nearest you, subject to the deduction of ten percent commission. In the US this process should take no longer than ten minutes. They charge according to the amount sent (ranging from $13 to wire $100, to $49 for $1000). *Western Union* offer a similar service, at slightly higher rates (US ☎1-800/325-6000; UK ☎0800/833833); if credit cards are involved they charge an extra $10.

If you have a few days' leeway, it's cheaper to mail a **postal money order**, which is exchangeable at any post office. The equivalent for foreign travellers is the **international money order**, for which you need to allow up to seven days in the mail before arrival. An ordinary cheque sent from overseas takes two to three weeks to clear.

Foreign travellers in real difficulties also have the final option of throwing themselves on the mercy of their nearest national consulate, who will – in worst cases only – repatriate you, but will never, under any circumstances, lend money.

Money: A Note for Foreign Travellers

US currency comes in bills of $1, $5, $10, $20, $50 and $100, plus various larger (and rarer) denominations. All are the same size and same green colour, making it necessary to check each bill carefully. The dollar is made up of 100 cents in coins of 1 cent (known as a penny), 5 cents (a nickel), 10 cents (a dime) and 25 cents (a quarter). Change – especially quarters – is needed for buses, vending machines and telephones, so always carry plenty.

Generally speaking, one **pound sterling** will buy between $1.50 and $1.70; one **Canadian dollar** is worth between 70¢ and 90¢; one **Australian dollar** is worth between 70¢ and 90¢; and one **New Zealand dollar** is worth between 60¢ and 75¢.

To report stolen travellers' cheques and credit cards, call:

American Express	
cheques	☎ 1-800/221-7282
American Express cards	☎ 1-800/528-4800
Citicorp	☎ 1-800/645-6556
Diners Club	☎ 1-800/234-6377
Mastercard	☎ 1-800/826-2181
Thomas Cook/Mastercard	☎ 1-800/223-9920
Visa cheques	☎ 1-800/227-6811
Visa cards	☎ 1-800/336-8472

Accommodation

For advice on **camping**, see the "Outdoors" section beginning on p.21.

On the whole, **accommodation** in the Southwest is relatively inexpensive. Most travellers simply want a bed for the night before moving on the next day, so **motels** everywhere provide clean, no-frills places to sleep without bothering to offer additional amenities. Basic room rates in rural areas are as low as $30 per night, while prices along the major highways and interstates start at more like $40. Only in the most popular summer destinations – cities such as Santa Fe, or "gateway" towns near the major national parks – will you find it hard to find a room for under $60. If you prefer a bit more comfort, it's almost always available, and in most areas covered by this book you can get a room in a top-class hotel for well under $100.

At the lower end of the spectrum, a fair number of budget **hostels** are scattered across the region, but with a single dorm bed usually costing between $10 and $15, groups of two or more will find them little cheaper than motels. Many motel rooms hold two double beds, and will accommodate three or four guests for slightly

over the normal two-person rate. On the other hand, the lone traveller has a hard time of it: a "single" room is just a double at a fractionally reduced rate.

Wherever you stay, you'll be expected to pay in advance, at least for the first night and perhaps for further nights too. Most places ask for a credit card imprint when you arrive, but they'll also accept cash or dollar travellers' cheques. Reservations – essential in busy areas in summer – are only held until 5pm or 6pm unless you've warned the hotel you'll be arriving late.

Hotels and motels

It is consistently easy to find a basic **motel** room in the Southwest. Drivers approaching any significant town are confronted by lines of motels along the highway, while the choice along major cross-country routes is phenomenal. Most towns mentioned in this book hold more motels than there's room to review; the very few that have none at all are clearly indicated.

Hotels and **motels** are essentially the same thing, although motels tend to be located beside main roads away from city centres, and thus are much more accessible to drivers. The budget ones are pretty basic affairs, but in general there's a uniform standard of comfort everywhere – each room comes with a double bed, a TV and phone, and an attached bathroom – and you

---

Accommodation Price Codes

Throughout this book, **room rates** in hotels, motels and B&Bs are indicated with the symbols below, according to the cost of their least expensive double rooms, **excluding taxes**, which can add between five and fifteen percent. Significant seasonal variations are indicated as appropriate, as are establishments that hold rooms at widely differing prices.

① up to $30	② $30–45	③ $45–60
④ $60–80	⑤ $80–100	⑥ $100–130
⑦ $130–175	⑧ $175–250	⑨ $250+

Hotel, Hostel and Motel Chains			
Best Western (③–⑤)	☎ 1-800/528-1234	Howard Johnson (②–④)	☎ 1-800/446-4656
Comfort Inn (④–⑤)	☎ 1-800/221-2222	Motel 6 (②)	☎ 505/891-6161
Days Inn (④–⑤)	☎ 1-800/329-7466	Ramada Inn (④ and up)	☎ 1-800/272-6232
Econolodge (②–④)	☎ 1-800/424-4777	Sleep Inn (②)	☎ 1-800/221-2222
Hilton Hotels (⑤ and up)	☎ 1-800/445-8667	Super 8 (②–③)	☎ 1-800/800-8000
Holiday Inn (④ and up)	☎ 1-800/465-4329	Travelodge (②)	☎ 1-800/578-7878
Hostelling International – American Youth Hostels (①)	☎ 1-800/444-6111	YMCA (①–②)	☎ 1-800/922-9622

don't get a much better deal by paying, say, $60 instead of $40. Over $60, the room and its fittings simply get bigger and more luxurious, and there'll probably be a swimming pool which guests can use for free.

The very cheapest properties tend to be family-run, independent motels, but there's a lot to be said for paying a few dollars more to stay in motels belonging to the national **chains**. After a few days on the road, you should find that a particular chain consistently suits your requirements (*Super 8* is a personal recommendation). You can then use its central reservation number, listed above, to book ahead, and possibly obtain discounts as a regular guest.

During off-peak periods many motels and hotels struggle to fill their rooms, and it's worth haggling to get a few dollars off the asking price. Staying in the same place for more than one night will bring further reductions. Additionally, look out for **discount coupons**, especially in the free magazines distributed by local visitor centers and interstate welcome centers. These can offer amazing value – $20 for a double room in a comfortable mid-range chain – but read the small print, as rates are often limited to midweek.

Not many budget hotels or motels bother to compete with the ubiquitous diners and offer **breakfast**, although many provide free self-service coffee and sticky buns.

Bed and breakfasts

Over the last decade or so, **bed and breakfast** has become an ever more popular option, often as a luxurious – if not necessarily any more expensive – alternative to conventional hotels. Some B&Bs consist of no more than a couple of furnished rooms in someone's home, and even the larger establishments tend to have no more than ten rooms, without TV and phone but often laden with flowers, stuffed cushions and an almost over-contrived homely atmosphere.

The price you pay for a B&B – which varies from around $50 to $130 – always includes a huge and wholesome breakfast. The crucial determining factor is whether or not each room has an en-suite bathroom; most B&Bs feel obliged to provide private bath facilities, although that can damage the authenticity of a fine old house. Those that do tend to cost between $60 and $80 per night for a double. At the top end of the price spectrum, the distinction between a "hotel" and a "bed and breakfast inn" may amount to no more than that the B&B is owned by a private individual rather than a chain.

In many areas, B&Bs have grouped together to form central **booking agencies**, making it much easier to find a room at short notice; we've given addresses and numbers for these where appropriate. Statewide organizations include the *Arizona Association of B&B Inns* (PO Box 7186, Phoenix AZ 85011; ☎ 1-800/284-2589), the *New Mexico B&B Association* (PO Box 2925, Santa Fe NM 87504-2925; ☎ 505/766-5380 or 1-800/661-6649), and the *Utah B&B Association* (PO Box 3066, Park City UT 84060; ☎ 801/595-0332).

Ys and youth hostels

Around twenty **hostels** provide accommodation for backpackers and budget travellers in the Southwest. Most work out little cheaper than motels, so there's little point staying in hostels unless you prefer their youthful ambience and sociability. Note also that many are not accessible on public transport, or particularly convenient for sightseeing in the towns and cities, let alone in rural areas.

Hostels belonging to the official **HI-AYH** (*Hostelling International–American Youth Hostels*) network tend to impose curfews and limited daytime hours, and segregate dormitories by sex. Most expect guests to bring sheets or sleeping bags. Rates range from $8 up to around $15 for *HI* members; non-members generally pay an additional $3 per night.

There's also a growing number of **independent hostels**, of which some may have failed to meet the *HI*'s (fairly rigid) criteria, but most simply choose not to be tied down by *HI* regulations. Many are no more than converted motels, where the "dorms" consist of a couple of sets of bunk beds in a musty room, which is also let out as a private room on demand; others may be purpose-built rural properties, or at least converted and modernized to a high standard.

In addition, **YMCA/YWCA** hostels (known as "Ys"), provide mixed-sex or, in a few cases, women-only accommodation, at prices ranging from around $12 for a dormitory bed to $20–35 for a single or double room. Ys offering accommodation (and not all do, many being basically health clubs) are often in older buildings in less than ideal neighbourhoods, but facilities can include a gym, a swimming pool and an inexpensive cafeteria.

Especially in high season, it's advisable to reserve ahead by writing to the relevant hostel and enclosing a deposit. The maximum stay is often restricted to three days, though this rule tends to be ignored if there's space. Few hostels provide meals but most have cooking facilities.

The *Hostel Handbook for the USA and Canada*, produced each May, lists over four hundred hostels and is available for $2 from Jim Williams, *Sugar Hill House International Hostel*, 722 St Nicholas Ave, New York, NY 10031 (☎212/926-7030). *Hostelling North America*, the *HI* guide to hostels in the USA and Canada, is available free of charge to any overnight guest at *HI-AYH* hostels or direct from the *HI National Office*, PO Box 37613, Washington DC 20005 (☎202/783-6161).

Overseas travellers will find a comprehensive list of hostels in the *International Youth Hostel Handbook*. In the UK, it's available from the *Youth Hostel Association* headquarters/shop, at 14 Southampton St, London WC2 7HY (☎0171/836 1036), where you can also buy a year's *HI* membership for £9 (under-18s £3).

Southwest Youth Hostels

Albuquerque, NM	p.160	Page, AZ	p.393
Antonito, CO	p.149	Panguitch, UT	p.364
Bryce, UT	p.369	Phoenix, AZ	p.203
Cedar Crest, NM	p.115	Pilar, NM	p.127
Durango, CO	p.72	Salt Lake City, UT	p.458
Flagstaff, AZ	p.260	Santa Fe, NM	p.97
Hurricane, UT	p.342	Silver City, NM	p.191
Kanab, UT	p.362	Taos, NM	p.137
Las Vegas, NV	p.448	Telluride, CO	p.74
Moab, UT	p.425	Truth or Consequences, NM	p.188
Oscuro, NM	p.172	Tucson, AZ	p.220

Getting Around

Attempting to tour the Southwest by public transport is an extremely bad idea. Buses and planes – and trains to a much lesser extent – connect the major urban areas, but public transport within the cities is minimal. The region's greatest attraction, its national parks and wide-open landscapes, simply can't be explored without your own vehicle. Unless you're an *extremely* energetic cyclist, therefore, you'll need a motorbike or car.

If you can't drive, the only itinerary that makes much sense is to cross northern Arizona and northern New Mexico by bus or train, flying in or out of **Albuquerque** in the east or **Las Vegas** in the west. Obvious stops would include **Flagstaff**, with a side-trip by bus to the Grand Canyon, and **Santa Fe**, the only city small enough to be seen on foot. Phoenix and Tucson are no fun at all without a car, while what little public transport exists in southern Utah is no use for seeing the parks. **Hitchhiking** is not recommended under any circumstances.

By car

To **rent** a car, you're supposed to have held your licence for at least one year; drivers under 25 years old may encounter problems, and have to pay higher than normal insurance premiums. Rental companies expect customers to have credit cards; if you don't, they may let you leave a cash deposit (at least $200), but don't count on it.

All the major rental companies have outlets at the main regional airports. Reservations are handled centrally rather than locally, so calling their national toll-free numbers is the best way to shop around for **rates**. Potential variations are endless; certain cities and states are consistently cheaper than others, while individual travellers may be eligible for corporate, frequent-flier or *AAA* discounts. In low season, you might find a tiny car (a "subcompact") for as little as $100 per week, but a typical budget rate would be more like $35–40 per day, and $150 per week. A car rented in Las Vegas, Nevada, can easily cost $100 less per week than one rented in Colorado, and prices in Arizona, New Mexico and Utah are ranged between the two.

Don't automatically go for the cheapest rate. Little-known local rental companies, such as *Ladki Rent-a-Car* in Las Vegas, may offer especially appealing prices, but if you break down several hundred miles from their offices it may be hard to get assistance. Even between the major operators, there can be a big difference in the quality of cars. Industry leaders like *Hertz* and *Avis* tend to have newer, lower-mileage cars, often with air-conditioning and stereo cassette decks as standard equipment – no small consideration on a 3000-mile desert drive. Always be sure to get free **unlimited mileage**, and remember that leaving the car in a different city to the one where you rent it can incur a drop-off charge of as much as $200.

When you rent a car, read the small print carefully for details on **Collision Damage Waiver** (CDW), sometimes called Liability Damage Waiver (LDW), a form of insurance which often isn't included in the initial rental charge but is well worth considering. This specifically covers the car that you are driving yourself – you are in any case insured for damage to other vehicles. At $10–15 a day, it can add substantially to the total cost, but without it you're liable for every scratch to the car – even those that aren't your fault. Some credit card companies offer automatic CDW coverage to anyone using their card; contact your issuing company for details.

Your rental papers should include an emergency number to call in case of breakdown or acci-

For advice on **driving in the desert**, see p.24.

Car Rental Companies

	USA	UK	Ireland	Australia
Alamo	☎ 1-800/354-2322	☎ 0800/272200		
Avis	☎ 1-800/331-1212	☎ 0990/900500	☎ 01232/240404	☎ 1-800/225 533
Budget	☎ 1-800/527-0700	☎ 0800/181181	☎ 01232/230700	☎ 13 2727
Dollar	☎ 1-800/421-6868	☎ 01895/233300		
Enterprise	☎ 1-800/325-8007			
Ladki Rent-a-Car	☎ 1-702/597-2900			
Hertz	☎ 1-800/654-3131	☎ 0990/996699	☎ 01/660 2255	☎ 13 3039
Holiday Autos		☎ 0990/300400	☎ 01/454 9090	
National	☎ 1-800/227-7368	☎ 01345/222525	☎ 01232/450904	
Rent-A-Wreck	☎ 1-800/535-1391			
Thrifty	☎ 1-800/367-2277	☎ 01494/442 110		
Value	☎ 1-800/468-2583			

dent. Contact the rental company before you arrange, or pay, for any repairs. Women in particular should also consider renting a mobile telephone with their car – you often only have to pay a nominal amount until you actually use it, and it can be a lifesaver should something go terribly wrong.

The *American Automobile Association*, or *AAA* (4100 E Arkansas Drive, Denver CO 80222; ☎ 1-800/222-4357), provides free maps and assistance to its members, and to members of affiliated associations overseas, such as the British *AA* and *RAC*.

Renting an RV

RVs, or Recreational Vehicles – those huge juggernauts that rumble down the highway complete with multiple bedrooms, bathrooms and kitchens – can be rented from around $400 per week (plus mileage charges) for a basic camper on the back of a pickup truck. Though good for groups or families travelling together, these can be unwieldy on the road. Also, rental outlets are not as common as you might expect, as people tend to own their RVs. On top of rental fees, take into account the cost of gas (some RVs do twelve miles to the gallon or less) and any drop-off charges. It is rarely legal simply to pull up in an RV and spend the night at the roadside; you are expected to stay in designated parks that cost up to $20 per night.

The *Recreational Vehicle Dealers Association*, 3251 Old Lee Highway, Fairfax VA 22030

(☎ 703/591-7130 or 1-800/336-0355), publishes a newsletter and a directory of rental firms. Among the larger companies offering RV rentals are *Cruise America* (☎ 1-800/327-7799), *Go! Vacations* (☎ 1-800/845-9888) and *Grand Travel Systems* (☎ 602/939-6909 or 1-800/849-9959).

Driving for foreigners

UK nationals can drive in the US on a full UK driving licence (International Driving Permits are not always regarded as sufficient). Fly-drive deals are good value if you want to rent a car (see pp.8 & 10), though you can save up to sixty percent simply by booking in advance with a major firm. If you choose not to pay until you arrive, be sure you take a written confirmation of the price with you. Remember that most standard rental cars have automatic transmissions, and that it's safer not to drive immediately after a long transatlantic flight.

It's also easier and cheaper to book **RV**s in advance from Britain. Most travel agents who specialize in the US can arrange RV rental, and usually do it cheaper if you book a flight through them as well. A price of £400 for a five-berth van for two weeks is fairly typical.

Buying a secondhand car, and selling it at the end of your trip, might sound like a money-saving idea. Quite apart from finding a reliable vehicle, however, registering and insuring it is a complicated and expensive business. Each state has different regulations; contact the *AAA* for details.

By bike

While riding a bike in the Southwest can be absolutely exhilarating, long-distance cyclists face a fearsome challenge, above all in the heat of summer. Neighbouring towns can be as much as a hundred miles apart, along desert highways that offer neither food, water nor shade. Quite apart from the high mountains and deep canyons, most areas covered in this book are a mile or more above sea level, so the altitude alone can be a real problem. The only road from A to B may well turn out to be a major interstate; when there's no alternative, cyclists are generally allowed to ride on interstate shoulders, but they have to battle the slipstream of mighty trucks.

If you have a good bike and know how to maintain it, however, and time your trip for the cooler months, it is feasible to explore the Southwest by bike. Specific regions that lend themselves to **cycle touring** are north-central New Mexico, where countless routes radiate from Santa Fe; the vicinity of Flagstaff and Sedona in Arizona; and southwest Utah, around Zion National Park. Other areas have seen a recent boom in **mountain-biking**, such as Moab, Utah – home of the gruelling Slickrock Bike Trail (see p.426) – and Durango, Colorado.

For general **information** and advice, contact the *New Mexico Touring Society*, 4115 12th St NW, Albuquerque NM 87107 (☎505/298-0085), the *Arizona Bicycle Club*, PO Box 7191, Phoenix AZ 85011 (☎602/264-5478), or ask the Utah Travel Council (see p.12) for a free *Bicycle Utah Vacation Guide*. The national, non-profit **Adventure Cycling Association** (formerly *Bikecentennial*), at 150 E Pine St, Missoula MT 59807 (☎406/721-1776), publishes maps ($6.95 each) of several 400-mile routes, detailing campgrounds, motels, restaurants, bike shops and sites of interest. Their *Southwest America Bicycle Trail* runs from Yuma up to Flagstaff and

the Grand Canyon, then crosses the Navajo and Hopi reservations to Gallup. *Backroads Bicycle Tours*, 1516 Fifth St, Berkeley CA 94704 (☎510/527-1555 or 1-800/462-2848), and the *HI-AYH* hostelling group (see p.17) also arrange group tours.

Greyhound, *Amtrak* and major airlines all carry passengers' bicycles – dismantled and packed into a box – for a small additional fee.

By train

Details of the very limited *Amtrak* **rail service** to and across the Southwest appear on p.5. There are also a number of **historic** and **scenic rail-roads** in the region – some of them steam-powered or running along narrow-gauge mining tracks – including the *Cumbres and Toltec* line in northern New Mexico (see p.149), the *Grand Canyon Railway* between Williams and the Grand Canyon in Arizona (see p.296), and the *Durango & Silverton Narrow Gauge Railroad* in Colorado (see p.71).

By bus

Greyhound **buses** link all major cities and many smaller towns in the Southwest; for fares, schedules and reservations, call ☎1-800/231-2222. Routes that are particularly useful for tourists – as well as services offered by other operators – are detailed at the relevant points in this book.

While scheduled buses can get you from city to city, they're of no use when it comes to enjoying the great outdoors. **Tour buses**, however, do set off into the wilderness from most major towns; they too are detailed throughout this book.

Commuter flights within the Southwest are detailed on p.5.

Outdoors

Cut by deep canyons, coated by dense forests and capped by great mountains, the Southwest glories in some of the most fabulous wilderness areas in the United States. By far the easiest way for visitors to enjoy this natural wonderland is to plot an itinerary that samples the countless national, state and county parks. These are not necessarily the most beautiful places of all – after all, some are simply lands that pioneer farmers, Indian tribes, and mining corporations alike never bothered or managed to grab – but they do offer the campgrounds and hiking trails that make backcountry exploration possible even for the least experienced tourists.

> For up-to-the-minute information on the national park system, access the official park-service **Web site** at *www.nps.gov/parklists/nm.html*. It features full details of the main attractions of the national parks, plus opening hours, the best times to visit, admission fees, hiking trails and visitor facilities.

National parks and monuments

The **National Park Service** administers both national parks and national monuments. The park service is sadly underfunded – it doesn't even get to keep park entrance fees, which are absorbed into the general Federal treasury – and in style and design most of its visitor centers and other facilities still date conspicuously from the 1950s. Nonetheless, its rangers do a superb job of providing information and advice to visitors, maintaining trails, and organizing such activities as free guided hikes and campfire talks.

Most parks and monuments charge an admission fee of between $4 and $20, which covers a vehicle and all its occupants. For $50, they also sell the *Golden Eagle* pass, which gives a named driver, and all passengers in the same vehicle, a year's unlimited access to (almost) every national park and monument. Separate passes are available for disabled travellers and senior citizens – see p.31 and p.32 respectively.

In theory, a **national park** preserves an area of outstanding natural beauty, encompassing a wide range of terrain as well as sites of historic interest, while a **national monument** is much smaller, focusing perhaps on just one archeological site or geological phenomenon and thus holding a narrower appeal for tourists. In practice, however, the distinction between the Southwest's national parks and national monuments is somewhat blurred. Most of the **parks** cover desert regions that have barely known human occupation, and thus boast little historic significance, and while the **Grand Canyon** and **Zion** are huge and very varied, parks such as **Bryce Canyon** and **Carlsbad Caverns** are essentially one-trick wonders. Many of the **monuments** do consist of a single Indian ruin or nineteenth-century fort, but several more are as diverse and spectacular as the parks. Arizona's **Canyon de Chelly** would surely be a national park were it not on the Navajo reservation, while the new **Grand Staircase-Escalante** monument in Utah is larger than any park.

Hotel-style **lodges** are found only in the major parks – specifically, the Grand Canyon, Zion, Bryce and Mesa Verde. However, both parks and monuments tend to have at least one well-organized **campground** for visitors. With appropriate free permits – subject to number restrictions in popular parks – backpackers can also usually

> ### Adventure Travel
>
> The opportunities for **active travelling** in the Southwest are all but endless. In the last few years, the former uranium mining town of **Moab**, Utah, has grown to become the region's major base for adventure travel of all kinds. Mountain biking is its speciality, with rafting and four-wheel-driving (universally abbreviated to 4WD) a close second; full listings can be found on p.426. Other towns popular with energetic visitors include **Durango**, Colorado (see p.71) and **Sedona**, Arizona (see p.269); guides, outfitters and local tour operators are recommended throughout this book.

camp in the **backcountry** (a general term for areas inaccessible by road, as opposed to the frontcountry).

While national parks tend to be perfect places to **hike** – almost all have extensive trail networks – they're all far too large to tour on foot. Canyonlands in Utah is an extreme example, with its different sections lying a hundred miles apart, but of all the parks in this book only the Grand Canyon could conceivably be visited using **public transport**. If you don't have a vehicle of your own, your only option is to join a sightseeing tour from some nearby town.

Other public lands

National parks and monuments are often surrounded by tracts of **national forest**, which are also federally administered, but are much less protected. While these too tend to hold appealing rural campgrounds, each is in the words of the slogan a "Land Of Many Uses", and usually allows some limited logging and other land-based industry – ski resorts more often than strip mines, fortunately.

Further government departments administer a whole range of wildlife refuges, national scenic rivers, recreation areas and the like – such administration consisting basically of leaving the natural landscape alone. The **Bureau of Land Management** (BLM) has the largest holdings of all, most of it open rangeland, such as in Utah, but also including some enticingly out-of-the-way reaches.

State parks and state monuments are a mirror-image of the federal system, preserving sites of more limited, local significance. Many are explicitly designed for recreational use, and thus hold better campgrounds than their federal equivalents.

Camping and backpacking

The ideal way to see the Southwest – especially if you're on a low budget – is to tour the region by car, and **camp** at night in state and federal campgrounds. These may lack the luxury of the commercially run campgrounds, found in abundance near the larger towns, but they tend to be far more peaceful, far more scenic, and far better positioned for days of hiking and canyoneering.

Camping on Public Lands

Mailing addresses for individual **national parks** are given throughout this book. For more general maps and information on camping on public lands, contact the following organizations:

National Forest Service
Southwest Regional Office
517 Gold Ave SW
Albuquerque NM 87102
☎505/842-3292

National Forest Service
Intermountain Regional Office
2501 Wall Ave
Ogden UT 84401
☎801/524-5030

Bureau of Land Management
Arizona State Office
3707 North Seventh St
Phoenix AZ 85011
☎602/650-0528

Bureau of Land Management
New Mexico State Office
1474 Rodeo Rd
Santa Fe NM 87502
☎505/438-7400

Bureau of Land Management
Utah State Office
PO Box 45155
324 S State St, #301
Salt Lake City UT 84145-0155
☎801/539-4001

Arizona State Parks Office
1300 W Washington, #150
Phoenix AZ 85007
☎620/542-4174

New Mexico State Park and Recreation Division
408 Galisteo St, PO Box 1147
Santa Fe NM 87504-1147
☎505/827-7465

Utah Division of Parks and Recreation
1636 W North Temple, #116
Salt Lake City UT 84116-3156
☎801/538-7221

Typical public campgrounds range in **price** from free (usually when there's no water available, which may be seasonal) to around $8 per night; commercial fees are more like $15–20, for campgrounds that can be more like open-air hotels, with shops, restaurants and washing facilities.

There may be plenty of campgrounds, but there are also plenty of people who want to use them: if you're camping during public holidays or the high season, you should either reserve in advance or avoid the most popular areas. By contrast, basic campgrounds in isolated areas may well be completely empty whatever time of year you're there, and if there's any charge at all you'll be expected to pay by leaving the money in the bin provided.

Backcountry camping in the national parks is usually free, by permit (see pp.21–22). Before you set off on anything more than a half-day hike, and whenever you're headed for anywhere at all isolated, be sure to inform a ranger of your plans, and ask about weather conditions and specific local tips. Carry sufficient food and drink to cover emergencies, as well as all the necessary equipment and maps. In summer in the national parks, you have to carry so much water – see below – that you'll need to lighten your load as much as possible, perhaps by sleeping in a lightweight sack rather than a sleeping bag.

When camping rough, check that **fires** are permitted before you start one; even if they are, try to use a camp stove in preference to local materials – in some places firewood is scarce, although you may be allowed to use deadwood. In wilderness areas, try to camp on previously used sites. Where there are no toilets, bury human waste at least six inches into the ground and a hundred feet from the nearest water supply and campground. Burn what trash you can, and take the rest away.

Desert survival

If you plan to go **hiking in the desert**, the crucial thing is to plan ahead. Tell somebody where you are going, and write down all pertinent information, including your expected time of return. Carry an extra two days' food and water and never go anywhere without a map. Try to cover most of your ground in early morning: the midday heat is too debilitating, and you shouldn't even think about it when the mercury goes over 90°F.

Stick to official trails in the national parks, as described throughout this book, and you shouldn't face any serious **technical difficulties**. However, many trails are marked only by occasional stone cairns, and if your concentration starts to wander your feet may do so too. If you do get lost, try your utmost to retrace your steps; if that fails, find some shade and wait. As long as you've registered, the rangers will eventually come and fetch you. There are two good reasons not to try to blaze your own trail. The first is the **cryptobiotic crust** – what looks like a faint coating of dead moss on the sand is the building block on which all desert life depends, and merely treading on it has serious ecological consequences. The other is the risk of becoming **rim-rocked**; picking your way across even a shallow gully, it's much easier to climb up than down, and you may well find yourself stuck above a drop you're unable to negotiate.

Top Ten Southwest Hikes

Mesa Arch Trail, Canyonlands Nat Park	one hour	p.406
Canyon Overlook Trail, Zion Nat Park	one hour	p.353
Delicate Arch Trail, Arches Nat Park	two hours	p.419
White House Trail, Canyon de Chelly Nat Mon	two hours	p.53
Betatakin Trail, Navajo Nat Mon	five hours	p.41
Horseshoe Canyon, Canyonlands Nat Park	five hours	p.409
Chesler Park Loop Trail, Canyonlands Nat Park	one day	p.414
West Rim Trail, Zion Nat Park	one day	p.354
Havasupai Indian Reservation	two days	p.314
Grand Gulch Primitive Area	one week	p.438

On a day-hike down into a **canyon**, allow more time to hike back up – when you're already tired, and the temperature is likely to be hotter – than you do to go down. Turn back after a third of your allotted time; if you plan a six-hour hike, reckon on two hours hiking down and four hours to hike up.

To stay cool during the day, wear full-length sleeves and trousers. Shorts and a vest will expose you to far too much sun – something you won't be aware of until it's too late. A wide-brimmed hat and a pair of good sunglasses will spare you the blinding headaches that can result from the desert light. You may also have to contend with flash floods, which can appear from nowhere: one innocent-looking dark cloud can turn a dry wash into a raging river. Never camp in a dry wash, and don't attempt to cross flooded areas until the water has receded.

Bear in mind too that much of the Southwest – such as the Colorado Plateau, home to the Grand Canyon and Utah's national parks – is more than a mile above sea level, and the **altitude** alone can impose severe demands on even the fittest of athletes. Be prepared for below-freezing temperatures at high elevations at night.

Water

It's essential to carry – and **drink** – large quantities of liquid in the desert. An eight-hour hike in typical summer temperatures of over 100°F would require you to drink a phenomenal **thirty pints** of water. Loss of appetite and thirst are early symptoms of heat exhaustion, so it's possible to become seriously dehydrated without feeling thirsty. Watch out for signs of dizziness or nausea, and if you feel weak and stop sweating, it's time to get to the doctor. You should always know whether water will be available on your chosen trail – park rangers keep abreast of the latest conditions – and carry at least a quart per person even if it is. Just to confuse things, there's also a risk of **water intoxication**, which can happen if you drink too much without eating; you must have regular snacks as well. Finally, watch your **alcohol** intake: if you must booze during the day, compensate heavily with pints of water between each drink.

Backpackers should never drink from rivers and streams, however clear and inviting they may look; you never know what unspeakable acts people – or animals – have performed fur-

ther upstream. **Giardia** – a water-borne bacteria that causes an intestinal disease, characterized by chronic diarrhoea, abdominal cramps, fatigue and weight loss – is a serious problem. Water that doesn't come from a tap should be boiled for at least five minutes, or cleansed with an iodine-based purifier (such as *Potable Aqua*) or a Giardia-rated filter, available from any camping or sports store.

Insects and allergies

Mosquitoes and biting insects are rarely a problem in the Southwest, though in springtime you may encounter them near rivers in parks such as Zion. *Avon Skin-so-soft* handcream or anything containing *DEET* are fairly reliable repellents. **Ticks** – tiny beetles that plunge their heads into your skin and swell up – can be a hazard. They sometimes leave their heads inside, causing blood clots or infections, so get advice from a park ranger if you've been bitten.

Beware, too, of **poison oak**, an allergenic shrub that grows all over the western states, usually among oak trees. Its leaves are in groups of three and are distinguished by prominent veins and shiny surfaces. If you come into contact, wash your skin (with soap and cold water) and clothes as soon as possible – and don't scratch. In serious cases, hospital emergency rooms can give antihistamine or adrenaline jabs.

Desert driving

Whenever you **drive** in the desert, be sure to have two gallons of water per person in the car. You should also carry flares, matches, a first-aid kit, and a compass, plus a shovel, air pump and extra gas. If the car's engine overheats, don't turn it off; instead, try to cool the engine quickly by turning the front end towards the wind. Carefully pour some water on the front of the radiator, and turn the air conditioning off and heating up full blast. In an emergency, never panic and leave the car: you'll be harder to find wandering around alone.

Flora and fauna

Though the popular conception of the Southwest sees it as an arid wasteland, in fact it holds a broad spectrum of plant and animal life. Scientists divide the earth into "**life zones**" according to climate and distance from the equator, each of which holds a different assortment of species. In the Southwest, altitude substitutes for latitude; the higher the elevation, the cooler the temperature. Within the Grand Canyon alone, the range of habitat is equivalent to that experienced in a trip from the deserts of Mexico to the forests of the Canadian mountains.

It's the lowest, hottest level, the **Lower Sonoran** zone, that's home to the rattlesnakes and cactuses you're probably expecting. Southern Arizona is the obvious example, with its dramatic saguaro and organ pipe cactuses, but a similar ecosystem can be found in the depths of the Grand Canyon.

By the time you reach a mile above sea level – the height of most of Utah's national parks – you're in the **Upper Sonoran** zone. This is characterized by smaller prickly pear cactuses and sagebrush, mammals such as rabbits and prairie dogs, and predators like coyotes and mountain lions (not that tourists are at all likely to encounter lions). Low rainfall results in a "pygmy forest" where gnarled, long-lived trees such as the piñon (also spelled pinyon) pine and Utah juniper grow to a maximum height of little more than twenty feet.

Around ten thousand feet up in the mountains of southern Colorado, northern New Mexico and central-southern Utah, the **Canadian** zone is even more densely forested, with Douglas firs joining the aspen and ponderosa, and bighorn sheep making an appearance in remoter areas. The Colorado Rockies, and Utah's Henry and La Sal ranges, rise higher still into the **Hudsonian** zone, between eleven and twelve thousand feet. Before the tree cover gives out altogether, ultra-resilient species such as the bristlecone pine, which can live for literally thousands of years, cling to the slopes.

The highest summits in the Southwest – places like the San Francisco Peaks near Flagstaff in Arizona (12,633ft), Wheeler Peak near Taos in New Mexico (13,161ft), and Uncompahgre Peak near Ouray in Colorado (14,309ft) – belong to the Arctic or Alpine zone, where the occasional tiny mammal scuttles through the tundra-like grasses and mosses.

Wherever and whenever **water** is abundant, however, the position changes. Southwestern riverbeds are lined with magnificent **cottonwood** and **aspen** trees, so many a canyon buried deep in the desert still manages a superb display of fall colours, while spring snowmelts help bring the mountain hillsides and the meadows of Zion alive with wild flowers.

Snakes and creepy-crawlies

Though the Southwestern deserts are home to an assortment of **poisonous creatures**, these are rarely aggressive towards humans. By observing obvious **precautions** – don't attempt to handle wildlife; keep your eyes open as you walk, and watch where you put your hands when scrambling over obstacles; shake out shoes, clothing and bedding before use; and back off if you do spot a creature, to give it room to escape – you should be able to avoid trouble.

If you are **bitten** or stung, current medical thinking rejects the concept of cutting yourself open and attempting to suck out the venom; whether snake, scorpion or spider is responsible, apply a cold compress to the wound, constrict the area with a tourniquet to prevent the spread of venom, drink lots of water, and bring your temperature down by resting in a shady area. Stay as calm as possible and seek medical help immediately.

> ******** **STOP PRESS** ********
>
> As this book went to press, sweeping price increases across the national park system seemed set to double virtually all park entrance fees, with the Grand Canyon rising to $20 per vehicle, Zion, Bryce, Canyonlands, Arches and Mesa Verde going up to $10 per vehicle, and other prices leaping accordingly.

Food and Drink

The international craze for modern **Southwestern cuisine** has done little to turn the Southwest itself into a gourmet's paradise. In **Santa Fe**, dozens of top-class restaurants have followed in the footsteps of Mark Miller's trail-blazing *Coyote Cafe* – see p.108 – while the upscale resorts of **Phoenix**, **Tucson**, **Taos** and **Sedona** all offer opportunities for fine dining.

Out there on the road, however, the great American diner still holds sway. With typical dinner prices starting well below $10, travellers happy to eat the same old steak or chicken, with baked potato and salad bar, can get excellent value for money. That said, southern Utah, for example, is the last place to go if lingering over an exquisite meal in atmospheric surroundings ranks high on your holiday wish list. Vegetarians in particular are in for a rough ride, unless macaroni strips with jelly bits consistently hit your spot.

The **Hispanic** regions of New Mexico and southern Arizona do at least have their own indigenous cuisine, broadly similar to **Mexican** food but influenced by the Pueblo Indians. The essential ingredient is the **chile** (New Mexicans insist it should never be spelled *chili* or *chilli*). You'll soon become familiar with the bright-red *ristras*, strings of dried peppers, that adorn doorways throughout the region, and are festooned on restaurant entrances as warnings of the fiery delights awaiting within. Both **green** and **red** chiles grow on the same plant; in principle the red is the mature version of the green, but confronted with a plateful there's no guarantee which will be the hotter variety. They in turn go to make spicy **salsa**, which at its most basic is simply dried peppers mixed with water, but more usually contains tomato and onion, *cilantro* (coriander) and other herbs, oil and lemon juice, and other secret ingredients. If it's too hot for you, the best remedy is to drink milk.

A basic meal in a New Mexican cafe or diner is broadly similar to what you'd eat south of the border, though it may well make more use of fresh meats and vegetables. The essentials are: lots of rice and pinto beans, often served refried as *frijoles* (ie boiled, mashed and fried), with variations on the **tortilla**, a very thin corndough or flour pancake that can be wrapped around the food and eaten by hand (a burrito); folded, fried and filled (a taco); rolled, filled and baked in sauce (an enchilada); or fried flat and topped with a stack of filling (a *tostada*). Meals are usually served with complimentary *nachos* (chips) and salsa dip, or with *sopaipillas*, deep-fried air-filled pastry "pillows", often sweetened with honey. The *chile relleno* is a good vegetarian option – a green pepper stuffed with cheese, dipped in egg batter and fried.

Here and there, you'll also find **Native American** restaurants, both on and off the reservations. The most ubiquitous dish, generally known as a **Navajo taco**, consists of a piece of **fry-bread** – a puffy deep-fried slab of bread – smothered with beans, lettuce and cheese. A Hopi taco, an Apache taco and a Pueblo taco are all surprisingly similar. **Corn** or maize, the first crop cultivated in the Americas, comes in some amazing multi-coloured varieties. Blue corn chips have spread beyond the Southwest, but you may also encounter blue cornflakes, and wafer-thin *piki* or *piiki* bread made with blue cornflour.

Drinking

In general, to buy and consume **alcohol** in the US, you need to be aged 21 or over; you may be asked for ID even if you look much older. In **New Mexico** and Arizona, most restaurants have liquor licences, and it's always easy to find a drink. In Mormon-dominated **Utah** – whose drinking laws are outlined on p.331 – things are a bit more complicated, though it's not quite the "dry" state of popular legend. Most small towns have at least one restaurant licensed to sell beer or wine to diners. On **Indian reservations**, however, alcohol is prohibited altogether; you can't have beer in your car, let alone in your motel room.

Tipping

Whatever you eat and wherever you eat it, service is usually enthusiastic – thanks in large part to the American institution of **tipping**. Waiting staff depend on tips for the bulk (and sometimes all) of their earnings; fifteen to twenty percent is the standard rate.

Telephones and the Mail

International Telephone Calls

The telephone code to dial **TO THE US** from the outside world (excluding Canada) is 1.

To make international calls **FROM THE US**, dial 011 followed by the country code:

Australia 61	Ireland 353
New Zealand 64	United Kingdom 44

call **toll-free** (☎1-800) numbers in America before they arrive in the US.

US mail

Post offices in the Southwest are usually open Monday to Friday from 9am until 5pm, and Saturday from 9am to noon, and there are blue mail boxes on many street corners. Ordinary mail within the US costs 32¢ for a letter weighing up to an ounce. Air mail between the US and Europe or Australia costs 50¢ for postcards or aerograms, 60¢ for letters weighing up to half an ounce (a single thin sheet), and generally takes about a week.

The last line of the address consists of two letters to denote the state (Utah is "UT", New Mexico is "NM", etc), and a five-figure **zip code**; you should also write a return address on the envelope. Mail that doesn't carry the zip code is liable to get lost or at least delayed. The additional four digits you sometimes see appended to zip codes are not essential.

Letters can be sent *c/o General Delivery* (what's known elsewhere as **poste restante**) to the relevant post office in each city, but must include the zip code and will only be held for thirty days before being returned to sender. If you're receiving mail at someone else's address, it should include "c/o" and the regular occupant's name.

Rules on sending **parcels** are very rigid: packages must be in special containers bought from post offices and sealed according to their instructions. To send anything out of the country, you'll need a green customs declaration form, available from a post office.

Telephones

It's usually easy to find a public **payphone** in the Southwest. As a rule, local calls cost 25¢, but you may have to feed in nine or ten quarters just to call the next town down the highway, and long-distance calls can cost far more. Some budget **motels** offer guests free local calls, but in general calls from **motel rooms** are even more expensive.

If you make a lot of calls when you're on the road, it's well worth getting a **charge card** of some kind, perhaps from your phone service provider at home. Americans can obtain these from *AT&T* (☎1-800/874-4000 ext 359); British travellers should contact *BT* (☎0800/800 838) or *Swiftcall* (☎0171/488 2001 or 0800/769 0800). Such cards also make it possible for foreigners to

Useful Numbers

Emergencies ☎911; ask for the appropriate emergency service: fire, police or ambulance

Long-distance directory information
☎1 (Area Code)/555-1212

Directory enquiries for toll-free numbers
☎1-800/555-1212

Festivals and Public Holidays

The box below lists the Southwest's major annual **festivals**. Specific annual events are described in the relevant town accounts, and you'll also find a full calendar of events in the **pueblos** of New Mexico on p.124. In addition, tourist offices for each state (see p.12) can provide full lists, or you can call local visitor centers ahead of your arrival and ask what's coming up. As a rule, only the **Indian Market** in Santa Fe and the **Balloon Festival** in Albuquerque attract large enough crowds to place a serious strain on accommodation and other facilities.

Public holidays

On national **public holidays** listed opposite, shops, banks and offices are liable to be closed all day.

Annual Festivals and Events

Jan to mid-Feb	Gem & Mineral Show	Quartzsite, AZ
Early Feb	Festival of the Arts	Tubac, AZ
Late May	Zuni Craftsmen Exhibition	Flagstaff, AZ
Late May	Iron Horse Bicycle Classic	Durango, CO
Early June	Bluegrass Festival	Telluride, CO
Late June	New Mexico Arts & Crafts Fair	Albuquerque, NM
June–Aug	Utah Shakespeare Festival	Cedar City, UT
Early July	Hopi Craftsmen Exhibition	Flagstaff, AZ
July 4	Nambe Falls Celebration	Nambe Pueblo, NM
July–Aug	Santa Fe Opera	Santa Fe, NM
July (2nd wk)	Taos Pueblo Pow-wow	Taos Pueblo, NM
July (last wk)	Spanish Market	Santa Fe, NM
July (last wk)	Navajo Craftsmen Exhibition	Flagstaff, AZ
Aug (3rd wk)	Indian Market	Santa Fe, NM
Late Aug	Central Navajo Fair	Chinle, AZ
Sept 2	San Esteban Feast Day	Ácoma Pueblo, NM
Early Sept	New Mexico State Fair	Albuquerque, NM
Early Sept	Hatch Chile Festival	Hatch, NM
Early Sept	Navajo Nation Fair	Window Rock, AZ
Sept (2nd wk)	Fiestas de Santa Fe	Santa Fe, NM
Sept (last wk)	Jazz on the Rocks	Sedona, AZ
Early Oct	International Balloon Fiesta	Albuquerque, NM
Early Oct	Northern Navajo Fair	Shiprock, NM
Mid Oct	Western Navajo Fair	Tuba City, AZ
Oct (3rd wk)	Helldorado Days	Tombstone, AZ
Late Oct	Fat Tire Festival	Moab, UT
Early Dec	National Finals Rodeo	Las Vegas, NV
Early Dec	Shalako ceremony	Zuni Pueblo, NM

The traditional **summer season** for tourism runs from Memorial Day to Labor Day; some tourist attractions are only open during that period.

Jan 1	**New Year's Day**
Jan 15	**Martin Luther King's Birthday**
3rd Mon in Feb	**President's Day**
	Easter Mon
Last Mon in May	**Memorial Day**
July 4	**Independence Day**
1st Mon in Sept	**Labor Day**
2nd Mon in Oct	**Columbus Day**
Nov 11	**Veterans' Day**
Last Thurs in Nov	**Thanksgiving Day**
Dec 25	**Christmas Day**

Travelling in Indian Country

There are around fifty separate **Indian reservations** in the Southwest, ranging in size from the vast **Navajo Reservation** (or "Navajo Nation"), which extends across three states in the Four Corners region, to the nineteen autonomous **pueblos** of **New Mexico**, many of which consist of one single village.

Some reservations make no effort to attract or inform visitors; some do the bare minimum to sate tourists' curiosity; some eagerly encourage paying guests to stay in tribal-run motels and campgrounds. Among the most compelling attractions on native American soil are **Monument Valley** and **Canyon de Chelly** and **Navajo national monuments**, all on the Navajo Reservation; the stupendous waterfalls of the **Havasupai Reservation**, deep in the Grand Canyon; and the adobe pueblos of **Taos** and **Ácoma** ("Sky City") in New Mexico.

Many outsiders – Americans and non-Americans alike – feel uncomfortable about entering Indian land, but so long as you behave with due **cultural sensitivity** you will almost always be made to feel welcome. In particular, travellers in "Indian Country" should respect the laws that bar the sale, possession and consumption of **alcohol** on the reservations. Always request permission before drawing or **photographing** people or personal property, and accept that you may be asked for a fee. As well as obeying explicit signs that ask you not to enter specific areas, such as shrines or *kivas*, you should also be aware that **off-road driving**, and **off-trail hiking** or **climbing**, is forbidden. If you

have to drive up to someone's home or *hogan*, stay in your car and wait to be approached, rather than blundering in.

On a more general note, attempts to make friends may run contra to what Native Americans regard as good **manners**. In the words of a leaflet issued by the Navajo, "the general exuberance many cultures define as friendliness is not considered such by the American Indians". Most Southwestern Indians regard **eye contact** as rude, and will avoid meeting your eye; they may also prefer not to shake hands. Your **clothing** may also be an issue; the Hopi for example request visitors not to wear shorts or hats, or to use umbrellas. Persistent, intrusive questioning is obviously liable to offend. In Pueblo communities especially, don't ask about religious matters when children are present, as children are only initiated into religious secrets at the appropriate age.

Buying Indian crafts

For many tourists, the quest to buy **Indian crafts** becomes a major focus of their visit to the Southwest. Museums and galleries throughout the region display beautiful Pueblo pots, Navajo rugs, Apache baskets, and silver and turquoise jewellery of all kinds, stimulating a desire for affordable gifts and souvenirs that stores everywhere can barely keep up with.

Much of what's widely seen as traditional Indian craftwork has in fact only developed in the last hundred years or so. The collapse of traditional tribal economies coincided with the nineteenth-century arrival of the railroads, and with them the Southwest's first wave of tourists. Enterprising traders encouraged Indians to adapt or learn craft techniques to make souvenirs; as one anthropologist put it, the resultant hybrid was "the Indian's idea of the trader's idea of what the white man thought was Indian design".

To ensure good prices and good quality, you should ideally buy specific Indian crafts as near as possible to where they're made. On the Navajo Reservation, head for the **Hubbell Trading Post** (see p.55); on the Hopi Reservation, try the **Hopi Cultural Center** and the nearby stores; **Ácoma**, **Taos** and **San Ildefonso** pueblos are also good bets. More accessibly, the Indian traders in front of the Palace of the Governors in **Santa Fe** are a reliable source, while that city's summer **Indian Market** is a showcase for the entire region. In addition, the Northern Arizona museum in Flagstaff, the Heard museum in Phoenix, and the Millicent Rogers museum in Taos all have excellent stores.

If you want to be sure that whatever you're buying was individually crafted by a Southwestern Indian, you're entitled to ask the vendor for a written Certificate of Authenticity. Only the phrase "Authentic Indian hand-made" has any legal force; words such as "real" and "genuine" mean nothing. The **Indian Arts & Crafts Association** (122 La Veta NE, suite B, Albuquerque NM 87108; ☎505/265-9149) can provide further detailed advice.

Jewellery

Jewellery is perhaps the oldest Southwestern craft of all. The ancient Anasazi made necklaces of disks cut from seashells; a single specimen unearthed near Kayenta was 36 feet long and held over fifteen thousand beads. Such necklaces are now known as *heishi*, and are the speciality of New Mexico's Santo Domingo pueblo.

Turquoise has always been prized by Southwestern Indians; the prehistoric city at Chaco Canyon (see p.78) was probably founded on the proceeds of the turquoise trade, while to this day the Navajo see turquoise as symbolizing the state of harmony and beauty known as *hozho*. Necklaces of raw and polished turquoise beads are widely available, and it also adds colour and character to the **silver** jewellery made by the Hopi, Zuni and Navajo in particular.

Silversmithing is a relatively recent tradition, probably introduced from Mexico in the mid-

Another Hopi speciality, the carving of the wooden statuettes known as *kachina* dolls, is described on p.59.

nineteenth century. For many years, acquiring chunky silver bracelets, or belts studded with solid-silver conches, was the standard Navajo way of accumulating wealth. Such items could be pawned for cash at trading posts on the reservation, and then redeemed when times got easier; now known as pawn jewellery, they count as valuable collectors' pieces. Casual buyers tend to prefer − and to be more able to afford − the more delicate **overlay** style, in which a stencilled design is cut from a thin sheet of silver then soldered onto a solid backing sheet. This originated in 1947, when returning Hopi servicemen were trained in the technique as a means of earning a living, and the Hopi remain its finest exponents. Overlay designs can be seen on earrings, belt buckles, rings, and, especially, the clasps of *bolo* (bootlace) ties.

Weaving

The best **weavers** in the Southwest are generally acknowledged to be the Navajo. In legend, they acquired the craft from Spider Woman, who lives atop Spider Rock in the Canyon de Chelly; in fact, they were probably taught by the Pueblo peoples after the Pueblo Revolt of 1680. That was also when they began to raise sheep, which had been introduced by the Spanish a century earlier.

Originally the Navajo wove blankets and clothing; **Navajo rugs** were the brainchild of nineteenth-century traders, who also suggested that using "earth" colours such as brown would appeal to tourists expecting a "natural" look. Many individual Navajo communities or families weave designs named for their own area, such as Teec Nos Pos, Ganado or Two Gray Hills. As a rule, the patterns have no religious significance, but most include an "escape route" or "spirit line", a line that runs to the very edge of the rug and ensures that the weaver's spirit is not trapped within it. Traditional rugs also left a hole in the centre, as in a spider's web.

Authentic Navajo rugs take months to create, and sell for thousands of dollars; anything you see cheaper is probably a mass-produced Mexican imitation. The monthly Navajo Rug

Auction at Crownpoint in New Mexico (see p.80) is the best opportunity to pick up a genuine bargain.

Pottery

Spanish explorers in 1540 spoke of Pueblo women as making "jars of extraordinary labor and workmanship, which were worth seeing". The **ceramic** tradition of northern New Mexico's pueblos remains as strong as ever, having been revitalized in the twentieth century by the San Ildefonso potter **Maria Martinez**. Although she consciously modelled her earlier work on designs found in ancient archeological sites, the black-on-black museum pieces for which she became famous are a far cry from the popular conception of Native American crafts. Many tourists prefer either the straightforward pots and jars, painted with rectilinear "pueblo motifs", created at Ácoma Pueblo, or the ubiquitous **"storyteller"** figures, showing a mother surrounded by children, that were first created at Cochiti Pueblo. A representative cross-section of styles can be seen at the roadside store run by **Pojoaque Pueblo**, twelve miles north of Santa Fe (see p.121).

Directory

AIRPORT TAX This is invariably included in the price of your ticket.

BANKS As explained on p.14, if you carry an ATM card and/or US dollar travellers' cheques, you won't need to visit a bank in the Southwest. However, normal banking hours are from 9am or 10am until 3pm or 4pm Monday to Thursday, and slightly longer on Friday.

DATES In the American style, the date 1.8.98 means not August 1, as in Europe, but January 8.

DISABLED TRAVELLERS For information on specific states, contact the tourism departments on p.12. *SATH* (☎212/447-7284), is a non-profit travel-industry referral service that passes queries on to its members as appropriate; allow plenty of time for a response. *Travel Information Service* (☎215/456-9600) is a telephone information and referral service. *Mobility International USA* (☎541/343-1284) offers travel tips to members ($25 a year) and operates an exchange programme for disabled people. *Wheelchair Getaways of New Mexico* (☎505/247-2626 or 1-800/408-2626) rents wheelchair- and scooter-accessible vans by the day, week and month. The *Golden Access* Passport, issued without charge to permanently disabled US citizens, gives free lifetime admission to all national parks. *Easy Access to National Parks*, published by the *Sierra Club* ($15; ☎415/776-2211), details every national park for people with disabilities, senior citizens and families with children. Various other useful publications are produced by *Twin Peaks Press* (☎360/694-2462 or 1-800/637-2256).

ELECTRICITY The US electricity supply is 110 volts AC. Plugs are standard two-pins − foreign visitors will need an adaptor and voltage converter for their own electrical appliances.

EMERGENCIES Dial ☎911.

FLOORS The first floor in the US is what would be the ground floor in Britain; the second floor would be the first floor, and so on.

GAY AND LESBIAN TRAVELLERS Resources for gay and lesbian travellers in the Southwest include the *Gay and Lesbian Community Center*, 3136 N Third Ave, Phoenix (☎602/234-2752); *Wingspan*, 422 N Fourth Ave, Tucson; (☎520/624-1779); *Utah Stonewall Center*, 770 South 300 West, Salt Lake City (☎801/539-8800); the *Gay Las Vegas* Web site (*www.gay-vegas.com*),; and the *Santa Fe Cares* hotline (☎505/982-3301)

HEALTH MATTERS Most travellers do not require inoculations to enter the US, though you may need certificates of vaccination if you're en route from cholera- or typhoid-infected areas in Asia or Africa – check with your doctor before you leave. The "mystery illness" that killed around fifty people in the Four Corners region in 1993 was eventually traced to a hantavirus spread by the droppings of deer mice; backpackers should take care to avoid camping near rodent nests.

ID Should be carried at all times. Two pieces should suffice, one of which should have a photo: a passport and credit card(s) are your best bets. Not having your licence with you while driving is an arrestable offence.

MEASUREMENTS AND SIZES US measurements are Imperial, though American pints and gallons are about four-fifths of Imperial ones. Clothing sizes are two figures less than in the UK – a British women's size 12 is a US size 10 – while British shoe sizes are half below American ones for women, and one size below for men.

PHOTOGRAPHY In the bright Southwestern sun, you should get better photographs if you use slower film; an ASA speed of 100 is recommended.

SENIOR TRAVELLERS Anyone over the age of 62, who can produce suitable ID, can enjoy certain discounts. *Amtrak* and *Greyhound*, for example, offer (smallish) percentage reductions on fares to older passengers. US residents aged over 50 can join the *American Association of Retired Persons*,

601 E St NW, Washington DC 20049 (☎202/434-2277 or 1-800/424-3410), which organizes group travel for senior citizens and can provide discounts on accommodation and vehicle rental. *Golden Age* passports, available to US citizens or residents aged 62 or older, allow free admission to national parks for life, for a one-off $10 fee.

TAX Sales tax is added to virtually everything you buy in a shop, but isn't included in the marked price. The actual rate varies from place to place, but in the states covered in this book it ranges between around five and seven percent – except on Indian reservations, which do not levy sales tax. Most towns also charge lodging taxes of between five and fifteen percent.

TEMPERATURES Always given in Fahrenheit.

TIME ZONES New Mexico, Utah, Colorado and Arizona all operate on **Mountain Standard Time**, which is two hours behind Eastern Standard Time and seven hours behind Greenwich Mean Time, so 2pm in Santa Fe is 4pm in New York City, and 9pm in London. Nevada and California are on **Pacific Standard Time**, another hour behind. Between the first Sunday in April and the last Sunday in October, New Mexico, Utah, Colorado and Nevada switch to **Daylight Savings Time**, and advance their clocks by one hour. Arizona, however, does not, so in summer it joins Nevada in being an hour behind New Mexico and Utah. Confusingly, the **Navajo Nation** in northeast Arizona does shift to Daylight Savings Time, making it one hour later than the rest of Arizona in summer, while the Hopi Reservation, entirely surrounded by the Navajo Nation, stays put. The time in the part-Navajo, part-Hopi town of Tuba City, Arizona – see p.39 – varies from street to street.

VIDEOS The standard format used for video cassettes in the US is different from that used in Britain. You cannot buy blank videos in the US compatible with a video camera bought in Britain.

The Guide

Chapter 1

The Four Corners

T he **Four Corners** region is the heartland of the Southwest, not because the states of Arizona, Utah, Colorado and New Mexico happen to meet here, but because it remains dominated by **Native American** cultures to an extent that's unique in the modern United States.

Quite possibly, the uplands of the Colorado Plateau – said to be the highest inhabited plateau in the world, bar Tibet – are now home to a smaller population than a thousand years ago. At that time, the people known to history as the **Anasazi** occupied settlements scattered throughout the region. They're chiefly remembered for their fabulous "**cliff dwellings**", which cling like eagle-nests to the walls of soaring red-rock canyons, but in fact they lived everywhere, from the valley floors to the mesa tops. After the Anasazi moved away, seven centuries ago, the nomadic **Navajo** took their place; now 250,000 strong, they're the largest single Native American group in the United States, and their reservation forms the bulk of the Four Corners area. Contrary to popular legend, however, the Anasazi did not vanish completely, and their descendants still live nearby, in the **Hopi** villages of Arizona, and the pueblos of **Zuni** and **Ácoma**, across the border in New Mexico.

The history of the Anasazi, whose name comes from a pejorative Navajo word meaning "enemy ancestors", is summarized on p.468.

The ruins left by the Anasazi have become the Four Corners' prime tourist destinations. Among the most significant are **Mesa Verde National Park** in southwest Colorado, where dozens of graceful pueblo complexes are tucked into high rocky alcoves, and the fully-fledged cities of New Mexico's remote **Chaco Canyon**, where Anasazi civilization reached its peak. For sheer beauty, however, **Canyon de Chelly National Monument** in Arizona, where Navajo farmers live alongside the ancient remains, far surpasses both. Elsewhere, the main appeal is the **scenery**, which ranges from the Western-movie deserts epitomized by **Monument Valley**, via lone outcrops such as **Shiprock**, to the snow-capped peaks of Colorado.

For general advice on "Travelling in Indian Country", see p.29.

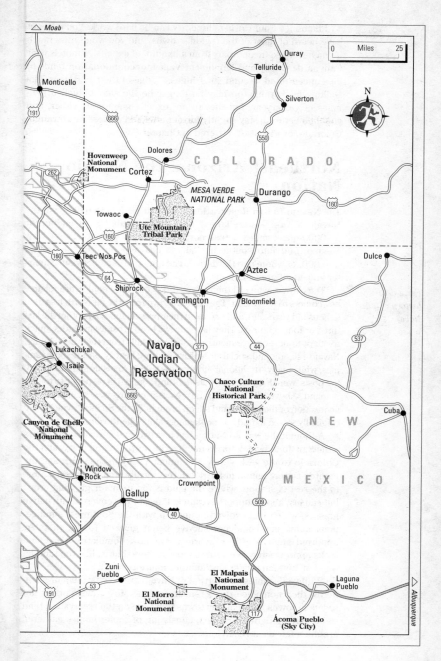

Planning a Four Corners itinerary can be hard work. You may not have heard of most of the region's towns, and you won't miss much if you never see them. Apart from a handful of expensive motels near Canyon de Chelly and Monument Valley, **accommodation** tends to be concentrated around its fringes. "Edge-of-the-res" towns like Gallup and Farmington may no longer be the alcohol-fuelled hell-holes of yesteryear, but they're not exactly glamorous either, and you'd do better to stay slightly further afield, in places like **Durango**, Colorado, or **Flagstaff**, covered in Chapter Five.

Northeast Arizona: the Navajo Nation

The **Navajo Indian Reservation** – or, as it prefers to be known, the **Navajo Nation** – is the largest reservation in the US, extending for 27,000 square miles across northeast Arizona and northwest New Mexico, and into southern Utah. It has a population of around 250,000, of whom two thirds are aged under 21, and between a quarter and a half are Christians.

For a detailed history of the Navajo, see p.486.

The Navajo, who call themselves the *Diné*, "the People", are relative newcomers to the region. They drifted down from the far North less than a thousand years ago, and occupied their present territory within the last three or four centuries. They have always been great assimilators, quick to adapt to new environments and acquire skills from their neighbours. Navajo religion and social organization draw heavily on Pueblo examples, while many "traditional" crafts, now sold in roadside stalls and trading posts, were learned from outsiders and adapted in response to tourist demand. Above all, contemporary Navajo culture was shaped by the acquisition of the **horses** and **sheep** brought by the Spanish, which were originally seized in raids on settlements along the Rio Grande.

Although the Navajo Nation has just two major year-round rivers – the **San Juan**, which forms much of its northern boundary, and the **Colorado** to the west – only Monument Valley in the north and the Painted Desert region in the south technically count as desert. Most of the rest is **steppe**, where the land is too poor for growing crops but can just about support livestock. It used to be covered with native grasses, which had evolved in tandem with the Southwest's indigenous fauna but could not survive being gnawed to the roots by imported animals. The sagebrush that now dominates the region looks appropriately Western to most visitors, but is, like the tumbleweed or Russian thistle, just another interloper.

While a declining proportion of Navajo are now farmers or shepherds, their nomadic origins remain evident. Most Navajo prefer not to live in towns, so what few towns there are on the reservation tend to be ugly modern accretions, consisting of trailer homes gathered around a few dishevelled lots.

For travellers, a day or two's driving across the Navajo Nation carries a real sense of adventure. Whether at supermarket check-outs or on the radio, you're sure to hear spoken Navajo, a language of such complexity that it was adapted during World War II as an uncrackable military code. You'll also get a chance to try the ubiquitous **Navajo taco**, a piece of open-topped fry-bread smothered with chile and/or refried beans that's another cultural borrowing, this time acquired during the years of exile in New Mexico.

The tourist infrastructure is however relatively minimal, with only half a dozen widely-scattered towns offering even a single motel. As a result, most visitors confine their attentions to the region's trio of indisputably top-class attractions – the stunning sandscape of **Monument Valley**, the Anasazi remains and Navajo *hogans* of the beautiful **Canyon de Chelly**, and the ancient cliff dwellings of **Navajo National Monument**.

Tuba City

Though it's the largest community on the western side of the Navajo Nation, you're only likely to stop at **TUBA CITY**, ten miles up US-160 from US-89, if you're too tired to drive any further. Don't expect any tubas; the town was named for Tuuvi, a Hopi from nearby Moenkopi, who upon converting to Mormonism in 1877 invited a group of Mormon families to settle here. Soon the Mormons were monopolizing the site's precious springs – fed by an aquifer that reaches to Monument Valley – and they were forced to move out when the area was added to Navajo lands in 1903.

Tuba City has two unusual claims to fame. The first is a set of petrified **dinosaur tracks**, near the highway five miles southwest of town. These 65-million-year-old sandstone imprints were left by a ten-foot creature known as Dilophosaurus, and were hugely significant in proving that dinosaurs could run, though there's no evidence to support the suggestion in *Jurassic Park* that Dilophosaurus also spat venom. It's hard to spot the tracks on your own – in truth, they're not all that riveting – but waiting Navajo guides can lead you to them for a small donation. Secondly, Tuba City straddles two separate **time zones**. Most businesses along the highway, such as *Basha's* supermarket, operate on Mountain Standard Time, while clocks in the town proper, a block or two north, are set in summer to Daylight Savings Time, an hour later.

Practicalities

In the centre of Tuba City, a mile north of the US-160/Hwy-264 intersection, the large, modern *Tuba City Motel* has its own RV park (☎520/283-4545, fax 283-4144; winter ③, summer ⑤). Next door, *Pancho's Family Restaurant* (☎520/283-5260) offers a long, inexpensive Mexican-American menu, and the *hogan*-shaped *Tuba City Trading Post* sells rugs, jewellery, books and groceries.

*Between early April and late October, when the Navajo Nation joins Utah and New Mexico on **Daylight Savings Time**, it's one hour later than the rest of Arizona, including the Hopi Reservation.*

*Tuba City hosts the three-day **Western Navajo Fair** in mid-October.*

*The **price codes** used here are explained on p.15.*

Back at the intersection, the *Tuba City Truck Stop Cafe*
(☎520/283-4975) is renowned for its cheese-and-chile-topped
Navajo tacos. In summer, **Grey Hills High School** – turn left off US-
160, half a mile northeast – becomes the *Grey Hills Inn* (☎520/283-
6271; ①/②). Its thirty basic twin-bedded rooms, which share bathrooms, are normally rented by the room, but members of hostelling
associations can rent a bed for $16 per night.

Navajo National Monument

Despite its name, **NAVAJO NATIONAL MONUMENT**, reached via a
ten-mile spur road that runs north from US-60 fifty miles northeast
of Tuba City and twenty miles southwest of Kayenta, has little to do
with the Navajo. Instead, it's among the most beautiful ancient sites
in the Southwest, with each of its three separate parcels preserving a
long-lost **Anasazi cliff dwelling**.

Betatakin, set in an enormous rocky alcove, can be admired from
an overlook near the visitor center, or entered on a six-hour ranger-
led hike. The even larger **Keet Seel** is a seventeen-mile round-trip
from the road, on foot or horseback, and thus only seen by a dedicated few. Finally, fragile **Inscription House** – named not for ancient
petroglyphs, but for the date "1661" carved on a wall, suggesting
that some seventeenth-century Spaniard passed this way – has been
closed to visitors for over thirty years.

Archeologists divide the Four Corners Anasazi into three sub-
groups. One centred on Mesa Verde, another on Chaco Canyon;
Tsegi Canyon, the focus of Navajo National Monument, is the
definitive **Kayenta Anasazi** site. Its inhabitants are seen as conservative, in that they still lived in pithouses long after the people
of Chaco and Mesa Verde started to construct sophisticated pueblos; they were however fine potters, and Kayenta ceramics are
now much-prized museum pieces. Tree-ring dating pinpoints
their move into the alcoves of Tsegi Canyon to around 1250 AD.
The first three of the still-standing dwellings in Betatakin were
erected in 1267; another was added in 1268, and a further ten or
more, plus a *kiva*, in 1275. By 1300 AD, intensive irrigation had
lowered the water table and rendered farming impossible, and the
canyon had been abandoned.

What became of the Kayenta people is no mystery. According
to the Navajo, Keet Seel was built by settlers from Navajo
Mountain, and Betatakin by a group from Chaco. That dovetails
with the **Hopi** legend that as many as eight of their clans lived
here for around fifty years, just before their migrations ended at
the Hopi Mesas, fifty miles south. A pictograph at Betatakin –
consisting of a bird-like figure within a large white circle – shows
Masaw, the symbol of the Hopi Fire Clan. Hopis regularly return
for ceremonies honouring their ancestors, and at the time of the
Oraibi dispute, in 1905 (see p.484), the breakaway Hopi faction

*In Navajo,
tsegi means
"rock". It's the
word that was
corrupted to
become
"Chelly" at the
Canyon de
Chelly; see
p.50.*

that eventually founded Hotevilla seriously considered re-settling here.

Navajo National Monument was established in 1909, after Navajo guides led members of the Weatherill family (of Mesa Verde fame; see p.68) to Keet Seel. Betatakin was "discovered" a year or two later, by chance already within the monument boundaries.

Practicalities

The paved section of Hwy-564 ends ten miles north of US-160, at the monument's **visitor center** (May to early Sept daily 8am–6pm; early Sept to mid-Dec & April daily 8am–5pm; mid-Dec to March daily 8am–4.30pm; ☎520/672-2366 or 672-2367). You can't see the ruins from here, but interesting displays include a traditional Navajo forked-stick *hogan* (see p.54) in the forest at the back.

The lovely little **campground** nearby is open year-round; all its first-come first-served sites are free, but water is only available from May to September. The closest **motel** is the simple *Anasazi Inn*, on US-160 ten miles east of the turn-off, halfway to Kayenta (☎520/697-3793, fax 697-8249; winter ③, summer ⑤), which has a small restaurant and no neighbours apart from its derelict predecessor.

Admission to Navajo National Monument is free; ordinary vehicles should not continue along the unpaved extension of Hwy-564, beyond the monument.

The Sandal Trail

If you only have time for a brief visit, all you can do is gaze across the canyon to **Betatakin** from the end of the **Sandal Trail**. This easy one-mile round-trip hike, which doubles as a nature trail, runs partly on a boardwalk and partly over level open rock.

The view at the end, where a sumptuous orange recess in the canyon wall arches above the hundred-room cluster of dwellings, is quite amazing. Their straight walls rise in tiers from a ledge above the canyon floor; hence the Navajo name Betatakin, or "house on ledges". It's all in such good condition – everything you see is original, except for the ladders and a few of the roof beams – that it's hard to believe the 120 or so inhabitants left not seven years but seven centuries ago.

Hiking to Betatakin

While it's worth visiting the monument for the long-distance view alone, to get any closer to Betatakin you have to join a free ranger-guided **hike**, which is also a great opportunity to learn more about the land and its history. The precise schedule depends on funding, but in principle hikes depart daily at 9am and noon between Memorial Day and Labor Day, and at 10am only during early May and from Labor Day until some time in October; remember the time difference if you're hurrying here from beyond the Navajo Nation. Only the first 25 people to register at the visitor center each day get to go; there are no advance reservations.

All hikers are expected to bring enough food and water (at least half a gallon) to last the six-hour round-trip. The hike starts not at the

Betatakin is best photographed in late afternoon, when direct sunlight penetrates the alcove.

visitor center but a mile or two's drive away, dropping steeply into the canyon from the top of Skeleton Mesa. Betatakin itself only comes into sight right at the end, as you head up a steadily narrowing side canyon, filled with delicate aspens that turn a gorgeous yellow in the fall. Closely monitored by the rangers, you climb right up into the alcove, whose full dimensions of 452ft high, 370ft wide, and 135ft deep are overwhelming. Anyone lacking a head for heights may well prefer to stay below. Most of the dwellings are off limits in any case, but sitting in the plaza of the ancient pueblo is an extraordinarily evocative experience.

Keet Seel

Getting all the way to **Keet Seel** – Arizona's largest cliff dwelling – is a major undertaking. The gruelling seventeen-mile self-guided round-trip **hike** is too much to attempt in a single day, so **hikers** have to spend the night at the primitive campground near the ruin. The alternative is to go on **horseback** with a Navajo guide, which can be arranged through the visitor center for $55 per person.

Unlike Betatakin, all hikers *must* make advance reservations through the visitor center, at least one day, but not more than two months, in advance. Up to twenty permits per day are issued from Memorial Day until Labor Day. There's no drinkable water en route, though you may well have to wade through muddy streams.

Visitors to Keet Seel can only enter the ruins with the ranger stationed nearby. The village reaches deep back into the hillside, so well sheltered that its 150-plus rooms have barely deteriorated. No more than half a dozen are *kivas*; the Kayenta were not relentless *kiva*-builders like their neighbours at Mesa Verde. Keet Seel was a longer-lasting and more dynamic settlement than Betatakin; its cliff dwellings date from the same era, but people lived in the vicinity from around 950 AD, and migrating groups came and went for the next few hundred years. Little now survives of the large free-standing pueblo that stood on the valley floor not far away.

Black Mesa

Immediately opposite the Navajo National Monument turn-off, a broad but poorly-surfaced road sets off south to climb **Black Mesa**. Only 4WD vehicles can get more than a mile or two down here, so few tourists see the gaping **strip mines** where the *Peabody Western Coal Company* extracts the prodigious coal deposits for which the mesa is named. While you may well pass one of the endless trains that ferry coal up to the **Navajo Generating Station** at Page (see p.392), neither will you see the underground pipeline that uses an extravagant billion gallons of pure water per year to slurry crushed coal on a three-day trip around the Grand Canyon and into Nevada. For many Navajo and Hopi, the mining of Black Mesa remains a deeply controversial issue, although the meagre payments the two tribes formerly received from *Peabody* increased after the mineral leases were renegotiated during the 1980s.

Kayenta

KAYENTA, where US-160 meets US-163 twenty miles northeast of Navajo National Monument, is not in any sense an historic town. Having begun life in the 1950s as a dormitory community for workers in the uranium mines to the north, it later became the main base for the miners of Black Mesa. Just twenty miles south of Monument Valley, it now also caters to ever-increasing numbers of tourists, but remains little more than a conglomeration of trailer homes.

Kayenta's zip code is AZ 86033.

Practicalities

Kayenta's new *hogan*-shaped **visitor center**, at the highway intersection (daily 10am–9pm; ☎520/697-3572), carries information on the whole Navajo Nation, holds several crafts stalls, and stages Navajo dances on summer Tuesdays (8pm). The *Burger King* next door has a large display on the war-time Navajo Code Talkers.

Both Kayenta's **motels** are quite upscale. South of the junction, facing drivers arriving from Monument Valley, the large *Holiday Inn* (☎520/697-3221 or 1-800/HOLIDAY, fax 697-3349; winter ④, summer ⑥), houses the distinctive and good-value *Wagon Wheel* restaurant. The *Wetherill Inn*, a mile north on US-163 (☎520/697-3231; winter ③, summer ⑤), is run by the same people as *Goulding's* in Monument Valley, so it's handy for arranging tours, and has the *Golden Sands Cafe* nearby (☎520/697-3684). There's also a good deli counter at the central *Basha's* supermarket.

*The **price codes** used here are explained on p.15.*

Monument Valley

The classic Wild-West landscape of stark sandstone buttes and forbidding pinnacles of rock, poking from an endless expanse of drifting red sands, has become an archetypal image. Only when you arrive at **MONUMENT VALLEY** do you realize how much your perception of the West has in fact been shaped by this one spot. Such scenery does exist elsewhere, of course, but nowhere is it so perfectly concentrated and distilled. While movie-makers have flocked here since the early days of Hollywood, the sheer majesty of the place still takes your breath away. Add the fact that it remains a stronghold of **Navajo** culture, little affected by tourism, and Monument Valley may well prove to be the absolute highlight of your trip to the Southwest.

Monument Valley Tribal Park straddles the Arizona–Utah state line, 24 miles north of Kayenta and 25 miles southwest of Mexican Hat. You can see the buttes for free – silhouetted on the skyline from fifty miles away, and towering alongside US-163 – but the four-mile detour to enter the park is rewarded with much closer views, while the tours beyond the end of the road are unforgettable.

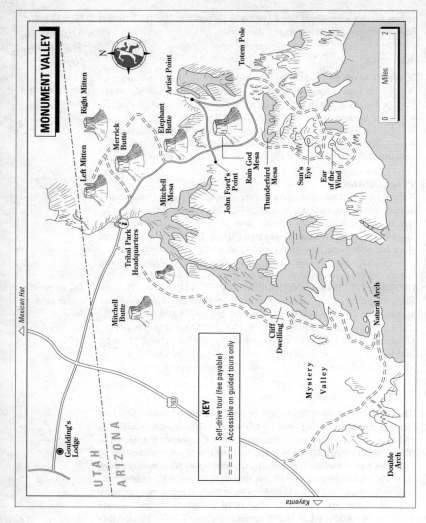

A history of Monument Valley

Monument Valley is not really a valley. There's no permanent stream, nor higher ground to either side, and no valley has buttes along its floor. This whole region was once a flat plain, concealing the top of what are now the tallest "monuments". In the last ten million years, the Monument Uplift – part of the general upthrust of the Colorado Plateau – has bulged that plain up from below, creating cracks that have since eroded to leave only isolated nuggets of harder rock.

On the surface, thanks to annual rainfall of under ten inches, this looks like an unpromising region in which to live. However, sand dunes are surprisingly efficient at conserving moisture, and a huge aquifer deeper down stretches all the way to Tuba City. Beneath the small **cliff dwellings** that burrow into the rocks, the slopes are littered with ancient potsherds, indicating that the Anasazi were here until around 1300 AD. After that, the area may have remained unoccupied until a band of Navajo retreated here to avoid Kit Carson's round-up in 1864 (see p.487). Their leader, **Hoskinnini**, is said to have discovered silver nearby. Two white prospectors sneaked some of the metal away in 1880, but were killed – by passing Paiutes, according to the Navajo – when they returned, at the bases of **Mitchell** and **Merrick** buttes respectively.

The Navajo, who named Monument Valley *Tse 'bü'ndisgaü'*, or "there is a treeless area amid the rocks", see the whole place as a *hogan*, with its "door" facing east at the visitor center, and the butte behind *Goulding's Lodge* as its central hearth. They say the whole area has become drier during the last century, perhaps because the spirit of the Totem Pole formation, which was regarded as a line of prayersticks capable of granting rain, was offended when it was climbed during the filming of *The Eiger Sanction* (see p.47).

Park practicalities

The park's **$2.50 admission fee** is payable a short way down the approach road off US-163, which ends about four miles along at the **visitor center** (May–Sept daily 7am–7pm; Oct–April daily 8am–5pm; Thanksgiving 8am–noon, closed Christmas Day and New Year's Day; ☎801/727-3287). As well as holding a small museum, and staging **dances** on summer evenings at 8pm, this is the site of the *Haskeneini* **restaurant** (Nov–March daily 6.30am–6pm; April–Oct daily 6am–10pm; ☎520/871-4602), which serves reasonable conventional meals, plus Navajo fry-bread. The exposed, summer-only *Mitten View* **campground** nearby operates on a first-come, first-served basis, with sites costing $10.

In the parking lot, among the crafts stalls, several Navajo-run outfits tout for customers for **valley tours**, by jeep or horse. These are very highly recommended; all can be booked in advance, but it's usually easy to turn up and get on a tour straight away. The going rate for a **jeep tour**, with operators such as *Roland's Navajoland Tours* (☎520/697-3524 or 1-800/368-3524) or *Nizhoni Homeland Tours* (☎801/727-3276) is around $15 for up to two hours, $20 for up to three hours, and $50 for a whole day. Typical **horseback tours** cost $35 (1hr 30min), $40 (2hr 30min), or $100 all day; possibilities include *Ed Black's Monument Valley Trail Rides* (☎801/739-4285 or 1-800/551-4039) and *Navajo Country Guided Trail Rides* (☎801/727-3210). *Roy Black's Hiking and Van Tours* (☎801/739-4226 or 1-800/749-4226), also do **hiking trips**, charging $75 for either a six-hour hike or an **overnight** backpack.

Monument Valley and the Mythic West

*The real star of my Westerns has always been the land . . . My
favourite location is Monument Valley. It has rivers, mountains,
plains, desert, everything that land can offer . . . I consider this the
most complete, beautiful, and peaceful place on earth.*

John Ford, *Cosmopolitan*, March 1964

In 1937, Harry Goulding, the owner of *Goulding's Lodge*, heard talk that
Hollywood producers were planning to shoot Western-themed movies in
the Southwest. Armed with a portfolio of photographs of Monument
Valley, he set off for California, and started knocking on doors. Within a
year, **John Ford** had brought a crew to Goulding's remote desert outpost,
and was filming *Stagecoach*.

From their first moment on screen, Monument Valley's emblematic
buttes served as a visual shorthand for the Wild West. The geographical
reality was irrelevant. *Stagecoach* supposedly followed a coach heading
through Apache territory from Tonto in southern Arizona to Lordsburg in
New Mexico. In fact it did no more than duck in and out of Monument
Valley; as John Wayne put it, "there's some things a man just can't run away
from". Wayne was at it again in *The Searchers* (1956), when he spent five
years scouring Texas for Scar's band of Comanche, although both he and
they were within the same five-mile radius of the Mittens all along. In *My
Darling Clementine* (1946), Henry Fonda as Wyatt Earp drove his cattle
across the floor of Monument Valley and into Tombstone, somehow transplanted from southern Arizona complete with (potted) saguaro cactuses;
the OK Corral perched on a mesa nearby. Monument Valley consistently
symbolized the untamed wilderness that lay beyond the ramshackle towns,
beleaguered forts, isolated cabins or crude fences of the West's earliest
white pioneers.

In total, John Ford made seven movies in Monument Valley, including
his increasingly turgid "cavalry trilogy" of *Fort Apache* (1948), in which

Guided jeep tours are also run from *Goulding's Lodge* (see p.48),
and the associated *Wetherill Inn* in Kayenta. **All-day** trips (adult
$60, under-8s $45) start from the *Lodge* daily at 9am in season; **half-
day** tours (3hr 30min; adult $30, under-8s $18) leave daily at 9am,
1.30pm and 4pm; and there are regular shorter trips (2hr 30min;
adult $25, under-8s $15).

Seeing the valley

The most prominent of the buttes visible from outside the visitor center are the pair known as **The Mittens**, of which the Left or West
Mitten is in Arizona and the Right or East Mitten is in Utah. Rising a
thousand feet from the desert floor, each has a distinct "thumb" that
splinters off from its bulkier central section.

A rough, **unpaved road** drops from the western end of the parking lot to run through Monument Valley. The 17-mile loop marked as
the **self-drive** route makes a bumpy but bearable ride in an ordinary

both Wayne and Fonda played opposite the adult Shirley Temple, *She Wore A Yellow Ribbon* (1949), and *Rio Grande* (1950). He worked closely with the Navajo, who featured as all-purpose Indians whenever necessary, camping out in wigwams in *The Searchers*, for example, at what's now known as John Ford's Point. Medicine man Hosteen Tso is said to have been kept on hand to control the weather, and is credited with producing a snowstorm and a sandstorm to order for *Stagecoach*. The construction of Monument Valley's first road, in the 1950s, spoiled Ford's hitherto pristine landscape, but he carried on filming here until *Cheyenne Autumn* (1963). He died shortly after announcing plans to make *Appointment at Precedence* in the valley, in 1972.

The spectacle of Henry Fonda's son smoking marijuana in Monument Valley, in *Easy Rider* (1969), may have marked an end to the days of the classic Western, but the valley itself has remained in demand. Clint Eastwood had some perilous moments on top of the Totem Pole in *The Eiger Sanction* (1975), and Michael J Fox's souped-up DeLorean outgunned pursuing Indian warriors in *Back to the Future III* (1989). Other recent visitors have included Mick Jagger in *Freejack* (1992) and Tom Hanks in *Forrest Gump* (1994), while in Mario van Peebles' hip-hop Western *Posse* (1993), Monument Valley was almost bursting with Sioux Indians, gold mines, railroads and buffalo soldiers.

Monument Valley's starring role as the setting for many *Roadrunner cartoons* probably stems from its appearances in the wildly popular *Krazy Kat* syndicated comic strip of the 1920s and 1930s. Despite the opinions of learned critics such as e e cummings, who referred to the strip's "strictly irrational landscape", and Umberto Eco, who spoke of "surrealistic inventions, especially in the improbable lunar landscapes", artist **George Herriman** was a regular visitor to *Goulding's Lodge*. The adventures of Krazy Kat and Ignatz Mouse – set in Coconino County – were played out against a backdrop of realistic depictions of Monument Valley formations.

vehicle, and takes something over an hour to complete (open summer daily 8am–6pm; winter daily 8am–4.30pm). You're allowed to stop en route to stretch your legs, but not hike for any distance.

At the main halt, **John Ford Point**, you can browse a few jewellery stalls, enter a *hogan*-cum-gift store, and enjoy the classic widescreen valley panorama. A Navajo man normally poses on horseback at the tip of the nearby promontory, while closer at hand children in traditional dress invite you to photograph them for a dollar or two. The road goes on to pass near the **Totem Pole** before heading back via **Artist Point** to the visitor center.

Guided tours, with the operators listed on p.45, follow the same route but also take visitors "behind the scenes", beyond the main road, and offer a fascinating Navajo perspective on the place. Likely stops on longer tours include the **Sun's Eye** – a very high natural arch, with petroglyphs at its base of bighorn sheep – and the similar, even more dramatic **Ear of the Wind**, as well as an obligatory visit to a *hogan* for a weaving demonstration. The most striking **Anasazi remains** are in adjacent **Mystery Valley**, which you're only likely to see if you take a full-day tour.

Goulding's Lodge

The price codes used here are explained on p.15.

The only **accommodation** within twenty miles of Monument Valley is two miles west of US-163, along a road that starts immediately opposite the park approach road. *Goulding's Monument Valley Lodge* (PO Box 360001, Monument Valley UT 84536; ☎801/727-3231, fax 801/727-3344; Jan to mid-March & mid-Oct to Dec ④, mid-March to May ⑤, June to mid-Oct ⑥) rises in tiers at the foot of a large sandstone bluff, with superb views across the valley. It began life as a 1920s trading post, opened by Harry Goulding and his wife "Mike", and has expanded to incorporate an upscale motel, a restaurant, an indoor pool, a general store and a gas station. All the motel rooms have balconies, as well as VCRs to watch the *Lodge*'s library of westerns; dinner at the *Stagecoach Dining Room* will set you back up to $20. There's also a **campground** (mid-March–Oct; same phone), where sites cost $14 per night.

The original lodge building has been preserved much as the Gouldings left it, and holds a small but entertaining **movie museum** (April–Nov Mon–Fri & Sun 7.30am–9pm, Sat 8am–9.30pm), where visitors are invited to make a $2 donation towards scholarships for Navajo students. Behind it stands the cabin used by John Wayne, as Captain Nathan Brittles, in *She Wore A Yellow Ribbon*. The nearby store, incidentally, sells *John Wayne Toilet Tissue*: "it's rough, it's tough, and it doesn't take crap off anyone".

From Monument Valley to Canyon de Chelly

*Alternative bases for Monument Valley, further afield, include **Mexican Hat** (see p.442), **Bluff** (see p440) and **Kayenta** (see p.43).*

The most direct, and also the most scenic, route between the Navajo Nation's two major tourist attractions, Monument Valley and Canyon de Chelly, is **Arrowhead Hwy-59**. This gorgeous drive heads south off US-160 eight miles east of Kayenta, and then spends almost fifty miles skirting the northern flanks of Black Mesa.

For most of the way, it runs across flat desert grasslands, like a slightly more fertile version of Monument Valley, with cracks in the plains to either side hinting at unfathomable canyons. Here and there, off to the south, villages such as **Chilchinbito** and **Rough Rock** nestle against the mesa, but the road steadfastly ignores them. When it finally drops down **Carson Mesa** to reach Chinle Valley, you're confronted by the unlikely waters of **Many Farms Lake**. The road meets US-191 at the community of **Many Rivers**, fourteen miles north of Chinle.

Canyon de Chelly

A short way east of **Chinle**, halfway between Kayenta and Window Rock, twin sandstone walls emerge abruptly from the desert floor, climbing with phenomenal speed to become the thousand-foot cliffs

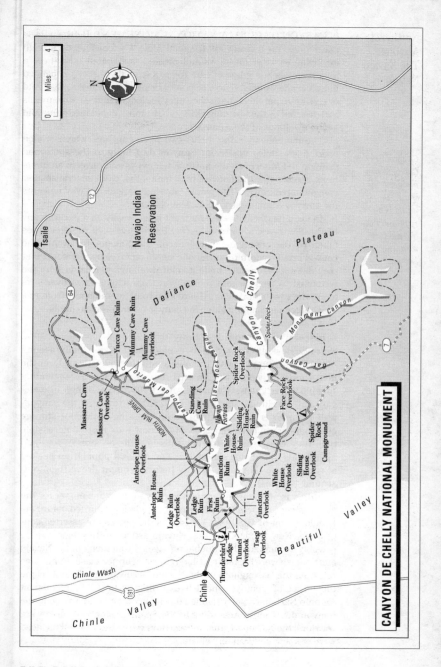

CANYON DE CHELLY NATIONAL MONUMENT

of **CANYON DE CHELLY NATIONAL MONUMENT**. Between these sheer sides, the cottonwood-fringed Chinle Wash meanders through an idyllic oasis of meadows and planted fields. Here and there a *hogan* stands in a grove of fruit trees, a straggle of sheep is penned in by a crude wooden fence, or ponies drink at the water's edge. And everywhere, perched above the valley on ledges in the canyon walls and dwarfed by the towering cliffs, are the long-abandoned stone and adobe dwellings of the **Anasazi**.

Canyon de Chelly is pronounced "de shay"; the name is a corruption of the Navajo tségi, *meaning "rock canyon".*

The monument in fact holds two main canyons, which branch apart a few miles upstream: **Canyon de Chelly** to the south and **Canyon del Muerto** to the north. Each twists and turns in all directions, scattered with immense rock monoliths, while several smaller canyons break away. The whole labyrinth threads its way upwards for thirty miles into the Chuska Mountains.

Canyon de Chelly is a magnificent place, easily on a par with any of the Southwest's national parks. Its relative lack of fame owes much to the continuing presence of the **Navajo**, for whom the canyon retains enormous symbolic significance, despite the fact that they did not themselves build its cliff dwellings. Casual visitors are restricted to peering into the canyon from above, from overlooks along the two "**rim drives**". There's no road in, and apart from one short hike you can only enter the canyons with a Navajo guide.

A history of Canyon de Chelly

Anasazi Basketmakers first occupied Canyon de Chelly around 300 AD, digging primitive pithouses into the valley floor. Over the next thousand years, the Anasazi moved first into free-standing "pueblo" apartment-style blocks, from 700 AD, and then into elegant cliff dwellings, starting in 1100 AD. Virtually all the canyon-wall complexes face south to catch the sun, with cool storage chambers set in deep recesses. Many now look more inaccessible than they were, thanks to rock falls and the erosion of toe- and hand-holds in the soft sandstone. The Anasazi population peaked at roughly one thousand, shortly before drought drove them out, around 1300 AD.

Hopis from the west farmed the canyon floor in summer for the next few centuries, but no permanent population returned before the Pueblo Revolt of 1680 (see p.474). As the Spanish re-asserted control over New Mexico, the first **Navajo** arrived in the region, quite possibly accompanied by Pueblo refugees. From then on, the Navajo and Spanish were locked in a bloody cycle of armed clashes and slave raids. As the "stronghold of the Navajo", Canyon de Chelly became the target of punitive **Spanish** expeditions. In 1805, Lieutenant Antonio Narbona's party gunned down over a hundred Navajo in the Canyon del Muerto. According to the Spanish, ninety of them were warriors; the Navajo say that the warriors were away, and all the dead were women, children and elders.

After the Yankees replaced the Mexicans in Santa Fe, the US Army in turn set about dislodging the Navajo. The process culminated in 1864, when General Carleton's men despatched all the Navajo they could round up on the "**Long Walk**" to Fort Sumner (see p.487). In Canyon de Chelly, **Kit Carson** starved the last Navajo warriors down from Navajo Fortress and destroyed their homes, livestock, and beloved peach orchards. Within a few years, however, Congress allowed the Navajo to return from their barbaric imprisonment. To this day, 25 Navajo families still farm the Canyon de Chelly in summer, the land having passed down from mother to daughter – as is usual for the Navajo – from the women between whom it was re-apportioned in the 1870s.

Arrival and information

The monument's **visitor center** is a little over two miles east of Chinle and US-191 (May–Sept daily 8am–6pm; Oct–April daily 8am–5pm; ☎520/674-5500). Set on the mound where Kit Carson signed the "treaty" that ended his siege of the canyon in 1864, it holds useful displays, and is the place to arrange unorthodox hiking or motorized expeditions (see p.52). No **public transport** runs closer to the canyon than the *Greyhound* buses and *Amtrak* trains that ply the I-40 corridor to the south.

*No **entrance** fee is charged at Canyon de Chelly.*

Accommodation and eating

For the moment, Canyon de Chelly remains remarkably unspoiled, but nearby facilities are overstretched in summer, and it's essential to book **accommodation** well in advance. None of the three options could be considered cheap. Much the best is *Thunderbird Lodge*, just past the visitor center near the canyon entrance (☎520/674-5841, 674-5842 or 1-800/679-2473, fax 674-5844; Nov–March ④, April–Oct ⑤). Its conventional motel rooms surround a century-old trading post, which houses a large, reasonably-priced self-service **cafeteria** (daily 6.30am–9pm) that's festooned with rugs from the well-stocked **giftshop** next door (daily 7.30am–9pm). If you take a *Thunderbird* sightseeing tour on the day you leave, check out of your room first; they charge $5 per hour extra after 11am.

Chinle's zip code is AZ 86503.

Locals had hoped the former **Garcia Trading Post**, half a mile short of the monument entrance, would be restored as an historic attraction. Instead, the site now holds the ersatz adobe *Holiday Inn* (☎520/674-500 or 1-800/23-HOTEL, fax 674-8264; winter ⑤, summer ⑥). This upscale hundred-room complex adjoins *Garcia's Restaurant*, which serves a breakfast buffet and full lunches and dinners. The *Best Western Canyon de Chelly*, just east of the US-191 intersection in Chinle (☎520/674-5875 or 1-800/327-0354, fax 674-3715; winter ④, summer ⑥), is an adequate but somewhat characterless alternative, again with its own restaurant.

No alcohol is sold in Chinle.

It's also possible to spend the night in one of several traditional *hogans* in the vicinity that belong to the Coyote Pass clan, and offer basic **B&B** lodging together with the opportunity for guided hikes (c/o Will Tsosie Jr, PO Box 91, Tsaile AZ 86556; ☎520/724-3383 or 602/674-9655; ⑤).

Chinle itself is a brief nondescript straggle on the highway, with service stations, *Taco Bell*, *Kentucky Fried Chicken*, a post office and a laundromat. In late August, it hosts the **Central Navajo Fair**.

No **camping** is permitted in the canyons. However, the first-come first-served *Cottonwood Campground* spreads among the trees beside *Thunderbird Lodge*. All sites are free, with a five-day maximum stay, but there are no showers, and when the water is cut off, from November to March, no restrooms either. The equally primitive, but less hectic Navajo-owned **Spider Rock RV & Campground** (☎520/674-5261) is near the end of South Rim Drive.

The view from above: the rim drives

To take the best photographs, tour the North Rim in the morning, the South Rim in the afternoon.

The monument's two rim drives are equally superb. The dead-end **South Rim Drive** traces the south rim of the Canyon de Chelly, while the **North Rim Drive** follows the north rim of the Canyon del Muerto and then heads off to the northeast. Both involve a round-trip drive of roughly forty miles from the visitor center, punctuated by overlooks where short walks across the mesa-top lead to views of natur-

---

Canyon de Chelly Tours

With the exception of the White House Trail (see p.53), taking a **guided tour** is the only way to get a close-up view of Canyon de Chelly's amazing Anasazi remains, or to see the Anasazi, Navajo and Hopi rock art that lines its walls. It's also unforgettable for the scenery alone, with the glorious, glowing cliffs towering far above you, and tranquil Navajo farms to either side.

The most popular are the **4WD** trips organized by *Thunderbird Lodge* (see p.51), which zigzag into either or both canyons, following the washes, which vary from two or three feet deep during the spring thaw to completely dry in summer. For most of the year, these "shake'n'bake" tours are in open-top flatbed trucks, lurching over the rutted riverbed, and the heat can be incredible; in winter they carry on in glass-roofed army vehicles with caterpillar tracks. A **half-day** trip (summer daily 9am & 2pm, winter daily 9am & 1pm; adults $34, under-13s $26) enables you to see a wide variety of sites and terrain, but to reach as far as Spider Rock, you have to take the **full-day** tour (late spring to early fall only, daily 9am; $55, no reductions). At the visitor center, you can also hire a Navajo guide to accompany you in your own 4WD vehicle for $10 per hour.

The visitor center can provide **hiking** guides for $10 per hour, and also arranges 4.5-mile, 4hr 30min, group hikes into the canyon, on no fixed schedule, for $10 per person. In addition, *Ernest Jones' Canyon Hiking Service* (☎520/674-5326) offers half-day, full-day and two-hour night hikes for between $12 and $20 per person.

Both *Justin's Horse Rental* (☎520/674-5678) and *Twin Trail Tours* (☎520/674-8425) organize **horseback** trips for $8 per person per hour, plus $8 an hour for a guide.

---

al or archeological wonders. Even if you don't stop at them all, each drive takes around half a day. Thefts from cars have been a major problem, so follow the prominent warnings.

The South Rim Drive

The first stop along the South Rim Drive, two miles up from the visitor center, **Tunnel Overlook** is a trailhead for guided hikes; unaccompanied travellers have no reason to stop. **Tsegi Overlook**, just beyond, is high above a sweeping curve in the canyon. Though the wash itself is seldom more than a trickle, its broad sandy floor clears a wide gap between the fringe of cottonwoods. Behind the *hogan* near the stream, fields and paddocks reach to the cliffs.

By now, as you look back west, Chinle is visible spreading across the valley, with the full stretch of Black Mesa beyond. Four miles up, **Junction Overlook** marks the meeting of the two main canyons. Canyon de Chelly narrows off to the right, behind a large monolith, while Canyon del Muerto to the left is much less conspicuous. Two tiny ruins indent the base of the canyon walls opposite.

At **White House Overlook**, six miles from the visitor center, Canyon de Chelly is 550ft deep, with its rim topped by strange whorls of slickrock. The majestic pale cliff that drops on the far side of the wash forms a stupendous backdrop for the photogenic **White House Ruin**. Squeezed into a tiny recess, well above the fields, this cluster of rooms originally stood above a larger pueblo on the valley floor, roughly half of which has now eroded away; it was probably reached by ladders on the roofs of the topmost towers.

The **White House Trail**, to the right of the viewing area, offers the sole opportunity for visitors to hike alone into the canyon. A beautiful if slightly precarious walk – some of it runs along ledges chiselled into the rock – it reaches the canyon floor through a tunnel that perfectly frames a Navajo *hogan* and its glowing attendant cottonwood. Thus far the ruin has been hidden from view, but once across the wooden footbridge that spans the wash you can admire it close up, separated only by a protective fence. Sixty feet above you, the ancient dwelling appears to be in almost perfect condition, still with the dazzling coat of plaster that gave it its name. Navajo traders nearby sell sodas and trinkets, and keep an eye out for hikers tempted to wander any further than the permitted hundred yards in either direction.

Allow at least two hours for the 2.5-mile round-trip hike on the White House Trail; 30 to 45 minutes to get down, and a good hour to get back up.

From **Sliding House Overlook** – separated from the road by a couple of hundred yards of cairned slickrock, twelve miles along – the **Sliding House Ruin** appears to be tucked into the slenderest of crevices in the cliff face. It's now steadily slipping down towards the ploughed Navajo fields below.

South Rim Drive ends after roughly twenty miles at the astonishing **Spider Rock**, where Monument and Bat canyons split away from Canyon de Chelly. These twin eight-hundred-foot pinnacles of rock

The Navajo Hogan

The traditional dwelling known as a *hogan* (pronounced *ho-wun*), as seen throughout Canyon de Chelly, is the focus of Navajo life, and the venue for all sacred ceremonies. Few Navajo may actually live in a *hogan* year-round, but every family has at least one, and those who still farm and raise sheep in the backcountry are likely to have several.

The earliest *hogans*, described by the Spanish in the sixteenth century and still widely used until the 1940s, were known as "**male** *hogans*". They consisted of three vertical forked sticks propped against each other, aligned to the north, south, and west, covered with logs, brush and mud, and with a door that faced east to greet the rising sun.

Virtually all the *hogans* on the reservation today are "**female**", larger six- or eight-sided structures made of cribbed horizontal logs and once again covered with mud. These became more popular at the end of the nineteenth century, with the advent of steel saws to cut the timber, and wagons to haul it; in fact many were made from salvaged railroad ties. The doorway still faces east, with a floor of hard-packed dirt to provide contact with the earth, and a smoke hole in the centre of the domed roof for access to the sky. Each area of the hogan has a particular significance; the south side "belongs" to the women and the north to the men, while the male head of the household sits to the west. Food is prepared and stored on the northeast side, and the southwest is the sleeping area.

Since the 1970s, more and more Navajo have chosen to live in trailers rather than face the labour of constantly renewing a *hogan*'s protective mud coating. It's also said that as many Navajo now die in hospital, the custom that a dwelling place in which a death has occurred must be abandoned has become less of a deterrent against building elaborate homes.

soar to within two hundred feet of the canyon rim, and are said by the Navajo to be home to Spider Woman. She taught them the art of weaving, but also steals misbehaving children – their bleached, chewed bones are strewn across the top of the double monolith.

The North Rim Drive

The **Ledge Ruin Overlook**, five miles along the North Rim Drive, is not among the monument's more significant moments, but both the viewpoints at **Antelope House Overlook**, five miles beyond that, are well worth seeing. The first faces across to **Navajo Fortress**, at the tip of the mesa that divides Canyon del Muerto from Black Rock Canyon. It took Kit Carson's besieging forces three months, from December 1863 onwards, to starve down a group of defiant Navajo warriors who had reached the summit of this solitary tower of rock by means of ladders which they then drew up behind them.

The other viewpoint looks down on **Antelope House Ruin**, at the base of a huge white overhang in a separate twist of Canyon del Muerto. This site was first occupied in 693 AD, and grew to comprise two square towers to the rear, plus a central plaza that held half a dozen dwellings. It's named after an antelope pictograph painted by the Navajo artist Dibé Yazhi, or Little Sheep, in the 1830s. He was also responsible for the "Spanish Mural" a little further along, which shows a Spanish lieutenant, priest and troops advancing through the canyon. Across the wash, in the **Tomb of the Weaver**, the embalmed body of an old man was found wrapped in golden eagle feathers.

The next, final spur road off the North Rim Drive splits to reach two separate overlooks. To the south, **Mummy Cave Overlook** offers a clear view of the single most striking ruin in the monument – **Mummy Cave Ruin**, which the Navajo call **House Under The Rock**. Inhabited for over a thousand years, from 300 AD until 1300 AD, it consists of two pueblo complexes deep in the shade of adjacent alcoves, with a prominent **Central Tower** on the spur in between. As the masonry of the tower is more sophisticated than the rest, and its construction has been dated to 1284 AD, archeologists believe it may have been built by migrants from Mesa Verde.

In the "cave" visible from **Massacre Cave Overlook**, to the north, Narbona's expedition of 1805 (see p.487) killed more than a hundred Navajo. It's more of a pitifully exposed ledge, far above the canyon floor, on which the huddled group were easily picked off by the Spanish, using ricochets off the overhang above. A short walk away – there's no sign or trail to guide you there – you can also see **Yucca House Ruin**, which unlike the rest of the monument's Anasazi sites is very near the mesa-top. It's an amazing location, set in a hollow in the rock above a sheer drop, with no conceivable way down to the valley floor, but almost none of the buildings survive.

As Hwy-64, the North Rim Drive continues for fifteen more miles to meet Arrowhead Hwy-12 in the small town of **TSAILE**. The upper floors of the Navajo Community College here hold the stimulating **Ned Hatathli Museum** of Navajo history (Mon–Fri 8am–noon & 1–5pm), which also sells craft items. It's possible to hike into Canyon del Muerto from this end, with a guide hired in Chinle.

Ganado and the Hubbell Trading Post

The village of **GANADO**, halfway between Chinle and the interstate, and thirty miles west of Window Rock, was named after Chief Ganado Mucho ("Won a lot"), one of the twelve signatories of the 1868 treaty that ended the Navajo's imprisonment at Fort Sumner.

After the Navajo returned from New Mexico, independent white entrepreneurs set up trading posts at the edge of the reservation, supplying the Indians with goods from the world beyond in return for craft items such as blankets and jewellery. The **Hubbell Trading Post**, founded by John Hubbell a mile west of Ganado, still functions today, now run by the Park Service (summer daily 8am–6pm; winter daily 8am–5pm; ☎520/755-3475). Located at the end of a tree-lined avenue beside the Pueblo Colorado Wash, it's a fascinating living museum, where you can watch Navajo weavers at work and wander out to the old stables, piled with hay and filled with venerable wooden wagons. Serious collectors pay premium prices for the best rugs and silverwork, but the groceries in the general store – pretty historic in themselves – make less expensive souvenirs.

Ganado has no **motels**, but the *Cafe Sage* is a good lunchtime stop. To the east, Hwy-264 climbs onto the thickly wooded Defiance Plateau and heads for Window Rock, while US-191 undulates for forty miles due south, through more forests, to Chambers on I-40.

Window Rock

*On the first
weekend after
Labor Day,
Window Rock
hosts the
Navajo Nation
Fair
(☎520/871-
6478).*

The capital of the Navajo Nation, **WINDOW ROCK**, sits on the Arizona–New Mexico border 25 miles northwest of Gallup. It only became capital in the 1930s, and remains much more of an administrative headquarters than a lively town. Most casual visitors simply pass through on Hwy-264, and spot a few malls and gas stations plus the showpiece *Navajo Nation Inn*. Technically, if you do that, you're not in Window Rock at all; you also won't see the rock itself.

Both "town" and rock are a mile or two north on Arrowhead Hwy-12. The **Window Rock**, an impressive, almost circular hole in a golden sandstone cliff, used to surmount a spring where water was collected for use in the Water Way ceremony. With the spring now dry, it has become the focus of a landscaped area with picnic tables, dedicated as the Navajo Nation Veterans Memorial in November 1995. Nearby stands the octagonal **Council Chamber** where the **Navajo Tribal Council** meets at least four times yearly.

*The **zip code**
for Window
Rock is AZ
86515.*

Back on Hwy-264, the small but comprehensive **Navajo Nation Museum** (winter Mon–Fri 8am–5pm; summer Mon–Sat 8am–6pm; donation) is housed in the *Navajo Arts and Crafts* store just east of the *Navajo Nation Inn*. Its well-arranged exhibits trace regional history from Pueblo times, covering the arrival of the Navajo, their exile at Fort Sumner and the contemporary crafts scene.

Practicalities

Regular **buses**, run by the *Navajo Transit System* (☎520/729-5458), connect Window Rock with Gallup, New Mexico (see p.82). The **Navajoland Tourism** office, in the Economic Development Building on Hwy-264 a couple of miles west of town, can supply general information on the region (PO Box 663; Mon–Fri 8am–5pm; ☎520/871-6436, fax 871-7381).

Much of the Navajo's day-to-day business is conducted in the **restaurant** and coffee shop of the *Navajo Nation Inn*, at 48 W Hwy-264 (☎520/871-4108 or 1-800/662-6189, fax 871-5466; ④), which is open for all meals daily. The rooms are good value, but can be hard to come by in summer; there are no other motels between Chinle and Gallup. Ask at the desk for details of local **tours**.

The rest of Window Rock holds few alternative places to **eat**, but in the Window Rock Shopping Center at the highway intersection, the friendly *Navajo Joes* (☎520/871-5775) is doing its best to introduce the Navajo to the joys of a morning espresso.

The Hopi Indian Reservation

The ten thousand inhabitants of the **Hopi Indian Reservation** can trace their ancestry back well over a thousand years, to the **Anasazi** people who dominated the entire Four Corners region. What's more, almost uniquely in the United States, the Hopi have occupied the same spot for at least eight hundred years.

To outsiders, it's not obvious why, with the whole Southwest to pick from, the Hopi should have chosen to live on three barren and unprepossessing fingers of rock, poking from the southern flanks of **Black Mesa** in the depths of northeast Arizona. There are two simple answers. The first is that while Black Mesa has no perennial streams, its subterranean rocks are tilted at just the correct angle to deliver a tiny but dependable trickle of water, and that the "black" in its name comes from the coal that gives the Hopi limitless reserves of fuel. The second is that the Hopi used to farm and hunt across a much wider area, and have only been restricted to their mesa-top villages by the steady encroachment of their Navajo neighbours. While the Hopi are celebrated for their skill at **"dry farming"**, managing to preserve enough precious liquid to grow corn, beans and squash on hand-tilled terraces laid out beneath the villages, this precarious and difficult way of life has nonetheless been forced upon them.

For a detailed history of the Hopi, see p.482.

The Hopi **language**, Hopic, belongs to the Uto-Aztecan group of languages, and is spoken in different dialects on each of the three mesas. While it bears similarities to the Ute and Paiute languages, the Hopi themselves have little in common with either tribe. Their culture and beliefs are instead closely related to those of the Pueblo peoples of New Mexico, to the east. Until the 1920s, the Hopi were known by a name coined by the people of Ácoma: **Moki**, or Moqui. Because that sounded too much like a Hopic word meaning "to have died", they then changed to *Hopi*, which means "well-behaved".

The Hopi are a matriarchal society, with homes, land and clan affiliation passing down the female line. They are not a united people; each of the thirteen villages or settlements, which belong to five main clusters, is an independent entity. As required by federal law, there is a Hopi Tribal Council, but it's currently recognized by the religious leaders of only two of the villages.

By their very survival, not to mention the persistence of their ancient beliefs and ceremonies in the heart of modern Arizona, the Hopi have long been a source of fascination to outsiders. Visitors are welcomed, but the Hopi have no desire to turn themselves into a

Hopi Religion: The Kachinas

The Hopi feel neither the urge nor the obligation to divulge details of their **religious beliefs** and practices to outsiders. To that end, they have resisted attempts to make Hopi a written language, or to expose it to scrutiny by teaching it in schools. Missionaries and anthropologists have gleaned what they can, but well-known accounts of Hopi spirituality, such as Frank Waters' *Book of the Hopi*, are based on the reports of informants not themselves initiated into the innermost secrets of the *kiva*. Inevitably, Hopi spirituality has been repeatedly mis-represented to the world, whether as barbarous devil-worship or New Age guff.

There is in any case no single unified Hopi religion; ceremonials vary from clan to clan and village to village. The most basic common element is the role of the **kachina** (often spelled *katsina*, with the plural *katsinum*). These "spirit messengers", which may represent the spirits of the dead, live in the San Francisco peaks north of Flagstaff, and return to the Hopi mesas in the form of rain-bearing clouds.

There are over three hundred different *kachinas*. At one time, they visited the mesas in person; now they come in the form of masked dancers. Not every village follows the same **ceremonial calendar**, but in general the *kachinas* arrive each year in early February for the *Powamuya* ceremony, or **Bean Dance**. Each matriarch receives a bundle of fresh bean sprouts to plant for the coming year, and the threats of the *so'so'yoktu* ogres to eat disobedient (*ka-hopi*) children are placated by gifts of food from their parents. The *kachinas* continue to visit throughout the growing season, before returning home after the *Niman* ceremony or **Home Dance** in July.

The Hopi do not worship the *kachinas*; their main significance is as examples and allegories for the children. All Hopi babies receive a *tihu* – what outsiders know as a **kachina** doll – at their first *Niman* ceremony, and the girls receive further dolls at each *Powamuya* and *Niman* ceremony thereafter. Most boys and girls alike are initiated into a **kachina society** at around the age of ten, when they discover that the *kachina* dancers are their own relatives, and begin to participate themselves.

All the Southwestern pueblos had some form of *kachina* cult, which is occasionally suggested to have arisen as a post-Hispanic mimicry of Catholicism. However, pottery, murals and rock carvings point to an earlier origin, around 1300 AD. Anthropologists have tended to argue that it spread east from the Hopi mesas or Zuni rather than west from the Rio Grande, though the *kachina* cult's virtual disappearance along the Rio Grande is probably due to vigorous Spanish attempts to stamp it out. In fact, it seems to have reached both regions from the **Mimbres** culture to the south, and to have developed in **Mexico**.

The role and iconography of specific Hopi *kachinas* strongly echo **Aztec** deities such as **Tlaloc**, the god of rain, and **Quetzalcoatl**, the plumed serpent, who was also the bringer of rain and corn. For the Aztec preoccupation with death, blood, and human sacrifice, however, the Hopi and other Southwestern people substituted an obsessive focus on **rain**.

Attending Hopi ceremonies

For much of the twentieth century, Hopi ceremonies were promoted as tourist attractions. Even after cameras were banned in 1916, occasions such as the **Snake Dance**, when members of the Snake clan dance with live snakes between their teeth, attracted as many as 2500 observers. In recent years, however, the Hopi have moved towards the **exclusion** of non-Indians. By 1989, Second Mesa had closed all its ceremonies to outsiders, and it was joined by all the First Mesa villages in 1992 after the publication of a *Marvel* comic that characterized the *kachinas* as violent avengers.

While spectators are now very unlikely to be allowed at any *kachina* dances, however, some **social dances**, held between August and January when the *kachinas* are away from the mesas, may still be "open". Held in the village plazas, these usually take place at the weekend, so that Hopi who live off the reservation can return. Specific timings tend not to be announced until a few days in advance; for information, ask at the Cultural Center or call ☎520/734-2441.

Kachina dolls

Kachina masks, worn by the dancers, are sacred objects, and the Hopi have successfully petitioned to remove them from museum displays. However, because a *tihu* (the plural is *ti'tihu*) is just an instructional tool, it has become acceptable for **kachina dolls** to be sold to outsiders as collectors' items.

The *ti'tihu* given to Hopi children were originally flat dolls that were intended to hang from beams or walls within the home. Made from kaolin clay, and thus white in colour, the basic shape was painted to show a head, plus a pair of arms folded over a kilt that represented rain. Local trading posts were stocking these simple dolls in the 1890s, and by 1900 they were being made specifically for sale.

Since then, they have acquired a much greater complexity of form and colour, as well as feet to enable them to stand. Most are carved from cotton-wood roots; the carving is seen as a prayer for water, symbolizing the root's own search for water. The artists themselves – who thanks to the art market's desire for signed pieces are no longer anonymous – became more interested in representing human anatomy, and also began to tailor their designs to suit the tastes of white collectors. Strictly speaking, only men should carve *ti'tihu*, but the rewards are great enough for some women now to be making them as well.

Not all *ti'tihu* represent *kachinas*. Some of the most popular designs depict the **clowns** who also appear during ceremonies, such as the black-and-white-striped *koshares*, and the knobbed "mudheads" or *koyemsi*. Just as the clowns may devise costumes to mock tourists, for example, certain *ti'tihu* are caricatures of recognizable figures, like basketball players or anthropologists.

The Hopi do however draw the line at attempts by others to cash in on the commercial success of the *kachina*-doll business. During the 1960s, the tribal council failed in a bid to copyright the word "*kachina*", and thus stop Navajo and other non-Indian copyists from using the name. Genuine hand-carved dolls are both exquisite and expensive, and a top-class carver will produce fewer than fifty per year, while fake *kachinas* are mass-produced in New Mexico at the rate of over 100,000 per year. People from Ácoma pueblo recently acceded to a Hopi request to stop working in one such factory, but the Navajo have refused to do so.

Good places to **buy** a *kachina* doll include the Hopi Cultural Center on Second Mesa, the Museum of Northern Arizona in Flagstaff (see p.261), and the Pueblo Cultural Center in Albuquerque (see p.162), though it's hard to find a reasonable-sized piece for under $300. The best bet of all is to take a tour of **Walpi**, and see what you're offered.

If you do get the chance to attend a Hopi ceremony, wear clothing that fully covers your body, keep your distance, and do not photograph, sketch or question either dancers or audience.

The Hopi
Indian
Reservation

For more
about Hopi
crafts, see
p.30.

tourist attraction. Two motels make it possible to stay on the reservation, and stores and galleries provide plenty of opportunity to buy much-prized Hopi **crafts** such as pottery, basketwork, silver overlay jewellery and hand-carved *kachina* dolls. However, tourists who arrive in the hope of extensive sightseeing – let alone spiritual revelations – are likely to leave disappointed, and quite possibly dismayed by what they perceive as conspicuous poverty.

Since 1986, when increased mining revenues finally placed the tribal economy on a relatively secure footing, non-Indians have been barred from almost all Hopi ceremonies. These days, the only way visitors can get a sense of traditional Hopi life is to take a guided tour of the magnificently situated village of **Walpi**, on First Mesa.

Arrival and information

The Hopi mesas – three distinct spurs along a 25-mile stretch of Black Mesa, numbered from east to west as **First**, **Second** and **Third** mesas – are roughly fifty miles north of I-40, fifty miles east of Tuba City, and ninety miles southwest of Canyon de Chelly.

Both the roads from the interstate up to the mesas, **Hwy-87** from Winslow and **Hwy-77** from Holbrook, run through a superbly desolate butte-studded segment of the Navajo reservation, on the western fringes of the Painted Desert. If you're coming from the Grand Canyon, take **Hwy-264** east from US-160. Once beyond the Hopi outpost of **Moenkopi**, just outside Tuba City (see p.39), this traverses some rugged canyonlands and then climbs onto Third Mesa after around fifty miles.

For tourist
information,
but not motel
reservations,
call ☎ 520/
734-2441 ext
190 or 520/
734-6648.

The essential first stop is the roadside **Hopi Cultural Center** below Second Mesa, which serves as motel, restaurant, gift store and information centre. If any forthcoming events are open to tourists, the friendly staff should be able to tell you about them. Otherwise, check out the wide-ranging historical exhibits, and the choice displays of Hopi arts and crafts, in the adjoining **museum** (summer Mon–Sat 8am–5pm, Sun 9am–4pm; winter Mon–Fri 8am–5pm; $3). The large single-storey shop next door is particularly good for silver.

Touring the Hopi mesas

Each of the mesa-top Hopi villages centres around a **plaza**, where successive generations have built new houses on top of the old ones as they crumble into sand. Often the main entrance is via the roof, reached by a wooden ladder. A few buildings are now constructed of grey concrete blocks, but they still blend almost imperceptibly with the ruins that trail away down the slopes. Several villages stand on open seams of coal, and large chunks of coal lie scattered around. Outhouses are dotted across the hillsides; all waste was traditionally thrown over the edge of the mesa to tumble down and fertilize the terraces – a conservationist policy that works less well now that refrigerators and old bedsteads are being thrown over too.

Fortunately, the most impressive village, **WALPI**, is the only one that offers **guided tours** to visitors (Mon–Fri 9.30am–4pm; donation). By Hopi standards, Walpi is not in fact that old; it was hastily thrown together in the immediate aftermath of the Pueblo Revolt of 1680, when the people of First Mesa decided to move to a more secure site in the face of possible Spanish or Navajo attack (see p.483). The spot they chose is absolutely stunning, standing alone at the narrow southernmost tip of the mesa, and connected to the other First Mesa villages by the merest slender neck of stone, with a drop of three hundred feet to either side. It's now home to around 35 people, who do without electricity or running water.

To see Walpi, take Hwy-264 to modern **POLACCA**, at the foot of First Mesa, then drive a mile up the twisting paved road until it ends in **SICHOMOVI**. Although you can't tell where one village stops and the next begins, you've just passed through **HANO**. Its inhabitants arrived during the Pueblo Revolt to offer their services as the defenders of First Mesa, and still speak the Tewa language.

The tours assemble in Sichomovi's small Ponsi Hall Community Center, setting off at regular intervals for a half-hour walk to and around Walpi. Depending on the time of year, you'll either be in a group of twenty or so, or on your own, but either way there's plenty of opportunity to ask questions, and to buy pottery, *kachina* dolls, and fresh-baked *piiki*, a flatbread made with blue cornflour.

Accommodation and eating

The best place to **stay** on the Hopi Reservation is the modern, mock-Pueblo *Hopi Cultural Center Motel* (☎520/734-2401; ④); in summer, its unexotic but adequate rooms are usually booked solid a week or more in advance. The cafeteria serves good solid meals, but be warned that there's precious little to do between the time it closes, at 9pm, and 7am the next morning, when you can indulge your curiosity by having blue cornflakes for breakfast.

*The **price** codes used here are explained on p.15.*

Extremely basic double rooms are also available at the *Keams Canyon Motel* (☎520/738-2297; ②), twenty miles along Hwy-264 at the eastern edge of the reservation. There's a free campground here too, as well as a popular cafe, open until 8pm on weekdays and 6pm on weekends and dishing up local-style fast food (watch out for *noqkwivi*, an exceptionally tough mutton stew).

Southwest Colorado

In ancient times, of course, the straight-line boundaries that divide the states of Arizona, New Mexico, Utah and Colorado – and mark the northeastern limits of the Navajo Nation – did not exist. As a result, while Colorado might not spring to mind as a "Southwestern" state, its far southwest corner holds some of the region's most

fascinating archeological sites. **Mesa Verde National Park** is
absolutely unmissable, and **Ute Mountain Tribal Park** offers adventurous travellers an even more exhilarating sense of discovery.

Once you've crossed the border into Colorado, it's hard to resist
the lure of the Rockies, looming along the skyline to the north.
There's no scope in this book to do more than sketch out a brief tour,
looping up the **San Juan Skyway** from lively **Durango** to historic
mining towns such as **Silverton** and **Ouray**.

Four Corners Monument Navajo Tribal Park

The **Four Corners Monument Navajo Tribal Park** (summer daily
7am–7pm, winter daily 8am–5pm; $1.50), reached by a short spur
road half a mile northeast of US-160, is the only place in the United
States where four states meet at a single point. However exciting you
may find the concept, the reality is bleak and dull. A steady stream of
visitors mooch around the pivotal brass plaque, ponderously con-
torting a limb into each state for demeaning photographs. Navajo
stalls on all sides sell crafts, T-shirts and fry-bread.

Ute Mountain Tribal Park

For a couple of centuries after **Ute Indians** acquired horses from the
Spanish, their hunting territory extended east from Utah as far as
what's now Nebraska. As miners pushed the Victorian-era frontier
westwards, however, the Ute were confined to ever decreasing areas
of poorer land. The creation of reservations split them into three separate groups: the **Northern Utes**, who now live in the mountains
near Utah's border with Wyoming; the **Southern Utes**, who occupy
a strip of southern Colorado south of Durango; and the **Ute
Mountain Utes**. These latter take their name from a long, low mountain ridge in Colorado's far southwestern corner, known to outsiders
as **Sleeping Ute Mountain** because of its uncanny resemblance,
when seen from the east, to a slumbering warrior.

Among the Southwest's poorest peoples, the Ute Mountain Utes
draw their income from mineral leases and a casino near the main
settlement of **Towaoc**. They also run the inaccessible but utterly
enthralling **Ute Mountain Tribal Park**, which abuts against Mesa
Verde National Park and preserves an equally extraordinary but far
less visited assortment of ancient **Anasazi** remains.

The park's **cliff dwellings**, such as the eighty-room Lion House,
and the precarious Eagle's Nest, were built at the same time as those
on Mesa Verde, and can only be seen on **Ute-guided tours**. These
start by arrangement from the tribe's **visitor center**-cum-museum
(no fixed hours; ☎970/565-3751 ext 282 or 1-800/847-5485),
housed in a former gas station at the intersection of US-160 and US-
666, twenty miles up from the Four Corners Monument. Full-day
tours (8.30am–4.30pm) cost $25, and involve walking three miles

and climbing five tall ladders; easier half-day trips are $15. Visitors should bring their own sturdy vehicles and all supplies.

Hovenweep National Monument

Hidden in the fifty-mile-wide swathe of no-man's-land that straddles the Utah–Colorado border, the Anasazi ruins at **HOVENWEEP NATIONAL MONUMENT** lack the scale and setting of the Mesa Verde cliff dwellings or similar Four Corners sites. Instead, sprouting from the rims of shallow desert canyons and dwarfed by the distant mountains, they offer a haunting sense of timeless isolation. They also have one distinctive and unusual feature, in the shape of the tall round **towers** that many archeologists regard as early astronomical observatories.

There is no admission fee at Hovenweep, which is named after a Ute word meaning "deserted valley".

Whatever most tourist maps may suggest, almost all the roads that lead to Hovenweep have now been paved, thanks largely to companies such as *Mobil*, drilling for oil and gas around Aneth. The monument is best reached by driving 35 miles due west from Cortez, leaving US-160 near the airport at the south end of town, or 25 miles east from US-191 via Hwy-262, which branches off halfway between Bluff and Blanding in Utah; it's also possible to follow a dirt road southwest from Pleasant View in Colorado.

Although Hovenweep preserves six distinct conglomerations of ruins, easy public access is restricted to the **Square Tower Group**, behind the monument's small **ranger station** (daily 8am–5pm; no phone). Until a few years ago, it was possible to walk among and even into several different structures, but the trail system now keeps visitors at a safe distance.

The shorter of the two main routes, the half-mile **Tower Loop Trail**, offers good views of the largest ruins, at the head of Little Ruin Canyon. The grandly named **Hovenweep Castle**, a four-square building just a few yards from the ranger station, was constructed around 1200 AD. It may well have stood guard over a much larger pueblo complex that nestled on the sandy floor of the canyon a mere thirty feet below, clustered around the perennial spring that was the site's only source of water. Only **Square Tower Ruin** now survives down there, while Hovenweep Castle has endured, a perfect illustration of the Biblical admonition that only a house built on rock shall stand.

The **Square Tower Ruins Trail** continues along the far side of the canyon, and eventually dips across it and loops back to the ranger station, a circuit that takes a little less than an hour to complete. Highlights along the way include a number of ruins perched on solitary boulders and pinnacles, as well as the fortress-like **Stronghold House** and the **Unit-type House**, where niches in the walls appear to line up with the angle of the sun at the summer and winter solstices.

No accommodation, gasoline or food is available at or anywhere near Hovenweep, but (funding permitting) the 31-site **campground** beside the ranger station remains open all year ($6; no reservations). In winter, water is only available at the ranger station.

Cortez

The town of **CORTEZ**, twenty miles north of the US-160/US-166 intersection, consists of little more than a long curve of over-developed highway. Were it not so close to Mesa Verde National Park, there would be no reason to visit; as it is, Cortez offers a large if not exactly broad selection of roadside motels and diners.

Practicalities

The zip code for Cortez is CO 81321.

The local **visitor center**, on the edge of City Park at 928 E Main St (daily 9am–6pm; ☎970/565-3414 or 1-800/253-1616) has information on the entire state. Both *Mesa Verde Tours* (☎970/ 656-1278 or 1-800/626-2066) and *Four Corners Tours* (☎970/882-8880 or 1-800/884-0591) offer full-day **tours** of Mesa Verde for around $60.

The price codes used here are explained on p.15.

Motels along the main strip include the *Arrow National 9 Inn*, 440 S Broadway (☎970/565-7778; ②), *Aneth Lodge Budget Six*, 645 E Main St (☎970/565-3453; ②), and the slightly more upmarket *El Capri*, 2110 S Broadway (☎970/565-3764; winter ②, summer ④). *Kelly's Place*, ten miles west at 14663 County Rd G (☎970/565-3125 or 1-800/745-4885, fax 565-3540; ④), has eight en-suite **B&B** rooms, with guided hikes and horse-rides available.

For an old-time Western **diner**, head for *Homesteaders*, 45 E Main St (☎970/565-6253; closed Sun in winter), where most of the barbecued meats and fish, and Mexican fry-ups, cost under $10. The nearby *Main Street Brewery*, 21 E Main St (☎970/564-9112) marks a newer Western tradition, as a **brewpub** selling microbrews plus simple meals. Part cafe, part ramshackle bookstore, *Earth Song Haven*, at 34 W Main St (☎970/565-9125), serves eccentric $5 lunch specials such as *pansit bihan* – containing rice, noodles, choc-chip cookies, melon and gherkins – and good smoothies.

Around Montezuma Valley

Cortez is very much Montezuma Valley's biggest town these days, but a thousand years ago the entire valley was densely populated. Those earlier occupants are commemorated in small museums and lesser-known sites dotted around the valley.

The **Anasazi Heritage Center**, three miles west of **DOLORES** and six miles due north of Cortez, centres on a couple of twelfth-century pueblos. Excavated and stabilized during the construction of nearby McPhee Dam, they're named for the eighteenth-century Spanish friars Domínguez and Escalante, who first noted the traces of prehistoric Indians in the area. Admission to both the well-equipped museum of Pueblo life (daily 9am–5pm), and the trail around the ruins themselves (daily 8am–5.30pm), is free.

From **Pleasant View** on US-666, fourteen miles northwest, an undulating straight road leads nine miles to **Lowry Pueblo Ruins** (no fixed hours; free). There's not a tremendous amount to see at this free-standing pueblo, but in summer it's noteworthy as the one of the few sites where at least part of an **Anasazi mural** remains in place on the walls of a "Great Kiva". In winter, on the other hand, the mural is taken away for preservation, and the gravel surface of the approach road's last four miles is often impassable to vehicles.

Southwest
Colorado

*For more
about Great
Kivas, see
p.77.*

Also in summer, **Crow Canyon Archeological Center**, five miles northwest of Cortez at 23390 County Rd K, runs day programmes for amateur archeologists (June to mid-Sept, Tues, Wed & Thurs 9am; mid-Sept to mid-Oct Tues & Thurs 9am; $40; ☎970/565-8975 or 1-800/422-8975). These provide the chance to assist on digs at Anasazi sites in the valley, such as **Sand Canyon Pueblo**, a walled city that once covered the cliff-tops at Crow Canyon, or the 1800-room **Yellow Jacket** further north.

The *Rio Grande Southern Hotel*, 101 S Fifth Street (PO Box 5162, Dolores CO 81323; ☎970/882-7527; winter ②, summer ③), is an inexpensive, atmospheric **B&B inn**, not far from the Anasazi Heritage Center in Dolores. There's more accommodation available in little **MANCOS**, ten miles east, including the *Mesa Verde Motel* (PO Box 552, Mancos CO 81328; ☎970/533-7741 or 1-800/825-MESA; winter ②, summer ③), which has its own restaurant.

*Yucca House
National
Monument
near Cortez,
shown on
many maps,
has never been
excavated and
remains closed
to the public.*

Mesa Verde National Park

MESA VERDE NATIONAL PARK, the only national park in the US to be exclusively devoted to archeological remains, is set high in the plateaux of southwest Colorado, off US-160 halfway between Cortez and Mancos. It's an astonishing place, so far off the beaten track that its extensive **Anasazi ruins** remained unseen by outsiders until late in the nineteenth century.

Mesa Verde itself – the "green table" – is a densely wooded sandstone plateau, cut at its southern edge by sheer canyons that divide the land into narrow fingers. Hundreds of natural alcoves, eaten high into the canyon walls by seeping water, served as homes for the Anasazi for over 700 years; by the time they were abandoned, around 1300 AD, several held multi-storey **cliff dwellings** that have remained virtually intact to this day.

By Southwestern standards, the mesa is not especially pretty, and it doesn't offer the same **hiking** opportunities as the region's other national parks. The relics however are compelling enough to make Mesa Verde an essential stop on any Four Corners itinerary. It can get very crowded in summer, so the **best months** to visit are in May, September and October. In **winter**, an elevation of over 8000ft means that most of the sights become inaccessible, though the park, its main museum, and one ruin – Spruce Tree House – remain open all year round. **Concessions** such as gas, food and lodging only operate between late April and mid-October.

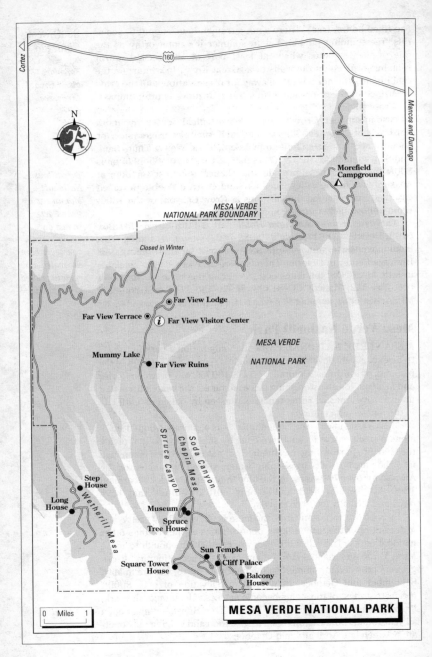

MESA VERDE NATIONAL PARK

A history of Mesa Verde

Although Archaic sites in Montezuma Valley down below date back to 5500BC, the Anasazi are thought to have been the only inhabitants that Mesa Verde has ever had. No one has lived here since the thirteenth century, and despite repeated searches the earliest trace of humans is a Modified Basketmaker pithouse from 550 AD.

People first moved to the mesa, therefore, at around the time they acquired the skill of pottery. They were not so much farmers as gardeners, who continued to gather wild plants and hunt deer and rabbits while also growing small fields of corn and owning domesticated dogs and turkeys. For 500 years, they lived in pithouses dug into the floors of sheltered caves; then, around 1100 AD, they congregated in walled villages up on the mesa tops. A century later, they returned to the canyon-side alcoves to build the "palaces" for which Mesa Verde is now famous.

As some rooms were exclusively used for storage, each settlement probably held roughly as many people as it had rooms. That would give the largest, Cliff Palace, a population approaching 250. Two or three people may have slept in a typical living room, measuring six feet by eight feet, while each family had its own *kiva* – see p.468 – which when not in ceremonial use was used for weaving and other domestic activities. Neither the architecture, nor the relatively few burials that have been found – some in sealed chambers, and some simply, if reverentially, in the trash heaps – indicate any rigid social hierarchy. Mesa Verde may well have been a peripheral community. While its population is thought to have peaked at around 2500, in the middle of the thirteenth century, there were at least eight larger surface pueblos in Montezuma Valley.

Ironically, archeologists regard the cliff dwellings that seem so elegant to modern visitors as signs of a declining culture. They say the mesa-top pueblos were more sophisticated in both design and construction, while the alcove complexes are haphazard accretions, forced into contortions by the constraints of the rock, and characterized by inferior craftsmanship. These were not ideal homes; older members of the community must have found it impossible to get in or out, while children lived in constant peril of fatal falls. In theory, each complex got its water from the seep or spring that had created its alcove in the first place, but many of those springs had run dry, leaving them with a constant cycle of fetching and carrying.

All of which begs the question of **why** the cliff dwellings were built. Some experts argue that they were primarily defensive, but there's no evidence they were ever attacked, and in any case dwellings such as Spruce Tree House lie exposed to assault, while the towers are of little use as lookouts. Agricultural space may have been at a premium, with the entire mesa top criss-crossed by dams, terraces and irrigation channels. In any case, Mesa Verde was completely abandoned by the end of the thirteenth century. The tradi-

Southwest Colorado

For a detailed history of Anasazi culture, see p.468.

tional explanation, that a drought lasting from 1276 until 1299 drove the Anasazi away, only tells part of the story, in that six previous droughts had been just as bad. The likely truth is that both firewood and game animals in the region had depleted to the point where survival became too much of a struggle.

Although Mesa Verde was named by the Spanish in the seventeenth century, the ruins themselves went unrecorded for two hundred more years. Photographer William Henry Jackson snapped some lesser sites in 1874, and a passing prospector spotted Balcony House in 1884, but the outside world first took notice when Richard Wetherill stumbled upon Cliff Palace in a snowstorm in 1888. The Wetherills, a local ranching family, took to finding and selling Anasazi artefacts as a way of life, and helped the Swedish Count Gustaf Nordenskïold to ship caseloads of ancient pottery to Europe in 1891. Their activities prompted the Antiquities Act of 1906, which prohibited dealing in archeological treasures, and the creation of Mesa Verde National Park in the same year.

Thanks to Nordenskïold, the National Museum of Finland holds the world's finest collection of Mesa Verde artefacts.

Arrival and information

The access road to Mesa Verde climbs south from US-160 ten miles east of **Cortez**, and 35 miles west of **Durango**. Once past the entrance station – where an **admission charge** of $5 per vehicle, $3 for motorcyclists, cyclists, and pedestrians, is payable – it twists and turns for fifteen miles to the **Far View visitor center** (late April to late Oct daily 8am–5pm; ☎529-4461). Exhibits inside cover Navajo, Hopi and Pueblo crafts and jewellery. Immediately beyond, the road divides to the two main constellations of remains: Chapin Mesa to the south, and Wetherill Mesa to the west.

To receive information by mail, write to Mesa Verde National Park, PO Box 8, Mesa Verde CO 81330.

To tour any of the three major ruins, as opposed to simply skimming around the overlooks, you must first buy **tickets** at the visitor center. The exact seasons and times of the tours vary according to both funding and climate; each costs $1.25, with tickets valid for one specific time only. On **Chapin Mesa**, as a rule, **Cliff Palace** is open between 9am and 5pm daily from late April until early November, with tours every half-hour in midsummer and every hour in low season, and **Balcony House** is open for hourly tours from late April until mid-October, during the same hours. You may well not be allowed to tour Balcony House and Cliff Palace on the same day (though many couples circumvent the regulations by queuing separately for tickets). If you're forced to choose, it is at least possible to see Cliff Palace without joining a tour, but on the other hand the Cliff Palace tours are much less strenuous than those of Balcony House. On **Wetherill Mesa**, which is generally accessible between late May and early September, hourly tours of **Long House** operate between 9am and 4pm daily. Allow several hours between tours on Chapin and Wetherill mesas. After the visitor center closes in late fall, tour tickets are sold for the remainder of the season at the museum on Chapin Mesa (see opposite).

*Mesa Verde tours from **Durango** are detailed on p.71, from **Cortez** on p.64.*

Park **bus tours** start daily in season from *Far View Lodge* and *Morefield Campground* (adults $16 for a half-day, $21 for a full day; under-12s $8 on either); contact either for details.

Accommodation and eating

The only **rooms** at Mesa Verde are at the summer-only *Far View Motor Lodge*, near the visitor center (PO Box 277, Mancos CO 81328; ☎970/529-4421 or 1-800/449-2288; winter ☎970/533-7731; late April to mid-June & early to mid-Oct ④, mid-June to early Oct ⑤). It's a peaceful place, away from the bustle of the park; guest rooms, which lack phones or TVs, are in two-storey units dotted around the mesa-top. The sweeping views reach into the Rockies to the north, and across nearby slopes blackened by a forest fire in 1996, but no archeological sites are visible. The *Metate Room*, in the mock-adobe main lodge, serves all meals daily.

Lodging in Cortez is detailed on p.64, and in Durango on p.72.

The park's official **campground** – the very large, never full *Morefield Campground* (late April to mid-Oct; ☎970/529-4421) – is four miles up from the entrance. No reservations are necessary, and a site for one or two vehicles costs $9.

Food is also available in season at the *Far View Terrace*, across from the visitor center – which serves espresso coffees and has a gas station – and all year round at *Spruce Tree Terrace* near the Chapin Mesa museum, which has a pleasant shaded terrace. Light snacks are sold at the end of the road on Wetherill Mesa.

Chapin Mesa

A couple of miles from the visitor center towards **Chapin Mesa**, you reach **Far View** itself, a mesa-top pueblo abandoned early in the thirteenth century. Thanks to the coal-burning power plants in the middle distance, it seldom lives up to its name. Archeologists used to think it drew its water from the artificial **Mummy Lake** nearby; now they wonder whether this large depression, capable of holding half a million gallons, was in fact an open-air plaza.

Another four miles on, **Chapin Mesa Archeological Museum** contains the park's best displays on the Anasazi, including several dioramas made in the 1930s (summer daily 8am–6.30pm, winter daily 8am–5pm). Hikers can register at the adjacent **park headquarters** for a couple of unremarkable two- to three-mile nature trails.

This is also the starting point for the short, steep hike down to **Spruce Tree House**, the only ruin that can be seen in winter. Consisting of several well-preserved three-storey structures, snugly moulded into the recesses of a rocky alcove and fronted by open plazas, the neat little village was occupied from 1200 AD until 1276 AD. One of its *kivas* has been re-roofed, and visitors can enter the dusty, unadorned interior by way of a ladder.

Ruins Road, beyond the museum area, is only open between April and early November, from 8am until sunset daily. The western of its two one-way, six-mile loops is the one to skip if you're pressed for time, but its overlooks are still interesting. At **Square Tower House**, a 500-foot stroll is rewarded by views of an 80-room alcove complex, focused around the four-storey Square Tower – at 26 feet, the tallest tower in the park. **Sun Point Overlook** looks across Spruce Canyon to as many as twelve distinct cliff dwellings, including Cliff Palace, making it clear just how crowded the canyon was in its heyday. Unlike the alcove sites, the mesa-top **Sun Temple**, next, was built to a premeditated design, and may have been a ceremonial centre for the whole community. It was never finished, however, and its shape and function can only really be appreciated from aerial photos; walking around its walls is not very thrilling.

*Details of Cliff Palace tours are on p.68. As with most of the ruins, the best time for **photography** is late afternoon.*

The first stop on the eastern portion of Ruins Road, **Cliff Palace**, is the largest Anasazi cliff dwelling to survive anywhere. Tucked a hundred feet below an overhanging ledge of pale rock, its 217 rooms once housed over two hundred people, while its 23 *kivas* suggest they were split between 23 families or clans. If you haven't managed to get a ticket for a tour (see p.68), you can still get a great view from the promontory where the tour groups gather, just below the parking lot. Entering the ruin itself, especially on a quieter day, provides a haunting evocation of a lost and little-known world, as you walk through the empty plazas, and peer down into the mysterious *kivas*. Fading Anasazi murals can still be discerned inside some of the structures. As you leave, climbing an unalarming metal stairway through a narrow crevice, you may spot the original toe- and footholds used by the Anasazi.

Technically, Ruins Road passes out of the national park just beyond Cliff Palace, and briefly enters **Ute Mountain Tribal Park**, where you can pick up information on tours (see p.62). It then arrives at **Balcony House**. This is one of the few Mesa Verde complexes that was clearly geared towards defence; access is very difficult, and it's not visible from above. Guided tours involve scrambling up three hair-raising ladders and crawling through a narrow tunnel, teetering all the while above a steep drop into Soda Canyon. Park authorities present it as being more "fun" than the other ruins, but unless you share the fearless Anasazi attitude to heights, you might prefer to give it a miss.

Distant views of Balcony House can be had from three quarters of a mile along the forested **Soda Canyon Overlook Trail**, which starts a short way further around Ruins Road.

Wetherill Mesa

The tortuous twelve-mile drive onto **Wetherill Mesa** from the visitor center is usually open from late May until early September. Access is then permitted between 8am and 4.30pm daily, though large vehicles such as RVs, and also cycles, are always banned.

From the parking lot at the far end of the road, where there's a ranger station and snack kiosk, a free **miniature train** loops around the tip of the mesa. Priority is given to visitors with tickets for the timed Long House tours (see p.68). Any time spent waiting can be occupied by walking down to examine nearby **Step House**, where a single alcove contains a restored pithouse, dated to 626 AD, as well as a pueblo from 1226 AD.

The mini-train stops at various trailheads from which hikers can walk to early mesa-top sites or alcove overlooks, but its principal destination is the **Long House**. The park's second largest ruin is set in its largest cave; hour-long tours descend sixty or so steps to reach its central plaza, then scramble around its 150 rooms and 21 *kivas*. These ruins are said to be especially authentic, having been "re-sta-bilized" in recent years, rather than subjected to the same extensive rebuilding as the better-known sites, earlier this century.

Durango

DURANGO, named after Durango Mexico and now also twinned with it, was founded in 1880 as a rail junction for the gold-rush com-munity of Silverton, 45 miles further north. **Steam trains** still run the same high-mountain route, through the Animas Valley, and are the foundation of the local tourist economy. From the depot at 479 Main Ave, at the south end of town, the **Durango & Silverton Narrow Gauge Railroad** operates up to four return trips daily between late April and October (all leave in early morning; $43 round-trip; reserve at least two weeks in advance; ☎970/247-2733). Shorter excur-sions, on the scenic section as far as Cascade Canyon, run between late November and late April (daily 10am; $36).

Durango has also become one of the West's latest boom towns, attracting a large influx of long-distance computerized teleworkers. Combine them with outdoors enthusiasts, who come to ride their **mountain bikes** on the gruelling back roads nearby, and in the morning at least the place has a youthful, energetic buzz. In the evening, they're all a bit too wiped out to do anything very much.

Arrival and information

Durango's **visitor center** is a block or two south of downtown near the train station (summer Mon–Fri 8am–7pm, Sat 10am–6pm, Sun 11am–5pm; winter Mon–Fri 8am–6pm, Sat 8am–5pm, Sun 10am–4pm; ☎970/247-0312 or 1-800/525-8855). *Greyhound* **buses** between Denver and Albuquerque call in at 275 E Eighth Ave.

Mountain bikes can rented from *Southwest Adventures*, 780 Main Ave (☎970/259-0370), or *Mountain Bike Specialists*, 949 Main Ave (☎970/247-4066), while the cheapest **4WD rentals** are from *RentAWreck*, 21760 US-160W (☎970/259-5858). *Mesa Verde Tours* (☎970/247-4161 or 1-800/626-2066) and *Durango Transportation* (☎970/259-4818) pick up from Durango motels at around 8am daily for $60 **Mesa Verde tours**.

Durango's zip code is CO 81301.

Southwest
Colorado

*The price
codes used
here are
explained on
p.15.*

Accommodation

Very few of Durango's many **motels**, and none of the budget ones,
are in walking distance of downtown, though a **free trolley** (Mon–Fri
7am–7pm) does run forty-block loops up and down Main Avenue.
Almost all the motels double their rates in summer.

Durango Youth Hostel, 543 E Second Ave; ☎970/247-9905. Handy downtown private hostel, with $12 dorms and a few basic private rooms. ①/②.

Scrubby Oaks, 1901 Florida Rd; ☎970/247-2176. Good-value mountain-view
B&B, three miles east of town. ④.

Siesta, 3475 Main Ave; ☎970/247-0741. Very inexpensive motel, well up the
highway from the centre. Winter ①, summer ②.

Strater Hotel, 699 Main Ave; ☎970/247-4431 or 1-800/247-4431, fax 259-
2208. Major downtown landmark, with almost a hundred antique-furnished
rooms, not far from railroad depot. Winter ④, summer ⑥.

Vagabond Inn, 2180 Main Ave; ☎970/259-5901, fax 247-5345. Inexpensive
but adequate motel, which looks smarter on the outside than it does once
you're inside. Winter ②, summer ③.

Eating

Main Avenue downtown, and the block or two to either side of it, are
filled with places to **eat** and **drink**, some with their sights set on afflu-
ent train passengers, others aimed at young bikers.

Carver's Bakery & Brewpub, 1022 Main Ave; ☎970/259-2545. Bustling
brewpub, open Mon–Sat 6.30am–10pm, Sun 6.30am–1pm, with a good menu
of big breakfasts and grilled specials during the day, and beer at night.

Lady Falconburgh's Barley Exchange, Century Mall, 640 Main Ave;
☎970/382-9664. Popular pub between Sixth and Seventh in the heart of
downtown, open daily 11.30am–2pm, with snacks of all kinds and over a hundred beers.

Red Snapper, 144 E Ninth St; ☎970/259-3417. Upmarket seafood and steak
joint, open nightly 5–10pm, with daily specials, a large salad bar – and plenty
of red snappers. With prices on the high side, at $14–20 per entree, you'd
expect the food to be better.

B W Shay's, 948 Main Ave; ☎970/247-4144. Downtown diner, open Mon–Sat
11am–10pm, serving standard but well-cooked Mexican and American food.

Steaming Bean Co, 915 Main Ave; ☎970/385-7901. Early-morning espressos
and pastries, speciality drinks, sandwiches and live music later on.

*The
Continental
Divide runs
along the
mountain-tops
east of
Silverton, with
the source of
the Rio Grande
on the far side.*

Silverton

North of Durango, the **San Juan Skyway** sets off to loop over two
hundred miles through the Rockies, up US-550 and then back via
Hwy-145 and US-160. Its first stretch, across invigorating high passes, is known as the **Million Dollar Highway**, for the amount of gold
in the ore-bearing gravel that was used in its construction.

The first town along the way, **SILVERTON**, spreads across a
small flat valley in the heart of the mountains fifty miles up, and
marks journey's end for the narrow-gauge railroad from Durango.

It's one of Colorado's most atmospheric mountain towns, with wide dirt-paved streets leading off towards the hills to either side of the one main road. Silverton's zinc and copper mining days only came to an end in 1991; the population has dropped since then, but those that remain have resisted suggestions that its future lies in legalizing gambling to draw in tourists. Meanwhile, the false-front stores along "Notorious Blair Street", paralleling the main drag, recall the days when Bat Masterson was the city marshal – and are the scene of a daily shoot-out at 5.30pm.

Practicalities

Silverton is heavily dependent on tourism, which makes it pretty quiet in off season. It's also geared more towards day-trippers than overnight guests, so to spend a night here is to step back a century. Bargain **accommodation** is to be had at the ugly but well-maintained *Triangle Motel*, 848 Greene St (☎970/387-5780; winter ②, summer ③), at the south end of town, which also offers good-value two-room suites and jeep rental, though the central, swanky *Grand Imperial Hotel*, 1219 Greene St (☎970/387-5527 or 1-800/341-3340; winter ②, summer ④) is not much more expensive. The *French Bakery*, 1250 Greene St (☎970/387-5976), serves **food** from sandwiches to full meals, and has the cheap, somewhat run-down *Teller House Hotel* upstairs (☎970/387-5423 or 1-800/342-4338; winter ②, summer ③). Nearby, *Romero's*, at 1151 Greene St (☎970/387-5561), is an enjoyable Mexican *cantina*.

Silverton's zip code is CO 81433.

Ouray

The equally attractive mining community of **OURAY** lies 23 miles north of Silverton, on the far side of the 11,018-foot **Red Mountain Pass**, where the bare rock beneath the snow really is red, thanks to mineral deposits. The Million Dollar Highway twists and turns, passing abandoned mine workings and rusting machinery in the most unlikely and inaccessible spots; back roads into the mountains offer rich pickings for hikers or 4WD drivers.

Ouray itself nestles into another cosy and verdant valley, with the commercially run **Ouray Hot Springs** beside the Uncompahgre River at the north end of town. A mile or so south, a one-way loop dirt road leads to **Box Canon Falls Park** (daily 8am–7pm; $2), where a straightforward 500-foot trail, partly along a swaying wooden parapet, leads into the dark, narrow Box Cañon. At the far end, the falls thunder through a tiny cleft in the mountain.

Practicalities

Ouray's **visitor center** is outside the hot springs (daily 8am–6pm; ☎970/325-4746 or 1-800/228-1876). *Switzerland of America* (☎970/325-4484 or 1-800/432-5337), and *Red Hot Ryders*, 700 Main St (☎970/325-4444 or 1-800/325-4385), rent **4WD vehicles**.

Ouray's zip code is CO 81427.

At *Box Canyon Lodge*, an old-style timber **motel** at 45 Third Ave below the park (☎970/387-4981 or 1-800/327-5080; ③), you can bathe in natural hot tubs; the luxurious **B&B** *St Elmo Hotel*, 426 Main St (☎970/325-4951, fax 325-0348; winter ④, summer ⑤), has a good **restaurant**. The central *Grounds Keeper Coffee House and Eatery*, 524 Main St (☎970/325-0550), serves espresso coffees and light lunches, while the *Ouray Brewing Co*, next door at 522 Main St (☎970/325-4265), is a non-smoking brewpub.

Telluride

TELLURIDE, 120 miles northwest of Durango on Hwy-145, is another former mining village. In the 1880s, it was briefly home to the young Butch Cassidy; he robbed his first bank here in 1889. Telluride is now better known as a **ski resort**, and rivals Aspen as the prime winter destination for the stars. It has, however, achieved this status without losing its character – the wide main street, a National Historic District with low-slung buildings on either side, still heads directly up towards one of the most stupendous mountain views in the Rockies. Healthy young bohemians with few visible means of support but top-notch ski equipment form the bulk of the 1200 citizens, while most of the glitzy visitors hang out two miles above the town in **Mountain Village**; the two places are connected by a free year-round gondola service.

Practicalities

Telluride's **zip** *code is CO 81435.*

Accommodation in Telluride is much less expensive in summer than during ski season, though prices do go up for the Bluegrass Festival in June, the Jazz Festival at the beginning of August and the Film Festival at the start of September. As well as being the town's official **information** service, *Telluride Central Reservations*, 666 W Colorado Ave (winter Mon–Fri 9am–5pm; summer daily 9am–7pm; ☎970/728-4431 or 1-800/525-3455) co-ordinates lodging and package deals, with free lift tickets for the first month of the season for guests in certain lodges. Skiing comes half-price if you stay in any of seven neighbouring towns.

Of specific places, the 1895 *New Sheridan Hotel*, 231 W Colorado Ave (☎970/728-4351 or 1-800/200-1891, fax 728-5024; winter ⑥, summer ③), offers some bargain rooms with shared bath, and the *Victoria Inn*, 401 W Pacific Ave (☎970/728-6601; winter ⑤, summer ③), has clean doubles. *Oak Street Inn*, 134 N Oak St (☎970/728-3383; ①/③), is an *AYH* **youth hostel** with private rooms.

Eddie's, 300 W Colorado Ave (☎970/728-5335), serves good Italian food and home-brewed ales; other **brewpubs** in town include the bakery-bar *Baked In Brewed In Telluride*, 127 S Fir St (☎970/728-4705), and the *San Juan Brewing Co* in the Historic Depot, 300 S Townsend St (☎970/728-0100).

Northwest New Mexico

Although **northwest New Mexico** formed the heart of the Dinetah, the Navajo's original homeland in the Southwest, the Navajo territories here are now less visited than their more scenic equivalents in Arizona. Archeology buffs are drawn to **Chaco Canyon** and **Aztec Ruins**, which while among the most significant Anasazi sites anywhere are, unfortunately for tourists, less photogenic than their better-known rivals. None of the towns nearby, whether on or off the reservation, holds any lasting interest.

Instead the region is notorious as the home of the **Four Corners plant**, near **Farmington**. After this coal-fired generating station opened in the 1960s, it was said to be the single greatest source of pollution in the United States, emitting more noxious gases than either New York City or Los Angeles. Regulations have been tightened since then, but with the **Navajo Mine**, the largest open-pit coal mine in the West, just a mile away, and several other generating plants in the immediate neighbourhood, there's no incentive for outsiders to linger. For the Navajo, of course, who provide much of the industry's workforce, it's a different story.

Shiprock

By far the most striking landmark in the dusty red plains of New Mexico's far northwestern corner is the craggy monolith known as **Shiprock**. In Navajo legend, as *Tsé bit'a'i* or "Rock Wing", this awesome 1500-foot peak was home to one or two monstrous birds, which were either killed by the hero Monster Slayer, or turned into an eagle and an owl. To Anglo eyes, it resembled instead a mighty ocean-going ship. Navajo medicine men continued to use it in sacred ceremonies until 1939, when it was defiled by being climbed by *Sierra Club* members including David Brower, the "Arch-Druid" who later founded *Friends of the Earth* (see p.391).

US-666 runs within a few miles of Shiprock's vast, eerie bulk. Signs at a roadside pull-out explain that the mountain is a volcanic plug, the hard central core of a volcano that has itself eroded away. There's no point trying to approach it any closer – you can't walk up to the base, let alone climb it – or in stopping at the sprawling mining town six miles north, also known as **Shiprock**.

Farmington

FARMINGTON, the largest town in northwestern New Mexico, lies roughly fifty miles west of the Four Corners Monument and fifty miles southeast of Durango, Colorado. Once you know that it was founded as "Farmingtown", in 1876, you know enough of its past; now that it's a mere ten miles west of both the Navajo Mine and the Four Corners Power Plant, you can imagine its present.

*In early October, the town of Shiprock plays host to the **Northern Navajo Fair**.*

USA Today rates USA-666 between Shiprock and Gallup – which bears the Number of the Beast – as the most dangerous highway in the country.

When the mineral boom was getting going, from the 1950s onwards, Farmington acquired a dreadful reputation as a definitive "edge-of-the-res" community, rife with racism and violence. In recent years, it has cleaned itself up and prospered accordingly, with new developments such as the **Animas Valley Mall**, 4601 E Main St, making it the principal business centre of a wide area.

Farmington's one concession to tourism is its **museum**, on the northern edge of downtown at 302 N Orchard St (Tues–Fri noon–5pm, Sat 10am–5pm; free), which traces its history from the geological "New Mexico Seacoast" up to trading-post times.

The **Bisti Wilderness**, thirty miles due south of Farmington on Hwy-371, is an area of weirdly eroded desert badlands where the Bureau of Land Management encourages hikers to indulge in "primitive types of recreation". If you want to exploit its considerable oil deposits, on the other hand, you'll need a permit.

Practicalities

*Farmington's
zip code is NM
87401.*

The local **visitor center** is at 203 W Main St (Mon–Sat 8am–5pm, Sun noon–4pm;   ☎505/326-7602 or 1-800/448-1240). *TNM&O Coaches*, 101 E Animas St (☎505/325-1009), run **buses** to Durango and Albuquerque, while the Four Corners Airport, west of town, has **flights** to Albuquerque (*Mountain West*; ☎505/326-3338 or 1-800/637-2247), Denver (*United Express*; ☎505/326-4495 or 1-800/242-6522), and Phoenix (*America West Express*; ☎505/326-4494 or 1-800/235-9292).

You may not set out with the intention of spending a night in Farmington, but with over twenty **motels** to choose from, including two *Motel 6*'s, you might as well stay. The best budget choice is the *Super 8*, southeast on US-64 at 1601 Bloomfield Hwy (☎505/325-1813 or 1-800/800-8000; ②). Upscale alternatives include *La Quinta*, 675 Scott Ave (☎505/327-4706 or 1-800/531-5900; ③), and the nearby *Best Western Inn at Farmington*, 700 Scott Ave (☎505/327-5221 or 1-800/528-1234; ④), which has a reasonable if predictable **restaurant**. *Clancy's Pub*, 2703 E 20th St (☎505/325-8176), is a youth-oriented pseudo-Irish **bar**, serving simple meals.

Aztec

The town of **AZTEC**, fourteen miles northeast of Farmington, is the county seat of San Juan County, but it's a lower-key and more enjoyable place to visit. On its leafy central thoroughfare, the homely **Aztec Museum**, 125 N Main Ave (summer Mon–Sat 9am–5pm; winter Mon–Sat 10am–4pm; $1) incorporates a pioneer village, with frontier-style buildings such as a schoolhouse, a jail and a bank.

The main reason anyone comes to Aztec, however, is to see **Aztec Ruins National Monument**, across the Animas River a mile north of town (summer daily 8am–6pm; winter daily 8am–5pm; $2; ☎505/334-6174). This preserves an **Anasazi pueblo** erroneously attributed by early Anglo settlers to ancient Mexicans. In fact it's a large "outlier" settlement, built from 1111 AD onwards by people from the Chaco culture (see p.80), and connected with Chaco Canyon, 64 miles south, by a die-straight road now only visible from the air. Aztec stands halfway between Chaco and Mesa Verde, and is thought to have been remodelled by a new wave of settlers from Mesa Verde around 1225 AD.

From the visitor center, which holds some interesting Anasazi artefacts, a short trail leads to the **West Ruin**, the only part of the site to have been excavated. This 500-room E-shaped structure was entirely walled, with only one entrance. Its **Great Kiva** – the technical term for a *kiva* used by an entire community rather than an individual clan or family – was reconstructed in 1934, making it the only Great Kiva in the Southwest that can be seen in anything approaching its original state. Aspects of the restoration remain conjectural, but there's no disputing the circular chamber's sheer size. It measured fifty feet across, with each of the four pillars that held up its 95-ton roof resting on four 375-pound limestone disks, carried here from forty miles away. Archeologists say that the *kiva* may have been in use when the *kachina* religion was first being developed, and that the fifteen side rooms, now connected with the main chamber by ladders, may have served as changing rooms from which masked figures would emerge during ceremonies.

For more about kachinas, *see p.58.*

Practicalities

Aztec's well-stocked **visitor center**, east of the river at 110 N Ash St (Mon–Fri 9am–noon & 1–5pm; ☎505/334-9951), even sells an *Aztecopoly* board game. *M.A.R.* (☎505/334-6675) offer tailor-made **tours** of the area for small groups, at $80 for half a day or $175 for a full day, and can take you to little-known sites such as the fortified "Pueblitos of Dinetah", where Pueblo peoples hid from the avenging Spanish after the Pueblo Revolt (see p.474).

Aztec's zip code is NM 87410.

Aztec has three **motels**: the shiny new *Step Back Inn*, where US-550 meets Main Avenue at 103 W Aztec Blvd (☎505/344-1200 or 1-800/334-1255; winter ③, summer ④); the smaller *Enchantment Lodge*, 1800 W Aztec Blvd (☎505/334-6143; ②); and a tiny budget option, *El Aztec Motel*, 221 S Main Ave (☎505/334-6300; ②), in the heart of town. The *Aztec Restaurant*, 107 W Aztec Blvd (☎505/334-9586), is a venerable steak-and-pancake diner opposite the *Step Back*, while the *Weary Traveler*, 103 N Main Ave (☎505/344-3881), a few doors down from the museum, is a gift store that also sells espresso coffees, pastries and sandwiches.

The price codes used here are explained on p.15.

Bloomfield

BLOOMFIELD, eight miles south of Aztec or twelve miles east of Farmington, is an unattractive little desert crossroads notable only for its **Salmon Ruin**, two miles west (April–Oct daily 9am–5pm;

Nov–March Mon–Sat 9am–5pm, Sun noon–5pm; $2; ☎505/632-2013). Built perhaps twenty years before its neighbour at Aztec, this outlying Chacoan pueblo went through the same cycle of abandonment and re-occupation by migrants from Mesa Verde. Homesteader George Salmon discovered it on his land during the 1880s, and his family spared it the usual looting until they sold it to the county in 1979. Excavations since then have unearthed well over a million artefacts, the best of which are displayed, together with reconstructed dwellings, in the on-site museum.

Practicalities

Bloomfield's
zip code *is NM*
87413.

If you find yourself in Bloomfield for the night, much the best of its few **motels** is the *Super 8*, at 505 W Broadway (☎505/632-2113 or 1-800/800-8000; ②). The *Triangle Cafe*, across the highway at 506 W Broadway (☎505/632-9918), is a traditional, friendly local **diner**.

Chaco Canyon

For casual visitors, the long, bumpy ride to the **Anasazi ruins** of **CHACO CANYON**, twenty miles off the nearest paved road, may seem more bother than it's worth. True, the site protected as the Chaco Culture National Historic Park is the **largest pre-Columbian city** in North America. For beauty and drama, however, it can't compete with lesser settlements such as Canyon de Chelly. The low-walled canyon is a mere scratch in the scrubby high-desert plains, and the Chaco Wash that runs through it is often completely dry.

Once you accept that you won't have amazing photos to show the folks back home, there's still plenty about Chaco to take your breath away. Over 3600 separate sites have been logged in the canyon, of which the thirteen principal ones are open to visitors. Six of these, arrayed along the canyon's north wall, are what's known as **great houses** – self-contained pueblos, three or four stories high, whose fortress-like walls concealed up to eight hundred rooms. The largest, **Pueblo Bonito**, is claimed to have been the largest single building in America until structural steel was developed in 1898.

Arrival and information

Both the **routes to Chaco Canyon** entail driving twenty miles over rough but passable dirt roads. Open all year, these should not be attempted during, or within a day of, a rainstorm. Whether you approach from the south – by following Hwy-57 up from **SEVEN LAKES**, eighteen miles northeast of **Crownpoint** – or from the north or east – by turning off Hwy-44 at **NAGEEZI**, 36 miles south of **Bloomfield** – you'll enter the park at its southeast corner.

Admission to
Chaco Canyon
costs $4 per
vehicle.

Park maps and brochures, plus schedules of summer-only ranger-led tours, are available in the **visitor center** (summer daily 8am–6pm; winter daily 8am–5pm; ☎505/786-7014). This also shows videos such as *Sundagger*, which explains how carefully sited rocks and petroglyphs atop nearby **Fajada Butte** plotted not only the annual solstices but also the moon's 18.5-year cycle.

The basic first-come, first-served *Gallo* **campground** ($8), a short way east of the visitor center, is the only visitor facility the park has to offer; from April to October it's usually full by 3pm. Bring any firewood you require. Backcountry camping is forbidden.

Seeing the park

The gates of the canyon's eight-mile one-way **loop road** are immediately north of the visitor center, and open the same hours. The major stop is at the far end, where **Pueblo Bonito** ("Beautiful town" in Spanish), can be explored on an easy half-mile trail. Work on this four-storey D-shaped structure, which is almost perfectly aligned east–west, started in 850 AD, and continued for around three hundred years. Speculation that hordes of slaves were forced to build it have been deflated by precise dating of its parts; even at its busiest time, a workforce of just thirty men, cutting and hauling trees for a full month each year, and quarrying and shaping stone for four months every two years, could have done the job.

The trail leads around the back of Pueblo Bonito, passing the spot where Threatening Rock, a colossal boulder whose collapse the Anasazi staved off with prayer sticks and supporting walls, finally destroyed thirty rooms in 1941. Entering the ruin via its lowest levels, the path reaches its central plaza, which held at least three **Great Kivas** of the kind restored at Aztec (see p.77). From there, you can walk through the passageways and chambers of the pueblo proper, where the rows of neatly finished doorways, each framed by the next, are Chaco's most photographed feature.

A separate trail from the same parking lot heads to the smaller complex of **Chetro Ketl**, a quarter of a mile to the east. Constructed over the course of a century, from 1010 AD onwards, this shows Chacoan masonry at its most sophisticated, with horizontal rows of large, squared-off stones chinked with smaller, flatter stones and set into a bed of adobe mortar with a mosaic-like precision. Many of its original beams (*vigas*) remain in place, and a vivid fragment of an ancient mural is protected behind a glass panel.

Pueblo del Arroyo, the next stop along the loop road, is the only great house to stand right beside Chaco Wash. Although it rarely holds much water, the stream channel is much deeper and broader than it was in Anasazi days, thanks to erosion of its bank caused by over-grazing. The pueblo, raised on a small hillock, was occupied between 1070 AD and 1105 AD. Only half of it has been excavated.

Casa Rinconada, perched on another mound not far beyond, is the canyon's largest **Great Kiva**, at 62 feet across. It now lies open to the sun, the subtleties of its precise astronomical alignments lost but its central features still clearly identifiable. Archeologists are

The Chaco Phenomenon

To archeologists, Chaco Canyon represents the apogee of Anasazi achievement. However, what they call the **Chaco Phenomenon** remains one of the Southwest's greatest puzzles. How can the canyon's apparent unsuitability for large-scale occupation – if anything it was slightly drier in Anasazi times than it is today – be reconciled with its massive structures, and demonstrable influence over an "empire" that covered at least 25,000 square miles ?

Pithouses built by early Anasazi Basketmakers are scattered around the canyon, but Chaco's surface pueblos began to appear during the ninth century. Sophisticated masonry techniques were either developed, or brought here by migrants from the Mesa Verde region, around 1000 AD, enabling the construction of larger multi-storey apartments. The canyon's heyday was between around 1050 AD and 1125 AD; its last definite tree-ring date is 1132 AD, and by 1200 AD it was abandoned altogether. A prodigious amount of work went into its construction; upwards of 200,000 tree trunks, mostly ponderosa pines and corkbark fir, were carried here from hillsides fifty or more miles away, without the use of animals or the wheel.

When Chaco became a national monument in 1907, archeologists estimated that it was once home to twenty thousand people. That figure was later revised down to five thousand, based on the number of rooms in the pueblos. Now, in view of the low number of burials that have been found, the lack of signs that the upper floors were ever inhabited, and the canyon's poor soil, modern theories suggest that Chaco never held more than two thousand inhabitants.

It's now thought that Chaco was not so much a residential community as a **ceremonial centre**. Huge quantities of **turquoise** have been discovered – harvester ants, who for some reason collect blue and green turquoise to adorn their nests, scavenged fifty thousand pieces in Pueblo Bonito alone. Turquoise, still precious to contemporary Indian cultures, was the most valuable trading commodity in the ancient Southwest. The Chacoans shipped in raw turquoise from distant mines – mostly to the east, in the Cerrillos region (see p.114) – and crafted it into sacred and ornamental objects. Ultimately, turquoise from Chaco passed from hand to hand down trading networks into the heart of Mexico; ninety percent of the turquoise

unsure whether the two large vaults in the *kiva* floor served as foot drums, or to propagate seedlings; both usages are suggested by modern Pueblo and especially Hopi practices. Minor house sites and unexcavated mounds are scattered on the canyon floor nearby.

Crownpoint

CROWNPOINT, almost forty miles southwest of Chaco Canyon and 24 miles north of the I-40 town of **THOREAU**, is the principal town along the eastern flank of the Navajo Nation. Its only conceivable appeal for tourists is as the site of the **Navajo Rug Auction**, held on the third Friday of each month at Crownpoint Elementary School. Viewing is from 3pm until 6pm, with the auction at 7pm, and prices found in the Aztec capital of Tenochtitlan was of Southwestern origin. Similarly, the parrots and scarlet macaws whose skeletons have been found here must have come from southern Mexico or beyond.

However, Chaco's primary significance was much more local. Having started as a small settlement that specialized in trading turquoise, it probably became a place of a pilgrimage, where individuals came, with appropriate rituals, to obtain the sacred stone. From there, it's a small step to picture regional **festivals**, held at regular intervals, when large crowds would assemble for public ceremonies. For most of the year, Chaco held a relatively small, high-caste population, and the upper floors of its pueblos were empty or used for storage; at festival times, they accommodated a large influx of temporary guests.

Evidence for this ceremonial role includes the extraordinary 450-mile network of **roads** that links Chaco with around 75 "outlier" communities. Averaging thirty feet in width, they were far wider than ordinary human foot-traffic could require; in fact they were often more like causeways, built of hard-packed stone and running arrow-straight across cliffs, mesas and canyons. Most are now only visible from the air. The longest to have been identified stretched all the way to Aztec Ruins, 64 miles north (see p.76), but if that same line is extended *south*, it makes a virtually perfect alignment with the site known as **Casas Grandes**, over 300 miles away in Mexico. Roadside beacons may have been lit to summon pilgrims to major festivals.

Navajo legends relate that Chaco was ruled by the despotic **Great Gambler**, who was born to a poor Chacoan woman, taught to gamble by his father, the Sun, and won control over the canyon and all it held. When he was eventually defeated, he was shot into the sky, where he once more accumulated great wealth, and returned to the region in the shape of the Spaniards. Meanwhile, freed of their oppressor, the people of Chaco had dispersed.

Trying to guess **why** the Chacoans left the canyon when they did – from 1230 AD onwards – is probably futile, although only a tiny reduction in rainfall might have been enough to drive them out. **Where** they went, however, is no great mystery. Aztec, which was at its peak between 1110 AD to 1275 AD, is an obvious possibility, as is Casas Grandes, occupied from 1250 AD to 1500 AD. Ácoma Pueblo (see p.86) is among many modern pueblos that show a clear continuity with Chacoan culture, while the Zuni say a medicine society known as the Sword Swallowers joined them from Chaco.

range from $100 up to perhaps $2000. For more details, contact Crownpoint Rug Weavers (☎505/786-7386).

Western New Mexico

Although the reality of today's **I-40** may not match the romance of its predecessor, **Route 66**, crossing **western New Mexico** still has its rewards. The interstate passes through some memorable desert scenery, while successive detours to the south lead to crucial sites in Southwestern history. At **Zuni Pueblo**, Spanish *conquistadores* first encountered the region's indigenous inhabitants, and **El Morro National Monument** records centuries of further incursions. Above all, Ácoma Pueblo, the superbly sited "Sky City", makes it worth spending a night in the dreary interstate towns of **Gallup** or **Grants**.

Gallup

As the largest town in I-40's 300-mile run between Albuquerque and Flagstaff, you might expect the famous Route 66 halt of **GALLUP**, 25 miles from the Arizona state line, to offer a diverting break in a long day's drive. Don't get your hopes up; cheap motels make it a handy overnight pitstop, but there's nothing to hold your interest.

Gallup sprang into being when the railroad arrived in 1881, and its role as the major railhead for the Navajo Nation has since been augmented by the construction of first Route 66, and later I-40. The interstate and the railroad tracks still run east–west through the heart of town, paralleled by a ten-mile stretch of the former Route 66 that's lined with endless budget motels and fast-food outlets.

In the week leading up to the second weekend in August, the Navajo and other local Native Americans come together in Gallup for the **Inter-Tribal Indian Ceremonial**, a six-day extravaganza centred on Red Rock State Park, four miles east of town. A two-day pow-wow is followed by four days of rodeo, craft shows and dancing, culminating in a Saturday morning parade through town. For information and tickets, call ☎505/863-3896 or 1-800/233-4528.

During the Inter-Tribal Indian Ceremonial, motel reservations are a must.

During the rest of the year, Gallup remains a major commercial centre for the Navajo. An estimated eighty percent of all **jewellery** sold in the Southwest passes through the hands of traders like *Shush Yaz*, 214 W Aztec Ave (☎505/722-0130), *Richardson's Trading Company*, 222 W 66 Ave (☎505/722-4762), and *Tobe Turpen's*, 1710 S Second St (☎505/722-3806 or 1-800/545-7958). For more mundane shopping, head to the **Rio West Mall**, near exit 20 off I-40, which has the usual mall stores and a movie theatre.

Practicalities

The *Amtrak* station at 201 E 66 Ave has one daily **train** to Flagstaff (7.50pm) and one to Albuquerque (10.33am). **Buses** along I-40 call in at the *Greyhound* station at 105 S Dean St (☎520/863-3761), which is also used by *Navajo Transit System* (☎520/729-5458) services to Window Rock, Arizona (see p.56). Gallup's **visitor center** is a mile from downtown, across the railroad tracks and the interstate at 701 Montoya Blvd (summer daily 8am–5pm; winter Mon–Fri 8am–5pm; ☎505/863-3841 or 1-800/242-4282).

El Rancho's original slogan was "The Charm of Yesterday and the Convenience of Tomorrow".

Absolutely *the* place to **stay** is *El Rancho Hotel and Motel*, 1000 E 66 Ave (☎505/863-9311 or 1-800/543-6351; ③–④), built in 1937 by the brother of movie mogul D W Griffith. From the murals in its opulent Spanish Revival lobby, to the photo gallery of celebrity Hollywood guests – John Wayne, Humphrey Bogart and Ronald Reagan among them – this sumptuous Route 66 roadhouse is bursting with atmosphere. Its **restaurant** serves burgers named after

Wayne and Bogart, plus (separate) Lucille Ball and Errol Flynn sandwiches, and the usual range of barbecue, steaks, and shrimp. There's also a bar and a gift store. Some guest rooms are in the original ranchhouse, the rest in a two-storey motel building alongside.

Even if you avoid the scuzziest of Gallup's other 1600 motel rooms, you can pay under $30 per night at places like the *Colonial*, 1007 W Coal Ave (☎505/863-6821; ①), and the *Ambassador*, 1601 W 66 Ave (☎505/722-3843; ①). The *Super 8*, 1715 W Hwy-66 (☎505/722-5300 or 1-800/800-8000; winter ②, summer ③), is not quite up to the chain's usual standards, but it's still a reliable option. The best place to **camp** is *Red Rock State Park* – see opposite – where a site for the night costs $8 (☎505/722-3829).

Western New Mexico

Gallup's zip code is NM 87301.

Zuni Pueblo

Although few tourists now bother to visit the dusty and unenthralling **ZUNI PUEBLO**, a short way west of Hwy-602 35 miles south of Gallup, it occupies a pivotal role in the Southwestern history. Here, in 1539, the black African **Esteban** became the first outsider to enter the Pueblo world, and was promptly killed and cut into strips by the Zuni. Fray Marcos de Niza, following close behind him, fled for his life back to Mexico, to report "this land . . . is the greatest and best of all that have been discovered". The Zuni call themselves *A:shiwi*, "the flesh", and their country *Shi:wona*, "the land that produces flesh". Fray Marcos, who garbled that name into Cíbola, announced that the six Zuni towns were the **Seven Cities of Cíbola**. Spanish *conquistadores* had long sought the legendary Seven Cities of Antilla, founded by bishops who sailed west to escape the Moorish invasion of Portugal in 714 AD, and rich in **gold**. In 1540, therefore, a Spanish expedition led by Francisco Vásquez de **Coronado** returned to Zuni. Turned back from the now-vanished town of Hawikku, the Spaniards defeated its inhabitants in the first battle ever fought between Europeans and Native Americans.

There was no gold at Zuni. The region had by that time been occupied for eight hundred years, and had become a major Pueblo trading centre, where the peoples of the Rio Grande exchanged turquoise for birds, feathers and shells brought up from the south. Life went on after Coronado departed, but, like the Hopi, the Zuni thereafter found themselves restricted to an ever smaller area by Navajo, Apache, Spanish and Anglo newcomers. Today's **Zuni Indian Reservation** encompasses around three percent of ancestral Zuni lands, and with agriculture rendered marginal by erosion and overgrazing, the Zuni now depend for most of their livelihood on the recently acquired skill of making **silver overlay jewellery**.

Esteban's extraordinary life story, and the full tale of the Coronado expedition, are told on p.83.

Visiting Zuni Pueblo

The dominant feature on the Zuni reservation is the red-and-white-striped mesa of **Corn Mountain**, a traditional refuge for the Zuni people in times of trouble. Immediately below, straddling Hwy-53 three miles west of Hwy-602, stands the main **village**, which was founded as *Halona*, or "Middle Anthill", around 1700 AD, when the Zuni came down from Corn Mountain after the Pueblo Revolt.

On the eastern edge of town, the **A:shiwi A:wan Museum and Heritage Center** (Mon–Fri 9am–4pm; donation; ☎505/782-4403), holds interesting displays on Zuni history and culture, and is the best place to pick up information of all kinds. The next few blocks west are lined with jewellery outlets, and there's also a supermarket, a *Taco Bell*, and a local diner, the *Seventh City of Cíbola*. There are however no **motels** on the reservation.

Turn south onto Malani Street, in the heart of town, and a walk or drive of two hundred yards brings you to **Our Lady of Guadalupe Mission Church**. This adobe church, erected by the Spanish in 1629, was derelict in the 1960s, but has now been restored to more or less its original appearance. In line with historical accounts, the interior once more holds "life-sized" murals of Zuni *kachinas* (Mon–Fri 8am–4.30pm; for a guide, call ☎505/782-4477; donation). An ancient five-storey "apartment block" still stands nearby, but it's completely concealed beneath modern additions; the only examples of traditional pueblo architecture you'll see are the beehive-shaped bread ovens scattered around the plaza.

General advice on visiting New Mexico's nineteen pueblos, and a calendar of annual events, appears on pp.28–9.

On a typical day, few visitors make it to Zuni, and even fewer stay very long. Special events can draw crowds, however, most notably the **Zuni Tribal Fair** in late August, and the all-night **Shalako** dance, held in late November or early December. Anthropologists believe that this winter-solstice celebration, in which the *kachina* cult appears to blend with Aztec elements, was introduced by Mexican Indians left behind by Coronado.

El Morro National Monument

The admission fee at El Morro is $4 per vehicle, or $2 per person.

Hidden away on Hwy-53 south of the Zuni mountains, 25 miles east of Zuni Pueblo and 42 miles west of Grants, **EL MORRO NATIONAL MONUMENT** feels as far off the beaten track as it's possible to be in the modern United States. It seems incredible, therefore, that this sheer sandstone cliff was a regular rest stop for international travellers before the Pilgrims landed at Plymouth Rock. The evidence is plain to see, however. It was first recorded by Spanish explorers in 1583 – *el morro* means "the headland" – and in 1605, **Don Juan de Onate**, the founder of New Mexico, carved the first of the many messages that earned it the American name of **Inscription Rock**.

Translations and explanations of El Morro's graffiti are displayed in the **visitor center** (summer daily 9am–7pm; winter daily 9am–5pm; ☎505/783-4226). You can see the real thing on a half-mile **trail**, which stays open until an hour before the visitor center closes.

El Morro is technically a cuesta, a long sloping mesa terminating in an abrupt bluff. The trail's first stop is the reason so many people passed this way: a cool, perennial pool of **water**, collected beneath a waterfall that tumbles through a cleft in the pale pink cliffs. In such a self-evidently sacred spot, it's no surprise to see ancient Anasazi **petroglyphs** scraped into the desert varnish nearby.

Not far beyond, Don Juan's chiselled signature celebrates "the discovery of the South Sea"; he was returning from an expedition that had taken him all the way to the mouth of the Colorado. Further inscriptions follow thick and fast, some detailing the minutiae of minor campaigns on the Spanish frontier, others recording moments such as the Reconquest after the Pueblo Revolt. Oddities from later years include the autograph of P Gilmer Breckenridge, who led a caravan of 25 **camels** past El Morro in 1857 (see p.245).

An optional and much more demanding two-mile hike climbs the cliff beyond the last of the inscriptions to see the recently excavated **A'ts'ina Ruins**, up on top. Its builders, who abandoned it in 1350 AD, were among the ancestors of the modern Zuni.

El Malpais National Monument

If you had to pick one federal park in the Southwest *not* to visit, **EL MALPAIS NATIONAL MONUMENT** would be the obvious choice. There was more than a whiff of the pork-barrel about its creation in the 1980s, which was bitterly opposed by neighbouring Ácoma Indians. They lost, in part, because they preferred not to reveal the locations of shrines they wanted to remain inviolate. For tourists, however, the problem with El Malpais is more basic: it's **dull**.

El Malpais is Spanish for "the **Badlands**", and preserves a tract of territory covered by **lava flows** from a volcanic eruption two or three thousand years ago – recent enough for the landscape to remain blackened and barren. Potholers delight in underground "lava tubes" up to seventeen miles long, but hiking any distance across the rough rock above is a pretty miserable business.

The map of El Malpais is a peculiar patchwork of desolate lava interspersed with pockets of grassland that the eruption somehow missed. Confusingly, only the lava areas belong to the **national monument**, which is run by the National Park Service, and served by a **visitor center** twenty miles east of El Morro on Hwy-53. The rest is administered as a **National Conservation Area** by the Bureau of Land Management, which has a **ranger station** on Hwy-17, nine miles south of I-40 exit 89. Each of those roads skirts the periphery of the badlands; in an ordinary vehicle you can only get from one to the other via Grants.

On **Hwy-17**, the more interesting drive of the two, **Sandstone Bluffs Overlook** near the ranger station commands views westwards across the flatlands to the jagged peaks of the **Cerritos de Jaspe**, and north to Mount Taylor. Displays illustrate the difference between the two main kinds of lava, known to geologists the world over by their Hawaiian names of *aa* and *pahoehoe*. Not far beyond, **La Ventana**

Arch is a chunky natural window three-quarters of the way up a cliff face east of the highway.

Grants

In general, **GRANTS**, sixty miles east of Gallup on I-40, looks a lot better by night than it does by day. Daylight exposes an air of dereliction along its old Route 66 frontage that's concealed when the neon signs come on after dark. Even so, Grants feels more characterful than Gallup, and is a handy base for detours off the interstate.

Like Gallup, Grants started out as a railroad town. In the 1950s, just as a half-hearted **carrot** boom fizzled out, it struck it rich in a rather less wholesome way. A Navajo shepherd, Paddy Martinez, picked up some yellow rocks on nearby Haystack Mountain, and Grants found itself sitting on half the US's reserves of **uranium**. Both *Anaconda*, which opened an enormous mine, and the *Santa Fe Railroad*, who owned the land, made a fortune; Martinez got a monthly pension and the title "official uranium scout".

Grants' uranium years have receded into history, but they're enjoyably recalled in the **New Mexico Museum of Mining** at 100 Iron St (summer Mon–Sat 9am–6pm, Sun 9am–4pm; winter Mon–Sat 9am–4pm; $3). Visits consist of a faked descent into a mock-up mine, where you can poke around with no fear of radiation.

Practicalities

*The **zip code** for Grants is NM 87020.*

Grants' **visitor center** (☎505/287-4802 or 1-800/748-2142), in the same building as the museum (see above), opens the same hours. Most of its more salubrious **motels** – the ones that charge by the night, not the hour – congregate east of downtown, across the railroad near exit 85 off the interstate. These include a good *Super 8*, 1604 E Santa Fe Ave (☎505/287-8811 or 1-800/800-8000; ②), and a slightly more upmarket *Holiday Inn Express*, 1496 E Santa Fe Ave (☎505/285-4676; ③). Back in town, the *Sands Motel*, 112 McArthur Ave (☎505/287-2996) is a presentable budget option.

The most popular place to eat is *Grants Station*, a railroad-themed family restaurant at 200 W Santa Fe Ave (daily 5.30am–11pm; ☎505/287-2334), which serves full dinners, including soup and salad bar, for under $10. The tiny *Uranium Cafe*, 519 W Santa Fe Ave (closed Mon & Tues; ☎505/287-7540), is a vintage adobe diner opposite the mining museum.

Ácoma Pueblo

The amazing **ÁCOMA PUEBLO**, south of I-40 fifteen miles east of Grants and fifty miles west of Albuquerque, encapsulates a thousand years of Native American history. Focused around the ancient village known as **"Sky City"**, perched atop a magnificent mesa, it has adapted to repeated waves of invaders while retaining its own strong identity. The Acomans have long been happy to take the tourist dollar – they run a large casino beside the interstate, and have hosted the *Miss America* swimsuit pageant – so visitors seldom feel the awkwardness possible at other Pueblo communities. Nonetheless, Ácoma is the real thing, and its sense of unbroken tradition can reduce even the least culturally sensitive traveller to awestruck silence.

Western
New Mexico

*General advice
on visiting
New Mexico's
nineteen pueb-
los, and a cal-
endar of annu-
al events,
appears on
p.124.*

A history of Ácoma Pueblo

Only certain Hopi villages (see p.57) can rival Sky City's claim to be the **oldest inhabited settlement** in the United States. This isolated mesa, 367 feet high and 7000 feet above sea level, was probably occupied by Chacoan migrants between 1100 and 1200 AD, when the great pueblos of Chaco Canyon were still in use.

The **Coronado** expedition of 1540 described the Acomans as "robbers, feared by the whole country round about". Noting the mesa's redoubtable defences – it could only be reached by climbing ladders through a narrow crevice – the Spaniards commented that "no army could possibly be strong enough to capture the village".

In October 1598, Don Juan de **Onate** visited Acoma in peace, while exploring his recently proclaimed colony of New Mexico. A month later, however, his nephew Juan de **Zaldivar**, following with reinforcements, arrived at the foot of the mesa, demanded food, and was rejected. Depending on which version you believe, the Spaniards either tricked their way onto the mesa, or the Acomans invited them up and then ambushed them. In the ensuing fight, all the Spaniards were killed, save four who survived being hurled off.

A punitive force of seventy men, equipped with cannons, stormed into the village in January 1599, and over eight hundred Acomans died in a three-day house-to-house battle. Five hundred women and children, and eighty men, were taken prisoner. All were sentenced to twenty years of penal servitude, and each man had a foot publicly chopped off, in the plazas of the Rio Grande pueblos.

Oñate was eventually called back to Mexico City and removed from office, in punishment for his savagery. By 1629, Ácoma had a resident Spanish friar – Fray Juan Ramírez is said to have been accepted after he caught a child who fell off the mesa – and the Acomans were hard at work building a huge mission church. Ramírez's successors were driven out during the Pueblo Revolt, and a tyrannical eighteenth-century priest was thrown to his death, but in theory the pueblo was permanently converted to Catholicism.

The people of Ácoma clearly never felt inclined to follow the architectural example of the mission, whose mighty beams were carried 25 miles from Mount Taylor without once being permitted to touch the ground. Instead they went on constructing the same multi-storey stone and adobe houses that can still be seen today.

The **Ácoma Indian Reservation** now has a population of six thousand, most of whom live in three communities that were originally sited for their proximity to fresh water but now stand conveniently close to I-40 – **ACOMITA, McCARTYS** and **ANZAC**. Only ten or twelve families, thirty people in all, live on the mesa itself, but others make daily trips to sell pottery or fry-bread, and many more return to their ancestral homes for feast days and other ceremonies. Eighty percent of Acomans call themselves Catholic, but the old religion endures; there are fourteen separate clans, and the Antelope Clan are still, as they have always been, in charge of everything. Even today, the non-Indian priest can only visit the mesa once a week, on Wednesdays.

Arrival and information

Sky City is twelve miles south of the interstate, via any of three connecting roads. For the most dramatic approach, come in from the west, leaving I-40 at exit 102. When the mesa comes into view, glowing in the sunlight as you drop down a hillside roughly three miles distant, you'll understand why the first Spanish explorers spoke of cities of gold.

Ácoma is closed to all visitors July 10–13, and during the first or second weekend in October.

Before you take any photographs, however, you must first pay the relevant fees at the **visitor center**, at road's end below the mesa. You can only see Sky City itself on an hour-long **tour**; buses take groups up at regular intervals (April–Oct daily 8am–7pm; Nov–March daily 8am–4.30pm; admission $6, plus $10 for photo permit, no video tripods; ☎505/470-4966 or 1-800/747-0181). While you wait, there's a small museum and snack-bar, and a gift store sells exquisite pottery.

Sky City

While the original walls of **Sky City**'s oldest houses lie concealed beneath several centuries of re-plastering, the overall appearance of the village can have changed little in the last millenium. The high windowless wall of the main pueblo, at the northern edge of the mesa, protected its inhabitants against both the chill north wind, and potential invaders. Three or four storeys of terraced "apartments" face south to maximize the winter sun. Just one room still has its original tiny "windowpane" of translucent crystal. Digging *kivas* down into the sandstone requires too much labour, so seven of the above-ground rooms are *kivas*, each shared by two clans and entered by a tall ladder pointing to the north. Ácoma's sparse rainfall collects in natural depressions in the rock; beside the largest of these cisterns is the mesa's only tree, a slender cottonwood.

Tour groups stroll more or less at will around the mesa-top, with plenty of opportunities to buy hand-made pottery or ears of multi-coloured corn. Don't expect to enter any individual dwellings, however. The main stop is the still-active mission church of **San Esteban del Rey**, which measures 120 feet long by forty feet wide, with seventy-foot-high walls that taper from ten feet thick at the base to six feet at the top. The floor is made of hard-packed earth, while the whitewashed interior walls are decorated with a mixture of Christian images and Pueblo motifs. Ácoma's greatest treasure hangs above the altar – a painting of **St Joseph**, said to grant prayers for rain, which was borrowed by Laguna Pueblo in 1800, and only returned after the Acomans took Laguna all the way to the US Supreme Court. As no photography is permitted, you won't be prepared for the sublime view as you turn around from the altar, and look back across the cavernous space to the glorious New Mexican light that streams in through the doorway.

There's no soil on the mesa-top, so all the adobe bricks of the church were made with mud carried up from below, and its **cemetery** was filled with endless basket-loads of sand. Only honoured elders can now be buried here – not in coffins, but "re-planted", facing east. At first, the churchyard wall looks crenellated, but in fact the bumps are "warriors", placed to guard the dead.

Legend has it that the forbidding **Enchanted Mesa**, visible to the east, once held its own Pueblo community; the only access to the top was via a spider's-web of ropes strung between the mesa itself and an adjoining rock pillar. When that pillar collapsed one day while the men were away from the village, the women and children on top were left stranded, their cries for help fading as they starved.

If you prefer, you can walk rather than ride back down from Sky City, following the ancient footpath through clefts in the rock.

Laguna Pueblo

LAGUNA PUEBLO, just north of the interstate six miles east of Ácoma and 44 miles west of Albuquerque, is the **youngest** of the New Mexican pueblos. It was established in 1698 by refugees from several different pueblos, driven here by the disruption of the Pueblo Revolt and the increasing threat of Navajo and Apache raids. It's also the **richest** pueblo, thanks to the presence of the world's largest **uranium** mine, *Anaconda*'s Jackpile mine. That closed in 1982, after operating for thirty years, but the Laguna people are still living off the royalties. They're also having to cope with the **pollution** it caused, having burrowed its way under the main Pueblo village; birth defects and cancers have become a major problem.

All of Laguna Pueblo, including its **San José Mission Church**, is visible from a rest stop on the west-bound side of the interstate, where traders sell crafts. There's no reason to explore any further.

Chapter 2

Santa Fe and Northern New Mexico

B asking in the magical "light" that artists – and tourist boards – rave about, stretching beneath the flame-red peaks of the Sangre de Cristo mountains, **Northern New Mexico** is the New Mexico of popular imagination, with its pastel colours, vivid desert landscape and adobe architecture. Quite apart from its ravishing **beauty**, nowhere else in North America can boast such a sense of unbroken **history**. Native American pueblos and Hispanic colonial settlements have stood side by side along the Rio Grande for four hundred years, and the Yankees who arrived on the Santa Fe Trail still seem like relative newcomers.

Adobe

For many visitors, the defining feature of New Mexico is its **adobe architecture**, as seen on homes, churches, and even shopping malls and motels. Ancient pueblo villages were constructed using blocks of mud, cut from the riverbeds and mixed with grass, but early Franciscan missionaries introduced moulded **adobe bricks**. The Spaniards had themselves learned the technique from the Arabs, in which a mixture of earth, sand, charcoal and chopped grass or straw is left to bake in the sun in a wooden frame known as an *adobero*. Built into walls, they are set with a mortar of much the same composition, and then plastered over with mud and straw. The colour of the soil used dictates the colour of the final building, and thus subtle variations can be seen all across the state. However, adobe is a far from convenient material: it needs replastering every few years, and turns to mud when water seeps up from the ground, so that many buildings must be sporadically raised and bolstered by the insertion of rocks at their base.

These days, most of what looks like adobe is actually painted cement or concrete, but even this looks attractive enough in its own semi-kitsch way, while hunting out such superb old adobes as the remote **Santuario de Chimayó** on the High Road between Santa Fe and Taos, the formidable church of **San Francisco de Asis** in Ranchos de Taos, or the multi-tiered dwellings of **Taos Pueblo**, can provide the focus of an enjoyable tour.

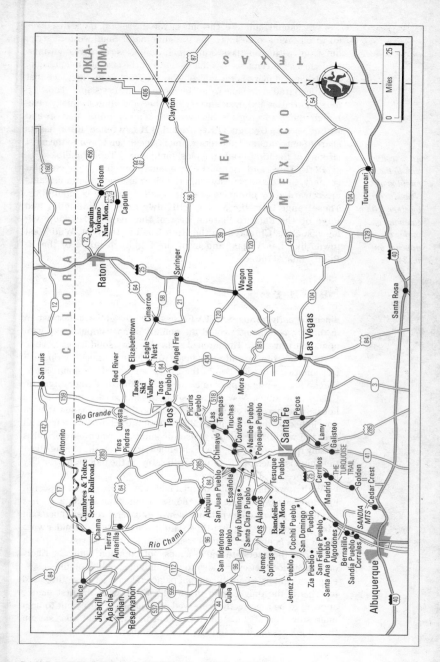

State capital **Santa Fe**, the only city in the region, more than lives up to its high-profile image as the epitome of Southwestern style, bursting with top-class museums, galleries and restaurants. Nonetheless, it remains less than a tenth of the size of Albuquerque, and its central plaza is recognizable as the frontier marketplace that welcomed trade caravans from Mexico and the Mississippi. **Taos**, 75 miles northeast and even smaller, has become almost equally celebrated thanks to a remarkable twentieth-century influx of artists and writers such as **Georgia O'Keeffe** and **D H Lawrence**. It too has its share of museums and amenities, and is a near-neighbour to the most striking of the Rio Grande pueblos, multi-storey **Taos Pueblo**.

*An introduction to the **pueblos** of New Mexico, together with a calendar of major events, appears on p.124.*

Both Taos and Santa Fe are surrounded by spectacular scenery, and detours away from the river and into the mountains are rewarded by glimpses of countless fascinating communities. These range from the ancient **cliff dwellings** of **Bandelier** and **Puyé** on the Pajarito Plateau west of the river, to Hispanic villages such as **Chimayó** on the **High Road** to the east, Wild-West towns like **Las Vegas**, and even the high-tech home of the H-Bomb, **Los Alamos**.

Santa Fe

Since the early 1980s, **SANTA FE** has been the chic-est destination in the US, consistently voted the country's most popular city with upmarket travellers. That appeal rests on a very solid basis; it's one of America's **oldest** and most **beautiful** cities, founded by Spanish missionaries a decade before the Pilgrims reached Plymouth Rock. Spread across a high plateau at the foot of the stunning **Sangre de Cristo** mountains, New Mexico's capital still glories in the adobe houses and baroque churches of its original architects, and they're now joined by museums and galleries that attract art-lovers from all over the world. The busiest season is **summer**, when temperatures usually reach into the eighties Fahrenheit; in winter, the average daytime high is a mere 42°F, though with snow on the mountains the city looks more ravishing than ever.

With upwards of a million and a half tourists every year descending upon a town of just sixty thousand inhabitants, Santa Fe has inevitably grown somewhat overblown; long-term residents bemoan what's been lost, while first-time visitors are inclined to wonder what all the fuss is about. The depressing urban sprawl as you approach town from the interstate makes a lousy introduction, while the rigorous insistence that every downtown building should look like a seventeenth-century Spanish colonial palace takes a bit of getting used to. This is the only city in the world where what on first glance appears to be a perfectly preserved ancient adobe turns out to be a multi-storey parking lot, and it would be illegal to build a gas station that didn't resemble an Indian prayer chamber.

There's still a lot to like about Santa Fe, however. Santa Fe style may have become something of a cliché, but even the clichés are changing; the pastel-painted **wooden coyotes** that were the obligatory souvenir five years ago have been replaced by cast-iron sculptures of Kokopelli, the hunch-backed Anasazi flute-player. In a town where the *Yellow Pages* list over 250 art galleries, you'll get plenty of opportunity to buy one.

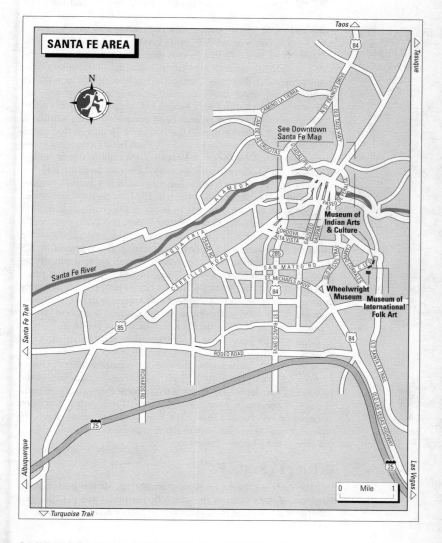

A History of Santa Fe

The first homes of **La Villa de Santa Fe** were erected on the ruins of an abandoned pueblo around 1607. In 1610, after previous settlements to the northwest had been deemed unsuitable, it became the third capital of the infant colony of **New Mexico**. Its name, "Holy Faith", was taken from the camp outside Granada where Spanish monarchs Ferdinand and Isabella stayed before the assault that drove the Moors from Spain in 1492. Santa Fe was laid out as an imposing administrative city; as the **Palace of the Governors**, the *casas reales* or "royal houses" that commanded its parade-ground plaza were to house Spanish, Pueblo, Mexican and American rulers.

For a detailed history of New Mexico, see p.473.

It was from Santa Fe that **horses** dispersed across America, and during its first two centuries the city presented an inviting target for mounted Apache, Ute and Comanche raiders. Relations with the **Pueblo** peoples whom the Spaniards had come to convert were initially stable, but growing antagonism led to the **Pueblo Revolt** of 1680, when Santa Fe was besieged and conquered by an alliance of many different Indian groups. One thousand Spaniards fled south, and lived in exile for twelve years at El Paso before returning under a new Governor, **Don Diego de Vargas**. Their fight to regain control of the city is still celebrated in the annual **Fiestas de Santa Fe**.

Santa Fe was always a neglected outpost of the Spanish empire; at the time of Mexican independence in 1821, its garrison was armed with bows and arrows. Attempts to improve the economy thereafter focused on the ever-expanding United States, and the despatch of a trade delegation to St Louis in 1824 resulted in the opening of the **Santa Fe Trail** across the plains. As American goods poured in, US citizens were forbidden to settle in the city, in a bid to avoid a repetition of the Yankee takeover of Texas. In 1843, the Mexican president ordered that the Santa Fe Trail be closed altogether, but a mere three years later New Mexico passed into American hands. A discreet payment of $50,000 to Governor Armijo ensured that there was no opposition to the entry of the US Army on August 18, 1846.

Although the Yankees set about transforming the squat, dusty Mexican town into something more conspicuously American, building in wood rather than adobe, the time-honoured traditions of Santa Fe were eventually reasserted. Since a preservation campaign in the 1930s, city mandates have ensured that almost every structure within sight of the plaza, even the downtown *Woolworth's*, has been designed or redecorated to suit the Pueblo Revival mode. Santa Fe today – at least at its core – looks much more like its original Spanish self than it did a hundred years ago.

Getting to Santa Fe

Despite its fame, Santa Fe is surprisingly far off the beaten path. Most out-of-state visitors **fly** into Albuquerque – see p.156 – and either rent a vehicle at the airport for the hour's drive up to Santa Fe, or take one of the dozen or so daily *Shuttlejack* buses direct to their hotel ($20; ☎505/982-4311). Santa Fe's **municipal airport**, ten miles southwest of town, is served only by commuter planes, including flights from Albuquerque on *Mesa Air* (☎1-800/637-2247), and Denver on *United Express* (☎505/473-4118).

Buses from all over the Southwest to the *Greyhound* terminal at 858 St Michael's Drive (☎505/471-0008), a long way from the plaza, include four daily buses to and from Albuquerque, which cost $10.50. There's no direct **rail** link. *Amtrak* trains arrive every afternoon at **Lamy**, seventeen miles southeast, from Albuquerque and Chicago – to be met by *Lamy Shuttle* vans (☎505/982-8829).

Information

Santa Fe's **visitor center**, two blocks northwest of the plaza in the lobby of the Convention Center, 201 W Marcy St (Mon–Fri 8am–5pm; ☎505/984-6760 or 1-800/777-2489), stocks a very limited selection of brochures, though its *Maps Guide* is well worth picking up. The **New Mexico Department of Tourism**, in the Lamy Building at 491 Old Santa Fe Trail (Mon–Fri 8am–5pm; ☎505/827-4000 or 1-800/545-2040), has racks of material on the whole state, and in summer, there's a small information kiosk in the plaza itself.

The main **post office** is also northwest of the plaza, at 120 S Federal Place (Mon–Fri 8am–4pm, Sat 9am–1pm; ☎505/988-6351).

Getting around

Most of what there is to see in Santa Fe lies within walking distance of the central plaza, but to get there from your hotel, or to see the further-flung attractions, you may need to use the *Santa Fe Trails* **bus service**. All nine routes start from the **Sheridan Transit Center**, a block northwest of the plaza on Sandoval Street (Mon–Fri 6.30am–10.30pm, Sat 8am–8pm; ☎505/438-1464), with a standard adult fare of 50¢, and monthly passes for $10. The most useful for visitors are routes #21–23, which run up **Cerrillos Road**, and route #10, which loops between the plaza and the **outlying museums**, roughly half-hourly in summer and hourly in winter.

The only **taxi** company in town is *Capital City Cabs* (☎505/438-0000), while **bikes** can be rented at *Palace Bike Rentals*, 409 E Palace Ave (☎505/986-0455).

Tours and excursions

Walking tours of town are conducted by *Afoot in Santa Fe*, based in the *Inn at Loretto*, 211 Old Santa Fe Trail (daily 9.30am & 1.30pm; ☎505/983-3701), and *Santa Fe Detours*, 107 Washington Ave (daily 9.30am & 1.30pm; ☎505/983-6565 or 1-800/338-6877). Both charge around $10 for a 2hr 30min walk, and also operate **coach tours** at similar prices.

Gray Line, 1330 Hickox St (☎505/983-9491), run ninety-minute ($8) and three-hour ($15) city bus tours, plus half-day trips to the ancient ruins at Bandelier ($40) and Puyé ($46), and full-day trips to Taos ($50). *Nambe Pueblo Tours* (☎505/820-1340 or 1-800/946-2623) have an extensive program of tours to modern and ancient Pueblo sites, and up to what they call O'Keeffe Country.

Excursion trains down to Lamy, drawn by diesel not steam, leave from the old *Santa Fe Southern Railway* depot at 410 S Guadalupe St (Tues, Thurs, Sat & Sun 10.30am, Fri 6pm; round-trip $21; ☎505/989-8600). The idea is for passengers to eat at Lamy's *Legal Tender* restaurant, but you can take a picnic if you prefer.

Accommodation

Even in winter, you won't find a room within walking distance of downtown Santa Fe for under $50, and in summer – when every bed in town is frequently taken – there's little under $80. **Cerrillos Road** (US-85), the main road in from I-25, holds most of the town's **motels** and its one **hostel**. Everything gets more expensive as you approach the centre, though **B&Bs** make an attractive alternative to paying the sky-high prices demanded by the plush plaza-area hotels. If you get stuck, call *Santa Fe Central Reservations* (☎505/983-8200 or 1-800/776-7669) or *Accommodations Hotline* (daily 4–10pm; ☎505/983-6565 or 1-800/338-6877).

Commercial **campgrounds** in the Santa Fe area, charging upwards of $20 for a tent site, include *Los Campos*, 3574 Cerrillos Rd (mid-May to Sept; ☎505/473-1949 or 1-800/852-8160), and the *KOA*, further east at I-25 exit 290 (March–Oct; ☎505/982-1419). Camping nearby in the **Santa Fe National Forest** is a cheaper and much more appealing prospect. The *Black Canyon* site ($5) is seven miles up Hwy-475, northeast of town, *Big Tesuque* (free) is five miles beyond that, and *Aspen Basin* (free) is another three miles on, at the ski area. All open in summer only; contact the forest headquarters, 1226 St Francis Drive (☎505/988-6940).

Inexpensive

*Unless otherwise specified, properties listed here share the **zip code** Santa Fe NM 87501.*

Budget Inn, 725 Cerrillos Rd at Don Diego; ☎505/982-5952 or 1-800/288-7600, fax 984-8879. The most centrally located of the chain motels; large, clean and a mile or so from the plaza. Winter ③, summer ④.

Cactus Lodge, 2864 Cerrillos Rd at Siler Rd; ☎505/471-7699. Small but perfectly adequate old-style motel, with some two-bedroom suites, well out from the centre. Winter ②, summer ③.

El Rey Inn, 1862 Cerrillos Rd at St Michael's Drive, Santa Fe NM 87502; ☎505/982-1931 or 1-800/521-1349, fax 989-9249. Most characterful and best-value of the Cerrillos Road motels, with surprisingly stylish Southwestern rooms, some nice suites, a pool, and a large garden. ④.

Luxury Inn, 3752 Cerrillos Rd at Rodeo Rd, Santa Fe NM 87505; ☎505/473-0567 or 1-800/647-1346. Clean, inexpensive motel, well south of downtown. Pool and hot tub, but no restaurant. Winter ③, summer ④.

Santa Fe International Hostel, 1412 Cerrillos Rd at Alta Vista, Santa Fe NM 87505; ☎505/988-1153. Old-style *HI-AYH* hostel, housed in a ramshackle former motel a couple of miles from the plaza. Young international travellers enjoy the enforced intimacy, but in winter it can be pretty damp and cold. Dorm beds for $12 ($15 non-members) and private rooms from $30. ①/②.

Santa Fe Motel, 510 Cerrillos Rd at N Guadalupe St; ☎505/982-1039 or 1-800/999-1039, fax 986-1275. Small, quiet, pleasant adobe motel near downtown. No connection to the *Hotel Santa Fe* next door. Winter ④, summer ⑤.

Silver Saddle, 2810 Cerrillos Rd at Siler Rd; ☎505/471-7663. Small, down-to-earth, characterful motel, well out from downtown. Winter ③, summer ④.

Super 8, 3358 Cerrillos Rd at Richards Ave; ☎505/471-8811 or 1-800/800-8000, fax 471-3239. Hundred-room chain motel, four miles from downtown, but a dependable bargain. Winter ②, summer ③.

Mid-range

Fort Marcy Compound Hotel Suites, 320 Artist Rd; ☎505/982-6636 or 1-800/745-9910, fax 984-8682. Plush one-, two- and three-bedroom suites an easy walk north of downtown, located on a mountain-view knoll once occupied by the city's first US Army fort. Winter ⑤, summer ⑥.

Garrett's Desert Inn, 311 Old Santa Fe Trail; ☎505/982-1851 or 1-800/888-2145, fax 989-1647. Large, rather dull-looking two-storey motel, but the rooms are well equipped, there's a pool and a French-style cafe, and the rates are good for such a convenient location. Nov–Feb ④, March–Oct ⑤.

Homewood Suites, 400 Griffin St; ☎505/988-3000 or 1-800/225-5466, fax 988-4700. Spacious, comfortable all-suite hotel, just off Paseo de Peralta a couple of blocks northwest of the plaza. Winter ⑥, summer ⑦.

Hotel Santa Fe, 1501 Paseo de Peralta at Cerillos Rd; ☎505/982-1200 or 1-800/825-9876, fax 984-2211. Attractive, very comfortable adobe hotel on the edge of downtown, within walking distance of the plaza, that's run and majority-owned by Picuris Pueblo, has its own *Blue Corn Cafe*, and features free lectures by local experts. Winter ⑤, summer ⑦.

La Posada de Santa Fe, 330 E Palace Ave; ☎505/988-6351 or 1-800/727-5276, fax 982-6850. Downtown's most peaceful option, with individual adobe *casitas* (cottages) set in spacious gardens. Sizes and furnishings vary, but the smaller cottages offer excellent value. Winter ⑤, summer ⑥.

Expensive

La Fonda de Santa Fe, 100 E San Francisco St; ☎505/982-5511 or 1-800/523-5002, fax 988-2952. Gorgeous old inn on the southeast corner of the plaza, marking the end of the Santa Fe Trail. Built to replace the century-old original in 1920, it features hand-painted murals and stained glass throughout, and a genuine O'Keeffe behind the front desk. Each opulently furnished room is different, and there's a good restaurant and a rooftop bar. ⑧.

Hilton of Santa Fe, 100 Sandoval St, Santa Fe NM 87504; ☎505/988-2811 or 1-800/336-3676, fax 986-6439. Attractive luxury hotel, a short walk west of the plaza, which incorporates three rooms of the 250-year-old adobe Casa de Ortiz as B&B-style honeymoon suites; there's also a good restaurant, and the airy *Chamisa Courtyard Cafe*. Winter ⑥, summer ⑦; suites ⑨.

Inn at Loretto, 211 Old Santa Fe Trail; ☎505/988-5531 or 1-800/727-5531, fax 984-7988. Upmarket hotel in the shape of a fully-fledged mock pueblo, ris-

As explained on p.15, accommodation prices, excluding taxes, are indicated throughout this book by the following symbols:

① *up to $30*
② *$30–45*
③ *$45–60*
④ *$60–80*
⑤ *$80–100*
⑥ *$100–130*
⑦ *$130–175*
⑧ *$175–250*
⑨ *$250+*

Downtown hotels and B&Bs are marked on the map on p.100.

ing in seven tiers between the plaza and the river, and adjoining the Loretto Chapel (see p.104). Winter ⑦, summer ⑧.

Inn of the Anasazi, 113 Washington Ave; ☎505/988-3030 or 1-800/688-8100, fax 988-3277. No-expense-spared hotel just north of the plaza, modelled on an ancient cliff-dwelling, and featuring a superb restaurant; a fabulous place to stay, although most rooms offer no views to speak of. ⑧.

B&Bs

Rural B&Bs within easy reach of Santa Fe include the charming Hacienda Vargas *(p.112).*

Dancing Ground of the Sun, 711 Paseo de Peralta; ☎505/986-9797 or 1-800/645-5673. B&B inn that offers a choice of five separate Southwestern-themed *casitas* set in a tranquil garden. Winter ④, summer ⑤.

El Paradero, 220 W Manhattan Ave; ☎505/988-1177. Converted Spanish-era farmhouse near Guadalupe Street. Eight rooms en-suite, four share baths. ④.

Grant Corner Inn, 122 Grant Ave; ☎505/983-6678. Incongruous New-England-style house, two blocks northwest of the plaza, where guests enjoy considerable luxury, and lavish breakfasts – summer's Sunday brunch features a string quartet. Not all rooms are en-suite. Winter ④, summer ⑤.

Preston House, 106 Faithway St; ☎505/982-3465. Large Queen Anne inn, in a peaceful garden behind the cathedral, with a mixture of rooms (not all en-suite) and cottages, all furnished with Pueblo and Mexican artworks. Winter ③, summer ④.

The City

Although it can be almost impossible to distinguish genuine historic buildings from modern counterfeits, there's a definite, romantic continuity between today's Santa Fe and the Spanish settlement of four hundred years ago. The most enjoyable way to start a visit is simply to stroll the narrow streets of the old town, but before long you'll find plenty of specific goals to capture your interest.

Once you've got your bearings in the **plaza**, the best places to get a sense of local history and culture are the five components of the Museum of New Mexico – the **Palace of the Governors**, the

---

The Festivals of Santa Fe

The first of the three major events in Santa Fe's annual calendar is the **Spanish Market**, during the last week in July, when examples of the traditional folk arts of Hispanic New Mexico are sold on the plaza, and contemporary works are on sale in the Palace of the Governors.

The **Indian Market** fills the plaza on the weekend after the third Thursday in August, attracting over 100,000 buyers and craftspeople from all over the world for the premier showcase of Southwestern Native American arts and crafts.

September's **Fiestas de Santa Fe**, which take place during the weekend after Labor Day, have been held annually since 1712 to celebrate the Spaniards' return after the Pueblo Revolt. The parades and processions begin with the ceremonial burning of *Zozobra* ("Old Man Gloom") in the plaza.

Museum of Fine Arts, and the new **Georgia O'Keeffe Museum** downtown, and the museums of **Indian Arts and Culture** and **Folk Art** a couple of miles southeast. Alternatively, set about exploring Santa Fe's distinct neighbourhoods, such as the old **Barrio Analco** just southeast of downtown, home to the **San Miguel Mission**; the **Canyon Road** arts district, just beyond; and the funkier **Guadalupe Street** district to the west.

The plaza

Santa Fe's central **plaza** has been the heart of the city ever since 1610, though the original rectangular parade ground of the Spanish garrison was twice as large as the neat, leafy square of today. It has witnessed many turning points of New Mexican history, from the public hanging of three Indian "witchdoctors" in 1675 (which helped to trigger the Pueblo Revolt five years later, when Pueblo Indians filled the plaza to lay siege to the Palace of the Governors), to the nineteenth-century celebrations of Mexican independence and annexation by the United States, and journey's end for countless weary travellers on the Santa Fe Trail. How contentious that history remains is illustrated by the **obelisk** at its centre, where unknown hands have chiselled the word "savage" out of an inscription that formerly honoured "the heroes who have fallen in the various battles with savage Indians in the territories of New Mexico".

The plaza now serves as a pleasant public park, where tourists and office workers alike picnic on the grass as they watch the latest bemused arrivals spill out of their coaches. Under the arcade of the Palace of the Governors, along its northern flank, **Native American traders** shelter from the summer sun or winter wind. They're strictly licensed, so the price, authenticity and quality of the craftworks and jewellery they sell all compare favourably with the stores and galleries that line the other three sides.

Palace of the Governors

The **Palace of the Governors**, which fills the north side of the plaza, often fails to make an immediate impression on visitors. It's a long single-storey structure that looks much like every other building in central Santa Fe – which is not surprising, since it served as a blueprint for the remodelling of the city. It's also as much of a fake, in that until 1913 it was a typical, formal, territorial building, with a square tower at each corner, and its subsequent adobe "reconstruction" was based on pure conjecture.

Nonetheless, the palace is the oldest public building in the United States, and now serves as a fascinating **historical museum**. It was constructed in 1610 as the headquarters of the Spanish colonial administration, and first occupied by Governor **Pedro de Peralta**. The name may now seem misleadingly grand, but it was originally much larger, an imposing adobe, with two towers and a sod roof, that

The Palace of the Governors is open Tues–Sun 10am–5pm. Admission is $5, or a four-day ticket to all five parts of the Museum of New Mexico costs $10.

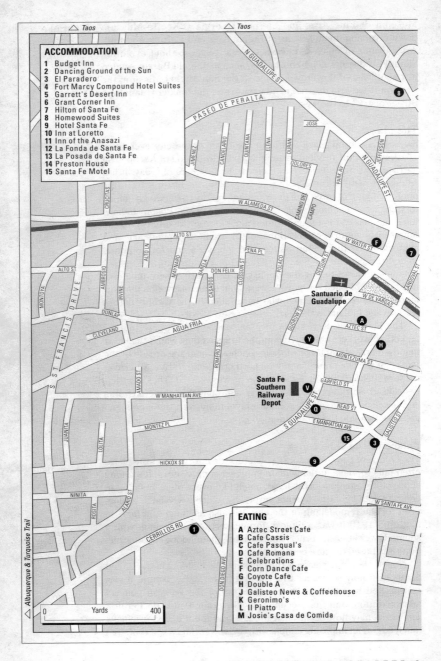

△ Taos   △ Taos

ACCOMMODATION

1 Budget Inn
2 Dancing Ground of the Sun
3 El Paradero
4 Fort Marcy Compound Hotel Suites
5 Garrett's Desert Inn
6 Grant Corner Inn
7 Hilton of Santa Fe
8 Homewood Suites
9 Hotel Santa Fe
10 Inn at Loretto
11 Inn of the Anasazi
12 La Fonda de Santa Fe
13 La Posada de Santa Fe
14 Preston House
15 Santa Fe Motel

Santuario de Guadalupe

Santa Fe Southern Railway Depot

EATING

A Aztec Street Cafe
B Cafe Cassis
C Cafe Pasqual's
D Cafe Romana
E Celebrations
F Corn Dance Cafe
G Coyote Cafe
H Double A
J Galisteo News & Coffeehouse
K Geronimo's
L Il Piatto
M Josie's Casa de Comida

△ Albuquerque & Turquoise Trail

0   Yards   400

DOWNTOWN SANTA FE

△ Tesuque

△ Santa Fe Ski Area

PASEO DE PERALTA
CATRON LN
CATRON ST
STAAB ST
MCKENZIE ST

Georgia O'Keeffe Museum

Sheridan Transit Center

Museum of Fine Arts

Palace of the Governors

Plaza

Institute of American Indian Arts

St Francis Cathederal

Loretto Chapel

San Miguel Mission

State Capitol

PASEO DE PERALTA

E SANTA FE AVE

ACEQUIA MADRE

BOOTH

CANYON RD

E ALAMEDA ST

E DE VARGAS

ORCHARD DR

PASEO DE PERALTA

BISHOP'S LODGE ROAD

ARTIST ROAD

MONTE

VISTA PL

OTERO ST

MAGDALENA

KEARNEY AVE

S FEDERAL PL

GRANT AVE

GRIFFIN

SHERIDAN AVE

LINCOLN

WASHINGTON AVE

W MARCY ST

E MARCY ST

CASTILLO P

NUSBAUM ST

PALACE AVE

SAN FRANCISCO ST

E WATER ST

GALISTEO ST

ORTIZ ST

SHELBY ST

CATHEDRAL PL

CIENEGA ST

PASEO DE PERALTA

FAITHWAY ST

CHAPELLE

JOHNSON ST

BURRO ALLEY

DON GASPAR AVE

OLD SANTA FE TRAIL

EATING

N Old Santa Fe Trail Books & Coffeehouse
O Ore House on the Plaza
P Paul's
Q Railyard Books & Coffee
R Santa Cafe
S The Pink Adobe
T The Shed
U Tia Sophia's
V Tomasita's Cafe
W Tribes Coffeehouse
X Woolworth's
Y Zia Diner

formed part of a bigger defensive complex. After the **Pueblo Revolt** of 1680, the palace was taken over by Pueblo peoples, who sealed its doors and windows, divided its rooms and dug storage pits into the floor, but it was soon back in Spanish hands, and later became home to first Mexican, and then American, governors of New Mexico. One, **Lew Wallace**, wrote part of *Ben Hur* here, during his term of office from 1878 to 1881. By then, the palace had turned Victorian, but its balustrades, elaborate windows and wallpaper were removed after it ceased to be the official Governor's residence in 1909, when it was restored as part of the **Museum of New Mexico**.

Displays in its well-preserved interior trace the entire era, from early pueblos right up to the A-bomb. They're especially strong on Hispanic New Mexico, featuring a reproduction nineteenth-century chapel with a genuine 1830 altarpiece, while the *Society Defined* section explores the daily lives of such citizens of 1790s Santa Fe as a farmer, a carpenter and a blacksmith. Be sure to visit the well-stocked bookstore, and to wander into the peaceful open-air courtyard beyond, where the restrooms still have their antique fittings, and the *Palace Print Shop* sells handprinted cards and booklets.

Museum of Fine Arts

As part of the Museum of New Mexico, the Fine Arts museum opens Tues–Sun 10am–5pm, with a $5 entrance fee, or a four-day, five-museum ticket for $10.

Across Lincoln Avenue from the palace, on the northwest corner of the plaza at 107 E Palace Ave, Santa Fe's **Museum of Fine Arts** is housed in a particularly attractive adobe, with ornamental beams and a cool central courtyard. Erected in 1917, this was Santa Fe's first example of the "Pueblo Revival" school of architecture. It was also one of the few major art museums to be established by artists rather than educators or collectors, and concentrates on painting and sculpture by mostly local artists. Since the Georgia O'Keeffe Museum opened, it has focused more than ever on changing exhibits of contemporary work, though the selections from its permanent collection displayed upstairs still include a few O'Keeffes.

Georgia O'Keeffe Museum

As part of the Museum of New Mexico, the O'Keeffe museum is open Tues–Sun 10am–5pm, but it also remains open until 8pm on Fri; it costs $5, or $10 for a combination ticket.

Santa Fe's showpiece new **Georgia O'Keeffe Museum**, a block northwest of the Museum of Fine Arts at 217 Johnson St, opened in summer 1997. Its ten galleries house the largest collection of O'Keeffe's work in the world, and include sculptures and drawings as well as paintings. The works range in date from 1914 – thus pre-dating her exposure to New Mexico, though a 1915 rendition of *Palo Duro Canyon* in Texas hints of the abstractions to come – up to 1982. Among the sun-bleached skulls and iconic flowers sold in print galleries throughout the Southwest, some less familiar New York cityscapes make a surprising contrast. Most of the desert landscapes were painted near **Abiquiu**, forty miles northwest of Santa Fe – see p.148 – where she lived from 1946 until her death in 1986.

Guadalupe Street

A few blocks southwest of the plaza, the stretch of **Guadalupe Street** that runs south from the tiny Santa Fe River has become the focus of one of Santa Fe's most characterful little districts, catering more to local students and artists than passing tourists. It centres around the small but exquisite **Santuario de Guadalupe** at Guadalupe and Agua Fria (May–Oct Mon–Sat 9am–4pm; April–Nov Mon–Fri 9am–4pm; donation), a shrine built between 1776 and 1795 to mark the end of the Camino Real highway from Mexico City. Restored as a museum for its (and the nation's) bicentennial in 1976, it also hosts dance and music performances.

In the late nineteenth century, the surrounding neighbourhood became the point of arrival into Santa Fe for trains on both the *Atchison, Topeka and Santa Fe* and the *Denver and Rio Grande* railroads. Old warehouses and small factory premises nearby have been converted to house boutiques, art galleries and restaurants.

For details of excursion trains on the Santa Fe Southern Railway, *see p.96.*

St Francis Cathedral

Santa Fe only acquired its first Catholic bishop in 1851, after New Mexico joined the United States and ceased to belong to the Mexican diocese of Durango. As described in Willa Cather's novel, *Death Comes For The Archbishop*, the arrival of **Jean Baptiste Lamy** – a Frenchman, previously resident in Kentucky – threw the overwhelmingly Hispanic church in New Mexico into turmoil.

Lamy's most lasting achievement, **St Francis Cathedral**, now makes an unlikely spectacle, looming at the top of San Francisco Street two blocks east of the plaza. Eschewing adobe, the first church west of the Mississippi to be designated a cathedral was built of solid stone, between 1869 and 1886, in the formal – and, frankly, dreary – Romanesque style of France. To enable services to continue during construction, its walls rose over and around those of its eighteenth-century predecessor, which was progressively removed as rubble. The only part of that structure to survive, the side chapel of **Our Lady of the Rosary**, gives pride of place to a statue of the Virgin known as **La Conquistadora**. Originally brought from Mexico in 1625, she was credited by the people of Santa Fe with facilitating both their escape from the Pueblo Revolt in 1680, and their subsequent reconquest, and is still paraded through the city each year, on the Sunday after Corpus Christi in June.

Institute of American Indian Arts

The stimulating **Institute of American Indian Arts** (Mon–Sat 10am–5pm, Sun noon–5pm; $4) is housed in a modern building that faces the cathedral. Don't confuse it with the Museum of Indian Arts and Culture on the edge of town (see p.105); as they insist on telling you before you come in, "we're contemporary, not historical", and most of the artwork on show is likely to be less than a year old.

Ranging across paintings, installations, collages and mixed-media pieces, it's all a long way from the usual stereotyped images of Native Americans. The sculpture garden is especially recommended.

Loretto Chapel

A block away from the plaza, at the start of Old Santa Fe Trail, the **Loretto Chapel** was built for the Sisters of Loretto under the auspices of Archbishop Lamy, from 1873 onwards (winter Mon–Fri 9.30am–4.30pm, Sun 10.30am–5pm; summer daily 9am–5pm; $1). Work was directed by Projectus Mouly, the 18-year-old son of the French architect responsible for St Francis Cathedral. In different accounts, he either drank himself to death, unable to take criticism of his design, or was killed by Lamy's cousin. Either way, when the chapel was completed it lacked any means of reaching the choir loft, twenty feet above the nave. Hence the legend of its **Miraculous Staircase**, an elegant wooden spiral – more of a spring, in a sense – which makes two complete 360° turns as it rises, and was built without a single nail, or any support at either the centre or the sides. It's said to be the work of a mysterious carpenter who arrived in answer to the nuns' prayers, and disappeared without demanding payment.

The story is more entertaining than the reality, however. The chapel is now deconsecrated, and belongs to the upmarket *Inn at Loretto*, with direct access from the hotel, so it's always packed with irreverent tourists. What's more, the nuns found the staircase too frightening to climb, so they disfigured it by adding banisters, while the whole thing is now propped up with a metal brace.

San Miguel Mission

Two blocks south of the **Loretto Chapel**, across the river along the Old Santa Fe Trail, **San Miguel Mission** is said to be the oldest church in the United States to have remained in continuous use (Mon–Sat 10am–4pm, Sun 2–4.30pm). The site is known to have been occupied in 1300 AD, while the church was built by Tlaxcalan Indians from central Mexico, who accompanied New Mexico's earliest Spanish settlers in 1610. Although its roof was destroyed during the 1680 Pueblo Revolt, parts of its graceful, sloping adobe walls survived. A hole in the floor beneath the altar reveals the foundations of an ancient pueblo, as well as the original steps of the sanctuary, while the pale-green *reredos* or altar-piece above was painted in 1798 to frame a statue of San Miguel brought by missionaries from Mexico. The mission also holds buffalo hides and deerskins, painted with religious scenes, that date from around 1630.

The claims of a nearby adobe – part of which is a pizzeria – to be the **Oldest House in the United States** are generally dismissed, though it too probably stands on the ruins of the former pueblo. This whole district, the **Barrio de Analco**, is now an appealing residential neighbourhood, abounding in two-hundred-year-old houses.

Canyon Road and Acequia Madre

Before Santa Fe ever existed, **Canyon Road**, which climbs a steady but shallow incline east from Paseo de Peralta, a few hundred yards east of San Miguel Mission, was an Indian trail that led to the pueblo at Pecos. Later it was the main route by which firewood from the mountains was brought to the city. Since the 1920s, however, it has been famous as the centre of Santa Fe's **art colony**. It's now dominated by snooty galleries and expensive stores – some of which are reviewed on p.111 – but even if you don't plan to buy anything it makes for an enjoyable half-day stroll out from downtown.

At Canyon Road's far eastern end, the 1940 **Cristo Rey** church is the largest adobe building in the US, and holds a huge carved-stone altarpiece from the long-demolished La Castrense chapel that once stood on the plaza. It's over three miles out, however, and most walkers prefer either to double back along Canyon Road at some earlier point, or return to town via **Acequia Madre**, one block south. The name of this ancient unpaved street literally means the "mother ditch"; following the course of the city's first irrigation canal, it's lined with beautiful adobe homes.

Museum of Indian Arts and Culture

The excellent **Museum of Indian Arts and Culture** is located on a raised plateau two miles southeast of downtown, with extensive views of the hills and mountains that almost entirely surround the city. Under the title *Here, Now and Always*, it comprehensively covers all the major Southwest tribes, including the 'O'odham, Navajo, Apache, Pai, Ute and Pueblo peoples. The section called *From This Earth* is the real highlight – holding a superb array of Native American pottery, from pristine thousand-year-old Anasazi and Mimbres pieces up to the works of twentieth-century revivalists, and using touch-screen CD-ROM technology to illuminate and explain the traditions and processes involved.

Museum of International Folk Art

The delightful **Museum of International Folk Art**, across the parking lot from the Indian Arts and Culture Museum, centres on the huge **Girard Collection** of paintings, textiles, and, especially, **clay figurines**, gathered from all over the world. These are arranged in colourful dioramas that include a Pueblo Feast Day, complete with dancing *kachinas* and camera-clicking tourists, and street scenes from countries such as Poland, Peru, Portugal, and Ethiopia, featuring fabulously ornate churches and cathedrals.

The **Hispanic Heritage Wing** is also fascinating, displaying the traditional New Mexican crafts you might expect, such as *santeros* and *retablos*, along with lesser-known contemporary works, like *paños* – handkerchiefs, decorated in magic marker or pencil with religious and secular images by often-anonymous prison inmates.

Like the rest of the Museum of New Mexico, the Indian Arts museum opens Tues–Sun 10am–5pm. Admission is $5, and a four-day combination ticket costs $10.

Santa Fe Trails *bus #10* loops *between the plaza and the museums described here, half-hourly in summer and hourly in winter.*

The Folk Art museum is the fifth part of the Museum of New Mexico; hours and prices as above. Its **gift store** *stocks some of the best ethnic souvenirs in town.*

Wheelwright Museum of the American Indian

The large, private **Wheelwright Museum of the American Indian** (Mon–Sat 10am–5pm, Sun 1–5pm; $2 donation), stands behind the folk art museum. Designed to resemble a Navajo *hogan* (see p.54), its original purpose was to record Navajo sand paintings and ceremonials. These days, however, its permanent collection is seldom on show, and it concentrates instead on changing exhibitions, usually of contemporary art that's little different to what you'll see in the galleries in town. The *Case Trading Post* downstairs sells jewellery, rugs, and *kachinas* of very high quality, at very high prices.

Rancho de las Golondrinas

Between April and October, guided tours of the ranch can be arranged by calling ☎505/473-4169.

The **Rancho de las Golondrinas**, fifteen miles south of Santa Fe, is an eighteenth-century *paraje*, or stopping place, on the Camino Real, which is now run as a living history museum (June–Sept Wed–Sun 10am–4pm; $3.50). To reach it, turn right onto Hwy-599 from exit 276 on I-25, then left onto Frontage Road, and right onto Los Pinos Road, which you follow for three more miles.

The "Ranch of the Swallows" holds Hispanic-era homes, workshops, watermills and chapels brought from all over New Mexico, and is staffed by "villagers" in period costume. The best time to come is for one of the monthly theme weekends ($5), starting with the Spring Festival in June and ending with October's Harvest Festival, but throughout the summer it provides an authentic feel of New Mexico's early days.

Eating

Santa Fe has been renowned as one of America's most exciting places to **eat** since the early 1980s, when a quite stupendous feat of marketing managed to make dishes such as banana-crusted sea bass seem quintessentially Southwestern. It's now said to have more quality restaurants per head than any US city – but that doesn't make it any easier to get a reservation at the latest hot spot in summer. In addition, the presence of so many tourists, and the fact that their clientele is constantly changing, makes it hard for restaurants to develop much character. Nonetheless, there's some memorable dining to be had, even if you don't pay the wallet-busting prices of the big-name attractions, and the sheer inventiveness of the city's menus makes up for its lack of interesting ethnic alternatives.

The **Santa Fe School of Cooking**, in the Plaza Mercado at 116 W San Francisco St (☎505/983-4511), holds lunchtime classes in preparing Southwestern specialities, culminating in the opportunity to eat the lot (2hr 30min; $30–60 depending on ingredients).

Coffeehouses

Aztec Street Cafe, 317 Aztec St; ☎505/983-9464. Counter-culture hangout in the Galisteo Street district, offering a travellers' notice board and a nice patio, as well as coffees, pastries, light meals and occasional live music. Open until well into the evening from 7.30am on weekdays, 8am weekends.

Galisteo News & Coffeehouse, 201 Galisteo St; ☎505/984-1316. Central, roomy downtown cafe, with plate glass windows to watch the world go by and the added bonus of plenty of out-of-state newspapers.

Old Santa Fe Trail Books & Coffee House, 613 Old Santa Fe Trail; ☎505/988-8878. Friendly, well-stocked bookstore, espresso cafe and all-purpose restaurant, open from 8am daily, for all meals except Sun dinner.

Railyard Books and Coffee, 340 Read St at Guadalupe; ☎505/995-0533. Interesting little Guadalupe Street bookstore, open from 8am weekdays, 10am Sat, and 11am Sun, with an espresso cafe at the back.

Tribes Coffeehouse, 139 W San Francisco St; ☎505/982-7948. Spacious downtown mall gallery that serves espresso coffees, plus soup, salad and sandwich lunches.

Downtown restaurants are marked on the map on p.100.

Inexpensive

Cafe Romana, 31 Burro Alley; ☎505/984-8804. Busy, authentic and very central *paninoteca* – sandwich-bar-cum-pasta-joint – with the feel of a real Italian local cafe. Almost everything costs under $10, there's live music at night, and it even has its own Sistine Chapel ceiling. Lunch and dinner daily.

Josie's Casa de Comida, 225 E Marcy St; ☎505/983-5311. Legendary local diner, in a tiny whitewashed house near the plaza. Open for weekday lunches only: spicy chiles, *tamales* and enchiladas, and an endless array of desserts.

Maria's New Mexican Kitchen, 555 W Cordova Rd at St Francis; ☎505/983-7929. Classic Mexican dishes and abundant tortillas, plus *mariachi* musicians and lashings of margaritas. Open for lunch and dinner daily.

Natural Cafe, 1494 Cerrillos Rd; ☎505/983-1411. Largely but not exclusively vegetarian place, near the hostel. Its menu, from all parts of the globe, may not always be authentic, but it's still tasty. Dinner entrees, such as East Indian *tempeh* curry, cost around $10. Open daily except Mon for lunch and dinner.

Tecolote Cafe, 1203 Cerrillos Rd at Cordova; ☎505/988-1362. This inconspicuous joint, a couple of miles south of downtown, is renowned for magnificent breakfasts – burritos, creamy eggs benedict, shirred eggs (poached on a bed of chicken livers). Open daily except Mon 7am–2pm.

The Shed, 113 E Palace Ave; ☎505/982-9030. Classic (New) Mexican diner just northeast of the plaza, serving a steady diet of chile enchiladas, blue-corn tortillas and even low-fat speciailties. Lunch Mon–Sat, dinner Wed–Sat.

Tia Sophia's, 210 W San Francisco St; ☎505/983-9880. Mexican diner, a block or two west of the plaza, that's so popular with lunching locals that you can expect to have to wait in line. Open Mon–Sat 7am–2pm.

Tomasita's Cafe, 500 S Guadalupe St; ☎505/983-5721. Lively, unpretentious place, cranking out quick-fire platefuls of tasty Mexican food for under $10, plus margaritas by the litre, in old railroad station. Lunch and dinner daily.

Woolworth's, 58 E San Francisco St; ☎505/982-1062. An only-in-Santa-Fe institution; the lunch counter at what's presumably the world's only adobe *Woolworth's*, right on the plaza, is famous for its *Frito* pies – spicy red chile poured over a bag of corn chips and topped with cheese. Daily 9am–4.30pm

Mid-range

Cafe Cassis, 103 E Water St; ☎505/989-1717. Good-value restaurant, with patio seating, one block south of the plaza. Lunchtime salads and sandwiches, dinners of wood-fired pizzas with Southwestern toppings for around $7, or pastas, grilled trout, or piñon-encrusted chicken for $8–12. Open for lunch and dinner daily, plus weekend breakfasts.

Cafe Pasqual's, 121 Don Gaspar Ave; ☎505/983-9340. All purpose Old/New Mexican bakery/restaurant that serves predictable if tasty (and large) eggy breakfasts, salads and Mexican standards for lunch, and fancier dinner entrees costing either side of $20. Open for all meals daily.

Celebrations, 613 Canyon Rd; ☎505/989-8904. Lively mock-adobe bistro, very popular with Canyon Road employees, specializing in inexpensive but good Southwestern dishes with a definite Cajun twist; they even do crawfish etouffé for $10. Open for breakfast and lunch daily, dinner Wed–Sat only.

Corn Dance Cafe, 409 W Water St; ☎505/986-1662. Slightly pricey tribal-owned restaurant, just off Guadalupe St, which serves Native American dishes from around the country – including buffalo steaks – to be enjoyed on a lovely garden patio. Lunch and dinner daily.

Il Piatto, 95 W Marcy St; ☎505/984-1091. Inexpensive but very good Italian restaurant, festooned with cooking utensils, and serving pasta galore, such as a calamari spaghetti for $10, plus specials like a $14 *cioppino* (a sort of Italian *bouillabaisse*). Open Mon–Fri for lunch and dinner, dinner only Sat.

Ore House on the Plaza, 50 Lincoln Ave; ☎505/983-8687. The food may not be desperately special – a mixed bag of salads, Mexican standards, and barbe-cued meats, including the $9 meat feast *Plato de Santa Fe*, with prime rib and Yucateca pork – but the prices are low, and the location unbeatable. From the tiled tables on its *ristra*-garlanded balcony, on the southwest corner of plaza, you can watch all the life of the city. Lunch and dinner daily.

Paul's, 72 W Marcy St; ☎505/982-8738. Unpretentious, but adventurous and well-priced downtown bistro, with delicous breads and salads, and entrees such as baked salmon in a pecan herb crust, for under $20. Open for dinner daily, lunch daily except Sun.

The Pink Adobe, 406 Old Santa Fe Trail; ☎505/983-7712. This 300-year-old adobe provides a deeply romantic setting for a not wildly inspiring hybrid New Mexican/Cajun menu. Open for lunch on weekdays only, with salads and sand-wiches for around $8, and dinner nightly, when entrees such as *poulet Marengo Pink Adobe* – a half chicken cooked in wine and brandy – cost $20.

Zia Diner, 326 S Guadalupe St; ☎505/988-7008. Stylish neo-chrome diner, offering all-American meat and fish dishes, plus breads and pastries from its own bakery. Daily 11.30am–10pm.

Expensive

The Anasazi Restaurant, *Inn of the Anasazi*, 113 Washington Ave; ☎505/988-3030. Very plush Pueblo-style hotel dining room, open for all meals daily and placing an emphasis on organic ingredients. The eclectic dinner menu features entrees such as filet mignon encrusted with chiles, or halibut with plan-tain, at well over $20; lunchtime specials serve as cheaper samplers.

Coyote Cafe, 132 W Water St; ☎505/983-1615. Celebrity chef Mark Miller's showcase restaurant, just off the plaza, remains as super-trendy as ever. The à la carte prices are ferocious, but the $39.50 set meal features signature dishes such as lamb fig sausage tamale and fried red-banana-crusted sea bass. It's possible to plot a vegetarian course through the menu, if a *polenta torta* is worth $40 to you and you can cope with the cowhide seats. For a cheaper taste, try the rooftop cafe upstairs. Both serve lunch and dinner daily.

Double A, 331 Sandoval St; ☎505/982-8999. Resembling an aircraft hangar from the outside, this postmodern dining-hall/refectory features more than a hint of Anasazi masonry amid the minimalism within. It's also one of Santa Fe's newest and finest restaurants, where $20 dinner entrees include such delights as braised lamb shanks *à la jardinière* or seared *ahi*, and there's a classy late-opening bar. Open for lunch and dinner daily except Mon.

Geronimo's, 724 Canyon Rd; ☎505/982-1500. With its separate small dining rooms, this converted ancient adobe is Santa Fe's most intimate upmarket restaurant, and offers a tasty menu of Mexican and Mediterranean specialities. Open for dinner daily, lunch daily except Mon.

Santa Cafe, 231 Washington Ave; ☎505/984-1788. Downtown courtyard cafe with a not entirely deserved reputation for gourmet cuisine; the menu's blend of Asian and Southwestern styles certainly looks enticing, but the quality can be patchy, and the service snooty in the extreme. So long as you're happy to spend well over $20 per entree, and you steer clear of the seafood, you may come out smiling. Open for dinner daily, lunch on weekdays only.

Nightlife and entertainment

Santa Fe has the range of **nightlife** you'd expect in a small city rather than a major metropolis, though its **cultural scene** livens up during the summer tourist season. For full **listings** of what's going on, check the free weekly *Reporter* or the *Pasatiempo* section of Friday's *New Mexican*.

The much-anticipated **Santa Fe Opera** season runs through July and August in a magnificent amphitheatre seven miles north of town (☎505/986-5900); tickets are sold in the *Eldorado Hotel*, 309 W San Francisco St. July and August is also the time to catch the six-week **Santa Fe Chamber Music Festival** (☎505/983-2075), and the free **Shakespeare in Santa Fe** alfresco productions held on weekend evenings at St John's College, 1160 Camino de la Cruz Blanca (☎505/982-2910). All year round, the **Center for Contemporary Arts**, 291 E Barcelona Rd at Old Santa Fe Trail (☎505/982-1338), puts on a varied programme of performances and arthouse movies.

Santa Fe's major annual festivals are detailed on p.98.

Some of the most atmospheric places to **drink** in town are in the old hotels – the downstairs lounge and rooftop bar of *La Fonda* on the plaza spring to mind – but otherwise conventional bars are surprisingly few and far between.

Clubs and bars

Catamount Bar, 125 E Water St; ☎505/988-7222. Downtown bar with plenty of microbrewed beers on tap, and live rock or blues most nights.

Club Dr No, 731 Canyon Rd; ☎505/988-7100. Spacious club in the (not at all bad) *Imperial Wok* Chinese restaurant, featuring funk, jazz and alternative sounds nightly except Sunday.

The Edge, 125 W Palace Ave; ☎505/986-1700. Gleaming mall nightclub just west of the plaza, with a huge bar, open nightly until 2am

El Farol, 808 Canyon Rd; ☎505/983-9912. Historic bar-cum-restaurant that serves Spanish *tapas* to a musical accompaniment from blues to flamenco.

Evangelo's, 200 W San Francisco St; ☎505/982-9014. The only good bare-bones bar in easy walking range of the plaza, with a pool table and a jukebox.

414, 414 Old Santa Fe Trail; ☎505/986-9971. Small, central gay and lesbian club, in spitting distance of the Capitol, that's not all that exciting except on Trash Disco nights, Wednesday and Saturday.

Rodeo Nites, 2911 Cerrillos Rd; ☎505/473-4138. Nonstop country music every night.

Shopping

Secure in the knowledge that many visitors come specifically to **shop**, central Santa Fe is bursting with (generally high-priced) stores and galleries. The galleries alone turn over more than $200 million each year. The city remains largely the preserve of independents, however; few of the international names that move in seem to last long, so you'll have to familiarize yourself with what's around.

For general advice on buying Indian crafts, see p.29.

Almost everyone agrees that the best place to buy **Indian crafts**, such as silver and turquoise **jewellery**, is from the Native American sellers outside the Palace of the Governors, ideally during August's Indian Market (see p.98). If you're interested in **Hispanic folk art**, take a look at the gift store in the Museum of International Folk Art before you shop around downtown.

The two main **malls**, neither of which is particularly large or interesting, are the **Villa Linda Mall**, southwest at 4250 Cerrillos Rd, and the **De Vargas Mall**, ten minutes' walk northwest of the plaza at N Guadalupe Street and Paseo de Peralta.

Downtown Santa Fe

Artesanos, 222 Galisteo St; ☎505/983-1743. Lots of tin mirrors and glassware, *ristras*, furniture, Mexican ceramics, and a room-full of tiles of all sizes.

The Chile Shop, 109 E Water St; ☎505/983-6080. Chile products galore – sauces, intricate *ristras*, etc – plus tasteful Anasazi- and Mimbres-influenced ceramic tableware.

Don't expect to make an early start when you're shopping in Santa Fe; most stores and galleries don't open until 10am.

Kent Galleries – The Contemporary Craftsman, 130 Lincoln Ave; ☎505/988-1001. Interesting assortment of works, mostly by local artists, including paintings, sculpture, furniture and ceramics.

Mira, 101A W Marcy St; ☎505/988-3585. Tongue-in-cheek religious kitsch (Virgin Mary snowstorms, etc), plus antique clothing and oddments, at very inexpensive prices. One block north of the plaza.

Old Santa Fe Trail Books & Coffee House, 613 Old Santa Fe Trail; ☎505/988-8878. Enjoyable bookstore, across Paseo de Peralta from the Capitol, with its own espresso cafe and restaurant.

Santa Fe Paint Party, Santa Fe Village, 227 Don Gaspar Ave; ☎505/984-2524. Fun spot selling inexpensive unfired pottery that for a $6 per hour fee you can paint yourself before it goes in the kiln.

Canyon Road

Hahn Ross Gallery, 409 Canyon Rd; ☎505/984-8434. Enjoyable fine art gallery, run by a children's book illustrator, and specializing in very bright paintings that blend the fantastic with the naive.

Kania-Ferrin Gallery, 662 Canyon Rd; ☎505/982-8767. Native American antiques, with baskets, rugs, and, especially, superb old Hopi *kachinas*, at prices that run into thousands of dollars.

Nambé Showroom, 924 Paseo de Peralta; ☎505/988-5582. Factory outlet at the foot of Canyon Road, with a large stock of Nambé ware – shiny, futuristic table- and ovenware made from a local alloy that looks like silver but has unique heat-retaining properties.

Pachamama, 223 Canyon Rd; ☎505/983-4020. Unusually cheap Hispanic craftworks, mainly from Mexico, including *retablos*, statues, and lots of tin.

Off the Wall, 616 Canyon Rd; ☎505/983-8337. Eccentric assortment of contemporary art objects, mostly functional, largely ceramic, many tea-oriented. There's a weird influence of medieval Judaica – and an espresso bar.

Silver Sun, 656 Canyon Rd; ☎505/983-8743. Native American arts and crafts, with a stand-out collection of beautiful turquoise jewellery.

South to Albuquerque

Travellers embarking on the sixty-mile drive southwest from Santa Fe to Albuquerque have a choice of two routes. The **interstate**, I-25, is fast and reasonably scenic, but for atmosphere and Old-West charm it doesn't begin to match the **Turquoise Trail**, which squeezes between the Sandia and Ortiz mountains to the east.

The interstate route

Commuters may not give it a second thought, but the hour-long journey from Santa Fe to Albuquerque on I-25 represents a major transition. When it drops down the escarpment known as **La Bajada**, twenty miles from downtown Santa Fe, the interstate leaves the Rocky Mountains and enters the desert. To the north, the Rio Grande was traditionally known as the **Rio Arriba**, or Upper River, and cuts through a deep rocky gorge; to the south, the **Rio Abajo** or Lower River meanders across a broad floodplain.

La Bajada also marks the dividing line between the northern and southern **pueblos**. Below it, the interstate runs through three separate Indian reservations. In 1996, when state legislators seemed poised to outlaw the Indian gaming that has finally brought the pueblos a degree of prosperity, Pueblo authorities retaliated by threatening to place **toll-gates** on the interstate at every boundary.

Cochiti Pueblo

COCHITI PUEBLO, ten miles west of the interstate on Hwy-16, at the foot of La Bajada, is home to a thousand Keresan-speaking Indians who trace their ancestry back to the cliff dwellers of

In the Keresan language, Kotyete means "stone kiva".

Bandelier (see p.118). Visitors have free access to the pueblo in daylight hours, but it holds no formal stores, and while the mission church of **San Buenaventura** still incorporates vestiges of its original adobe form, it has been greatly modified over the years, and the contemporary frescoes within are not all that enthralling.

A Cochiti potter, Helen Cordero, fashioned the first ceramic "**storyteller**" here in 1946. Depicting a mother with up to thirty children, they're among New Mexico's best-selling souvenirs, and are made by over two hundred Indians, including around fifty Cochiti.

In the 1970s, the tribe leased land to the federal government for the creation of nearby **Cochiti Lake**, which attracts a million recreational visitors each year. A planned residential community went bankrupt, however, and the loss of Cochiti agricultural land has left the pueblo sceptical about further "developments".

Santo Domingo and San Felipe pueblos

*Advice on
visiting the
pueblos, and
a calendar of
major feast
days, appears
on p.124.*

Six miles on from Cochiti, **SANTO DOMINGO PUEBLO** is the largest Keresan pueblo. For many centuries, its people have been renowned for making **jewellery**, and especially necklaces of delicate shell and turquoise *heishi* beads, By some accounts, they taught the art of silversmithing to the Navajo in the nineteenth century, and they're now prominent among the Indian traders of Santa Fe.

The **visitor center** in the plaza at Santo Domingo doubles as a crafts store and tribal museum (daily 8am–5pm; ☎505/465-2214), while the all-purpose *Santo Domingo Trading Post* to the north ranges from food to jewellery.

The next of the southern pueblos, a few miles downriver, is **SAN FELIPE PUEBLO**. Until 1250 AD, the San Felipeans were a single tribe with their fellow Keresan speakers the Cochiti. Their subsequent migrations only ended in 1693, when they settled here for good after the Pueblo Revolt. Daytime visits are always permitted.

Algodones

The village of **ALGODONES**, stretching languidly beside the river five miles southwest of San Felipe, makes a tranquil base for visits to both Santa Fe and Albuquerque. *Hacienda Vargas*, 1431 El Camino Real (☎505/867-9115; ④), is one of New Mexico's most relaxing rural **B&Bs**, set in a lovely adobe trading post.

Coronado State Monument

BERNALILLO, five miles on from Algodones, is an unexciting satellite community at the edge of Albuquerque's urban sprawl, noteworthy only as the site of **CORONADO STATE MONUMENT** (May–Sept daily 8am–5pm; Oct–April daily 8.30am–4.30pm; $2). In a spectacular setting on the west bank of the Rio Grande, a mile west of the interstate, this preserves what remains of the ancient pueblo of **Kuaua**. The Spaniards knew this region as **Tiguex**, and described it as a "broad valley planted with fields of maize and dotted with cottonwood groves"; Francisco de Coronado may well have spent the winter of 1540 here. Kuaua was then a thriving community of well over a thousand rooms; now it's a ruin, of which a few eroded adobe walls have been exposed by archeologists. The central feature is a restored *kiva*, decorated with vivid reproductions of its multicoloured **murals**. The faded originals, preserved in the visitor center, include scenes of a rabbit hunt – the animals are still abundant in the undergrowth by the river.

Near the monument entrance, the state maintains a large but attractive riverfront **campground** (☎505/867-5589), where rates depend on what degree of comfort you require. One of New Mexico's finest **restaurants** is a mile or so northwest. The *Prairie Star*, 1000 Jemez Canyon Dam Rd (☎505/867-3327), which opens for dinner daily and brunch on Sunday, serves contemporary Southwestern cuisine at upwards of $20 per entree.

South to
Albuquerque

*Rabbits often represent the **moon** in Pueblo art, as Pueblo peoples saw a "rabbit in the moon" rather than a "man in the moon".*

Sandia Pueblo

SANDIA PUEBLO, between Bernalillo and Albuquerque, dates back to around 1300 AD, and was visited by Coronado in 1540. *Sandía* is the Spanish for watermelon; the Spaniards mistook the squashes they saw growing here for watermelons. The village's Tiwa name – **Nafiat**, meaning "dry or sandy place" – seems more appropriate to its dusty central plaza. After it was destroyed in 1692, by Spaniards returning after the Pueblo Revolt, many of its inhabitants took refuge with the Hopi, far to the west, and it was not rebuilt for fifty years. The main preoccupation of the three hundred present-day Sandians is the protection of their sacred sites in the nearby mountains from blundering hikers, but they also operate the *Bien Mur Trading Post* **crafts centre** and **restaurant**, on Tramway Road near the interstate (☎505/821-5400), which has a herd of buffalo.

The Turquoise Trail

The **Turquoise Trail** – less glamorously known as **Hwy-14** – is a modern name for what may be one of the oldest thoroughfares in north America, connecting **mines** along the eastern flanks of the Sandia Mountains with the settlements of the Rio Grande Valley. In the last two hundred years, these mines have yielded considerable quantities of copper, coal, and even gold, but **turquoise** production dates back perhaps ten times as far. Long before the coming of the Spaniards, traders carried local stone all over the Southwest and down into Mexico, and wealthy pueblos lined the nearby streams.

Until a recent influx of artists, craft-workers and small-scale entrepreneurs, communities along the trail had dwindled to become little more than **ghost towns**, but now **Madrid** in particular is one of the most appealing day-trip destinations for visitors to Santa Fe.

Cerrillos

CERRILLOS, the northernmost Turquoise-Trail town, is just over twenty miles south of Santa Fe, reached simply by continuing south on Cerrillos Road, which becomes Hwy-14, for fifteen miles beyond its intersection with I-25. The dusty rolling hillocks that surround it – the "little hills" of its name – hold one of the world's greatest concentrations of **turquoise**.

Archeologists have estimated that ninety percent of the fabled turquoise treasures seized by the Spaniards from the Aztec capital of Tenochtitlan came from this unprepossessing spot. With basic tools, prehistoric miners scooped a hundred thousand tons of rock from **Mount Chalchihuitl**, two miles northeast, leaving a cavern 300 feet wide and 200 feet deep. Early Spanish settlers may have forced the Indians to work for them; it's said that a mine collapse around 1680, which killed up to eighty Indians, helped to precipitate the Pueblo Revolt. By the time the Spaniards returned, the Indians had deliberately hidden many of the shafts, and tales of fabulously wealthy "lost mines" still abound.

The unpaved streets and falsefront wooden buildings of Cerrillos made it an ideal location for the 1988 bratpack Western Young Guns.

Today's Cerrillos, nestled amid the giant cottonwoods along the bank of the broad but usually dry Galisteo River, has changed little since its last boom, during the 1890s. Mining not only turquoise but gold, silver, copper and lead, it was briefly rich enough to support eight daily newspapers and numerous hotels and saloons. There's still a bit of life in the old town; as recently as 1983 robbers made off with $500,000 worth of gold from the nearby Ortiz Mines. Tourists, however, have to content themselves with the **Casa Grande Trading Post, Turquoise Mining Museum and Petting Zoo**, an endearing shop-cum-museum that offers a random assortment of old bills and letters, porcupine quills, rattlesnake skins and petrified wood, plus the chance to pet a llama or pull on a string to make a plaster Indian hammer on a rock.

Madrid

Between 1869 and 1959, the village of **MADRID** (pronounced *MADrid*), three miles south, made a good living from mining **coal**. The hills here are unusual in holding deposits of both bituminous (soft) and anthracite (hard) coal, which in the early days was hauled by wagon as far as St Louis, and later was consumed in vast quantities by the *Santa Fe Railroad*. A mine shaft directly beneath the main street can now be seen in the **Old Coal Mine Museum** at the south end of town (daily 9am–5pm; $3).

After the mine closed down, the whole town was auctioned off piecemeal, and the straggle of wooden cottages to either side of the narrow highway have progressively been taken over by New-Agey newcomers. Several hold genuinely interesting crafts and antiques stores; if you're close enough to home to carry **furniture**, there are some real bargains to be had. Among the best stores are *Primitiva*, on the raised boardwalk at 500 Main St, which has two spacious floors of artefacts from around the world, and the *Turquoise Trail Trading Post* nearby, which concentrates more on Pueblo crafts.

One attractive old mining home, *Java Junction* (☎505/438-2772; ③), houses a **coffee shop** downstairs and a **B&B** apartment upstairs, with kitchen and bathroom, while the lively *Mine Shaft Tavern*, in front of the museum (☎505/473-0743), claims to have the longest **bar** in New Mexico, and puts on live **music** at weekends.

Golden

GOLDEN, fifteen miles beyond Madrid, was the site in 1825 of the Wild West's first-ever gold rush. It has yet to revitalize to any great extent, and you might hardly notice it was there as the highway races down its former main street. Look out, however, for the tumbledown **adobe church** on the hill at the north edge of town, which served the mining camp of **Tuerto**, and has preserved its pioneer graveyard.

Sandia Crest and Cedar Crest

Ten miles on from Golden, the **Sandia Crest Scenic Byway** branches west from Hwy-14, to climb for eight tortuous miles up to the razorback ridge atop the Sandia Mountains. From the mile-high **observation deck** at road's end, you can survey the sprawling city of **Albuquerque**, with the Rio Grande flowing in from the north, and also look east across the endless plains, beyond the Ortiz Mountains. The adjacent *Sandia House* sells tasteless snacks and useless gifts. A fee of $3 is charged for day-use of the nearby trails, but most visitors stay for barely ten minutes before heading back down the hill; there's no through route to Albuquerque.

In winter, **skiers** exploring the eastern Sandia slopes base themselves down below, in **CEDAR CREST** at the foot of the Scenic Byway. The *Sandia Mountain Hostel* (☎505/281-4117; ①) offers dorm accommodation, while the *Kokopelli Cafe* (☎505/281-2002) serves all meals. The Turquoise Trail ends six miles south at the intersection with I-40, which sweeps the final dozen miles west to Albuquerque through **Tijeras** – "Scissors" – **Canyon**.

West of Santa Fe

The **Jemez Mountain Trail**, which loops through the mountains west of Santa Fe, can be enjoyed as a long day's excursion, or a roundabout route down to Albuquerque. Communities along the way range from modern **Los Alamos** – the top-secret Town That Never Was – to the ancient dwellings of **Bandelier National Monument**; the scenery encompasses mountain meadows and desert canyons.

The **Pajarito Plateau**, the dominant feature of the landscape, was created just over a million years ago, when colossal **volcanic eruptions** buried four hundred square miles of land beneath a thousand feet of ash. This solidified into the easily-eroded rock known as **tuff**, which has been eaten away by wind and rain ever

Pajarito
*means "little
bird" in
Spanish; it's a
direct transla-
tion of the
Tewa tsirege,
the name of an
abandoned
local pueblo.*

since to form an intricate tangle of deep gorges and forested mesas. Only one road climbs onto the plateau, **Hwy-502**, which branches west from US-84 near Pojoaque Pueblo, fifteen miles north of Santa Fe.

Los Alamos

*Visitors to Los Alamos and Bandelier should avoid the **rush hour** traffic that heads up Hwy-502 until around 9am, and comes back down again from 3pm onwards.*

LOS ALAMOS, eighteen miles up Hwy-502, is not so much a town as the overgrown campus of the **Los Alamos National Laboratory**. Home during World War II to the **Manhattan Project**, which first developed the atomic bomb, it has remained the leading US centre for the research and development of nuclear weapons. With the laboratory now run by the University of California, Los Alamos has become in the process New Mexico's wealthiest enclave.

It's a confusing place to visit. The layout – sprawling along several "fingers" at the edge of the Pajarito Plateau, separated by deep canyons – is bizarre in the extreme, and the fact that most of the complex is off limits to the public doesn't help. Most tourists call in at one of the two local **museums**, then head on to Bandelier.

The **Bradbury Science Museum**, at Central and 15th (Tues–Fri 9am–5pm, Sat–Mon 1–5pm; free), presents the authorized version of the laboratory's history. Opponents of nuclear proliferation are given space to state their case, but visitors inevitably gravitate towards the central exhibits – full-sized 1940s replicas of "Little Boy", which devastated Hiroshima, and "Fat Man", dropped on Nagasaki. The **visitors' book** is fascinating enough to have been published in the past. Americans tend to be resolutely gung-ho; international travellers – of which a sizeable percentage seem to come from Hiroshima and Nagasaki – rather less so. The excellent *Otowi Station* **bookstore**, alongside, is open daily for longer hours.

Los Alamos Historical Museum, adjoining the visitor center at 2132 Central Ave (winter Mon–Sat 10am–4pm, Sun 1–4pm; summer Mon–Sat 9.30am–4.30pm, Sun 11am–5pm; free), is housed in the former dining hall of Los Alamos Ranch School. As well as displays on the school, and local geology and prehistory, it too covers the bomb in some detail. Exhibits range from a 360° aerial photo of Hiroshima, to classic examples of atomic kitsch, such as a picture of the commander of the 1946 tests at Bikini cutting a mushroom-cloud shaped cake, some earrings made with "atomsite" fused glass from the Trinity site, and an A-bomb-shaped lamp.

Practicalities

*Los Alamos' **zip code** is NM 87544.*

Los Alamos' **visitor center** is a couple of blocks west of the Bradbury Museum, at 2132 Central Ave (Mon–Fri 8am–5pm; ☎505/662-8105). As well as a couple of nondescript upmarket **motels** that cater largely for visiting scientists – the *Hilltop House*, 400 Trinity Drive

The Town That Never Was: Los Alamos and the Bomb

In 1942, the American and British governments decided to amalgamate the nine research efforts then racing to build the **atomic bomb**. Albert Einstein had suggested the idea to President Roosevelt three years earlier, and a team led by Enrico Fermi was achieving promising results in a laboratory beneath a disused football stadium in Chicago. The search was on for a suitable location, in a sparsely populated area, away from the sea, with a reasonable year-round climate. **J Robert Oppenheimer**, the scientific chief of the **Manhattan Project**, had backpacked before the war in New Mexico. He recommended the Los Alamos Ranch School, an exclusive private school on the Pajarito Plateau, and the site was duly bought out. When its final class graduated in February 1943, the scientists moved in.

It took just over two years, working in the utmost secrecy – the words "Los Alamos" were forbidden, and newcomers were told merely to report to 109 Palace Avenue in Santa Fe – for the bomb to become a reality. The first successful test took place at the **Trinity Site**, two hundred miles south (see p.171), on July 16, 1945. Three weeks later, bombs were dropped on the cities of **Hiroshima**, on August 6, and **Nagasaki**, August 9; a complete Japanese surrender followed immediately.

For Oppenheimer, who described the development of the bomb with a quotation from the *Bhagavad Gita*, "I am become Death, the shatterer of Worlds", Los Alamos had served its purpose, and the laboratory could now close. Instead, as the Cold War set in, its energies were devoted towards the construction of the **H-Bomb**. Though security was more paramount than ever, ideologically motivated spies such as **Klaus Fuchs** and **David Greenglass** (whose sister and her husband, **Ethel** and **Julius Rosenberg**, were later executed) soon betrayed Los Alamos' secrets to the Russians. Paranoia grew to the point that employees were instructed to *Watch Your Liberal Friends*, and Oppenheimer himself was barred by his successor Edward Teller from access to privileged information.

The gate house on the road up from Santa Fe that denied outsiders access to Los Alamos was finally removed in 1957, and the ownership of private property on the plateau was allowed in 1962. The laboratory business is still booming, however. Of its 1993 budget of $1,122 million, just over half, $589 million, was spent on the research and development of nuclear weapons. While it has also drilled a 12,000-foot hole to "mine" heat from hot rocks deep in the earth, and worked on the Human Genome project which aims to map the entire DNA structure of human beings, its public image remains firmly linked with nuclear experimentation, and constantly changing plans for the disposal of its radioactive waste are among New Mexico's hottest political issues.

(☎505/662-2441 or 1-800/462-0936, fax 662-5913; ④), and *Los Alamos Inn*, 2201 Trinity Drive (☎505/662-7211 or 1-800/279-9279; ④) – it has a handful of **B&Bs**, such as the *Orange Street Inn*, 3496 Orange St (☎505/662-2651 or 1-800/662-3180; ③). The *Trinity Sights Restaurant*, upstairs in *Hilltop House*, is the best place to **eat** in town, though the *Cafe Allegro*, 800 Trinity Drive (☎505/662-4040), serves a mean espresso.

Bandelier National Monument

*For details of
Gray Line **bus
tours** to
Bandelier
from Santa Fe,
see p.96.*

Long before the scientists descended upon Los Alamos, the "finger canyons" of the Pajarito Plateau were home to Native Americans. At **BANDELIER NATIONAL MONUMENT**, ten miles south of Los Alamos – a fifty-mile drive from Santa Fe – the ancient **Anasazi** enlarged natural cavities in the soft volcanic rock to create **cliff dwellings**, and built free-standing **pueblo** communities beside the streams on the valley floors. Set amid delightful woodlands, framed against the rose-pink canyon walls, Bandelier's intriguing remains provide an ideal introduction to New Mexico's prehistoric roots.

Although the Anasazi are often said to have "disappeared" around 1300 AD, there's little mystery about where they went. Bandelier is a "missing link", occupied between roughly 1150, at the time the Four Corners region was being abandoned, and 1550, when many of today's pueblos were established. As successive itinerant groups streamed in, perhaps fleeing drought or invasion, they may have amalgamated here to create the modern Pueblo culture. The peoples of **Cochiti** and **San Ildefonso** in particular trace their ancestry back via Bandelier to Mesa Verde, and it was a Cochiti guide who led amateur archeologist **Adolph Bandelier** to this site in 1880.

The monument covers fifty square miles, but all **backcountry** areas have been closed to the public since the devastating **Dome Fire** of April 1996, when a backpacker's campfire consumed 44,000 acres of forest, and may remain so for up to eight years. **Frijoles Canyon**, home to the main ruins, was unaffected.

Frijoles Canyon

*The Frijoles
Canyon trails
are open daily
dawn to dusk;
admission is
$5 per vehicle.*

The major sights of Bandelier are concentrated along a 1.5-mile loop trail through **Frijoles** ("Beans") **Canyon**. The **visitor center**, at the bottom of a narrow switchback road down from Hwy-4, gives an excellent overview, with displays of pottery and jewellery, models of the ruins, full-scale reconstructions of pueblo interiors, and century-old photographs of Indian life (winter daily 8am–5pm; summer daily 8am–6pm; ☎505/672-3861).

Beyond the visitor center, the trail leads swiftly to the remains of **Tyuonyi**, a circular, multi-storey village of four hundred rooms, of which only the ground floor and foundations survive. Its name means "place of agreement", and it's seen as a centre for trade and storage, common to the **Keresan**-speaking peoples, whose pueblos lay to the south, and the **Tewa** speakers to the north. Local obsidian was traded as far as the Dakotas and the Mississippi. Tyuonyi may have still been in use when Coronado's first expedition reached the Southwest (see p.472), though they didn't reach this far.

A side path from Tyuonyi leads up to dozens of **cave dwellings**, their rounded chambers scooped into the warmer, south-facing wall of the canyon. Ladders and walkways mean visitors can scramble up to, and even enter, some of them, to peer out across the valley.

The main trail continues to the **Long House**, an 800ft series of two- and three-storey houses built side by side against the cliffs. Though most of the upper stories have collapsed to expose the plastered walls, you can still see the morticed holes that held up their pine roof beams or *vigas*. Above these are rows of petroglyphs and pictographs, mostly depicting figures and abstract symbols.

Though the main trail doubles back to the visitor center, keen hikers can follow the stream for another half-mile, to the point where **Ceremonial Cave** nestles in a rocky overhang 150 feet above the canyon floor. Reaching it entails climbing three hair-raising ladders, as well as steep stairways hacked into the crumbling rock. At the top, you can see by the *viga*-holes that the cave once held several structures, but it's now bare except for a reconstructed *kiva*, set down in its sloping sandy floor, and entered by ladder.

Another trail drops south from the visitor center, coming out after a mile and a half at the **Lower Falls** – at their best in late spring – and then reaches the Rio Grande in another ten minutes.

Snacks and sodas are available at the visitor center, but there's no **accommodation** at Bandelier apart from the very pleasant *Juniper Campground*, just off Hwy-4 up on Frijoles Mesa (March–Nov; first-come, first-served; $6).

Valle Grande and Spence's Hot Spring

Hwy-4 climbs west of Bandelier and Los Alamos, bursting unexpectedly out of the forests to skirt the long rim of **Valle Grande**. This 500-foot-deep, 176-square-mile basin is the world's largest extinct caldera, and its wide meadows form a lush counterpoint to the dry-as-dust terrain of most of New Mexico.

Vestiges of the volcanic past can be seen in the form of the numerous **hot springs** that bubble from beneath the ground. Among the most irresistible is **Spence's Hot Spring**, on a promontory above the Jemez River between mileposts 24 and 25, half an hour out of Los Alamos. Half a dozen waterfall-connected pools provide a range of temperatures to suit anybody, from the high 90°sF in the lower pools to a blissful 104°F at the top; local custom calls for bathing suits on weekend nights, otherwise it's clothing optional. To get there, cross the river over a fallen tree and then climb up the canyon, keeping to the left for about ten minutes' walk uphill.

Jemez Springs

Five miles down from Spence's Hot Spring, Hwy-4 runs past the bizarre **Soda Dam**, where calcified deposits all but block the Jemez River, to enter **JEMEZ SPRINGS**. This appealing hamlet, where the river is lined by glowing cottonwoods, and flows between high canyon walls that flame gold and red, was once the site of the Towa-speaking pueblo of **Giusewa**, the "Place of the Boiling Waters".

*If Bandelier captures your imagination, don't miss the similar **Puyé Cliff Dwellings** (see p.123).*

What little remains of the mission church of **San Jose de los Jemez**, built by Franciscans in 1621 only to be destroyed almost immediately by Navajo raiders, is now preserved in **Jemez State Monument** (daily 8.30am–5pm; $2.50). Walls that once held bright frescoes are now just ruined stumps, but the principal doorway has been reconstructed.

Practicalities

*Jemez
Springs' zip
code is NM
87025*

Jemez Springs offers several small-scale **accommodation** options, including the beautiful river-view *Dancing Bear B&B* (PO Box 128; ☎505/829-3336 or 1-800/422-3271, fax 829-3395; ④–⑥), and the *Jemez River B&B Inn*, 16445 Hwy-4 (☎505/829-3262 or 1-800/809-3262; ④–⑥), which doubles as a hummingbird sanctuary. The *Laughing Lizard Cafe* (☎505/829-3692) serves espresso coffee and full meals on a nice terrace above both highway and river, while the late-opening *Los Ojos Restaurant and Saloon* (☎505/829-3547) has food, pool tables and cheap beer.

Jemez Pueblo

*Advice on
visiting the
pueblos, and a
calendar of
major feast
days, appears
on p.124.*

After Giusewa Pueblo was abandoned in 1630, its inhabitants built **JEMEZ PUEBLO**, fifteen miles downstream. There they participated in the Pueblo Revolt of 1680, sacking their church and killing its priest; when the Spaniards returned, they briefly retreated northwest, establishing cultural and family links with the Navajo that endure to this day. They also assimilated the last twenty survivors of Pecos Pueblo in 1838 (see p.131). Jemez now has a population of around 2500, and is the only surviving Towa-speaking pueblo. Its people successfully resisted plans to develop a geothermal power plant in the Jemez mountains in 1982.

In honour of the surrounding scenery, the Jemez Indians call themselves **Walatowa**, "people of the canyon", and that's also the name of their village. A **visitor center** nearby (daily 8am–5pm; ☎505/834-7235) holds displays on their history and crafts, but the pueblo itself is only open to visitors on August 2 and November 12. On summer weekends, the **Jemez Pueblo Open Air Market**, on Hwy-4 at **Red Rock** three miles north, sells foods and artworks.

Zia and Santa Ana pueblos

Little **ZIA PUEBLO**, which also overlooks the Jemez River, a dozen miles further downstream – reached by a short spur road off Hwy-44 – is best known for the **sun symbol** that features on New Mexico's flag and licence plates. Now 750 strong, the Zia Indians have occupied this spot since the sixteenth century, when they were visited by early Spanish explorers. Their neighbours at the equally small **SANTA ANA PUEBLO**, eight miles southeast along Hwy-44, are also Keresan speakers, who moved in after the Pueblo Revolt.

There's little reason for outsiders to visit either pueblo; the road into Santa Ana, in fact, is barred except for the occasional feast day.

The Jemez Mountain Trail ends ten miles on from Santa Ana, when Hwy-44 meets the I-25 interstate at **Bernalillo**, home to the **Coronado State Monument** (see p.112). Downtown Albuquerque is a sixteen-mile drive south – though the suburbs start almost immediately – while Santa Fe is forty miles northeast, a drive described on p.111 onwards.

From Santa Fe to Taos: the northern pueblos

The quickest route between Santa Fe and Taos follows US-84 as far as the Rio Grande, then continues northeast beside the river on Hwy-68 – not that the switch from one to the other, at **Espanola**, is discernible to the naked eye. US-84 passes through the heartland of the **northern pueblos**, a cluster of tiny Tewa-speaking villages that have survived for over five hundred years. The most interesting for casual visitors are **Santa Clara**, where the **Puyé Cliff Dwellings** are among the Southwest's least-known ancient ruins, and **Nambe**, near the impressive **Nambe Falls**. **Pojoaque** on the highway can provide a quick taste of Pueblo culture and a souvenir or two, but serious collectors head instead for **San Ildefonso** and its famous pottery.

For a detailed history of the Pueblo peoples, see p.471; general advice on visiting the pueblos appears on p.124.

Tesuque Pueblo

Nine miles north of Santa Fe, west of US-84, the traditional community of **TESUQUE PUEBLO** studiously turns its back on the city, overlooked by the remarkable **Camel Rock**. Its name means "place of the cottonwood trees", and its people were the first to strike against the Spaniards during the Pueblo Revolt. They now operate a **campground**, geared mainly towards RVs (☎505/455-2661).

Pojoaque Pueblo

POJOAQUE PUEBLO, twelve miles out of Santa Fe, was once one of the largest pueblos, but its original settlement was abandoned after a smallpox epidemic in 1895. Though some ceremonial activities have resumed in the last twenty years, most of the tribe's attention is devoted to running a busy roadside complex just east of US-84. As well as a **visitor center** covering all the Tewa peoples (daily 8.30am–5.30pm), which sells a wide range of Native American artefacts, this includes the **Poeh Museum** (Tues–Sat 8am–noon & 12.30–4.30pm; $1), whose displays are little different from those in the store, and the *Po Suwae Geh* **restaurant** (daily 7am–8pm; ☎505/455-7493). On summer Saturdays and Sundays, it's also the venue for **dance** performances at 11am and 1pm. The *Cities of Gold* **casino** stands alongside.

Nambe Pueblo

The most beautifully sited of the northern pueblos is **NAMBE PUEBLO**, up the hillside five miles east of Pojoaque. Apart from a large *kiva*, not much remains in its old plaza area, but the triple-decker **Nambe Falls**, another four miles on, are well worth seeing (April, May & Oct daily 7am–7pm; June–Sept daily 6am–9pm; free). You can **camp** beside the reservoir below the falls ($8).

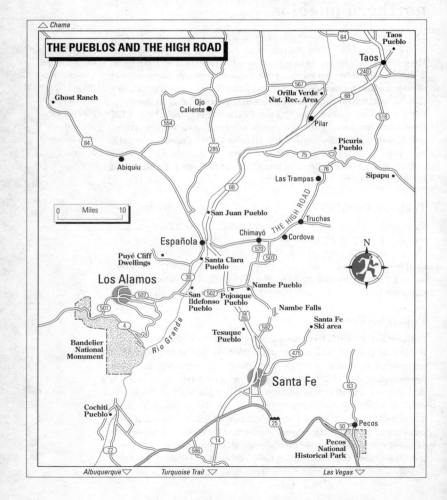

San Ildefonso Pueblo

Five miles west of Pojoaque, before Hwy-502 crosses the Rio Grande and climbs up to Los Alamos, **SAN ILDEFONSO PUEBLO** is best known as the former home of potter **Maria Martinez**. From 1919 onwards, together with her husband Julian, she was responsible for revitalizing the Pueblo ceramic tradition. The people of San Ildefonso trace their ancestry back to Mesa Verde, by way of the Pajarito Plateau. In 1694, when the Spaniards returned after the Pueblo Revolt, refugees from San Ildefonso and its neighbours held out on a nearby mesa, **Black Rock**, until they were starved down.

San Ildefonso now consists of two distinct plazas, one of which holds a replica of its original mission church. Individual artesans sell pottery from their own homes – look out for signs – or you can buy from the selection in the **visitor center** (Feb–Oct daily 8am–5pm; Nov–Jan Mon–Fri 8am–4.30pm) when you pay your $3 admission fee. The nearby **tribal museum** (Mon–Fri 8am–4pm) holds some of Martinez' original works.

The finest collection of pottery made by the Martinez family is in Taos' Millicent Rogers Museum; see p.141.

Santa Clara Pueblo and Puyé Cliff Dwellings

Five miles north of San Ildefonso, or five miles west of Española, **SANTA CLARA PUEBLO** is known to its 1500 inhabitants as Kapo, "where the roses grow near the water". They too now sell black pottery from houses around the central plaza, but the main reason to visit is to see where they *used* to live: the dramatic **PUYÉ CLIFF DWELLINGS** in Santa Clara Canyon, an eleven-mile drive on paved roads west of the pueblo (April–Sept daily 8am–8pm, Oct–March daily 9am–5pm; $5, or $7 for a guided tour, summer Mon–Fri 9am).

Like the similar but better-known ruins at Bandelier (see p.118), the ancient community of Puyé was set against the south-facing cliffs at the edge of the Pajarito Plateau, and occupied between 1250 and 1550. Two tiers of "apartments" were hollowed into the upper canyon wall – so soft that it could be shaped with wooden tools – while a large free-standing pueblo occupied the mesa-top just above. The trail up from the visitor center is easy at first, but seeing the whole thing involves climbing at least one steep ladder, plus some deeply worn "staircases" in the rock. What seem like cosy little cave dwellings were originally interior rooms in larger complexes; each was fronted by several adobe-walled rooms, as the countless holes that once supported roof-beams now testify. Intriguingly, petroglyphs above the entranceways appear to mark specific homes.

Puyé means "where the rabbits meet" in Tewa.

If you're reluctant to tear yourself away from this gorgeous spot, there's a **cafe** in the visitor center that serves snacks on weekdays, and it's even possible to **camp** six miles further along Santa Clara Canyon (April–Oct; $8; ☎505/753-7326).

From Santa Fe to Taos: The Northern Pueblos

Visiting the Rio Grande Pueblos

The first Spaniards to explore what's now New Mexico, in 1540, encountered a settled population of around a hundred thousand people, living in perhaps a hundred villages and towns. They named them the **Pueblo Indians**, *pueblo* being the Spanish for "village". Smallpox, war, and general disruption have taken their toll, but New Mexico is still home to around forty thousand Pueblo Indians. They live in nineteen autonomous pueblos, each with its own laws and system of government.

Fifteen of those pueblos are concentrated along the Rio Grande north of Albuquerque. There's a long-standing division between the seven **southern pueblos**, south of Santa Fe, most of which speak **Keresan**, and the group to the north, which mostly speak **Tewa** (pronounced *tay-wah*), and jointly promote themselves as the **Eight Northern Indian Pueblos** (☎505/852-4265 or 1-800/793-4955). The remaining four pueblos are **Ácoma** (see p.86), **Isleta** (p.185), **Laguna** (p.89), and **Zuni** (p.83).

Despite their fascinating history – outlined on p.471 – most pueblos aren't really the tourist attractions they're often touted to be. The best-known, **Taos** and **Ácoma**, retain their ancient defensive architecture, but the rest tend to be dusty adobe hamlets scattered around a wind-blown plaza. Unless you arrive on a feast day, or are a knowledgeable shopper in search of Pueblo crafts (most have their own specialities), visits are liable to prove disappointing. In addition, you'll certainly be made to feel unwelcome if you fail to behave respectfully – don't go "exploring" places that are off limits to outsiders, such as shrines, *kivas* or private homes.

Visitors to each are required to **register** at a visitor center; some charge an admission fee of around $3, and all charge additional fees of $5 for still photography, $10–15 for video cameras, and up to $100 for sketching. There's no extra charge for feast days or dances, but photography is often forbidden on special occasions. The recent explosion of Native American gaming has seen many open their own **casinos**, usually along the major highways, well away from residential areas.

For details of **guided pueblo tours**, contact *Nambe Pueblo Tours* (112 W San Francisco St, Santa Fe; ☎505/820-1340 or 1-800/946-2623).

Southern Pueblos		Northern Pueblos	
Cochiti; p.111	☎465-2244	Nambe; p.122	☎455-2036
Jemez; p.120	☎834-7235	Picuris; p.126	☎587-2519
San Felipe; p.112	☎867-3381	Pojoaque; p.121	☎983-2667
Sandia; p.113	☎867-3317	San Ildefonso; p.123	☎455-3549
Santa Ana; p.120	☎867-3301	San Juan; p.126	☎852-4400
Santo Domingo; p.112		Santa Clara; p.123	☎753-7326
	☎465-2214	Taos; p.133	☎758-1028
Zia; p.120	☎867-3304	Tesuque; p.121	☎455-3460

All the above numbers share area code ☎505

A Pueblo Calendar

Jan 1	Transfer of Canes	Most pueblos
Jan 6	King's Day	Most pueblos
Jan 22–23	San Ildefonso Pueblo Feast Day	San Ildefonso
Jan 25	St Paul's Feast Day	Picuris
March 19	St Joseph's Feast Day	Laguna
April 1	Spring Corn Dance	Many pueblos
Easter	Dances	Most pueblos
May 1	Green Corn Dance	San Felipe
May 3	Santa Cruz Feast Day	Cochiti, Taos
June 8	Buffalo Dance	Santa Clara
June 13	Sandia Pueblo Feast Day	Sandia
June 13	St Anthony's Feast Day	Most pueblos
June 23–24	San Juan Pueblo Feast Day	San Juan
June 20	Governor's Dance	Isleta
June 24	Corn Dances	Santa Ana, Taos
June 29	San Pedro Feast Day	Most pueblos
July 4	Nambe Falls Celebration	Nambe
July 14	San Buenaventura	Cochiti
July (2nd wk)	Taos Pueblo Pow-wow	Taos
July (3rd wk)	Northern Pueblo Artist & Craftsman Show	varying northern pueblos
July 25–26	Corn Dances	Taos
July 25–26	Santa Ana Pueblo Feast Day	Santa Ana
Aug 2	Pecos Bull Dance	Jemez
Aug 4	Corn Dance	Santo Domingo
Aug 9–10	San Lorenzo Feast Day	Picuris
Aug 12	Santa Clara Pueblo Feast Day	Santa Clara
Aug 15	Zia Pueblo Feast Day	Zia
Aug (3rd wk)	Indian Market	Santa Fe
Aug 28	St Augustine Feast Day	Isleta
Sept 2	San Esteban Feast Day	Ácoma
Sept 4	Isleta Pueblo Feast Day	Isleta
Sept 19	Laguna Pueblo Feast Day	Laguna
Sept 22	Harvest Dance	San Juan
Sept 29–30	Feast of San Geronimo	Taos
Oct 3–4	San Francisco Feast Day	Nambe
Nov 12	San Diego Feast Day	Jemez, Tesuque
Early Dec	Shalako ceremony	Zuni
Dec 12	Guadalupe Feast Day	Jemez, Pojoaque
Dec 25	Matachina Dance	most pueblos
Dec 26	Turtle Dance	San Juan
Dec 26	Children's Dances	Picuris, Santa Clara

Española

The only sizeable Hispanic settlement between Santa Fe and Taos is
ESPANOLA, roughly halfway between the two, where US-84 veers
west across the river towards Chama. Other than watching the local
youth cruising the streets in their customized "low-riders", or joining
them in one of the dozens of neighbourhood fast-food joints,
Española has little to offer tourists. However, it's central enough to
make an inexpensive alternative base, with a strip of budget **motels**
that includes a *Super 8*, 298 S Riverside Drive (☎505/753-5374 or
1-800/800-8000, fax 753-5339; winter ②, summer ③).

San Juan Pueblo

SAN JUAN PUEBLO, the largest of the Tewa pueblos, is set amid the
cottonwoods on the east bank of the Rio Grande off Hwy-68, five
miles north of Española. It's the third village to have stood in this
vicinity since 1250, all of which have been called **O'ke**, meaning "we
are the brothers". The first two capitals of the colony of New Mexico
were also built here in 1598. Before they relocated to Santa Fe in
1610, the Spanish started out by taking over O'ke and calling it **San
Juan**, and then occupied nearby Yunge and renamed it **San Gabriel**.
Later that century, San Juan was the birthplace of **Popé** ("ripe
squash"), the medicine man who led the Pueblo Revolt.

The centrepiece of the plaza today is the much-restored **mission
church**, which was the first building in the Southwest to be made
with adobe bricks as opposed to simple chunks of mud. It's flanked
by two rectangular *kivas*, as well as a smaller Catholic chapel.
Admission is free in daylight hours, but photography is by permission only. The *Tewa Indian Restaurant* serves weekday lunches.

Picuris Pueblo

*Picuris Pueblo
owns and runs
the excellent
Hotel Santa Fe
in Santa Fe;
see p.97.*

Tiny **PICURIS PUEBLO**, tucked away in a side valley ten miles off
the Rio Grande, twenty miles south of Taos, was the last pueblo to be
"discovered" by the Spanish, and proudly insists that it has never
signed a treaty with any other government, the US included. Its population has never risen much above two hundred, and Picuris today
remains no more than a cluster of adobe houses, spreading across
the hillside around a whitewashed church.

There's a model of the pueblo and a reconstructed *kiva* in the village **museum** (daily 11am–8pm). The same building also holds a gift
store and the *Hidden Valley Restaurant*, a snack bar with views
over a small blue lake. A self-guided **pueblo tour**, which leads past a
few active *kivas*, costs $1.75, or $5 with a photo permit.

Pilar

Once an Apache farming village, later occupied by Hispanic settlers,
PILAR, perched above the Rio Grande fifteen miles southwest of

Taos, is now a base for summer **rafting** trips. **Accommodation** at the attractive *HI-AYH Rio Grande Gorge Hostel*, perilously close to the highway (☎505/758-0090; ①), consists of two six-bed dorms, where a bed for the night costs $9.50 in summer and $11.50 in winter, two private en-suite rooms at $29 for members, and two strange domes in the garden. Reservations are essential in summer, when the little *Pilar Cafe* next door serves basic meals.

A minor road leads along the riverside away from the highway, into the **Orilla Verde Recreation Area**, where developed **campsites** cost $7 per vehicle.

The High Road

Though the most direct route from Santa Fe to Taos heads straight up the Rio Grande Valley – see p.121 onwards – the "High Road" over the forested Sangre de Cristo Mountains to the east makes a rewarding alternative if you have a couple of hours to spare. Winding its way through timeless **Hispanic villages**, it passes some splendid old **adobe churches**, and offers good opportunities to buy locally produced folk art, or sample traditional New Mexican food.

Chimayó

The first and most famous of the High Road towns, **CHIMAYÓ**, is 25 miles north of Santa Fe, eight miles northeast of **Pojoaque Pueblo** via Hwy-592 and Hwy-503, or eight miles east of **Espanola** on Hwy-76. Stretching luxuriantly through the fertile upland meadows that line the Santa Cruz River, and backed by scrubby red-tinged hills, it feels more of a piece with the Rio Grande Valley below than with the mountains in the distance to the east.

Chimayó was founded in 1740, as a sort of penal colony for Hispanic troublemakers. In Tewa, the word *tsimayo* means "good flaking stone", and Indians from San Juan Pueblo quarried obsidian here, which they chipped to form sharp blades. They held a dried-up hot spring nearby sacred, claiming that the mud from around it, when eaten, had healing properties. That spring, in the *barrio* (district) at Chimayó's southern end known as **El Potrero**, is now the site of a spell-binding colonial chapel, the **Santuario de Chimayó** (May–Sept daily 9am–6pm; Oct–April daily 9am–4pm).

The church was built between 1813 and 1816, after the landowner, **Bernardo Abeyta**, was told by a visiting priest of the shrine at Esquipulas in Guatemala, which had arisen at a similar spring venerated by Guatemalan Indians. As a result, Abeyta's church too centred on a crucifix known as **Nuestro Senor de Esquipulas**, supposedly found locally in 1810 (conceivably it had been buried during the Pueblo Revolt).

The church, the crucifix, and the still-exposed *posito*, or dust pit, swiftly became the focus of **pilgrimages** not only by Hispanic peas-

ants, but also by Pueblo Indians, for whom the sacred hole in the
earth clearly echoed the ancient concept of the *sipapu* (see p.468).
To this day, it remains the "**Lourdes of America**". Devout New
Mexican Catholics resent state advertising campaigns that seem to
reduce festivals such as the Good Friday ceremonies, and the re-
enactment of the conquest of Spain by Santiago Matamoros (Saint
James the Moor-killer), held during the fourth weekend in July, to the
status of picturesque tourist attractions.

*Mass is said
in the
Santuario at
noon on Sun,
plus Mon–Sat
11am in sum-
mer, Mon–Sat
7am in winter.*

However, the Santuario is an undeniable delight to visit, a ravishing little round-shouldered, twin-towered, tin-roofed adobe beauty,
set in a walled churchyard beneath the rolling Sangre de Cristo
foothills. At the heart of the altar within, the crucifix is framed by a
gorgeous *reredos* painted by the nineteenth-century *santero*
Molleno, with a small equestrian statue of Santiago to the right. Two
smaller **side chapels** are filled with a mind-boggling array of votive
offerings – paintings, photographs, statues, press cuttings, even discarded crutches. The hole containing the "Holy Dirt" is in the floor at
the rear; pilgrims are allowed to take a scoop, as it's replenished regularly with earth from the hills.

The smaller and more ramshackle **Santo Niño Chapel** (same
hours), across the plaza, contains a diminutive statue of Santo Niño,
the Lost Child – more of a doll, if truth be told – to whom expectant
mothers bring offerings such as tiny pairs of shoes.

Chimayó has specialized in weaving since 1805, when two
weavers sent as teachers from Spain chose to live here in preference
to Santa Fe. Outlets scattered through the village sell hand-woven
goods; other galleries concentrate on wood-carving and religous art.

Practicalities
Two properties belonging to the long-established Jaramillo family
make Chimayó an appealing overnight destination. The *Rancho de
Chimayó*, Hwy-503 (☎505/351-4444), must be the best traditional
New Mexican **restaurant** in the state, serving superb *flautas* and a
mouthwatering *sopaipilla*, stuffed with meat and chiles, on a lovely
sun-drenched outdoor patio. Across the road, the rambling adobe
Hacienda Rancho de Chimayó (PO Box 11, Chimayó, NM 87522;
☎505/351-2222; ④), has lovely **B&B** rooms.

Truchas

By the time you reach **TRUCHAS**, eight miles up from Chimayó on
Hwy-76, you're well into the mountains; the views from the highway
down and across the Rio Grande Valley are tremendous. Villagers
from Las Trampas, further up, were granted permission to establish
Truchas in 1754, on condition that it was enclosed within a walled
square, to defend against Comanche attacks. It took on its present
form almost immediately, however, consisting of separate individual
farms arrayed along a high ridge above the Río de las Truchas, or

The Penitentes

During the nineteenth century, the remote hills above Chimayó were
renowned as the heartland of the mysterious Hispanic Catholic sect known
as the **Penitentes**. Anglo newcomers claimed to have glimpsed hooded figures filing along the ridges at dawn, **whipping** themselves as they went.

A large grain of truth lay beneath the lurid speculation. Self-mortification –
the infliction of pain in order to share the suffering of Christ – was widespread
in medieval Europe. The Spanish expedition that founded New Mexico performed public self-flagellation on Good Friday 1598, as it marched up through
Mexico, and similar acts by early Franciscan missionaries attracted Pueblo
Indian scorn. The Penitentes as such, however, emerged after Mexico achieved
independence in 1821. Cut off from Spanish funding, the Franciscans vanished
from New Mexico within twenty years, leaving the region almost devoid of
priests. Hispanic Catholics formed **lay brotherhoods** to keep their faith alive.

The Penitentes – **Los Hermanos de Nuestro Padre Jesús Nazareno**, or
the Brothers of Our Father Jesus of Nazareth – may well have modelled
themselves on a Guatemalan example, introduced at the same time as the
Guatemalan-influenced pilgrimages to Chimayó. From an initial emphasis
on individual prayer and penance, they extended to developing a complex
system of rituals; they never administered the sacraments, but brought
solace to Catholics forced to live – and die – in the absence of priests. The
Penitente brotherhood in each village soon became a mutual-aid society
for the community, a cultural and political force as well as a spiritual one.

After the American takeover of New Mexico in 1846, the Penitentes
were suddenly outsiders not only in their own country, but even in their
own church. The first Catholic bishop of Santa Fe, Jean-Baptiste **Lamy**
(see p.103), had little sympathy for the unorthodoxies of his Hispanic
flock, and denied the sacraments to their most prominent spokesman,
Father **Martínez** of Taos (see p.134). The Penitentes were forced into
secrecy, and began to gather at night in remote spots. Denied access to
official church property, they met instead in plain adobe structures known
as *moradas* – not necessarily distinguished with crosses or towers, but
adorned with the hand-made sacred images known as *santos*.

The focus of ritual activity was **Lent**, when all Catholics practise some
form of self-denial, and the Penitentes attempted to experience the passion and death of Christ. For processions, they divided into *Los Hermanos
de Luz* – the **Brothers of Light**, responsible for the candles and music –
and *Los Hermanos de Sangre*, the **Brothers of Blood**, who scourged
themselves with yucca whips or carried giant wooden crosses. Participants
were hooded to ensure humility. Some re-enacted the **crucifixion**, though
tied rather than nailed to the cross, while others dragged a **Death Cart** – a
wooden wagon holding an effigy of Death, armed with a bow and arrow –
laden with stones. The Death Cart also figured in the Penitentes' elaborate
funeral processions. The wayside stone cairns, topped with crosses, seen
throughout the High Country are not graves, as outsiders supposed, but
descansos – places where the coffin-bearers would pause to rest.

A century of conflict ended in 1947, when the Penitentes were officially recognized by the Bishop of Santa Fe. Those that remain now regard
themselves as members of the **Third Order of St Francis**, a lay branch of
the Franciscan monastic order, and the most lasting Penitente legacy in
New Mexico is the *santero* tradition of religious folk art.

"river of trout". As one of New Mexico's least changed Hispanic communities, it served in 1987 as the location for Robert Redford's movie of John Nichol's *Milagro Beanfield War* (see p.495).

Hwy-76 makes a right-angle bend to avoid Truchas, but a detour east onto the minor road up the valley takes you along a narrow street of adobe homes and barns – interspersed with the odd incongruous gallery – and past the fields towards the 13,103ft **Truchas Peak**. Besides its gorgeous desserts, the *Truchas Mountain Cafe*, on the highway (☎505/689-2444), fries up fine *sopaipillas*.

Las Trampas

Truchas' parent community, the quiet hamlet of **LAS TRAMPAS**, is another eight miles along Hwy-76. This started life as an outpost used by fur-trappers pursuing beaver – hence its name, "the traps" – which by attracting Comanche raids doubled as an early-warning system for Santa Fe. Though no longer walled, its dusty central plaza, right alongside the highway, still holds the powerfully evocative adobe church of **San Jose de Gracia** (June–Aug daily 9am–5pm). Built in 1760, it features a choir loft that extends both inside and out, so that singers could accompany ceremonies on the square as well as in the church. Note the unattached *morada* – Penitente meeting place (see p.129) – beside the cemetery to the east.

Five miles on from Las Trampas – which holds a couple of gift stores, but nowhere to eat or sleep – Hwy-76 meets Hwy-75 at **Picuris Pueblo** (see p.126), ten miles west of Hwy-68. The quickest route to Taos, twenty miles north, is via Hwy-518 to the east; more Hispanic villages line the way, but none is of interest to tourists.

East of Santa Fe

Modern visitors tend to gravitate northwards after seeing Santa Fe, up the Rio Grande towards Taos. Pueblo Indian traders, pioneers on the **Santa Fe Trail**, and transcontinental train travellers, however have all crossed the mountains to the **east**. Now followed by the **I-25** interstate, the traditional route between New Mexico and the plains still holds a number of intriguing historical sites, including the ancient pueblo at **Pecos** and the Wild-West town of **Las Vegas**.

Pecos National Historical Park

A short way north of I-25, twenty-five miles east of Santa Fe, a long, low ridge in the heart of the Sangre de Cristo mountains served for over a thousand years as one of the most significant cultural rendezvous in the Southwest. Since 1920s excavations so precisely chronicled changes in pottery and architecture that it became the model for all other such digs, **PECOS NATIONAL HISTORICAL PARK** has been famed as the "birthplace of Southwestern archeology".

Santuario de Chimayó, NM

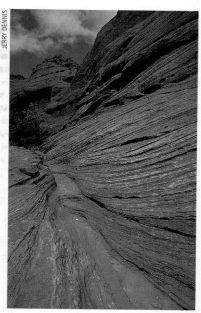

White House Trail, Canyon de Chelly, AZ

Taos Indians in Santa Fe plaza, NM

TONY YEATES

Pueblo church, NM

GREG WARD

JERRY DENNIS

Taos Pueblo, NM

John Ford Point, Monument Valley, AZ

GREG WARD

GREG WARD

Navajo *hogan*, Monument Valley, AZ

Navajo National Monument, AZ

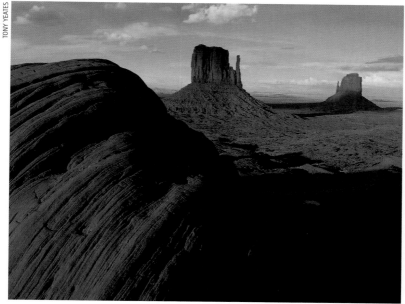

Cliff Palace, Mesa Verde National Park, CO

Monument Valley, AZ

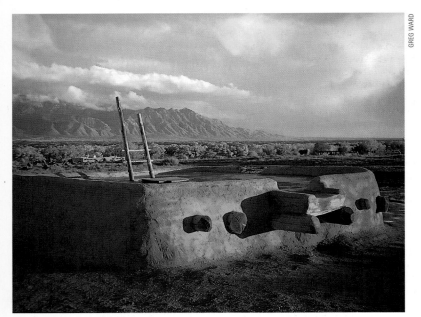

Kiva at Coronado State Monument, NM

Betatakin, Navajo National Monument, AZ

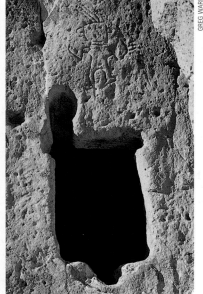

Petroglyph at Puyé Cliff Dwellings, NM

Ninth-century Basketmakers (see p.468) were the first to inhabit this spot, but between 1450 and 1550, as the pueblo of **Cicuyé**, it was home to over two thousand people, including five hundred warriors. Protected behind four-storey walls, it was a major **trading centre**, where Pueblo peoples exchanged turquoise, axes, and shells from as far west as the Pacific for bison meat, hides, and wood for bows brought by plains nomads who camped outside the walls. **Coronado** stayed here in 1541, and met a captive from the plains who lured his expedition east in search of the nonexistent gold of Quivira.

The full story of Coronado's expedition is told on p.472.

After Franciscan missionaries built a church alongside what they called **Pecos Pueblo** sixty years later, Spaniards too came to trade, but Apache and Comanche raids eventually forced Pecos into decline. Its last twenty survivors migrated 65 miles west to join Jemez Pueblo in 1838. Their descendants continue to elect a governor of Pecos Pueblo, and return for ceremonies.

The whole story is well told in the **visitor center** (daily 8am–5pm; $2), from where a mile-long trail loops onto the ridge itself. Much of the former pueblo area remains unexcavated, though some walls are exposed, and large buried structures are obvious everywhere. Beyond it, the trail leads around and through the high roofless walls of the **mission church**, stark in the bright sunlight, and surrounded by the ruined *convento* buildings where its priests once lived. The *kiva* in the heart of the church was dug as a deliberate act of sacrilege during the Pueblo Revolt.

Two newly acquired parcels of the park, not expected to open to visitors in the near future, incorporate the site of the **Battle of Glorieta Pass**. Fought on March 28, 1862, it was the turning point of the **Civil War** in the Southwest, when four thousand Union soldiers repelled three thousand Confederate invaders who had already briefly occupied Santa Fe.

Las Vegas

LAS VEGAS, New Mexico, has more in common with its upstart Nevada namesake than may be immediately obvious. Though now a sleepy backwater, it was once a wild, lawless frontier outpost, where almost anything went. It consists of two distinct sections. The **old Plaza** area, above the fertile meadows (*vegas*, in Spanish) that line the Gallinas River, was established in 1835, when Hispanic settlers drove away the Comanche and set about capturing trade on the burgeoning **Santa Fe Trail**. When the **railroad** arrived in 1879, the focus of town shifted across the river to the grid of streets around the new station. Incomers included the legendary **"Doc" Holliday**, who briefly owned a saloon on Center Street before scurrying back to Dodge City to escape a murder charge, and in one month alone Las Vegas witnessed 29 gunshot deaths.

At the end of the nineteenth century, Las Vegas was the principal city in New Mexico, and almost all its buildings still date from the

Victorian era. The conspicuous lack of adobe makes it easy to forget you're in the Southwest, but it ranks among the state's most authentic Wild-West towns, and while it offers no particular standout tourist attractions it's a real delight to stroll around.

Grand Avenue – the main business drag – and I-25 alike now closely parallel the railroad, leaving the **Plaza** high and dry a mile to the west. Its four-square layout resembles something from the Deep South, though a Victorian bandstand rather than a courthouse stands at its centre. The only significant building on the perimeter is the *Plaza Hotel* (see below), but **Bridge Street**, which leads up from the highway, is lined with antique stores and cafes.

Theodore Roosevelt recruited around forty percent of his volunteer **Rough Riders**, who invaded Cuba in 1898, in Las Vegas. Their exploits, plus the minutiae of local history, are recorded in the **City Museum**, 727 Grand Ave (Mon–Fri 9am–noon & 1–4pm; free).

Practicalities

Las Vegas' **zip code** is NM 87701.

Two *Amtrak* **trains** still pull into Las Vegas each afternoon, from Albuquerque and Chicago. Brochures at the **visitor center**, in the museum at 727 Grand Ave (same hours; ☎505/425-8631 or 1-800/832-5947), detail **walking tours** of town.

The nicest place to **stay** is a restored, antique-furnished en-suite room at the *Plaza Hotel*, 230 Old Town Plaza (☎505/425-3591 or 1-800/328-1882, fax 425-9659; ④), where the *Landmark Grill* is Las Vegas' classiest **restaurant**. There are also plenty of **motels**, such as the *Super 8*, 2029 Grand Ave (☎505/425-5288 or 1-800/800-8000, fax 454-8481; ②), and the *Inn at Las Vegas*, 2401 Grand Ave (☎505/425-6707; ②). Local students huddle over lunchtime espressos at *Bridge Street Books and Coffeehouse*, 131 Bridge St (☎505/454-8211), while the nearby *Rialto*, 141 Bridge St (☎505/454-0037), is more of a traditional diner.

Mora

While I-25 heads northeast into the grasslands from Las Vegas, towards **Raton** (see p.152), **Hwy-518** leads due north into some of New Mexico's most appealing mountain scenery, and serves as an eighty-mile short cut to **Taos**.

The village of **MORA**, thirty miles out, is the seat of Mora County, which has a population of fewer than five thousand, and has been ranked by the *Wall Street Journal* as one of the three poorest counties in the US. Mora itself is the closest thing New Mexico now has to a traditional, unspoiled Hispanic farming community, and its inhabitants are determined to keep it that way. The one concession to tourism, the former flour mill preserved in working order as the **Cleveland Roller Mill Museum** (summer daily 10am–5pm; $2), is unlikely to change things.

Sipapu

Twenty miles up from Mora, not long before Hwy-518 is joined by Hwy-75, the "High Road", for the final run down to Taos, the tiny **ski resort** of SIPAPU is tucked into the pretty mountain valley known as **Tres Ritos Canyon**. *Sipapu Lodge*, along the highway to either side of the Rio Pueblo (Rt Box 29, Vadito NM 87579; ☎505/587-2240; ①–④), offers every conceivable grade of accommodation, from $8.50 dorm beds through private camping cabins, motel rooms and luxury duplexes.

East of
Santa Fe

*The **High Road** between Santa Fe and Taos is described on p.127 onwards.*

Taos

Part Spanish colonial outpost, part hangout for bohemian artists and New-Age dropouts, and home to one of the oldest Native American communities in the United States, tiny TAOS has become famous out of all proportion to its size. Just six thousand people live in its three component parts: **Taos** itself, around the old plaza; sprawling **Ranchos de Taos** three miles south; and the Indian village of **Taos Pueblo** two miles north.

"Taos" rhymes with "house".

Like Santa Fe, Taos stretches languidly across a glorious high-desert plateau. The approach from the south is especially spectacular, as you cross a final bluff on Hwy-68 to be confronted by the pine-forested Sangre de Cristo mountains soaring above the sunbleached foothills. This far up, the **Rio Grande** is not yet meandering through a well-watered valley, but lies deep in a craggy canyon west of town, occasionally glimpsed as a crack in the plateau.

Beyond the usual unsightly highway sprawl, Taos is a delight to visit. As well as museums, galleries and stores to match Santa Fe, it still offers the unhurried pace and charm, and the sense of a meeting place between Pueblo, Hispanic and American cultures, that attracted figures such as Georgia O'Keeffe and D H Lawrence.

A history of Taos

Taos Pueblo is around a thousand years old, and its first Franciscan mission was established in 1598. However, the modern town of Taos dates from the 1630s, when an uprising at the pueblo persuaded Spanish colonists to found the separate community of **Fernando de Taos** a few judicious miles south. Although its early history was dogged by Pueblo rebellions, the Spaniards and Pueblos eventually united to resist raids by "horse Indians" such as the Apache and Comanche. In the early nineteenth century, despite attempts by the Mexican authorities in Santa Fe to restrict contact with the outside world, Taos was the venue for annual **rendezvous**, at which "mountain men" and trappers from the Rockies traded with Indians from the Pueblos and Plains, and New Mexican merchants.

After the US takeover of New Mexico, Taos' Hispanic and Pueblo citizens once more found common cause. In **1847**, the territory's first American governor, Charles Bent, was killed in his Taos home,

The history of Taos Pueblo is summarized on p.142.

but the revolt failed to spread to Santa Fe, and the US Army launched an assault on the Pueblo that suppressed further resistance. For long after that defeat, local priest **Antonio Jose Martínez** – sometimes alleged to have been complicit in the uprising, and the villain of Willa Cather's *Death Comes For The Archbishop* – continued to champion the rights of the Hispanic population.

Taos' reputation as an **arts colony** began at the end of the nineteenth century, with the arrival of the painter Joseph Henry Sharp. He was soon joined by two young New Yorkers, Bert Phillips and Ernest L Blumenschein; legend has it that their wagon lost a wheel outside Taos as they headed for Mexico in 1898, and they liked it so much they never got round to leaving. The three men formed the nucleus of the **Taos Society of Artists**, established in 1915. Soon afterwards, society heiress and arts patron Mabel Dodge arrived, and married an Indian from the Pueblo to become **Mabel Dodge Luhan**. She in turn wrote a fan letter to English novelist **D H Lawrence**, who visited three times in the early 1920s; his widow **Frieda** made her home in Taos after his death. New generations of artists and writers have "discovered" Taos ever since, but the most famous of all was **Georgia O'Keeffe**, who stayed for a few years at the end of the 1920s before moving to Abiquiu (see p.148). Her renditions of the church at Ranchos de Taos in particular were a major influence on contemporary Southwestern art.

Arrival and information

Hwy-68, the main route up to Taos from Santa Fe and Albuquerque, passes first through Ranchos de Taos, and is then lined by an uninspiring strip of motels as it approaches downtown and becomes **Paseo del Pueblo Sur**. The well-equipped **visitor center**, two miles south of the plaza at the intersection of Hwys 68 and 64, stocks all the brochures and maps you could possibly require (daily 9am–5pm; ☎505/758-3873 or 1-800/732-8267).

Shuttle buses from Albuquerque airport are run by *Shuttlejack* ($30; ☎505/243-3244), *Twin Hearts Express* ($30; ☎505/751-1201), and *Faust Transportation* (one-way $35, round-trip $65; ☎505/758-3410). *Faust* also continue to Taos Ski Valley ($40), connect Taos to Santa Fe ($25), and operate local **taxis**. *Greyhound* and *TNM&O* **buses** from Albuquerque ($20) and Santa Fe ($15) arrive at **Taos Bus Center**, at the *Chevron* station opposite the visitor center on Hwy-68 (☎505/758-1144).

Taos Post Office is north of the plaza at 318 Paseo del Pueblo Norte (Mon–Fri 8am–4pm, Sat 9am–1pm; ☎505/758-2081).

Getting around

Walking is the best way to get around the compact centre of Taos, though a public **bus** service, the *Chile Line* (☎505/751-2000), makes hourly runs along a five-mile stretch of Hwy-68, between

TAOS AREA

| 0 | Yards | 800 |

Ranchos de Taos and the *Kachina Lodge*, with a loop around the plaza in the middle (June–Aug & Dec–March Mon–Sat 7am–10pm, Sun 9am–6pm; April, May & Sept–Nov Mon–Sat 7am–7pm, Sun 9am–6pm; 50¢ one-way, $1 all day). Another option is to rent a **bike** from *Native Sons Adventures*, 715 Paseo del Pueblo Sur (☎505/758-9342 or 1-800/753-7559).

Tours and excursions

For a **guided walk** around town, contact either *Taos Historic Walking Tours* (June–Aug, Mon–Sat 10am from the Mabel Dodge Luhan House, 240 Morada Lane; ☎505/758-4020; $10) or the *Taos Inn* (Tues–Thurs & Sat 10am & 5pm, Sun, Mon & Fri 5pm; ☎505/776-2562; $15). In summer, open-air **trolley tours** cover the plaza, Taos Pueblo and Ranchos de Taos (*Pride of Taos*; April–Oct daily 10.30am from visitor center, 10.45am at plaza; ☎505/758-8340 or 1-800/273-8340; $15, under-12s free).

Out of ski season, from April to mid-October, many visitors go **whitewater rafting** instead, through the Taos Box Canyon of the Rio Grande. Operators based at Pilar, south of town – see p.126 – include *Far Flung Adventures* (1-day trips $91; ☎505/758-2628 or 1-800/359-2627), and *Rio Grande Rapid Transit* (half-day $30, full-day $65; ☎505/758-9700 or 1-800/222-RAFT). *Taos Indian Horse Ranch* (☎505/758-3212 or 1-800/659-3210) run **horseback** excursions on Pueblo lands; a short beginners' ride costs around $65. *El Paseo Llama Expeditions* (half-day $49, full day $70, multi-day treks $125 per day; ☎505/758-3111 or 1-800/455-2627) operate **mountain hiking** trips, with a llama to carry your pack.

Rafting, horse riding, and, in winter, snowmobiling can also be arranged through *Native Sons Adventures*; see above.

Accommodation

Taos has **accommodation** to meet all needs, at prices well below those of Santa Fe, However, midwinter rates are no lower than midsummer, and for properties close to the ski area they can even be considerably higher. There are no real **budget** options near the plaza, but the *Abominable Snowmansion* and the *New Buffalo* to the north, and the *Rio Grande Gorge Hostel* to the south all offer bare-bones bunks or simple rooms. Otherwise, chain motels line Hwy-68 south of town, while three or four amusingly adobe-styled motels on Kit Carson Road just east of the plaza provide quieter alternatives. For a few dollars more, you can avail yourself of atmospheric B&B inns or luxury hotels. **Agencies** that reserve lodging in advance include *Taos Central Reservations* (☎505/758-9767 or 1-800/821-2437), *Taos Accommodations Unlimited* (☎505/758-8899 or 1-800/548-2146), and the *Taos Bed & Breakfast Association* (☎505/758-4747 or 1-800/876-7857).

The **Rio Grande Gorge Hostel** *at Pilar is only a dozen miles south-west of Taos;*

see p.126.

The best places to **camp** in the vicinity are the ten summer-only campgrounds in **Carson National Forest**, reached by following Kit Carson Road east until it becomes Hwy-64 (☎505/758-6200).

Hostels, motels and hotels

Abominable Snowmansion Hostel/HI-Taos, Taos Ski Valley Rd, Arroyo Seco; ☎505/776-8298, fax 776-2107. Pleasant, friendly *HI-AYH* hostel-cum-ski lodge, at a very tight curve in the road as you enter Arroyo Seco village on Hwy-150 up to the ski valley, five miles north of downtown. Office hours daily 8–10am & 4–10pm, so don't arrive at midday; membership not required. Dorm beds $15.50 in summer, $22 in winter; teepees and camping space out back; and bargain private rooms. ①/③.

Best Western Kachina Lodge de Taos, 413 Paseo del Pueblo Norte; ☎505/758-2275 or 1-800/522-4462, fax 758-9207. Large, tasteful, family-oriented motel at the Taos Pueblo turn-off, with lots of Southwestern art, a good restaurant, live music, and nightly Pueblo dance performances in summer. ⑤.

El Monte Lodge, 317 Kit Carson Rd; ☎505/758-3171 or 1-800/828-8267. Rural 1930s motel half a mile east of the plaza, offering comfortable en-suite accommodation in a complex of adobe cottages. Low ④, high ⑤.

El Pueblo Lodge, 412 Paseo del Pueblo Norte; ☎505/758-8700 or 1-800/433-9612, fax 758-7321. Southwestern-themed motel, half a mile north of downtown near the Taos Pueblo turn-off. Low ③, high ④.

Koshari Inn, 910 E Kit Carson Rd; ☎505/758-7199. Inexpensive and hospitable adobe motel, a couple of miles from the plaza on the east side of town. ③.

La Fonda de Taos, 108 South Plaza; ☎505/758-2211. Throwback 1930s hotel on the plaza, with a gallery of DH Lawrence paintings (see p.140); not the cheapest place in town, but among the most charming. The rooms are not as large or lavish as in modern motels – and lack TVs – but with their bright hand-painted furniture they're infinitely more characterful. Low ④, high ⑤.

Quail Ridge Inn Resort, Ski Valley Rd; ☎505/776-2211 or 1-800/624-4448, fax 776-2949. Rooms and suites in luxury adobe cottages near the start of the Ski Valley Road, five miles north of downtown, with a good on-site restaurant, mountain views, swimming pool and hot tub, tennis courts and fitness centre. Low ⑤–⑨, high ⑤–⑧.

Sagebrush Inn, 1508 Paseo del Pueblo Sur; ☎505/758-2254 or 1-800/428-3626, fax 758-5077. Attractive three-storey adobe inn, well south of the centre near Ranchos de Taos, which was briefly home to Georgia O'Keeffe and is filled with Southwestern arts and crafts. Swimming pool, tennis, and live music in the lobby bar nightly. ⑤.

Taos Inn, 125 Paseo del Pueblo Norte; ☎505/758-2233 or 1-800/826-7466, fax 758-5776. Gorgeous central Taos landmark, where several ancient adobes have been welded together to create an atmospheric and very Southwestern hotel; the lobby area was originally an open-air courtyard. Both *Doc Martin's* restaurant (see p.145), and the *Adobe Bar* are packed nightly, while each of the 37 rooms plays a variation on the Pueblo theme. ④–⑧.

Taos Super 8 Motel, 1347 S Hwy 68; ☎505/758-1088 or 1-800/800-8000, fax 758-2685. Among the least expensive of the franchise motels that line Hwy-68 south of town, and making a half-hearted attempt to look adobe. Low ③, high ④.

*High season in Taos is Christmas to mid-April and mid-June to mid-Oct; **low season** is mid-April to mid-June and mid-Oct to Dec.*

*Unless otherwise stated, all the properties listed here share the **zip code** Taos NM 87571.*

*As explained on p.15, **accommodation prices**, excluding taxes, are indicated throughout this book by the following symbols:*

① *up to $30*
② *$30–45*
③ *$45–60*
④ *$60–80*
⑤ *$80–100*
⑥ *$100–130*
⑦ *$130–175*
⑧ *$175–250*
⑨ *$250+*

B&Bs

Casa de las Chimeneas, PO Box 5303, 405 Cordoba Rd; ☎505/758-4777, fax 758-3976. Grand four-room B&B, set in adobe-walled gardens a couple of blocks southeast of the plaza. ⑥.

El Rincon, 114 Kit Carson Rd; ☎505/758-4874. Hispanic-flavoured rooms of differing standards, in peaceful adobe B&B not far east of the plaza. ④–⑥.

Laughing Horse Inn, 729 Paseo del Pueblo Norte; ☎505/758-8350 or 1-800/776-0161, fax 758-8350. Former print shop, half a mile north of the plaza, turned 11-room B&B inn. Rooms, suites and cottages of varying degrees of luxury, plus Jacuzzi, psychic readings and free mountain bikes. ③–⑥.

New Buffalo, 108 Lower Hondo Rd, Arroyo Hondo NM 87513; ☎505/776-2015. Former 1960s hippy commune, on large estate ten miles north of town, that now offers inexpensive, comfortable B&B rooms, plus $12 dorm beds in teepees, private teepees, and space for tent camping. ①–③.

Taos Country Inn, PO Box 2331, Upper Ranchitas and Karavas roads; ☎505/758-4900 or 1-800/866-6548. Vintage Spanish *hacienda* a couple of miles west of the plaza, amid the cottonwoods beside the Rio Pueblo, now offering nine luxurious en-suite rooms and sumptuous breakfasts. ⑥.

Taos Ski Valley

Amizette Inn, PO Box 756, Taos Ski Valley NM 87525; ☎505/776-2451 or 1-800/446-8267. Small but comfortable ski lodge, with sweeping views from its verandahs. Rates include breakfast. Low ③, high ⑤.

Hotel Edelweiss, PO Box 83, Taos Ski Valley NM 87525; ☎505/776-2277 or 1-800/I-LUV-SKI, fax 776-2533. Intimate, luxurious hotel at the foot of the slopes, with its own French restaurant, plus sauna, Jacuzzi and in-house masseuse. Low ④, high ⑦.

Thunderbird Lodge, PO Box 87, Taos Ski Valley NM 87525; ☎505/776-2280 or 1-800/776-2279, fax 776-2238. Lively ski lodge – south-facing, so sunnier than most – with a few quieter and plusher chalets. Low ④, high ⑥.

The Town

Downtown Taos still centres on the old Spanish **plaza**, which has been remodelled several times over the years, and migrated slightly eastwards in the process. The tiny square is now ringed by galleries and souvenir stores, but its tree-shaded benches make a pleasant spot from which to watch the world go by. The Stars and Stripes have flown day and night from the flagpole at its heart ever since it was erected by Kit Carson during the Civil War; the nearby bandstand was a gift from Mable Dodge Luhan.

While there's little to see on the plaza itself, apart from the **D H Lawrence paintings** in *La Fonda* and the murals in the old **Courthouse**, a short walk along the narrow, winding streets that stretch away in all directions will be rewarded with glimpses of Taos as it used to be. The best of the central museums is the **Kit Carson House**, but the **Millicent Rogers Museum**, a few miles north, holds a superb collection of Native American and Hispanic artworks.

La Fonda

La Fonda hotel, on the south side of the plaza, was built in 1937, well after **D H Lawrence**'s death, but a gallery in the lobby holds a unique collection of paintings by the Nottinghamshire novelist (irregular hours; $3). Bought from his widow Frieda's second husband, most were painted in Italy rather than Taos; one, *The Holy Family*, was his first ever canvas, and it shows. Apart from one landscape (a "collaboration" with Frieda and their friend Dorothy Brett), they depict sweaty, fleshy wrestlings such as *The Rape of the Sabine Women*. When first exhibited, at London's *Warren Gallery* in 1929, they were regarded as obscene, and banned from further showing in Britain. They now seem tame, though the *Sunday Times*' original verdict remains accurate: "he can do rather less with a paintbrush than a child of seven without any natural flair".

La Fonda hotel is reviewed on p.137; D H Lawrence's ashes are held in a memorial chapel north of Taos; see p.150.

The Courthouse and the Harwood Foundation

After much of the north side of the plaza was destroyed by a fire in May 1932, Taos' **Courthouse** was rebuilt in the prevalent Pueblo Revival style (Mon–Fri 10am–5pm, Sat 10am–4pm; $3). Four artists, led by Emil Bisttram, a former student of Diego Rivera, were commissioned by the *WPA* to decorate its interior with **murals** depicting the use and misuse of law. The Courthouse itself closed in 1970, but the murals have now been restored, and make an interesting diversion as you tour the plaza.

The murals are exhibited under the auspices of the **Harwood Foundation**, whose main gallery is two blocks southwest of the plaza at 238 Ledoux St (same hours, same ticket). This combines works by twentieth-century Taos artists such as Bert Phillips and wood-carver Patrocino Barelo with *santos* and *retablos* by their nineteenth-century Hispanic counterparts.

Ernest L Blumenschein Home and Museum

Near the Harwood Foundation at 222 Ledoux St, the **Ernest L Blumenschein Home and Museum** preserves the much-restored 1790 house of the co-founder of the Taos Society of Artists (daily 9am–5pm). Paintings by Blumenschein, his daughter Helen, and Zuñi and Hopi artists such as Fred Kabotie (see p.250) are on display, but the real star is the house itself. Though Taos has grown to obscure its original uninterrupted views, Blumenschein's studio, made gloriously light by its raised ceiling and enlarged windows, still commands a fine prospect of the mountains.

*The Blumenschein Home is one of the three **Kit Carson Historic Museums**, each of which charges $4 admission, with combined tickets at $6 for two museums, and $8 for three.*

Governor Bent House and Museum

Bent Street, a block north of the plaza, takes its name not from any irregularities but from the first American governor of New Mexico, Charles Bent, whose former home at no. 117 is now the **Governor Bent House and Museum** (daily 10am–5pm; $2). The imposition of American rule was resented by Taos' Hispanic and Indian population alike, and Bent was killed here by an angry mob on January 19, 1847. You can still see the hole hacked into the adobe walls through which most of his family attempted to escape; they were captured, but their lives were spared. The rest of the small house serves as a ramshackle museum of frontier Taoseño life, holding Indian artefacts, antiquated rifles, and even an eight-legged lamb.

Kit Carson Home and Museum

Just east of the plaza, across the highway at the end of Taos' sole sur-viving stretch of wooden boardwalk, is the dusty but evocative adobe home of "mountain man", mason and part-time US cavalry officer **Kit Carson** (May–Oct daily 8am–6pm; Nov–April daily 9am–5pm; $4). Born in Kentucky in 1809, Carson left home to join a wagon train to Missouri in 1826 – a one cent reward was offered for the return of the teenage runaway – and spent the ensuing winter in Taos. He was to return repeatedly throughout his life, in between escapades like scouting for the 1840s Frémont expeditions, and campaigning against the Navajo in the 1860s (see p.487).

Carson bought the house at the heart of today's museum in 1843, upon his marriage to a local woman, Josefa Jaramillo, and it was sold after their deaths in 1868 to support their seven orphaned children. Much of it is now filled with run-of-the-mill Wild-West paraphernalia, such as rifles with crude wooden handles, and the accoutrements of fur trappers. However, press cuttings and photos relating to Carson himself, and the mock-up of a typical Hispanic home of the period, complete with *fogon de campaña* – a bell-shaped adobe fireplace – make for a fascinating hour's visit.

Carson's house is one of the Kit Carson Historic Museums; see opposite.

Millicent Rogers Museum

Four miles north of the plaza, well past the Taos Pueblo turning and reached by a dirt road that angles into a tricky five-way intersection, the **Millicent Rogers Museum** is among New Mexico's very finest galleries (April–Oct daily 10am–5pm; Nov–March daily except Mon 10am–5pm; $6). Millicent Rogers – a former fashion model who was the granddaughter of a founder of Standard Oil, and is said to have been "close" to Cary Grant – lived here until her death in 1953.

The museum focuses on both Native American and Hispanic art, and traces how those cultures have been perceived. Its undoubted highlight is the family collection of San Ildefonso Pueblo potter **Maria Martinez**, whose black-on-black ceramics are the most famous (and valuable) Native American artworks of the twentieth century. It also outlines the unbroken thousand-year tradition of Pueblo pottery, from pieces produced by the prehistoric Mimbres and Anasazi peoples through Rio Grande works from the fourteenth and fifteenth centuries. Other crafts include turquoise jewellery,

*For more on
Death Carts
and the like,
see p.129; see
also the
Glossary on
p.496.*

Navajo blankets, and some amazing *kachinas* (see p.58), such as a Zuñi buffalo *kachina* from 1875, made of hide, fur and feathers.

The development of Spanish Colonial religious art in the New World is shown through an array of rugs, looms, carved wooden furniture, *bultos*, and *retablos*, plus a couple of "**Death Carts**", in which a skeleton holding a bow and arrow, known as Doña Sebastiana, rides in a rickety wooden carriage. The earliest relic is a faded representation of *Christ Washing the Feet of the Disciples*, painted on buffalo hide by an unknown Franciscan around 1700.

Taos Pueblo

Tiwa-speaking peoples have lived at **TAOS PUEBLO**, just over two miles north of Taos plaza, for almost a thousand years. While they may have originally arrived from the east, across the plains, they have long been at the forefront of the **Pueblo Indian** cultural tradition, which can be traced back to the Anasazi of the Four Corners. Together with Ácoma (see p.86) and the Hopi mesas (see p.57), the pueblo can claim to be the oldest continuously occupied settlement in the United States. It's also stunningly beautiful, centring on two multi-storey adobe "apartment blocks" framed beneath the shining forested peak of Taos Mountain.

The northernmost New Mexican pueblo, Taos is among the few not to have been displaced by the coming of the Spaniards in the sixteenth century. Its survival has taken a long hard struggle; the pueblo was abandoned for two years in the 1630s, to escape retaliation after the killing of a priest, and it later played a central role in the **Pueblo Revolt** of 1680. When the Spanish subsequently reconquered New Mexico, Taos Pueblo was almost completely destroyed. It revolted again under both Mexican and American rule. In 1837, Taos Indians cut off the head of the Mexican governor of New Mexico and used it as a football, and their leader José Gonzalez briefly usurped the governorship until he was himself executed. Ten years later, they were heavily implicated in the rebellion against Charles Bent (see p.133); over 150 Taos Indians were killed when the US Army besieged and burned the pueblo's church.

*For more on
the Pueblo
Revolt, see
p.474.*

In the twentieth century, the pueblo was forced to campaign for the return of the sacred **Blue Lake**, high in the mountains. The source of the Río Pueblo de Taos that flows through the heart of the village, and the focus of an annual three-day pilgrimage, Blue Lake was unexpectedly incorporated into a federal forest reserve in 1906. When Richard Nixon finally handed it back in 1970, it marked the first time that land had ever been returned to Native Americans for religious reasons; access is now forbidden to outsiders.

Visiting the pueblo

Taos Pueblo is reached via two approach roads off Hwy-68. One continues north as the highway veers west at the *Best Western Kachina*

Lodge, half a mile north of the plaza, the other branches off at *Jackie's Trading Post*, another half-mile on. After entering the reservation, they meet and run together to the pueblo plaza, where you pay the **entrance fee** ($5 per vehicle, plus $1 per person, $5 per still camera, $10 per video camera). Pueblo residents lead guided **walking tours** at regular intervals, which can help overcome any awkwardness you may feel but won't take you beyond the limited public areas through which you're free to wander alone.

Visits focus on the two large **adobe complexes** – Hlauuma, the north house, and Hlaukwima, the south house – to either side of the Río Pueblo de Taos. In their current form, they almost certainly date from the uncertain years that followed the Pueblo Revolt, at the start of the eighteenth century. This architectural design, consisting of individual dwellings stacked like dice and entered via rooftop ladders, was originally adopted for defence, and has been abandoned as unnecessary by most other pueblos. At Taos, the homes have been adapted to include ground-level doorways and windows, but their hundred or so occupants still choose to live without toilets, running water or electricity. The remainder of the reservation's two thousand inhabitants live in newer homes nearby. Several rooms facing the plaza function as **craft shops**, but you can't penetrate any further, and you'll only glimpse the *kivas* (ceremonial chambers), distinguished by their long ladders, from a distance.

Visitors are encouraged to enter, but not photograph, the pretty little **Church of San Gerónimo** on the edge of the plaza. The latest incarnation of the pueblo's Catholic mission church – the ruins of the previous version stand beside the pueblo cemetery, to the west – is decorated inside with murals that feature traditional corn and sun motifs. In the plaza itself, what look like makeshift awnings to shelter parked cars are in fact *ramadas*, wooden racks used for drying corn and chile peppers.

For most of the year, Pueblo life continues with scant regard for the intrusion of tourists, though (camera-less) outsiders are welcome at certain spectacular feast days and dances. Most of these take place in summer; the biggest are the **Corn Dances** (June 13 and 24, July 25 and 26), the **Taos Pueblo Pow Wow** (second weekend in July), and the **Feast of San Gerónimo** (Sept 29 and 30).

Taos Pueblo is one of the many pueblos to have rushed to build its own **casino**, located on Hwy-68 several miles northwest of the pueblo itself. As one unapologetic elder remarked, "poverty was never a part of Pueblo life until the Europeans came".

Ranchos de Taos

The distinct community of **RANCHOS DE TAOS**, which spreads to either side of Hwy-68 three miles southwest of central Taos, was originally an area of Indian farmlands. These were later taken over by

Taos

Taos Pueblo is generally open daily 8am–5.30pm, but may be closed for tribal events such as festivals or funerals; call ☎505/758-1028 to check.

the Spanish to grow the crops that fed the townspeople of Taos. Each *rancho* or farm had its own main house, or *hacienda*, and even today Ranchos de Taos retains the feel of a rural village; you can still buy fresh hay for your animals from lots along the highway.

San Francisco de Asis

The reredos *at Ranchos de Taos is the work of the nineteenth-century san-tero Molleno, who was also responsible for the altarpiece of the Santuario de Chimayó; see p.127.*

In Rancho's small unpaved plaza, the mission church of **San Francisco de Asis** turns its broad shoulders, or more accurately its massive adobe buttresses, to the passing traffic on Hwy-68. Built around 1776, it's one of colonial New Mexico's most splendid architectural achievements, with subtly rounded walls and corners disguising its underlying structural strength. Encountering genuine adobe, which crumbles away after heavy rain or snow, can come as a shock after so much fakery elsewhere in the state; the local congregation is obliged to replaster the whole thing yearly.

Though the ever-changing interplay of light and shade across the church's golden exterior has fascinated painters from Georgia O'Keeffe onwards, its **interior** is equally intriguing. Amid a clutter of devotional objects and artworks, a magnificently ornate green-and-red *reredos* (altarpiece) frames several naive paintings. The **plaza** outside – remarkably peaceful considering that the highway is thirty yards away – holds a handful of restaurants and gift stores.

Hacienda Martínez

The Hacienda Martínez is one of the Kit Carson Historic Museums; see p.140.

Two miles west of the highway, roughly halfway between San Francisco de Asis and the downtown plaza on Ranchitos Road, the **Hacienda Martínez** is one of the few Spanish *haciendas* anywhere to be preserved in anything approaching its original state (daily 9am–5pm; $4). It was built in 1804 by Don Antonio Martínez, an early mayor of Taos who was also the father of Padre Antonio Jose Martínez (see p.134). Within its thick, windowless, adobe walls – the place could be sealed like a fortress against still-prevalent Indian raids – two dozen rooms are wrapped around two separate patios, holding animal pens and a well. Trade goods of the kind Don Antonio once carried south along the Rio Grande are displayed alongside tools, looms and simple furnishings of the era.

Taos Ski Valley

Selected accommoda-tions in Taos Ski Valley are listed on p.138.

Fifteen miles north of Taos, reached via an attractive road that winds up through a narrow gap in the mountains from the village of Arroyo Seco, lie the precipitous slopes of **TAOS SKI VALLEY**. Located on the north flank of **Wheeler Peak** – at 13,161 feet the highest point in New Mexico – the runs are usually open to skiers from late November until early April (daily lift tickets $26 in December, $41 in high season; information ☎505/776-2291, reservations ☎1-800/776-1111). Experts rate Taos one of the most challenging ski resorts in the

Rockies, but the highly-rated *Ernie Blake Ski School* (same number) teaches novices aged three and upwards on the nursery slopes. Snowboarding is not permitted.

Several hotels and condos in the Ski Valley remain open year-round, but there wouldn't be a lot of point staying in summer.

Eating and drinking

Taos is too small to offer much **nightlife**, but it does have a fine selection of **restaurants** in all price ranges, and several **coffeehouses**. If your main priority is to **drink**, the *Adobe Bar* in the *Taos Inn* (see p.137), with its roaring log fire and regular live music, is the cosiest spot in town, while *Eske's*, a short way south at 106 Des Georges Lane (☎505/758-1517), is a **brewpub**, open nightly until 10.30pm, that also serves simple stews and snacks.

Apple Tree Restaurant, 123 Bent St; ☎505/758-1900. Eclectic international cafe, very near the plaza, where the menu ranges from Thai to Mexican, and evening entrees cost up to $20. The courtyard seating is ideal for a summer's evening. Open for lunch and dinner daily, and all afternoon for light snacks.

Bent Street Deli & Cafe, 120 Bent St; ☎505/758-5787. Airy, partly outdoor place, just north of the plaza; good-value breakfasts, sandwich lunches, and tasty dinners for well under $20. Try the *ceviche* appetizer and the Mexican-style *pollo con molé* (chicken in chocolate). All meals daily except Sun.

Casa Fresen Bakery, Arroyo Seco; ☎505/776-2969. Unlikely gourmet deli, in a tiny village on the road up to Taos Ski Valley, that serves espresso coffees, pricey but tasty pastries, and sandwiches daily 7.30am–6pm.

Doc Martin's, *Taos Inn*, 125 Paseo del Pueblo Norte; ☎505/758-1977. Delicious, inventive New Mexican food in romantic old adobe inn, on the main road just east of the plaza. Most dinner entrees, such as Southwest lacquered duck or smoked lamb sirloin, are $15–20. Open daily for all meals.

La Luna, 223 Paseo del Pueblo Sur; ☎505/751-0023. Top-quality modern Italian-influenced cooking a few blocks south of the plaza, past *McDonald's*. Good-value wood-fired pizzas for around $10, plus pricier specials such as wild mushroom pate or tuna steaks. Dinner only, daily except Wed 5–10pm.

Lambert's of Taos, 309 Paseo del Pueblo Sur; ☎505/758-1009. Stylish contemporary diner half a mile south of the plaza, serving New American rather than New Mexican cuisine, with grilled meat or fish entrees for around $15, and opulent desserts. Open for dinner nightly, lunch Mon–Fri only.

Michael's Kitchen, 304C Paseo del Pueblo Norte; ☎505/758-4178. Inexpensive Mexican and Southwestern dishes in old adobe kitchen a few blocks north of the plaza. Daily 7am–8.30pm, closed April and Nov.

Renegade Cafe, *Quail Ridge Inn Resort*, Taos Ski Valley Rd; ☎505/776-1777. Attractive Southwestern restaurant with an Italian flavour, five miles north of town; good pizzas and salads, plus fancier specials. Daily 7am–10pm.

Stakeout Grill and Bar, Outlaw Hill off Hwy-68; ☎505/758-2042. Well-hidden, unpretentious and popular dinner-only restaurant in a truly stunning setting, specializing in big, good-value steaks. Only accessible by car, 4 miles south of Ranchos de Taos up a dirt track east of the highway. Daily 5–10pm.

Tapas de Taos, 136 Bent St; ☎505/758-9670. Friendly, central cafe in old adobe that serves an extensive Mexican menu – with $6–8 Mexican brunches on weekends – plus snacks and *tapas* from all over the world, including Thai and Vietnamese noodle dishes, and also espresso coffees. Open daily from mid-morning until around 9pm.

Downtown Taos restaurants are marked on the map on p.139.

Tiwa Kitchen, Taos Pueblo; ☎505/751-1020. Indian-run restaurant on the road into Taos Pueblo, serving strong chile-flavoured stews, traditional *horno*-baked bread, Indian fry bread, and lots of blue corn meal. Closed Tues.

Wild and Natural Cafe, 812 Paseo del Pueblo Norte; ☎505/751-0480. Tasty three-course vegetarian dinners for $8, plus espresso and dessert bar. A mile north of town near the second Taos Pueblo turning. Mon–Sat 7am–9pm.

Coffeehouses

The Bean, 900 Paseo del Pueblo Norte; ☎505/758-7711. Serious coffee roasters, selling espressos and pastries to a clientele composed largely of forty-somethings, including Indians from the nearby pueblo.

Caffe Tazza, 122 Kit Carson Rd, ☎505/758-8706. Trendy central cafe with nice sunlit terrace, next door to *Taos Book Shop*, selling coffees and light veggie meals to students and assorted crazies. Live entertainment most evenings, with anarchic open-mike nights.

Rio Raye's Coffee Bar, 814 Paseo del Pueblo Norte; ☎505/751-4857. Espresso coffees, hot double-chocolate muffins and light lunches, geared towards Taos' New Age community.

Teos Espresso and Juice Bar, 4141 Hwy-68; ☎505/751-7081. Tiny little place, an inch or so north of San Francisco de Asis on the main highway in Ranchos de Taos, selling espressos and smoothies.

Shopping

If you're **shopping** for souvenirs, Taos may not have quite Santa Fe's range of stores, or anything like so many upmarket galleries, but it's just as much fun to walk around. Most of the shops on the plaza itself are very predictable, but the area immediately north, towards Bent Street, is more diverting, and there are some genuine oddities elsewhere. As ever, the **museum stores** – especially at the Millicent Rogers Museum – are among the best in town.

Gift stores and galleries

Blue Rain Gallery, 115 McCarthy Plaza; ☎505/751-0066. The very best in Native American arts and crafts, on the east side of the plaza; unfortunately, the exquisite *kachinas* can run into thousands of dollars.

Coyote Moon, 120C Bent St; ☎505/758-4437. Taos' best selection of Mexican folk art, with plenty of colourful Oaxacan carved animals.

Françoise, 103-H East Plaza; ☎505/758-9255. The plaza's strongest collection of turquoise and silver jewellery, both new and antique.

FX-18, 1018 Paseo del Pueblo Norte; ☎505/758-8590. Quirky crafts, from jewellery to metalwork, plus unusual gifts, a couple of miles north of town.

Hacienda de San Francisco Galeria, 4 St Francis Plaza, Ranchos de Taos; ☎505/758-0477. Also known as *Colonial Antiques*. Antique *retablos* and furniture, mostly from South America, in gorgeous old adobe beside the church at Ranchos.

Silver Eagle, 113 Paseo del Pueblo Norte; ☎505/758-7709. Enjoyable, inexpensive assortment of mostly South American crafts, just south of *Taos Inn*.

Taos Artisans Co-op, 107A Bent St; ☎505/758-1558. Individually styled jewellery, clothing and sculpture by an assortment of Taoseño artists.

Bookstores

The Brodsky Bookshop, 218 Paseo del Pueblo Norte; ☎505/758-9468. Very helpful store, a couple of blocks north of the plaza, with a huge array of Southwest-related material, and lots of maps.

Moby Dickens, 124A Bent St; ☎505/758-3050. Copious selection of local fiction and history, plus New Age material.

Taos Book Shop, 122D Kit Carson Rd; ☎505/758-3733. Friendly, venerable store with a large stock of rare and out-of-print volumes but a surprisingly small selection of current titles.

West of Taos

While the obvious day-trip drive from Taos follows the **Enchanted Circle** to the northeast – see p.150 – a longer and wilder route heads west on US-64, across the Rio Grande and over the dramatic **San Juan Mountains**. Branching west off Hwy-68 four miles out of downtown Taos, this reaches the awesome, 650-ft high **Rio Grande Gorge Bridge** seven miles on. After a magnificent seventy-mile mountain run, punctuated by scenic overlooks, US-64 finally drops into **Chama Valley**. From there, either head south into Georgia O'Keeffe country around **Abiquiu**, or north to **Chama** itself, the base for excursions on New Mexico's best-known **steam railroad**.

The Rio Grande Gorge Bridge featured in the wedding scene in the movie Natural Born Killers.

Tierra Amarilla

US-64 meets the north–south US-84 in **TIERRA AMARILLA** ("yellow earth"), at the foot of the sheer, furrowed **Brazos Cliffs**. This pastoral village, founded in 1832 when the valley was prone to constant Ute, Apache and Navajo raids, provides a classic example of how New Mexico's Hispanic population suffered after the American takeover of the territory. In 1860, the US Congress refused to recognize that shared grazing lands belonged to the community as a whole, and instead sold them off to a Yankee landowner from Santa Fe.

Bitter disputes have raged ever since, culminating in an incident commemorated by a defaced roadside marker in the heart of the village. In 1967, a group led by Chicano activist **Reies López Tejerina** – a Texan Protestant – seized a nearby campground in the Kit Carson National Forest. Declaring independence from the United States, they burned down Tierra Amarilla's Rio Arriba Courthouse, destroying land-grant records and injuring a policeman and a jailer. The government responded by sending in two hundred military vehicles, including tanks. After a controversial trial, Tejerina was acquitted of any involvement by an Albuquerque court.

Although Tierra Amarilla remains the county seat, it has declined in the last thirty years. Parts are now all but derelict, but the community continues to resist the construction of weekend homes for wealthy outsiders, and the possible development of a ski resort on Brazos Peak. In the nearby village of **LOS OJOS** – the scene of major civil disobedience in 1989 – one co-operative effort to revitalize the local economy has proved a resounding success. **Tierra Wools** maintains local **weaving** traditions by breeding Spanish Churro sheep in the valley, and selling hand-dyed rugs and clothing from the clearly signposted *Los Ojos Trading Post* (☎505/588-7231), a mile or so west of US-84.

Abiquiu and Ghost Ranch

The Rio Chama curves southwest from Tierra Amarilla, but US-84 heads due south for around forty miles before rejoining the river amid the definitive Southwestern red-rock splendour immortalized by **Georgia O'Keeffe**. These cliffs and mesas of Chinle, Entrada and Windgate sandstone, rising above corrugated hillocks of grey, brown and red clays, are strongly reminiscent of southern Utah and the Navajo badlands of northeast Arizona, and disappear well before the Chama flows into the Rio Grande 25 miles southeast.

From 1946 until she died, aged 98, in 1986, O'Keeffe lived and worked in the pretty adobe village of **ABIQUIU**, originally a settlement of *genízaros* (the Christianized descendants of Plains peoples captured by eighteenth-century Spaniards). Her former home is now open for limited tours (Tues, Thurs & Fri, by appointment; $15; ☎505/685-4539). Nearby, the *Trade Routes Coffee House* (☎505/685-4790) serves espresso coffees and snacks, and it's possible to stay (and dine) at the twenty-room *Abiquiu Inn*, half a mile north (☎505/685-4378 or 1-800/447-5621; ④).

Several religious groups have established retreats in the Abiquiu region, including the international Moslem community that erected the **Dar al-Islam mosque** on the mesa above the village, and the Presbyterian ministry at **Ghost Ranch**, fourteen miles north, where there's also a **Living Museum** of local natural history (daily except Mon 8am–4.30pm; $3). The Benedictine brothers of the **Monastery of Christ in the Desert**, thirteen miles west of Ghost Ranch on the unpaved Hwy-151, have attracted a lot of recent attention by selling their services designing Internet sites.

Chama

Tiny **CHAMA**, set in the meadows at the head of the Chama Valley, a dozen miles north of Tierra Amarilla and a total of 85 miles northwest of Taos, is a former mining camp that has re-invented itself as a base for summer hunters and winter skiers.

Chama's major appeal for out-of-state visitors is that the pretty yellow station just below the town centre is the western terminus of the narrow-gauge **Cumbres and Toltec Scenic Railroad** (Memorial Day to mid-Oct; ☎505/756-2151). This exhilarating, if not wildly comfortable, 64-mile steam-train ride crosses the High Brazos mountains into Colorado by way of **Cumbres Pass**, then runs through the deep **Toltec Gorge** and out onto the plains at **Antonito**. You can't do the entire round-trip by train in one day; passengers either go by van to Antonito, and return by train (dep Chama 8am; $52), or take the train through the most scenic segment as far as Osier, and pick up a return train there (dep Chama 10.30am; $34).

West of Taos

Wrap up warm if you ride the Cumbres and Toltec; *it gets pretty cold in the mountains.*

Practicalities

Chama's **visitor center**, half a mile south of town at the junction of US-64 and Hwy-17 (daily 8am–5pm; ☎505/756-2235), can provide details of the many **riverfront lodges** along US-64/84 to the south, such as the comfortable new *Vista del Rio* (☎505/756-2138 or 1-800/939-9943; ④). Back in town, *Gandy Dancer*, 299 Maple St (☎505/756-2191 or 1-800/424-6702; ⑤), is a **B&B** in a purple clapboard mansion with seven en-suite rooms and a hot tub, while the venerable *Fosters Hotel* (☎505/756-2296; ②) is opposite the station, and holds an all-day diner and lively saloon. Nearby, the menu at the cheerful, inexpensive *Whistle Stop Cafe* (☎505/756-1833), includes a few vegetarian options. The most convenient place to **camp** is the *Rio Chama RV Campground*, beside the river at the north end of town (☎505/756-2303).

Chama's **zip** *code is NM 87520.*

The Cumbres Pass and Antonito, Colorado

North of Chama, **Hwy-17** follows much the same route as the railroad, first climbing far above the single track and then crisscrossing it repeatedly as it makes its way up to the 10,022-foot **Cumbres Pass**. In July 1848, legendary "mountain man" Bill Williams was injured here in a confrontation between the US Army and a combined force of Utes and Apaches.

Beyond the pass, highway and railroad part company, not to meet again until they reach **ANTONITO**, Colorado, fifty miles out of Chama – a dreary, depressing little town that's home to the reasonable *Narrow Gauge Railroad Inn* (☎719/376-5441 or 1-800/323-9469; ②) and a few basic cafes. If you're looking for a place to stay in the vicinity, the *Conejos River Hostel* (☎719/376-2518; ①) – a cluster of green cabins on the far side of the Conejos River, ten miles west of Antonito where forest-service road FDR-103 branches south from Hwy-17 – is a far more enticing prospect.

Dulce

US-64 and US-84 join forces for twelve miles **west of Chama**, then US-64 continues alone for another fifteen miles to **DULCE**, the headquarters of the **Jicarilla Apache Indian Reservation**. Today's three-thousand-plus Jicarilla are descended from separate Apache groups who lived further east, some as Plains nomads in the Cimarron area, and some in adobe villages near the pueblos of the Rio Grande. Their name is often said to come from the little baskets (*jicarillas*) they now sell to tourists, but the Jicarilla themselves suggest that they started making baskets when they were confined to this remote reservation in the nineteenth century, and that the name comes from a Mexican word connected with chocolate.

There's little for tourists to see or do on the Jicarilla reservation, whose economy is based on oil and gas revenues and raising sheep. However, Dulce's roomy and attractive *Best Western Jicarilla Inn* (☎505/759-3663 or 1-800/742-1938, fax 759-3170; ④), is regarded as a model for Indian-owned businesses. It has a good restaurant, and offers special deals on train trips from Chama.

The Enchanted Circle

The driving circuit through the Sangre de Cristo range northeast of Taos doesn't quite live up to its tourist-brochure billing as the **Enchanted Circle**, though it does pass a handful of long-abandoned ghost towns amid the mountain scenery. While Oklahomans and Texans flock to the closest **ski slopes** to home, visitors from further afield are more likely to make the brief detour east to the hard-bitten frontier town of **Cimarron**.

The Lawrence Ranch

Starting seventeen miles north of Taos on Hwy-222, a rutted, muddy road climbs for five miles east to the **Lawrence Ranch**. The English novelist **D H Lawrence** made three six-month visits to Taos in the early 1920s, having been enticed across the Atlantic by Mabel Dodge Luhan (see p.134). Staying at her mountain cabin, then known as Kiowa Ranch, he wrote "there are all kinds of beauty in the world, but for greatness of beauty I have never experienced anything like New Mexico". **Georgia O'Keeffe** was also a guest here, in 1929, when she painted the tree right in front of the main cabin as *The Lawrence Tree*.

Lawrence died in France in 1930, but five years later his widow Frieda shipped his ashes back to New Mexico. They now rest in a small **shrine** that enjoys panoramic views of the upper Rio Grande valley, at the top of a zigzag cement footpath cleared through the forest. Frieda is said to have acquired the ranch from Mabel Dodge Luhan in exchange for the manuscript of *Sons and Lovers* – which Mabel in turn used to pay her psychiatrist – and lived in it until her death in 1956. It now belongs to the University of New Mexico, which holds weekend retreats in the main cabin; only the shrine is accessible to visitors, with no fixed hours or admission fee.

Red River

Half a dozen miles beyond the Lawrence Ranch turn-off, as Hwy-522
gathers itself for the final climb into Colorado, **Hwy-38** follows Red
River east from **QUESTA**, an ugly little village ravaged by opencast
mining. After twelve more attractive riverside miles, it reaches **RED
RIVER** itself, a former gold-mining town whose rough-shod timber
architecture is more authentic than it looks. Summer visitors hike in
the surrounding forests, but Red River is at its busiest during the winter **ski** season, when there's cross-country skiing down in the valley
and a downhill resort in the mountains to the south.

Red River claims to have more **hotel** rooms than Santa Fe, though
it's hard to see where they might be. Appealing options include the
Riverside Lodge, 201 E Main St (☎505/754-2252 or 1-800/432-
9999; ③), and the *Lodge at Red River*, PO Box 189, W Main St
(☎505/754-6280 or 1-800/915-6343; ④); there's also a central
reservations service (☎505/754-2223 or 1-800/348-6444).

*Red River's **zip
code** is NM
87558.*

Cimarron

Beyond Red River, Hwy-38 negotiates the 9820-foot **Bobcat Pass**
– often closed in winter – then drops by way of the ruins of long-
abandoned **ELIZABETHTOWN** down to **EAGLE NEST**. Just a
cluster of cabins and RV parks, Eagle Nest sprang up around a
lake formed when the **Cimarron River** was dammed in 1920, and
is popular with fishing enthusiasts. US-64 parallels the river to
enter impressive **Cimarron Canyon** four miles east, beneath the
towering 800-foot **Palisade Cliffs**. This route provided access to
Taos for nineteenth-century travellers who split from the Santa
Fe Trail's "mountain branch" at **CIMARRON** itself, 24 miles east
of Eagle Nest.

Cimarron means "wild" or "untamed", and in its heyday the town
was as wild as the West could be. It stood at the heart of the 1.7-mil-
lion-acre **Maxwell Land Grant**, the largest private landholding in the
United States, accumulated by Lucien Bonaparte Maxwell in the
years following the American takeover of New Mexico. Maxwell's
main business was cattle ranching, but with gold and silver mines
booming and busting all over the mountains, Cimarron lured a vast
profusion of gamblers, gunfighters, outlaws and cowboys.

Cimarron's old downtown area now stands relatively intact half
a mile or so south of the main highway. Its history is lovingly chronicled in the **Old Mill Museum** (May–Oct Mon–Wed, Fri & Sat
9am–5pm, Sun 1–5pm; $3), where visitors can pick up a walking
tour map of other nearby relics. The most famous of all is the *St
James Hotel* opposite, built by President Lincoln's former White
House chef in 1873, and said to have witnessed 26 murders
(☎505/376-2664 or 1-800/748-2694, fax 376-2623; motel ③,
hotel ⑤). Names in the guest register include Jesse James and

Buffalo Bill, who stayed here while organizing his Wild West Show. It now has its own grand, atmospheric restaurant, and a less romantic motel annexe.

Angel Fire

The Enchanted Circle loops back to Taos from Eagle Nest along US-64, passing after ten miles through the part-**golf**, part-**ski** resort of **ANGEL FIRE** in Moreno Valley. First developed in the late 1960s, Angel Fire shows no signs of maturing beyond its current brash, unappealing sprawl, though the creature comforts of its centrepiece *Legends Hotel* cannot be faulted (☎505/377-6401 or 1-800/633-7463; ④–⑥).

Northeast New Mexico

As I-25 heads north from Las Vegas (see p.131) into New Mexico's **northeast corner**, the Sangre de Cristo mountains gradually recede below the western horizon, and the Great Plains begin to unfurl in all their relentless monotony. There's no great reason to stray off the interstate until the Rockies start to loom above **Raton**, a hundred miles on, though with time to spare the detour to **Capulin Volcano** at that point is worth making.

Raton

*Raton's zip
code is NM
87740.*

Appealing little **RATON** is tucked into the foothills of the Rockies around a hundred miles north of Las Vegas on I-25, a mere eight miles south of the Colorado border. Once a way-station on the Santa Fe Trail, it reached its present size after becoming the site of a railroad repair shop in 1880, and can have changed little since then.

*Trinidad,
twenty miles
north of Raton
in Colorado,
makes an
equally divert-
ing stop.*

Few passengers now bother to dismount from the sleek *Amtrak Starliner* that pulls into the Santa Fe Depot at noon daily, but an hour or two's stroll in **downtown Raton** can be fun. Photos and oddments in the **Raton Museum**, facing the station at 216 S First St (May–Sept Tues–Sat 10am–4pm; Oct–April Wed–Sat 10am–4pm; free), recall highlights from Raton's first century. Until 1938, it was dominated by the seven-storey *Hotel Swastika*, which then "found it necessary to change its name" to the *Yucca*, and is now a bank.

The *Red Violet Inn*, 344 N Second St (☎505/445-9778 or 1-800/624-9778; closed Feb; ③), is a friendly downtown **B&B**, though you can get a cheaper room a few blocks north in the *Melody Lane Motel*, 136 Canyon Drive (☎505/445-3655 or 1-800/421-5210; ②).

Capulin Volcano National Monument

CAPULIN VOLCANO NATIONAL MONUMENT, thirty miles east of Raton on US-64/87 and then three miles north on Hwy-325, preserves the neatest and most symmetrical of a chain of cinder cones that last exploded around ten thousand years ago.

Displays explaining its formation can be examined in the **visitor center** (summer daily 8am–8pm; winter daily 8.30am–4.30pm; ☎505/278-2201; $4 per vehicle), but most visitors drive straight on up the spiral two-mile road that leads to its summit. Once there, a thousand feet above the surrounding plains, you can **hike** for a mile around the rim, enjoying views to the Sangre de Cristo mountains in the west and Oklahoma to the east, or pick your way down to the vent where it all began.

FOLSOM, six miles north of the volcano, is renowned in scientific circles as the place where 1920s archeologists first identified a type of spearpoint known as the **Folsom point**. Some were found wedged between the ribs of a species of bison that has been extinct for ten thousand years, proving that Paleo-Indians were here around 9000 BC – much earlier than had previously been thought. Such points have since been found at sites all over the Southwest. The original excavation site at Folsom is not open to the public.

Clayton

The town of **CLAYTON** stands fifty miles on from Capulin in the far northeast corner of the state, just short of both Oklahoma and Texas. Early Spanish explorers named this region the **Llano Estacado**, or "Staked Plains", on the basis that they could only find their way through the high grasslands by hammering a trail of wooden stakes into the ground. Clayton was founded when the railroad came through in the 1880s, and it's still hard to imagine that anyone would set out on a journey with this as their goal.

The fenced-in dinosaurs on the lawn of the local **visitor center**, 1003 S First St (Mon–Fri 9am–5pm; ☎505/374-9253), are a reference to the dinosaur footprints in the fossilized lakeside muds at **Clayton State Park**, twelve miles north. As well as rock-bottom **motels** in town, like the *Clayton Motel*, 422 Monroe St (☎505/374-2544; ①), there's a *Super 8* to the south at 1425 US-87 (☎505/374-8127 or 1-800/800-8000, fax 374-2598; winter ②, summer ③).

Chapter 3

Albuquerque and Southern New Mexico

C entral and southern New Mexico are not wholly devoid of interest, but it's not surprising that they see fewer visitors than the prime tourist destinations to the north. Despite being the state's capital and largest city, **Albuquerque** holds less to encourage a long stay than Santa Fe or Taos, while few of the towns that lie along the monotonous I-40 highway to the **east**, or in the endless desert expanses to the **south**, are worth going out of your way to see.

Much of the region remained under the domination of the nomadic Apache until well into the nineteenth century. Even Albuquerque was founded long after Santa Fe, while towns such as **Silver City**, **Mesilla** and **Lincoln** didn't really get going until New Mexico joined the United States in 1846. All three went on to play significant roles in the career of **Billy the Kid**, and all still look today much like the frontier outposts Billy must have known. Together with the pre-Columbian remains of the **Gila Cliff Dwellings** in the remote southwest corner, they're the most appealing historic attractions in the region, but there are also a couple of **geological** wonders. The subterranean labyrinths of **Carlsbad Caverns National Park** lure a million tourists across the plains each year, while the dazzling dunes of **White Sands National Monument** make an extraordinary spectacle against the San Andres Mountains. Top-secret missile tests and bomb blasts give this desolate landscape an added sense of mystery, making its role in popular myth as the site of the notorious **Roswell Incident** a tiny bit more plausible.

Albuquerque

Sprawling at the heart of New Mexico, where the main east–west road and rail routes cross both the Rio Grande and the old road south to Mexico, **ALBUQUERQUE** is with half a million people the state's only major metropolis. Though many tourists race straight from the

airport up to Santa Fe, without a thought for Albuquerque, the "**Duke City**" has a good deal going for it. Like Phoenix, it's grown a bit too fast for comfort in the last fifty years, but the original Hispanic settlement is still discernible at its core, and its diverse, cosmopolitan population gives it a rare cultural vibrancy. Even if its architecture is often uninspired, the setting is magnificent, sandwiched between the Rio Grande, lined by stately cottonwoods, and the dramatic, glowing **Sandia Mountains**. Specific highlights for visitors include the intact **Spanish plaza**, the neon-lit **Route 66** frontage of Central Avenue, the excellent **Indian Pueblo Cultural Center**, and October's **hot-air balloon** extravaganza.

A history of Albuquerque

The Spanish colonists who founded a new town beside a sweeping curve of the Rio Grande in 1706 named it in honour of the Spanish **Duke of Alburquerque**. Its earliest surviving adobe buildings, still the nucleus of **Old Town**, date from the 1790s, when Albuquerque occupied a pivotal position on the **Camino Real** – the "Royal Road" from Chihuahua to Santa Fe – which later connected with the **Santa Fe Trail** from the Mississippi. Modern Albuquerque began to grow with the arrival of the railroad in 1880, when its epicentre shuffled a couple of miles east towards the new station.

The extra "r" in Alburquerque got lost somewhere along the way, possibly thanks to a misspelling by a railroad signpainter.

What really transformed Albuquerque was the decentralization of **defence** industries during World War II. Weapons research at **Sandia National Laboratories**, on the Kirtland Air Force Base, brought a massive influx of money and jobs. In the 1950s, "Atomic City" was the best educated city in the nation, in terms of PhDs per capita, and acquired enough federal offices to earn the nickname "Little Washington". It also achieved the dubious distinction of surviving an **H-bomb**: in 1957, a B-36 bomber accidentally dropped a 42,000-pound nuclear device near the air base. Its conventional explosives went off, creating a sizeable crater, but failed to trigger the intended one-megaton thermonuclear blast.

Arrival and information

*For details of **flights** to and within the Southwest, see p.3 onwards.*

Albuquerque's **International Sunport**, New Mexico's principal airport, is four miles southeast of downtown. *Mesa Airlines* (☎1-800/637-2247) and *Southwest* (☎1-800/435-9792) run commuter flights throughout the state.

All the **rental car** chains (see p.19) have outlets at the airport, while a **taxi** into the centre with the *Albuquerque Cab Co* (☎505/883-4888) costs around $10, and *Checker Airport Express* (☎505/765-1234) run door-to-door shuttles. Many hotels and motels also have their own free shuttles. Up to a dozen daily *Shuttlejack* (☎505/243-3244) vans make the 70-minute drive north to Santa Fe ($20), and *Twin Hearts Express* (☎505/751-1201) go to Santa Fe ($20), Taos ($30) and Red River ($45). The *Sun Tran* **city bus** network (☎505/843-9200) is of more use to commuters than tourists; bus #50 connects the airport with downtown, but like all routes it operates no later than 6pm, and not at all on Sundays.

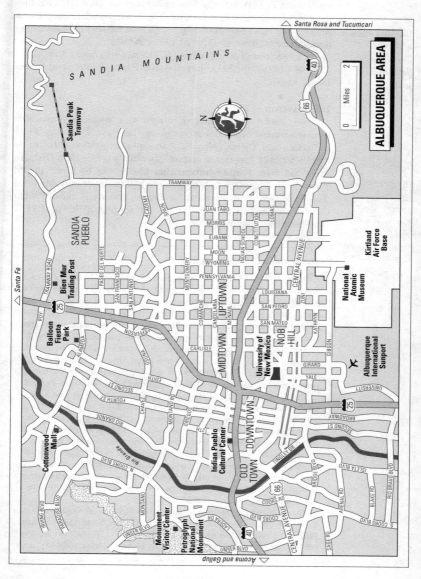

Albuquerque

Walking tours *of the Old Town are detailed on p.160.*

Both *Amtrak* and *Greyhound* are located in an otherwise deserted area, five easy minutes' walk south of downtown. The modern *Greyhound* **bus terminal**, 300 Second St SW (☎505/243-4435), is used by long-distance east–west services, as well as four daily buses up to Santa Fe ($10.50) and Taos ($30), and has good-sized left-luggage lockers. Two *Amtrak* **trains** daily – one heading west to Los Angeles, the other east to Chicago – call in at the small station immediately behind *Greyhound*, at 214 First St.

For a **city tour** of Albuquerque ($21), call *Gray Line* (☎505/242-3880 or 1-800/256-8991); they also go to Santa Fe ($35) and Ácoma Pueblo ($29).

Information

The free, useful *Art of Visiting Albuquerque* magazine is available from the **tourist office** downtown in the Galeria mall, 20 First Plaza at Second and Tijeras (Mon–Fri 8am–5pm; ☎505/842-9918 or 1-800/284-2282). Americana enthusiasts will also enjoy their *Historic Route 66* map. Further **information kiosks** can be found in Old Town, in the Plaza Don Luis on Romero NW (summer only, Mon–Sat 9am–7pm, Sun 10am–5pm); at the airport; and at the Indian Pueblo Cultural Center (see p.162). The city's main **post office** is at 1135 Broadway NE (daily 7.30am–6pm).

The Balloons of Albuquerque

First held in 1972, Albuquerque's annual **International Balloon Fiesta**, a photographer's dream that lasts from the first Saturday until the second Sunday of October, has grown to become the most important event in world ballooning. By a freak of geography, the **"Albuquerque Box"** offers ideal conditions for balloonists. After take-off, the prevailing winds consistently blow balloons towards the east, until they clear the top of the Sandia Mountains. Then stronger winds propel them back westwards, making it possible to land more or less where they were launched. As a result, Albuquerque regularly hosts major gas and hot-air ballooning championships, such as the unlikely-sounding Coupe de Gordon Bennett.

The Balloon Fiesta, now sponsored by *Kodak*, attracts around a thousand balloons and well over a million visitors. Book several months in advance if you need a room, or even a rental car, in early October. The fun focuses on **Balloon Fiesta Park**, half a mile west of I-25 seven miles north of downtown. Admission costs $4, and the busiest times are the dawn mass launchings on the four weekend mornings, as well as the "Special Shapes" events, when balloons in shapes ranging from beer bottles to dumptrucks, and dragons to doughnuts, take to the air. Volunteers are always welcomed to help set the things up, and may be rewarded with a quick flight. For a full festival programme, call ☎505/821-1000.

Among companies running hot-air balloon flights year round, at around $100 per person, are *Discover Balloons* (☎505/842-1111), *Adam Family Flying Services* (☎505/883-5874), *Rainbow Ryders* (☎505/293-0000) and *Hot Air Extraord-in-Air* (☎505/266-9744).

Accommodation

The easiest way to find a place to stay in Albuquerque is to cruise the twenty-mile length of **Central Avenue**, the old Route 66, which is lined with the flashing neon signs of dozens of $30-a-night motels. Try to have a good look in daylight, to spot those that may turn scary at night. If you want to escape your car for a while, you'll have to pay a little extra to stay in the heart of Old Town – which holds few accommodation options – or downtown. Larger convention hotels are congregated along the interstates, while a handful of B&Bs are scattered across the city.

Albuquerque Hilton, 1901 University Blvd NE, Albuquerque NM 87102; ☎505/884-2500 or 1-800/274-6835. Midtown high-rise, near the intersection of I-40 & I-25. Good rooms, three restaurants – the *Casa Chaco* serves tasty Southwestern cuisine – and several busy bars. ⑥.

Barcelona Suites Uptown, 900 Louisiana Blvd NE, Albuquerque NM 87110; ☎505/255-5566 or 1-800/223-0888. Spacious suite-only hotel, three miles east of downtown and two blocks south of I-40 at exit 162. All the suites have kitchens, and there are indoor and outdoor pools. ⑤.

Best Western Airport Inn, 2400 Yale Blvd SE, Albuquerque NM 87106; ☎505/242-7022 or 1-800/528-1234, fax 243-0620. Pleasant courtyard motel, quieter than you might expect, and offering a free airport shuttle. ④.

Casa del Granjero, 414 C de Baca Lane NW, Albuquerque NM 87114; ☎505/897-4144 or 1-800/701-4144, fax 897-9788. Adobe farmhouse in three-acre gardens, converted into tasteful, upmarket non-smoking B&B inn, with three rooms and four suites. ④–⑦.

Casas de Sueños, 310 Rio Grande Rd SW, Albuquerque NM 87104; ☎505/247-4560 or 1-800/242-8987, fax 842-8493. Beautifully furnished, exotic – as in the extraordinary Caracol room coiled above the entrance – and friendly B&B, very close to Old Town, with themed cottages and smaller rooms. One of New Mexico's most appealing places to stay. ⑤–⑧.

Comfort Inn–Airport, 2300 Yale Blvd SE, Albuquerque NM 87106; ☎505/243-2244 or 1-800/221-2222. Good-value motel, served by free shuttles from the airport across the road, and offering complimentary breakfasts. ④.

Crossroads Motel, 1001 Central Ave NE, Albuquerque NM 87102; ☎505/255-7586. Simple, good-value budget motel, between Old Town and the University on Route 66, and complete with pool. ②.

El Vado Motel, 2500 Central Ave SW, Albuquerque NM 87104; ☎505/243-4594. Vintage adobe Route 66 motel, within easy reach of Old Town. ②.

Holiday Inn Crowne Plaza Pyramid, 5151 San Francisco Rd NE, Albuquerque NM 87109; ☎505/821-3333 or 1-800/544-0623, fax 828-0230. Gigantic pyramid (stepped not smooth) near exit 232 off I-25 north of town, with a waterfall in the lobby and over three hundred rooms. President Clinton holed up here to prepare for his second debate with Bob Dole in 1996. ⑥.

Monterey Nonsmokers Motel, 2402 Central Ave SW, Albuquerque NM 87104; ☎505/243-3554. Clean, fifteen-room motel, two blocks west of Old Town, with pool, laundry, and a strict non-smoking policy. ③.

As explained on p.15, accommodation prices, excluding taxes, are indicated throughout this book by the following symbols:

① *up to $30*
② *$30–45*
③ *$45–60*
④ *$60–80*
⑤ *$80–100*
⑥ *$100–130*
⑦ *$130–175*
⑧ *$175–250*
⑨ *$250+*

Hotels and B&Bs are marked on the map on p.161.

Old Town Bed and Breakfast, 707 17th St, Albuquerque NM 87104; ☎505/764-9144. Friendly, very small-scale B&B in mock-adobe home a couple of blocks from the heart of Old Town. ④.

Conrad's restaurant in La Posada *is reviewed on* p.165.

La Posada de Albuquerque, 125 Second St NW, Albuquerque NM 87102; ☎505/242-9090 or 1-800/777-5732. Historic, elegant hotel in convenient downtown location, built in Mexican style by Conrad Hilton in 1939. Plush, renovated rooms, a superb restaurant, and a spacious, atmospheric bar. ⑥.

Route 66 Hostel, 1012 Central Ave SW, Albuquerque NM 87102; ☎505/247-1813. Albuquerque's only hostel, a friendly place on the outskirts of Old Town, a mile west of downtown, offers dorm beds for $13 ($11 members), kitchen facilities, and bargain private doubles. ①.

The City

Albuquerque consists of several distinct districts, interspersed between anonymous residential areas, and threaded through by the twenty-mile artery of **Central Avenue**, the most authentic surviving remnant of the classic Route 66, alive with flashing neon. **Old Town** remains the most interesting area for visitors, with **downtown** two miles to the east, and the **university district** and the fashionable **Nob Hill** area beyond that. Further east, the **Sandia Mountains** finally call a halt to the Sunbelt sprawl. The city has begun instead to push west of the Rio Grande, where only **Petroglyph National Monument** holds any interest for tourists.

Old Town

Albuquerque's tree-filled **Old Town Plaza** may lack the cachet of its Santa Fe equivalent, but it makes an appealing focus for explorations of the old Spanish settlement. After decades of decline, the adobe buildings on all four sides have been restored as souvenir stores and tourist restaurants, and they're still presided over by the twin-towered facade of **San Felipe de Neri church** to the north.

To get a sense of the city's past, spend an hour or two at the **Albuquerque Museum**, a couple of blocks northeast of the plaza at 2000 Mountain Rd (daily except Mon 9am–5pm; free). As well as an impressive array of the armour and weaponry carried by the Spanish conquistadors, it holds delicate religious artefacts, plus paintings and photos showing Albuquerque through the centuries. It's also the starting point for Old Town **walking tours** (mid-April to mid-Nov, daily except Mon 11am; $2).

Another two blocks east, the **New Mexico Museum of Natural History and Science**, 1801 Mountain Rd NW (daily 9am–5pm; closed Mon in Jan & Sept; $4), primarily appeals to kids. Star attractions include full-size animatronic dinosaurs, a simulated volcanic eruption, and a replica of an Ice Age snow cave, plus an engaging, handleable collection of fossils and dinosaur bones.

Southeast of the plaza at 202 San Felipe St NW, the bizarre **American International Rattlesnake Museum** has live rattlers on

CENTRAL ALBUQUERQUE

GRAND AVE
TIJERAS AVE
BROADWAY
COMMERCIAL
MARTIN LUTHER KING JR BLVD
FIRST ST
SECOND ST
LOMAS BLVD
THIRD ST
MARQUETTE AVE
FOURTH ST
TIJERAS AVE
FIFTH ST
ROMA AVE
COPPER AVE
SIXTH ST
CENTRAL AVENUE (ROUTE 66)
SEVENTH ST
GOLD AVE
EIGHTH ST
SILVER AVE
KELEHER
LEAD AVE
COAL AVE

Galeria Mall
Explora Science Center
i
Amtrak
Greyhound
KiMo Theater

2
C
B
A
E
3

FIRST ST

N

0   250   Yards

Old Town Plaza (1.1 miles) ▷
Old Town Plaza (1.2 miles) ▷

OLD TOWN

NINETEENTH ST
NINETEENTH ST
SAN PASQUALE AVE
OLD TOWN ROAD
MOUNTAIN ROAD
CHARLEVOIX
SAN FELIPE ST
ROMERO ST
N PLAZA
SOUTH PLAZA
OLD TOWN
LOMAS
RIO GRANDE BLVD
CENTRAL AVE
66

New Mexico Museum of Natural History & Science
Albuquerque Museum
San Felipe de Neri
G
D
i
F
Turquoise Museum
2

0   100   Yards

ACCOMMODATION

1 Casa de Sueños
2 La Posada de Albuquerque
3 Route 66 Hostel

EATING

A Artichoke Cafe
B Gold Street Caffè
C Hyperion Coffee and Tea
D La Placita
E M & J Restaurant
F Restaurant Antiquity
G Zane Graze

display and rattlesnake curios for sale (daily 10am–6.30pm; $2). *Gus' Trading Post*, across the highway nearby at 2026 Central Ave SW, stocks a well-priced assortment of Indian crafts and jewellery.

Still on Central Avenue, in the Old Town Shopping Center half a block west of the plaza, the intriguing little **Turquoise Museum** (Mon–Sat 9.30am–6pm; $2) looks like just another mall store. Once you step inside, you find that in fact you've entered a fortified bank vault, filled with rare and beautiful turquoise nuggets. The story of worldwide turquoise production is told in copious detail, and there's lots of useful advice on the tricks of the trade; unfortunately, the only way to tell if a piece of turquoise is genuine involves destroying it. Of course, visits end with the chance to buy a few trinkets.

Indian Pueblo Cultural Center

The good-quality Pueblo Kitchen **cafe** *in the Cultural Center is reviewed on p.165.*

The **Indian Pueblo Cultural Center**, at 2401 12th St NW, across I-40 a few blocks north of Old Town (daily 9am–5.30pm; $3; ☎505/843-7270 or 1-800/766-4405), is a stunning museum and crafts market collectively run by the nineteen New Mexican pueblos. Its horseshoe-shaped design deliberately echoes the architecture of the ancient Anasazi city of Pueblo Bonito, in Chaco Canyon (see p.78).

This is New Mexico's one major museum about Native Americans to be curated by Native Americans, and the displays downstairs, under the banner *Our Land, Our Culture, Our Story*, have a clear and distinct point of view. The shared Anasazi heritage at the root of Pueblo culture is explained in detail, as is the impact of the Spanish conquistadors. Describing the Pueblo Revolt of 1680 as the "first civil war", it states that by allowing the defeated Spaniards to leave unharmed, the Pueblo peoples "showed them more mercy than they showed us". There's also as good an explanation as you're ever likely to get of a topic Pueblo Indians rarely discuss with outsiders; how indigenous Pueblo religion has managed to co-exist with imported Catholicism. Videos illustrate modern Pueblo life, and an outstanding selection of pottery and jewellery is sold in the stores upstairs. For most of the year, **Pueblo dances** take place in the central courtyard on weekends (April–Dec, Sat & Sun 11am & 2pm; free).

The riverfront

The Rio Grande has shifted its course in the last three hundred years, so there's an unexpectedly low-key gap **west** of Old Town, much of it left undeveloped in deference to the unruly river. Along the wooded eastern riverbank, north of where Central Avenue crosses the river, the **Bio Park** holds two attractions that focus on the natural world.

Not for the squeamish, the **Albuquerque Aquarium** (daily 9am–5pm; $4.50) offers such diverse experiences as eating in a restaurant beside a glass-walled tank filled with live sharks, and walking through a tunnel surrounded on all sides by fierce-eyed moray eels. Across the way, the **Rio Grande Botanic Garden** (same hours, same ticket) consists of two giant conservatories – one holding rare plants from the Sonoran and Chihuahua deserts, the other more temperate Mediterranean species – plus a series of formal walled gardens.

Two miles north of Old Town, by way of Rio Grande Boulevard, the **Rio Grande Nature Center** (daily 10am–5pm; $1) has informative displays describing local wildlife. Two short but very welcome nature trails follow the riverside, feeling far removed from the city.

Downtown

Downtown Albuquerque may be where New Mexico's largest city conducts its daily business, but it holds little that's likely to detain tourists for long. If you call at the visitor center in the small **Galeria** mall (see p.158), you might also stop by the **Explora Science Center** in the same building (Wed–Sat 10am–5pm, Sun noon–5pm; $2). Its hands-on displays and experiments are mainly designed to keep kids occupied while their parents shop.

The University District

A couple of miles east of downtown, the campus of the **University of New Mexico** stretches along the northern side of Central Avenue. The 25,000-strong student body keeps the southern side of the highway – lined with funky hangouts of all kinds, from bookstores to laundromats by way of cafes and diners – lively right around the clock, but there's not all that much scope for sightseeing.

Of the six museums on campus, non-academic visitors are most likely to enjoy the **Maxwell Museum of Anthropology** (Mon–Fri 9am–4pm, Sat 10am–4pm, Sun noon–4pm; free), which holds a wide range of displays on the *Peoples of the Southwest*, past and present. There's some fine Mimbres pottery (see p.193), as well as material from Chaco Canyon, while the *Ancestors* segment traces human evolution from the three-million-year-old Lucy, just 3ft 7in tall, unearthed in Ethiopia.

The National Atomic Museum

On the fringes of the giant Kirtland Air Force Base, southeast of the city, the **National Atomic Museum** (daily 9am–5pm; free) delights in its "impressive array of American fission weapons". Visitors enter the base via gates on Wyoming or Gibson boulevards, where you have to stop to pick up a free pass and map. Once you find the museum, you'll be soothed to learn how much more precise and sophisticated today's weapons are compared to the "primitive city-busting concepts" of the Cold War era, just how surprisingly safe nuclear waste disposal can be, and a host of other little-known facts.

The Sandia Mountains

The forested 10,500ft peaks of the **Sandia Mountains** tower over Albuquerque to the east; the view from the summit is especially beau-

*Manzano Mountain, entirely enclosed by Kirtland Air Force Base, is said to be **hollow**, stuffed full of more nuclear weapons than any other site on earth.*

tiful at and after sunset, when the city lights sparkle below. In summer it's a good 25°F cooler up here than in the valley, while in winter you can go downhill or cross-country **skiing** (mid-Dec to mid-
March; lift tickets $30 per day; ☎505/242-9133).

High Finance,
the restaurant
at the top of
the tramway,
is reviewed
opposite.

The most exciting way to reach the top is by riding the world's
longest tramway, the 2.7-mile **Sandia Peak Aerial Tram**, which
departs from the end of Tramway Road a dozen miles northeast of
town. During the uppermost 1.5 miles of its exhilarating 15-minute
climb, not a single support tower interrupts the progress of the cable
car (summer daily 9am–10pm; spring and fall Thurs–Tues
9am–8pm, Wed 5–8pm; winter Mon, Tues, Thurs & Fri 9am–8pm,
Wed noon–8pm, Sat & Sun 8.30am–8pm; $13).

If you'd rather **drive** to the top of the mountains, you have to circle around the back and approach from the east, by way of the
Turquoise Trail – a route described on p.113.

Petroglyph National Monument

Beneath a chain of burned-out cinder cones thrown up by a 150,000-
year-old volcanic eruption, a low seventeen-mile escarpment west of
the Rio Grande has recently become the **PETROGLYPH NATIONAL
MONUMENT**, to protect its unusually accessible ancient Indian **rock
art**. Apart from spectacular views of the valley and the Sandia
Mountains, however, there's no great need to go to its **visitor center**
(winter daily 8am–5pm, summer daily 9am–6pm; ☎505/839-4429),
reached by crossing the river on I-40 then driving four miles north on
Unser Boulevard. Instead, continue to the petroglyphs themselves,
another mile north in **Boca Negra Canyon** (same hours; Mon–Fri $1
per vehicle, Sat & Sun $2 per vehicle).

Three short trails off its one-way loop road lead up to the escarpment, which on close inspection turns out to consist of tumbled
black lava boulders; only the half-hour **Mesa Trail** demands any
energetic climbing. Most of the crudely scratched images you'll pass,
ranging from simple spirals to masked figures and eagles with Bart
Simpson hairdos, date from 1300 to 1680 AD. During the eighteenth
century, shepherds from the nearby Hispanic settlement of Atrisco
added a number of Christian crosses and symbols.

Eating

The chefs of Santa Fe may be trying to redefine Southwestern cuisine, but Albuqerque still knows what it likes – mountainous
Mexican meals. This is the place to get to grips with what real New
Mexican food is all about, with family diners all over the city competing to create the spiciest *chile rellenos*, enchiladas and *sopaipillas*. If you prefer to stick with the familiar, there are also 25
McDonald's, and a number of gourmet restaurants where prices on
the whole are well below those in Santa Fe.

Budget restaurants and diners

Chef du Jour, 119 San Pasquale St SW; ☎505/247-8998. Sandwiches and inventive light meals, in a plain cafe an easy walk from Old Town Plaza, with some outdoor seating. Open Mon–Fri for lunch only.

Duran Central Pharmacy, 1815 Central Ave NW; ☎505/247-4141. Mexican dining counter attached to a working drugstore, not far from Old Town. Open daily for breakfast and lunch only, with delicious, inexpensive tortillas, enchiladas and plenty of chile.

Frontier, 2400 Central Ave SE; ☎505/266-0550. Legendary 24-hour diner across from the university, where an unceasing parade of characters chow down on burgers, burritos and great vegetarian enchiladas.

M&J Restaurant, 403 Second St SW; ☎505/242-4890. Family-run Mexican diner near the *Greyhound* station, boasting fresh-made tortillas and *sopaipillas*, blue-corn enchiladas and pork *adovada*. Breakfast and lunch daily except Sun, dinner Thurs–Sat only.

Pueblo Kitchen, Indian Pueblo Cultural Center, 2401 12th St NW; ☎505/843-7270. Indian fry-bread and other Pueblo specialities, plus good guacamole burgers. Open daily 7.30am–4pm.

La Placita, 208 San Felipe St NW; ☎505/247-2204. Attractive centuries-old adobe hacienda on the Old Town Plaza, where a predominantly tourist crowd enjoy Mexican meals at surprisingly reasonable prices. Open daily 11am–9pm, with live Mexican music most evenings.

66 Diner, 1405 Central Ave NE; ☎505/247-1421. Classic Fifties diner near the university, with white-capped waiting staff, a soda fountain and a lively late-night clientele. Lunch and dinner daily, breakfast on weekends only.

Albuquerque restaurants are marked on the map on p.161.

Fine dining

Artichoke Cafe, 424 Central Ave SE; ☎505/243-0200. Simple but classy restaurant in the heart of downtown, with indoor and outdoor seating. Good, varied menu of California-influenced modern American cuisine; most entrees well under $20. Open for dinner daily except Sun, lunch on weekdays only.

Cafe Oceana, 1414 Central Ave SE; ☎505/247-2233. Oyster bar and seafood restaurant, across from the *66 Diner* near the university, cooking fresh fish and shellfish in a hybrid Southwestern/Cajun style. Most entrees cost under $20. Open for dinner daily except Sun, lunch on weekdays only.

Conrad's, *La Posada de Albuquerque*, 125 Second St; ☎505/242-9090. Classic Thirties Art-Deco hotel diner, modernized and serving excellent Hispanic-influenced dishes, including tasty salads and *tapas*, plus the signature dish, a superb seafood paella, complete with lobster and saffron rice, at $20 for one person or $34 for two. Open daily for all meals.

High Finance, 40 Tramway Rd NE; ☎505/243-9742. Pricey seafood and steak place in unparalleled location, at the top of the Sandia Peak Tramway – see opposite – with eagle's-eye views of Albuquerque. Entrees range from $15 to $35. Open daily for lunch and dinner.

Monte Vista Fire Station, 3201 Central Ave NE; ☎505/255-2424. Upmarket haunt, housed in one of Nob Hill's unlikeliest buildings – a restored Art-Deco Pueblo Revival fire station. Fancy grilled meats and fish at under $20 per entree, with specialities like crab cakes and even ostrich *fajitas*. Dinner nightly, lunch on weekdays only.

Restaurant Antiquity, 112 Romero St NW; ☎505/247-3545. Old Town cottage turned romantic French restaurant, open nightly for dinner only, with a changing menu of gourmet dishes at around $20.

Coffeehouses

Double Rainbow, 3416 Central Ave SE; ☎505/255-6633. Nob Hill coffee bar, with indoor/outdoor seating, a lively student clientele, a stupendous array of breads and pastries, and a huge stock of magazines. Daily 6.30am–midnight.

EJ's Coffee & Tea Co, 2201 Silver Ave SE; ☎505/268-2233. Slightly grungy student hang-out, one block south of Central near the university. Open daily from espresso-fuelled breakfasts until late, with vegetarian lunches and somewhat fancier pasta dinners.

Gold Street Caffè, 218 Gold St SW; ☎505/765-1633. Oddly formal downtown espresso cafe, offering "a unique coffee experience" and wonderful pastries. Mon–Fri 6.30am–5.30pm.

Hyperion Coffee & Tea, 215 Central Ave NW; ☎505/242-7766. Sidewalk cafe in downtown's *First National Bank* building, serving espresso coffees, light breakfasts, and sandwiches and salads from 7am until mid-afternoon on weekdays, and 8am–1pm Sat.

Zane Graze, 308 San Felipe NW; ☎505/243-4377. Old Town coffee bar, open for breakfast and lunch daily, with salads and desserts as well as espressos.

Drinking and nightlife

Most of Albuquerque's more reputable **bars** and **nightclubs** are inside the larger chain hotels, but there are also plenty of small theatres and music venues. Two free magazines, the weekly *NuCity* and the monthly *On The Scene*, can tell you everything you need to known about what's coming up or going down.

Assets Grille & Brewing Company, 6910 Montgomery Blvd NE; ☎505/889-6400. Lively microbrewery with indoor and outdoor seating, plus Italian food – dinner nightly, lunch daily except Sun.

Caravan East, 7605 Central Ave NE; ☎505/265-7877. Enormous honky-tonk, where tenderfeet can do the two-step with throngs of urban cowboys.

Dingo Bar, 313 Gold St SW; ☎505/243-0663. Basic bar where you'll hear predominantly blues, plus R&B or TexMex performed by local musicians.

El Rey Theatre, 620 Central Ave SW; ☎505/243-7546. Live music from salsa to country, and all points in between.

Golden West Saloon, 620 Central Ave SW; ☎505/243-7546. The venue of choice for Albuquerque's metal maniacs, and host to touring indie bands.

KiMo Theatre, 423 Central Ave NW; ☎505/848-1370. Gorgeous city-owned "Pueblo Deco" theatre, dating from the late 1920s, which puts on an eclectic programme of opera, dance and theatre performances, kids' movie shows, and also regular live bands.

University Draft House, 318 Central Ave SW; ☎505/843-7078. Hectic no-cover downtown bar, always packed with students, open Tues–Sat until 2am.

East of Albuquerque

The first twenty miles of I-40's eastward run from Albuquerque are
deceptively scenic, with the interstate threading its way between the
Sandia Mountains. Once through the hills, however, unless you then
turn north onto the **Turquoise Trail** towards Santa Fe – see p.113 –
you're in for a long hard slog out into the plains. The only place
before Texas which might conceivably pique your curiosity is **Fort
Sumner**, which played a heart-rending role in Navajo history and
also holds the grave of **Billy the Kid**.

Santa Rosa

A hundred unutterably boring miles east of the Sandia Mountains,
weary drivers reach their first potential overnight stop. South and
west of the interstate, a four-mile stretch of the former Route 66
runs through **SANTA ROSA**. As **Parker Avenue** in the small
downtown, and **Will Rogers Drive** further east, it's dotted with
diners and motels, but there's nothing worth going out of your
way to see. **Scuba-divers** desperate for a desert dip cross the
plains to plunge into Santa Rosa's **Blue Hole**, a crystal-clear natural pool that's sixty feet across and eighty feet deep, though to
anyone who's seen the ocean it may come as an anti-climax.
You'll find it by turning left off Fifth Street, south of the main
drag, onto Blue Hole Road.

In 1541, the first Spanish expedition into the Southwest is said to
have crossed the Pecos River at **Coronado's Bridge**, ten miles south
of Santa Rosa on the dead-end Hwy-91. Following the lush river-
banks makes a welcome break from the interstate, and the village of
PUERTO DE LUNA at road's end is pretty enough, but of the bridge
itself not a trace remains.

Practicalities

*Santa Rosa's
zip code is NM
88435.*

Santa Rosa's **visitor center** is at 486 Parker Ave (Mon–Fri
9am–5pm, Sat 9am–1pm; ☎505/472-3763). Of its dozen or so
motels, the large, new *Super 8*, 1201 Will Rogers Drive (☎505/472-
5388 or 1-800/800-8000; winter ②, summer ③) is clean and comfortable, while the *Sun'n'Sand*, 1124 Will Rogers Drive (☎505/472-
5268; ②), is cheaper and has its own predictable but reasonable
diner next door. The best place to **camp** is Santa Rosa Lake State
Park, seven miles north of town on Hwy-91 (☎505/472-3110).

The *Lake City Diner*, downtown at 101 Fourth St
(☎505/472-5253), is a spotless cafe straight out of a Norman
Rockwell painting. Housed in a converted bank, and run by a
dynamic young man enthused by a year in Barcelona, Spain, it
serves an enticing menu of sandwiches, daily specials, Coca Cola
cake and espresso coffees.

Tucumcari

Sixty miles east of Santa Rosa, **TUCUMCARI** is the definitive
Route 66 pit-stop. If you expect its abundant truck stops, diners,
and motels to yield a kitsch fascination, you'll be sorely disappointed, but their glittering neon signs make a welcome sight as
dusk descends on the plains. No one in their right mind stays two
nights in Tucumcari; an hour spent admiring the barbed-wire collection of the **Tucumcari Historical Museum**, 416 S Adams St
(June–Aug Mon–Sat 9am–6pm, Sun 1–6pm; Sept–May Tues–Sat
9am–5pm, Sun 1–5pm; $2), should convince you it's time to hit
the road again.

Practicalities

*Tucumcari's
zip code is NM
88401.*

Tucumcari Boulevard cuts a broad five-mile swathe through town,
passing 34 motels along the way, as well as the local **visitor center**
at 404 W (Mon–Fri 8am–noon & 1–5pm; ☎505/461-1694). Among
the more salubrious places with **rooms** for well under $30 are the
Palomino, 1215 E (☎505/461-3622; ①), and the *Blue Swallow*,
815 E (☎505/461-9849; ①). Classier options include the *Super 8*,
4001 E (☎505/461-4444 or 1-800/800-8000; ②), and the more central *Rodeway Inn East*, 1023 E (☎505/461-0360; ②).

More fun than the plentiful highway fast-food outlets is the *Big
Dipper*, an old-fashioned diner and soda-fountain in the heart of the
old downtown at 101 Second at Main (☎505/461-4430). A popular
local rendezvous, it opens daily around 9am.

Fort Sumner

A 45-mile detour south of I-40 between Santa Rosa and Tucumcari
brings you to modern **FORT SUMNER**. This small town was
named after a nineteenth-century Army outpost that stood seven
miles southeast, on what's now **Fort Sumner State Monument**
(daily 8.30am–5pm; $1). The fort was infamous as the headquar-
ters of the **Bosque Redondo Indian Reservation**, where nine
thousand Navajo and Mescalero Apache captives were incarcerat-
ed during the 1860s (see p.487). The idea was for the reservation
to be self-sufficient, and for the Indians to become accustomed to
an agricultural lifestyle. In fact, the Pecos River proved too salty
to drink, let alone use for irrigation. Over three thousand prisoners died before the experiment was abandoned in 1868, and the
survivors were allowed to return home. In the words of Navajo
headman Barboncito:

> *Whatever we do here causes death. Some work at the acequias,
> take sick and die; others die with the hoe in their hands; they go
> to the river to their waists and suddenly disappear; others have
> been struck and torn to pieces by lightning. A rattlesnake bite*

here kills us; in our country a rattlesnake before he bites gives warning which enables us to keep out of its way and if bitten, we readily find a cure – here we can find no cure.

For the full saga of Billy the Kid, see p.174.

Only a low ridge of adobe bricks on the eastern riverbank remains of the fort the Navajo built for their captors, while the dead are honoured by a brass plaque nearby inscribed in Navajo.

After the reservation closed down, the fort and the surrounding land was bought by rancher Lucien Maxwell. **Billy the Kid** was hiding in his son Peter's bedroom here in 1881 when **Pat Garrett** tracked him down and shot him dead. His **grave** is located in the backyard of the **Old Fort Sumner Museum**, a few hundred yards east of the fort (daily 9am–5pm; $2). Billy was buried alongside two fellow outlaws Tom O'Folliard and Charlie Bowdre; all remain imprisoned to this day, as their joint tombstone, poignantly inscribed "*PALS*", is protected from would-be thieves behind steel bars. The museum itself holds a jumble of items that may or may not have belonged to Billy, together with displays relating to local history. In that respect, it's indistinguishable from the rival **Billy the Kid Museum**, back in town at 1601 E Sumner Ave (mid-May to mid-Sept daily 8.30am–5pm, closed Sun in winter; $2).

Practicalities

If you're trapped by a desert thunderstorm, you might choose to shelter in one of Fort Sumner's two rudimentary **motels** – the *Oasis*, 1704 E Sumner Ave (☎505/355-7414; ①), or the *Coronado*, 309 W Sumner Ave (☎505/355-2466; ①). Later on, you'd probably end up eating a cheap Mexican **meal** at the *Rodeo Cafe*, 112 E Sumner Ave (☎505/355-9986).

Clovis

The midsized railroad and ranching community of **CLOVIS**, on the border with Texas sixty miles east of Fort Sumner and 85 miles southeast of Tucumcari, has twice entered the history books. In 1932, the remains of prehistoric mammoth hunters found at nearby **Blackwater Draw** provided the first firm evidence that humans were present in North America as much as twelve thousand years ago. Although archeologically speaking it was a sensational discovery, the **Blackwater Draw Museum**, en route to **PORTALES** a dozen miles southwest of town on US-70 (summer Mon–Sat 10am–5pm, Sun noon–5pm; winter closed Mon; $2), is not wildly exciting. The excavation site, ten miles east on Hwy-467, is open to visitors in summer (same hours and ticket).

Clovis' other brush with fame came in 1958, when a bespectacled teenager, **Charles "Buddy" Holly**, crossed the state line from Lubbock, Texas, to record a few tunes with his band, the Crickets – *Peggy Sue*, *That'll Be the Day* and a dozen others. Call the visitor

East of Albuquerque

center in advance (see below), to arrange a tour of Norman Petty's original **studio** – which also gave Roy Orbison his first break – at 1313 W Seventh St.

Practicalities

Clovis' **visitor center** is downtown at 215 N Main St (Mon–Fri 9am–5pm; ☎505/763-3435), near the huge, derelict old *Hotel Clovis*. **Motels** interspersed between the Mexican diners and fast-food specialists along US-60/84 further east include the *Days Inn*, 1720 Mabry Drive (☎505/762-2971; ②), and the *Clovis Inn*, 2912 Mabry Drive (☎505/762-5600; ②).

Southeast of Albuquerque

While the Rio Grande Valley, south of Albuquerque – and covered on p.185 onwards – has always held a larger human population, the terrain that lies **southeast** of the city is of far greater scenic and historic appeal. Here you'll find the ancient pueblos of **Salinas National Monument**, the eerie gypsum wastelands of **White Sands**, and the mountain resorts of **Ruidoso** and **Cloudcroft**. Most compelling of all, however, is the rough-hewn frontier town of **Lincoln**. Scene of the bloodiest exploits in the saga of **Billy the Kid**, it has remained all but untouched in the century since his death.

Salinas National Monument

The precious salt deposits of **Salinas Valley**, east of the Manzano Mountains around seventy miles southeast of Albuquerque, were regarded by early Spanish colonists as one of New Mexico's greatest treasures. Franciscan missionaries targeted the Pueblo peoples of the valley, erecting massive churches atop their existing settlements, but thanks to epidemics and Apache raids the entire region had been abandoned by the time of the Pueblo Revolt of 1680. Three separate ruined pueblos now form **SALINAS NATIONAL MONUMENT**. Each has its own "contact station" (all daily 9am–5pm; free), and they share a **visitor center** (daily 8am–5pm; free; ☎505/847-2585) in **MOUNTAINAIR**, 36 miles east of I-25 on US-60. Mountainair itself is a small community whose one claim to fame is that fifty years ago it was the "Pinto Bean Capital of the World".

Visiting Gran Quivira in 1598, Juan de Oñate reported that its inhabitants painted stripes on their noses.

The largest of the Salinas pueblos, **Gran Quivira**, stands on a low hill 26 miles south from Mountainair along Hwy-55. It's the only one where the pueblo itself has been more than minimally excavated, to reveal an impressive 300-room structure complete with hidden *kivas*, built in secret to avoid the wrath of the Spanish priests. The adjoining Mission of San Buenaventura church was probably not yet completed by the time the pueblo was abandoned.

The main feature of **Quarai**, a mile west of Hwy-55 eight miles
north of Mountainair, is the fortress-like stone church of La Purísima
Concepción, whose golden walls tower above the rubble-strewn
mounds that conceal the pueblo village. At **Abó**, just north of US-60
nine miles west of Mountainair, the church of San Gregorio dominates an even more tantalizing expanse of ruins.

Carrizozo and the Valley of Fires

Fifty miles southeast of Gran Quivira, where US-54 meets US-380,
CARRIZOZO is a parched desert outpost that replaced better-known
Lincoln as the seat of Lincoln County in 1909. Apart from a couple
of **motels** – the *Four Winds*, at the crossroads (☎505/648-2356;
②), has its own restaurant – there's nothing much to it.

The **Valley of Fires Recreation Area**, four miles northwest (daily
dawn–dusk; $6; ☎505/648-2241), preserves a jet-black river of lava
that poured for over forty miles down the Tularosa Valley, around 1500
years ago. Though it ranges from four to six miles wide, and up to 150
feet deep, the one trail across the lava is less than a mile long. It's so
rough underfoot, and so exposed to the sun, that you're unlikely to want
to hike any further, but there's a good **campground** alongside ($8).

*At its southern
end, the lava
flow abuts the
utterly con-
trasting White
Sands
National
Monument; see
p.179.*

Three Rivers Petroglyphs

Five miles east of US-54, halfway from Carrizozo to Alamogordo, an
extensive if not wildly enthralling collection of pre-Columbian **rock
art** now forms the **Three Rivers Petroglyph National Recreation**

Trinity Site

Twice each year, sightseers make a peculiar pilgrimage to the **Trinity Site**,
out on the **White Sands Missile Range** in the desert thirty miles west of
Carrizozo, where the first **atomic bomb** was detonated at 5.30am on July
16, 1945. Brought by road from Los Alamos (see p.116), the bomb, code-
named **Fat Man**, was not dropped, but placed atop a steel tower. The blast
was strong enough to shatter windows in Silver City, 120 miles west, and
to fuse the sands below "Ground Zero" into a thick slab of radioactive
glass, known as **trinitite**.

The Missile Range has witnessed thousands more weapons tests since
then, and remains off limits to non-military personnel except for the
first Saturdays of April and October. Visitors on those days can either join a
"caravan" of vehicles that sets off from **Alamogordo** at 8am, or enter the
range unaccompanied via the **Stallion Gate** (9am–2pm), on US-380 fifty
miles west of Carrizozo. You're forbidden to stop or take photos other than
at the site itself, or to make political speeches, and encouraged to resist
the temptation to pick up any trinitite you may spot. Not only is it part of
a National Historic Landmark, it's radioactive.

For full tour information, contact Alamogordo's visitor center. If you'd
like to known more about the range itself, drop in at the White Sands
Missile Range Museum, described on p.179.

Area (daily dawn–dusk; $3). Between 1000 and 1400 AD, agricultural Mogollon villagers hacked over twenty thousand petroglyphs into boulders at the foot of the Capitan Mountains, depicting bighorn sheep, stylized masks and geometric patterns. A representative sample can be admired from a half-mile trail, while a separate, easier trail leads to the remains of three Mogollon dwellings. This area once belonged to Susan Barber, "Cattle Queen of New Mexico" and widow of Alexander McSween, killed in the Lincoln County War (see p.174). She's said to have "rode as hard and shot as straight as any man".

The closest lodging is in one of New Mexico's few budget **hostels**, in **OSCURO**, a dozen miles north on US-54. The *High Desert Hostel Ranch* (PO Box 798, Carrizozo NM 88301; ☎505/648-4007; ①), has $12 dorm beds and $26 private rooms. Its friendly owners run local tours, and offer a weekly shuttle service to their *Route 66 Hostel* in Albuquerque.

Capitan

A twenty-mile drive up into the mountains east of Carrizozo brings you to the crossroads known as **CAPITAN**, notable only as the birthplace of a little bear named **Smokey**. Rescued from a forest fire in 1950, the five-month-old Smokey was taken to the National Zoo in Washington DC, where he survived another 26 years. His words of wisdom, seen on anti-fire billboards across the country – "Only YOU Can Prevent Forest Fires" – live on. Smokey's grave is the centrepiece of **Smokey Bear Historical State Park**, which also features exhibits on his life, and a short nature trail (daily 9am–5pm; 50¢).

Capitan is plagued by a running feud between people who say "Smokey Bear" (good), and wilful misfits who insist on "Smokey the Bear" (bad).

Capitan's adobe *Hotel Chango* has no guest rooms; it's a top-class **restaurant**, serving a changing menu of gourmet delicacies amid an eclectic collection of folk art (Wed–Sat, dinner only; ☎505/354-4213). The small *Smokey Bear Motel* (☎505/354-4213; ②), does however offer basic **accommodation** near the park.

Lincoln

Though not strictly speaking a ghost town, tiny **LINCOLN**, twelve miles east of Capitan on Hwy-380, is as perfectly preserved a Wild-West settlement as it's possible to imagine. During the late nineteenth century, as a cattle-ranching centre and the site of the Army outpost of **Fort Stanton**, it was home to around 750 people, including the legendary Billy the Kid. Bypassed by the railroads, however, it lost its role as seat of Lincoln County to Carrizozo in 1909; the population soon dwindled to well under a hundred, and time seems to have stood still ever since. No new buildings have joined the venerable false-front structures that line Main Street, and the entire town is now **Lincoln State Monument**. Visitors can stroll its length at any time, while admission to its various historical sites is via a joint ticket sold at each (daily 8.30am–5pm; $5; ☎505/653-4372).

The **Lincoln County Historical Center**, towards the east end of town, is the most modern museum, and its short opening video makes a good introduction to Lincoln's complicated story. After displays covering Hispanics, cowboys, "Buffalo Soldiers" – the black cavalrymen stationed at Fort Stanton – and Apaches, the museum moves on to the Lincoln County War. Prize exhibits include Billy the Kid's knife, holster and what may have been his gun, as well as the coroner's handwritten report on the men shot during his April 1881 escape. Movie posters celebrate celluloid Billies such as Paul Newman, Kris Kristofferson and Val Kilmer, and the museum store has a fun selection of Western souvenirs.

Alongside the museum stands Lincoln's oldest building, the **Torréon**. This circular masonry tower may resemble the handiwork of the ancient Anasazi, but was in fact erected as a refuge against Apache raids by 1850s Hispanic settlers. It's too small to admit visitors; a glance from the street makes it easy to imagine quite how cramped and airless it must have been, and speaks volumes about the miserable, unglamorous reality of frontier life.

A few yards further west, the **Tunstall Store** is an extraordinary time capsule. The "mercantile" over which the Lincoln County War was fought – and which passed from the Tunstall to the Dolan factions as a result – must have failed to sell a single item in the ensuing century. It remains stocked with dusty date-expired groceries, plus Victorian storekeeping paraphernalia like weighing scales and cash registers, cases of photos and artefacts, and even Lincoln County's first-ever light bulb, installed in 1914 and allegedly still capable of burning. The wounded Billy the Kid is said to have hidden beneath the floorboards after shooting Sheriff William Brady on the street outside, on April 1, 1878.

After Dolan took over Tunstall's operation, L G Murphy's original store, across the road and a hundred yards west, became the **Lincoln County Courthouse**, and served as Billy's prison when he was brought back from Mesilla to be hanged. It's hardly surprising that Billy felt he was being railroaded, as evidenced by his increasingly bitter letters to Governor Lew Wallace, displayed downstairs. A bullethole at the foot of the stairs shows where he shot Deputy Bell during his famous escape, while you can stand at the upstairs window through which he then shot Marshal Olinger. Stones in the garden mark where the two men died. That the Courthouse is now so old and musty merely adds to the atmosphere of it all.

Practicalities

Lincoln doesn't have its own visitor center; call the monument offices for general information. On the first weekend of August, the town fills up, and its streets echo with gunfire once again, during the three-day **Old Lincoln Days** festival.

Near the courthouse, the *Wortley Hotel* – once owned by Pat Garrett – had to be rebuilt to its original appearance following a fire in the 1930s

Billy the Kid and the Lincoln County War

The Hispanic farming community of Las Placitas del Río Bonito, founded during the 1850s, was renamed **Lincoln** in 1869. It became the seat of **Lincoln County**, which occupied a quarter of New Mexico – itself much larger than it is today – and was at 27,000 square miles the largest county in the United States. At that time, rival Anglo ranchers and their political allies were competing for economic control throughout the Wild West. What some historians call the **Western Civil War of Incorporation** pitted large cattle-raising conglomerates, federal lawmen and Republican capitalists against small-scale Democrat ranchers and cowboys. Such tensions were everywhere exacerbated by individual antagonisms; Tombstone's **Gunfight at the OK Corral** is a classic example (see p.236).

Lincoln in the 1870s was dominated by a "ring" of men that centred on the mercantile (store) of **Lawrence G Murphy**, an alcoholic Irish former theology student whose business affairs were run by **James J Dolan**. Their racketeering included rustling cattle from local rancher, **John Chisum**, to supply beef at knock-down prices to the US Army at nearby Fort Stanton. The arrival of a wealthy 23-year-old Englishman, **John Tunstall**, who opened a rival mercantile in Lincoln with lawyer **Alexander McSween**, triggered the **Lincoln County War**.

On February 18, 1878, Tunstall was murdered on the road to Ruidoso by a posse of Dolan's men. Among Tunstall's hired hands who witnessed the slaying was the gunslinger history remembers as **Billy the Kid**. Born Henry McCarty in Brooklyn in late 1859, he had been brought west by his mother, who married William Antrim in Santa Fe in 1873. Within a year, she had died in Silver City, and young Billy Antrim was cast adrift. A life of petty teenage crime culminated with the shooting in August 1877 of a bullying Irish blacksmith in Fort Grant, Arizona. Now calling himself **Billy Bonney**, the fledgling outlaw fled to Lincoln.

After Tunstall's death, his men formed the **Regulators**, and were deputized by the local justice of the peace to seek out his killers. Ten of them, including Billy, killed the two chief culprits in March, then gunned down **Sheriff William Brady**, a Dolan man, on Lincoln's main street on April 1. That July, forty of Dolan's supporters laid siege to the Regulators in the adobe home of Alexander McSween; after five days, they summoned soldiers from Fort Stanton, who trained a Gatling gun on the house and set it ablaze. McSween and three Regulators were killed trying to escape the flames, but Billy and around ten others sprinted to safety.

Billy spent two years on the run, mostly rustling cattle near Fort Sumner, where he also dealt cards in the saloon of Texan buffalo hunter

Lincoln's zip code is NM 88338.

(PO Box 96; ☎505/653-4300; ④). It now offers eight plain but appealing hotel rooms, furnished with functional rather than twee Victorian antiques, and its dining room serves simple stews and sandwiches at lunchtime only. If you like a bit more comfort, head to the *Casa de Patrón*, another former store and hideout of Billy the Kid that's now a friendly, romantic B&B, with three en-suite rooms in an 1860 house, two more in a modern annex, and a couple of individual *casitas* (PO Box 27; ☎505/653-4676 or 1-800/524-5202, fax 653-4671; ④–⑥).

Pat Garrett. In 1880, New Mexico's governor **Lew Wallace** offered an amnesty to all participants in the Lincoln County War who would testify against Dolan. Billy accepted the deal and surrendered, only to escape when he realized that Wallace – then busy writing *Ben Hur* – was not going to keep his word. Later that year, Pat Garrett was elected as sheriff of Lincoln County, on a pledge to recapture Billy (who naturally lobbied for his opponent). Garrett knew exactly where to look. Just before Christmas, after ambushing and killing two of Billy's friends at Fort Sumner, he duly captured Billy himself at nearby Stinking Springs. Reporting his arrest, the *Las Vegas Gazette* made the first-ever reference to "Billy the Kid".

Billy was taken by train to Santa Fe and on to **Mesilla** (see p.189), where he was convicted of Sheriff Brady's murder in the only successful prosecution relating to the Lincoln County War. As he awaited the hangman's noose in Lincoln's courthouse – which ironically was the former Murphy store, its owner James Dolan having by now taken over the Tunstall mercantile down the street – Billy committed his most daring **escape**, on April 28, 1881. Taking advantage of a trip to the outhouse, he shot Deputy J W Bell with his own gun. Meanwhile, Marshal Bob Olinger, a long-time Dolan ally, was having lunch with a group of prisoners in the *Wortley Hotel*. Hearing the shots, he raced across the street, to be felled by a blast from an upper window. Eyewitness accounts relate how Billy struggled unsuccessfully for an hour to break his shackles, and repeatedly fell off the horse he was attempting to commandeer, watched all the while by a crowd of onlookers who dared not intervene.

With a $500 reward on his head, Billy fled back to Fort Sumner. Late on the night of July 14, Pat Garrett crept into Pete Maxwell's bedroom to ask if he had seen his friend Billy. Moments earlier, Billy had climbed through the window to find out if Maxwell knew Garrett's whereabouts. Garrett recognized the voice that called *"quien es ?"*– who's there ? – and shot him dead.

The next year, Garrett wrote a bestseller, *The Authentic Life of Billy The Kid, the Noted Desperado of the Southwest*. He was not re-elected as sheriff, however, and embarked on a life of wandering that saw him ranching in Texas, a guest of Theodore Roosevelt at the White House, and a customs collector in El Paso, before he was eventually murdered for no apparent reason near Las Cruces in 1908. Strangely enough, the man who shot him, William Brazel, was the uncle of the main "witness" of the Roswell UFO crash in 1947 (see p.180).

Ruidoso

For visitors from the flatlands of West Texas and Oklahoma – not to mention valley towns like Alamogordo – the hill-top community of **RUIDOSO**, nestling amid the forested Sacramento Mountains thirty miles southwest of Lincoln, offers an enticing weekend retreat from the heat of summer. As a result, it's the fastest-growing resort in the Southwest, with motels and mountain lodges lining several miles of the Ruidoso ("Noisy") River. Tourists from further afield, however, may well find it lacking in interest, though it makes a reasonable overnight stop en route to Carlsbad.

Ruidoso's major claim to fame is the **All-American Futurity**, which was until the 1980s the world's richest **horse race** of any kind, and with prize money totalling over $2.5 million remains the highest-paying event for quarter horses. It's held on Labor Day each year at the **Ruidoso Downs** racetrack, just east of town, as the climax of a 77-day racing season that runs from early May.

All matters equine are celebrated in the **Museum of the Horse**, alongside the racetrack (May to Labor Day daily 9am–5.30pm; Labor Day to Oct daily 10am–5pm; Nov–April Tues–Sun 10am–5pm; $5). Displays on the natural and human-related history of horses plot their arrival in north America – which was really a return, as horses had become extinct on the continent around 7000 BC – and there's a selection of memorabilia from around the world such as horse-drawn Russian sleighs, English road coaches and Wild West stagecoaches. By the time you reach "Anne's Attic", holding collector Anne Stradling's riding trophies and copies of *Black Beauty*, it's all getting a bit sickly, while the huge statue that stands outside – *Free Spirits of Noisy Water*, portraying eight lifesize horses – is too sentimental for words.

In winter, attention turns to the 12,000ft slopes of **Ski Apache** (☎505/336-4565), a downhill ski area northwest of town where lift tickets cost around $40 per day. Though operated by the Mescalero Apache, it's not on tribal land – they bought it as a going concern.

Practicalities

Brochures from Ruidoso's **visitor center**, 720 Sudderth Ave (Mon–Sat 9am–5pm, Sun 1–4pm; ☎505/257-7395 or 1-800/253-2255), list dozens of **motels**, but supply still fails to meet demand on big race days. Among inexpensive options are the *Apache Motel*, 344 Sudderth Ave (☎505/257-2986 or 1-800/426-0616; ②), and the *Super 8*, beside US-70 at 100 Cliff Drive (☎505/378-8180 or 1-800/800-8000; ②), which has separate male and female saunas. **B&Bs** in the immediate vicinity include the welcoming *Sierra Mesa Lodge*, ten miles north near the ski area at Fort Stanton Rd in the village of Alto (PO Box 463, Alto NM 88312; ☎505/336-4515; ⑤).

The real local showpiece, however, is the glitzy *Inn of the Mountain Gods*, on Carrizo Canyon Road (PO Box 269, Mescalero NM 88340; ☎505/257-5141 or 1-800/545-9011, fax 257-6173; winter ⑤, summer ⑥). Owned and run by the Mescalero Apache, it offers ski packages, casino gambling, golf, fishing, tennis and horse riding, while its excellent *Dan Li Ka* ("good food") **restaurant** serves steak and seafood entrees for under $20, and nightly specials with a more thoroughly Southwestern (read hot) twist.

Other dining possibilities range from the classy French cuisine of *La Lorraine*, 2523 Sudderth Ave (closed Sun; ☎505/257-2954), to the steaks at the *Inncredible*, near Ski Apache on Hwy-48 in Alto (closed Sun; ☎505/336-4312) and the wholesome snacks at the *Hummingbird Tearoom*, in the Village Plaza at 2306 Sudderth Drive (lunch only, closed Sun; ☎505/257-2100).

Mescalero Apache Indian Reservation

Immediately south of Ruidoso, US-70 runs for around fifteen miles through the highlands of the **Mescalero Apache Indian Reservation**. The Mescalero as a distinct Apache group trace their history back to the early eighteenth century, when like the Jicarilla of northern New Mexico (see p.149) they were driven from the plains by the Comanche and turned to a lifestyle partly of farming and partly of raiding Pueblo and Hispanic settlements. After being rounded up by Kit Carson in 1862 and confined with the Navajo at Fort Sumner (see p.168), they were granted this small reservation in the 1880s, which was too high to grow or gather many of their traditional foods. The Mescalero were later joined by other Apache refugees, such as those remnants of Geronimo's Chiricahua who in 1913 chose to return to the Southwest from their enforced exile in Oklahoma. Together with their successful investment in Ski Apache, revenues from gaming at the *Inn of the Mountain Gods* (see opposite), have greatly strengthened the tribal economy in recent years, while Apache cowboys ride the open range between Ruidoso and Cloudcroft in pursuit of their errant cattle.

Cloudcroft

Much smaller and cosier than Ruidoso, forty miles north, the picturesque mountain village of **CLOUDCROFT** has been a vacation resort from the word go. It was built in 1898, after a railroad spur was pushed up into the Sacramento Mountains in order to carry mountain timbers down to El Paso, and immediately began to attract day-trippers from the sweltering valley below. These days the railroad has gone, so drivers who have never rounded a curve in their lives now twist their wary way up US-82 to find a pretty little Western town with no great history or significance but plenty of appealing souvenir stores and cafes to while away an afternoon.

Practicalities

Cloudcroft's **visitor center** is on US-82 as you approach from the west (Mon–Sat 10am–5pm, Sun 11am–3pm; ☎505/682-2733), but the main focus of interest is the boardwalk of **Burro Avenue**, one block north of the highway. Here you'll find an assortment of restaurants, such as the lively Mexican/American *Kokopelli's*, upstairs at no. 306 (☎505/682-2009), and the sandwich-and-espresso cafe *Backstreet Eats*, behind the *High Altitude* bike store nearby.

Across the highway, up the slope from the visitor center, *The Lodge at Cloudcroft* ranks among the Southwest's most prestigious

Cloudcroft's
zip code is NM
88317.

historic hotels (PO Box 497; ☎505/682-2566 or 1-800/395-6343 in
NM, fax 682-2715; ④–⑨). As well as surprisingly well-priced B&B
rooms, it features some absurdly plush suites and private cottages,
and is home to *Rebecca's*, an attractive continental restaurant with
panoramic views.

Several motel-style clusters of wooden cabins along the highway
provide cheap accommodation for hikers and skiers, including the
bright red *Buckhorn Cabins*, where each cabin can sleep four guests
(☎505-682-2421; ③). In addition, the Forest Service runs summer-
only **campgrounds** along Hwy-244 towards Ruidoso; the closest to
town, about a mile northeast of the centre, is *The Pines* (mid-May to
mid-Sept; ☎505/682-2551).

Alamogordo

ALAMOGORDO, sprawled at the foot of the Sacramento Mountains
seventy miles northeast of Las Cruces, is like Los Alamos a child of
the Bomb. Once a quiet ranching centre, it has grown since World
War II to a town of thirty thousand inhabitants, most of whom owe
their living to the various military bases and research facilities
tucked away in the surrounding deserts. Its original central streets
remain oddly atmospheric, but they're now a neglected backwater
compared to the frenzy of commercial activity along the five-mile
strip of US-54, here known as **White Sands Boulevard**.

Given pride of place at the **Alamogordo Museum**, 1301 N White
Sands Blvd (Mon–Sat 10am–4pm; free), an old electric toaster from
Howards Cafe bears witness to quite how little ever happens round
these parts. Other exhibits include a headdress worn by Geronimo,
and the stuffed head of a grizzly bear.

Any five-storey building in Alamogordo would probably be a tourist
attraction; that the gleaming glass cube on the hillside east of town
holds the **International Space Hall of Fame** is gilding the lily (summer daily 9am–6pm; winter daily 9am–5pm; museum $2.50, theatre
$4.50, combined ticket $6). Displays inside trace the history of rock-
etry from eleventh-century China onwards, covering New-Mexico-
based pioneers Robert Goddard (see p.181) and Wernher von Braun
(see p.180) – one snap of von Braun's cheery crew sitting astride a V-
2 rocket is straight out of *Dr Strangelove* – up to the futuristic Delta
Clipper, designed to replace the Space Shuttle and offer the first commercial spaceflights. A diorama depicts the unfortunate Ham, who
became the first chimp in space in 1961, and was trained at
Alamagordo by receiving electric shocks or banana-flavoured pellets
according to which lever he moved. There's also a mock-up Martian
landscape – not something it's all that hard to create in New Mexico.
The adjoining **Clyde W Tombaugh Omnimax Theater** shows giant-
screen movies and doubles as a state-of-the-art **planetarium**, while
the "garden" of abandoned rockets outside was used by Bob Dole for
a rally during the dying moments of his 1996 Presidential bid.

Practicalities

Alamogordo's **visitor center** is alongside the local museum at 1301 N White Sands Blvd (Mon–Sat 8.30am–5pm, Sun 1–5pm; ☎505/437-6120 or 1-800/826-0294 in NM, 1-800/545-4021 elsewhere). **Motels** along US-54 range from the *Super 8*, north of town at 3204 N White Sands Blvd (☎505/434-4205 or 1-800/800-8000; ②), to the large, low, stylish *Holiday Inn*, to the south at 1401 S White Sands Blvd (☎505/437-7100 or 1-800/465-4329; ④).

As for **food**, *Keg's Brewery*, a mile west of the highway at 817 Scenic Drive (closed Sun; ☎505/437-9564), is a Fifties-themed diner that has successfully re-invented itself as a microbrewery while still serving good meals. If coffee and a snack will do, head for *Mastroddi's Espresso Cafe & Bagels*, appropriately at 804 New York Ave (☎505/437-2323) in the heart of downtown.

White Sands National Monument

The glistening, three-storey dunes of **White Sands** fill 275 square miles of the broad Tularosa Basin, between the Sacramento and San Andres Mountains. Though their whiteness is beyond dispute, they're not in fact sand, but fine **gypsum**, deposited on an ancient seabed 250 million years ago. Anywhere else, they'd have dissolved, and been carried off by rivers; here, however, they're trapped in a riverless ring of mountains. The southern portion of this surreal landscape has been set aside as **WHITE SANDS NATIONAL MONUMENT**, entered north of US-70 fourteen miles west of Alamogordo.

*Roughly twice each week, both US-70 and the Dunes Drive **close** for up to two hours while missile tests are underway.*

Beside the highway, the **visitor center** (summer daily 8am–7pm; winter daily 8am–4.30pm; ☎505/479-6124) illustrates the unique bleached life-forms that have adapted to suit this pallid environment. From there, the eight-mile paved **Dunes Drive** (summer daily 7am–10pm; winter daily 7am–sunset; $4), loops through the heart of the dunes. At first, as you drive beyond the entrance station and get your first glimpses of white sand beneath the scrubby vegetation, you may wonder what the fuss is about. Gradually, however, the plants thin out, and you come to an utterly surreal landscape of dazzling white knife-edge ridges and graceful slopes. The west winds that constantly replenish the dunes pile sand across the pavement in luxuriant drifts. Plentiful pull-outs enable you to leave your vehicle and plough through pristine sand to the top of the ridges, which offer long-range mountain views. Slipping and sliding back down again is even better.

There's no developed **campground** at White Sands, but backcountry camping is allowed, by permit only.

White Sands Missile Range Museum

A couple of miles north of the national monument boundary, on the top-security White Sands Missile Range, the **White Sands Space Harbor** holds one of the three seven-mile runways where the **Space**

Shuttle is able to land. A back-up facility to the regular landing sites in California and Florida, it has only been used once, in 1982.

For the full story, head for the **White Sands Missile Range Museum**, thirty miles west of the monument en route to Las Cruces, and four miles south of US-70 (Mon–Fri 8am–4.30pm; free). The open-air **Missile Park** alongside offers a chance to inspect "the weapons that won the cold war", and displays all the missiles ever tested at White Sands. These date back to "Vengeance Weapon 2", the **V-2** rocket, almost four thousand of which were fired across the English Channel by the Nazis during World War II. After the war, the weapon's designer, Dr Wernher von Braun, directed the firing of sixty more V-2s at White Sands – one went astray and crashed across the border near Ciudad Juarez, Mexico – before he moved on to Huntsville, Alabama in 1950.

The southeast corner

East of the mountains, at the edge of the Great Plains, **southeast New Mexico** has little in common with the rest of the Southwest. It's not quite as dull as it looks, however; all its treasures are tucked away under the ground, in the shape not only of the oil and mineral wealth that keeps its economy ticking over, but also of the fairy-tale labyrinth of **Carlsbad Caverns National Park**, which is the only reason tourists ever stray this way.

Roswell

Seventy-five miles north of Carlsbad, the small ranching town of **ROSWELL** is renowned as the spot near which an **alien spacecraft** supposedly crashlanded on the night of July 4, 1947. The commander of the local air force base authorized a press statement announcing that they had retrieved the wreckage of a flying saucer, which had been taken away for examination. Despite a follow-up denial within a day, claiming that it was in fact a weather balloon, the story has kept running. As 100,000 *X-Files* fanatics descended upon Roswell for a six-day festival to mark the "Incident's" fiftieth anniversary, in 1997, the US Air Force revealed that the errant balloon had been monitoring the atmosphere for evidence of Soviet nuclear tests. Witnesses were also said to have confused the balloon crash with a series of parachute experiments in 1953, which involved the dropping of dummies from high-altitude planes. UFO theorists, however, remain unconvinced. Considerable vagueness surrounds exactly where the crash took place, incidentally. Since a local entrepreneur bought up one purported site, the original witnesses have started to "remember" that it all happened somewhere else entirely.

Each of the two **museums** in town devoted to the "Roswell Incident" has its own particular lunacies to offer. Despite its best intentions, and the wishful thinking of the truly weird clientele who drift in from the plains, the central **International UFO Museum**, 400–402 N Main St (daily 11am–5pm; free), inadvertently exposes the whole tawdry business as transparent nonsense. Run by the military press officer responsible for the 1947 announcement, it reveals such gems as that John Kennedy was shot because he was about to reveal the secret, and that Neil Armstrong, astonished at encountering flying saucers on the moon, blurted out "Boy, were they beige!" (You'd have to assume that "big" was the word he was fumbling for.) Its showpiece is a model of the **"alien autopsy"**, said to have taken place at the Wright-Patterson Airforce Base in Dayton, Ohio, later the venue for the Bosnian peace talks (conspiracy theorists see that as no coincidence). Built for the movie *Roswell*, you can't help suspecting it also featured in the grainy "documentary" autopsy footage that created a brief international sensation in 1995.

There's another chance to have your photo taken with a "little grey", as those who know their aliens like to call them, at the even tackier **UFO Enigma Museum**, a long way south at 6108 S Main St (Mon–Sat 9am–5pm, Sun noon–5pm; $1). Here it's not dead on a slab, but alive and keen to make friends – unlike two of its unfortunate hand-knitted companions, which lie strewn in silver jumpsuits beside their disabled spaceship nearby.

By way of contrast, the long-standing **Roswell Museum**, 100 W 11th St (Mon–Sat 9am–5pm, Sun 1–5pm, free), boasts an excellent, multi-faceted collection with nary an alien corpse to be seen. Its most sensational section celebrates pioneer rocket scientist **Robert Goddard** (1882–1945), one of whose early experiments prompted the newspaper headline *'Moon Rocket' Man's Test Alarms Whole Countryside*. His entire laboratory has been reconstructed, and an entertaining video shows him wheeling a rudimentary rocket in a wagon to the launch pad, then racing to escape the blast in a model T Ford. Elsewhere, historical artefacts range from armour and pikes brought by Spanish conquistadors, by way of an Apache Ghost Dancer's shirt, to astronaut Harrison Schmitt's spacesuit. There's also a huge, top-quality **art gallery**, displaying Southwestern landscapes by Henriette Wyeth and Peter Hurd, and Georgia O'Keeffe's *Ram's Skull With Brown Leaves*.

Practicalities

Roswell's **visitor center** is near the Roswell Museum at 912 N Main St (Mon–Sat 9am–5pm; ☎505/623-5698). The finest **motel** in town, the *Best Western Sally Port Inn*, 2000 N Main St (☎505/622-6430 or 1-800/548-5221, fax 623-7631; ④), also has a good restaurant; if you just want a place to lay your head the *Super 8*, 3575 N Main St (☎505/622-8886 or 1-800/800-8000; ②), and the *Frontier Motel*, 3010 N Main St (☎505/622-1400 or 1-800/678-1401; ②), are

cheaper. The *Cattle Baron*, 1113 N Main St (☎505/622-2465), is a
large, good-value **steakhouse** with an extensive salad bar, while the
Blues Coffee Bar, 305 N Main St, serves a decent espresso.

Carlsbad

Considering that a million tourists per year pass through **CARLS-
BAD** en route to Carlsbad Caverns National Park – covered below –
the town itself is astonishing in its mundanity. A century of ranching
and potash-mining has given it a sizeable if characterless downtown
area, but the one significant attraction is the **Living Desert State
Park**, a couple of miles northwest (summer daily 8am–8pm, winter
daily 9am–5pm; last admission 1hr 30min before closing; $3). This
botanical garden of desert plants doubles as a zoo that houses elk,
bear, rattlesnakes, and a prairie dog village.

Practicalities

Carlsbad's **visitor center**, at 302 S Canal St (Mon–Fri 8am–5pm;
☎505/887-6516 or 1-800/221-1221), can supply copious lists of
local **motels**. Central options include the *Holiday Inn*, 601 S Canal
St (☎505/885-8500 or 1-800/742-9586, fax 887-5999; winter ③,
summer ④), while cheaper alternatives like the clean, comfortable
Super 8, 3817 National Parks Hwy (☎505/887-8888 or 1-800/800-
8000; winter ②, summer ③), line US-62/180 to the southwest.

*Carlsbad's **zip
code** is NM
88220.*

   Decent places to **eat** are much harder to find, but at least *Beaver's
Restaurant*, 1620 S Canal St (closed Mon & Tues; ☎505/885-
4515), has a big menu, with three-course dinners for just $6, lots of
breaded seafood, and the usual Mexican options. *Le Chelle's*, 807 N
Canal St (closed Sun; ☎505/885-1572), serves espresso coffees and
lunchtime "subwiches".

Carlsbad Caverns National Park

*Note that
there's no
camping at
the national
park; the near-
est camp-
grounds and
motels are at
White's City
and Carlsbad.*

CARLSBAD CAVERNS NATIONAL PARK consists of a tract of the
Guadalupe Mountains that's so riddled with underground caves and
tunnels as to be virtually hollow. Tamed in classic park-service style
with concrete trails and electric lighting, this subterranean wonderland is now a walk-in gallery, where tourists come in droves to marvel at its intricate limestone tracery. Before you decide whether to
join them, however, be sure to grasp that the park is a *long* way from
anywhere else – three hundred miles southeast of Albuquerque, and
150 miles northeast of El Paso, Texas.

   The Guadalupe Mountains are the remnants of the **Capitan Reef**, a
400-mile-long horseshoe-shaped reef that formed beneath the waters
of a primeval ocean. Made up of algae and sponges rather than coral,
it was thrust above the plains a mere three million years ago. In the
process, cracks were created through which surface moisture has
trickled ever since, gnawing at the rock within. Almost all park visitors

confine their attention to the main cave, **Carlsbad Cavern** itself, and the summer crowds can get pretty intense. In a strange way, though, that's part of the fun – coming to Carlsbad feels like a real throwback to the great 1950s boom in mass tourism. If you're not convinced, wait until you see the gloriously kitsch Underground Lunchroom.

The
southeast
corner

Arrival and information

The park headquarters is reached by driving twenty miles southwest of the town of Carlsbad on US-62/180, then turning west at **White's City** to climb another seven miles. This narrow, twisting road ends atop the mountains, with sweeping views east across the plains. Part of a complex that includes a restaurant, a gift store, a crèche and even a kennel, the **visitor center** is the place to pay entrance fees, and pick up details of the day's programme of tours (summer daily 8am–7pm; winter daily 8am–5.30pm; ☎505/785-2232).

To receive information by mail, write to Carlsbad Caverns National Park, 3225 National Parks Hwy, Carlsbad NM 88220.

The standard park fee of $5 for three days covers access to **Carlsbad Cavern** by elevator or on foot. For additional fees that range from $4 to $12 you can also join guided tours to otherwise inaccessible parts of the main cavern, or of **Slaughter Canyon Cave**, as detailed on p.184. Some tours require participants to carry flashlights, or even to wear kneepads. All tours can be reserved in advance, using *Visa* or *Mastercard*, on ☎505/785-2232 ext 429.

Carlsbad Cavern

The centrepiece of Carlsbad Cavern, the **Big Room**, lies 750 vertical feet below the visitor center – though being inside the mountain, in places it's also 400 feet horizontally from the open air. Measuring up to 1800 feet long and 250 feet high, it's festooned with stalactites, stalagmites, and countless unnameable shapes of swirling liquid rock. All are a uniform stone grey; the rare touches of colour are provided by slight red or brown mineral-rich tinges, improved here and there with gentle pastel lighting. Most visitors take an hour or so to complete the reasonably level trail around its perimeter. Whatever the weather up top – and summer highs exceed 100°F – the temperature down here is always a cool 56°F, so dress warm.

Golden Eagle passes (see p.21) are not accepted at Carlsbad Caverns; Golden Access and Golden Age passes (see p.31 and p.32) earn fifty percent discounts.

Direct **elevators** drop to the Big Room from the visitor center (summer first down 8.30am, last up 6.30pm; winter first down 8.30am, last up 4.55pm). They arrive alongside the **Underground Lunchroom**, a vast formation-free side cave paved over in the 1950s to create a diner-cum-souvenir-store that sells indigestible lunches in polystyrene containers, plus Eisenhower-era souvenirs like giant pencils and *Viewmaster* reels. To modern eyes, this strange installation seems absurd, but moves to close it down have been stymied by its place in popular affections.

To get a better sense of the cavern's depth, eschew the elevator and **walk** down via the **Natural Entrance Route** (last entry summer 3.30pm, winter 2pm). This steep paved footpath switchbacks into

All visitors to the cavern are obliged to ride the elevator back out.

the guano-encrusted maw of the cave, a short way from the visitor center, taking fifteen minutes to reach the first of the formations and another fifteen to reach the Big Room itself. 50¢ rents a "radio stick" that delivers a crackling commentary as you go.

The main appeal of walking down used to be that the trail meandered through beautiful side caves such as the **King's Palace** and the **Queen's Chamber**, filled with translucent "draperies" of limestone. These were however closed to casual visitors in 1993, as formations were being broken at the rate of two thousand per year. They're now open on guided tours only, which start from the Big Room (daily 9am, 11am, 1pm & 3pm; $4).

The rest of the park

The park's other readily accessible cave is **Slaughter Canyon Cave**, 25 miles southwest of the visitor center. Much less frequented, and much less developed, it can only be explored on two-hour guided tours (usually summer daily 10am & 1pm, winter Sat & Sun 10am & 1pm; call for exact schedule; $8). To get there, drive five miles south of White's City on US-62/180, then eleven miles west on Hwy-418, and finally hike the steep half-mile up to the cave entrance.

Slaughter Canyon Cave still appears as "New Cave" on some maps, but it's been renamed to avoid confusion since the discovery of **Lechuguilla Cave**. Revealed after cavers cleared a thirty-foot plug of bat dung and rubble in 1986, the astonishing Lechuguilla cave system is not only deeper than Carlsbad Cavern but at 1600 feet has turned out to be the deepest in the US. Sixty miles of tunnels have been mapped so far, but they're so dangerous that Lechuguilla is off limits to all but the experts. It's expected to remain a "wilderness cave" – even its location is kept secret – so the rest of us will have to content ourselves with the marvellous pictures of its delicate crystalline formations in the visitor center.

White's City

WHITE'S CITY, twenty miles southwest of Carlsbad at the turn-off for Carlsbad Caverns, is not a town but a privately owned tourist complex that provides the closest accommodation and camping to the national park. All its components share the same address and phone number (17 Carlsbad Caverns Hwy, White's City NM 88268; ☎505/785-2291 or 1-800/CAVERNS). They include the mock-adobe *Best Western Cavern Inn*, on both sides of the highway (④), the *White's City RV Park*, which has tent camping space, and the *Velvet Garter Restaurant*. The minivan shuttles up to the park ($15 round-trip) might be convenient for passengers arriving on the thrice-daily *Greyhound* Carlsbad–El Paso **buses** (☎505/887-1108).

White's City also boasts the ultra-tacky **Million Dollar Museum** (daily 7am–8pm; $2.50), an assortment of decrepit dolls' houses, two-headed snakes, old shoes and arrowheads, and human corpses, in the nauseating form of a "7000-year-old cliff dwelling baby".

Hobbs

Unless it's on your route home, it's hard to know what impulse might carry you seventy miles east of Carlsbad to **HOBBS**, in New Mexico's far southeastern corner. Surrounded by endless dusty flatlands punctuated only by dementedly bobbing oil-pumps, this 30,000-strong community holds nothing to divert visitors. If you're sure there must be more to it than meets the eye, a handful of cheap motels – such as the *Super 8*, 722 N Marland Blvd (☎505/397-7511 or 1-800/800-8000; ②) – will be baffled to accept your custom.

The Rio Grande valley

The 260-mile route **south from Albuquerque**, to El Paso, Texas, and the Mexican border, follows one of America's oldest and most romantic trails. For 250 years, the **Camino Real** or "Royal Road" beside the Rio Grande gave the Hispanic colonists of New Mexico their one tenuous link with the outside world. Now, however, it's a monotonous four-hour drive on I-25, with little to divert the eye apart from distant views of the mountains that rear to either side. You don't even see much of the river itself, except where it's been dammed to form incongruous turquoise lakes around **Truth or Consequences**. Of the old way stations en route, only **Socorro** in the north and **Mesilla** in the south are particularly worth visiting.

Isleta Pueblo

The only New Mexican pueblo south of Albuquerque, **ISLETA PUEBLO**, lies just off the interstate a dozen miles from downtown. The sole survivor of the many pueblos encountered by early Spanish

The Rio Grande valley

explorers along the lower Rio Grande, it served in the seventeenth century as a refuge where Tiwa peoples gathered to resist the threat of Apache raids. At the time of the Pueblo Revolt, those Isletans who chose not to accompany the Spanish retreat southwards – where they founded the pueblo of **Tigua**, outside El Paso – fled west to join the Hopi in what's now Arizona. Isleta itself was repopulated in 1718, and remains home to almost four thousand people.

For more about visiting New Mexico's pueblos, and a full calendar of festivals, see p.124.

Although the tribal lands mark a verdant interruption amid the dormitory communities that line the interstate's first fifty miles, the reservation is plagued by river-borne pollution from the industries of Albuquerque. Economically it's dependent on its huge neighbour; a high proportion of Isletans work in the city, and the tribe also runs a 24-hour **casino** (11000 Broadway Blvd SE). Every day during daylight hours, visitors have free access to the principal pueblo village – also known as **SHIAW-IBA** – where the main attraction is the white-walled **mission church** of San Agustín de Isleta. In addition, Isleta stages major festivals on August 28 and September 4.

Socorro

Historic **SOCORRO**, eighty miles south of Albuquerque, received its unusual name – "help", in Spanish – from Don Juan de Oñate in 1598, after local Pueblo peoples fed his expeditionary party from their reserves of corn. The first Hispanic settlement was destroyed during the Pueblo Revolt of 1680, whereafter the site was abandoned for over a century. Both the picturesque **plaza** at its core, and the imposing adobe church of **San Miguel** a couple of blocks north (daily 6am–6pm; free), were re-built during the 1820s. Sixty years later, triggered by the arrival of the railroads and the discovery of extensive **silver** deposits nearby, Socorro briefly became New Mexico's largest town. When the silver ran out, so too did most of the population, leaving behind some fine Victorian architecture.

Practicalities

Socorro's zip code is NM 87801.

For a self-guided walking tour of Socorro, call in at the **visitor center**, north of the centre at 103 Francisco de Avondo (Mon–Fri 8am–5pm, Sat 9am–5pm; ☎505/835-0424). The most central **budget motel** is the *Sands*, 205 California St NW (☎505/835-1130; ②); the smarter *Super 8* is further out at 1121 Frontage Rd NW (☎505/835-4626 or 1-800/800-8000; winter ②, summer ③), while *Eaton House*, 403 Eaton Ave (☎505/835-1067; ⑤), is a luxurious central **B&B** with three en-suite rooms and two guest *casitas*. As for **food**, the atmospheric *Val Verde Steak House*, housed in a former hotel east of the plaza at 203 Manzanares Ave (☎505/835-3380), is open daily for lunch and dinner.

The Jornada del Muerto

Early Hispanic travellers on the Camino Real were so prone to Apache attack if they followed the curve of the Rio Grande between Socorro and Las Cruces that they preferred to take a hundred-mile shortcut behind the mountains that lie east of the river. This route too had its perils – not least a complete lack of water – and became known as the **Jornada del Muerto**, or Dead Man's Route, after Juan de Oñate's chaplain Fray Cristóbal de Salazar died here in the early 1600s. A long litany of subsequent deaths gave it a terrible reputation, and to this day there's no north–south road through the desert.

The point where the old trail crossed the river, twenty miles south of Socorro on Hwy-1, is now the **Bosque del Apache Wildlife Refuge**, the Southwest's most spectacular **bird-watching** site (Nov–March daily 7am–5pm; April–Oct Mon–Fri 7am–5pm; ☎505/835-1828). As migratory birds arrive for the winter, in early December, it can hold as many as twenty thousand sandhill cranes and almost fifty thousand snow geese; even in summer, its riverine marshes and forests are bursting with birds and mammals.

Truth or Consequences

Until 1950, the minor spa town seventy miles south of Socorro was appropriately known as **Hot Springs**. Then the radio show *Truth or Consequences* promised that any community prepared to change its name would receive the meagre reward of hosting its tenth anniversary edition. Hot Springs prostituted itself for fifteen minutes of fame, and **TRUTH OR CONSEQUENCES** was saddled with the world's worst name – though locals habitually abbreviate it these days to "**T or C**".

Many of the region's **thermal springs** – where Apache warriors such as Geronimo once soaked away the worries of the warpath – are now run as private bathhouses, with prices starting at around $3 for a twenty-minute session. Native American memorabilia, including Mimbres pottery (see p.193) form a prominent part of the historical collection at the **Geronimo Springs Museum**, 211 Main St (Mon–Sat 9am–5pm, Sun 1–4pm; $2). You can also learn fascinating snippets about **Ralph Edwards**, presenter of the long-defunct *Truth or Consequences* show, who still returns each year for the **Truth or Consequences Fiesta**, on the first weekend in May.

Practicalities

T or C's small downtown consists of a couple of blocks sandwiched between two busy one-way streets, Broadway and Main Street. That's where you'll find the **visitor center**, just off Main St at 201 Foch St (Mon–Fri 9am–5pm; ☎505/894-3536 or 1-800/831-9487), but most of the better **motels** are well to the north, near

Carrie

6 pm Conf 241 924 908

interstate exit 79. These include the *Best Western Hot Springs Inn*, 2270 N Date St (☎505/894-6665 or 1-800/528-1234; ④), where there's a pool and a steakhouse, and the *Super 8*, 2151 N Date St (☎505/894-7888 or 1-800/800-8000, fax 894-7883; ③). Beside the Rio Grande in the heart of town, however, the lovely *Riverbend Hot Springs Hostel*, 100 Austin St (☎505/894-6183; ①–②), offers $12 dorm beds, private rooms and suites, and even individual tepees, and also has spring-fed hot tubs. *La Cocina*, 280 Date St (☎505/894-6499) is a good Mexican **restaurant**, while *Touch of Seattle*, 1806 S Broadway (closed Sun; ☎505/894-9460), is an appealing coffee- and snack-bar adjoining the *Downhome Laundry* in the suburb of Williamsburg.

Hillsboro

Hwy-152 branches west from I-25 fifteen miles south of T or C, crossing the Mimbres Mountain en route to **Silver City** (see p.191). **HILLSBORO**, less than twenty miles off the interstate in the fertile foothills, is a former gold-mining settlement that has since turned its hand to apple-growing instead. Now no more than a village, with a small crop of arts-and-crafts galleries, it also boasts the *Enchanted Villa* (PO Box 456, Hillsboro NM 88042; ☎505/895-5686; ③), a bright and attractive whitewashed adobe **B&B**.

Hatch

Forty miles south of T or C, halfway down I-25 towards Las Cruces, tiny **HATCH** is noteworthy only as the home of New Mexico's leading **chile farms**. All year, roadside stalls sell fresh peppers and the dried garlands known as *ristras*, while Labor Day weekend sees a **Chile Festival** with fiercely competitive chile cook-offs. *Dora's*, 401 E Hall St (☎505/267-9294), is renowned for fiery Mexican cuisine.

For advance details of the Chile Festival, call ☎505/267-5050.

Las Cruces

Named after "the Crosses" that marked the graves of early travellers killed by the Apache, **LAS CRUCES** is now a major crossroads, where the east–west I-10 meets the north–south I-25. Once a riverside farming community, it has grown beyond recognition in recent years, but the boom in industrial and military employment has been at the expense of any scenic beauty it may once have possessed. Now Las Cruces is simply a place to hurry through, with any time you can spare for sightseeing better spent in neighbouring Mesilla.

Practicalities

Las Cruces' downtown **visitor center**, 211 N Water St (Mon–Fri 8am–5pm, Sat 9am–1pm; ☎505/524-8521 or 1-800/343-7827), has lists of all the **motels** you'd expect, including a couple of

*Super 8*s – the handiest is at 245 La Posada Lane (☎505/523-8695 or 1-800/800-8000; ②) – and the *Best Western Mission Inn*, 1765 S Main St (☎505/524-8591 or 1-800/528-1234; ③). The *Inn of the Arts*, 618 S Alameda Blvd (☎505/526-3326 or 1-888/526-3326; ④), is a **B&B inn** where each room is named for regional artists such as Maria Martínez or Georgia O'Keeffe, and furnished appropriately.

Las Cruces'
zip code is NM
88005.

The slogan of *Nellie's Cafe*, 1226 W Hadley Ave (☎505/524-9982) – "*Chiles with Attitude*" – tells you what to expect: sublimely spicy Mexican food. Blander snacks are readily available in the fast-food court of **Mesilla Valley Mall**, west of I-25 at Lohman Avenue.

Mesilla

The little-changed Hispanic village of **MESILLA** stands just south of I-10 two miles west of Las Cruces, an easy drive down the Avenida de Mesilla from downtown. When New Mexico passed into American hands in 1846, the Mesilla Valley still belonged to Mexico, and Mesilla itself was founded in 1850 by New Mexicans who preferred to remain Mexican. Under the **Gadsden Purchase**, however, signed here in 1853, it passed to the US, and soon became one of the Southwest's largest towns, with over eight thousand inhabitants. During the Civil War, Mesilla even served briefly as the Confederate capital of the territory of Arizona, but it went into swift decline when the railroad bypassed it in favour of Las Cruces in 1881.

Mesilla's delightful Old-West **plaza** has a real frontier feel to it, even though most of the old adobes that surround it – including the former courthouse where **Billy the Kid** was tried and sentenced to death in 1881 – now house art galleries and souvenir shops. Gift stores such as *La Zia* and *Del Sol* stock interesting Southwest souvenirs and jewellery leavened with some much cheaper Mexican crafts, while the *Mesilla Book Center* has an excellent selection of local literature. Two blocks east, the small **Gadsen Museum** (Mon–Sat 9–11am & 1–5pm, Sun 1–5pm; $2), recounts the town's history and details the events that lead to the Gadsen Purchase.

For more on
Billy the Kid,
see p.174.

Practicalities

The *Mesón de Mesilla*, 1803 Avenida de Mesilla (PO Box 1212, Mesilla NM 88046; ☎505/525-9212 or 1-800/732-6025; ③–⑥), is a luxury thirteen-room **B&B** five minutes' walk east of the plaza, offering gorgeous mountain views, an outdoor pool and a top-class gourmet dining room. **Restaurants** on the plaza itself include the *Double Eagle* (☎505/523-6700), which has indoor and outdoor seating and serves steaks, shark, and even ostrich for lunch and dinner daily, and *El Patio*, a Mexican *cantina* in the former offices of the Butterfield Stage Coach (closed Sun; ☎505/524-0982).

Southwest New Mexico

Most of New Mexico's sparsely populated **southwest corner** – also known as the *"Bootheel"*, for the way it steps down into Mexico – consists of open rangeland that's devoid of interest for travellers. Interstate towns like **Deming** and **Lordsburg** are entirely forgettable, though a detour north into the mountains takes you to the mining town of **Silver City**, and the ancient **Gila Cliff Dwellings**.

Deming

DEMING, sixty miles due west of Las Cruces, is a typical desert outpost, scattered with motels and diners. If you're ready for a break, however, the **Deming Luna Mimbres Museum**, 301 S Silver Ave (Mon–Sat 9am–4pm, Sun 1.30–4pm; free), has some surprisingly good displays, including cabinets of Mimbres pottery (see p.193) and a great show of minerals and gemstones. Assuming you have a pick-axe handy, you're allowed to take away whatever agates, onyx or geodes you can prise from the arid slopes of **Rock Hound State Park**, ten miles southeast (daily 7.30am–dusk; $3).

Practicalities

Deming is served by *Amtrak* **trains** – daily except Friday, in alternate directions but always at around 2.30pm – and more frequent *Greyhound* **buses**, 300 E Spruce St (☎505/546-3881). The **visitor center** is at the east end of downtown, 800 E Pine St (daily 9am–5pm; ☎505/546-2674 or 1-800/848-4955). Budget **motels** along the main drag, parallel to the interstate, include a *Super 8*, 1217 W Pine St (☎505/546-0481 or 1-800/800-8000; ②), and the *Deming Motel*, 500 W Pine St (☎505/546-2737; ①).

Pancho Villa State Park

In sleepy **COLUMBUS**, thirty miles south of Deming, just north of the Mexican border, the site where the thousand-strong forces of Mexican revolutionary Pancho Villa did battle in 1916 against the US cavalry, is now **Pancho Villa State Park** (daily 8am–5pm; $3). A small museum chronicles the last invasion of the US, and the adjoining sixty-acre desert botanical garden makes a nice place to **camp** (except in summer, when it's baking hot).

If you fancy a *cerveza* or two, the frontier with neighbouring **LAS PALOMAS**, three miles south in Mexico, remains open day or night. Border formalities are minimal, though foreign travellers must be sure to carry their passports.

Silver City

Six thousand feet up in the Mogollon mountains, **SILVER CITY** stands roughly fifty miles northwest and northeast respectively from the I-10 towns of Deming and Lordsburg. As you drive up from the interstate, however, it's easy not to notice that you're climbing – the region has been so extensively **mined** that many of the hills that lay to the south of Silver City have been completely carved away.

Ancient peoples knew this region as a source of top-quality **turquoise**, but the Hispanic settlement of La Cienaga de San Vicente was only founded in 1804, soon after some friendly Apaches showed the Spanish soldier Jose Manuel Carrasco where to find **copper**. The Santa Rita copper mine was however repeatedly attacked by the Apache, and was abandoned altogether in 1838. Only when **silver** was discovered after the Civil War was the town re-established, with a new name and a rip-roaring reputation. **Billy the Kid** spent most of his childhood here; according to some stories he committed his first robbery here, on a Chinese laundry, and also his first murder.

Things calmed down when the silver ran out, so Silver City today is a somewhat run-down, but nonetheless appealing, Victorian relic, scattered with ornate old buildings. The two thousand students of Western New Mexico University, whose campus is on the western edge of downtown, keep things reasonably lively for most of the year, and they're replaced in summer by a large influx of tourists. Copper mining, meanwhile, continues unabated; neighbouring Santa Rita, which had become a fully-fledged community in its own right, and was the birthplace of Apollo 17 astronaut Harrison Schmitt, disappeared into the bowels of an open-pit copper mine in 1966.

Silver City's zip code is NM 88061.

Arrival and information

Silver City's **visitor center** is on Hwy-90 a few blocks northeast of downtown, at 1103 N Hudson St (April–Oct Mon–Sat 9am–5pm, Sun noon–5pm; Nov–March Mon–Fri 9am–5pm; ☎505/538-3785 or 1-800/548-9378).

Accommodation

Room rates are surprisingly inexpensive in Silver City, but with most of the **motels** strung along US-180 east of town there's a dearth of options within walking distance of downtown.

Bear Mountain Guest Ranch, Bear Mountain Rd; ☎505/538-2538 or 1-800/880-2538. A 1920s ranch house four miles northwest of downtown, charging all-inclusive rates to stay in very pleasant rooms and eat three full meals per day. Myra McCormick, who has run the place for almost forty years, regularly guides bird-watching trips and can suggest or arrange multi-day cycling, mountain-biking, or cross-country skiing tours of the surrounding area. ⑤.

The Carter House B&B, 101 N Cooper St; ☎505/388-5485. Downtown *HI-AYH* youth hostel that doubles as a B&B, with $12 dorm beds ($15 non-members) and some nice little private rooms. ①/④.

As explained on p.15, **accommodation prices***, excluding taxes, are indicated throughout this book by the following symbols:*

① up to $30
② $30–45
③ $45–60
④ $60–80
⑤ $80–100
⑥ $100–130
⑦ $130–175
⑧ $175–250
⑨ $250+

Holiday Motor Hotel, 3420 US-180 E; ☎505/538-3711 or 1-800/828-8291. Good-value motel rooms on the eastern approaches to town, with a pool and a good Italian restaurant, *Michael's*. Winter ②, summer ③.

Palace Hotel, 106 W Broadway; ☎505/388-1811. Small, nicely restored nineteenth-century hotel, downtown; most but not all rooms are en-suite. ②.

Super 8, 1040 US-180 E; ☎505/388-1983 or 1-800/800-8000. Reliable chain motel near the Gila Cliff Dwellings turn-off. Winter ②, summer ③.

The Town

A massive flood ripped the heart out of downtown Silver City in 1895, washing away its original Main Street. That site is now occupied by **Big Ditch Park**; stand on its eastern edge, at 11th and Hudson, and you're on the spot where **Billy the Kid** grew up, in a simple one-room cabin. Billy's mother is buried in the town cemetery, on Memory Lane a couple of miles east. After her death, Billy found work as a busboy in the *Star Hotel*, which survives in much-altered form at Broadway and Hudson, but soon turned to crime. The jail where he was imprisoned, and from which he made the first of his many escapes, stood at 304 N Hudson St.

Two good museums explore local history in considerable depth. The **Silver City Museum**, 312 W Broadway (Tues–Fri 9am–4.30pm, Sat & Sun 10am–4pm; free) concentrates on the boom-and-bust mining years, with photos of the frontier years and personal accounts of the vanished community of Santa Rita, though it also holds Indian pottery, rugs, and basketry. The emphasis at the **Western New Mexico University Museum**, 12th and Alabama (Mon–Fri 9am–4.30pm, Sat & Sun 10am–4pm; free), is on a remarkable collection of **Mimbres pottery**, tracing its development over a thousand-year period.

Eating

Inexpensive **diners** are two-a-penny in the downtown area – not to mention a few hair-raising **bars** – but don't expect to find anything more exciting along the highways further out.

Buck Horn Saloon, 62 Main St, Pinos Altos; ☎505/538-9911. Enjoyable Wild-West-themed steakhouse in the ghost town of Pinos Altos, seven miles north of Silver City. Open Mon–Sat for dinner only; live music on weekends.

Jalisco Cafe, 100 S Bullard St; ☎505/388-2060. One of the few options in the heart of downtown, serving Mexican meals daily except Sun.

Red Barn Family Steakhouse, 708 Silver Heights Blvd; ☎505/538-5666. Exactly what it sounds like; a large steakhouse, painted a lurid red, on Hwy-180 near the Gila turn-off at the eastern end of town.

Silver Cafe, 514 N Bullard St; ☎505/388-3480. New Mexican dishes in atmospheric saloon surroundings. Closes at 7.30pm Mon–Sat, and all Sun.

Into the mountains

North of Silver City, the volcanic **Mogollon** and **Mimbres mountains** are among the remotest wilderness areas in the US. Until the late nineteenth century, they were an Apache stronghold;

The Mogollon and the Mimbres

Archeologists identify the three major cultures of the prehistoric Southwest as the **Anasazi** of the Colorado Plateau, the **Hohokam** of the Salt River Valley around modern Phoenix, and the **Mogollon**, based in the **Mogollon mountains** of what's now southwest New Mexico. Thanks to their proximity to Mexico, Mogollon peoples were the first to acquire both **agriculture** – in the shape of corn and squash, around 1200 BC – and **pottery** – around 200 AD.

For more about the Mogollon, see p.470.

At its peak, between 100 AD and 1300 AD, the Mogollon culture extended well into modern Arizona and Mexican Chihuahua. Its heartland, however, remained the **Gila** and **Mimbres** rivers, north and east of modern Silver City, and the Mogollon sub-group known as the **Classic Mimbres** culture is considered to represent the ancient Southwest's finest artistic flowering. Above all, the Mimbres people – their name comes from the Spanish for "willows" – were superb **potters**. While the intricate stylized borders of their plates and bowls are typical of many pueblo peoples, their vivid naturalistic images of birds, insects and animals are quite extraordinary. Usually executed in black on white, they also hint at a complex mythology; some show bees or rabbits juxtaposed with strange humanoid creatures, others what may be prototype *kachina* figures (see p.58), and there are even scenes of decapitation suggesting human sacrifice.

The Mimbres culture reached its apogee around 1100 AD, with around five thousand people farming beside the Mimbres River. As well as a dozen or so walled villages, each of which held up to 200 rooms, they occupied several smaller, more isolated settlements. Depictions of fish that live only in the Pacific would suggest they travelled extensively, but there's little evidence of trade. No Mimbres ceramics have been discovered elsewhere, and it's believed that the finest bowls were created for specific individuals at birth, used in ceremonies throughout their lifetime, and finally **buried** with them. The bowl would be inverted over the head of the corpse, always with a "**kill hole**" punched through it which according to modern Pueblo Indians released its "spirit" to accompany that of the deceased. As a result, undamaged Mimbres bowls are extremely rare, and Mimbres pottery in general is so valuable that the few known Mimbres sites have been extensively looted, rendering the detective work of archeology almost impossible. As far as anyone can tell, the Mimbres stopped producing pottery around 1150 AD, and left the valley soon afterwards, possibly because over-use had depleted its soil.

Geronimo was born at the headwaters of the Gila River, and returned throughout his free adult life. Before that, they were home to the **Mogollon** peoples, and the main reason to make the fifty-mile dead-end trip into the mountains on **Hwy-15** these days is to see the dramatic Mogollon ruins of the **Gila Cliff Dwellings National Monument**.

Gila is pronounced "heela", and comes from an Apache word meaning mountain.

Hwy-15 is however a beautiful drive in its own right, albeit a slow one. It's never especially steep, let alone dangerous, but the twists and turns seem endless. Potential stops along the way include **Pinos Altos** – a fun little ghost town in the woods just a few miles out of Silver City – and the **Vista Viewpoint** above the

Gila River near the far end. Most of this region belongs to the **Gila National Forest**. If you know what you're doing, it offers magnificent opportunities for wilderness adventure; first-time backpackers, climbers or canoers would do better to join an expedition with *Southwest Mountain Adventures* (☎505/538-2338 or 1-888/482-4453).

Gila Cliff Dwellings National Monument

Occupied for just a brief moment in history, between 1270 AD and 1300 AD, the Mogollon pueblo now preserved as the **GILA CLIFF DWELLINGS NATIONAL MONUMENT** is southern New Mexico's most spectacular archeological site. While not on the scale of the Anasazi "cities" of the Four Corners region – see Chapter One – it's also nothing like so heavily visited, and you may well be lucky enough to have the place to yourself. To modern eyes, ancient Southwestern peoples often seem to have chosen to live in inhospitable places, but here there's no such problem. The dwellings are tucked into sheltered south-facing recesses along the wall of a shallow canyon, just a couple of hundred feet above a perennial creek and thus in earshot of running water and the constant rustle of small game.

You won't have time to see the monument if you set off from Silver City later than 4pm in summer, 2pm in winter.

Even when there's no traffic, driving the full fifty miles from Silver City can take two hours. The final eight miles are along the broad valley of the Gila River, with the monument's **visitor center** poised near the confluence of its Middle and West forks (summer daily 8am–5pm; winter daily 8am–4.30pm; free; ☎505/536-9461).

The **trail** to the dwellings (summer daily 8am–6pm; winter daily 9am–4pm) starts a mile further on, crossing the Gila on a long footbridge. Only once you've followed the creek for half a mile do you get your first glimpse of the pueblo. What look from below like three separate caves turn out when you climb the hillside to be a single deep, long alcove with three entrances. Each entrance was sealed with stones and mortar, but behind them lay around forty interconnected rooms, sharing a communal – and presumably very dark – plaza at the rear. As the trail leads into and through the complex, keep an eye out for the pictographs that mark certain dwellings, as well as a granary that still holds a dessicated cache of tiny corn.

The monument maintains a small free **campground** beside the Gila River, equipped with running water in summer only, and there's another pretty campground at the *Gila Hot Springs Vacation Center*, eight miles south (☎505/536-9551).

Lordsburg

Sixty miles down the interstate from Deming, twenty miles short of Arizona, **LORDSBURG** is southwest New Mexico's last gasp. John Wayne went to a lot of trouble to get here in *Stagecoach*, but seeing its desultory strip of gas stations and motels today you wonder why he bothered. Far more redolent of the old West is **SHAKESPEARE**, two miles south, a privately-owned **ghost town** that's only open for infrequent guided tours (every other Sat & Sun, 10am–2pm; $3; ☎505/542-9034).

Practicalities

The **New Mexico Welcome Center**, south of the interstate at the west end of town (daily 8am–5pm; ☎505/542-8149), is the best place to pick up information on Lordsburg and the region. If you need a **bed**, head for the *Aloha Friendship Inn*, 816 E Motel Drive (☎505/542-3567; ①), or the slightly plusher *Super 8*, 110 E Maple St (☎505/542-8882 or 1-800/800-8000; ②). *Kranberry's*, 1405 S Main St (☎505/542-9400), is the best of a humdrum crop of **diners**.

Chapter 4

Phoenix and Southern Arizona

S outhern Arizona may lack the compelling scenery of the state's northern half, but more than makes up for it in sheer weight of numbers. Despite every conceivable geographic and climatic disadvantage, ninety percent of Arizonans live here, mainly concentrated in two of the most ludicrous cities on earth – **Phoenix** and **Tucson**. What makes them ludicrous is that there's no logical reason for their existence; neither has anything like enough **water** to support itself, but both have accrued sufficient political leverage to persuade the federal government to spend ever larger amounts of money on vast canal projects to meet their needs.

Phoenix in particular can be seen as the bloated spider at the centre of the web, sucking the juices from the rest of the state. By far the largest city in Arizona, it holds only minimal appeal for tourists. **Tucson** at least has a spark of life, thanks to its long and fascinating history; it started out as a Mexican frontier outpost, and is still surrounded by relics of the Spanish missionary era such as the churches of **San Xavier del Bac** and **Tumacacori**. It's also at ease with its desert surroundings, accessible in **Saguaro National Park** and the **Arizona-Sonora Desert Museum**. Scattered among the "sky islands" of **southeast Arizona** are some evocative Wild-West sites, including **Tombstone**, now an entertaining if slightly tacky theme park, and the mining settlement of **Bisbee**.

Phoenix's fragile grip on reality is highlighted by the fact that it was built on the ruins of a long-lost desert civilization. The valleys of southern Arizona were until 1350 AD home to the **Hohokam** people, and crisscrossed by a sophisticated network of irrigation canals. It's thought that the Hohokam eventually overreached themselves, depleting the land too much for their way of life to endure. Their name means "people who have vanished", in the language of the **'O'odham** (once known as the Pima and the Papago) who later took their place. The 'O'odham now occupy vast reservations in southwest Arizona, while their old enemies, the **Apache**, dominate the mountains to the east.

Phoenix

*Although the entire Phoenix area is known colloquially as the **Valley of the Sun**, the term has no official meaning.*

When it began life in the 1860s, **PHOENIX** must have seemed like a good idea. The sweltering little farming town stood in the heart of the **Salt River Valley**, which measures forty miles east to west, and twenty miles north to south, with a ready-made irrigation system left by ancient Indians, and plenty of room to expand. Within a century, however, Phoenix had turned into what writer Edward Abbey called "the blob that is eating Arizona", acquiring as it did so the money and political clout to defy all notions of common sense, and just keep on growing. Today, Arizona's capital has filled the entire valley, and is the eighth largest city in the US, with over a million people within the city boundaries and more than two million in the metropolitan area. The state's financial and industrial epicentre may be just getting into its stride; boosters claim the megalopolis will one day stretch 150 miles, from Wickenburg to Tucson.

The city's phenomenal rise was originally fuelled by its image as a healthy oasis, where the desert had been tamed and transformed into a suburban idyll. While retirees still flock to enclaves such as **Sun City**, however, it now has a deserved reputation as the most unpleasant city in the Southwest – Las Vegas with no casinos, or LA with no beach. Its endless sprawl has long since covered the "golden fields of ripened grain" described in one 1940s guidebook, and swallowed a host of neighbouring communities, such as **Scottsdale**, **Tempe** and **Mesa**. The TB and asthma sufferers who came to the valley's sanatoriums would now choke on its polluted air. Above all, Phoenix is **hot**; between June and August daytime highs average over 100°F, making it the hottest city outside the Middle East.

Phoenix epitomizes the Western maxim that "water flows uphill to money", with a history that revolves around its manoeuvrings to obtain ever more water, from ever further afield. Despite dams and diversions, the drainage of the Salt River soon proved insufficient, so, absurdly enough, the city is now dependent on aqueducts that cross the deserts from the Colorado River. Since the 1980s, when Phoenicians used a profligate 250 gallons of water per person per day, a note of realism has crept in, and it's no longer legal to adorn your latest real-estate development with an artificial lake. The obsession with liquid remains; pedestrians clutch bottled water in the street, and you can't fill your gas tank without the digitized gas pump telling you "Wow it's hot. Wouldn't a cold drink taste good ?"

In winter, when temperatures rarely drop below 65°F, **tourists** from colder climes still arrive in Phoenix in large numbers. They pay vast sums to warm their bones in the luxury resorts and spas, concentrated especially in Scottsdale, that are the modern equivalent of the 1930s dude ranches. Unlike golf, tennis and shopping, **sightseeing** rarely ranks high on the agenda – which is just as well, since there's a good deal of truth in the charge laid by Phoenix's older

---

Excursions from Phoenix

If a family visit or business trip to Phoenix brings you to Arizona for the first time, and you'd like to see a little more of the state, you'll have to rent a car to get anywhere interesting.

Great **day-trips** include driving a hundred miles north on I-17, and visiting some combination of **Montezuma Castle** (see p.279), **Sedona** (p.269) and **Jerome** (p.276), or following the **Apache Trail** northeast from Mesa, as described on p.211.

With a **weekend** to spare, the **Grand Canyon** is an obvious possibility, though it is a 450-mile round-trip. Alternatively, **Flagstaff** is a good base for several lesser known attractions (see p.258), while Wild West fans will enjoy **Tombstone**, 180 miles southeast (p.235). Best of all, if you're up to driving 300 miles each way, is northeast Arizona's stupendous **Canyon de Chelly** (p.48).

---

archrival, Tucson, that the city is sorely lacking in culture and history. Apart from the **Heard Museum**'s excellent Native-American displays, and Frank Lloyd Wright's architecture studio at **Taliesin West**, Phoenix is short of must-see attractions. In fact, if you're on a touring vacation, you'd miss little if you bypassed it altogether, and a day at one of the city's plentiful upscale **malls** is probably as authentic and enjoyable an experience as Phoenix has to offer.

A history of Phoenix

Although no American settled in the Salt River Valley until **1865**, when John Smith began supplying hay to Camp McDowell, thirty miles northeast, it was clear to all that the valley had once supported a large population. Traces still remained of over three hundred miles of **canals** – up to fifteen feet wide, ten feet deep and twenty miles long – dug by the ancient **Hohokam** people. Confederate deserter Jack Swilling cleared one such canal in 1867, and thereby established **Phoenix**. The infant city was named by British adventurer "Lord" Darrel Duppa, who saw it as rising from the ashes of the Hohokam civilization much as the mythical bird regenerated from the flames that consumed it.

For more about the Hohokam, see p.470.

Phoenix was laid out in 1870 on a 98-block grid that stretched one mile long by half a mile wide. Avenues and streets (now numbered) were named for Indian tribes, and cross streets for presidents. By 1889, it was **capital** of Arizona, and in 1890 there were eleven thousand people in the valley. Catastrophic floods and droughts along the Salt River during the 1890s drove many farmers to abandon their fields, and convinced the city-dwellers that their future depended on ensuring a safe, dependable source of **water**. The building of the **Roosevelt Dam** in the mountains to the east, in 1911 (see p.212) was the first step in a process that culminated in the 1990s with the completion of the **Central Arizona Project**.

METROPOLITAN PHOENIX

N

LONE MTN RD

DYNAMITE RD

RIO VERDE DR

Verde River

PEAK RD

SCOTTSDALE RD

Fort
Mc Dowell
Indian
Reservation

MC DOWELL MTN RD

TONTO

NATIONAL

FOREST

FRANK LLOYD WRIGHT DR

• Taliesin West

CACTUS RD

PIMA RD

SHEA BLVD

Salt River
Indian Reservation

BEELINE HWY

BUSH HWY

DISE
LEY

DR

CAMELBACK
MOUNTAIN

Salt River

DALE

Fashion
Square

RD

HAYDEN RD

MC DOWELL RD

USERY PASS RD

• Phoenix
Zoo

Mesa
Southwest
Museum

MC KELLIPS RD

COUNTRY CLUB DR

MESA

UNIVERSITY AVE

MAIN ST

BROADWAY RD

Superstition
Springs Center
•

SUPERSTITION FREEWAY

BASELINE RD

TEMPE

GILBERT

ELLIOT RD

56TH ST

HURAL RD

MC CLINTOCK RD

PRICE RD

DOBSON RD

CHANDLER

ARIZONA AVE

POWER RD

VINEYARD RD

CHANDLER BLD

WILLIAMS FIELD RD

GREENFIELD RD

ELLSWORTH RD

QUEEN CREEK RD

OCOTILLO RD

10

CHANDLER HEIGHTS RD

HIGGS RD

Phoenix

By the 1920s, Phoenix was promoting itself as the "winter playground of the Southwest", a healthy refuge from the smog-laden cities of the East that was home to "forty thousand people and the best kind of people, too. A very small percentage of Mexicans, negroes or foreigners." Its citizens were exhorted to landscape their properties with gardens, under the slogan "**Let's Do Away With the Desert**", and lavish resort hotels began to open. Meanwhile, the black neighbourhoods of southwest Phoenix were classified by the federal government as holding the worst slums in the US.

World War II triggered the city's exponential growth, with the acquisition of three major air bases, and **industrialization** continued apace during the 1950s, when *Motorola* built a huge plant. The development of **air-conditioning** finally made the desert heat bearable, and half the "evaporative coolers" in the country were made in Phoenix. Between 1950 and 1960 alone, the population swelled from 107,000 to 439,000, and by the time it topped one million, around 1990, the city had grown by over four hundred square miles in forty years. That made it prey to some of the most rapacious speculators in the country, including the infamous **Charles Keating**, among whose projects were the no-expense-spared *Phoenician Resort* and the "masterplanned community" of Estrella – his arrest and ruin in 1989 coincided with the bankruptcy of ten of Arizona's eleven savings and loans – and state governor **J Fyfe Symington**, charged with corruption in 1997 following his intricate dealings with downtown developments such as the Mercado Mall.

Arrival, information and getting around

For details of ***flights*** *to and within the Southwest, see p.3 onwards.*

Sky Harbor International Airport (☎602/273-3321), three miles east of downtown, receives flights from all over the US and even direct from Europe. All the major **rental car** chains, listed on p.19, are represented. *Phoenix Transit System* **buses** (☎602/253-5000) connect the airport with downtown (#13; Mon–Sat), Tempe and Mesa (Mon–Fri), but it's easier to take a door-to-door **shuttle bus**, at up to $10 for downtown destinations or $20 for Scottsdale, with a company such as *SuperShuttle* (☎602/244-9000 or 1-800/331-3565). *Arizona Shuttle Services* (☎520/795-6671 or 1-800/888-2749) run south to Tucson, while *Nava-Hopi* (☎520/774-5003 or 1-800/892-8687) head north to Flagstaff and the Grand Canyon.

Amtrak ***trains*** *no longer serve Phoenix, though they still call at Tucson (see p.218).*

Greyhound buses arrive at 525 E Washington St (☎602/271-2426 or 1-800/231-2222), opposite the Civic Plaza. **Getting around** without a car is not ideal – it can take hours to cross town – but it's not impossible. The *Phoenix Transit System*'s commuter routes charge $1.25 per ride; pick up a schedule at the downtown terminal, First and Washington. Tourists are more likely to use the purple *DASH* buses (Mon–Fri 6.30am–6pm; 30¢), which ply between the Arizona Center and the Capitol downtown. For a **cab**, call *Checker Cab* (☎602/257-1818) or *Ace Taxi* (☎602/254-1999).

Phoenix's **visitor center** is at 400 E Van Buren St in the Arizona Center (Mon–Fri 8am–5pm; ☎602/254-6500; 24hr visitor hotline ☎602/252-5588); there's also an information kiosk at Adams and Second downtown (Mon–Fri 8am–4.30pm). The main **post office** is at 4949 E Van Buren St, though the branch at 522 N Central Ave is more convenient for downtown.

Phoenix

Contact Gray Line *(☎602/495-9100) for details of city tours.*

Accommodation

Metropolitan Phoenix is so huge that it's worth paying a bit extra to ensure that your **accommodation** is near the places you want to visit. Oddly enough, **downtown Phoenix** is not one of the more expensive areas, with cheap motels lining the somewhat rundown W Van Buren Street a few blocks north of the centre. Room rates are considerably more expensive in **winter**, when snowbirds from all over the US fill the upscale **resorts** of Scottsdale in particular.

Central Phoenix

Arizona Biltmore Hotel, 24th St & Missouri Ave, Phoenix AZ 85016; ☎602/955-6600 or 1-800/950-0086, fax 381-7646. Extraordinarily lavish 500-room resort, built under the influence of Frank Lloyd Wright in the 1930s, and recently renovated while retaining its Art-Deco trimmings. June–Sept ⑥, Oct–May ⑨.

Budget Lodge Motel, 402 W Van Buren St, Phoenix AZ 85003; ☎602/254-7247. Reasonably attractive rooms at very attractive rates – not far from the centre, but you'll feel safer if you drive rather than walk here. ②.

HI-Phoenix, *The Metcalf House*, 1026 N Ninth St above Roosevelt St, Phoenix AZ 85004; ☎602/254-9803. Dorm beds at $10 for *HI/AYH* members, $13 non-members, a 15min walk north of the Arizona Center. No phone reservations, but space is usually available. No curfew, cheap bike rental. ①.

Howard Johnson Lodge, 124 S 24th St, Phoenix AZ 85034; ☎602/244-8221. Standard doubles near the airport. Summer ③, winter ④.

San Carlos Travelodge Hotel, 202 N Central Ave, Phoenix AZ 85004; ☎602/253-4121 or 1-800/528-5446, fax 253-6668. Atmospheric, very central Twenties hotel, with tasteful good-value rooms, a nice cafe (see p.209) and a rooftop swimming pool. June–Sept ④, Oct–May ⑥.

Super 8 Phoenix Airport, 3401 E Van Buren St, Phoenix AZ 85008; ☎602/244-1627 or 1-800/800-8000, fax 275-1126. Dependable chain motel, a mile north of the airport, with free shuttle connection. Summer ③, winter ⑤.

YMCA, 350 N First Ave; ☎602/253-6181. Grungy but central single rooms for men and women, with shared bathrooms. Very low weekly rates. No reservations: first come, first served. ①.

Scottsdale

Days Inn Scottsdale Fashion Square Resort, 4710 N Scottsdale Rd, Scottsdale AZ 85251; ☎602/947-5411 or 1-800/325-2525, fax 946-1324. Standard hotel, well priced by local standards, and handily located at Fashion Square Mall, within walking distance of downtown. Summer ③, winter ⑤.

As explained on p.15, **accommodation prices**, *excluding taxes, are indicated throughout this book by the following symbols:*

① *up to $30*
② *$30–45*
③ *$45–60*
④ *$60–80*
⑤ *$80–100*
⑥ *$100–130*
⑦ *$130–175*
⑧ *$175–250*
⑨ *$250+*

Phoenician Resort, 6000 E Camelback Rd, Scottsdale AZ 85251; ☎602/423-2530 or 1-800/888-1234, fax 947-4311. Gorgeous 130-acre resort, arrayed at the base of Camelback Mountain at the northern end of Scottsdale, and offering every conceivable luxury, with golf course, waterfalls and lush gardens as well as lavish rooms and restaurants. Mid-June to Aug ⑦, Sept to mid-June ⑨.

Scottsdale Pima Motel, 7330 N Pima Rd, Scottsdale AZ 85258; ☎602/948-3800 or 1-800/344-0262, fax 443-3374. Relatively inexpensive motel, a few miles northwest of central Scottsdale but offering free local shuttles, with comfortable conventional rooms and pricier suites. Summer ②, winter ④.

Tempe and Mesa

Arizona Golf Resort, 425 S Power Rd, Mesa AZ 85206; ☎602/832-3202 or 1-800/528-8282, fax 981-0151. Pleasant rooms and suites in individual *casitas*, mainly intended for golfers using the adjoining course, but handy for forays into the mountains to the east. Summer ④, winter ⑤.

Motel 6, 630 W Main St, Mesa AZ 85201; ☎602/834-0066. The most central of Mesa's three *Motel 6*'s; there are three more in Tempe. All offer dull double rooms at budget rates. ②.

Super 8 Mesa Town Center, 3 E Main St, Mesa AZ 85201; ☎602/834-6060 or 1-800/800-8000. Budget motel in the heart of downtown Mesa, a couple of blocks from the Southwest Museum. Summer ②, winter ④.

Super 8 Tempe/Scottsdale, 1020 E Apache Blvd, Tempe AZ 85281; ☎602/967-8891 or 1-800/800-8000, fax 968-7868. Chain motel, within half a mile of the university and five miles of the airport. Summer ③, winter ④.

Central Phoenix

Downtown Phoenix – defined as the few blocks east and west of Central Avenue, and north and south of **Washington Street** – is too hot, too run-down, and too spread out to walk around in any comfort. Nominally it's still the headquarters of Arizona Inc, but the major corporate offices and institutions are now scattered throughout the Valley of the Sun. The latest downtown **mall** – the **Arizona Center**, on Van Buren Street between Third and Fifth – has finally brought some retail business back to the centre, but it's still a pale imitation of the mega-malls further north (see p.210).

What little remains of Phoenix's nineteenth-century architecture now constitutes **Heritage Square**, a couple of blocks southeast of the Arizona Center at 115 N Sixth Street. Rather than original adobe ranch houses, however, it preserves a twee assortment of Victorian homes, converted into tea rooms and toy museums. You can get a better impression of the early days at the new **Phoenix Museum of History**, across the street at 105 N Fifth St (Mon–Sat 10am–5pm, Sun noon–5pm; $5), which starts with a "calendar stick" used by Pima Indians, and features the city's first jail – a rock with a chain attached – as well as early town plans and a steam-powered bicycle.

Twenty sun-baked blocks west, the sparkling copper dome of the disused **Arizona State Capitol** dominates the low-level sprawl.

Documents in the dull, dry museum within do little to bring the state's political history to life (Mon–Fri 8am–5pm; free).

Two more significant attractions lie a mile or so north of downtown (and north of I-10, though you won't see the interstate as it burrows beneath Central Ave). The **Phoenix Art Museum**, 1625 N Central Ave (Tues & Thurs–Sat 10am–5pm, Wed 10am–9pm, Sun noon–5pm; free, with charges for special exhibitions), was being extensively remodelled as this book went to press, with the intention of highlighting its extensive contemporary collections and making room for further controversial exhibtions such as 1996's *Old Glory: The American Flag in Contemporary Art*. Its permanent displays should include paintings by Georgia O'Keeffe and Rufino Tamayo, as well as *de rigueur* Western art by Russell and Remington and some middleweight Old Masters; the top-quality gift shop stocks Mexican crafts items and jazzy modern ceramics.

DOWNTOWN PHOENIX

ACCOMMODATION
1 Budget Lodge Motel
2 HI-Phoenix
3 San Carlos Travelodge
4 YMCA

EATING
A All That Jazz
B Sam's Cafe

Three blocks north and a block east, the **Heard Museum**, 22 E Monte Vista Rd (Mon, Tues & Thurs–Sat 9.30am–5pm, Wed 9.30am–9pm, Sun noon–5pm; $5, free Wed 5–9pm), offers a fascinating introduction to the **Native Americans** of the Southwest, and their arts and crafts in particular. The pottery is especially good, ranging from stunning Mimbres bowls, a parrot-headed and -tailed Salado jar from 1350 AD, and clay dolls made by the Quechan and Mohave peoples as souvenirs for nineteenth-century railroad passengers, to modern Hopi ceramics. You'll also find a complete Navajo *hogan*, some fine old Havasupai baskets, Apache beadwork, and painted buffalo-skin shields from New Mexican pueblos. The real highlight, however, is a refrigerated room filled with *kachina* dolls – 400 of them donated by arch-conservative Arizona senator Barry Goldwater – arranged according to the Hopi sacred calendar. Look for a haunting photo of the *so'so'yoktu*, the ogres who scare Hopi children into good behaviour, taken at Walpi in 1900 before photographers were banned from the Hopi reservation.

*For more on the **Mimbres** culture, see p.193; Navajo **hogans** are discussed on p.54; and the **kachina** religion is described on p.58.*

Scottsdale

Having grown to house well over 150,000 people, and stretch almost twenty miles from north to south, the town of **SCOTTSDALE**, founded ten miles northeast of Phoenix in the 1880s, is a remarkable success story in its own right. Despite being almost wholly subsumed into the metropolitan maw, it has carved itself an eccentric double niche as both the city's chic-est destination, home to opulent resorts and designer-led malls, and its most determinedly "Western" quarter.

Southeast of **Camelback Mountain** and the grand **Scottsdale Fashion Square** mall, downtown Scottsdale focuses on a few pleasant blocks of sidewalk cafes and souvenir stores. West of Scottsdale Road counts as the **Main Street Arts and Antiques District**; to the east, **Old Town** plays the Wild West theme for all it's worth.

If you doubt whether the people who named Camelback Mountain had ever seen a real camel, see p.245.

Whatever its general appearance may suggest, Phoenix has managed to attract some visionary designers. Notable among them is **Frank Lloyd Wright**, who came to the city to work on the *Biltmore Hotel*, and stayed for most of the 25 years before his death in 1959. His winter studio, **Taliesin West** – located at 114th Street and Frank Lloyd Wright Boulevard, at Scottsdale's northeastern edge – is now an architecture school and a working design studio, with regular multimedia exhibits of the man's life and work (Oct–May daily 9am–4pm; June–Sept daily 7.30–11am; ☎602/860-2700). It's open for up to five hour-long tours each morning ($8), followed by three 1hr 30min "Insights" on winter afternoons ($12).

Less well known, but in many ways more compelling, is the **Cosanti Foundation**, four miles southwest at 6433 Doubletree Rd (daily 9am–5pm; $1 donation). The buildings, designed by **Paolo Soleri**, an Italian-born ex-student of Wright, and constructed out of rammed earth and concrete, have a much more organic feel than

Taliesin. Crafts workshops cast bells and bronzes, and a small museum shows drawings and models of Soleri's life work: the planned community of **Arcosanti**, described on p.281.

Papago Park at the south end of Scottsdale is home to the **Desert Botanical Garden** (Oct–April daily 8am–dusk; May–Sept daily 7am–10pm; $6), filled with an amazing array of cactuses and desert flora from around the world, and **Phoenix Zoo** (May to Labor Day daily 7am–4pm; winter daily 9am–5pm; $7), which offers four monkey islands and a half-hour ride on a Safari Train. At the **Big Surf water park**, not far east at 1500 N McClintock Ave (May–Sept only, Mon–Sat 10am–6pm, Sun 11am–7pm; $12.50), you can ride five-foot waves or careen down multistorey waterslides into a giant freshwater lagoon.

Tempe

As the site of **Arizona State University**, the community of **TEMPE**, across I-60 south of Scottsdale, and around six miles east of downtown Phoenix, is probably the liveliest portion of the Valley of the Sun. Several minor museums and galleries are dotted across the college campus, but the main reason to visit is to hang out in the cafes and clubs of **Mill Avenue**, immediately west. For an overview of local history – Tempe started out as a ferry post for travellers crossing the Salt River – call in at the spruced-up **Tempe Historical Museum** (Mon–Thurs & Sat 10am–5pm, Sun 1–5pm; $2.50).

Mesa

Built on the site of the Mormon settlement of Fort Utah, which lasted for three years from 1877, **MESA**, east of Tempe, is now Arizona's third-largest city. Covering more than a hundred square miles, it has a population of over 300,000. Hidden among its endless broad boulevards are twenty golf courses, several large malls, some of Phoenix's most affordable residential districts, and dozens of cheap motels, and with the Superstition Mountains rising to the east it's not a bad base for passing visitors.

As well as displays on dinosaurs and the Hohokam, the enjoyable **Mesa Southwest Museum**, 53 N MacDonald St (Tues–Sat 10am–5pm, Sun 1–5pm; $4), features a reconstruction of a block of Mesa's Main Street as it looked a century ago. Stars of the show, however, are the crudely carved **Peralta Stones**, believed by some to hold the key to the legendary Lost Dutchman Mine (see p.211); four to six major expeditions each year use them as their guide.

Eating

Most of the **restaurants** in greater Phoenix seem to have retreated to the malls in recent years, so unless you're prepared to pay resort prices, it's hard to find a good restaurant with very much atmosphere. The mall places aren't at all bad, however, and there's plenty of variety. Apart from a block or two in central Scottsdale, no area of the metropolis is small enough to walk around while you look for a place to eat, but if you're happy to drive neighbourhood diners – especially Mexican – can still be found, and the major thoroughfares are the usual fast-food heaven.

Central Phoenix

All That Jazz, 333 E Jefferson St; ☎602/256-1437. Very central, somewhat upmarket Caribbean restaurant, open daily for lunch and dinner, with a menu of tasty, spicy West Indian specialities, and live jazz at weekends.

Cafe Brazil, 3239 E Indian School Rd; ☎602/955-0060. Unusual mid-priced Brazilian restaurant – try the meaty *feijoada* stew, thickened with mashed-up black beans. Open daily for lunch and dinner, with live samba at weekends.

Ed Debevic's Short Orders Deluxe, 2102 E Highland Ave; ☎602/956-2760. Burgers and fries, malts and cokes, served amid frenetic retro-Americana that includes a mini-jukebox on every table.

The Fish Market, 1720 E Camelback Rd; ☎602/277-3474. Two-tier fish restaurant on the way to Scottsdale, which shares its premises with a real fish-monger – always a good sign. The large downstairs dining room, open for lunch and dinner daily, includes an oyster and sushi bar, while the cooking in the pricier dinner-only *Top of the Market* upstairs is more adventurous.

There's another Sam's Cafe *in the Biltmore Fashion Park, north of downtown at 24th and Camelback;* ☎ *602-954-7100.*

Sam's Cafe, Arizona Center, 455 N Third St; ☎602/252-3545. Hectic downtown mall joint, with patio seating, that's nonetheless a great place to try out modern Southwestern cuisine – grilled fish is the best low-cal option – at old-fashioned prices. Lunch and dinner daily.

Such is Life, 3602 N 24th St; ☎602/955-7822. Classy cooking from southern and central Mexico, including Yucatecan specialities such as the delicious chicken-and-lime dish *pollo pibil*, and authentic *mole* sauces. More expensive than a typical neighbourhood Mexican, but still good value. Open for lunch and dinner Mon–Fri, dinner only Sat.

Roxsand, Biltmore Fashion Park, 2594 E Camelback Rd; ☎602/381-0444. Eclectic, futuristic restaurant in upmarket uptown mall, where entrees drawn from the major world cuisines – especially Asian, with plenty of spicy Thai and Chinese sauces – start at around $20. Lunch and dinner daily.

Wright's, *Arizona Biltmore Hotel*, 24th St & Missouri Ave; ☎602/955-6600. Very stylish resort restaurant, serving modern American food in gorgeous Art-Deco surroundings; entrees like wood-smoked venison cost around $30. Open for dinner daily, breakfast and lunch Mon–Fri only.

Scottsdale

Coyote Grill, 3202 E Greenway Rd; ☎602/404-8966. Good, inexpensive Southwestern restaurant, with a healthy menu of grilled meats and fish, and lighter lunchtime snacks. Dinner only Mon–Thurs, lunch and dinner Fri–Sun.

Daa's Thai Room, 7419A East Indian Plaza; ☎602/941-9015. Top-quality Thai food at very reasonable prices, just off Camelback Road. Open Tues–Fri for lunch and dinner, Sat & Sun for dinner only.

Phô Dong Phuong, 8123 E Roosevelt Rd; ☎602/949-5251. Neat neighbourhood Vietnamese diner, specializing in great beef or vegetarian noodle soups at very low prices. Lunch and dinner daily.

Windows on the Green, *Phoenician Resort*, 6000 E Camelback Rd; ☎602/423-2530. This bright, attractive resort dining room – overlooking the golf course, it's the *Phoenician*'s "casual" alternative to the formal and very elegant *Mary Elaine's* – is a fine restaurant in its own right. The Southwestern menu concentrates on grilled and roasted fish and meat, at $20–25 per entree. Open for lunch and dinner Tues–Sun, lunch only on Mon.

Tempe

House Of Tricks, 114 E Seventh St; ☎602/968-1114. Tiny little modern-American place in the University district, named for chefs Robin and Robert Trick, with lots of vegetarian options. Open Mon–Sat for lunch and dinner.

La Cascio's, 2210 N Scottsdale Rd; ☎602/949-0334. Friendly, filling south-ern-Italian restaurant, with everything comes with lashings of creamy tomato sauce, and the desserts are never less than succulent. Lunch and dinner daily.

Monti's La Casa Vieja, 3 W First St; ☎602/967-7594. Tempe's oldest adobe house, built beside the Salt River ferry landing in 1873, is now an atmospher-ic Western-themed diner, serving a conventional steak-and-chicken menu at extraordinarily low prices. Lunch and dinner daily, until at least 11pm.

Mesa

Annabelle's, *Arizona Golf Resort*, 425 S Power Rd; ☎602/832-3202. Attractive resort restaurant, serving good-quality deli lunches for well under $10, and more formal dinners, usually with seafood specials, at $10 and up. Open for all meals daily.

The Landmark Restaurant, 809 W Main St; ☎602/962-4652. Classic mid-American diner housed in a former Mormon church, serving hearty baked and roasted meats for $10–15, including a trip to the excellent salad bar. Open for lunch and dinner Mon–Fri, dinner only on Sat, brunch only on Sun.

The Seafood Market, 1318 W Southern Ave, suite #11; ☎602/890-0435. A feast of fresh fish, flown in from all over the world, and prepared simply at rea-sonable prices, for lunch and dinner daily.

Coffeehouses

Espresso coffee has swept across Phoenix like wildfire in the last few years, with speciality coffeehouses in the trendier districts and chain outlets in all the malls. The local coffee set even have their own free magazine, *Java Monthly*. As well as the cafes below, look out for the popular *Coffee Plantation* chain, whose locations include the Biltmore Fashion Park, Fashion Square in Scottsdale, Fiesta Mall in Mesa, and 680 S Mill St in Tempe.

The Art of Coffee, *San Carlos Hotel*, 202 North Central Ave; ☎602/254-1566. The best downtown cafe, in historic hotel, with some sidewalk seating.

Espressions, 4407 N Saddlebag Trail, Scottsdale; ☎602/946-9840. Coffee and tea in every imaginable flavour, at temperatures from frozen to searing.

Orbit Cafe, Uptown Plaza, Central & Camelback; ☎602/265-2354. Large mall cafe doubling as a gallery and performance space, with an emphasis on jazz.

The Picnic Company, 1415 E University Blvd, Tempe; ☎602/968-7740. Coffees, bagels and snacks, with live music at weekend lunchtimes. Open from 10am daily.

The Willow House, 149 W McDowell Rd; ☎602/252-0272. Single-storey house, a mile north of downtown, that offers snacks and desserts, poetry and comedy, as well as coffee. Open Mon–Fri 7am, Sat & Sun 8am, until late.

Nightlife, entertainment and sports

Not surprisingly, **nightlife** in Phoenix tends toward cowboy dance halls and Top 40 discos in the big hotels. For a rundown of what's on musically, pick up the free weekly *New Times* in local record- or bookstores, or check out the bars and clubs listed below.

Both the **Phoenix Symphony Hall**, 225 E Adams St (☎602/262-7272), and the **Scottsdale Center for the Arts**, 7380 E Second St (☎602/994-2787), put on classical music, theatre and ballet. The **Phoenix Suns** play NBA basketball at the America West Arena, 201 E Jefferson St (☎602/379-7867), and football's **Arizona Cardinals** are based at the university's Sun Devil Stadium (☎602/379-0102.)

Balboa Cafe, 404 S Mill Ave, Tempe; ☎602/966-1300. Jazz, offbeat rock and acoustic artists near the university.

Char's Blues, 4631 N Seventh Ave; ☎602/230-0205. Phoenix's longest-standing, best-loved blues venue, attracting big-name touring stars.

Coyote Springs Brewing Company, Town & Country Shopping Center, 4883 N 20th St; ☎602/468-0403. Mall microbrewery that puts on R&B several nights of the week.

See also Cafe Brazil *and* All That Jazz, *reviewed under* Eating *on p.208.*

Electric Ballroom, 1216 E Apache Blvd, Tempe; ☎602/894-0707. A steady diet of rap, dance and indie rock, in two rooms, for the college crowd.

The Mason Jar, 2303 E Indian School Rd; ☎602/956-6271. Headbanger heaven, hosting mostly metal seven nights a week.

Memphis Blues and Barbecue, 1264 W University Drive, Mesa; ☎602/668-9334. Meaty R&B, with a gospel brunch on Sundays.

Mr Lucky's, 3660 NW Grand Ave; ☎602/246-0686. Massive country-music honky-tonk, featuring real-life bull riding at weekends.

Phoenix Live!, Arizona Center, 455 N Third Ave; ☎602/252-2112. Anodyne but very central alliance of three separate clubs under a single roof, with a single cover charge.

Shopping

Space does not permit a detailed listing of individual stores in Phoenix, but with the city's great outdoors too hot and sprawling to take for more than a few minutes at a time, you'll probably find yourself looking for a nice cool **mall** at some point.

The biggest of the lot – in the whole Southwest, for that matter – is the **Metrocenter**, just east of I-17 at 9617 Metro Parkway, nine miles north of downtown. The central mall building holds all the usual outlets, plus four large department stores, while countless more stores and restaurants line the oval ring road around it. When you tire of shopping, try the rollercoaster in **Castles and Coasters**, alongside (daily 10am until at least 10pm; pay per ride).

The **Biltmore Fashion Park**, north of Camelback Road at 24th Street, halfway between downtown Phoenix and Scottsdale, concentrates on designer names, but does have a giant *Borders* bookstore, while the **Scottsdale Fashion Park**, further east at 7000 E Camelback Rd, is (slightly) more affordable. Also in Scottsdale, a couple of miles north, the smaller **Borgata** mall is notable for its extraordinary mock-Italian architecture. Finally, the downtown **Arizona Center** is a bit short on interesting shops but is at least livening the place up a little. Some day, it may be helped in that task by Fyfe Symington's white elephant **Mercado** mall, to build which the state governor is said to have siphoned off $10 million of the city's pension fund; currently it's all but empty.

t Phoenix

East of Phoenix

Almost two hundred miles of mountainous terrain stands between Phoenix and New Mexico to the east, much of it belonging to two huge Apache reservations. Although sweltering Phoenicians spend summer weekends in hill towns such as Payson and Pinetop to the northeast (both covered in Chapter Five), there's little to detain ordinary tourists on the long drive east.

US-60 and US-70 are the quickest routes to New Mexico, but if you want a quick escape from the desert heat, head instead up the Apache Trail into the **Superstition Mountains**. An enduring Arizona legend makes these the site of the **Lost Dutchman Mine**. Two German prospectors, Jacob Waltz and Jacob Weiser, supposedly discovered rich deposits of gold around 1870, and turned up repeatedly in the town of Florence bearing priceless nuggets. Before his death in Phoenix in 1890, Waltz is said to have murdered not only Weiser but another seven men who tried to shadow him back to the motherlode. Ever since, countless expeditions have attempted to follow his deathbed directions to the mine – guarded, according to different accounts, by pygmies or a never-discovered group of Apaches – and an estimated thirty gold-seekers have lost their lives.

The Apache Trail

The closest accessible wilderness to central Phoenix lies along **Hwy-88**, which climbs northeast into the Superstition Mountains from Apache Junction, almost twenty miles east of Mesa and a good thirty miles from downtown. This fifty-mile highway was constructed in 1904 to provide a direct route to the site of the Roosevelt Dam, then being built at the confluence of Tonto Creek and Salt River. After the dam's completion in 1911, it was re-named **The Apache Trail** by the Southern Pacific Railroad in a bid to drum up tourists, and became a popular scenic drive. It's still a long, slow haul, tortuous enough to take around two hours end to end.

r

Many day-trippers go no further than **Canyon Lake**, created by a
subsequent dam fifteen miles up, but old enough to look as though it
belongs amid the scrubby surrounding hills. It's narrow enough to
frustrate pleasure boaters, who find themselves having to turn
around every time they get up a bit of speed, but if you're happy to
take it easy, a ninety-minute cruise on *Dolly's Steamboat* is an
enjoyable way to pass a morning (☎602/827-9144; $12).

TORTILLA FLAT, at the east end of the lake, is not so much a
town as a hundred-yard stretch of boardwalk that holds the *County
Store*, the *Dutchman's Inn* and the *Superstition Saloon*, all operated by the same management (☎602/984-1776). It was named for
the nearby flat-topped boulders, not the Steinbeck novella.

Beyond Tortilla Flat, the mountains finally start to get serious,
while Hwy-88 responds by turning to gravel. After a few hair-raising
hairpin bends, with stomach-lurching views across the saguaro-stud-
ded canyons, it returns to undulating gently along beside the river.
An optional detour drops down to **Apache Lake**, another busy boating and picnicking spot. Keep going to reach **Roosevelt Dam** itself,
which was recently raised and strengthened to cope with Phoenix's
bottomless thirst for water.

Tonto National Monument

Three miles east of Roosevelt Dam, the **cliff dwellings** of **TONTO
NATIONAL MONUMENT** stand high above Hwy-88, overlooking
Theodore Roosevelt Lake. From the visitor center (daily 8am–5pm;
$4 per vehicle; ☎520/467-2241), a very steep trail, which shuts an
hour before closing time, climbs half a mile upwards. Not a walk to
schedule for the middle of a summer's day, it leads to the remarkably
complete **Lower Ruin**, set in a deep alcove near the top of the rocky
ridge, with great saguaro cactuses standing sentinel.

This large pueblo was built in the mid-fourteenth century by a
people now known as the **Salado** Indians, who are regarded as less
sophisticated than the Anasazi to the north. Their masonry is much
cruder, using lumps of rock that had fallen from the cliff face and
were then thickly plastered with mud that still bears thousands of
ancient fingerprints. Visitors can walk right through several rooms of
the ruin, some of which retain their original beams and saguaro-rib
ceilings. "Shelves" and storage niches are tucked into the cave walls,
as well as notches that once supported additional rooms.

Between November and April only, rangers lead guided hikes to
the **Upper Ruin**, reached by a separate trail up the next ridge along.

Globe

Hwy-88 rejoins US-60, the direct route east from Phoenix, thirty
miles on from Tonto National Monument, just outside **GLOBE**. This
still-functional mining town sprang into being in the 1880s, when a

twelve-mile strip of land on which a globe of pure silver had just been discovered was stripped from the Apache reservation; since the silver and gold ran out, it has made its living from copper.

The central few blocks of downtown Globe still hold several brick-built Victorian-era structures, though the claim that these include "the West's oldest *Woolworth's*" betrays quite how little there is of any great interest. On the northern outskirts, the small **Gila County Historical Museum**, 1330 N Broad St (Mon–Fri 10am–4pm; free), explores local history in punitive detail.

That Native American occupation of the region predated the Apache is shown by the ruins of **Besh-Ba-Gowah**, a mile southeast of town, which were home first to the Hohokam and later to the Salado; their modern Apache name is said to mean "metal-its-house". Visitors can enter reconstructed living quarters and a *kiva* (daily 9am–5pm; $2).

If you like your Wild West to be utterly unvarnished and unromantic, head a mile or two west of Globe to the twin communities of **CLAYPOOL** and **MIAMI**. All but engulfed by monstrous mountains of copper-mine tailings, these flyblown towns are packed with gun stores, all-day saloons and pick-up trucks.

Practicalities

Globe's **visitor center** stands in front of the county museum on Hwy-88, at 1360 N Broad St (Mon–Fri 8am–5pm; ☎520/425-4495 or 1-800/804-5623). Of the dozen or so **motels**, *El Rey*, 1201 E Ash St (☎520/425-4427; ②), and the *Ember*, 1105 N Broad St (☎520/425-5736; ②), which has a pool, offer the best value. Downtown **cafes** include the Mexican bakery *La Luz del Dia*, 304 N Broad St (☎520/425-8400; ②), where the burritos are made with fresh tortillas, while *Better Life Center*, 201 N Broad St, makes great smoothies. On the third weekend in October, Native Americans from all over the Southwest pour in for the three-day **Apache Days** fair.

*Globe's **zip code** is AZ 85502.*

San Carlos Indian Reservation

The two-million-acre **San Carlos Indian Reservation**, which extends a hundred miles east and north of Globe, was created by President Grant in 1872, to protect the **Apache** from such outrages as the Camp Grant massacre of 1871 (see p.214). In the words of one tribal member, it was "the worst place in all the great territory stolen from the Apache. If anybody ever lived there permanently, no Apache knew of it . . . The heat was terrible. The insects were terrible. The water was terrible."

Around eight thousand Apache now live on the reservation, which offers few activities for tourists apart from sailing or fishing on **San Carlos Lake**, twenty miles east of Globe, or **camping** beside it at *Soda Canyon Point* (☎520/475-2756; $5). The original reservation town of **SAN CARLOS** was drowned – despite strong Apache opposition – when the lake arose behind the new Coolidge Dam in 1930, whereupon the community previously known as **Rice**, ten miles north, was simply renamed San Carlos. It's just an administrative centre; if you want to learn more about the Apache, take time to study the displays on their religion and history at the **San Carlos Apache Cultural Center** in **PERIDOT**, on US-70 nearby (Tues–Sat 9am–5pm, Sun 11am–4pm; $3).

Aravaipa Canyon

One of the most notorious tragedies in the whole sorry tale of Anglo-Apache relations took place in the deceptively beautiful **ARAVAIPA CANYON**, just below the southern boundary of the San Carlos reservation. In 1871, when it was home to a semi-permanent Apache encampment under the nominal protection of the US army, 144 women and children were slaughtered in the **Camp Grant Massacre**. Their killers, an unholy party of Tucson vigilantes who called themselves the Committee of Public Safety, consisted of a hundred Tohono 'O'odham, fifty Hispanics and six Anglos.

Reached along a well-maintained eleven-mile dirt road that heads east from Hwy-77 fifty miles south of Globe, Aravaipa Canyon is now a **wilderness area** managed by the federal government and the Arizona Nature Conservancy. The terrain ranges from sun-drenched hillsides covered with saguaros to the deep red gorge carved by Aravaipa Creek – a rare perennial desert stream – and lined by giant cottonwoods. Visitors keen to experience the desert in its wild state need to come prepared; the canyon has no trails, no established campgrounds and no signs, and is home to rattlesnakes and scorpions. Only fifty people can enter the thirty-square-mile wilderness at any one time; obtain a **permit** ($1.50 per day, with a maximum two-night stay) from the *Bureau of Land Management*, 711 Fourteenth Ave, Safford AZ 85546 (☎520/428-4040).

Safford

The farming community of **SAFFORD**, 77 miles southeast of Globe, is the only sizeable town north of I-10 in southeast Arizona. There's no significant reason to visit, but if you're ready to stop for the night, it holds around a dozen motels, as well as a pleasant **B&B**, *Olney House*, 1104 Central Ave (☎520/428-5118; ④).

Morenci and Clifton

At its southern end, the **Coronado Scenic Road** – described on p.253 – twists its way down past a vast tiered pit, where the Gila Mountains still yield 175,000 tons of copper a day. **MORENCI**, at the bottom, is a modern-looking company town that was built in the 1960s to replace a predecessor swallowed up by the mine, and is absolutely dominated by the *Phelps Dodge* company. The *Morenci Motel and*

Restaurant (☎520/865-4111; ③) stands on a knoll opposite the *Phelps Dodge Mercantile Company Store*.

A few miles further on, the older town of **CLIFTON** has become seriously run-down, and is too derelict to be worth a stop.

From Phoenix to Tucson

The hundred-mile sprint from Phoenix to Tucson along the **I-10** interstate is one of Arizona's less inspiring drives, though it is at least over quite quickly. If you don't mind taking a slightly more circuitous route, however, it's possible to break the journey at a couple of equally unlikely and enigmatic structures – ancient **Casa Grande**, and ultra-modern **Biosphere 2**.

Casa Grande Ruins National Monument

Near **COOLIDGE**, fifteen miles east of exit 185 on the interstate, or twenty miles north of exit 210, **CASA GRANDE RUINS NATIONAL MONUMENT** preserves the most substantial surviving example of the architecture of the **Hohokam** people (daily 8am–5pm; $4 per vehicle; ☎520/723-3172). The Casa Grande itself – the name is Spanish for "Great House" – is a four-storey building that was completed in the early fourteenth century. Made of the concrete-like natural stone known as caliche, it stood at the centre of a walled compound in the flood-plain of the **Gila River**. The villagers used a well-developed network of canals to grow crops, harvested fruit from saguaro cactuses, and traded for shells and macaws with peoples from the south. The exact purpose of the Casa Grande is unknown, however; archeologists speculate that it was an astronomical observatory that doubled as a fortress in case of attack. Now protected beneath a spider-like canopy, it's not open to visitors, who have to content themselves with the historical displays in the visitor center, and strolling through other less identifiable ruins.

Casa Grande National Monument shares a name, but little else, with the I-10 pit stop of Casa Grande, thirty miles southwest, and the much larger ancient site of Casas Grandes, far south in northern Mexico.

Biosphere 2

Hwy-79 heads southeast from the small farming community of **FLORENCE**, ten miles west of Casa Grande monument, to meet **Hwy-77** roughly thirty miles north of Tucson. Turning east towards Oracle at this point gives tourists the chance to catch up with the latest developments in the extraordinary science-fiction saga of **BIOSPHERE 2**, at mile-marker 96.5 on Hwy-77 (daily 9am–4.30pm; $12.95; ☎520/896-6200 or 1-800/828-2462).

When it was completed, in 1991, this vast complex of plexiglass pyramids was trumpeted as a major laboratory for experiments in applied environmental science. Containing five separate "**biomes**", or self-contained ecosystems – rainforest, marsh, savannah, desert and a 25-foot-deep ocean – it was designed as a miniature working model of Biosphere 1, planet Earth itself, and stocked like a real-life Noah's Ark with almost four thousand species of plants and animals. Investigative journalists soon revealed, however, that it was staffed largely by ex-actors from an obscure experimental theatre group, the "Theater of All Possibilities", assembled by John Allen, or "Johnny Dolphin", at the *Synergia Ranch* outside Santa Fe, to colonize Mars and thus escape the impending nuclear holocaust on Earth. A hundred million dollars' worth of support from Texas oil tycoon Ed Bass got this far-fetched scheme off the ground, and top academics were recruited to add a veneer of respectability.

Eight "Biospherians" were sealed into Biosphere 2 in September 1991, their "mission" being to survive in isolation for two full years. This they more or less did, although emergency oxygen twice had to pumped in as carbon dioxide levels rose, and one member briefly exited for medical treatment (and was seen to return with a suspiciously full bag of belongings). They grew 88 percent of their own food, and lost 13.65 percent of their body weight. Much of what transpired was replete with irony; hungry Biospherians soon found themselves planting bananas and papayas in what they had resolved would be the inviolate wilderness of the rainforest, and destroying parts of the desert to boost oxygen, while the ocean proved impossible to keep clean. As for their fellow inhabitants, the bush babies caught the hummingbirds, and the only birds to survive were unwanted sparrows that sneaked in during construction. "Crazy ants" killed all the pollinating insects, so the Biospherians were reduced to the tedious task of pollinating all their plants by hand.

By the time the next crew moved in, conditions at Biosphere 2 had degenerated into farce. Two of the original crew, who had been acrimoniously fired, sneaked back and broke the Biosphere's seals from the outside, thus aborting the second mission after just six months; they later sued and won compensation. Ed Bass remains in charge, but Biosphere 2 has since 1996 operated in conjunction with **Columbia University**. Presented with this vast, expensive tool – now referred to as a campus – they seem to be trying to think of something to do with it. The line these days is that the problems are what makes it interesting.

In its brief heyday, Biosphere 2 was one of Arizona's most popular tourist destinations. Now that no one is locked inside, the crowds have dwindled, but the two-and-a-half-hour **tours** are still worth taking. Most of that time is spent peering into the greenhouses hoping to spot any sign of life larger than an ant, and marvelling at the fact that whatever you may have assumed Biosphere 2 is not solar powered, but depends on an external natural-gas power plant. Visitors are also allowed into the Biospherians' wilfully futuristic living quarters, tacked like a space capsule onto the back of the main block, and topped by a tower holding a spherical library.

The Biosphere compound holds the *Canyon Cafe*, which serves good meals on an appealing terrace, as well as a cybercafe, and offers good-value **lodging** at its own motel, the *Inn at Biosphere 2* (☎520/825-6222; May–Sept ③, Oct–April ⑤).

Tucson

TUCSON has been southern Arizona's leading city for over two hundred years, during which time it has lived under five separate flags. Spreading across a mountain-ringed basin at the northern limits of the **Sonoran Desert**, its 750,000-plus inhabitants pride themselves on being more cosmopolitan, cultured and liberal than those of its upstart rival Phoenix. Like Phoenix, the "Old Pueblo" has grown way past the point where the flow of the region's rivers, such as the Santa Cruz, is sufficient to quench its thirst. All are now dry sandy washes for most of the year, though flash-floods still rage through the cross-town culverts after summer thunderstorms. However, unlike Phoenix, Tucson embraces rather than denies the desert, eschewing lawns and fountains in favour of directing visitors towards the authentic landscapes of **Sabino Canyon** and the **Arizona-Sonora Desert Museum**, and the cactus-strewn hillsides of **Saguaro National Park**.

*Tucson is
pronounced
too-sawn.*

By Southwestern standards, Tucson is a diverse, attractive and lively city, home to the 35,000 energetic students of the **University of Arizona** as well as a large recent influx of retirees, and tempered by its long association with Mexico, a mere sixty miles south. Although it suffers from the same Sunbelt sprawl as Albuquerque and Phoenix, it still has a compact and recognizably historic centre, some good parks and museums, affordable accommodation and enjoyable restaurants, and even a pretty good nightlife.

A history of Tucson

The valley of the Santa Cruz had already been inhabited for many centuries by the time Spanish priest Eusebio Kino passed through in 1700, and visited the **Pima Indian** settlement of *Stjukshon*, or "dark spring". In 1776, under the direction of **Hugo O'Conor**, one of the Catholic "Wild Geese" who had fled English-controlled Ireland to fight for Spain, the Spanish relocated their main Arizonan fortress here from Tubac (see p.230). That forty-mile move northwards brought them closer to **Apache** territory, and the energies of the Hispanic and Pima citizens of **San Agustín de Tucson** were largely devoted to resisting Apache raids and sieges. The severed heads of Apache warriors were displayed as trophies on the city walls.

When Tucson was sold to the US government as part of the **Gadsden Purchase** of 1854, the incoming Anglos were generally welcomed as a stabilizing presence. Not only did most of the valley's Mexican farmers remain in Arizona, but they were joined by more of their former compatriots. Soon, however, travellers were describing Tucson as "a place of resort for traders, speculators, gamblers, horse-thieves and vagrant politicians . . . a paradise of devils".

Although the **Confederates** who occupied southern Arizona in 1862 were swiftly driven away by Union forces from California, suspicions of lingering Confederate sympathies ensured that Tucson was passed over as capital of the new Territory. Conflict with the Apache continued, and a vigilante force of Mexicans, Anglos and 'O'odham Indians from Tucson was responsible for the notorious **Camp Grant Massacre** of 144 Apaches in Aravaipa Canyon in 1871 (see p.214). US army commanders came to believe that a shadowy "**Tucson Ring**" of businessmen were consistently provoking the Apache, in order to profit from the resultant military spending.

The end of the Apache Wars in the 1880s coincided with the coming of the transcontinental **railroad**, and the re-orientation of the commerce of Tucson along east–west routes. Its role as an entrepot for trade with Mexico rapidly declined, and the Mexican merchants who had been its wealthiest citizens were driven out of business. Ever since, Mexican labourers have streamed back and forth across the border as the economy expands and contracts, but Tucson has become ever more American. Outstripped by Phoenix during the 1920s, and home to under forty thousand people (in an area of just nine square miles) as recently as 1940, by conventional standards the city has nonetheless grown at a phenomenal rate.

Arrival, information and city tours

Tucson International Airport, eight miles south of downtown (☎520/573-8100), receives flights from all over the Southwest, but as far as long-distance services are concerned it very much plays second fiddle to Phoenix. It's connected to the city by *Sun Tran* **bus** #25 (75¢), and the $11 shuttle vans of *Arizona Stagecoach* (☎520/889-1000). For **taxi** service, call *Allstate Cab* (☎520/798-1111), or *Yellow Cab* (☎520/624-6611).

The *Amtrak* station, downtown at 400 E Toole Ave, is served by three **trains** weekly in each direction between Los Angeles and points east; connecting *Amtrak* buses run north to Phoenix. *Greyhound* **buses** also stop centrally, at 2 S Fourth Ave (☎520/792-3475 or 1-800/231-2222). *AZ Flying Coach* (☎520/887-8788 or 1-800/723-1200) run seven $15 shuttle vans daily between Tucson, with pick-ups at Park Mall, the university and their office at 3013 N First Ave, and **Phoenix**'s Sky Harbor airport.

Most of downtown can be explored on foot, but if it's getting hot you can ride the **Old Pueblo Trolley** ($1) from Fourth Avenue out to the university, a mile east of the centre, on weekday lunchtimes, Friday evenings, all day Saturday, and Sunday afternoons.

METROPOLITAN TUCSON

EATING
A Blue Willow
B Cafe Terracotta
C Daniel's Restaurant
D Jack's Original Barbeque
E Kingfisher
F Ranchers Club
   The Good Earth

△ Phoenix

△ New Mexico

△ Nogales

SANTA CATALINA MOUNTAINS

▲ Mt. Lemmon

SAGUARO NATIONAL PARK (EAST)

RINCON MOUNTAINS

FREEMAN ROAD
HOUGHTON
BROADWAY
HARRISON ROAD
IRVINGTON ROAD
WILMOT ROAD
ALVERNON WAY
OLD SPANISH TRAIL
SPEEDWAY BLVD
TANQUE VERDE BLVD
MOUNT LEMMON HWY
SABINO CANYON ROAD
SUNRISE DR
PANTANO ROAD
KOLB ROAD
WILMOT ROAD
GOLF LINKS ROAD
CRAYCROFT ROAD
SWAN ROAD
COUNTRY CLUB RD
CAMPBELL AVE
FIRST
SIXTH AVENUE
AVENUE
STONE AVE
FORT LOWELL BLVD
RIVER
ROGER ROAD
ORACLE RD
WETMORE ROAD
ORANGE GROVE RD
INA ROAD
LA CANADA ROAD
MAGEE RD
HARDY RD
NARANJA
LAMBERT
LA CHOLLA ROAD
TANGERINE
THORNEYDALE ROAD
PICTURE ROCKS ROAD
GATES PASS ROAD
GOLDEN GATE RD
KINNEY ROAD
MISSION ROAD
VALENCIA ROAD
DREXEL ROAD
AJO WAY
W ANKLAM
GRANT ROAD
SPEEDWAY BLVD
W ANGAM
CAMINO D'OESTE
AVRA VALLEY ROAD
TWENTY-SECOND ROAD

Tucson Mall
Tohono Chul Park
University of Arizona
See Downtown Tucson Map
'A' Mountain ▲
Old Tucson
TUCSON MOUNTAINS
SAGUARO NATIONAL PARK (WEST)
Arizona-Sonora Desert Museum

0   Miles   3

ACCOMMODATION
1 Arizona Inn
2 Best Western Ghost Ranch Lodge
3 Econolodge
4 Loews Ventana Canyon Resort
5 Tanque Verde Ranch
6 Travelodge Flamingo Sun Motel
   & Super 8 Downtown
7 Westward Look Resort
Downtown Accommodation and Restaurants
are marked on the 'Downtown Tucson' Map

Tucson

Tucson's downtown **visitor center**, 130 S Scott Ave (Mon–Fri 8am–5pm, Sat & Sun 9am–4pm; ☎520/624-1817 or 1-800/638-8350), has free maps and information. The *Southwest Parks and Monuments Association* bookstore, three blocks away at 223 N Court St (Mon–Fri 10.30am–5.30pm, Sat & Sun 11am–4pm; ☎520/792-0239) in the El Presidio district, stocks Arizona's best selection of historical, hiking and wildlife guides. The main **post office** is at 141 S Sixth Ave.

Tucson Tours (☎520/297-2911) offer 1hr 30min **city tours** for $15, excursions to Mission San Xavier, the Arizona-Sonora Desert Museum, or Old Tucson for $18, and an extensive programme of trips further afield from around $30 for a half-day, $60 per full day.

Accommodation

Tucson offers a broader range of **accommodation** than Phoenix, with plenty of reasonably priced **hotels** and **motels** downtown as well as some atmospheric B&Bs both in the historic centre and out in the surrounding desert. It also has its fair share of **resorts**, which can be every bit as expensive as their counterparts in Phoenix (if, as a rule, much less stuffy), and **dude ranches**. Once again, rates drop when the mercury rises, and some places are open only in the peak winter and spring seasons.

Hotels, motels and B&Bs

As explained on p.15, accommodation prices, excluding taxes, are indicated throughout this book by the following symbols:

① *up to $30*
② *$30–45*
③ *$45–60*
④ *$60–80*
⑤ *$80–100*
⑥ *$100–130*
⑦ *$130–175*
⑧ *$175–250*
⑨ *$250+*

Casa Tierra, 11155 W Calle Pima, Tucson AZ 85743; ☎520/578-3058. Secluded, three-room, desert-edge B&B near the Arizona-Sonora Desert Museum, modelled on an adobe hacienda, with outdoor spa. Sept–May only, ④.

Econolodge, 3020 S Sixth Ave, Tucson AZ 85713; ☎520/623-5881 or 1-800/623-5881. Inexpensive motel, west of the airport. Summer ②, winter ③.

El Presidio Inn, 297 N Main Ave, Tucson AZ 85701; ☎520/623-6151 or 1-800/349-6151. Three tastefully furnished Spanish colonial suites in historic downtown adobe B&B, with spacious wrap-around verandah. ⑤.

Hotel Congress, 311 E Congress St, Tucson AZ 85701; ☎520/622-8848 or 1-800/722-8848, fax 792-6366. Central, bohemian downtown hotel, an easy walk from *Amtrak*, with vintage Art Deco furnishings. In the 1930s, bank-robber Dillinger was arrested here after pleading for his strangely heavy luggage to be rescued from a blaze on the third floor; now it offers $12 hostel beds for HI/AYH members (no reservations) and simple private rooms for just over $30. There's a small breakfast cafe and a lively bar downstairs, and at night it's one of the hottest spots in town, with loud music and dancing. ①/②.

Park Inn Santa Rita, 88 E Broadway Blvd, Tucson AZ 85701; ☎520/622-4000 or 1-800/622-1120, fax 620-0376. Large if anonymous hotel that's an unexpected downtown bargain, and has a good Mexican cafe downstairs. ③.

Super 8 Downtown, 1248 N Stone Ave, Tucson AZ 85705; ☎520/622-6446 or 1-800/800-8000. Adequate, if not wildly prepossessing, chain motel, a mile northwest of the university not far from downtown. Summer ②, winter ③.

Travelodge Flamingo Sun Motel, 1300 N Stone Ave, Tucson AZ 85705; ☎520/770-1910 or 1-800/300-3533, fax 770-0750. Attractively renovated motel, barely a mile north of downtown Tucson. Summer ②, winter ④.

Ranches and resorts

Tucson

The Arizona Inn, 2200 E Elm St, Tucson AZ 85719; ☎520/325-1541 or 1-800/933-1093, fax 881-5830. Elegant desert oasis that's been a winter favourite for numerous presidents, Rockefellers and the Duke and Duchess of Windsor, but remains surprisingly unstuffy and not all that expensive in low season. Rates include gourmet breakfast. Summer ⑤, winter ⑦.

Best Western Ghost Ranch Lodge, 801 W Miracle Mile, Tucson AZ 85705; ☎520/791-7565 or 1-800/456-7565, fax 791-3898. Charming old-fashioned resort, roughly ten miles north of town, with south-of-the-border stylings, a cactus-filled garden, and amazingly low rates. Summer ②, winter ④.

Loews Ventana Canyon Resort, 7000 N Resort Drive, Tucson AZ 85750; ☎520/299-2020, fax 299-6832. Grand red-brick resort, reaching majestically across a hundred acres at the foot of the Santa Catalina mountains northeast of the city, with its own on-site waterfall. Four restaurants, two golf courses, plus tennis and spa, and the desert on your doorstep. Summer ⑤, winter ⑨.

Tanque Verde Ranch, 14301 E Speedway Blvd, Tucson AZ 85748; ☎520/296-6275 or 1-800/234-DUDE, fax 721-9426. Arizona's most authentic dude ranch, an irresistibly romantic 400-acre spread adjoining Saguaro National Park twenty miles east of downtown, offers luxury accommodation in individual *casitas* and a stable of over a hundred horses. Rates include all meals and a full programme of rides, from early-morning cowboy cookouts to all-day pack trips; there's also tennis, swimming and hiking. Summer ⑧, winter ⑨.

Westward Look Resort, 245 E Ima Rd, Tucson AZ 85704; ☎520/297-1151 or 1-800/722-2500, fax 297-9023. Plush modernized resort in attractive landscaped grounds north of the city, offering extra-large rooms and suites in low-slung *casitas*. The emphasis on physical fitness, and tennis in particular, doesn't preclude having a top-quality restaurant. Summer ④, winter ⑥.

Downtown Tucson

Downtown Tucson, which centres on the area where the east–west Congress Street and Broadway Boulevard cross the north–south Stone Avenue, is characterized by undistinguished modern architecture. The adobe fortress of San Agustín de Tucson occupied what's now the four-block **El Presidio Historic District**, a couple of blocks northwest. None of its original structures is still standing, but several of their nineteenth-century successors, dating from the period when Tucson passed into American hands, have been restored as cafes, art galleries and B&Bs.

Access to much of El Presidio is controlled by the new **Tucson Museum of Art**, alongside at 140 N Main Ave (Sept–May Mon–Sat 10am–4pm, Sun noon–4pm; June–Aug Tues–Sat 10am–4pm, Sun noon–4pm; $2, free Tues). Its oldest house, **La Casa Cordova** at 175 N Meyer Ave (same hours), now contains displays on the city's Mexican heritage, and between October and April, free **walking tours** leave at 11am on Wednesday and Thursday mornings from the museum's tree-shaded courtyard.

The museum itself has an excellent collection of pre-Columbian artefacts, including ceramics with extraordinarily life-like faces pro-

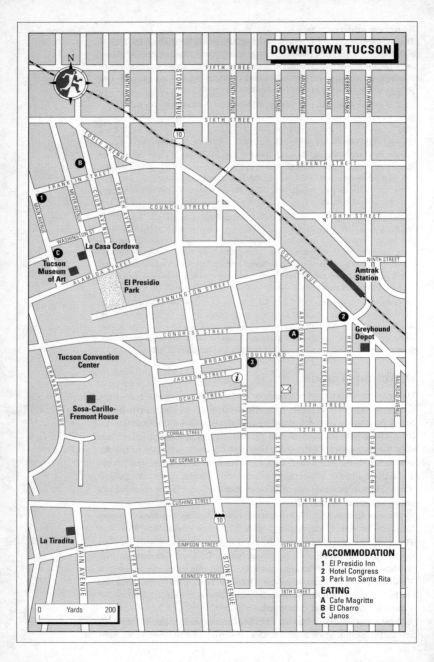

DOWNTOWN TUCSON

FIFTH STREET
NINTH AVENUE
STONE AVENUE
SEVENTH AVENUE
SIXTH STREET
SIXTH AVENUE
ARIZONA AVENUE
FIFTH AVENUE
HERBERT AVENUE
FOURTH AVENUE

SEVENTH STREET

TOOLE AVENUE
10

B

FRANKLIN STREET
CHURCH AVENUE
COUNCIL STREET

EIGHTH STREET

1
MEYER AVENUE
COURT AVENUE

NINTH STREET

WASHINGTON ST
C
La Casa Cordova

TOOLE AVENUE
Amtrak
Station

Tucson Museum
of Art
ALAMEDA STREET
El Presidio
Park
PENNINGTON STREET

CONGRESS STREET

A
ARIZONA AVENUE
2
Greyhound
Depot

Tucson Convention
Center
BROADWAY BOULEVARD
3
FIFTH AVENUE
HERBERT AVENUE
RAILROAD AVENUE

JACKSON STREET
i
SCOTT AVENUE

OCHOA STREET
11TH STREET

Sosa-Carillo-
Fremont House
GRANADA AVENUE

CORRAL STREET
12TH STREET
SIXTH AVENUE

MC CORMICK ST
13TH STREET
FOURTH AVENUE

CONVENT AVENUE
CUSHING STREET

10

La Tiradita
SIMPSON STREET
15TH STREET

MAIN AVENUE
MEYER AVENUE
STONE AVENUE
KENNEDY STREET

16TH STREET

0   Yards   200

ACCOMMODATION
1 El Presidio Inn
2 Hotel Congress
3 Park Inn Santa Rita
EATING
A Cafe Magritte
B El Charro
C Janos

duced by the Mochica culture of northern Peru from 100 BC onwards, textiles from the later Peruvian Chancay culture, and gold from Colombia and Costa Rica. Mexican artefacts range from masks and effigies created by the ancient Olmec and Mixtec peoples, via eighteenth-century religious pieces, to nineteenth-century oil-on-tin family portraits. A large gallery that spirals down into the basement is used for changing exhibitions of modern painting and sculpture, and the gift shop stocks some interesting contemporary crafts.

Three blocks south, engulfed by the Tucson Convention Center complex, the solitary adobe **Soza-Carrillo-Fremont House** (Wed–Sat 10am–4pm; free) is the sole survivor of a neighbourhood torn down during the 1960s in the name of urban renewal. Built for merchant Leopoldo Carrillo in 1858, it was briefly rented by former explorer John C Frémont when he was Governor of Arizona in 1878. Though much restored, it offers a vivid sense of the more civilized side of frontier life, from the high-quality furniture and the saguaro-rib ceilings to the fig-tree-shaded rear courtyard gardens.

Still within walking distance, **Cushing Street**, three more blocks south, marks the start of the **Barrio Historico**. The city's 1880s business district holds plenty of century-old adobes, but its most notable landmark is the sidewalk shrine of **El Tiradito**, "the castaway". Said to mark where a young man was killed by his father-in-law for committing adultery with his mother-in-law, and was buried where he fell, it's famous as the **Wishing Shrine**. Light a candle that burns through the night, and your prayers will be answered.

The University district

The other main area of interest in central Tucson is the **University of Arizona**, which spreads between Sixth Street and Speedway Boulevard a mile east of downtown. Park Avenue, on its western flank, is lined with funky cafes and stores that cater to students.

On campus, the highlight is the two-part **Arizona State Museum** (Mon–Sat 10am–5pm, Sun noon–5pm; free). Its southern wing concentrates on archeology, with a diorama of a mammoth hunt, an exhibit on cave-dwellers, and pottery and a macaw skull unearthed during university-sponsored excavations at the abandoned Hopi site of Homolovi (see p.257). The recently remodelled north wing is more innovative, housing the fascinating *Paths of Life* exhibition, which illuminates the history and beliefs of all the major Native American peoples of the Southwest.

Just to the north, the **Center for Creative Photography** holds one of the world's finest photography archives (Mon–Fri 11am–5pm, Sun noon–5pm; free). Ansel Adams left his personal negatives, prints and journals to the university on condition that they be available to the public, and his collection has since been complemented by photographs from all eras. Temporary exhibitions can only show a tiny selection, however, and the archive is primarily intended for serious

Fruitissimo, opposite the main university gate at 998 E University Blvd, sells delicious fruit smoothies.

scholars who know what they wish to see. Next door, the eclectic **UA Museum of Art** (winter Mon–Fri 9am–5pm, Sun noon–4pm; summer Mon–Fri 10am–3.30pm, Sun noon–4pm; free) has some morbid Spanish *retablos* and assorted modern pieces, with canvases by Rembrandt, Picasso, O'Keeffe and Warhol, and some fine cubist sculpture by Jacques Lipchitz.

The **Arizona Historical Society Museum**, across Park Avenue at 949 E Second St (Mon–Sat 10am–4pm, Sun noon–4pm; free), is a tired and somewhat humdrum ragbag of a place, currently in the process of being updated, where reconstructed rooms trace the history of Tucson *"From Shelter to Showplace"*.

Northern Tucson and the Santa Catalina Mountains

Metropolitan Tucson's northern boundary is formed by the natural barrier of the **Santa Catalina Mountains**, whose bare, dusty slopes are eventually crowned with pine forests. At the edge of the mountains, eight miles north of downtown, **Tohono Chul Park**, a block west of Oracle Road at Ina Road, is a former private estate that has been converted into a desert garden (daily 7am–sunset; $2 donation; ☎520/742-6455). The name means "desert corner" in the Tohono 'O'odham language, and it's now filled with yucca, prickly pear and other cactuses, and a-flutter with hummingbirds.

The park's Tohono Chul Tea Room is reviewed on p.227.

For an enjoyable taste of the mountains, head to **Sabino Canyon**, at the far end of Sabino Canyon Road in the Coronado National Forest, ten miles northeast of downtown (daily 8am–4.30pm; free; ☎520/749-2861). The canyon was cut into the lower reaches of Mount Lemmon by Sabino Creek, which manages to flow for up to eleven months of the year, and is lined by green vegetation. Assorted trails lace into the hills from the four-mile riverbank road – barred to private vehicles, but served by jump-on, jump-off **tram rides** ($5) – which is popular with early-morning joggers.

The 9157-foot summit of **Mount Lemmon**, which towers above Sabino Canyon, is a two-day hike beyond the canyon, or a one-hour drive on the recently upgraded **Mount Lemmon Highway**. After branching off Tanque Verde Road, an eastward continuation of Grant Road, a few miles east of the Sabino Canyon turn-off, this winds for 25 slow miles up the mountain, with countless panoramic viewpoints to either side.

Western Tucson

Twelve miles west of the university on Speedway Boulevard, en route to Saguaro, **Old Tucson**, 201 S Kinney Rd (daily 9am–9pm; $11.95) is an entertaining if contrived Wild West theme park. Its focus is a movie-set mock-up of the "Old Pueblo" that was constructed for a 1939 western, and has been used for TV shows and movies up to such recent productions as *Tombstone* and *Geronimo*. Visitors can ride a stagecoach or a coal-fired steam train, and watch gunfights on Main Street or a bawdy music-hall show in the saloon. Kids love it, though since Old Tucson had to be almost entirely rebuilt after being gutted by fire in April 1995, it's now even more spurious than ever.

Part zoo, part garden, the much more worthwhile **Arizona-Sonora Desert Museum** stands two miles further west in Tucson Mountain Park (Oct–Feb daily 8.30am–5pm; March–Sept daily 7.30am–6pm; adults $8.95, ages 6–12 $1.75). Gallery displays in the museum proper explain regional geology and history, and a series of dioramas are filled with tarantulas, rattlesnakes and other creepy crawlers. In enclosures along the loop path beyond – a hot walk in high summer – bighorn sheep, mountain lions, jaguars and other seldom-seen desert denizens prowl in credible simulations of their natural habitats, and a colony of impish prairie dogs goes about its impenetrable business. Hawks and bald eagles fly about their own large aviary, thankfully separated from the greenhouse-full of hummingbirds. The museum also serves as an animal rescue centre: almost all the animals you see were injured in some way before ending up here, and would be unable to survive on their own.

The outdoor terrace of the museum's Ironwood Tree restaurant makes a great stop-off for a light lunch.

Saguaro National Park

Flanking Tucson to either side, the two sections of **SAGUARO NATIONAL PARK** offer visitors a rare and enthralling opportunity to stroll through strange desert "forests" of monumental, multi-limbed **saguaro** (pronounced *sa-wah-row*) **cactuses**. Both tend to be seen on short forays from the city; in summer, it's far too hot to do more than pose for photographs, dwarfed beneath some especially eccentric specimen, and there is in any case no lodging, or even permanent campground, in either segment.

Saguaro prefer sloping foothills, which offer a little run-off after rain, to level desert, so both sections include rugged mountain tracts. Most of the **Rincon Mountain District** in the east, which became a national monument in 1933, is much higher, and the one road only penetrates its low-lying fringes. It was joined in 1961 by the **Tucson Mountain District** in the west, which incorporates the world's densest stand of saguaro. The two together were upgraded to national park status in 1994.

To receive information by mail, write to Saguaro National Park, 3693 S Old Spanish Trail, Tucson AZ 85730.

The western park: Tucson Mountain District

The **Tucson Mountain District** of Saguaro National Park stretches north from the Desert Museum around fifteen miles west of downtown Tucson, and charges no admission fee to visitors. Beyond the Red Hills **visitor center** (daily 8am–5pm; ☎520/733-5158), the nine-mile **Bajada Loop Drive** is not fully paved but is always passable to ordinary vehicles. It loops through a wonderland of weird saguaro, offering plentiful short hiking trails and photo opportunities. The easiest walk is the half-mile **Desert Discovery Nature**

The Saguaro Cactus; a Desert Saga

As the mighty, multi-armed **saguaro cactus** is unique to the Sonora Desert, and Tucson stands near the desert's northeastern extremity, the Tucson region is one of very few places in the Wild West where real-life saguaro grow. Whatever you may have seen in the movies, you can drive a long way in Arizona without seeing a saguaro; the thrill when you finally encounter a thousand at once is deeply satisfying.

Each saguaro can grow up to fifty feet tall, and weigh up to eight tons, but it reaches that size at the slowest of rates. A teenage cactus is a foot high, a fifty-year-old more like seven feet. At 75, it sprouts the first of what may amount to forty "arms", and it only reaches its full height at around 150, with perhaps another fifty years to go before it dies. Its roots radiate as much as a hundred feet in all directions, barely three inches below the surface, and can draw enough water from one rainstorm to last the plant for two years.

Each year from the age of thirty onwards, between late April and June, a saguaro grows up to a hundred white flowers, each of which blossoms for a single night and dies by the next afternoon. In its lifetime, each saguaro produces as many as forty million seeds, though few if any are likely to germinate and thrive. It's also home to an intricate community of birds, insects, mammals and reptiles. Woodpeckers and owls burrow holes into the trunk for their nests, which the cactus heals over with hardened "scar tissue" to create permanent hollows. The **Tohono 'O'odham** Indians traditionally cut away these depressions for use as bowls; they also mashed the saguaro's succulent crimson fruit to make jam, syrup and even wine, and used its long wood-like ribs to construct dwellings and fences.

Contact park rangers in either section for details of ***backcountry camping*** *(by permit only).*

Trail, but gluttons for punishment can follow the longer **Hugh Norris Trail** up a ridge to the 4687-foot summit of Wasson Peak.

Branching onto Golden Gate Road from the northeastern limit of the loop drive brings you in around five miles to Picture Rocks Road, which joins **Ina Road** a few more miles along and thus makes an alternative route back to northern Tucson.

The eastern park: Rincon Mountain District

To reach the eastern section of Saguaro National Park, the **Rincon Mountain District**, drive seventeen miles east of town along first Broadway Boulevard and then Old Spanish Trail. An **admission fee** of $4 per vehicle is collected at the **visitor center** at the end of the road (daily 8am–5pm; ☎520/733-5153); national park passes are both sold and accepted.

Although short trails such as the quarter-mile **Desert Ecology Trail** lead off the eight-mile **Cactus Forest Drive** (Nov–March daily 7am–5pm; April–Oct daily 7am–7pm), many visitors come specifically to hike far from the road, up into the mountains. The saguaro cactuses thin out almost as soon as you start climbing the **Tanque Verde Ridge Trail**, which leads in due course to a hundred-mile network of remote footpaths through thickly forested canyons.

Eating

Though downtown Tucson shuts down pretty early each evening –
it's hard to find anywhere open after 9pm – the city has a fine selection of **restaurants**. Mexican joints and cowboy-style Wild-West
steakhouses abound in the central districts, while fancier restaurants
congregate in the exclusive St Philip's Plaza, a few miles north, as
well as in the resort hotels.

Coffeehouses

Coffee, Etc, 2830 N Campbell Ave; ☎520/881-8070. Hectic but attractive 24-
hr cafe, serving burgers and sandwiches as well as fresh-ground coffee.

Cup Cafe, *Hotel Congress*, 311 E Congress St; ☎520/798-1618. Jazzy downtown cafe, straight out of the 1930s but updated to include an espresso bar,
and serving a bewilderingly broad menu from 8am until after midnight daily.

Cuppuccinos, 3400 E Speedway Blvd; ☎520/323-7205. Espresso bar that
does its best to turn Tucson into Seattle, with pastries in the week and
omelettes at weekends. Daily until late, from 7am Mon–Fri, 8am Sat & Sun.

Cafes and diners

Blue Willow, 2616 N Campbell Ave; ☎520/795-8736. Tasty, fruity breakfasts
and light lunches and dinners, served on a pleasant garden patio. Open daily
until late, from 7am on weekdays and 8am weekends.

Cafe Magritte, 254 E Congress St; ☎520/884-8004. Self-consciously arty
downtown cafe, with an eclectic – but not expensive – menu to match its offbeat clientele. Great desserts, coffees and digestifs, plus sandwiches and pasta
for under $10. Daily except Mon, 11am until late.

El Charro, 311 N Court Ave; ☎520/622-1922. Housed in the same El Presidio
building since 1922, this claims to be the oldest Mexican restaurant in the US,
and now has its own lively bar next door. The food is good, though not especially fiery; specialities include fine *chimichangas,* said to be a Tucson invention, and the *topopo* salad, piled like a pyramid atop a tortilla. Open from 11am
daily for lunch and dinner.

The Good Earth, El Mercado Mall, 6366 E Broadway at Wilmot; ☎520/745-
6600. Healthy, if not exclusively vegetarian, hangout, with cactus-filled courtyard and its own bakery. Pizzas, Mexican dishes, salads and grilled chicken.
Open daily for all meals; lunch specials cost around $6, dinner more like $10.

Jack's Original Barbeque, 5250 E 22nd St; ☎520/750-1280. Drive-in barbecue pit with a fifty-year tradition of serving tangy pork ribs followed by down-
home peach cobbler or sweet potato pie. Open daily for lunch and dinner.

Ranchers Club, *Hotel Park Tucson*, 5151 E Grant Rd; ☎520/323-6262.
Tucson's best and biggest cuts of beef – starting under $20, and rising to 48-
oz steaks for $50 – grilled over desert mesquite or cherrywood flame, plus
excellent soups and salads, all served beneath the horrified gaze of generations
of stuffed animals. Open for lunch and dinner Mon–Fri, dinner only Sat.

Tohono Chul Tea Room, Tohono Chul Park, 7366 N Paseo del Norte;
☎520/797-1711. Attractive adobe cafe in small desert park on the northern
fringes of town, operated by the *Cafe Terra Cotta* (see overleaf). Open daily
8am–5pm, and ideal for breakfast, a light lunch or a scones-and-jam afternoon tea.

Fine dining

Cafe Terra Cotta, St Philip's Plaza, 4310 N Campbell Ave; ☎520/577-8100. Inventive Southwestern cuisine in smart mall surroundings. The menu ranges from gourmet pizzas cooked in a wood-burning oven to meats grilled with chiles, all at under $20. Open daily for lunch and dinner, until late.

Daniel's Restaurant and Trattoria, St Philip's Plaza, 4340 N Campbell Ave; ☎520/742-3200. North Italian specialties served amid stylish black decor, lightened with Art-Deco mirrors. The sauces are kept light, and the breads are delicious. Open for dinner only, daily from 5pm.

The Gold Room, *Westward Look Resort*, 245 E Ina Rd; ☎520/297-1151. Bright, relatively casual resort restaurant, offering health-conscious breakfasts and lunches, and a dinner menu of richer delights such as braised ostrich in cherry sauce, at around $20 per entree. Open daily for all meals.

Janos, 150 N Main St; ☎520/884-9426. This immaculate El Presidio adobe is one of Tucson's trendiest spots. Open for dinner only, with an imaginative selection of Southwestern-themed dishes. Entrees cost up to $30, but in summer there's a $13 sampler menu. Closed Sun, and also Mon in summer.

Kingfisher, 2564 E Grant Rd; ☎520/323-7739. Upmarket new fish restaurant that serves seafood from Maine lobsters and Maryland soft-shelled crabs to Oregon oysters, with an eclectic mix of American cooking styles from Cajun to New Pacific. Open for lunch and dinner daily.

Ventana Room, *Loews Ventana Canyon Resort*, 7000 N Resort Drive; ☎520/299-2020. Showcase resort dining room, commanding a panoramic view from the northern foothills. Continental-style grilled meats and fish from $20 per entree, or pick the *prix fixe* menu. Opens for dinner nightly at 6pm.

Entertainment and nightlife

Tucson **nightlife** focuses on Congress Street downtown, with its gaggle of arty cafes and nightclubs; most venues double as bars or restaurants. A handful of studenty places can be found near the university, and there are half a dozen country and western saloons on the outskirts of town. For a full rundown, check the listings in the free *Tucson Weekly*. The Tucson Convention Center Music Hall, 260 S Church Ave (☎520/791-4266), features orchestral concerts, opera and ballet, while the city's prime drama venue is the Temple of Music and Art, 330 S Scott Ave (☎520/622-2823). The Tucson Jazz Society (☎520/743-3399) promotes jazz gigs all over town.

Cafe Sweetwater, 340 E Sixth St; ☎520/622-6464. Casual, thirty-something place with regular live jazz.

Club Congress, *Hotel Congress*, 311 E Congress St; ☎520/622-8848. Hectic, trendy, late-opening bar, with live music a couple of nights each week.

Cushing Street Bar and Restaurant, 343 S Meyer Ave; ☎520/622-7984. Good live music of all sorts, in a hundred-year-old Barrio Historico building.

Gentle Ben's Brewing Co, Tyndall Ave & University Blvd; ☎520/624-4177. Micro-brewery, regularly packed out with students, which serves simple food.

The Maverick, King of Clubs, 4702 E 22nd St; ☎520/748-0456. Old-fashioned country-music honky-tonk, well out from the centre and brimming with stetsons.

The Rialto Theatre, 318 E Congress St; ☎520/740-1986. 1920s vaudeville theatre that's re-opened as Tucson's hottest venue for touring bands.

South to Mexico: the Mission Trail

The tract of southern Arizona that lies between Tucson and the
Mexican border was the first part of the state to be settled by the
Spanish, and it remained Arizona's most populous region until well
into the nineteenth century. The Spanish called this region **Pimería
Alta**, and its scattering of **mission churches** and abandoned forts
still testify to their efforts to Christianize its **Pima** inhabitants from
1692 onwards. Epidemics and Apache raids meant that only Tucson
of the early towns grew to any size, but as recently as 1870, the
Pima were still Arizona's largest ethnic group.

Twelve thousand Pima – now known as the **Akimel 'O'odham**
– survive on the **San Xavier Reservation** a few miles south of
Tucson. The magnificent church of San Xavier – the "White
Dove of the Desert" – is the prime attraction for modern travellers who drive the 65 miles down to Mexico on the **I-19** interstate, but the artistic community at **Tubac**, and the atmospheric frontier town of **Nogales**, help to make for an entertaining
international day-trip.

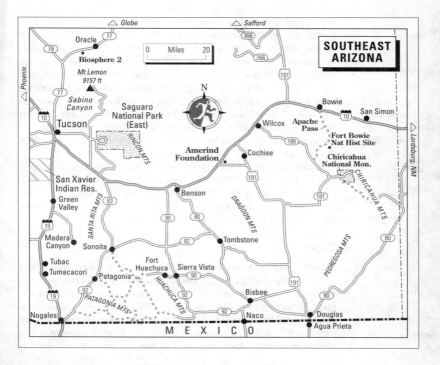

San Xavier del Bac

Even today, the white-plastered walls and towers of **San Xavier del Bac**, the best-preserved mission church in the United States, seem like a dazzling desert mirage. How much more dramatic they must have been two centuries ago, when to Christian missionaries and Apache warriors alike they symbolized the Spanish quest to subdue and convert the native peoples of the Southwest.

Located a mere nine miles south of downtown Tucson, just west of I-19, the church stands on the eastern fringes of the arid San Xavier Reservation. It was founded by the Jesuit **Father Eusebio Kino** in 1700, beside the Santa Cruz River and next to the Pima village of Bac. Kino's church was destroyed by Apaches in 1767; what survives is its replacement, built for the Franciscans between 1783 and 1797. No one knows the name of the architect responsible for its Spanish Baroque, even Moorish lines – it consists almost entirely of domes and arches, making only minimal use of timber – let alone the 'O'odham craftsmen who embellished its every feature.

Although the church attracts a constant stream of tourists (daily 9am–6pm; donation), the ideal time to come is on Sunday morning, when four separate masses attract large congregations of Indians from the reservation. As you approach the main entrance across the dusty plaza, with saguaro cactuses to the right and ocotillo to the left, take a moment to appreciate its ornate facade. On the top level, a cat squats on the spiral flourish to the right, eyeing a mouse in the corresponding position on the left. The tower on the right was never completed, possibly to avoid the need to pay a levy to the authorities back in Mexico. Inside the church, the left alcove holds a recumbent, articulated statue of **St Francis Xavier**, covered with metal *milagros* – images of healed bodyparts – and photographs of children. Devout Catholics are permitted to lean in and lift his head. The approach to the main altar is guarded by two naive gilt-headed lions, representing the royal lions of Leon and Castille in Spain.

The major feast days at San Xavier Mission are those of St Francis of Assissi, on October 4, and St Francis Xavier, December 3.

Still within the mission walls, to the right of the church, a small **museum** displays a gigantic illuminated sheepskin psalter, and photos of other remote churches on the Tohono O'odham reservation. The little hillock immediately to the east is topped by a replica of the shrine of Saint Bernadette at Lourdes, France.

Tubac

TUBAC, fifty miles south of San Xavier, was the first permanent Spanish settlement in what's now Arizona, founded in 1752 as a **presidio** or fortress to guard against repetitions of the previous year's Pima Revolt against the Jesuits. In 1775, its commander, Juan Bautista de Anza, launched the expedition that established **San Francisco**, but Tubac declined after 1776, when its garrison was shifted to the new city of Tucson. For the next century, it was alternately abandoned and resettled as Apache raids permitted; in the 1850s it even briefly became a **Mormon** colony.

South to Mexico: the Mission Trail

Since World War II, Tubac has redefined itself as an **arts colony**; it's a tiny little place, where dust-devils whirl down unpaved streets filled with crafts and jewellery stores. Most sell folk items from south of the border, but the **Tubac Center of the Arts**, 9 Plaza Rd (Oct–May Tues–Sat 10am–4.30pm, Sun 1–4.30pm; free), holds exhibitions by local artists.

Although the foundations of the original adobe fortress now lie beneath an earthen mound in the **Tubac Presidio State Historic Park** (daily 8am–5pm; $2), they can be admired from a cool underground viewing gallery. The large museum alongside contains pieces from all periods of Tubac's long history, including some beautiful naive *retablos*, the press used to print Arizona's first newspaper, *The Weekly Arizonan*, in March 1859, and a crucifix depicting the black "Christo Negro" – a Native American Christ.

The highlight of Tubac's annual calendar is early February's week-long Festival of the Arts.

Practicalities

For information on Tubac, ask at the state park or call the local **chamber of commerce** (☎520/398-2704). The nicest of the **B&Bs** in the old centre is the *Tubac Country Inn*, a small blue wooden house at 409 Burruel St (☎520/398-3178; closed Aug; ④), with four en-suite rooms. Nearby, the flower-bedecked *Tosh's Hacienda de Tubac*, Camino Otero and Burruel (☎520/398-3008), is a clean Southwestern and Mexican **restaurant**, open daily for lunch and dinner. The *Burro Inn*, west of the interstate at 70 W El Burro Lane (☎520/398-2281; summer ④, winter ⑤), is a steakhouse-cum-motel with a well-priced selection of comfortable two-room suites.

Tubac's zip code is AZ 85646.

Tumacácori National Historical Park

A **Spanish mission** founded by Father Kino in 1691, before its more celebrated neighbour at San Xavier (see opposite), is now the focus of the **TUMACÁCORI NATIONAL HISTORICAL PARK**, three miles south of Tubac and nineteen miles north of the border (daily 8am–5pm; $2; ☎520/398-2341). Like San Xavier, the church here was built at the end of the eighteenth century, but Tumacácori soon proved unable to withstand Apache raids, and was abandoned in 1848, five years before the region passed into US control.

It's now an evocative ruin, topped by a restored whitewashed dome but home only to the birds that fly down from the Patagonia Mountains. Behind its red-tinged weatherbeaten facade, the plaster has crumbled from the interior walls to reveal bare adobe bricks. A few traces of a mural can still be discerned in the raised sanctuary, but little remains of the priests' living quarters alongside.

A fascinating **museum** holds a replica of a banner carried by missionaries; one side depicts the Madonna and Child, the other shows Indians burning in hell. Opposite the gate, the *Tumacacori Mission Restaurant* serves Mexican and Greek specialities.

Nogales, Arizona and Nogales, Mexico

Twenty miles south of Tumacácori , an hour from Tucson, sits the
largest of the Arizonan–Mexican border towns, **NOGALES** – in effect
two towns, one in the US and one across the border in Mexico.
Known jointly as *Ambos Nogales* (both Nogales), they were founded
in 1880 to handle the frontier formalities necessary on the main
route between their two countries, and still see vast quantities of
freight traffic daily. Tourists too pass through in considerable numbers, though with cheap Mexican crafts now so widely available in
the US, the day-trippers these days tend to be looking for cut-price
medicines rather than rugs or hammocks.

There's nothing in particular to see on either side of the border,
though the contrast between the sedate, ordered streets of the
American town and the jumbled whitewashed houses clinging to the
slopes in Mexico hits you as soon as you come in sight. Nogales,
Arizona – the birthplace of iconoclastic jazz great **Charles Mingus** –
is a dreary little community, while Nogales, Mexico is basically a lively, large-scale street market.

Crossing the border is straightforward, as Mexican visas are
only required by travellers heading more than 21km south of the
border. US citizens should, however, ideally carry their passports
or birth certificates – drivers' licences are not always sufficient –
while foreign visitors should check that their visa status entitles
them to re-enter the US; if you're on or eligible for the Visa
Waiver Scheme (see p.8), you're fine. There's no need to **change
money**; US dollars are freely accepted by stores and businesses in
Mexico.

If you do plan to set off south, pick up a **tourist visa** just beyond
the border crossing. Then take a taxi (around $6) a couple of miles
to the **long-distance bus station**, from which regular buses head to
Hermosillo, **Guaymas** on the Pacific (a good overnight stop), and
Los Mochis, the start of the Copper Canyon Railroad.

Practicalities

Nogales' **visitor center** is in Kino Park at the north end of town (winter Mon–Fri 8am–5pm; summer Mon–Fri 8am–1pm & 2–5pm;
☎520/287-3685). Hourly direct **buses** to Tucson are operated by
Citizens/Grayline Bus, 35 N Terrace Ave (☎520/287-5628).

*Nogales' zip
code is AZ
85621.*

None of the Arizona-side **motels** stands within a mile of the border; the closest is the *Best Western Siesta Motel*, 673 N Grand Ave
(☎520/287-4671, fax 287-9616; ③), while the cluster near the
interstate three miles out includes a *Super 8*, 543 W Mariposa Rd
(☎520/281-2242 or 1-800/800-8000; ③).

Most visitors prefer to **eat** in Mexico, where abundant cafes and
diners line the busy central streets. Classier dining is offered by the
unusual *La Roca*, hollowed into the rocky hillside just east of the railroad, a couple of blocks from the border at c/Elias 91, where a full

seafood meal still costs well under $20. The best restaurant on the Arizona side is *Mr C's Supper Club*, above town at 282 W View Point Drive (☎520/281-9000), which specializes in fish.

The Patagonia-Sonoita Creek Sanctuary

A longer but even more attractive route back from Nogales to Tucson avoids the interstate by following highways 82 and 83 northeast from Nogales through the lush **Sonoita Valley**, in the craggy mountains of the Coronado National Forest.

Thanks to the **Patagonia-Sonoita Creek Sanctuary** (Wed–Sun 7.30am–3.30pm; donation; ☎520/394-2000), the mining and cattle-ranching town of **PATAGONIA**, twenty miles up from Nogales, now attracts weekend crowds of **birdwatchers**. Located at the far southwestern end of a mile-long dirt road that leads off Fourth Street, this dense riverbank stand of oaks and cottonwoods is home to an amazing range of songbirds and raptors, including finches and flycatchers, kingbirds and kestrels, and woodpeckers and cardinals. With all this colourful collection to choose from, the sighting most prized by twitchers from all over the world is a drab little specimen called the northern beardless tyrannulet.

Twelve miles north of Patagonia, Hwy-83 veers northwest to rejoin I-10 two miles east of Saguaro National Park; Hwy-82 cuts east toward Tombstone, 35 miles away (see p.235).

Practicalities

Welcoming little **B&Bs** in Patagonia include the three-room *Duquesne House*, a century-old adobe boarding house at 357 Duquesne St (☎520/394-2732; ④), and the two-room *Little House*, 341 Sonoita Ave (☎520/394-2493; ③). The best place for a lunchtime snack is the **bakery/cafe** *Ovens of Patagonia* on Hwy-82 (☎520/394-2483)

Patagonia's
zip code *is AZ 85624.*

The southeast corner

Although the **I-10** interstate somehow manages to plot a dull and monotonous course across **southeast Arizona**, the rugged territory to the south holds some of the state's most spectacular scenery and memorable historic sites. The much-mythologized Wild-West outpost of **Tombstone** is the best known, and does its best to entertain the hordes of cowboy fanatics who troop this way, but the mining town of **Bisbee** is in many ways a more evocative relic of frontier times.

Further east, the **Chiricahua Mountains** witnessed the final saga of Native American resistance to federal encroachment, in the 1880s guerrilla campaign of Geronimo's **Apaches**. These mountains are merely one of around a dozen separate ranges that soar from the deserts, known as "**sky islands**" because each wilderness harbours its own unique ecosystem of plants, bird and animals.

Benson, Willcox and the Amerind Foundation Museum

The one point of interest on the barren interstate run to New Mexico comes 65 miles east of Tucson at exit 318, in the shape of the excellent **Amerind Foundation Museum** (June–Aug Wed–Sun 10am–4pm; Sept–May daily 10am–4pm; $3). This private anthropological museum covers native cultures from North, Central and Southern America, but specializes in the Southwest, and features fine Apache, Navajo and Hopi crafts, plus a gallery of Western art.

The museum stands in remote Texas Canyon, halfway between the nondescript communities of **BENSON** and **WILLCOX**. Both have several budget motels and little else, though the red-painted *Dining Car*, a genuine railroad car now serving as a diner, makes a fun stop for lunch in Willcox.

The long-delayed opening to the public of **Kartchner Caverns**, ten miles south of Benson on Hwy-90 – a complex of "live" limestone caves said to rival New Mexico's Carlsbad Caverns – was said to be imminent as this book went to press.

Sierra Vista

SIERRA VISTA, 25 miles south of the interstate on Hwy-90, is a characterless modern town that has grown in tandem with the Army base at **Fort Huachuca**, one of the few nineteenth-century military outposts to survive into the modern era. Once home to detachments of Apache scouts and Buffalo Soldiers, the fort still employs over thirteen thousand people, now working on high-tech electronic early-warning systems and the like. Its oldest buildings house dull displays on its early years (Mon–Fri 9am–4pm, Sat & Sun 1–4pm; free).

Sierra Vista's zip code is AZ 85635.

Plenty of **motels** in town cater to visiting service families and nature-lovers. The *Windermere Hotel*, 2047 S Hwy-92 (☎520/459-5900 or 1-800/825-4656, fax 458-1347; ④) is the newest and largest; the *Super 8*, 100 Fab Ave (☎520/459-5380 or 1-800/800-8000; ③), among the most reasonably priced. Seven miles south, the *Ramsey Canyon Inn*, 31 Ramsey Canyon Rd (☎520/378-3010; ⑤), is a plush six-room B&B where a battery of sugar-water feeders ensures the constant presence of countless colourful **hummingbirds**.

Coronado National Memorial

Tucked into the southernmost notch of the Huachuca Mountains, five miles off Hwy-92 twenty miles from Sierra Vista, **CORONADO NATIONAL MEMORIAL** commemorates the approximate spot where in May 1540 the expedition of **Francisco Vasquez de Coronado** first entered what's now the United States. A short video and some interesting displays in the **visitor center** (daily 8am–5pm; ☎520/366-5515) explain the history, but the memorial basically exists to offer a selection of scenic **hiking trails**.

The story of Coronado's expedition is told on p.472.

The best short hike climbs south from the washboard dirt road west of the visitor center at its highest point, **Montezuma Pass**. The 0.4-mile **Coronado Peak Trail** culminates in huge views in all directions, and especially to the pyramidal Mexican mountains across the border. Heading north from the same trailhead, you can hike for twenty miles up the western flank of the Huachucas. If the weather's good enough – check with rangers – ordinary vehicles can continue west on unpaved roads all the way to **Nogales** (see p.232), fifty miles distant beyond the Patagonia Mountains.

The
southeast
corner

Tombstone

Perhaps the most famous town in the Wild West, **TOMBSTONE** lies 22 miles south of I-10 on US-80, 67 miles southeast of Tucson. More than a century has passed since its mining days came to an end, but "The Town Too Tough to Die" clings to an after-life as a tourist theme-park. With its dusty streets, wooden sidewalks and swinging saloon doors, it's surprisingly unchanged. Most adults, however, have seen too many inauthentic replicas and movie re-creations for the real thing to retain much appeal, and so Tombstone is reduced to trying to divert kids with tacky dioramas and daily shoot-outs.

When **Edward Schieffelin** began prospecting in the Dragoon Mountains in 1877, he was told by soldiers stationed nearby that all he'd find would be his own tombstone. Hence the name of the town that rose from the desert when he made Arizona's largest **silver** strike, in March 1878. Schieffelin sold his stake for $500,000, but the mine produced $30 million in the next seven years, and by 1880 Tombstone was home to over ten thousand people. Drifters arrived from the played-out gold fields of Canada and Australia, and gamblers came in from Dodge City, only for the mine to hit water 500 feet below ground in 1886, and be flooded beyond repair.

Most of the buildings that fill modern Tombstone's simple grid date from the early 1880s. Decaying wagons are parked on the street corners, and signs along the boardwalks mark the sites of famous shoot-outs. Although the gunfight at the OK Corral in fact took place on Fremont Street, the **OK Corral** itself remains the major attraction for visitors (daily 8.30am–5pm; $2). As you enter the corral building, on Allen Street between Third and Fourth, the first thing you see is the hearse used to take the victims away. In the second of two baking-hot adobe-walled courtyards beyond, crude dummies show the supposed locations of the Earps and the Clantons, in complete contradiction to contemporary reports of the fight. The original studio of photographer C S Fly stands alongside, displaying his pictures of Geronimo and other Apache warriors, and you can also visit the room from which Big Nose Kate, Doc Holliday's girlfriend, is said to have witnessed the shootings.

A couple of blocks along Allen Street, the **Bird Cage Theater** (daily 8am–6pm; $3.50) was Tombstone's leading venue for entertainment of all kinds. Seven "bird cages", much like theater boxes but

Regular
Tombstone
shoot-outs
include re-
enactments at
the OK Corral
at 2pm on
alternate
Sundays, and
Helldorado
***Days**, held on*
the third week-
end in
October.

The southeast corner

Tombstone's Episcopalian minister at the time of the shoot-out, Endicott Peabody, went on to be Franklin Roosevelt's White House chaplain.

The Gunfight at the OK Corral

Despite the world-wide fame of the shoot-out with which it ended – the legendary **Gunfight at the OK Corral** – how the feud between the **Earps** and the **Clantons** began remains obscure. To Hollywood, the Earps have always been the heroes, with Wyatt played by firm-jawed stars like Henry Fonda and Kevin Costner. They were, after all, officers of the law, although it was **Virgil** who was Tombstone's marshal, and his brothers **Wyatt** and **Morgan** merely temporary deputies. Ike Clanton, his brother Billy and their "gang" were freebooting cattle rustlers, who raided Mexican ranches for beef to feed Tombstone's hungry miners.

Such family-based clans were typical of the West, where it was hard for individuals to prosper alone but trustworthy partners were few and far between. Equally typically, both factions had allied themselves with more powerful forces. The Earps dreamed of establishing their own cattle empire, but in Tombstone they were the hired guns of the town's **Republican** elite. For the owners and managers of the local mines, a federally imposed end to Arizona's frontier anarchy was essential for future investment. Their mouthpiece was the Republican mayor, John Clum, who was also editor of the *Tombstone Epitaph*. The Clantons, like most cowboys and small-scale ranchers, were aligned with the county sheriff, **Democrat** John Behan.

In the spring of 1881, masked gunmen held up a *Wells Fargo* stagecoach near Tombstone, and killed two passengers. Some sources say the robbers were Clanton associates; others, that a familiar cough betrayed one to be **John "Doc" Holliday**, a consumptive dentist from Georgia who was close to the Earps, and that the victims were Clanton's men. The holdup may even have been a joint operation by both groups, who fell out when the plan went awry.

By October, each faction had sworn to shoot the other on sight. The showdown finally came at 2pm on **October 26, 1881**. Virgil, Wyatt and Morgan Earp, together with Doc Holliday, confronted the Clanton brothers, Tom and Frank McLaury, and Billy Claiborne, not in the OK Corral itself, but on Fremont Street nearby. Two of the Clanton group were unarmed, whereas all the Earps had pistols, and Holliday was carrying a shotgun. The Earps fired first. When the shooting stopped, Billy Clanton and the McLaury brothers were dead; Virgil and Morgan Earp, and Doc Holliday, had been wounded, and Ike Clanton had fled.

Under the headline "Three Men Hurled Into Eternity in the Duration of a Moment", the next day's *Tombstone Epitaph* reported that "the feeling among our best citizens is that the Marshal was entirely justifiable." However, Wyatt and Holliday were charged with murder, and were held in jail before being acquitted towards the end of November.

In March 1882, Morgan Earp was killed by a shot fired through the window as he played billiards in Tombstone's *Campbell & Hatch* saloon. Three days later, Wyatt Earp shot the chief suspect, Clanton associate Frank Stilwell, in Tucson. He's said to have killed two more of the Clanton gang that summer before leaving Tombstone for good, with his surviving brothers. Warrants were issued for his arrest, but the governor of Colorado refused to authorize his extradition to Arizona on the grounds that he faced lynching if he returned to Tombstone. Instead, Wyatt Earp moved to Los Angeles, where he was lionized by early movie-makers, and died in 1929.

curtained off and said to have been used by prostitutes, hang from either side of the main hall. Those on the left were frequented by the Earps and their cronies, while the ones on the right were the preserve of Sheriff Behan and the Clantons. The theatre now holds a motley collection of curiosities, including a revolting foot-long "merman" from China and another ornate hearse, while downstairs you can see the old gaming tables and bordello rooms.

Tombstone's role as the seat of Cochise County – before it was supplanted by Bisbee – is recalled at the **Tombstone Courthouse State Historic Park**, Third and Toughnut (daily 8am–5pm; $2). Among displays on the Apache and early outlaws, the sheriff's office here holds the coroner's report on John Heith, a robber lynched in 1884 by a Bisbee mob: "I find that the deceased died of emphysima of the lungs which might have been caused by strangulation, self-inflicted or otherwise". Upstairs, you can watch a video reconstruction of a notorious 1897 murder trial in the former courtroom, while admiring the gallows in the high-walled yard outside.

Boothill Graveyard, half a mile north on US-80, closed in May 1884, having been filled by 276 burials. In keeping with the souvenir store that now guards the entrance, several of the graves bear dubious jokey epitaphs, but you can see where the losers at the OK Corral still rest in peace (daily 7.30am–6pm; free).

Practicalities

Tombstone's **visitor center** is at Allen and Fourth (Mon–Sat 9am–5pm, Sun 2–5pm; ☎520/457-3929 or 1-800/457-3423), while the *Territorial Book Trader* (☎520/457-3170), at the same intersection, has a fine stock of books on local history.

Central **motels** include the basic *Hacienda Huachuca*, 320 Bruce St (☎520/457-2201 or 1-800/893-2201; ②), and the *Adobe Lodge*, 505 Fremont St (☎520/457-2241 or 1-800/893-2201; ③). The classier mountain-view *Best Western Lookout Lodge* is a mile north on US-80 W (☎520/457-2223 or 1-800/652-6772, fax 457-3870; summer ③, winter ④). *Priscilla's*, 101 N Third St (☎520/457-3844; ③), and *Buford House*, 113 E Safford St (☎520/457-3969; ④), are similar antique-filled **B&Bs**.

Tombstone's zip code is AZ 85638.

Among old-style **saloons** serving steaks and beer in as raucous an atmosphere as they can manage are the *Crystal Palace* at Fifth and Allen, the *Longhorn Restaurant* at 501 Allen St, and *Big Nose Kate's* at 417 E Allen St, where you can still join an ongoing card game. The *Old West Coffee Co*, slightly back from the street at 509 Allen St (☎520/457-2526) serves espresso coffees and pastries.

Bisbee

Crammed into a narrow gorge 25 miles south of Tombstone, the town of **BISBEE** is rivalled only by Jerome, near Sedona (p.276) as Arizona's most atmospheric Victorian relic. Like Jerome, its fortunes were built on a century of mining mundane, dependable **copper** from the surrounding mountains, rather than a few ephemeral years of gold and silver. Its solid brick buildings still stand as an enduring testament to the days when Bisbee's population of twenty thousand outstripped both Phoenix and Tucson to make it the largest city between New Orleans and San Francisco.

George Warren first discovered copper in Mule Pass Gulch, the site of modern Bisbee, in 1877. So little did he value his claim that he lost it in a fit of drunken bravado, betting he could outrun a man on horseback. The *Copper Queen* and *Phelps Dodge* companies soon moved in, then amalgamated rather than face a legal battle over which owned a vast ore body found between their two mines.

The most notorious incident in local history came at the height of World War I, when demand for copper was at its peak. On July 12, 1917, two weeks into a miners' strike, a story in the *Bisbee Daily Review* under the headline "All Women and Children Keep Off Streets Today", announced the formation of a 2200-strong posse to arrest "strange men". In the so-called **Bisbee Deportation**, 1286 alleged members of the International Workers of the World – the **"Wobblies"** – were packed into railroad boxcars and dumped in the desert near Columbus, New Mexico. Following a national outcry, Bisbee's Sheriff Wheeler was tried for kidnapping in 1920, but the charges were dropped.

Phelps Dodge finally closed down its Bisbee operations in 1975, having extracted over six billion dollars' worth of metals. As the miners moved away, however, artists and retirees moved in, preserving Bisbee's original architecture while turning it into a thriving, friendly little community that caters to tourists without being overwhelmed by them.

Walking Bisbee's narrow central streets, lined with galleries and antiques stores, is a pleasure in itself, but if you'd like to know more of the background it's well worth calling in at the **Bisbee Mining and Historical Museum**, 5 Copper Queen Plaza (daily 10am–4pm; adults $3, under-18s free). You can also tour the actual mines, with *Queen Mine Tours*, 111 Arizona St (☎520/432-2071). Hour-long **underground tours** of the Queen Mine leave daily at 9am, 10.30am, noon, 2pm & 3.30pm (adults $8, ages 7–11 $3.50, ages 3–6 $2), while **van tours** of the opencast Lavender Pit, a massive hole that ended up swallowing many of Bisbee's earliest homes, set off at 10.30am, noon, 2pm & 3.30pm ($7 all ages).

Practicalities

Bisbee's **visitor center**, at 7 Main St (Mon–Fri 9am–5pm, Sat & Sun 10am–4pm; ☎520/432-5421), has details of **B&Bs** like the quirky *School House Inn*, in a converted school at 818 Tombstone Canyon (☎520/432-2996 or 1-800/537-4333; ③). Much the grandest place to stay, however, is the venerable *Copper Queen Hotel*, in the heart of town at 11 Howell Ave (☎520/432-2216 or 1-800/247-5829 in

Bisbee's zip code is AZ 85603.

AZ, fax 432-4298; ④), which has a plush bar and a good restaurant with terrace seating. The equally central *High Desert Inn*, 8 Naco Rd (☎520/432-1442 or 1-800/281-0510; ④), a more modern equivalent in the former county jailhouse, offers slightly fancier dining.

Once-notorious **Brewery Gulch**, which runs north from Main Street, still holds a handful of spit-and-sawdust saloons and diners, while the less atmospheric **Bisbee Convention Center** to the south holds its own brewpub and espresso cafe.

Douglas

As you'll see from the endless tailings that spill from the canyons to the south, room to build in or near Bisbee was extremely limited. In 1900, therefore, a new town was constructed 25 miles to the east, to hold a smelter to process copper from Bisbee's mines. Nestled against the Mexican border, **DOUGLAS** too depended on the world demand for copper. Although it has diversified into ranching and industry, since *Phelps Dodge* moved out following a bitter strike at the end of the 1980s its economy has remained too depressed for Douglas to make an appealing stop for tourists. Illegal trade with the much larger city of **AGUA PRIETA** across the border – home to almost 100,000 people – is a major source of income. In one recent case, a drug smuggler with houses in both towns hired surveyors and labourers to dig a deep tunnel between the two, and then had them executed to preserve his secret.

Cars and pedestrians alike cross into Mexico at the foot of Pan American Avenue, a mile or so southwest of downtown Douglas; US citizens don't need to carry passports. With its whitewashed adobe homes and churches, Agua Prieta is a considerably more attractive place to stroll around than Douglas, and offers plenty of opportunities to eat spicy Sonoran food and buy cheap souvenirs.

Practicalities

The only building of any interest in Douglas is the 160-room *Gadsden Hotel*, 1046 G Ave (☎520/364-4481; ②–⑤), which opened in 1907 and still boasts an extraordinarily opulent lobby, with a white marble staircase leading to a 42-foot Tiffany glass window. The guest **accommodation** is not nearly so classy, but the *Saddle and Spur Lounge* and *El Conquistador* **restaurant** both have a real frontier-town air about them. A few more downmarket **motels** are scattered along Hwy-80 to the east.

Chiricahua National Monument

Stretching northeast of Douglas towards New Mexico, the **Chiricahua Mountains** were renowned in the nineteenth century as the homeland and stronghold of the **Chiricahua Apache**. Led by such legendary warriors as **Cochise** and **Geronimo**, the Chiricahua were

The southeast corner

For more about the **Apache**, see p.489.

*Birds in the Chiricahua Mountains include a colony of thick-billed **parrots**, once common here and re-introduced in 1986.*

The monument stays open 24 hours, with an admission fee of $4 per vehicle.

the last Native Americans to hold out against the US Army. The 25-year **Apache Wars** began at Apache Pass in 1861, when Cochise met Lt George Bascom under a flag of truce, and was falsely accused of kidnapping a twelve-year-old boy. He escaped into the mountains, but his brother and two nephews were hanged, precipitating a vicious cycle of raids and killings that only ended with Geronimo's fourth and final surrender in 1886.

Had the small Chiricahua band not fought so long and hard, they might still be permitted to live on the **Chiricahua Reservation**, established during a period of relative peace in 1872. It centered on **Fort Bowie**, built to guard Apache Pass in 1862, whose ruined walls still stand at the end of a 1.5 mile trail that leads from the unpaved Apache Pass Road a mile north of the pass itself (daily 8am–5pm; free). The reservation measured 55 miles on each side, and occupied the entire southeastern corner of Arizona, but was disbanded in 1876, when the Chiricahua were forcibly de-camped to join their distant cousins on the San Carlos reservation to the north.

Although no visible sign of the Apache presence remains, the core of the former reservation now constitutes **CHIRICAHUA NATIONAL MONUMENT**, entered off Hwy-186 27 miles southeast of Willcox. The monument was designated instead to protect the bizarre **rock formations** created in the 27 million years since colossal volcanic eruptions covered the landscape with a 2000-foot coating of dark rhyolite rock. That layer has now cracked and fragmented into strange towers and columns of stacked and balanced stones, a bewildering maze that always defeated Army attempts to pursue the Apache into the mountains.

Chiricahua National Monument is not as spectacular as the desert canyons of Utah, which is presumably why the 1994 movie *Geronimo*, for all its much-vaunted authenticity, was filmed in Moab. However, this remote fastness preserves a tract of barely touched wilderness that conjures up haunting images of the Wild West, and it's also a sanctuary for rare animals and birds.

Just one paved road – the eight-mile **Bonita Canyon Drive** – penetrates, but does not cross, the mountains. From the monument entrance it runs for two miles to the **visitor center** (daily 8am–5pm; ☎520/824-3560), then follows Bonita Canyon east before climbing south to reach **Massai Point**, 6870 feet up. This high vantage point looks out over the main concentration of rocky pinnacles, in **Echo Canyon** and **Heart of Rocks**. If you're prepared to hike a minimum of three miles, you can loop down into the labyrinth; a walk of just over four miles gets you back to the visitor center.

No food, gas or lodging is available in the monument, and overnight backpacking is forbidden, but you can **camp** year-round at the small *Bonita Canyon Campground* (first-come, first-served; $7).

Southwest Arizona

Two interstates, I-8 and I-10, run west across central and southern
Arizona towards California, 35 miles apart near Phoenix and more
than twice that by the time they reach the state line. There's virtually nothing of interest in these vast desert plains, apart perhaps from
the strange prototype military airplanes glimpsed above the Barry M
Goldwater Air Force Range, which stretches south from I-8 to
Mexico. A long detour south will take you to the wild terrain of **Organ
Pipe Cactus National Monument**, but the only town you might conceivably want to visit is **Yuma**, a venerable river crossing on the far
southwest frontier with California whose mundane present fails to
live up to its wild past.

Papago Indian Reservation

The high country to the east of Tucson, known as **Papaguería** to the
Spanish, is now dominated by the **Papago Indian Reservation**. One
of three related groups who together call themselves the **'O'odham** –
"The People" – the Papago are now known as the **Tohono 'O'odham**,
which means "desert people". Unlike the Pima, or Akimel 'O'odham,
the "river people" who lived in permanent villages such as San Xavier
(see p.230), the Tohono 'O'odham were traditionally "two-villagers",
who divided their time between a summer "field" village in the valleys
and a winter "well" village near a spring in the foothills. Eighteen
thousand Tohono 'O'odham now live on the reservation, which was
established in 1916. They share it with the less numerous **Hia C–ed
'O'odham**, formerly known as the Sand Papago – desert nomads who
in 1976 accepted $26 million as compensation for the loss of the
lands now enclosed by Organ Pipe Cactus National Monument and
the Barry Goldwater Air Force Base.

For tourists, the only reward in driving the hundred-mile width of
the reservation, which starts 25 miles out of Tucson on **Hwy-86**, is
its sheer sense of desolation. The only signs of human occupation are
a handful of roadside buildings at **SELLS**, the administrative headquarters, and **QUIJOTOA**.

Organ Pipe Cactus National Monument

Hwy-86 eventually meets **Hwy-85**, fifty miles south of Gila Bend, at
a "Y"-shaped intersection that has over the years acquired the formal
name of **WHY**. A twenty-mile detour south from here through the
straight, flat **Sonoyta Valley**, between the jagged ridge of the dry Ajo
Mountains to the east and the lower Puerto Blanco Mountains to the
west, climbs in due course to reach **ORGAN PIPE CACTUS
NATIONAL MONUMENT**, right on the Mexican border.

Located at the heart of the Sonoran Desert, the five-hundred-
square-mile monument is a treasure-trove of rare desert plants and

animals, but focuses especially on the **organ pipe**, found almost nowhere else in the United States. Where the saguaro stands alone, the organ pipe grows in clusters of tubular "pipes", thrusting up from a shared central root system.

From the **visitor center**, just west of the highway (daily 8am–5pm; $4 per vehicle; ☎520/387-6849), two separate **scenic drives** loop off into the mountains. Both are unpaved and steep, but generally passable for ordinary vehicles; the 21-mile **Ajo Mountain Drive** takes around two hours to complete, the 53-mile **Puerto Blanco Drive** at least half a day.

In summer, **hiking** anything more than the hundred-yard nature trail at the visitor center would be far too gruelling to consider, but between October and April several short trails lead further afield. That's the only time when the **campground** (first-come first-served; $8), a mile south of the visitor center, is likely to fill up.

Ajo

Thirty miles north of the Organ Pipe monument, almost halfway to Gila Bend and the interstate, **AJO** is a former copper-mining town that belies its ugly outskirts – the huge open-pit mine to the south is a hideous spectacle – by having a spruce and attractive Spanish-style plaza at its core. Hispanic settlers were digging for copper by 1750; they named the town in honour of the garlic (*ajo*) that grows wild in the hills nearby.

Since *Phelps Dodge* closed the mine in 1984, after a bitter year-long strike, Ajo has defied the sceptics and clung to life by attracting a steady trickle of tourists and retirees. There's a welcoming bustle about its grassy plaza, surrounded by palm trees and holding two whitewashed Spanish-colonial churches, even if the streets behind hold little of interest.

Practicalities

Two clean, simple **motels** stand either side of the highway a couple of miles north of town. The *Marine Resort* is tucked behind a screen of cactuses at 1966 N Hwy-85 (☎520/387-7626; summer ②, winter ③), while *La Siesta* is on the west side a little further along at 2561 N Hwy-85 (☎520/387-6569; summer ②, winter ③). Back in town, the *Guest House Inn*, 3 Guesthouse Rd (☎520/387-6133; ③), is a comfortable **B&B** with four en-suite rooms. The *Copper Kettle* on the plaza is the best **restaurant**, serving mainly Mexican dishes.

Ajo's zip code is AZ 85321.

Gila Bend

At the intersection of Hwy-85 and I-8, **GILA BEND** is a minor farming community whose hopes of prosperity were dashed when the early twentieth-century spate of dam-building all but dried up the Gila River. While not a destination in itself, it has the widest selection of **motels** in almost 200 miles of interstate, with some run-down options offering rooms for little more than $20. The *Best Western Space Age Lodge*, 401 E Pima St (☎520/683-2273 or 1-800/528-1234; summer ③, winter ④), however, is irresistible. It's a classic Fifties motel, extensively updated, where the Sputnik motif extends to a giant neon flying saucer sign, and huge murals of the lunar landings both inside and out. The adjoining *Outer Limits* restaurant maintains the theme and so too does the swimming pool.

Twenty miles west of Gila Bend, the petroglyphs of the **Painted Rock Mountains** are said to mark the boundary between the traditional territories of the Maricopa and Yuma Indians.

Yuma

Although the sheer size of **YUMA**, a hundred miles west of Gila Bend, surprises most visitors, Arizona's third largest city ranks among the state's oldest communities. Commanding the confluence of the Gila and Colorado rivers, the site's significance was recognized as early as 1540, when **Hernando de Alarcon**, in charge of the naval wing of Coronado's pioneering expedition (see p.495), sailed past its high bluffs. It later became the major river crossing for California-bound travellers, though Spanish attempts to establish a permanent mission settlement were destroyed by the **Yuma Revolt** of 1781, when **Quechan** Indians (known to the Spaniards as the Yuma) massacred over 150 settlers during mass.

At the height of California's **Gold Rush**, sixty thousand passengers in a single year paid $2 each to be ferried across the Colorado at **Yuma Crossing**. This lucrative trade was at first controlled by the Quechan, but freebooting entrepreneurs wrested it out of their hands, with the US Army at Fort Yuma on hand to stifle Indian resistance. Known initially as Colorado City, and later Arizona City, Yuma took on its current name in 1873, by which time it was experiencing a gold rush of its own.

Now that intricate hydraulic engineering has tamed the Colorado – one canal feeding California's Imperial Valley actually siphons beneath the river – it would take a major dam-burst to cause a repeat of the river's formerly devastating floods. As seen in 1993, however, when it inundated Yuma's riverfront to a depth of six feet, the Gila remains as dangerous as ever. In theory, Arizona could use its share of the Colorado's water to irrigate the land around Yuma and create a rival to nearby **Imperial Valley**, one of the world's richest farming areas; instead it's channelled across the desert at absurd expense to Phoenix and Tucson.

Yuma is not a vacation destination in the usual sense, but its warm, dry winters, when temperatures seldom drop below the mid-70°s F, have made it a goal for hordes of "**snowbirds**", who keep an astonishing 72 local RV and trailer parks busy. During summer, on the other hand, when you can expect daytime highs of over 110°F, Yuma is too much of an inferno for anyone to linger very long.

Cormac McCarthy's novel **Blood Meridian** *features a phenomenally bloodthirsty account of the struggle to control Yuma's river traffic; see p.495.*

Southwest Arizona

The best place to get a feel for Yuma's tempestuous past is the **Yuma Territorial Prison State Historic Park**, set high above the Colorado a few blocks east of downtown (daily 8am–5pm; $3). Built in 1876, and known as the "Hell Hole of Arizona", this was the state's principal prison for 33 years. The restored wooden guard tower outside gives great views of the green-lined river meandering in from the north; inside the compound's adobe walls, built by the earliest inmates, fascinating displays tell the stories of its three thousand prisoners. These ranged from teenage burglars to Harvard lawyers, and included nine Mormon polygamists, several Mexican revolutionaries, and a handful of women, such as the colourful Pearl Hart, who served five years for committing Arizona's last stagecoach robbery in 1899. You can also enter several individual cells, many of which were occupied by homeless migrants during the 1930s. Each held six bunks, apart from the pitch-black "dark cell", where unruly prisoners, such as women spotted "flirting", were punished with spells in isolation.

In due course, the entire riverfront at Yuma is scheduled to become **Yuma Crossing Park**, which will extend from the prison to the **Quartermaster Depot**, on Fourth Ave near the river bridge. All Yuma's supplies originally reached the town by a fifty-mile river journey from the river from Port Isabel on the Gulf of California; the depot still holds two of the three warehouses where the Colorado paddle steamers used to moor.

Yuma's most unusual attraction has to be the **Saihati Camel Farm**, south of town on Ave 1E (tours Oct–May Mon–Sat 10am & 2pm, Sun 2pm; June–Sept Mon–Sat 10am, by reservation; $3; ☎520/627-2553). The centrepiece here is a large camel herd, but the farm raises a cross-section of the wildlife of the Arabian desert.

Finally, many visitors like to take a day-trip south into **Mexico**, whether to little **Algodones**, across from California a mere ten miles east, or to the much larger city of **San Luis**, 23 miles south. Both offer the usual array of souvenir stores and restaurants, together with cut-price drugstores.

Practicalities

Yuma River Tours run Colorado cruises from Fisher's Landing, 32 miles upstream from Yuma (half-day $32, full day $49; ☎520/783-4400).

Yuma's **visitor center** is a couple of blocks east of downtown at 488 S Maiden Lane (Mon–Sat 9am–5pm, Sun 10am–1pm; ☎520/783-0071). *Amtrak* **trains** from LA to Tucson stop nearby at 291 Gila St, at hideously unsocial hours. *Greyhound* **buses** run from 170 E 17th Place (☎520/783-4403), to Phoenix, Tucson and San Diego.

Besides its plethora of RV parks, Yuma has twenty or more **motels**. Budget options include *Motel 6*, 1445 E 16th St, Yuma AZ 85365 (☎520/782-9521, fax 343-4941; ②), and *Super 8*, 1688 S Riley Ave, Yuma AZ 85365 (☎520/782-2000 or 1-800/800-8000, fax 782-6657; ③). The more central *Radisson Suites*, 2600 S Fourth Ave, Yuma AZ 85364 (☎520/726-4830 or 1-800/333-3333, fax 341-1152; ⑤), consists solely of plush two-room suites.

The high spot of a poor bunch of places to **eat** is the *Garden Cafe*, 250 S Madison Ave (closed Mon & July–Sept; ☎520/783-1491), open for breakfast and lunch only, and serving salads, sandwiches and espresso coffees in a cool garden. The *Crossing*, 2690 Fourth Ave (☎520/776-5551), is typical of several run-of-the-mill diners along the main drag, while the *Coffee Bean*, 2450 S Fourth Ave (☎520/317-0284), is a friendly coffee-and-pastries joint.

North from Yuma: Quartzsite

North of Yuma, three **wildlife refuges** – the Kofa, Cibola and Imperial – line the Colorado River. Established to protect herds of mule deer and bighorn sheep as well as migratory Canadian geese, the parks aren't really designed for human visitors and are virtually inaccessible without a four-wheel-drive vehicle.

Granted that you'd rather not get caught up in the tank battles staged by the army in its **Yuma Proving Grounds**, there's nowhere to stop on the main north–south highway, **US-95**, until you reach **QUARTZSITE**, eighty miles out of Yuma.

With the Colorado now twenty miles to the west, Quartzsite is even bleaker and drier than Yuma, and has a nominal population of around two thousand, but it too experiences a major winter influx of snowbirds. Literally hundreds of thousands of RV-owners descend on this desert outpost between early January and mid-February each year, ostensibly to bargain for precious, semi-precious and merely pretty stones, but also to ride out the coldest months with like-minded fellow retirees.

In Quartzsite's dusty **cemetery**, north of the main drag in the heart of town, a pyramidal monument, topped by a brass camel, commemorates one of the odder episodes in Southwestern history. Inscribed "The last camp of **Hi Jolly**, born somewhere in Syria about 1828, died Quartzsite December 16 1902", it marks the grave of Haiji Ali, who arrived at Indianola, Texas, in February 1856, in charge of 33 **camels** that had been requisitioned by the then Secretary of War, Jefferson Davis. The idea was to see if they might prove suitable for use as beasts of burden; while they adapted well to the desert, army mule handlers and cowboys lacked the patience or inclination to care for them properly, and the experiment petered out during the Civil War. "Hi Jolly" became just another prospector; the abandoned camels continued to breed in the wild into the first years of the twentieth century.

To this day, it remains against the law to shoot a camel in Arizona.

Despite its endless expanse of RV parks, Quartzsite has just three tiny **motels**, with fewer than ten rooms each.

Parker

Quartzsite's winter crowds spill over to **PARKER**, beside the river 35 miles north. The main activity here is boating on the placid waters downstream of the **Parker Dam**, a Depression-era project designed

**Southwest
Arizona**

to divert Colorado water to the thirsty cities of southern California. Arizona's governor, Benjamin Moer, was so indignant at losing precious state resources that he sent a detachment of the Arizona National Guard – six men in a boat, nicknamed the Arizona Navy – to halt its construction in 1934. Such differences were soon resolved, however, and since 1985 the dam has also provided water for the **Central Arizona Project**, whose 336 miles of aqueducts stretch as far as Phoenix and Tucson. Almost twenty miles out of Parker, it's the deepest dam in the world, dug 235 feet into the riverbed. Jetskiers glide up to its base for a closer look, and it can also be seen on free self-guided **tours** (daily 7.30am–4pm).

Before serving as the headquarters for the building of the dam, Parker started life in 1905 as the principal settlement on the **Colorado River Indian Reservation**. Not far from the dam, clearly signposted from Hwy-95, visitors can examine prehistoric rock art, or **intaglios**, made by "carving" the darker top layer of rock away from the desert floor, to reveal lighter layers of sand beneath (daily 8am–sundown; $3). The figures are so huge (up to 160ft) that it's hard to tell what you're looking at, but gaze long enough and you can discern a four-legged animal, and a human and spiral design.

The most appealing **place to stay** in Parker is the vaguely Moorish *Holiday Kasbah Motel*, not far from the California border at 604 California Ave (☎520/669-2133; Sun–Thurs ②, Fri & Sat ③).

Chapter 5

Flagstaff and Central Arizona

With the state's northernmost hundred miles, from the rugged Navajo and Hopi reservations across to the Grand Canyon, impassable to east–west traffic, the **I-40 corridor** is the focus of a huge tract of north and central Arizona. Before the interstate was pushed through, legendary Route 66 followed much the same path; before either road, there was the *Santa Fe Railroad*; and before the railroad arrived, little more than a century ago, there were no significant Anglo settlements in the region at all.

Even today, only **Flagstaff** of the I-40 towns amounts to much more than an overnight pit stop. No doubt the contrast with the deserts to the east makes Flagstaff seem especially attractive, but set in the world's largest stand of sweet-smelling ponderosa **pine forest**, it's one of the Southwest's most characterful and charming towns. It also makes a great base for visits not only to the Grand Canyon (detailed in Chapter Six), but to the dramatic ancient sites of **Wupatki** and **Walnut Canyon** and the superbly positioned (if over-hyped and at times even deranged) New-Age mecca of **Sedona**.

The highlight of the long drive from Flagstaff to New Mexico is **Petrified Forest National Park**, where giant fossilized remains lie strewn like matchsticks across the eerie desert badlands. To the west, the road to California is less inspiring, so it makes sense to detour south by way of the historic hilltop mining town of **Jerome**, and pristine Victorian **Prescott**, or, further west, to take a timewarp spin along Route 66 to the ghost town of **Oatman**.

East of Flagstaff

During its 150-mile run west from the New Mexican border to Flagstaff, **I-40** passes few towns of any size, let alone of any interest. The **landscape** however, while barren in the extreme, is consistently beautiful, with double rainbows reaching across the desert plain and

Note that the Navajo and Hopi reservations, north of the interstate, are covered in Chapter One.

fiery dawns blazing along the horizon. The most accessible section of this **Painted Desert** lies within **Petrified Forest National Park**, which makes an intriguing half-day detour.

Most tourists feel that this relentless desolation is exactly what they came to see; few join the locals in escaping south to the cool uplands of the **White Mountains**.

Chambers

Arizona's easternmost I-40 town – CHAMBERS, 25 miles in from New Mexico – is also where you'll hit the interstate as you drive south from Ganado (see p.55) or Canyon de Chelly. It's not so much a town as a speck on the windscreen, consisting of three gas stations, each with its own small grocery, and the *Best Western Chieftain* motel (☎520/688-2754; ④), which has a restaurant.

Petrified Forest National Park

PETRIFIED FOREST NATIONAL PARK, which straddles the interstate 25 miles east of Holbrook, kills two birds with one stone. While its chief purpose is to protect a prehistoric "forest" of fossilized trees, south of I-40, it also stretches north to include some of the most picturesque stretches of the **Painted Desert**, an ill-defined area of multi-coloured badlands that covers much of northeast Arizona. Its blue-tinged clays and crumbling sands support little vegetation, or life of any kind, but continue to erode at a fearsome rate. Each year, more and more lithified logs are exposed to view, lying in haphazard profusion on the barren slopes. Petrified wood is not in fact all that rare, but its sheer abundance here is extraordinary; the wood-bearing layer, which is also rich in dinosaur bones and other fossils, extends for 300 feet beneath the ground.

The gigantic trees of Petrified Forest, drawn from long-extinct species such as *Auracarioxylon*, *Woodworthia* and *Schilderia*, date back 225 million years. This is not, however, a genuine forest. Its mighty trunks are horizontal, not vertical; they didn't grow here, they accumulated as a vast log jam in an ancient river. Settling onto the riverbed, they were buried by layers of silt and ash, which drastically slowed the processes of decay. Bit by bit, silica seeped in and replaced the original wood cells, then crystallized into quartz.

Cross-sections of petrified wood, cut through with diamond saws and then polished, look stunning; prize specimens are displayed in the park's two visitor centers, and lesser examples of all sizes are sold in commercial outlets nearby. As seen on the ground, however, from trails along the park's **27-mile Scenic Drive**, the trees themselves are not all that exciting. Segmented, crumbling and very dark, when all's said and done they're just a bunch of logs lying in the sand, even if they are stone logs.

Petrified Forest became a national park when large-scale **pilfering** threatened to deplete its stocks of wood altogether. A similar park in the Dakotas had to close in the 1930s after visitors carried off all its fossil treasures, and even today an estimated twelve tons of rock disappears from the Petrified Forest each year. In theory, rangers can search your vehicle as you leave, and impose heavy fines on anyone caught with a pocketful of petrified wood-chips. They rarely bother, however, preferring the subtler approach of displaying letters in the visitor centers from repentant rock thieves who have been punished by the loss of hair, health, pets or progeny.

Arrival and information

Although the main road through the park crosses I-40, there's no access to or from the interstate at that point. Instead, where you enter the park will depend on where you're heading afterwards. If you're coming from New Mexico, turn north off the interstate at exit 311, 22 miles west of Chambers, and within a mile you'll come to the **Painted Desert Visitor Center** (daily 8am–5pm; ☎520/524-6228). Drivers heading east should leave I-40 at Holbrook (see p.252) and take US-180 for twenty miles southeast to the southern entrance, near the **Rainbow Forest Museum** (daily 8am–5pm).

To receive information by mail, write to Petrified Forest National Park, AZ 86028.

Displays at both visitor centers explain the geology of the park and forest. The **admission fee** of $5 per vehicle, or $3 for motorcyclists, cyclists and pedestrians, is levied at roadside kiosks nearby, where you can also buy *Golden Eagle* passes (see p.21).

You can pick up simple snacks at the Rainbow Forest Museum, but the Painted Desert Visitor Center holds most of the park's few facilities, including a *Fred Harvey* **restaurant** that serves over-priced cafe meals all day, a large gift store, and a gas station. Note that there are no **lodges** or **campgrounds** in the park; the only way to spend a night here is by camping in the backcountry, with a free permit issued by the visitor center.

Seeing the park

Petrified Forest effectively divides into three sections, with an area rich in ancient Indian remains separating the desert in the north from the forest in the south. To see its full range, you have to drive the entire 27-mile scenic drive, but there's no need to stop at every one of the overlooks along the way.

Assuming you enter the park in the north, beyond the Painted Desert Visitor Center, you'll find that you're soon skirting the edge of a giant mesa, which drops away northwards to reveal long-range views across the **Painted Desert** itself. At different times of day, the undulating expanse of clay-topped mounds takes on different colours, with an emphasis on blueish shades of grey and reddish shades of brown. It's best admired through the panoramic windows of the **Painted Desert Inn** (daily 8am–4pm), a mile or two along. This defunct adobe hotel, now being restored as a museum, holds Mexican-style murals, painted by Hopi artist Fred Kabotie in 1948, of Hopi pilgrimages and dances. A stone slab bears a thirteenth-century petroglyph depiction of a fierce-clawed mountain lion. From the promontory behind the inn, **Kachina Point**, backcountry trails drop down into the Painted Desert Wilderness. That's the only way to appreciate the scale of the place, but even the shortest hike involves a hot climb back up again.

After six miles of similar overlooks, the road crosses first the interstate, and then, in quick succession, the *Santa Fe Railroad* and the broad but usually dry Puerco River. At the **Puerco Indian Ruin**, just beyond, a short trail leads around a small, partially excavated Anasazi pueblo, abandoned in 1300 AD. Patches of black desert varnish on nearby rocks show some well-preserved petroglyphs, including one you'd swear depicted a stork bringing a baby.

East of Flagstaff

Utah's Newspaper Rock is described on p.412.

A little further along, a bunch of bigger petroglyph-covered boulders – known collectively, like many such sites, as **Newspaper Rock** – lie at the foot of a rocky incline. Closer access is forbidden, but free binoculars allow you to peer at the indistinct scribbles. In time, some resolve themselves into male and female figures.

By the time you've passed the bizarre pyramidal hillocks of the **Teepees**, you've finally reached the **Petrified Forest**. At roadside halts from here on, rough concrete walkways have been laid over the terrain – and often over the tree trunks themselves – to enable visitors to ramble through the larger concentrations of logs. At **Blue Mesa**, certain treetrunks are raised on muddy "pedestals" above the surrounding desert; at **Agate Bridge**, one even spans a little gully.

The park's busiest trail, the **Long Logs Walk** near the southern entrance, is so popular that its parking lot is closed in the mornings, and hikers have to walk an additional few hundred yards up from the Rainbow Forest Museum. Here at the edge of the desert, a little grass manages to survive, which somehow makes the half-mile main trail especially surreal. The large, shattered logs – which when alive resembled ponderosa pines – are simply strewn across the grasslands, with not another stone or rock in sight. A side trail leads in another half mile to a knoll holding the remains of a seven-hundred-year-old Indian pueblo constructed entirely from petrified wood. **Agate House** sounds amazing, but, thanks perhaps to its rather clumsy restoration, it's oddly banal.

Holbrook

Halfway between Gallup and Flagstaff, **HOLBROOK** was for the last two decades of the nineteenth century the rowdy headquarters of the "Hashknife" cattle outfit, the third largest in the country. Not much seems to have happened since then, but Holbrook has been kept ticking over by traffic on Route 66 and I-40.

Unless you're ready to stop for the night, there's no great reason to stray off the interstate, though a romantic patch of Route 66 frontage survives along **Navajo Boulevard**, squeezed between the Little Colorado River and the railroad to the south, and the interstate to the north. The **Historic Courthouse Museum**, 100 E Arizona St (summer Mon–Fri 8am–8pm, Sat 8am–5pm; winter Mon–Fri 8am–5pm; free) is an appealing small-town melange of Anasazi pots, fading photographs, and dioramas of Wild-West shootouts.

Practicalities

*The price
codes used
here are
explained on
p.261.*

Holbrook's **visitor center** is in the museum (same hours; ☎520/524-2459 or 1-800/524-2459). By far the most unusual, if not exactly luxurious, place to **stay** is the *Wigwam Motel*, 811 W Hopi Drive (☎520/524-3048; ②), a Route 66 relic in which each room is a miniature concrete wigwam. There's also a *Super 8*, up the hill north of the interstate at 1989 E Navajo Blvd (☎520/524-2871 or 1-800/800-8000, fax 524-3514; winter ②, summer ③), with a *Bashas* supermarket nearby, and a dozen other chain motels.

Three of Holbrook's **diners** – including the *Arizona Country Cafe* at Hwy-77 and I-40 (☎520/524-2686), where the menu runs to just about anything – remain open 24 hours a day. The dinner-only *Butterfield Stage Co*, 609 W Hopi Drive (☎520/645-2467), serves espresso coffees.

The White Mountains and the Mogollon Rim

Though the spell-binding northern Arizonan desert appears to stretch away forever to either side of I-40, the southern limit of the Colorado Plateau is just beneath the horizon – the 2000-foot escarpment of the **Mogollon Rim**, curving 200 miles from west to east, and extending well into New Mexico. As you approach from the north, it feels as though you're heading into the back of beyond, but you're soon within a hundred miles of the megalopolis of **Phoenix**.

For sweltering city-dwellers, the highland forests – especially in the **White Mountains**, near **Show Low** – make ideal targets for weekend breaks. Visitors from beyond the Southwest rarely stray

this way, and unless you're looking to hunt, fish, or, in winter,
ski, the only point in doing so is if you want to get to **southern
Arizona** without passing through Phoenix. While none of the
Mogollon Rim towns amounts to more than the sum of its dreary
parts, they do at least offer an abundance of motels. Both roads
south, **US-60** and **US-191**, are exhilarating drives, passing
through untamed mountainous terrain that evokes the early days
of the Wild West.

Springerville and Eagar

The easternmost White Mountain towns, **SPRINGERVILLE** and
neighbouring **EAGAR**, stand near the edge of the plains in **Round
Valley**, just a few miles west of New Mexico. Their only significance
is as base camps for trips into the mountains, which you'll encounter
a couple of miles south on US-191, or ten miles west on Hwy-260, on
the far side of the innocuous Little Colorado River.

Springerville's **visitor center**, 148 E Main St (Mon–Sat
9am–5pm; ☎520/333-2123), can give details of nearby attractions,
including a couple of minor Indian ruins. The best value of its half-
dozen **motels** is the plain but friendly *Super 8*, Hwy-60 on the north
side of town (☎520/333-2655 or 1-800/800-8000, fax 333-5450;
②). As for **restaurants**, the *Safire*, 411 Main St (☎520/333-4512),
serves meats and beers to match any hunter's appetite, while *Booga
Red's*, 521 Main St (☎520/333-2640), is an all-day diner that offers
Mexican specialties such as *chimichangas* as well as steaks.

Coronado Trail Scenic Road

South of Springerville, US-191 is designated as the **Coronado Trail
Scenic Road**, though it doesn't so much follow the route taken by
Francisco de Coronado in 1540 – see p.472 – as vaguely parallel it.
It's such a tortuous high-mountain highway that driving all the way
to **Clifton**, 120 miles south (see p.215), can take up to four hours,
but so long as you fill up on gas first you're sure to enjoy it.

At the only village to interrupt the pine woods – **ALPINE**, 25
miles south – US-180 branches off west into New Mexico. Just a
tiny T-junction in a meadow, Alpine is said to be the chilliest spot
in Arizona. It holds a handful of motels, including the
Sportsman's Lodge near the intersection (☎520/339-4576; ②),
and *Tal-Wi-Wi Lodge*, three miles north (☎520/339-4319; summer ③, winter ④).

Beyond Alpine, US-191 is liable to be closed by snow between
mid-December and mid-March. When it's open, roadside trailheads,
used mainly by hunters, make it possible to hike into the **Apache-
Sitgreaves National Forest**, which also holds several rudimentary
campgrounds (call ☎520/339-4384 for details). The most scenic
spot is the **Blue Vista** pull-out, in the twistiest stretch of road twenty
miles south of Alpine, which commands sweeping views of the misty

mountains. It lies just south of the **Hannagan Meadow** clearing, where the big red-timber *Hannagan Meadow Lodge* is a restaurant that rents out cabins in summer (☎520/339-4370; ④).

Show Low

SHOW LOW, fifty miles south of Holbrook on Hwy-77, and 43 miles west of Springerville, is the largest town on the Mogollon Rim. It stands on the site of a 100,000-acre ranch, whose co-founders played cards in 1876 to decide who should get to keep it. With the game all square, one invited the other to "show low and take the ranch"; his rival drew the deuce of clubs and duly took possession. He went on to sell the ranch to the Mormon church, which built a small settlement before selling it on again.

Show Low today is basically a strip of motels and diners ranged along US-60, or **Deuce of Clubs Avenue**. For a full list, stop by the **visitor center**, 951 W Deuce of Clubs Ave (Mon–Fri 9am–5pm, Sat & Sun 10am–2pm; ☎520/537-2326). Inexpensive places to stay include the *Super 8*, 1941 E Deuce of Clubs Ave (☎520/537-7694 or 1-800/800-8000, fax 537-1373; winter ②, summer ③), and the more basic *Thunderbird*, 1131 E Deuce of Clubs Ave (☎520/537-4391; ②). No matter how hard you look, there's nowhere distinctive to **eat**, so you might as well settle for a pizza at the run-of-the-mill *Pat's Place*, 981 E Deuce of Clubs Ave (☎520/537-2337).

Pinetop and Lakeside

Half a dozen miles southeast of Show Low, and a thousand feet higher, the Mormon communities of **PINETOP** and **LAKESIDE** have long since merged into a single amorphous entity. Set deep in the woods, they're a marginally more attractive proposition than Show Low, though once again you have to bring your own entertainment.

The joint **visitor center**, 592 W White Mountain Blvd (summer Mon–Fri 8.30am–5pm, Sat & Sun 9am–noon; winter Mon–Fri 9am–5pm; ☎520/367-4290), has details of stables, fishing lakes and sporting facilities. There are some pricey luxury ranches around, but if you're just passing through, either the *Blue Ridge Motel*, 2012 E White Mountain Blvd (☎520/367-0758; winter ②, summer ③), or the *Best Western Inn of Pinetop*, 404 E White Mountain Blvd (☎520/367-6667 or 1-800/528-1234, fax 367-6672; winter ④, summer ⑤), should match your needs. The best **restaurant** around is *Creasey's*, 984 E White Mountain Blvd (☎520/367-1908), which cooks up some fancy Italian dishes, though *Porky's Memphis-Style BBQ*, behind the conspicuous *Arby's* at 1417 S Timber Lane (☎520/367-0252), makes a change from Arizona's usual offerings.

Fort Apache Indian Reservation

One reason why the mountains of eastern Arizona are not better known is that a large proportion of the central massif still belongs to the **Apache**. As a study of the intricacies of the Apache Wars soon reveals, the Apache are not a single "tribe" in the way outsiders like to imagine, and there are two separate but contiguous reservations here. The **FORT APACHE INDIAN RESERVATION**, which starts just a mile or two out of Pinetop and Show Low, stretches south to the Salt and Black rivers, while beyond it the **San Carlos Indian Reservation** extends for another hundred miles past Globe.

East of
Flagstaff

*For more
about the
Apache, see
p.489.*

The headquarters of the Fort Apache reservation is in the town of **WHITERIVER**, cupped in a mile-high valley twenty miles south of Pinetop, and home to the *White Mountain Apache Motel & Restaurant* (☎520/338-4927; ③). What few visitors make it this far, however, are drawn a few miles further southwest, to **FORT APACHE** itself, at the confluence of the North and East forks of the White River. This US Army outpost was founded in 1870 to support the campaigns of General Crook, who was allied with the White Mountain Apache but wanted to keep an eye on them nonetheless. Several buildings survive in reasonable condition, and hold displays on the period (Mon–Sat 10am–4pm; $2). The **tourist office** in the post office nearby can direct you towards crafts stores and other sites (Mon–Fri 8am–4.30pm, Sat 8–10.30am; ☎520/338-1230).

Two much more contemporary attractions form the backbone of the reservation's tourist trade. The **Hondah Casino** (☎520/3698-0299), at the junction of Hwys 260 and 73 outside Pinetop, is a 24-hour gaming facility, while the **Sunrise Resort** (☎520/735-7600; ③–⑧), at the top of Hwy-273 thirty miles east, is Arizona's most popular **ski resort**, open as a rule between November and April.

Hwy-60, the only north–south road across the reservation, is also the most direct route between northeast Arizona and Tucson. All of the 87-mile run from Show Low to **Globe** (see p.212) is awe-inspiring, but the most dramatic moment comes roughly fifty miles along, where it takes five miles of switchbacks to get the highway down to the bottom of the gaping **Salt River Canyon**.

Payson

Until 1959, **PAYSON**, ninety miles west of Show Low on Hwy-260, was a sleepy cowboy town that had started out in a gold-rush frenzy and then relaxed into a lifestyle where the yearly round of ranching was punctuated only by the odd rodeo. Then the paving of Hwy-87 placed Payson within two hours' drive of Phoenix, eighty miles southwest. Ever since then, it has been a mountain retreat whose population doubles or triples at weekends, as urban refugees flock to their second homes, or at least rent cabins in the forest.

On first glance, Payson is if not exactly appealing then at least mildly impressive, but somehow as you drive down its long, broad streets, passing representatives of every national fast-food and lodging chain, you never seem to find a compelling reason to stop. Follow the signs for "historic Main Street", and it's a fairly sorry story; you can see that this is a prosperous community, with plenty of new residential developments, but its former central thoroughfare, now bypassed by the highway, is desultory and run-down.

Payson's **visitor center**, at 100 Main St (Mon–Fri 8am–5pm, Sat 8am–2pm, Sun 10am–2pm; ☎520/475-4515 or 1-800/672-9766), can supply details of its many **motels**. Among reasonable options are the bright, white, ersatz Alpine *Swiss Village Lodge* (☎520/474-3241, fax 472-6564; ④), which dominates the eastern side of Hwy-89 north of town, and the *Payson Pueblo Inn*, 809 E Hwy-260 (☎520/474-5241 or 1-800/888-9828, fax 472-6919; ③).

The garden of *Oaks Restaurant*, 302 W Main St (☎520/474-1929), is a good spot to **eat** a sandwich lunch or steak or seafood dinner, or you can pick up coffee and pastries on the patio of the *Pony Espresso* (☎520/474-1822), opposite *Swiss Village Lodge*.

Tonto Natural Bridge

The world's widest and longest (but not quite highest) **travertine bridge** is preserved in **TONTO NATURAL BRIDGE STATE PARK**, fifteen miles north of Payson on Hwy-87 (winter daily 9am–5pm; summer daily 8am–6pm; $5). In 1877, a Scottish gold prospector, David Gowan, supposedly hid here as he fled the Apaches who used the surrounding meadows as a summer camp, then returned to build a cabin nearby. When a description of the bridge appeared in an English newspaper in 1896, David Goodfellow spotted the name of his long-lost uncle and wrote to Gowan, who offered him the site. Goodfellow's ten-room lodge no longer accepts guests, but still serves as the park's gift shop and visitor center.

The bridge itself, reached by a network of short trails and formed from minerals deposited by constantly flowing springs, doesn't really live up to the build-up. Spanning a gully that's roughly 150 feet wide, it's more of a tunnel, or a dank cave with openings at both ends. With effort, you can scramble down to a boardwalk at the base, but you can't go through it.

Pine and Strawberry

It must have taken the Mormon settlers who established a village in the forest five miles north of Tonto Bridge all of five seconds to hit on a name – **PINE**. Together with its neighbour and contemporary, **STRAWBERRY**, it's not a place you'd go far out of your way to visit, but both these tiny hamlets make very pleasant overnight stops if you're lost in the woods. Pine's *High Country Inn* rents out a couple of nice new **cabins** (☎520/476-2150; ③), and adjoins the friendly *Last Tortilla* **restaurant**, while a little further along Hwy-87, the *Frontier Deli* (☎520/476-3705) does good light lunches.

Winslow

Back on I-40, thirty miles east of Holbrook and 56 miles west of
Flagstaff, **WINSLOW** is another Route 66 town that's kept alive by
transcontinental truckers. It's also the closest the interstate comes to
the Hopi mesas (see p.57), which jut from the desert across sixty
miles of butte-studded wilderness to the north.

Winslow was founded as a railroad halt in 1882, not far from the
recently-established Mormon community of **Brigham City**, now
lying derelict a mile northeast. Such history as it has witnessed since
then is recalled in the diverting **Old Trails Museum**, 212 Kinsley St
(winter hours irregular; summer Tues–Sat 1–5pm; free).

Three miles northeast of town, **Homolovi Ruins State Park** (daily
8am–5pm; $3 per vehicle; ☎520/289-4106) holds four pueblo vil-
lages, and hundreds of lesser sites, that were occupied by the
Hisatsinom people, the ancestors of today's **Hopi**, until perhaps the
fourteenth century. Most remain unexcavated, though archeologists
are usually hard at work between June and July, when visitors are
welcome to join them.

Practicalities

Winslow's *Amtrak* station still sees one daily **train** west to Flagstaff,
and one east to Albuquerque. *Greyhound* **buses** along I-40 stop at
1000 E Third St. The local **visitor center** is near I-40 exit 253, at 300
W North Rd (Mon–Fri 8am–5pm; ☎520/289-2434).

Most of the older **motels** in town are now pretty decrepit, so
unless you're determined to pay rock-bottom rates you'd do better to
head a little further west to either the *Best Western Town House
Lodge*, 1914 W Third St (☎520/289-4611 or 1-800/528-1234;
winter ②, summer ③), or the *Super 8*, 1916 W Third St (☎520/289-
4606 or 1-800/800-8000; winter ②, summer ③). The pick of the
all-day **diners** is the *Falcon Restaurant*, 1113 E Third St
(☎520/289-2342), while the best **campground** is at Homolovi Ruins
(see above), where water is available in summer only.

*Winslow's **zip
code** is AZ
86047.*

Meteor Crater

Around 22,000 years ago, a meteorite slammed into northern
Arizona, blasting a huge hole, nearly a mile across and over five hundred feet deep, into the scrubby plateau. The site of that impact,
METEOR CRATER (daily 6am–6pm; $8, under-18s $2), can now be
reached by a six-mile spur road that heads south of the interstate
eighteen miles west of Winslow and 38 miles east of Flagstaff.

Though the staff dress up in mock Park-Service uniforms, Meteor
Crater is privately owned and operated, and frankly offers poor value
for money. A modern gallery beside the parking lot holds the
unimaginative **Astronauts Hall of Fame**, which commemorates the
fact that the first men on the moon were trained on the cavity's oth-

erworldly surface (some sceptics claim that they faked their entire mission here). Walkways from there climb to the lip of the abyss, where you'll probably find that there's a limit to how long you can spend staring at a featureless hole in the ground. You cannot hike into the actual crater.

Flagstaff

Despite having a population of little over fifty thousand, and barely a building that rises more than three storeys, the likeable college town of **FLAGSTAFF** is the most important community on Arizona's major east–west corridor. Its main thoroughfare, Santa Fe Avenue, was once **Route 66**, and before that, the pioneer trail west, while for more than a century the *Santa Fe Railroad* has run right alongside. All too many tourists race through, en route to the Grand Canyon eighty miles northwest, but Flagstaff is a worthwhile destination in its own right, with a couple of good museums, some wonderful scenery and ancient sites nearby, and, above all, a lively downtown whose old streets are still redolent with Wild West charm.

Flagstaff's first white settlers arrived in 1876, lured from Boston by widely publicized accounts of mineral wealth and fertile land. Although they soon moved on, disappointed, towards Prescott, they stayed long enough to celebrate the centenary of American independence by flying the Stars and Stripes from a towering pine tree. This flagpole became a familiar landmark on the route west, and as the town grew it inevitably became known as Flagstaff. Right from the start, it was a cosmopolitan place, with a strong black and Hispanic population working in the (originally Mormon-owned) lumber mills and in the cattle industry, and Navajo and Hopi Indians heading in from the nearby reservations to trade.

Today, Flagstaff makes an ideal base for travellers, with hotels, restaurants, bars and shops aplenty within easy strolling range of the centre, plus outlets of the national food and lodging chains a couple of miles away beside the interstate. Students from **Northern Arizona University**, whose campus is a mile or so south of downtown, ensure that there's always something going on.

Arrival and information

*Steam trains
to the Grand
Canyon still
run from
Williams, 32
miles west of
Flagstaff; see
p.296.*

Though the *Santa Fe Railroad* is still busy with freight, only two passenger **trains** stop at Flagstaff's venerable wooden stationhouse, in the heart of town – the daily 6.44am for Albuquerque and the nightly 9.14pm to Los Angeles. Connecting **buses** to the Grand Canyon's South Rim, run for *Amtrak* by *Nava-Hopi*, 114 W Route 66 (☎520/774-5003 or 1-800/892-8687), are detailed on p.297.

Both *Nava-Hopi* and *Greyhound*, a few blocks south of downtown at 399 S Malpais Lane (☎520/774-4573 or 1-800/231-2222), run four daily buses between Flagstaff and **Phoenix**, for a one-way

DOWNTOWN FLAGSTAFF

EATING
A Alpine Pizza
B Beaver Street Brewery
C Brix Grill
D Cafe Espress
E Chez Marc Bistro
F Hassib's

ACCOMMODATION
1 Birch Tree Inn
2 Downtowner
3 Hotel Monte Vista
4 Motel Du Beau
5 San Francisco Street B&B
6 The Inn at Four Ten
7 Weatherford Hotel

△ Museums & Grand Canyon

Amtrak Station

Northern Arizona University

Lowell Observatory

▽ Sedona & Phoenix

Yards 0 400

fare of around $20, while *Greyhound* services also head west to Las Vegas and LA, and east towards Albuquerque.

The helpful local **visitor center** is at 101 W Santa Fe Ave, a minute's walk west of the station (summer Mon–Sat 8am–7pm, Sun 8am–5pm; winter Mon–Sat 8am–6pm, Sun 8am–5pm; ☎520/774-9541 or 1-800/842-7293).

Tours and rentals

Nava-Hopi (see p.258) also operate a wide range of **one-day tours** from Flagstaff, to destinations including the Grand Canyon ($38 by bus, $64 for a combination bus-and-train tour via Williams); Sedona and Jerome ($38), the Hopi mesas ($62), Monument Valley ($74), and the Marble Canyon float trips detailed on p.298 ($89). Two local hostels – the *Motel du Beau* and the *Downtowner*, listed below – arrange inexpensive excursions for backpackers. *Flagstaff Jeep Tours* (☎520/522-0592) run off-road local **jeep tours**, with the possibility of hiking as well, from $19 per person.

The least expensive **car rental**, which for a group travelling to the Grand Canyon should cost less than the bus, is *Budget Rent-a-Car*, 100 N Humphreys St (☎520/779-0307); *Avis*, *Hertz* and *National* also have outlets.

Cosmic Cycles, 113 S San Francisco St (Mon–Sat 9am–6pm; ☎520/779-1092) rent out **mountain bikes** for $20 per day, or $75 per week. *Arizona Mountain Bike Tours* (☎520/779-4161 or 1-800/277-7985) run **cycling tours** for $25 (3hr) or $45 (5hr).

Accommodation

Flagstaff is something more than an interstate pit stop, so its dozens of **motels** and **B&Bs** get away with charging higher rates than the Southwest's other I-40 towns. They're still not bad value, however, and **budget** travellers can choose between four hotels that offer hostel-style dorm beds as well as private rooms. Most of the major chain motels are congregated well to the east, along Butler Avenue and Lucky Lane, but staying nearer downtown is much more fun. On summer weekends, when everywhere is likely to be booked solid, the privately-run *Flagstaff Central Reservations* may be able to help (☎520/527-8333 or 1-800/527-8388).

The best local **campground** is three miles south on US-89A, at *Fort Tuthill County Park* (☎520/774-5139), though continue further south and you're soon in Oak Creek Canyon (see p.268).

Flagstaff's zip code is AZ 86001.

Birch Tree Inn, 824 W Birch Ave; ☎520/774-1042 or 1-800/645-5811. Former frat house converted to upmarket B&B, with five tastefully themed guest rooms, fancy breakfasts, and a wrap-around verandah. ④–⑤.

Downtowner Grand Canyon International Hostel, 19 S San Francisco St; ☎520/779-9421. Independent hostel, across the tracks from *Amtrak*; dorm beds $8–10 winter, $12 summer, plus private rooms. Grand Canyon tours, $15 shuttle to sister hostel in Page (see p.393), and car rental discounts. ①.

Econolodge West, 2355 S Beulah Blvd; ☎520/774-2225 or 1-800/553-2666. Relatively appealing chain motel, with good facilities, south of downtown near the interstate. Winter ③, summer ④.

Holiday Inn, 2320 E Lucky Lane; ☎520/526-1150, fax 779-2610. Large motel, just off the interstate in a rather characterless area, with a handful of nearby diners. Winter ④, summer ⑤.

The Inn at Four Ten, 410 N Leroux St; ☎520/774-0088 or 1-800/774-2008. Bright ranch home that's now an antique-furnished eight-room B&B. ⑥–⑦.

Hotel Monte Vista, 100 N San Francisco St; ☎520/779-6971 or 1-800/545-3068, fax 779-2904. Flagstaff's best bargain; a very pleasant little 1920s hotel in the heart of downtown, restored to offer accommodation that ranges from dorm beds ($10 winter, $16 summer) through double rooms of varying sizes, with and without attached bathrooms. Several are named for celebrity guests such as Humphrey Bogart, John Wayne and Jane Russell; room rates rise by up to $15 at weekends. ①–④.

Motel du Beau International Hostel – HI/AYH, 19 W Phoenix Ave; ☎520/773-1656 or 774-6731 or 1-800/398-7112. Hostel offering $12 dorm or beds and budget doubles for around $25, or tent camping in the yard for $6. It's also the base of *Blue Goose Backpackers Tours*, who run a $22 shuttle to the Grand Canyon, $32 tours of the Grand Canyon, and tours down to Sedona and Montezuma Castle for $15 half-day, $25 full day. ①.

Motel 6, 2440 E Lucky Lane; ☎520/774-8756, fax 774-2067. The cheapest of several *Motel 6*s on the outskirts of town. ②.

San Francisco Street B&B, 622 N San Francisco St; ☎520/779-2257. Homely, inexpensive B&B a few blocks' walk north of downtown, where the three guest rooms share the use of a single bathroom. ③.

Super 8 Motel, 3725 Kasper Ave; ☎520/526-0818 or 1-800/800-8000, fax 526-8786. Standard, good value motel east of town. Winter ③, summer ④.

Weatherford Hotel, 23 N Leroux St; ☎520/774-2731. Very central *HI-AYH*-approved hostel, upstairs in a once-grand railroad hotel, with $12 dorm beds and private doubles for just over $30. ①–②.

*As explained on p.15, **accommodation prices**, excluding taxes, are indicated throughout this book by the following symbols:*

① *up to $30*
② *$30–45*
③ *$45–60*
④ *$60–80*
⑤ *$80–100*
⑥ *$100–130*
⑦ *$130–175*
⑧ *$175–250*
⑨ *$250+*

The Town

Flagstaff's atmospheric **downtown** stretches for a few red-brick blocks north of the railroad. Filled with cafes, bars, and stores selling Route 66 souvenirs and Indian crafts, it's a fun place to stroll around, even if it holds no significant tourist attractions or historic buildings. Your most lasting impression is likely to be of the magnificent **San Francisco Peaks**, rising smoothly from the plains on the northern horizon, and topped by a jagged ridge.

The exceptional **Museum of Northern Arizona**, however, three miles northwest of downtown on US-180, rivals Phoenix's Heard Museum as the best museum in the state (daily 9am–5pm; $5). Although it covers the geology, geography, flora and fauna of the Colorado plateau, its main emphasis is on documenting **Native American** life. It provides an excellent run-through of the Anasazi past and contemporary Navajo, Havasupai, Zuni and Hopi cultures, with a marvellous assortment of pots, rugs, silver and turquoise jewellery, and *kachina* dolls that makes a welcome contrast to the low standards seen in so many of the region's crafts stores. There are also temporary shows of local (not always Native American) arts and crafts, a well-stocked bookstore, and a **nature trail** that runs through the small canyon outside.

Ever since it was established, in 1928, the Museum of Northern Arizona has actively encouraged the development of traditional and even new skills among Native American craftworkers. The exquisite inlaid silver jewellery now made by the Hopi, for example, is the result of a museum-backed programme to find work for Hopi servicemen returning from World War II. During its annual Indian Craftsmen Exhibitions, every item is for sale. The **Zuni** show lasts for five days around Memorial Day weekend in late May, the **Hopi** one is on the weekend closest to July 4, and the nine-day **Navajo** event is at the end of July and the start of August.

On the road back towards town, the **Coconino Center for the Arts** is a gallery and concert hall specializing in works by local artists, while just behind it the co-operatively run **Art Barn** (daily 9am–5pm) sells a wide selection of crafts.

Call ☎520/774-2096 for details of evening stargazing sessions at the Lowell Observatory, held with varying frequency all year except January.

Set in the pine forest atop Mars Hill, a mile west of downtown, the **Lowell Observatory** (daily 9am–5pm; $3) is famous as the place where the existence of the planet Pluto was first confirmed. Many of the necessary calculations were performed by Dr Percival Lowell, who founded the observatory in 1894 and deluded himself that he'd discovered canals on Mars. Lowell died in 1916, however – he's buried in a small domed mausoleum of blue glass on the hilltop – and the ninth planet was eventually spotted by Clyde Tombaugh in 1930. Tombaugh himself lived on until January 1997.

From the **visitor center**, where technically minded visitors can play with computers and watch explanatory videos, the **Pluto Walk** footpath climbs up to the tiny original observatory. Signs tick off the relative positions of the planets, but if it kept going on the same scale, it would have to extend over 600 miles, beyond Boise Idaho, to show position of the nearest star, Alpha Centauri.

Eating

There's enough money around in Flagstaff to support several upscale **restaurants**, but what really gives eating in town an unusual edge is the presence of all those **students**. The area around San Francisco Street, both north and south of the tracks, is filled with vegetarian cafes and espresso bars, while snack places near the university further south include a *Cyber Cafe* in the *Bookmans* used bookstore at 1520 S Riordan Ranch Rd.

Alpine Pizza, 7 N Leroux St; ☎520/779-4109. Raucous student hangout downtown, with decent pizzas and lots of beer.

Beaver Street Brewery & Whistle Stop Cafe, 11 S Beaver St; ☎520/779-0079. Inventive sandwiches and salads, wood-fired pizzas, and outdoor barbecue in the beer garden in summer; ales and lagers brewed on the premises.

Black Barts, 2760 E Butler Ave; ☎520/779-3142. Enjoyable western-themed steakhouse on the east edge of town, with a delicious smell of burning wood and waiting staff who sing and dance on stage in between serving up barbecued steaks, ribs and chickens, for $15–20.

Brix Grill, 801 S Milton Rd; ☎520/779-5117. Fashionable restaurant in a former mall store, where the menu has an imaginative, Southwestern flair. Grilled meats come with plenty of chiles, peppers and avocado. Open for lunch and dinner Mon–Sat, dinner only on Sun.

Cafe Espress, 16 N San Francisco St; ☎520/774-0541. Great vegetarian breakfasts, then salads, sandwiches and veggie specials for the rest of the day, plus espresso coffees.

Charly's Pub and Grill, *Weatherford Hotel*, 23 N Leroux St; ☎520/779-1919. Cafe-restaurant which makes a classy if unlikely contrast with the hostel rooms upstairs, serving good, inexpensive meals accompanied by live music (cocktail piano at lunch, bands at night).

Chez Marc Bistro, 503 N Humphreys St; ☎520/774-1343. Fancy French restaurant in converted historic house, with patio seating. Crepes and pasta for lunch, with plenty of vegetarian options, for $6–9; delicious French dinner entrees like veal with lobster, halibut braised with cider, or buffalo with sundried cranberries, all for (just) under $20.

Hassib's, 211 S San Francisco St; ☎520/774-1037. Mainly Middle-Eastern specialities, like hummus, falafel and pitta-pocket sandwiches; ideal for a cheap healthy lunch. Open Mon–Fri 11am–7pm only.

Pasto, 19 E Aspen Ave; ☎520/779-1937. Downtown dinner-only Italian joint, with pasta specials plus chicken, shrimp or vegetarian entrees for $10–13.

Sakura, *Woodlands Plaza Hotel*, 1175 W Route 66; ☎520/773-9118. Japanese restaurant in upmarket hotel, which specializes in "flashing knives" Teppanyaki cuisine, where the food is chopped and grilled on your table.

Nightlife

Its streets milling with international travellers in summer, and students for the rest of the year, Flagstaff has to be the liveliest **nightspot** between Las Vegas and Santa Fe. Wander a block or two to either side of San Francisco Street downtown, and you can't go far wrong. Hotel bars which feature live music most nights include *Charly's* at the *Weatherford*, and the *Monte Vista Lounge*.

Flagstaff Brewing Company, 16 E Route 66; ☎520/773-1442. Popular downtown pub, with outdoor seating, big windows, and live music nightly.

The Mad Italian, 101 S San Francisco St; ☎520/779-1820. Highly sociable downtown bar with several pool tables.

The Monsoons, 22 E Route 66; ☎520/774-7929. Downtown music venue, opposite *Amtrak*, with live local bands most nights, plus barbecue.

The Museum Club, 3404 E Route 66; ☎520/526-9434. A real oddity; this log-cabin taxidermy museum somehow transmogrified into a classic Route 66 roadhouse, saloon and country music venue, that's a second home to hordes of dancing cowboys. Open daily noon–1am. Call ☎520/774-4444 for a free shuttle service from and to your motel.

Around Flagstaff

The area around Flagstaff is extraordinarily rich in natural and archeological wonders, with three national monuments – **Sunset Crater**, **Wupatki**, and **Walnut Canyon** – within 25 miles, and the **San Francisco Peaks** overshadowing them all. All are generally seen as day-trips from Flagstaff, however, as no accommodation is available; only Sunset Crater has even a campground.

The San Francisco Peaks

The **San Francisco Volcanic Field**, north of Flagstaff, consists of around four hundred distinct volcanic cones, which have appeared within the past two million years. During that time, the region has also been covered by glacial ice on three separate occasions, shaving around three thousand feet off the top of the volcanoes.

The serrated **SAN FRANCISCO PEAKS**, visible from downtown Flagstaff, are the remnants of a single mountain; their highest point today, at 12,643 feet, is the summit of **Mount Humphreys**. They were named by Spanish missionaries in honour of St Francis of Assisi, though the Hopi already knew them as *Nuvatukya'ovi*, the home of the *kachina* spirits (see p.58), and to the Navajo they were *Dook'o'oosliíd*, one of the four sacred mountains (see p.486). Seen from afar, topped by a semi-permanent layer of clouds, it's obvious why the Hopi and Navajo regarded them as the source of life-giving rain. It's because they were sacred to both that they now belong to neither; federal law dictates that Indian reservations can only include lands of which a tribe can prove it has "exclusive use". The Hopi in particular still make annual pilgrimages on foot from their mesas, 65 miles east, to shrines hidden in the mountains.

Considering that the San Francisco Mountain, which has not erupted for 220,000 years, is dormant rather than extinct, the time may come when the gods decide that the **Arizona Snowbowl** is a desecration no longer to be tolerated. For the moment, it survives, nestling between Mount Humphreys and Mount Agassiz at the end of a seven-mile spur road north of US-180, and featuring ski runs such as *Boo-Boo* and *Bambi*. There's not enough water up here to make artificial snow – another early name for the peaks was the **Sierra Sin Agua**, or "waterless range" – so the season typically runs from mid-December to early April. Lift tickets cost $31 per day, and a couple of lodges offer meals and equipment rental, but not overnight accommodation; for more information, call ☎520/779-1951.

In summer, the longest of the Snowbowl's five chair lifts, which climbs to within a few hundred feet of the 12,350-foot summit of Mount Agassiz, remains open as the **Scenic Skyride** (May–Oct daily 10am–4pm; ☎520/779-1951; $9). To protect the fragile vegetation, you can't hike any further from there, but there are plenty of other trails in the mountains, all intended for day-use only. One switch-backs right to the top of Mount Humphreys, giving seventy-mile views to the Grand Canyon and beyond.

Sunset Crater National Monument

The focus of **SUNSET CRATER NATIONAL MONUMENT**, three miles down a side road that heads east off US-89 twelve miles north of Flagstaff, is the youngest of the San Francisco volcanoes. Its most recent eruption, in 1065 AD, had a profound impact on the local population and economy. Thick deposits of ash for miles around opened up previously infertile land to cultivation, accelerating if not triggering a land rush that threw different Indian cultures into contact and competition for the first time.

*The combined
entry fee to
Sunset Crater
and Wupatki
national mon-
uments is $4
per vehicle, $2
for pedestrians
and cyclists.*

John Wesley Powell named Sunset Crater for its multi-coloured cone, which swells from a black base through reds and oranges to a yellow-tinged crest. Unfortunately, however, its shifting cinders are too unstable to allow hikers to climb up to the rim. Instead, the one-mile **Lava Flow Trail** at its base offers a close-up look at the jagged black lava that streamed out across the desert, and the steeper one-mile **Lenox Crater Trail** ascends a lesser cone nearby.

All is explained in the **visitor center** near the start of the road (daily 8am–5pm; ☎520/526-0502), opposite the forest service's *Bonito* **campground** (late May to mid-Oct; $8; ☎520/526-0866).

Wupatki National Monument

A dozen miles north of Sunset Crater, the ancient ruins at **WUPATKI NATIONAL MONUMENT** appear to show different tribal groups living side by side in harmony. After the Sunset Crater eruption, the Sinagua people already present here – who surely witnessed the explosion – were joined by many others, including the Anasazi and the Hohokam. When the rich new soil had been exhausted, around 150 years later, they all moved on once more.

The first of the five separate pueblo complexes along the road from Sunset Crater has been named **Wukoki**, a modern Hopi word meaning "big house". Reminiscent of the castle-like structures at Hovenweep (see p.63), it stands within sight of a procession of rounded cinder cones, but was probably positioned for its commanding prospect of the Painted Desert to the north and east. Windows in its central tower, which is moulded to the contours of a red-rock outcrop, and built with bricks of the same material, look out in all directions; the floor is deep in crumbling sand. With the Little Colorado River five miles distant, its inhabitants must have been desperately short of water.

The monument's **visitor center** (summer daily 8am–7pm, winter daily 8am–5pm; ☎520/679-2365), a short way on, holds some rather antiquated displays that have been updated by stick-on modern captions. Thus an original label that speaks of the Sinagua having "disappeared", is now called "inappropriate", in view of the fact that the Hopi are their obvious descendants.

A paved loop trail leads down from the visitor center to the main three-storey, hundred-room pueblo block of **Wupatki** ("tall house") itself. The site's most intriguing features, however, lie a little further along. First comes what seems to be an amphitheatre, a walled circular plaza whose purpose remains unknown. Beyond it is an oval **ball court**, the northernmost such court ever found. Similar arenas throughout central America were used for a game – part ritual, part sport – in which players tried to propel a rubber ball through a stone hoop high on a wall, using their knees and elbows alone. Much like modern basketball; except that the losers were sacrificed at the end. Alongside the ball court, cracks in the ground have created a natural **blowhole**, through which air is either sucked or blown depending on pressure and temperature. The audible "breathing" of the earth clearly made this a sacred shrine for Wupatki's ancient inhabitants.

The loop road past Sunset Crater and Wupatki rejoins US-89 twenty miles south of Cameron (see p.319). Outcrops along its final few miles hold more pueblos, such as one known for obvious reasons as the Citadel, perched on and fully occupying a hilltop.

Walnut Canyon National Monument

Another Sinagua site, even more spectacular than Wupatki, can be seen at **WALNUT CANYON NATIONAL MONUMENT**, just south of I-40 ten miles east of Flagstaff. Between 1125 and 1250 AD, this shallow canyon was home to a thriving Sinagua community, who lived in small family groups rather than in communal pueblos. Literally hundreds of their **cliff dwellings** still nestle beneath over-hangs in the sides of the canyon. They simply walled off alcoves where softer strata of rock had eroded away, and put up partitions to make separate rooms.

A large scenic window in the **visitor center** (June–Aug daily 8am–6pm; March–May & Sept–Nov daily 8am–5pm; Dec–Feb daily 9am–5pm; $4 per vehicle, $2 for pedestrians and cyclists; ☎520/526-3367) gives an excellent overall view. **Walnut Creek** itself, long since diverted to provide Flagstaff's drinking water, now runs very dry, but you can still see how fertile this valley must have been when the Sinagua first arrived. Trees cling to the porous rock to shade the ancient dwellings, and the vegetation thickens down to a valley floor dense with black walnut and oak.

The mile-long **Island Loop Trail** drops steeply down from the visitor center and crosses a narrow causeway to an isthmus of rock high above a gooseneck of the creek. Along the path, you can go inside several Sinagua homes; note the T-shaped door-ways, which could only be entered head first, and the ceilings blackened by the smoke of generations of fires. Petroglyphs have been found in the other ruins visible on all sides, but none remain on the trail.

Another trail follows the rim of the canyon. Its main purpose is to provide a less strenuous walk, which leads to a picnic area and to some surface ruins (in the dissimilar pueblo style, consisting of large clusters of rooms), though you could keep going to turn this into a lengthy hike. There is no accommodation, and only minimal snack food, available at the canyon.

Between June and August each year, rangers lead two- to three-hour **guided hikes** to lesser-known and otherwise inaccessible sites within the monument (Wed, Sat & Sun at 10am; call to confirm).

South of Flagstaff

US-89A threads its way south from Flagstaff down **Oak Creek Canyon** to emerge after 28 miles at **Sedona**, on the threshold of the extraordinary **Red Rock Country**. Up from the valley rise giant mesas and buttes of stark red sandstone, where Zane Grey set a number of his Wild West adventures. The boom-and-bust mining town of **Jerome** looks down from a mountainside to the south, while back beside I-17 towards Phoenix are the haunting Sinagua ruins of **Tuzigoot** and **Montezuma Castle**.

Oak Creek Canyon

Claims that **OAK CREEK CANYON**, the largest of several slender chasms that cut into the 2000-foot escarpment of the **Mogollon Rim**, is a serious rival to the Grand Canyon are somewhat exaggerated. However, you *can* drive right through it, and with its sheer walls striped in vivid horizontal bands of colour, its sparkling streams and densely wooded glens, and its facilities for camping, eating and generally playing around, anywhere else in the world this would be an unmissable attraction.

Lookout Point, its northern end, appears suddenly a dozen forested miles out of Flagstaff. Native-American craft stalls surround the parking lot, and several overlooks within easy walking distance command prospects of the narrow gorge below. The road then switchbacks sharply down to run alongside Oak Creek itself. The lowest level in the rocks to either side, often obscured by maples, cedars, oaks and pine, is the bright red Supai sandstone. Above that, layers of white sandstone, buff limestone, and finally black basalt testify to a geological history which has fluctuated from harsh desert to sea bottom. Temperatures are cool enough to make fishing, picnicking and hiking expeditions welcome escapes.

Seven miles before Hwy-89A reaches Sedona, **Slide Rock State Park** is a natural water chute, where you can swim and slide across smooth boulders set in the river bed (mid-May to mid-Oct daily 8am–7pm; March to mid-May daily 8am–6pm; mid-Oct to Feb daily 8am–5pm; $5 per vehicle). The absence of still water in Oak Creek means that it's almost insect-free.

Practicalities

The canyon floor is quite narrow, and has been heavily developed with leisure facilities, though at least careful landscaping makes most of these inconspicuous; good places to stay include the well-equipped log huts at *Don Hoel's Cabins* (☎520/282-3560 or 1-800/292-4635; ⑤). **Campgrounds** at river (and road) level include *Bootlegger* and *Pine Flat* (both mid-May to Sept; first-come first-served; $10; ☎520/282-4119). Despite its tiny size, erratic opening hours and off-the-beaten-track location, the most popular place to eat is *Garland's*, half a mile north of Slide Rock (April to mid-Nov; ☎520/282-3343), which has a different small menu each night.

Sedona

Though local boosters make much of its setting, amid some definitive Southwestern canyon scenery, the New-Age resort of **SEDONA** adds nothing to the beauty of its surroundings. Architecturally, it's a real mess, with several miles of ugly red-brick sprawl interrupted by the occasional mock-historical mall monstrosity. To the artists, healers, walking wounded and wealthy retirees who have flocked here in the last two decades, however, Sedona is "the next Santa Fe". Whether you love it or hate it will probably depend on whether you share their wide-eyed awe for angels, crystals and all matters mystical – and whether you're prepared to pay over-the-odds prices for the privilege of joining them. Whatever your attitude, Sedona is still a fascinating place to visit, where even the hardest-nosed commercial operation can seem a front for the real business of holding earnest conversations about the state of each other's psyches.

Established in 1902 by Theodore Schnebly, and named after his wife, Sedona remained for most of the twentieth century a small farming settlement, unmarked on most maps. German surrealist painter **Max Ernst** moved here in the 1940s – the bizarre backdrops of his later canvases seem less surreal once you've seen where they were painted – and Hollywood movie-makers filmed in the area from the 1950s onwards. However, Sedona's big break came in 1981, when Page Bryant, author and psychic, "channelled" the information that Sedona is in fact "the heart *chakra* of the planet". Since she pinpointed her first **vortex** – a point at which, it is claimed, psychic and electro-magnetic energies can be channelled for personal and planetary harmony – the town has achieved its own personal growth, and blossomed as a focus for New-Age practitioners of all kinds. Huge crowds came to Sedona in 1987 for the "Harmonic Convergence", paying up to $75 for a seat on Bell Rock at the time when it was supposed to launch itself to the galaxy of Andromeda. (Dissatisfied customers are said to have included one gentleman who brought his mouth-organ, under the impression that it was a harmonica convergence.)

Arrival and information

Sedona is 28 miles south of Flagstaff on Hwy-89A, and 120 miles north of Phoenix. It centers on the intersection known as the **"Y"**, above Oak Creek, where Hwy-89A branches southwest towards Cottonwood and Prescott, and Hwy-179 continues by way of the village of Oak Creek to meet I-17, fourteen miles south.

Just north of the "Y", in the area known as **uptown** – the one part of Sedona where the stores and businesses are close enough togeth-

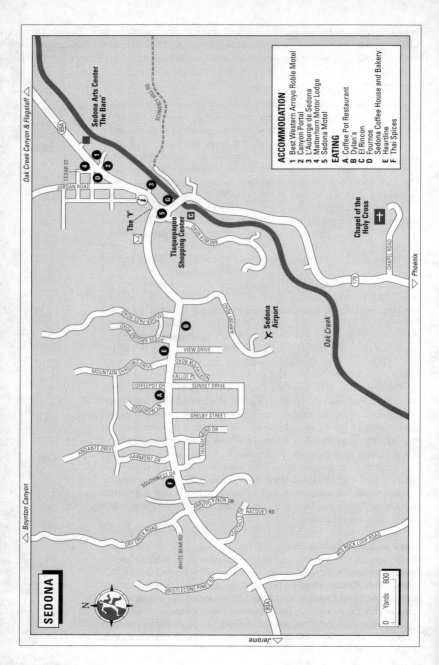

SEDONA

N

⬁ Boynton Canyon
⬁ Oak Creek Canyon & Flagstaff
⬁ Phoenix
Jerome ⬁

ACCOMMODATION
1 Best Western Arroyo Roble Motel
2 Canyon Portal
3 L'Auberge de Sedona
4 Matterhorn Motor Lodge
5 Sedona Motel

EATING
A Coffee Pot Restaurant
B Dylan's
C El Rincon
D Fournos
Sedona Coffee House and Bakery
E Heartline
F Thai Spices

Sedona Arts Center 'The Barn'

SCHNEBLY HILL RD

CEDAR ST
JORDAN ROAD
The 'Y'
Tlaquepaque Shopping Center
BREWER ROAD
AIRPORT ROAD
Sedona Airport
Oak Creek
Chapel of the Holy Cross
CHAPEL ROAD
179

SOUTH PASS ROAD
POSSE GROUND ROAD
VIEW DRIVE
MOUNTAIN SHADOWS DRIVE
KALLOF PL
NORTH VIEW ROAD
COFFEEPOT DR
SUNSET DRIVE
GOODROW LN
SHELBY STREET
ANDANTE DRIVE
THUNDERBIRD DR
HARMONY DR
SOUTHWEST DR
ARROYO PIÑON DR
RACQUET RD
FOOTHILLS DR
DRY CREEK ROAD
WHITE BEAR RD
RED ROCK LOOP ROAD
BRISTLECONE PINES RD
89A
89A

0   Yards   800

er to make walking a possibility – the **visitor center**, Hwy-89A and Forest Rd, has full listings of lodgings and tour operators (Mon–Sat 9am–5pm, Sun 9am–3pm; ☎520/282-7722 or 1-800/288-7336).

Three daily **flights** to and from Phoenix are operated by *Scenic Airlines* (☎520/282-7935 or 1-800/535-4448), with one-way fares starting at around $60. The *Sedona–Phoenix Shuttle* (☎520/282-2066 or 1-800/448-7988 in AZ), a six-daily **bus** service between Sedona and Phoenix Airport, costs $30 one way. Some *Greyhound* buses between Flagstaff and Phoenix call in at Sedona.

For a quick overview of the area, pick up either of the two different 45-minute **tours** run by the *Sedona Trolley* (daily 10am–5pm; hourly tours, $6; ☎520/282-5400), at the visitor center. Two companies rent **bikes**: *Canyon Country Mountain Bikes*, 245 N US-89A (☎520/282-6985), and *Sedona Mountain Bike Rental*, 376 Apple Ave (☎520/282-2164). **4WD** vehicles are available from *Sedona Jeep Rentals*, up at the airport (☎520/282-1234)

Accommodation

Sedona is an expensive place to **stay**, and apart from the immediate area of the "Y" it's too spread out to walk around in the evening. If you're watching your budget, you can get better deals nearby at Cottonwood, Jerome and Camp Verde; if you don't mind spending $100 or more, however, Sedona has some extremely fancy options, including at least a dozen upscale **B&Bs** and several full-service **resorts**. **Agencies** specializing in local accommodations and tours include *Sedona Central* (☎520/282-1518 or 1-800/445-4128) and *Red Rock Reservations* (☎520/284-3627 or 1-800/890-0521).

Bell Rock Inn, 6246 Hwy-179, Sedona AZ 86351; ☎520/282-4161 or 1-800/881-7625, fax 284-0192. Upmarket, pastel-painted motel six miles south of town, with two pools and two spas. Winter ④, summer ⑤.

Best Western Arroyo Roble Motel, 400 N US-89A, Sedona AZ 86339; ☎520/282-4001 or 1-800/528-1234. Comfortable multi-tiered motel, stacked up above Oak Creek not far north of uptown Sedona. Winter ⑤, summer ⑥.

Canyon Portal, 210 N US-89A, Sedona AZ 86339; ☎520/282-7125 or 1-800/542-8484, fax 282-1825. Fairly dismal joint just north of the "Y", which offers some of the cheapest rooms in town. ③.

The Canyon Wren, Star Route 3, PO Box 1140, Sedona AZ 86336; ☎520/282-6900. Individual two-person cabins, each with a whirlpool tub, six miles north of Sedona in Oak Creek Canyon. ⑥.

Cathedral Rock Lodge, 61 Los Amigos Lane, Sedona AZ 86336; ☎520/282-7608, fax 282-4505. Small, friendly B&B in spacious grounds on the Red Rock Loop Road, with two double rooms, a suite and a separate cabin. ④.

Cozy Cactus B&B, 80 Canyon Circle Drive, Sedona AZ 86351; ☎520/284-0082 or 1-800/788-2082. Ranch house B&B at the edge of the woods near the foot of Castle Rock, offering five themed, en-suite double rooms. ⑤.

Enchantment Resort, 525 Boynton Canyon Rd, Sedona AZ 86336; ☎520/282-2900 or 1-800/826-4180, fax 282-9249. Extremely luxurious

*Sedona's major annual event is the **Jazz On The Rocks** festival, held on the last Saturday of September; ☎520/282-1985.*

*As explained on p.15, **accommodation prices**, excluding taxes, are indicated throughout this book by the following symbols:*

① *up to $30*
② *$30–45*
③ *$45–60*
④ *$60–80*
⑤ *$80–100*
⑥ *$100–130*
⑦ *$130–175*
⑧ *$175–250*
⑨ *$250+*

Within You or Without You: Experiencing Red Rock Country

Dozens of Sedona-based operators compete to offer close encounters with red rock country. The most popular option is a **jeep tour**, but you can also take scenic **flights**, in balloons, airplanes or helicopters, ride on **horseback**, or trek with a llama. There's also a choice between a traditional tour, on which you'll see formations such as "Snoopy" and "Garfield", and a New-Age **vision quest**, in which the same rock may be a "sacred energy area" or a "beacon vortex". Some guides even eschew vehicles altogether, in favour of taking you on a **spiritual journey** instead.

Air Safari Charter & Tours; ☎520/282-3485. Quick flights over Sedona – 15min for $25 per person, up to 25min for $40 – plus longer tours by arrangement.

Creative Passages; ☎520/204-2549. Personalized experiences, from *Harley Davison* bike tours to "deep healing through the power of love" or "journey within yourself and your birthchart".

Crystal Light Centers; ☎520/282-2733. Tour the vortex sites; "use the earth energies for personal transformation". Half day $45, full day with lunch $75.

Don Hanson; ☎520/204-2235. Don "tunes into Universal Intelligence and talks to it out loud"; "you will experience tremendous relief . . . and gratitude".

Dorian Tours; ☎520/282-4562 or 1-800/728-4562. Ranges from

3hr $54 vortex tours to the full-scale Pilgrimage – "An interuniversal cosmic, historical adventure for those destiny reservists who have a call of service to humankind in these crucial years ahead".

Earth Wisdom Tours; ☎520/282-4714. "More than ordinary tours, these are journeys. . . in the way of our Native American friends . . . learn of the ancestral secrets of the Medicine Wheel"; costs $27 to $65.

Kachina Riding Stables; ☎520/282-7252. Horseback trips, largely geared around eating (in traditional cowboy style); 3hr rides in the vicinity of Red Rock State Park for $50–60, plus customized expeditions at $295 per day.

Legends of Sedona Ranch; ☎520/282-6826 or 1-800/848-

resort, equipped with four pools and twelve tennis courts, that has taken over ravishing Boynton Canyon eight miles west of town. Accommodation is in fully equipped one- and two-bedroom adobe *casitas*. ⑧.

L'Auberge de Sedona, 301 L'Auberge Lane, PO Box B, Sedona AZ 86336; ☎520/282-1661 or 1-800/272-6777, fax 282-2885. Plush two-part resort in the heart of the town, with fancy French-themed motel rooms looking out at the red rocks at road level and a cable-car connection to the individual guest cottages ranged along the tranquil banks of Oak Creek below. ⑦/⑧.

Matterhorn Motor Lodge, 230 Apple Ave, Sedona AZ 86336; ☎520/282-2176, fax 282-0727. Small, central mock-adobe motel, on the right as you come into town on Hwy-89A from the north, with two tiers of rooms that face across to the red rocks at sunset. Winter ③, summer ④.

Quality Inn King's Ransom, 771 Hwy-179, PO Box 180, Sedona AZ 86339; ☎520/282-7151 or 1-800/221-2222. Predictable upper-range motel, south of

7728. "Where horses are free . . . but rides ain't"; 1hr $35, 2hr $45.

Michele Celeste Renee Chaney; ☎520/282-2239. Angelic Visions Emissary, who channels the entity known as "I AM, the one with no name" for $1 per minute.

Natural Cultural Adventures; ☎520/462-3356 or 1-800/350-2693. 10hr tours of Sedona area for $90; 12hr tours to Hopi mesas ($125); two days to Canyon de Chelly with Navajo guide ($285).

Northern Light Balloon Expeditions; ☎520/282-2274 or 1-800/230-6222. Relatively unspiritual balloon trips, with champagne picnics.

Pink Jeep Ancient Expeditions; ☎520/282-2137 or 1-800/999-2137. Off-road jeep tours, up to 2hr 30min to ancient ruins or sacred places for $55.

Pink Jeep Tours (☎520/282-5000 or 1-800/8SEDONA). You can't miss this lot in uptown Sedona. Quite exceptionally garish "4-wheelin' vehicles" crunch around in 1- to 3-hr off-road tours that cost $18 to $42 per person.

Sedona Adventures; ☎520/282-3500 or 1-800/888-9494. 2hr

30min tours for around $40, plus the 3hr Vortex Adventure, to "discover your own unique energy and power", for $48.

Sedona Helicopter Adventures; ☎520/282-0904 or 1-800/282-5141. Chopper flights from 10min *Famous Formations* ($32) to 40min *Grand Mogollon* ($130).

Sedona Nature Tours; ☎520/282-3735. Transformational experiences in Coconino National Forest.

Sedona Red Rock Jeep Tours; ☎520/282-6826 or 1-800/848-7728. Jeep trips from 1hr ($22) up to 3hr Sacred Earth Tours ($65). As you bomb around the desert, you can "learn to smudge and walk in balance", to "work with crystals and . . . tap the energy of the earth's power spots to enhance personal growth" and "focus on the need to offer love and healing to our earth, as well as each other".

Sedona Sky Treks; ☎520/284-2998. 35min local tours for $49 per person, plus such tailor-made excursions as the Grand Canyon ($129), Monument Valley ($235), or Canyon de Chelly ($195).

town, with slightly small rooms but a nice garden and a reasonable restaurant. Winter ④, summer ⑤.

Sedona Motel, 218 Hwy-179, PO Box 1450, Sedona AZ 86339; ☎520/282-7151 or 1-800/221-2222. Small, relatively inexpensive motel, in an ideal and attractive location close to the "Y" uptown. ④.

Exploring Sedona

Sedona itself has little to detain sightseers, though strolling the two or so blocks that count as **uptown**, just north of the "Y", is pleasant enough. Even above the roar of the traffic, you can usually still hear the synchronized chirruping of the crickets in **Oak Creek** down below, while your eyes are repeatedly drawn to the superb red rocks that tower above the banal buildings along Hwy-89A. A little way south of the "Y", on Hwy-179, **Tlaquepaque Shopping Center** is a very upscale mall, modelled on a Mexican village near Guadalajara, that offers Sedona's most distinctive (and expensive) shopping.

The prevailing pay-no-taxes ethos of Sedona's ardent libertarians has ensured that few of the side roads off the main highways are paved. That dovetails neatly, of course, with the booming business in off-road tours, as listed on p.272. Nonetheless, a lot of the best scenery is visible from the highway, and in any case many of the jeep roads are perfectly passable in ordinary vehicles. So long as you're happy to remain in ignorance as to which rocks are really electro-magnetic tuning forks vibrating in harmony with Alpha Centauri, there's no great need to take a commercial tour.

The closest **vortex** to town is on **Airport Mesa**. Turn left up Airport Road from Hwy-89A as you head west, about a mile past the "Y", and the vortex is at the junction of the second and third peaks, just after the cattle grid. Further up, beyond the precarious airport, the **Shrine of the Red Rocks** looks out across the entire valley.

Three and four miles further along Hwy-89A, two successive turn-ings to the left mark the Upper and Lower sections of the seven-mile **Red Rock Loop Road**, all of which is paved barring a bumpy but not too difficult mile or so in the middle. Its prime attraction is reached via a spur road a couple of miles down Lower Red Rock Loop Road. **Red Rock State Park** (summer daily 8am–6pm; winter daily 8am–5pm; $5) may be the obvious name for a park in the Sedona area, but it's not in fact the best place to see red rocks. Instead it preserves a sweeping curve of **Oak Creek**, both of whose banks at this point used to belong to a private ranch. The riparian environment thus survives reasonably intact – its flora and fauna are explained in the well-equipped **visitor center**, which holds stuffed hawks and owls and some live fish in tanks – and can be explored on an assortment of short trails. Two miles from the highway on Upper Red Rock Loop Road, the site known as **Red Rock Crossing** is a small picnic area beside a picturesque ford in Oak Creek that has featured in many movies (daily 9am–8pm; $2). **Cathedral Rock**, on the far side of the stream, is another vortex.

Dry Creek Road, which heads north off Hwy-89 a mile closer to town, runs north past **Capitol Butte** to reach **Boynton Canyon**. The presence of the lavish *Enchantment Resort* has spoiled some of the magic of Boynton Canyon itself – which has its own vortex – but sev-eral neighbouring canyons are still perfect for short desert hikes. The resort office can provide trail maps showing the locations of Sinagua ruins in **Red Canyon**, while climbing **Doe Mesa**, or up into **Loy Butte Canyon**, gives great views of the whole Sedona valley.

South from the "Y", Hwy-179 is soon barrelling through the Coconino National Forest. Turn left as soon as you cross Oak Creek, onto the unpaved **Schnebly Hill Road**, to enjoy the area's most spec-tacular scenic drive. In summer, the road remains open all the way to I-17, twelve rough miles east. Alternatively, continue south for three miles and then take Chapel Road to the left, which soon brings you

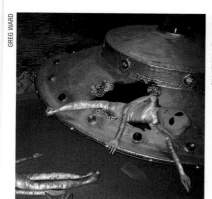
Alien encounter, 1947, Roswell, NM

Saguaro cactus, AZ

Biosphere 2, AZ

Chiricahua National Monument, AZ

Bisbee, AZ

San Xavier del Bac Mission, AZ

Havasupai Indian Reservation, AZ

Havasupai Indian Reservation, AZ

Grand Canyon, AZ

London Bridge, Lake Havasu City, AZ

Grand Canyon, AZ

to the **Chapel of the Holy Cross**. This tall and very narrow concrete chapel, whose facade is shaped like a massive cross, is squeezed into a cleft in the red cliffs (daily 9am–5pm). Another two miles down the highway, **Bell Rock**, on the east as you enter the village of Oak Creek, is Sedona's fourth major vortex.

Eating

Sedona is bursting with expensive Southwestern-style **restaurants**, not all of which are particularly good, and still has a smattering of old-fashioned diners. There's a shortage of places where you can just sit and watch the world go by over a coffee and a sandwich; most of its cafes are twee little places intended mainly to entice tourists into pastel-trimmed gift stores.

Coffee Pot Restaurant, 2050 W Hwy-89A; ☎520/282-6626. Sedona's largest, oldest diner, open daily from 6am until late, has a sports lounge, a hundred kinds of omelette, and all the burgers and fried specials you could hope for.

Dylan's, 1405 W Hwy-89A; ☎520/282-7930. American diner where sandwiches and *quesadillas* are served all day for under $10, while a complete steak or seafood dinner costs more like $20.

El Rincon, Tlaquepaque Shopping Center, Hwy-179; ☎520/282-4628. Authentic Mexican food in classy surroundings, with entrees costing up to $15 and indoor and outdoor seating. Tues–Sat 11am–9pm, Sun noon–5pm.

Fournos, 241 N Hwy-89A; ☎520/282-3331. Lovely little Greek restaurant, offering traditional dishes with all the right ingredients – feta cheese, *kalamata* olives, and so on. Open Thurs–Sat, when dinner is served at 6pm & 8pm, and Sun for brunch at noon; reservations compulsory, no credit cards.

Heartline, 1610 W Hwy-89A; ☎520/282-0785. Tasteful white-table-linen restaurant, with an attractive courtyard, that serves determinedly healthy – though not exclusively vegetarian – Southwestern cuisine. Open Mon–Sat for lunch and dinner, and dinner only on Sun.

L'Auberge, *L'Auberge de Sedona*, 301 L'Auberge Lane; ☎520/282-1667. Exquisite, river-view French dining at sky-high prices; individual entrees are around $30, a full set menu is $50. Open daily for all meals.

The Muse Literary Café, Artesania Plaza, 251 Hwy-179; ☎520/282-3671. Not desperately literary, but delicious fluffy breakfast *beignets* and coffees, salad lunches, and pizzas and pasta for around $10 in the evening – plus live music nightly. Opposite Tlaquepaque, just down from the "Y", with patio seating overlooking the creek.

Sedona Coffee House & Bakery, 283 N Hwy-89A; ☎520/282-2241. Popular breakfast hang-out near the "Y", serving espresso coffees and pastries, and graduating to soup and salad later on. Open daily 8am–5pm.

Thai Spices, 2986 W Hwy-89A; ☎520/282-0599. West of downtown, near the road out to Boynton Canyon; tasty, healthy Thai food, with meat or seafood green or red curries or *Pad Thai* noodles for under $10, plus vegetarian and even macrobiotic choices. Open for dinner nightly, lunch on weekdays only.

Yavapai Dining Room, *Enchantment Resort*, 525 Boynton Canyon Rd; ☎520/282-2900. Showcase resort restaurant, serving top-class Southwestern cuisine for lunch and dinner daily at up to $25 per entree; plenty of beans and chile to go with the freshest meats and fish. Open daily for all meals.

Cottonwood

Describing **COTTONWOOD**, eighteen miles southwest of Sedona in
the heart of the Verde Valley, the 1930s *WPA* guide to Arizona wrote
that "Familiar figures in the town are the cowboys from the range
and the prospector or 'desert rat' who wanders in from his camp in
the mountains to break the monotony of his lonely life". Today's
Cottonwood is not nearly so romantic, though it's grown much larger thanks to an influx of retirees. It's not really even the same place,
as the former downtown is stranded a couple of miles north of Hwy-
89A, now lined with modern strip development.

Cottonwood does, however, make an inexpensive base for trips to
Sedona and Jerome, and its old main street still possesses a certain
charm. Tucked around a flower-filled courtyard, the *Sundial Motel*, 1034
N Main St (☎520/634-8031; ②), is a pretty – albeit pretty basic – old-
style motel, while the nearby *Bell'Espresso*, 1025A N Main St (closed
Wed; ☎520/634-3300), is a friendly little espresso and snack bar housed
in a small gallery. If you prefer dependable chain lodgings, the *Best
Western Cottonwood Inn* is on Hwy-89A at 993 S Main St (☎520/634-
5575 or 1-800/350-0025 in AZ, fax 634-5576; winter ③, summer ④).

Tuzigoot National Monument

At the start of the fourteenth century, the Verde Valley held around
fifty major pueblo sites, occupied by the ancient Indian people now
known as the **Sinagua**. One of the largest, now **TUZIGOOT
NATIONAL MONUMENT**, perches on a hillock across the Verde
River from **CLARKDALE**, three miles west of Cottonwood.

The ground floor alone had 86 rooms, and shows signs of repeated additions; with fifteen more rooms on the upper level, it may have
been home to around 225 people. Some archeologists think it was a
final enclave, where the Sinagua gathered against encroaching
drought before abandoning the area early in the fifteenth century.
Artefacts at the **visitor center** (summer daily 8am–7pm; spring & fall
daily 8am–6pm; winter daily 8am–5pm; $2; ☎520/634-5564)
include turquoise mosaics and shell jewellery.

Unfortunately, Tuzigoot is one of the least satisfying such sites in
the Southwest. When it was restored as part of a 1930s make-work
programme, a little too much work was done, and its authenticity
was all but destroyed by laying a broad cement trail over, across, and
through the pueblo. Furthermore, while the river, lined with cottonwoods, still flows past the pueblo, the "fields" below are just a sickly
orange mass of tailings from the nearby copper mines.

Jerome

The former mining town of **JEROME**, once the fourth largest
community in Arizona, stands high above the Verde Valley on
Hwy-89A. It's conspicuous from quite a distance; not only is an

enormous letter "J" etched deep into the hillside above it, but a large chunk of that hillside is missing altogether, having been blown apart for **opencast copper mining**. This land abounds in mineral wealth – thick veins of copper are interspersed with gold and silver, and an endless supply of limestone is still extracted for cement – but serious exploitation only started in 1876. The **United Verde** mine was partly financed by New Yorker Eugene Jerome (a cousin of Winston Churchill's mother, Jennie Jerome), who insisted that the new town bear his name. The United Verde has been called "the richest mine ever owned by an individual"; it made William Clark $100 million, and by 1953, had produced enough copper to give a thirteen-pound lump to every person on earth. Until the tortuous highway was built, the only way up to Jerome was the rail line that corkscrewed down from the mine to the world's largest copper smelter, at Clarkdale.

With its disproportionate population of young males, Jerome was known as a hard-drinking and hard-living town. The young **Pancho Villa** started out in life by supplying its drinking water, using a relay of two hundred burros, and for a brief period the International Workers of the World (the "**Wobblies**") were a strong presence; several hundred miners and "outside agitators" were literally railroaded out of town in July 1917 and dumped unceremoniously in the remote deserts of southwest Arizona.

Harsh economic realities have always determined local fortunes. Plenty of copper remains in the earth; although the Depression hit hard, the mine was only closed when cheap imported copper in the early 1950s made it uneconomic to continue, and there's every possibility that as prices rise, it will reopen. To keep the mineral rights from reverting to the state, the present owners are obliged to keep on researching and prospecting; in fact they do more than they have to, and reportedly find enough gold to cover their expenses.

As recently as the 1970s, Jerome was a **ghost town** in which it was possible to turn up and move into an empty house. Many of those who did so are still here, making a living from arts and crafts, and the town itself has made a dramatic recovery. It's a bit of a tourist trap, but is nonetheless fascinating to explore.

Arrival and information

Though on paper at least Hwy-89A is a direct through route between **Sedona**, thirty miles northeast of Jerome, and **Prescott**, thirty miles southwest, the formidable **Mingus Mountain** makes reaching Jerome a slow business. Coming from Cottonwood, it's a painstaking switchback climb; if you approach from Prescott, you're descending back down by the time you come to Jerome, with gorgeous views of the valley spread out below.

*Jerome's **zip** code is AZ 86331.*

Hwy-89A branches in two in the heart of town, where a one-way system takes westbound traffic along **Hull Avenue**, and eastbound along **Main Street**. Pending the completion of a new visitor center, the **chamber of commerce** is housed in *Blue Heron Gifts*, next to the post office at 116 Main St (☎520/634-2900).

Accommodation

There's no room to build **motels** on Jerome's uncertain slopes, so accommodation is restricted to a couple of turn-of-the-century hotels and a few former homes that have been converted into **B&Bs**.

The **price** *codes* used *here are explained on p.271.*

Ghost City Inn, 541 N Main St; ☎520/634-4678. Century-old house, at the entrance to town as you come up from Cottonwood, with huge views from its wooden verandah. Four of the themed rooms share baths, one is en-suite; one is crammed with hot-air balloon memorabilia. ④.

The Inn at Jerome, 309 N Main St; ☎520/634-5094 or 1-800/634-5094. Atmospheric eight-room hotel in the heart of town, offering accommodation with and without en-suite bathrooms. ③.

Surgeon's House B&B, 101 Hill St; ☎520/639-1452 or 1-800/639-1452. Smart, upmarket B&B with dramatic views from the top of town; the en-suite rooms are especially plush. ⑤.

Wheeler's B&B, 3 Juarez St; ☎520/634-3270. Small antique-filled B&B, perched above the valley two blocks below Main Street. ⑤.

The Town

Thanks to the steep angle of the hillside, Jerome's streets are effectively stacked one on top of the other, and its stone houses – it was far too expensive to haul timber up here – tend to have two storeys at the front and four or five at the back. Under the repeated concussion of over two hundred miles of tunnels being blasted into the mountainside, the whole town used to slip downhill at the rate of five inches per year, and the **Sliding Jail** on Hull Avenue came to rest 225 feet from where it was built (it's still there, but not open to the public).

Built for mine owner "Rawhide Jimmy" Douglas in 1917, the **Douglas Mansion**, on Mine Museum Road below town, is now open as **Jerome State Historical Park** (daily 8am–5pm; $2). Given the sweeping views over the valley, it can be hard to concentrate on the displays that detail the history and workings of the mines, and the lifestyles of the bosses.

Up in town, the **Mine Museum** is housed beneath the pressed tin ceiling of the former *Fashion Saloon* at 200 N Main St (daily 9am–4.30pm; 50¢). Its amateurish but enjoyable collection of oddities include paintings that record different eras in mining, a chicken-wire stretcher once used for accident victims, and the primitive calculator used to calculate the *United Verde Copper Company*'s payroll.

Many of the **shops** only stock souvenirs, but there are some interesting **crafts** showrooms around, such as the *Knapp Gallery* on Lower Main Street and *Made in Jerome Pottery* next door.

Eating and drinking

Day-trippers tend to fill the tearooms and snackbars of Jerome at
lunchtime – especially on weekends – but come the evening you can
still get a faint sense of its riproaring past.

English Kitchen, 119 Jerome Ave; ☎520/634-2132. Built in 1899, this claims
to be Arizona's oldest restaurant. Under Chinese ownership, it was an opium
den; later the Wobblies held meetings downstairs. Now it's open for breakfast
and lunch Tues–Sun, and its terrace offers a commanding view of the valley.

Flatiron Cafe, 416 N Main St; ☎520/634-2733. Small, friendly joint at the
apex of the one-way system. Espresso coffees, scrambled-egg breakfasts and
fancy salad-and-sandwich lunches for around $7. Open daily 8am–5pm.

Paul & Jerry's Saloon, 206 N Main St; ☎520/634-2603. Old-style saloon dating from 1889, with glorious ornate pool tables and a fine old bar with period
trimmings.

Wedge on the Edge, 412 N Main St; ☎520/634-5554. Homemade sourdough
pizzas for $10 and upwards, with views out to both sides and off down the
mountains. Open Tues–Thurs & Sun 11am–7pm, Fri & Sat 11am–9pm.

Montezuma Castle National Monument

Towards the east end of the Verde Valley, two dramatic ancient sites
jointly constitute **Montezuma Castle National Monument**. Roughly
five miles apart, each now stands a short way east of I-17, around
forty miles south of Flagstaff and twenty miles southeast of Sedona.

The northernmost of the two, **Montezuma Well**, is a natural lake
that measures 368 feet across by 55 feet deep. Set like a volcanic
crater into a small hill, it was formed when the roof of an underground cave collapsed 11,000 years ago. It's still fed by a spring that
produces a phenomenal 1.9 million gallons per day of warm water,
heated to a constant 75°F.

Not surprisingly, the well was sacred to Native Americans; the
Yavapai people (see p.314) say that this was where they emerged
into the world. The **Hohokam** are thought to have moved here
around 600 AD, and were the first to divert its water for irrigation,
while the **Sinagua** replaced them in 1125 AD. Traces of ruined
Sinagua pueblos can be discerned on the hilltop, reached by a five-
minute walk from the parking lot, and a more complete **cliff
dwelling** is set into the inner crater wall. It's now inaccessible,
though you get a good view from the foot of the staircase that
leads down to the lakeside. A couple more dwellings stand at
ground level here, next to the hole or "swallet" through which the
water spills out of the lake and flows through the hillside to join
Beaver Creek outside.

Five miles south, **Montezuma Castle** itself is a superbly preserved
cliff dwelling in an idyllic setting above Beaver Creek. Filling an
alcove in the hillside with a wall of pink adobe, and originally reached
by three separate ladders from the valley floor, its five storeys taper
up to fit the contours of the rock. Apparently the sycamore beams are

still in place, and the fingerprints of the masons are still visible on the bricks, but visitors are not permitted to climb up.

The ruins of a much larger, though now much less photogenic, dwelling "next door" were exposed to view by a fire in around 1400 AD. Once again you can't go inside, but the exposed honeycomb of holes in the limestone rock show that it had around 45 rooms, as well as little "cupboards" recessed into the walls, and might have housed as many as a hundred people.

The **visitor center** at the castle (summer daily 8am–7pm; winter daily 8am–5pm; $2; ☎520/567-3322) has informative displays on the Sinagua, including a macaw skeleton which suggests trade with the Mexican civilizations thousands of miles to the south. There is no connection with the Aztec ruler Montezuma, though the well is said to appear on a deerskin map that belonged to Cortes himself.

Camp Verde

The scrappy little town of **CAMP VERDE**, a mile or so east of I-17 another two miles south of Montezuma Castle, is noteworthy only as the site of **Fort Verde**. Built in 1871 to succeed a neighbouring fort established in 1865, it served as headquarters for General George Crook's campaign against the Tonto Apaches. Crook failed to grasp the fact that the Yavapai and the Apache were separate peoples, but his massacre of the Yavapai at Skeleton Cave convinced the Apache to surrender. Both groups were rounded onto a reservation at Camp Verde, and later marched east to the San Carlos Reservation. Some ultimately returned, and a few pockets of land are now set aside for Yavapai-Apache joint use.

For a history of the Apache Wars, see p.489.

Fort Verde was damaged by fire in 1881, and decommissioned ten years later. The four crumbling adobe buildings that remain are now the **Fort Verde State Historic Park** (daily 8am–5pm; $2), with an interesting museum in the commanding officer's house and a few more exhibits – stuffed birds, old wheelchairs, fearsome medical instruments – in the former doctor's quarters. The fort was never walled, the Apaches always preferring to ambush soldiers in the mountains than attack defensive positions, so it bears little resemblance to movie depictions of Wild-West military outposts.

Practicalities

*Hwy-260 climbs east of Camp Verde towards **Pine** and **Strawberry**, in the woods thirty miles up; see p.256.*

While there's no great reason to spend a night in Camp Verde, the *Best Western Cliff Castle Casino*, 333 Middle Verde Rd (☎520/567-4262; ④), is a classic Southwestern hybrid: a luxury hotel built in what might conceivably have been Anasazi style, had the Anasazi ever felt the urge to build enormous hotels, and now run as a casino by the Yavapai-Apache Nation, featuring 24-hour slots. Cheaper rooms can be had at the *Super 8*, at the Montezuma Castle exit off I-17 (☎520/567-2622 or 1-800/800-8000; ③).

Arcosanti

South of
Flagstaff

Two miles east of the interstate at **Cordes Junction**, 25 miles south
of Camp Verde, the space-age project known as **ARCOSANTI** is
gradually rising from the rim of a beautiful high desert canyon.
Designed (someday) to be a self-sufficient community of five thousand people, Arcosanti is the clearest embodiment of **Arcology**, an
ideal blend of architecture and ecology created by Italian architect
Paolo Soleri, a former student of Frank Lloyd Wright.

*Paolo Soleri's
bell foundry at
Cosanti, near
Phoenix, is
described on
p.206.*

Though far from any sizeable settlement, Arcosanti is intended as
a model of future urban environments. Part construction site, part
theme park, with buildings shaped to maximize the benefit of the
sun's energy, it can be seen on hour-long guided tours (daily
9am–5pm; hourly tours 10am–4pm; $5; ☎520/632-7135). A spa-
cious **cafe** serves healthy and tasty meals, and you can stay in the on-
site **motel** for as little as $25 for a basic double room; if you like what
you see, you can even sign up for one of the month-long workshops
and help out with the construction. In summer, Arcosanti also hosts
a very popular series of outdoor **concerts**.

Prescott

The neat little Victorian town of **PRESCOTT** makes an unlikely sight
in the Arizona wilderness, a hundred miles north of Phoenix by way
of Hwy-69, which leaves I-17 at Cordes Junction, and fifty miles
south of Ash Fork on I-40. In 1863, when President Lincoln acceded
to pressure from mining interests in the central mountains and granted Arizona territorial status, he chose to establish a new capital well
away from Tucson, which he saw as a hotbed of Confederate sympa-
thizers. His first choice, **Fort Whipple**, was replaced in 1864 when
gold was discovered near Prescott nearby, which became the site of
both fort and capital. It was named in honour of William H Prescott,
the author of *A History of the Conquest of Mexico*.

Though Tucson duly supplanted it as capital within three years,
Prescott survived, with cattle ranchers joining the gold miners to
make it the rowdiest, hardest-drinking town within a hundred miles.
Those days are long gone, however, and while Prescott refused to die
it hasn't grown either. Its downtown, focused around the kind of
courthouse square you'd expect to find in the Deep South, now feels
prettified for tourists rather than the heart of a living community. For
out-of-state visitors, Prescott doesn't really merit a substantial
detour, but if you're passing this way anyway it makes a far more
characterful halt than a typical interstate truckstop.

To get a feel for Prescott's past, head to the **Sharlot Hall
Museum**, 415 W Gurley St (April–Oct Mon–Sat 10am–5pm, Sun
1–5pm; Nov–March Mon–Sat 10am–4pm, Sun 1–5pm; $2 donation;
☎520/445-3122). Sharlot Hall, a former official historian of Arizona
who arrived in Prescott with her pioneer parents in 1882, at the age

of twelve, put together the nucleus of this collection, which has expanded since her death to fill a dozen buildings and an entire city block. As well as the modern museum headquarters, it includes the 1864 Governor's Mansion – more of an oversized log cabin – plus a blacksmith's shop and a garage filled with vintage vehicles.

Practicalities

Prescott's **visitor center**, on Courthouse Plaza at 117 W Goodwin St (Mon–Sat 9am–5pm, Sun 10am–4pm; ☎520/445-2000 or 1-800/266-7534), has listings of around twenty **B&Bs** in Victorian homes. Among the nicest are the rambling *Victorian Inn*, 246 S Cortez St (☎520/778-2642 or 1-800/704-2642; ⑤–⑦), which offers a Teddy Bear Room and lavish breakfasts, and the Queen-Anne-style *Marks House*, 203 E Union St (☎520/778-4632; ④–⑥). The restored *Hotel St Michael*, 205 W Gurley St (☎520/776-1999 or 1-800/678-3757, fax 776-7138; winter ②, summer ③), is an inexpensive but atmospheric – some say haunted – old downtown hotel, while the *Hassayampa Inn*, 122 E Gurley St (☎520/778-9434 or 1-800/322-1927; winter ④, summer ⑤), is a grander Art-Deco alternative.

*Prescott's zip
code is AZ
86303.*

The finest **dining** in town is at the *Siena Restaurant*, 111 Grove Ave (closed Mon; ☎520/771-1285), which offers exquisite Italian cuisine in an elegant former private home. For an experience more in keeping with Prescott's early days, try the *Prescott Brewing Company* instead, at 130 W Gurley St (☎520/771-2795), where as well as home-brewed beers they have a bakery and a full menu. The *Caffe St Michael* in the *Hotel St Michael* (see above) serves espresso coffees.

Wickenburg

WICKENBURG, sixty miles southwest of Prescott and the same distance northwest of Phoenix, is another former mining and ranching town now kept ticking over by tourism. It's only a little higher, and a little cooler, than Phoenix, so the main visitor season is in winter, between November and April.

*Hassayampa
means "river
that runs
upside down"
in Apache, a
reference to
the fact that it
often flows
underground.*

Wickenburg stands beside the **Hassayampa River**, on the "pumpkin patch" where Prussian prospector Henry Wickenburg built a mill in 1864 to process the gold he'd discovered in the Vulture Mountains, fifteen miles south. Though it yielded substantial quantities of gold, thanks to geological peculiarities and its general inaccessibility the **Vulture Mine** was seldom profitable. After years of passsing from hand to hand, it finally closed down in 1942. By then, however, Wickenburg had established a successful sideline in running **dude ranches**, where well-heeled Easterners could dabble with the Wild-West lifestyle for a few carefree days.

In the heart of town, the wooden sidewalks and false-front stores along **Frontier Street** must look much as they did in Wickenburg's heyday. You can still see the mesquite tree that served as the town "jail"; miscreants were simply chained to its trunk. Local history is

recalled at the **Desert Caballeros Western Museum**, 21 N Frontier
St (Mon–Sat 10am–4pm, Sun 1–4pm; $4), which as well as paintings
by Remington and Russell, and the usual barbed-wire collection, features a re-created 1900s street scene.

Three miles south, the **Hassayampa River Preserve** (summer
Wed–Sun 6am–noon; winter daily 6am–noon; $5 donation) marks a
spot where the river bubbles from its sandy streambed to irrigate a
lush stretch of woodland that's home to innumerable bird species.

The **Vulture Mine** itself can also be visited, up in the mountains
at the southern end of the 12-mile Vulture Mine Road (May–Aug Mon
& Thurs–Sun 8am–4pm; Sept–April daily 8am–4pm; $5). Its long-
abandoned workings rear up from the streets of the well-preserved
ghost town of **Vulture City**. Stick to the walking trail as you wander
round; the various buildings, which include a blacksmith's shop and
the mine's head office, are not as sturdy as they appear.

Practicalities

Wickenburg's **visitor center** is housed in the former railroad station
at 216 N Frontier St (summer Mon–Fri 9am–5pm; winter Mon–Fri
9am–5pm, Sat 10am–3pm, Sun 1–4pm; ☎520/684-5479).

Only one working cattle ranch now accepts paying guests, the
Flying E Ranch, 2801 W Wickenburg Way (Nov–April only;
☎520/684-2173, fax 684-5304; ⑧). *Rancho de los Caballeros* is a
purpose-built luxury resort, complete with its own golf course and stables, at 1551 S Vulture Mine Rd (Oct to early May; ☎520/684-5484, fax
684-2267; ⑨). Of conventional motels, the *Best Western Rancho
Grande*, 293 E Wickenburg Way (☎520/684-5445 or 1-800/854-
7235, fax 684-7380; summer ③, winter ④), is the most attractive, part
genuine adobe and part Spanish colonial mock-up, while *La Siesta*,
486 E Wickenburg Way (☎520/684-2826; ②) is a budget alternative.
For a slap-up ranch-style feed, head out to *Charley's Steakhouse*, 1187
W Wickenburg Way (Oct–April only, closed Mon; ☎520/684-2413).

*Wickenburg's
zip code is AZ
85358.*

West of Flagstaff

Though the two hundred miles of I-40 that run **west from Flagstaff**
to California are kept busy by traffic heading to, from and between
the Grand Canyon and Las Vegas, few of the towns along the way are
especially interesting in themselves. However, most became reliant
on tourism during the heyday of **Route 66**, and driving through any
one of them can bring on a frisson of that era's romance.

If you have the time to indulge your 1950s fantasies, then take the
120-mile side trip on the longest surviving section of the "**Mother
Road**", which starts at **Seligman**, loops back down to **Kingman**, and
then crosses some wild and mountainous country to the ghost town
of **Oatman**. Otherwise, it makes little difference where or even if you
choose to take a break from the interstate.

Williams

Although Flagstaff is generally regarded as the obvious base for visitors to the Grand Canyon, **WILLIAMS**, 32 miles west, is in fact the closest interstate town to the national park. It's also a nice little place in its own right, filled with Route-66-era motels and diners but retaining a certain individuality despite the constant stream of tourists. Its setting helps, cupped in a high grassy valley amid pine-covered hills; the largest peak is the 9264-foot **Bill Williams Mountain** to the south, which was named after pioneer trapper and "mountain man" Bill Williams (1787–1849), and gave its name in turn to the town, founded thirty years after his death.

Like Flagstaff, Williams originally based both its architecture and its economy on the ponderosas of the surrounding forests. Ever since 1901, however, when the *Santa Fe Railroad* first connected it with the canyon rim, sixty miles due north, Williams has lived off tourism. Though the railroad was driven out of business in 1968, it re-opened again in 1989, promoted as a fun ride rather than a serious means of transportation, and most people who spend the night in Williams are here to take the morning train up to the canyon.

Practicalities

Schedules and prices for the *Grand Canyon Railway* (☎520/773-1976 or 1-800/THE-TRAIN) are listed on p.296; when it's running, which is daily in summer, the train sets off from the centre of town at 9.30am. Williams' **visitor center**, at 200 W Railroad Ave (daily 8am–5pm; ☎520/635-4061), hands out all the usual brochures, including a town walking tour, and doubles as an entertaining **museum** of neighbourhood history.

The two main streets, Railroad Avenue and Bill Williams Avenue, form a one-way loop through town that incorporates all Williams' former Route 66 frontage. Several **motels**, such as the *Downtowner Motel*, 201 E Bill Williams Ave (☎520/635-4041 or 1-800/441-8828; winter ①, summer ③), stretch between the two. Other inexpensive options include the British-owned *Norris Motel*, 1001 W Bill Williams Ave (☎520/635-2202 or 1-800/341-8000; winter ①, summer ③), and the *Super 8*, 2001 E Bill Williams Ave (☎520/635-4700 or 1-800/800-8000; winter ②, summer ④), a mile north of town near the interstate. There are also plenty of **B&Bs**, like the plush *Red Garter*, 137 W Railroad Ave (☎520/635-1484 or 1-800/328-1484), above a downtown bakery, and the cheaper *Johnstonian*, a little way south at 321 W Sheridan Ave (☎520/635-2178; ③–⑥). If you're **camping**, ask at the Chalender Ranger Station, 501 W Bill Williams Ave (☎520/635-2676), for details of secluded mountain sites in the Kaibab National Forest.

The most authentic of the Route 66 **restaurants** to survive is *Rod's Steakhouse*, 301 E Bill Williams Ave (☎520/635-2671). By contrast, *Java Junction*, 125 W Bill Williams Ave (☎520/635-2080), serves espressos, juices, pastries and sandwiches.

The zip code for Williams is AZ 86046.

Twin highlights of Williams' annual calendar are **Rendezvous
Days**, on the Memorial Day weekend, when locals dress up as pioneer "buckskinners", and the **rodeo** on Labor Day.

Ash Fork

The ranching community of **ASH FORK**, another twenty miles west
of Williams, is smaller, less picturesque and far less involved in catering to travellers. By this point I-40 has pulled clear of the forests, and
downtown Ash Fork is characterized by buildings constructed with
the yellowish local sandstone rather than timber.

The major **motel** chains haven't bothered to set up shop here, but
there are still a few homespun alternatives, including the *Stage
Coach*, 823 Park Ave (☎520/637-2551; ②), and the *Hi Line*, 124 E
Lewis Ave (☎520/637-2766; ②).

Seligman

Starting a few miles west of Ash Fork, the old Route 66 parallels its
modern replacement at a discreet distance for the twenty or so miles
to **SELIGMAN**. This flyblown desert halt now feels more than a little
stranded, a mile or two north of the interstate, but if you're in the
mood to be seduced by its kitsch diners and drive-ins, it makes a
mildly diverting stop in a long day's drive.

You might even choose to follow Route 66's original course as
it curves northwards, through a dozen fading villages and part of
the **Hualapai Indian Reservation**, and back south to Kingman.
That's a total drive of 88 miles, as opposed to the dreary 65-mile
run west on I-40. It also provides access to **Havasu Canyon**, in the
depths of the Grand Canyon – one of the Southwest's least-known
marvels.

*For a full
account of the
wonders of
**Havasu
Canyon**, see
p.313.*

Whichever way you drive, Seligman has the only **accommodation**
between Ash Fork and Kingman, though motels like the *Canyon
Shadows*, 114 E Chino Ave (☎520/422-3255; ②), and the *Romney*,
122 W Chino Ave (☎520/422-3294; ②) are all much of an indifferent muchness. The *Copper Cart*, in the former railroad station on
Chino Ave (☎520/422-3241), is the most popular **diner**.

Kingman

With a population of over thirty thousand, **KINGMAN**, 65 miles on
from Seligman and thirty miles short of California, ranks second to
Flagstaff among Arizona's I-40 towns. As all traffic between Phoenix
or the Grand Canyon and **Las Vegas** – a mere hundred miles northwest on US-93 – is obliged to pass this way, Kingman also welcomes
enough tourists to keep thirty or more motels busy year-round. The
best that can be said for it, however, is that it's not particularly ugly,
and it's not lifeless; apart from that, it's a humdrum little pit stop
with a slight tinge of Route-66 quaintness.

*Carole
Lombard and
Clark Gable
were married
in Kingman on
March 29,
1939.*

Kingman's main street, curving alongside the railroad tracks, is named in honour of native son **Andy Devine**, the actor who drove the eponymous *Stagecoach* in John Ford's 1939 movie. His career, the culture and basketwork of the Hualapai Indians, and sundry other unlikely components of Mohave County's heritage, are explored in the **Mohave Museum of History & Arts**, 400 W Beale St (Mon–Fri 10am–5pm, Sat & Sun 1–5pm).

Practicalities

Regular *Greyhound* **buses**, between Phoenix and Las Vegas as well as east–west, use a terminal up near the interstate at 3264 E Andy Devine Ave. The old station in the centre of town still sees *Amtrak* **trains** between Flagstaff and LA, but only at unearthly hours of the night. The **visitor center** is nearby at 333 W Andy Devine Ave (summer Mon–Fri 8am–7pm, Sat & Sun 9am–5pm; winter Mon–Fri 8am–5pm, Sat & Sun 9am–3pm; ☎520/753-6106)

Motels in the heart of town include the basic *Ramblin' Rose*, 1001 E Andy Devine Ave (☎520/753-5541; ②). More comfortable chain options, a couple of miles northeast near I-40 exit 53, range from the *Super 8*, 3401 E Andy Devine Ave (☎520/757-4808 or 1-800/800-8000; ②), to the *Best Western A Wayfarer's Inn*, 2815 E Andy Devine Ave (☎520/753-6271 or 1-800/548-5695, fax 753-9608; winter ③, summer ④). Timothy McVeigh spent a week at the very *un*-seedy *Hill Top Motel*, 1901 E Andy Devine Ave (☎520/753-2198; ②), shortly before he bombed the Alfred P Murrah building in Oklahoma City, in April 1995. There's beautiful **camping** in the hills southeast of town in the county-run **Hualapai Mountain Park** (☎520/757-3859), which also holds the *Hualapai Mountain Lodge Resort* (☎520/757-3545; ③).

The most conspicuous **restaurant** in Kingman is *Mr D'z Route 66 Diner*, 105 E Andy Devine Ave (☎520/718-0066); it may be new, but its lurid neon signs are in the best traditions of Route 66, and so too are its burgers, shakes and fries. The *Old Town Coffeehouse*, on the eastern fringes of downtown at 616 E Beale St (closed Sun; ☎520/753-2244), is a more refined affair, serving espressos, soups and sandwiches on its small outdoor patio.

Chloride

Fifteen miles northwest of Kingman, as US-93 tears through the flat, prosaically-named **Detrital Valley** towards Las Vegas, a paved road climbs away into the mountains to the right. Its goal is the former silver mining centre of **CHLORIDE**, four miles up, which was established in 1864 and boasts Arizona's oldest still-functional post office. As well as silver, vast quantities of gold, copper, lead and turquoise were also extracted from the roadless **Cerbat Mountains** beyond, but Chloride these days lives by its wits, exploiting its ramshackle Wild-West appearance to attract tourists. Some of its erstwhile neighbours – such as **CERBAT** and **MINERAL PARK** – have foundered altogether, to become genuine **ghost towns**.

The epicentre of Chloride's visitor industry is *Shep's* (☎520/565-3643; ②), a gallery, dance hall and antiques store that also runs a four-room **B&B**.

Bullhead City and Laughlin

While both the old Route 66 and the interstate head southwest from Kingman, Hwy-68 barrels due west for thirty miles to **BULLHEAD CITY** on the Colorado. Built as a work camp for the construction of nearby Davis Dam, Bullhead City somehow survived the dam's completion in 1953, and has prospered recently due to its proximity to the casinos of **LAUGHLIN**, Nevada, just across the river.

In terms of temperature, **Bullhead** is the hottest town in the US, exceeding 120°F on day after day each summer. In most other respects, however, it's not the least bit hot. Nearly thirty thousand people now live along a ten-mile riverfront stretch of Hwy-93; why on earth you'd join them, even for a night, is hard to imagine.

Not that **Laughlin** is much better, despite the endless hype of its tourist authorities. If you've never been to Las Vegas, you may well be impressed by the sheer size of the dozen or so glittering **casinos** that jostle for position beside the Colorado. They lack the panache of their Vegas counterparts, however, as well as the will to cater to anyone other than hardened gamblers.

Practicalities

Both *Tri State Super Shuttle* (☎520/704-9000 or 1-800/801-8687) and *Best-Way Shuttle* (☎520/758-1200 or 1-800/248-8744) run daily **bus services** between Bullhead City, Laughlin and Las Vegas, for around $20 one way. Several companies, such as *Guaranteed Tours* (☎702/369-1000) also run **free** day-trips to Laughlin from Las Vegas, subsidized by the casinos.

At least seven casinos offer well over a thousand rooms each, with weekday rates that drop as low as $15 per room, plus half a dozen restaurants ranging from buffet joints whose all-you-can-eat specials start at well under $5 to dimly-lit Italian schmoozeries. The oldest, which traces its ancestry all the way back to an eight-room motel that opened in 1966, but has consistently kept pace with the rest, is *Don Laughlin's Riverside Resort Hotel*, 1650 S Casino Drive (☎702/298-2535 or 1-800/227-3849; Sun–Thurs ①, Fri & Sat ②). Neighbours include the counterfeit Mississippi steamboat that is the *Colorado Belle*, 2100 S Casino Drive (☎702/298-7111 or 1-800/237-1739; Sun–Thurs ①, Fri & Sat ③); the sleeker *Edgewater Hotel*, 2020 S Casino Drive (☎702/298-2453 or 1-800/677-4837; Sun–Thurs ①, Fri & Sat ②); and the *Ramada Express*, 2121 S Casino Drive (☎702/298-4200 or 1-800/2RAMADA; Sun–Thurs ①, Fri & Sat ③), with its oddly uninspired railroad trimmings.

For general information on Laughlin, call ☎702/298-3321 or 1-800/452-8445.

Oatman

If you're in no great hurry to get to California from Kingman, following Route 66 over the **Black Mountains** is much more enjoyable than skirting south then west on I-40. While **Needles**, California, is only fifty miles away on what John Steinbeck called the "Mother Road", however – as opposed to 64 on the interstate – it's a long slow drive, and you need to be confident that your vehicle can handle tricky mountain bends.

The eastern approaches to the mountains, at the edge of the Sacramento Valley, are guarded by a splendid solitary rock pinnacle that served as a beacon to early travellers. Following a laborious climb up to a gap between the peaks, the road twists down the far side and eventually enters **OATMAN**. This former gold-mining community, which was established in 1906, and went bust in 1942, is one of Arizona's most appealing **ghost towns**; a second career as an all-purpose movie backdrop and tourist stop-off has ensured that it's never truly been abandoned. The streets are still roamed by semi-wild burros descended from animals left by the miners.

Oatman is built on such a slope that the raised wooden boardwalk is a necessity to keep your footing as you browse its gift and craft stores, pausing perhaps to snack on rattlesnake at *Cactus Joe's* (☎520/768-3242). The *1902 Oatman Hotel* (☎520/768-4408; ②) – a restored adobe that was in fact rebuilt after a fire in 1920 – still rents out basic **rooms**, including the one where Clark Gable and Carole Lombard spent their wedding night in 1939.

Lake Havasu City

Forty miles southwest of Kingman on I-40, ten miles from the California border, a twenty-mile detour south on Hwy-95 brings you to the most incongruous sight of the Southwestern deserts. At **LAKE HAVASU CITY**, the old grey stones of **London Bridge** reach out across the stagnant waters of the dammed Colorado River.

Californian chainsaw manufacturer **Robert P McCulloch** moved his factory to this unlikely spot – occupied by a disused military airstrip – in 1964, so he could try out his new sideline in outboard motors on the waters of Lake Havasu. Three years later, he heard Johnny Carson mention that London Bridge was up for sale; in the words of the nursery rhyme, it really was falling down, unable to cope with all those new-fangled automobiles. McCulloch bought it for $2,460,000, and painstakingly shipped ten thousand numbered blocks of granite across the Atlantic. Lacking anything for the bridge to span, he dug a channel that turned a riverbank promontory into the island of **Pittsburg Point**. Despite the jibes that McCulloch thought he was buying picturesque Tower Bridge – the turreted one that opens in the middle – instead of merely the latest in a long line of London Bridges, dating only from 1831, his investment paid off handsomely. The bridge now ranks second among Arizona's tourist attractions, after the Grand Canyon, and

London Bridge is listed in the Guinness Book of Records as the largest antique ever sold.

Lake Havasu City has become a major vacation resort and retirement centre, with a population of thirty thousand.

That said, it's not often you see anything quite as **boring** in Arizona as London Bridge; unless you've never seen a bridge before, it's one to miss. Once again, Lake Havasu City is one of those places with an undeniable attraction for the parched urbanites of Phoenix, who flock to fish on the lake, or charge up and down in motorboats and on jet-skis, but minimal appeal for travellers from further afield.

Only when you cross the bridge onto the island, and then look back, do you appreciate how large Lake Havasu City has grown, sprawling up the gentle slope away from the river. Most of those broad hillside streets are lined with condo blocks and minor malls; the only place tourists bother to visit is the **English Village**, a mock-Tudor shopping mall, which also holds a handful of riverview restaurants, at the base of the bridge. Out on the island, if you head south from the bridge past the *Island Inn Resort*, you'll soon come to **London Bridge Beach**. The "beach" is more grit than sand, and few people swim from it. With its bizarre fringe of date palms, however, and its panorama of weird desert buttes and the Chemehuevi Mountains, it does at least linger in the memory.

Practicalities

The local **visitor center** is up from the river at 1930 Mesquite Ave (Mon–Fri 9am–5pm; ☎520/453-3444 or 1-800/242-8278); there's also an information kiosk at 420 English Village (daily 10am–4pm; ☎520/855-5655).

Several operators, such as *Blue Water Charters* (☎520/855-7171) and *Dixie Belle Cruises* (☎520/453-6776), offer short **river cruises** from the quayside of the English Village, charging around $12 for an hour-long trip focusing on the bridge, or $20 for a two-hour excursion to see rock formations upriver. Companies renting **jet-skis** (at around $40 per hour) and the like include *Arizona Jet Ski* (☎520/453-5558 or 1-800/393-5558), and *Fun Time Boat Rentals* (☎520/680-1003 or 1-800/680-1003).

Lake Havasu City has a good 25 or so **motels**, though relatively few of them are immediately obvious from Hwy-95. They range from the perfectly adequate *Windsor Inn Motel*, 451 London Bridge Rd (☎520/855-4135 or 1-800/245-4135; winter ①, summer ②), by way of the fancier, all-suite *Pioneer Hotel*, 271 S Lake Havasu Ave (☎520/855-5169 or 1-800/528-5169; ③), to the frankly ridiculous riverfront *London Bridge Resort*, 1477 Queen's Bay Rd (☎520/855-0888 or 1-800/624-7939; ④), where everything has a British-royalty theme.

*Lake Havasu City's **zip code** is AZ 86403.*

As for **nightlife**, most of Lake Havasu City seems to be tucked up in bed by 9pm. For a night out, the Island Fashion Mall, at the island end of London Bridge, is your best bet. The dining room at *Shugrue's* here (☎520/453-1400) looks out out over the bridge, and serves fresh fish (even sushi), salads and pasta, and a new **microbrewery** was due to open as this book went to press.

Chapter 6

The Grand Canyon

Although five million people come to see the **GRAND CANYON OF THE COLORADO** every year, it remains beyond the grasp of the human imagination. No photograph, no set of statistics, can prepare you for such vastness. At more than one mile deep, it's an inconceivable abyss; at from four to eighteen miles wide it's an endless expanse of bewildering shapes and colours, glaring desert brightness and impenetrable shadow, stark promontories and soaring never-to-be-climbed sandstone pinnacles. Somehow it's so impassive, so remote – you could never call it a disappointment, but at the same time many visitors are left feeling peculiarly flat. In a sense, none of the available activities can quite live up to that first stunning sight of the chasm. The **overlooks** along the rim all offer views that shift and change unceasingly from dawn to dusk; you can **hike** down into the depths on foot or by mule, hover above in a **helicopter** or raft through the **whitewater rapids** of the river itself; you can spend a night at **Phantom Ranch** on the canyon floor, or swim beneath the waterfalls of the idyllic **Havasupai Reservation**. And yet that distance always remains – the Grand Canyon stands apart.

Mapping and defining precisely what constitutes the "Grand Canyon" has always been controversial; **Grand Canyon National Park** covers a relatively small proportion of the greater Grand Canyon area. Only in the last 25 years has it included the full 277-mile length of the Colorado River from Lees Ferry in the east to Grand Wash Cliffs near Lake Mead in the west, and even now for most of that way it's restricted to the narrow strip of the inner gorge. Ranchers whose animals graze in the federal forests to either side, mining companies eager to exploit the mineral wealth hidden in the ancient rocks, engineers seeking to divert the river to feed the deserts of southern Arizona, and Native Americans who have lived in the Canyon since long before the first Europeans reached north America, have combined to minimize the extent of the park.

The vast majority of visitors arrive at the **South Rim** – it's much easier to get to, there are far more facilities (mainly at

Admission to the national park, valid for seven days on either rim, costs $10 per vehicle or $4 per pedestrian or cyclist. All the park-service passes detailed on p.21 are both valid and sold.

The Formation of the Grand Canyon

Although the Grand Canyon could be called the world's clearest geological textbook, scientists continue to argue over how to read the story written in the stone. Layer upon layer of different rocks, readily distinguished by colour, and each with its own fossil record, recede down into the canyon and back through time, until the river bed lays bare some of the oldest exposed rocks on earth. Almost all of the successive strata of sandstone and limestone were deposited during periods when the entire region was submerged beneath shallow primeval seas. The bottom layer, the two-billion-year-old **Vishnu Schist**, is so ancient that it contains no fossils; it dates back to the Precambrian era, when life had barely begun.

That same tale of sedimentation, of course, holds true for much of the planet. What until five million years ago was an unremarkable landscape was transformed into the Grand Canyon thanks to two major factors. First of all, it was a **desert**; the chronic shortage of rain prevented the development of vegetation to bind the brittle surface together. Secondly, there was the fast-flowing **Colorado River**, cascading down from the Rocky Mountains with a gradient over 25 times steeper than the Mississippi. In full flood, charged with mighty boulders, it can blast deep crevices into the earth.

However, a crucial mystery remains. The Colorado Plateau at this point is not flat; it's an enormous hill, known to the Paiute Indians as the **Kaibab**, or mountain with no peak. Why, or how, the Colorado River cuts straight through that hill, rather than flowing around it, has long taxed the imaginations of geologists. The hypothesis currently in favour, "**stream piracy**", suggests that until five million years ago, the river did indeed skirt the Kaibab. Having reached what's now the eastern edge of the national park it flowed southeast along the present channel of the Little Colorado River. Then the headwaters of a minor stream that flowed west down the Kaibab cut their way way back sufficiently to breach a gap in the mountain, through which the Colorado was able to surge.

Crudely speaking, while the river is responsible for the **depth** of the canyon – and continues to scour its way ever deeper – it did little to create its **width**. The fantastic pyramids and mesas that tower above the central gorge are the result of erosion by wind, and extreme cycles of heat and cold; in particular, vast slabs of stone are chiselled away when water that trickles into cracks in the earth later freezes and expands. Some layers are much harder than others; thus the solid Tapeats Sandstone of the **Tonto Platform**, a mile-wide shelf above the river that runs through most of the national park, was left behind when the weaker Bright Angel Shale above it eroded away. Because the general slope of the Kaibab runs from north to south, rain that falls north of the canyon flows down towards the gorge, while rainfall to the south flows away. As a result, the **North Rim** is deeply cut by tributary streams, and pushed back further from the Colorado, while the lower **South Rim** is much more regular.

The most striking features were named for their supposed resemblances to the great temples of India and China – **Brahma Temple**, **Shiva Temple**, **Vishnu Temple**, and so on – by Clarence Dutton, a student of comparative religion who wrote the first Geological Survey report on the canyon in 1881. The tradition was followed by such cartographers as François Matthes, who named **Krishna Shrine** and **Walhalla Plateau**.

Grand Canyon Village, inside the park), and it's open all year round. Another lodge and campground are located at the **North Rim**, which by virtue of its isolation can be a lot more atmospheric, but at one thousand feet higher this entire area is usually closed by snow from mid-October until May. Few people visit both rims on a single trip; to get from one to the other demands either a two-day hike down one side of the canyon and up the other, or a 215-mile drive. On both rims, the main activity consists of gazing over the gorge from lookouts placed at strategic intervals along the canyon-edge roads. Whereas in the 1920s the average visitor stayed for two or three weeks, these days it's more like two or three hours – of which forty minutes are spent actually looking at the canyon.

Finally, there's a definite risk that on the day you come the Grand Canyon will be invisible beneath a layer of **fog**; many people blame the 250 tons of sulphurous emissions pumped out every day by the Navajo Generating Station, seventy miles upriver at Page.

A history of the Grand Canyon

It may look forbidding, but the Grand Canyon is not a dead place. All sorts of desert **wildlife** survive here – sheep and rabbits, eagles and vultures, mountain lions, and, of course, spiders, scorpions and snakes. The earliest signs of any **human** presence are twig figurines of animals, found hidden in caves in the canyon walls. Dated to around 2000 BC, they were probably created to ensure successful hunting. Remains of later dwellings built by the **Anasazi** are scattered throughout the canyon – the most accessible to modern visitors is Tusayan Ruin (see p.306) – while the **Havasupai** (see p.314) are thought to have arrived around 1300 AD.

In 1540 – less than twenty years after Cortés conquered the Aztecs of Mexico – the first **Spaniards** reached the Southwest. At the Hopi mesas, a detachment of Francisco Vázquez de Coronado's company were told of a great river not far to the west, inhabited by people with very large bodies (presumably the Havasupai, who tend to be significantly bigger than the Hopi). A small party, led by García López de Cárdenas, was despatched to investigate. Their Hopi guides led them to a spot somewhere near Grandview Point, but chose not to reveal the trails down to the river. The Spaniards spent three days on the South Rim, only appreciating the scale of the Canyon after an abortive attempt to reach the river. They identified the Colorado as being the Tíson or "Firebrand" River, up which a simultaneous naval expedition was attempting to sail (it managed 225 miles, reaching what's now the site of the Hoover Dam).

When jurisdiction over the Grand Canyon passed from Mexico to the United States, in 1850, it had never been surveyed, and did not even have a fixed **name**. To the Havasupai, it was Wikatata ("Rough Rim"); Spanish maps showed it as Río Muy Grande ("Very Big River"); and trappers and prospectors knew it as the Big Cañon. The name Grand Canyon, first used on a map in 1868, was popularized by the one-armed Civil War veteran **John Wesley Powell**, whose expeditions along the fearsome and uncharted Colorado, in 1869 and 1871–72 – see p.401 – captured public imagination.

As the Grand Canyon was being recognized as the most extraordinary natural wonder in the US, American settlers arrived in the vicinity in ever greater numbers. Tensions have arisen ever since between this new permanent population, seeking ways to survive in such an unforgiving environment, and visitors hoping to find unspoiled wilderness. Broadly speaking, **logging** and **grazing** interests have retained control of the plateau forests, while in the canyon itself most attempts at **mining** were defeated by the difficulty of the terrain, and **tourism** soon proved a far more lucrative proposition.

Nineteenth-century proposals to run a **transcontinental railroad** *beside the river at the bottom of the Grand Canyon were defeated not by the engineering problems but by the lack of towns – and therefore customers – along the way.*

When the **railroad** first crossed northern Arizona in 1882, visitors were taken by stagecoach from the nearest station to the Grand Canyon, at **Peach Springs**, to stay at the *Diamond Creek Hotel* by the river. With the growth of the timber towns to the east, that soon declined; by the 1890s, **Flagstaff** was the main terminus, connected with the canyon by three weekly stages. The railroad reached the canyon itself, via a branch line from **Williams,** in September 1901. That triggered the growth of **Grand Canyon Village**, built under the auspices of the *Fred Harvey Company*, a subsidiary of the *Santa Fe Railroad*, and dependent on water carried in 120 miles by rail from Del Rio. The company's grand *El Tovar Hotel* – still the showpiece canyon-edge lodging – opened in January 1905, and its early marketing strategies influence the experience of Canyon visitors to this day. Following an internal memo to "get some Indians to the Canyon at once", the *Hopi House* souvenir store was built, modelled on the Pueblo village of Old Oraibi (see p.482), and staffed with Hopi craftspersons. Similarly, Navajo weavers were exhorted to produce rugs to suit tourist tastes, using previously unfavoured "earth" colours such as brown. Pseudo-Pueblo architecture became the dominant theme, with a single architect, Mary Jane Colter designing such structures as Hermit's Rest (1914), the Desert Watchtower (1932; see p.307) and *Bright Angel Lodge* (1935).

Late nineteenth-century proposals to create a **Grand Canyon National Park** aroused vigorous local opposition. In due course, however, naturalist **John Muir** – who had earlier championed Yosemite Valley in California, and declared the Grand Canyon to be "unearthly . . . as if you had found it after death, on some other star" – found a powerful ally in President **Theodore Roosevelt**. Only entitled to protect sites of historical, rather than geological, interest, Roosevelt used the pretext of preserving Anasazi ruins to proclaim Grand Canyon National Monument in 1908. Having failed to persuade the Supreme Court to overrule the president, Arizonan politicians finally came round to the idea after Arizona achieved statehood in 1912. Even then, by the time the boundaries of the Grand Canyon National Park were fixed in 1919, they had trimmed away large tracts of grazing land. The new park covered around 1000 square miles, and included just 56 miles of the actual canyon.

Since 1890, **Ralph Cameron** had been accumulating bogus mining claims along the South Rim, which enabled him to charge a toll of $1 to use the Bright Angel Trail. In 1905, he built his own hotel alongside the railroad terminal, thereby forcing *Fred Harvey* to relocate the station out of sight of the upstart rival. Cameron continued to be a thorn in the side of the new national park. Elected to the US Senate in 1920, he spent a few years hacking at its budget before his mining claims were eventually invalidated. His presence had by then spurred the development of the **Kaibab Trail**, stretching from rim to rim of the canyon by way of the Kaibab suspension footbridge (see p.311). Plans to pave that route never materialized, but a small enlargement of the park in 1927 permitted the construction of a road east to Desert View, which with the completion in 1928 of the Navajo Bridge across Marble Canyon reduced the previous 600-mile drive between the rims to a more feasible 215 miles.

In the early years of the national park, the role of the park system in protecting the environment had yet to be defined, and techniques of **wildlife** management were in their infancy. Bitter rivalry over grazing lands pitted the park service against the forest service, while the decision to eliminate mountain lions on the North Rim during the 1920s resulted in ecological disaster. Free from predators, the deer population boomed from 4000 to 100,000, stripped the Kaibab Plateau bare, then starved to death en masse.

The first **automobile** arrived at the Canyon in 1902, despite running out of gas twenty miles short. By 1926, more visitors were coming by car than by train, and Flagstaff was once again the major point of access. Advance reservations for both mule rides and lodging have been necessary since 1938; annual visitor numbers first exceeded a million in 1956, and now run at over five million, with over 800,000 in each of June, July and August.

Green activists horrified by the damming of Glen Canyon (see p.390) forced the abandonment of proposals to dam the Colorado within the park itself during the 1960s, and commercial logging and mining were finally banned when its boundaries were redrawn and enlarged in 1975. With the exception of the Indian reservations, the Grand Canyon is now run exclusively for the benefit of visitors, though maximizing their enjoyment while minimizing their environmental impact is an all but impossible task. Current park proposals include the introduction of a daily quota system for the North Rim, under which only visitors with advance reservations would be admitted, and the banning of private cars from the South Rim, with the expansion of rail services from Williams. Although the park service has in the past objected to the presence of the sprawling community of **Tusayan**, six miles from the South Rim, it now envisages its transformation into **Canyon Forest Village**, holding two new railroad stations, as well as 5000 hotel rooms, 2600 homes for park employees, and a large shopping mall.

The South Rim

The **Coconino Plateau**, which fills the sixty-mile gap between the I-17 interstate and the Grand Canyon, is covered by the largest **ponderosa pine forest** in the world. Crossing this undramatic landscape, you get no sense of the impending abyss until you reach the very edge of the **South Rim**, near Mather Point. That comes roughly five miles beyond the simple wooden kiosk that marks the park entrance station, which is itself shortly beyond the small but heavily commercialized community of **Tusayan**.

One mile west of Mather Point, **Grand Canyon Village** holds the main park facilities. This is the principal destination for day-trippers, and also has the bulk of the overnight accommodation. In addition to the canyon panoramas visible from the village itself, the eight-mile **West Rim Drive** and 23-mile **East Rim Drive** offer countless differing vantage points. **Hiking trails** set off down into the canyon from trailheads scattered along the way.

Getting to the South Rim

The vast majority of visitors make their way to the South Rim by way of either **Williams** (58 miles south; see p.284) or **Flagstaff** (81 miles southeast; see p.258), both on I-17. Flagstaff is served by *Amtrak* trains, while a separate **rail** service connects Williams with the canyon itself. If you're travelling by **road**, AZ-64 from Williams joins US-180 from Flagstaff thirty miles south of the canyon itself. The route from Flagstaff, by way of the San Francisco Peaks (see p.264), is the more scenic of the two, and it's also the one followed by most commercial **buses**.

It's also possible to drive to Grand Canyon Village from the east, by turning onto AZ-64 from US-89 at Cameron (see p.320), and there are direct **flights** to Tusayan from Las Vegas and other points in the Southwest.

By train
Amtrak services from Chicago and points east arrive at Flagstaff at 9.14pm daily, and from Los Angeles at 6.38am daily. **Bus** connections are detailed opposite.

The restored **steam trains** of the *Grand Canyon Railway* (☎520/773-1976 or 1-800/THE-TRAIN) run for 64 miles from **Williams** to the picturesque station at Grand Canyon Village; bear in mind that most of the route is through the forest, so it has few scenic delights to offer. In **February**, the train runs on Friday, Saturday and Sunday; in **March** it runs from Wednesday to Sunday; from **late March until October** it's daily; in **November** it reverts to Friday, Saturday and Sunday; and in **December** it runs on Saturday and Sunday only, except for the week from December 26 until January 1, when it's daily again. Services leave Williams at 9.30am, arriving at Grand Canyon Village at 11.45am, and Grand Canyon Village at 3.15pm to arrive back in Williams at 5.30pm. The round trip costs **$55** for adults, $29.50 for ages thirteen to nineteen, and $15.73 for under-thirteens; a one-way ride is $45.23, $24.67, or $12.45 respectively. Note that *Amtrak* passes are not accepted.

By bus

Nava-Hopi **buses** (☎520/774-5003 or 1-800/892-8687) run twice daily between **Flagstaff** (departing from both the *Amtrak* station and the nearby *Nava-Hopi* terminal at 114 W Route 66) and the *Bright Angel Lodge* in Grand Canyon Village. The first leaves Flagstaff at 8am, calls at **Williams** at 8.50 am, and arrives at the canyon at 10.10am; the second runs straight from Flagstaff to the canyon, departing at 2.45pm and arriving 4.40pm. Return trips leave *Bright Angel Lodge* at 10.30am – a direct service to Flagstaff, arriving at 12.30pm – and 5pm, reaching Williams at 6.15pm and Flagstaff at 7pm. The fare to and from Flagstaff is $12.50 one way, $25 round-trip; for Williams it's $9 and $18; and under-sixteens travel half price.

Nava-Hopi also operate **one-day tours** to the Canyon from Flagstaff, costing $38 (under-16s $19) for a bus-only tour, and $64 (under-16s $32) for a combined bus-train tour.

By air

The small **airport** at Tusayan – just outside the park boundary, and used primarily by "flight-seeing" tour companies (see p.299) – also welcomes scheduled services, especially from **Las Vegas**. Unlike the tours, these flights do not pass directly above the park, but they still give good views, and can cost as little as $60 one-way.

The major Vegas operator is *Scenic Airlines* (☎702/739-1900 or 1-800/634-6801), which also offers day trips from Las Vegas that include a half-hour *Papillon Helicopters* flight for $269 per person (under-12s $230). Others include *Air Nevada* (☎702/736-8900 or 1-800/634-6377), *Las Vegas Airlines* (☎702/647-3056 or 1-800/634-6851), *Tri-Star Airline* (☎702/638-3010 or 1-800/218-8777) and *Adventure Airlines* (☎702/736-7511).

Budget and *Dollar* rent **cars** at the airport, while between late May and late September hourly **shuttle buses** run the seven miles to Grand Canyon Village.

The South Rim

A full account of the town of **Williams** *appears on p.284.*

For more on **Flagstaff**, *including details of* **car rental** *outlets, see p.258.*

For taxi service in and around Grand Canyon Village, call ☎*520/638-2822.*

Grand Canyon Tours

Fred Harvey

For details of, and reservations for the tours below, run by the *Fred Harvey Company*, contact the "transportation desks" in the lodges, or call ☎520/638-2401 or 297-2757.

Park Bus Tours

Desert View 3hr 45min rim tour east of the village (2 daily; $17, under-16 $8.50).

Hermit's Rest 2hr rim tour west of the village (2 daily; $11, under-16 $5.50).

Sunset Tour 1hr 30min tour to watch the sunset near Yavapai Point (late May to Sept only, 1 daily; $7.50, under-16 $4).

Horse Riding

Apache Stables (☎520/638-2891), based at *Moqui Lodge*, charges $22 for a 1hr trail ride through the Kaibab Forest, and $36 for 2hr, and in the evening offers campfire rides on horseback for $27, or by wagon for $7.50. To see the canyon itself, you have to take the 4hr East Rim ride, costing $57.50.

Smooth Water Rafting

Good-value full-day excursion, including an 8hr round trip to Marble Canyon by bus, plus 4hr floating through the spectacular gorge on an inflatable raft, with a picnic lunch. Probably your only chance of a trip along the river at short notice (April–Oct daily 7am from *Maswik Lodge*; $80, under-12 $50).

Long-distance Bus Tours

Ancient Ones 10–11hr bus tour to Flagstaff and nearby national monuments (1 daily; $80, under-12 $50).

Monument Valley All-day, 360-mile excursion, available year-round; 11–13hr in off-road vehicle ($80, under-12 $50), or 6hr 30min with flight and ground tour ($245 per person).

Railroad Express Round-trip excursion to Williams, by bus one way and on the Grand Canyon Railway the other (2 daily; $40, under-17 $20).

Mule Rides

Mule rides down the Bright Angel Trail tend to be reserved up to a year in advance. A one-day round trip to Plateau Point, including lunch, costs $100; the round trip to Phantom Ranch, beside the river, takes a full day in each direction. A one-night trip, including cabin accommodation and all meals, costs $252 for one person, $448 for two persons; two-night trips, available mid-Nov to March only, cost $353 for one, $594 for two. For more on Phantom Ranch, see p.311.

Grand Canyon Field Institute

Between April and November each year, the *Grand Canyon Field Institute* (PO Box 399, Grand Canyon AZ 86023; ☎520/638-2485, fax 638-2484), co-sponsored by the Grand Canyon Association and the National Park Service, offers an extensive programme of guided tours and hikes in and around the canyon. Different tours, some restricted to women only, specialize in geology, history, natural history, photography, wilderness techniques, and other topics. Some involve camping and backpacking, others include lodge accommodation; all are graded according to the difficulty of any hiking involved. The fees are remarkably low, with four-day backpacking tours costing around $175, and six-day van tours for under $500.

Flight-seeing Tours

Controversy has surrounded air tours of the Grand Canyon in recent years. An alarming safety record has led to a ban on all flying below rim level, while restrictions on the total number of overflights are being introduced to limit the barrage of noise within the park. Nonetheless, for many visitors such flights remain the highlight of their trip. **Prices** range from $65 ($30 child) for 30min in an airplane, or $95 ($70 child) for 30min in a helicopter, up to as long as you like for as much as you've got; all are subject to an additional $6 Federal Airspace Fee. All the operators below are based in **Tusayan**, though some helicopter companies take off from their own landing fields rather than using the airport proper.

Air Grand Canyon; ☎520/638-2686 or 1-800/247-4726.

AirStar Airlines; ☎520/638-2139 or 1-800/962-3869.

AirStar Helicopters; ☎520/638-2622.

Grand Canyon Airlines; ☎520/638-2307 or 1-800/528-2413.

Kenai Helicopters; ☎520/638-2412 or 1-800/541-4537.

Papillon Grand Canyon Helicopters; ☎520/638-2419.

Windrock Aviation; ☎520/638-9591 or 1-800/247-6259.

Papillon *also run excursions to the Havasupai reservation; see p.316.*

Whitewater Rafting

As the park service only allows around twenty thousand people to float through the canyon of the Colorado River each year, and there's a waiting list of almost ten years for permission to do so in your own boat, places on **commercial whitewater rafting trips** tend to be reserved as much as a year in advance. These vary in length from three days to three weeks, with the main choice being whether to cut the 300-mile voyage from Lees Ferry to Diamond Creek in half by leaving or joining the expedition at Phantom Ranch. An estimated 161 sets of rapids interrupt the full route.

Lobbyists for the industry have so far defeated park plans to ban motorized rafts, so you can also choose between a quieter, slower oar-powered trip or a motorized expedition; both tend to cost around **$200 per person, per day**. In addition to the operators listed below, virtually all of whom offer trips of both kinds and of varying lengths, the tribal-run *Hualapai River Runners* (☎520/769-2219 or 1-800/622-4409) arrange one- or two-day Colorado float trips on the Hualapai Reservation, starting at Diamond Creek.

Aramark-Wilderness River Adventures; ☎520/645-3296 or 1-800/992-8022.

Arizona River Runners; ☎602/867-4866 or 1-800/477-7238.

Canyon Explorations; ☎520/774-4559 or 1-800/654-0723.

Canyoneers; ☎520/526-0924 or 1-800/525-0924.

Diamond River Adventures; ☎520/645-8866 or 1-800/343-3121.

Grand Canyon Expeditions; ☎801/644-2691 or 1-800/544-2691.

Moki Mak River Expeditions; ☎801/268-6667 or 1-800/284-7280.

Outdoors Unlimited; ☎520/526-4546 or 1-800/637-7238.

Tour West; ☎801/225-5705 or 1-800/453-9107.

Western River Expeditions; ☎801/942-6669 or 1-800/453-7450.

Grand Canyon Village

Since the arrival of the railroad in 1901, **GRAND CANYON VIL-
LAGE**, ranged along the South Rim six miles in from the park
entrance station, has been the main centre for tourism at the canyon.
The self-consciously rugged log-and-boulder buildings from that era,
such as the *El Tovar* hotel and the Kolb photographic studio, have
since been joined by a plethora of less attractive but stylistically similar structures, and the whole place is carefully laid out to avoid
seeming too crowded.

Most visitors get their first proper look at the canyon from the
paved, railed **terrace** that follows the rim for the length of the village. The Colorado itself is too deep in the Inner Gorge to be visible
from here, but the Bright Angel Trail can clearly be seen as it heads
out to Plateau Point (see p.309), and at night you can usually pick
out the few lights over on the North Rim.

Tucked away in the woods across the road, well back from the
canyon, lie several more lodges, stores, restaurants, and the campground, together with the well-hidden residential area used by park
employees. It's normally possible to find a **parking space** somewhere in the village, but driving around can be incredibly slow.

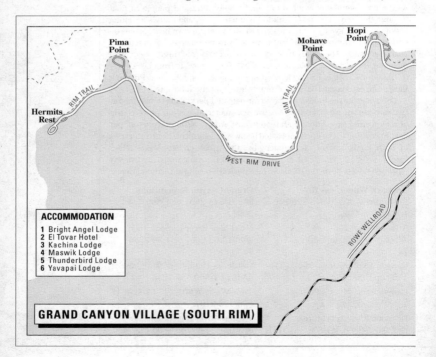

ACCOMMODATION
1 Bright Angel Lodge
2 El Tovar Hotel
3 Kachina Lodge
4 Maswik Lodge
5 Thunderbird Lodge
6 Yavapai Lodge

GRAND CANYON VILLAGE (SOUTH RIM)

Between late May and late September, free **shuttle buses** operate every fifteen minutes within the village and along West Rim Drive.

Information

The main park headquarters and **visitor center** (daily 8am–6pm; ☎ 520/638-7888) is half a mile from the rim, a mile east of the *El Tovar* and *Bright Angel* hotels. Ultra-patient rangers are happy to advise on how to make the most of your visit, handing out free brochures plus details of an extensive programme of **talks** and ranger-led **tours**. Informative displays explain canyon geology and wildlife, and the courtyard at the back houses a small museum of boats used by assorted twentieth-century river runners. Further information desks, with similar hours, operate at Kolb Studio, Yavapai Observation Station (see p.306), Tusayan Museum (see p.306), and Desert View (see p.307).

Most of these places, as well as several of the lodges and souvenir stores, sell a wide range of **books** about the canyon, including invaluable guides to the various hiking trails. None of the free **maps** on offer is adequate for backcountry hiking, so invest in the detailed hiking maps produced by *Earthwalk Press* ($3.95) or *Trails Illustrated* ($8.95). Canyon-related books and maps can be ordered

For details of the Backcountry Office, which issues permits for backpacking and camping in the canyon, see p.308.

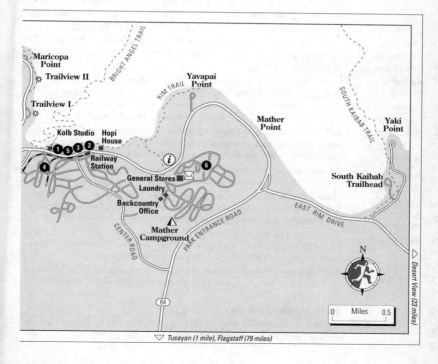

The South Rim

For details of staying at **Phantom Ranch**, *at the bottom of the canyon, see p.312.*

There is no longer a **youth hostel** *in or near the park.*

As explained on p.15, **accommodation prices**, *excluding taxes, are indicated throughout this book by the following symbols:*

① *up to $30*
② *$30–45*
③ *$45–60*
④ *$60–80*
⑤ *$80–100*
⑥ *$100–130*
⑦ *$130–175*
⑧ *$175–250*
⑨ *$250+*

All in-park **accommodation reservations**, including those for Phantom Ranch and for RV camping, are handled by *Amfac Parks & Resorts*, 14001 East Iliff, #600, Aurora CO 80014 (same-day ☎520/638-2631; advance ☎303/297-2757, fax 303/297-3175). The best rooms are often booked as much as a year in advance, and your chances of turning up without a reservation and finding a place in summer are minimal.

from the *Grand Canyon Association*, PO Box 399, Grand Canyon AZ 86023 (☎1-800/858-2808, fax 520/638-2484).

For free copies of the information-packed **newspapers**, *The Guide* and the *Trip Planner*, write to Grand Canyon National Park, PO Box 129, Grand Canyon AZ 86023; the park also has a homepage on the **Internet**, at www.thecanyon.com/nps/index.html.

Accommodation

Unless you're prepared to spend well over $150 for a deluxe room at the *El Tovar*, or $100 for a rim-side cabin at the *Bright Angel*, the **accommodation** available in Grand Canyon Village is not all that special. Neither does the village itself make a very stimulating place to spend the night. However, the *Fred Harvey*-run "lodges" are not bad value, and since prices in **Tusayan** (see p.304) are much the same, there's no cheaper accommodation within sixty miles. If you are stuck, other possibilities include **Cameron** (p.320), **Flagstaff** (p.258), and **Williams** (p.284).

As for seeing the canyon, it makes little difference where in the village you stay. Even in the "rim-edge" places, few rooms offer much of a view, and in any case it's always dark by 8pm.

Bright Angel Lodge. Individual "rustic" but comfortable log cabins, clustered around an imposing 1935 lodge that also holds some more basic rooms. Its fireplace displays all the principal types of rock found in the Grand Canyon, in the correct chronological sequence. Rooms ③; rim-side cabins ⑤.

El Tovar Hotel. Canyon-edge hotel, named for an early Spanish explorer, that still displays the same combination of rough-hewn charm and elegant sophistication that made it the very peak of fashion when it opened in 1905. ⑥.

Kachina Lodge. Anonymous but perfectly adequate rooms in newer block, near the rim and run in conjunction with *El Tovar Hotel*. ⑤; rim-side ⑥.

Maswik Lodge. Larger complex, a few minutes' walk from the rim at the west end of the village. A wide range of rooms, plus some basic summer-only cabins, some of which can sleep up to four guests. Cabins ③, rooms ④.

Thunderbird Lodge. Long, low, box-like lodge that shares the lobby of, and is run with, *Bright Angel Lodge*. Well-equipped if characterless rooms, separated by twenty yards of grass from the canyon edge. ⑤; rim-side ⑥.

Yavapai Lodge. 350 reasonable rooms in two motel-type buildings, well back from the rim in the woods near the visitor center. Open mid-March to Oct. ⑤.

Eating and drinking

There's a reasonably wide choice of places to **eat** in Grand Canyon Village, and the prices in the budget cafeterias are not bad considering the canyon's remoteness and lack of water. However, summer crowding can lead to endless queueing, and it's worth bringing at least some food with you. A few stores – notably *Babbitt's*, opposite the visitor center, which has a deli counter – sell basic supplies.

Both the *Bright Angel* and the *El Tovar* have atmospheric traditional **bars** open until 12.30am nightly, while *Maswik Lodge* has a "sports lounge" with big-screen TV.

Arizona Steakhouse, *Bright Angel Lodge*. Informal, good-quality restaurant, only a few yards from the rim but without views to speak of, and specializing in conventional meat and seafood dishes. No reservations accepted, so you may have to wait 2 hours or more. Dinner only, daily 5–10pm.

Bright Angel Coffee House, *Bright Angel Lodge*. All meals of the day, and pretty much anything you might want, from snacks and salads to steak. No reservations, daily 6.30am–10pm.

Canyon Cafe, *Yavapai Lodge*. Large family cafeteria, with attractive glassed-in seating area, which sells burgers for around $3 and chicken dinners for more like $5. Mid-March to mid-Nov daily 6am–10pm.

El Tovar, *El Tovar Hotel*; ☎520/638-2631 ext 6432. Very grand, enormously expensive dining room, looking right out over the canyon; reservations are accepted for dinner only, and tend to be grabbed days in advance. The sumptuous menu includes such unlikely desert dishes as a mixed plate of lobster, mussels and scallops. Breakfast is the most affordable option; lunch and dinner can easily cost upwards of $40 per person. Daily 6.30am–10pm.

Maswik Cafeteria, *Maswik Lodge*. Self-service fast food; breakfast for under $5, Italian and Mexican specialities later on at around $7. Daily 6am–10pm.

Other in-park facilities

Bank Opposite visitor center. Mon–Thurs 10am–3pm, Fri 10am–3pm & 4–6pm.

Camping Equipment Can be bought or rented at *Babbitt's General Store*, opposite visitor center.

Disabled Travellers Pick up the *Accessibility Guide* at the visitor center, or call ☎520/638-2631 for advice and details of wheelchair tours.

Gas Opposite visitor center. Summer daily 6am–9.30pm, winter daily 7am–8pm. Also available at Desert View, April to mid-May daily 8am–5pm, mid-May to Aug daily 7am–7pm, and in Tusayan.

Laundromat Near backcountry office and *Mather Campground*. Daily 7am–9pm, last wash 7.45pm.

Medical Help Call ☎911 for emergencies; ☎520/638-2551 for the village clinic; ☎520/638-2460 for the pharmacy; and ☎520/638-2395 for dentist.

Post Office Opposite visitor center. Mon–Fri 9am–4.30pm, Sat 11am–1pm.

Tusayan

There's no earthly reason to stay in **TUSAYAN**, which sprawls along the highway just over a mile south of the park entrance, rather than Grand Canyon Village, but it's the nearest alternative if all the park accommodations are full. It's also the site of an **IMAX Theater** specialising in stomach-lurching views of the canyon (March–Oct daily 8.30am–8.30pm; Nov–Feb daily 10.30am–6.30pm; $7.50).

Reservations for the large *Moqui Lodge* (mid-Feb to Nov; ④), set back in the woods just outside the park entrance, are handled by *Amfac Parks & Resorts* (see p.302). Otherwise, most of Tusayan's hotels are cast from the same anonymous but reasonably pleasant mould. *Seven Mile Lodge* (☎520/638-2291; ④), is the least attractive but least expensive, while alternatives include the pastel-painted *Quality Inn* (☎520/638-2673 or 1-800/221-2222; ⑥), the *Grand Canyon Squire Inn* (☎520/638-2681 or 1-800/622-6966; ⑥), the *Red Feather Lodge* (☎520/638-2414 or 1-800/538-2345; ⑥), and the *Holiday Inn Express* (☎520/638-3000; ⑥). Each has its own **restaurant**, while Tusayan also holds a handful of fast-food places and the good, if pricey, *We Cook Pizza* (☎520/638-2278).

Camping

*For details of
**backcountry
camping** in
the park, see
p.308.*

Sites at the year-round **Mather Campground**, south of the main road through Grand Canyon Village a couple of hundred yards from the visitor center, can be reserved up to five months in advance through *DESTINET* (☎1-800/365-2267), and cost $12 per night. Rangers at park service areas and visitor centers have details of daily availability both here and at the summer-only, first-come first-served **Desert View Campground**, near the lookout 26 miles east (see p.307). Reservations for **RV hookups** at the **Trailer Village** alongside *Mather Campground* are handled by *Amfac Parks & Resorts* (see box on p.302), and cost $18 per night for two people.

In addition, the forest service runs the minimally equipped, first-come first-served **Ten-X Campground** (May–Sept; $10 per night) in the Kaibab National Forest, outside the park entrance near Tusayan, and there's a commercial campground, **Camper Village** (☎520/638-2887; some RV hookups; $15–22), in Tusayan itself. Twenty miles further south, in **VALLE** at the junction of Hwys 64 and 180, **Flintstone's Bedrock City** (mid-March to Oct; ☎520/635-2600; some RV hookups; $12–16) has its own prehistoric theme park.

Exploring the South Rim

*On average
three or four
people fall into
the Grand
Canyon each
year; the
record is ten,
of which seven
were accidents
and three
suicides.*

Grand Canyon Village is set at the inward end of a curved recess in the South Rim, with long rocky promontories reaching out to either side. Thus, although the views from the village are stupendous, you can see a greater span of the canyon from the various **overlooks** perched on and beyond the headlands. Many also offer glimpses of the Colorado River, which cannot be seen from the village.

The **West** and **East Rim Drives** extend along the South Rim for several miles in either direction from Grand Canyon Village, paralleled for a couple of miles to either side of the village by paved and railed footpaths on the very lip of the canyon. No one overlook can be said to be the "best", but there are far too many to stop at them all. Obvious short walks include excursions to see the **sunrise** – head east, perhaps to Mather Point – and the **sunset** – particularly magical at Hopi Point, to the west.

The West Rim Drive

Thanks to the crowds, the **West Rim Drive** is closed to private vehicles between late May and late September. Instead, free **shuttle buses** call every fifteen minutes at each of the major overlooks. Walking is an easy, pleasant alternative; the four-mile round-trip from the village to Hopi Point, for example, takes under two hours.

The first two viewpoints along the way, known as **Trailview I** and **II**, let prospective Bright Angel Trail hikers (see p.309) see exactly what they're in for, with its red-dirt switchbacks clearly etched against the canyon walls below. After just over a mile, as you round the corner to pass out of sight of Grand Canyon Village, the railed, rocky overlook at **Maricopa Point** commands an almost 360° view, though only the tiniest sliver of the churning Colorado is visible. This is a prime spot for identifying the majestic buttes on the far side of the river, such as the Brahma and Zoroaster "temples", each with its capping layer of hard red sandstone. It's also easy to see from here why Bright Angel Canyon, cutting deeply in from the north, provides the best hiking route to the river from the North Rim (see p.327).

Beyond Maricopa, road and trail alike detour inland around a high fence, festooned with solemn radiation warnings. In the heart of this enclosure stands the hulking headframe of the **Orphan Mine**, which started out as a copper mine in 1893 but became America's largest uranium producer in the 1950s. Production stopped in 1969, and the mine was acquired by the park in 1988. There are however still significant uranium deposits in the vicinity, located by no coincidence at all in areas that remain outside the protection of the park. At the far end, **Powell Point** marks the spot where the park was officially dedicated on April 30, 1920, and holds a memorial to the crews of John Wesley Powell's two Colorado expeditions.

For more about John Wesley Powell, see p.401.

Beneath the curved terrace at **Hopi Point**, two miles out from the village, several distinct stretches of the Colorado are exposed to view. The most dramatic lies immediately below Plateau Point (see p.309), the last few yards of the trail to which are also visible. It's hard to believe that the river is 350 feet wide down there, lying at the foot of gnarled and impossibly ancient walls of black schist, streaked through with vertical pink faults.

By the time you reach **Mohave Point**, another three quarters of a mile along, huge views have opened up to the west. The river threads its tortuous way towards the ocean between interleaved spurs of red rock, and a maze of lesser canyons twists among the mighty buttes.

Pima Point is four miles further on, beyond another sheer-walled recess known as The Abyss. The river is by now less than two miles from the South Rim – look almost straight down to admire the three-quarter-mile Granite Rapids – but from the far bank it's another twelve labyrinthine miles to the North Rim.

The West Rim Drive ends one mile down the road, at **Hermit's Rest**, where you'll find a small, seasonal snackbar and the trailhead for the rudimentary Hermit Trail (see p.313).

The East Rim Drive

A 1.5-mile walk along the rim trail from *Bright Angel Lodge*, or a mile from the visitor center via the spur trail that leads to the canyon rim, the promontory **east** of the village ends at **Yavapai Point**. From this vantage point, you can see right down into the gorge, to a tiny stretch of the Colorado that happens to include both the suspension footbridge across the river and Phantom Ranch (see p.311). Nearby, if you can tear your eyes away from its panoramic bay windows, the **Yavapai Geologic Museum** (summer daily 9am–7pm; free) has illuminating displays on how the canyon may have been formed. Similar views can be enjoyed from **Mather Point**, half a mile further along what by now is a rough-and-ready rim-edge trail. The platform here is angled more towards the east, so the sunrise can be spectacular.

Mather Point is as far as most people would bother to walk from the village, but plenty of equally dramatic viewpoints are located along the 23-mile **East Rim Drive**, which branches off the park entrance road just beyond. The first of these, **Yaki Point**, commands prospects of several inner canyon trails, including the South Kaibab Trail, which can be spotted switchbacking down an exposed scree slope of red rock between two buttes, far below – a long way from its trailhead near the parking lot (see p.312). Across the canyon, Vishnu Temple is silhouetted against the skyline, while the Watchtower at Desert View (see opposite) stands stark on its promontory almost fifteen miles east.

En route to **Grandview Point**, nine miles out from the village, East Rim Drive first veers away from the canyon edge, then passes several unnamed roadside lookouts. Grandview Point is thought to have been where Europeans first saw the Grand Canyon, in 1540 (see p.293), and for the ten years after 1895, the *Grandview Hotel*, a mile or so from the existing overlook, was a major tourist destination. Long views both east and west make this in many ways a better site than Grand Canyon Village, but the railroad swiftly drove the hotel out of business, and little trace of it now remains.

Tusayan Ruin, ten miles further east, in the forest just south of the highway (and not to be confused with modern Tusayan), is an open-air archeological site that centres on the remains of a genuine **Anasazi pueblo**. One of two thousand such sites so far identified in the Grand Canyon area, it may not be comparable in scale to relics found elsewhere in the Southwest, but its very existence enabled President Teddy Roosevelt to accord National Monument status to the entire Grand Canyon (see p.294). Only low stone walls survive of the original complex of buildings, thought to have been occupied for perhaps 25 years by a group of up to thirty people, around 1185 AD. A small museum, staffed by park rangers, holds displays on the contemporary Navajo and Hopi peoples, as well as well as 4000-year-old twig figurines and Anasazi pottery found nearby.

For more about the Anasazi, see p.468.

Desert View, 23 miles out from the village and three miles east of Tusayan Ruin, is at 7500 feet the highest point on the South Rim. That's still lower than the North Rim, but at least as you look across you get a real sense of the tree-covered plateau on the far side. Down in the canyon, the Colorado River can be seen four miles away, flowing in from the north and just about to make its sudden westward turn, at the point where the "stream piracy" described on p.292 may have taken place. Just north of the last visible curve lies the confluence of the Colorado and Little Colorado rivers. Not far up the Little Colorado River from there lies the legendary *sipapu*, the hole through which the Hopi believe that human beings first entered this, the Third World (see p.482). You won't find this natural dome, topped by a permanent spring, marked on any map; only the Hopi are allowed access, or even to know where it is.

*Groups of **tarantulas** are often seen in the evenings at Desert View, scuttling back into the warmth of the canyon for the night.*

The flat summit of **Cedar Mountain**, perched above the rim just east of Desert View, marks the original, pre-erosion ground level of this entire vast landscape. Beyond it, the north wall of the Little Colorado Canyon, running east, is the one stark break in the endless flatlands of the Navajo Nation, which stretch right to the horizon. Ninety miles northeast, beyond the Vermillion and Echo Cliffs, lies the grey bulk of Navajo Mountain.

The odd-looking cylindrical construction on the very lip of the canyon is **Desert View Watchtower**, built for *Fred Harvey* by Mary Jane Colter in 1932. Beneath the Anasazi-style masonry exterior it's held together by a solid framework of steel and cement, but it's still attractive, and well worth visiting. Pay 25¢ at the turnstile in the gift store at its base (daily 8am–7pm) to climb through three successive circular chambers, decorated with authentic murals by the Hopi artist Fred Kabotie, as well as reproduction petroglyphs.

*The road **east of Desert View**, to Cameron and beyond, is described on p.320 onwards.*

South Rim hikes; into the canyon

Hiking any of the trails that descend into the Grand Canyon offers something more than just another view of the same thing. Instead you pass through a sequence of utterly different landscapes, each with its own distinct climate, wildlife and topography. However, while the canyon can offer a wonderful wilderness experience, it's essential to remember that it can be a hostile and very unforgiving environment, gruelling even for expert hikers.

More detailed advice on desert hiking can be found in the Basics, on p.23.

The South Rim

The best seasons to hike in the Grand Canyon are spring and fall.

In summer, Trans Canyon Shuttle *(☎520/638-2820) operate shuttle buses between the South and North rims.*

Park rangers have one simple message for all would-be hikers: **don't try to hike to the river and back in one day**. It might not look far on the map, but it's harder than running a marathon. Up to fifteen hikers each year die in the attempt, and several hundred more receive emergency medical treatment. If you do want to reach the Colorado, it's best to reserve campgrounds for two nights, so you have a day to recover before the trek out.

The South Rim is 7000 feet above sea level, an altitude which most people is fatiguing in itself. Furthermore, all hikes start with a long, steep descent – which can come as a shock to the knees – and unless you camp overnight you'll have to climb all the way back up again when you're hotter and wearier. As a rule of thumb, keep track of how much time you spend hiking down, and allow twice that much to get back up again. Average summer temperatures inside the canyon exceed 100°F; to hike for eight hours in that sort of heat, you have to drink an incredible thirty pints of water. Always carry at least a quart per person, and much more if there are no water sources along your chosen trail. You must have food as well, as drinking large quantities without also eating can cause water intoxication.

Several trails lead into the canyon from the South Rim, but most either start from inaccessible places or are in poor condition. Traffic is heaviest on the **Bright Angel** and **South Kaibab** trails, the two "**Corridor Trails**" that link up in the gorge to lead to Phantom Ranch, and can be combined with the North Kaibab Trail to form a continuous route between the South and North rims. These trails also offer the best **day-hikes** in the canyon; down the Bright Angel Trail as far **Indian Garden**, or at most out to **Plateau Point**, and down the South Kaibab Trail to **Cedar Ridge**.

Backcountry camping

To camp overnight below the canyon rim, or at undeveloped campsites on the rim, you must have a **free permit** issued by the **Backcountry Office** near *Mather Campground* in Grand Canyon Village (daily 8am–noon; information ☎520/638-7875 Mon–Fri 1–5pm). If you put your name down as soon as you arrive at the canyon there's a chance of getting a cancellation, but it's best to reserve as far in advance as possible. Guests with reservations at Phantom Ranch do not need permits; anyone else found in the canyon without a permit is subject to a heavy fine.

Mailed applications (Backcountry Office, PO Box 129, Grand Canyon AZ 86023) are accepted for dates until the end of the fourth month following the date of the postmark; thus in January you can apply for nothing later than the end of May. Fax or phone applications are not accepted, and all applications have to specify the number in your party, its leader, and an exact itinerary with named campgrounds; alternative dates and routes can be suggested. The office has full lists of campgrounds; much the most popular are the three along the rim-to-rim "Corridor Trails" – *Indian Garden* on the Bright Angel Trail, *Bright Angel Campground* near the river, and *Cottonwood Campground* on the North Kaibab Trail.

The Bright Angel Trail

The **Bright Angel Trail**, followed on foot or mule by thousands of
visitors each year, starts in Grand Canyon Village, alongside the
wooden shack that once served as the Kolb photographic studio. An
old Havasupai route, it was improved by miners a century ago, and
then operated as a toll trail when the mines failed to prosper.

Although the side canyon immediately below the village makes
access to the Tonto Platform relatively straightforward, it's still a
long hard climb. Most **day-hikers** content themselves with walking to
either of the two resthouses in the first three miles, but with an early
start you should be able to manage the round trip of nine miles to
Indian Garden, or even twelve miles to Plateau Point. In summer, you
can obtain water along the trail, and only need to carry one quart of
water per person; in winter, when there is none, you should carry
two. Only try to reach the river – 7.8 miles from the trailhead, with
Phantom Ranch almost two miles beyond that – if you've reserved a
campsite for the night.

The trail begins with a long, exposed set of switchbacks down the
dry rocky hillside, which changes in colour from pale pink to sheer
red. There are two short tunnels in its first mile. After another mile,
you start to see more wildlife around – deer, rodents and the ubiquitous ravens – while rock surfaces at various points along the way
hold a few pictographs, all but obscured by graffiti. Basic **resthouses**, built in the 1930s, are located after 1.6 and 3.1 miles. Both have
water in summer (mid-May to Sept) and emergency phones, but only
the 1.6-mile one has restrooms.

Beyond the second resthouse, a set of switchbacks known as
Jacob's Ladder carry you down the sheer Redwall cliff, a major
obstacle throughout almost the entire canyon. Then, finally, the trail
starts to level out, and the vegetation gets greener, with a scattering
of yellow- and red-blossomed cacti to either side. Soon you hear the
astonishing sound of trickling water in Garden Creek, lined by dazzling green trees.

The spring at **Indian Garden**, 4.6 miles from the rim, is the reason this trail exists. Native peoples really did have a garden here,
originally planted in prehistoric times and continuously used by the
Havasupai from around 1300 AD until the nineteenth century. Now
this unexpected little oasis holds a ranger station, restrooms, separate camping and day-use areas, and a staging post for mules.

Plateau Point

From Indian Garden, the Bright Angel Trail continues to the river
(see p.311 while the **Tonto Trail** runs both east and west along
the flat, arid Tonto Platform. A spur trail off the Tonto Trail –
reached by heading left at Indian Garden, crossing Garden Creek,
and then turning right at an obvious intersection three quarters of
a mile along – threads its way out to **Plateau Point**, a superb

GRAND CANYON HIKING TRAILS

overlook above the Inner Gorge from which it is not possible to descend any further. Constructed to give day-tripping mule riders a view of the river, this trail makes an ideal route for hikers. The desert landscape, barren even by inner-canyon standards, is spectacular, with agave and yucca plants shooting up from the sandy soil, and the mighty red buttes and mesas of the canyon now framed against the blue sky.

Shortly after you get your first awesome glimpse of the black tumbling walls of the gorge, the trail comes to an end. Precariously perched on the rocky outcrops, you can see a long stretch of the dark-green Colorado, though both the bridges and Phantom Ranch lie out of sight around the next promontory to the east. With binoculars, you can just make out the buildings back at the top of the rim, six miles away.

Devil's Corkscrew and the Colorado River
The continuation of the Bright Angel Trail beyond Indian Garden first drops through the fertile margins of Garden Creek, then switchbacks down the **Devil's Corkscrew**, hacked into the rock to create a shortcut to the river during the 1930s. Once beside the Colorado, dwarfed beneath thousand-foot walls of dark-grey granite, it undulates through sand dunes scattered with yucca and prickly pear.

Hikers can cross the river around a mile along, using the 1960s **Silver Bridge**; mules, which quite sensibly balk at the prospect of seeing the river between its slats, have to continue a little further. The 400-foot **suspension bridge** they prefer was set in place in 1928, hanging from twin cables that were carried down the Kaibab Trail on the shoulders of 42 Havasupai. Close to the bank on the far side are the mule corral and Bright Angel Campground, with Phantom Ranch a short way up Bright Angel Creek beyond.

The temperature at river level tends to be around 20°F higher than on the South Rim, and there's significantly less rainfall. The **ecology** down here is changing fast since Glen Canyon Dam was completed in the mid-1960s (see p.390). Previously, up to a million tons of earth and rock hurtled past Phantom Ranch each day. Now it's more like 80,000; trees are establishing themselves that would previously have been swept away, and fish are becoming extinct.

Phantom Ranch
Bright Angel Creek, which flows down Bright Angel Canyon from the North Rim, and is several hundred feet wide by the time it meets the Colorado below Grand Canyon Village, was first spotted by John Wesley Powell in 1869. His journals record "We discover a stream entering from the north, a clear beautiful creek coming down through a gorgeous red canyon"; he named it to contrast with the muddy Dirty Devil upriver in Utah.

Allow at least eight hours for the day-hike to Plateau Point and back.

All the water for Grand Canyon Village is piped from the North Rim, by way of the Silver Bridge.

The South Rim

*Reservations for **Phantom Ranch** are handled by Amfac (☎303/297-2757, fax 297-3175); see p.302.*

Since then, the terrain just east of the confluence has been landscaped to create the welcoming glade now occupied by **Phantom Ranch**, the only accommodation option inside the canyon itself. Clustered around a central lodge, its various cabins, corrals and outbuildings stand amid huge cottonwoods and fruit orchards. These were planted early in the twentieth century, to shade *Rust's Camp*, renamed *Roosevelt's Camp* after a visit by Theodore Roosevelt in 1913. That in turn was replaced by Phantom Ranch itself, designed by Mary Jane Colter for the *Fred Harvey Company* in 1922, using uncut river stone to blend in with the surroundings.

The fully-equipped individual **cabins** at Phantom Ranch are reserved for the use of riders on *Fred Harvey* mule trips – full details, including prices, appear on p.298. In addition, there are four ten-bunk **dormitories**, intended for hikers, which cost $22 with bedding provided. Do not hike down without a reservation; even if you do have one, you must **re-confirm** before 4pm on the day before your stay, either at the *Bright Angel* transportation desk or by calling ☎520/638-3283. Phantom Ranch tends to be booked way in advance, but cancellations for dorm beds and, conceivably, cabins, are handed out first-come, first-served at the *Bright Angel* early each morning. Check what time they'll be opening the night before – it can be as early as 6am. All supplies reach *Phantom Ranch* the same way you do, so **meals** are expensive, a minimum of $12 for breakfast and $17 for dinner.

South Kaibab Trail

*An account of the **North Kaibab Trail**, which connects Phantom Ranch with the North Rim, appears on p.327.*

The **South Kaibab Trail**, the most direct route from the South Rim to Phantom Ranch, is never as busy as the Bright Angel Trail. And no wonder – taking just six miles to drop to the river, it's an even steeper haul, while hikers have to drive over four miles east of Grand Canyon Village to reach the trailhead. Set aside the time for a short day-hike, however, and you'll be rewarded by superb views.

If you're combining the Bright Angel and South Kaibab trails, the Kaibab is the one to descend.

The trail starts by descending slightly west of **Yaki Point**, but once past the end of the promontory it runs along the top of **Cedar Ridge**. This high crest surveys a thirty-mile stretch of the canyon in both directions, and also faces straight up Bright Angel Canyon towards the North Rim. In the absence of any water en route, most hikers turn back after 1.5 miles. If you keep going, down a precipitous and very exposed slope, you meet the **Tonto Trail** 4.4 miles down. A long if level trek east enables backpackers to connect with the Grandview Trail (see opposite) but the obvious way to go is west. At a spot known as the **Tipoff**, a few hundred yards along, you're poised to plunge down into the Inner Gorge. The river, and the 1928 suspension bridge that leads to Phantom Ranch, are little more than a mile away. Alternatively, continue on the Tonto Trail for four miles to **Indian Garden** (see p.309), and climb back up to the village from there.

Grandview Trail

The **Grandview Trail**, which starts from the parking lot at Grandview Point (see p.306), was built during the 1890s to aid copper mining at the *Last Chance* mine, out on **Horseshoe Mesa**. One of Ralph Cameron's less fictitious claims (see p.295), the *Last Chance* was nonetheless played out by 1907, and the trail was used by guests at the nearby hotel until that too folded in 1916.

Now officially an "unmaintained" trail, it's a very demanding hike, on which some of the most difficult switchbacks consist of wooden walkways pegged to the rock face. The chief appeal is to camp overnight on the mesa, three miles down, and explore (with care) the derelict mine workings, but it is possible to descend the far side to reach the Tonto Trail. Too hot and dry in summer, the Grandview Trail gets icy in winter, so the best months to come are April, May and October.

Hermit Trail

Named in honour of Louis Boucher, a nineteenth-century prospector, the **Hermit Trail** is another unmaintained trail that dates from the days when the obstreperous Ralph Cameron controlled access to most of the prime rim-edge sites (see p.295). Built in 1912 by *Fred Harvey*, for mule riders from the *El Tovar*, and abandoned in 1931, much of its engineering remains in good shape. Once more, it's used mainly by solitary types, setting off on long backcountry camping expeditions away from the crowds.

Before hiking unmaintained trails such as the Hermit, ask at the park visitor center about current conditions.

From the Hermit's Rest parking lot at the end of West Rim Drive (see p.306), the trail drops into a side canyon, then switchbacks into Hermit Gorge and slowly descends a high rock wall far above Hermit Creek. Rockfalls tend to make for slow progress, but eventually views of the Inner Gorge start to open up. *The Hermit Camp* campground is not far west of the junction with the Tonto Trail, 12.6 miles along. Turning right (north) shortly before the campground brings you to the Colorado itself, just over fourteen miles from the trailhead, at **Hermit Rapid**, where the wave-like surge of the river can reach over twenty feet high.

The Havasupai Reservation

Havasu Canyon, one of the most spell-bindingly beautiful places in the entire southwest, nestles deep in the Grand Canyon a mere 35 miles west of the park headquarters. The only approach is from the east, however, so it's a road trip of almost two hundred miles, the last ninety miles, once you leave the interstate, across the endless Coconino Plateau.

Those visitors who brave the eight-mile desert hike down into the canyon are rewarded by a stunning oasis of turquoise waterfalls and lush vegetation, a Shangri-La that has been home for centuries beyond record to the same small group of Native Americans. They're here thanks to a geological fluke; although the canyon receives only nine inches of rain each year, all the water that falls for three thousand square miles around funnels down into this one narrow gorge, to create the year-round torrent of Havasu Stream.

The Havasupai

The **Havasupai** – the "people of the blue-green water" – can trace their occupation of Havasu Canyon back at least as far as 1300 AD. The word "**Pai**" means people, and refers to a Yuman-speaking group that reached the Southwest via California well over a thousand years ago. They soon quarrelled, splitting to form the **Hualapai** ("Pine-clad Mountain People") of northwest Arizona, and the **Yavapai** ("Almost-People", who no longer quite deserved to be regarded as people) who settled along the Colorado further south. The Hualapai established close links with Pueblo groups such as the Hopi and Zuñi, from whom they eventually acquired the art of raising sheep, horses, and imported crops such as peaches. Until the Havasupai were allocated their own reservation towards the end of the nineteenth century, they regarded themselves not as a separate "tribe" but as just another band of Hualapai.

Although the Havasupai took their name from the turquoise river that watered their fields, they only lived on the canyon floor in summer, in houses of hide-covered branches. In winter, the canyon made a cold, miserable home, lacking big game and wood for fuel and receiving as little as five hours of sunlight per day. Instead the Havasupai moved up onto the plateau to hunt deer, elk, and antelope, using artificial water holes to lure them closer. Their territory extended beyond the San Francisco Peaks (near modern Flagstaff) and took in the region now occupied by Grand Canyon Village.

In the summer of 1776, as the Declaration of Independence was being signed in Philadelphia, the Havasupai welcomed their first white visitor. **Father Francisco Tomás Garcés**, a missionary from San Xavier del Bac near Tucson (see p.230), was greeted by five days of feasting. Describing the Grand Canyon as a "calaboose of cliffs and canyons", he dubbed it the Puerto de Bucareli; more enduringly, he was the first to name the Río Colorado. Meanwhile, as Garcés explored the canyon, the rest of his expedition blazed a trail to California, where they founded San Francisco.

The Havasupai then remained undisturbed for a further eighty years, before Anglo prospectors and surveyors began to enter the region. Conflict arose in 1866, when to encourage the spread of the railroads Congress granted the Atlantic and Pacific Railroad company ownership of swathes of land adjoining its tracks across northern Arizona. Native resistance soon escalated into **war**, and the defeated Hualapai spent several years confined to a reservation near Ehrenberg on the Colorado. Because the Havasupai did not participate in the fighting, they were allowed to remain in their traditional territory. In negotiations over the extent of a permanent Havasupai reservation, the US government was as usual only prepared to acknowledge Native American "ownership" of land that held permanent settlements and cultivated fields. Areas used for hunting, gathering or even grazing, especially if use was shared by more than one band, was never included in reservations. Fearful of being deported themselves, the Havasupai settled in

Havasu Canyon forms the heart of the **Havasupai Reservation**, said by a 1930s anthropologist to be "the only spot in the United States where native culture has remained in anything like its pristine condition". Since then, tourism has become the mainstay of the tribal economy, but visitor numbers are kept deliberately low, at around 35,000 per year. Suggestions of building a road – or even a tramway

1882 for a tiny 518-acre plot at the bottom of Havasu Canyon. Restricted to a fraction of their former range, they were obliged to farm what little land they were granted as intensively as possible.

A century of hardship was to follow, during which the Havasupai repeatedly petitioned to have their reservation enlarged. Suffering great spiritual uncertainty, both the Havasupai and Hualapai took part in the **Ghost Dance** movement in the 1890s, when Native Americans throughout the West joined in trance-like rituals designed to ensure that white men would vanish from the land and the old ways would return. The Havasupai also briefly adopted the rain-making *kachina* dances of the Hopi (see p.58), until a catastrophic **flood** on January 1, 1910 destroyed their village, which then stood half a mile from its current site.

At first, the creation of **Grand Canyon National Park** placed yet more restrictions on Havasupai use of traditional lands. One early supervisor avowed that the "Grand Canyon should be preserved for the everlasting pleasure and instruction of our intelligent citizens as well as those from foreign countries; I therefore deem it just and necessary to keep the wild and inappreciable Indians from off the Reserve". Although Coconino National Forest takes its name from the Hopi word for the Havasupai, tribal members could only graze animals there by annual permit. The Havasupai survived largely through disobeying whatever unenforceable regulations outsiders sought to impose, continuing to spend their winters up on the plateau. Many Havasupai in due course found jobs in Grand Canyon Village, while tourism to Havasu Canyon itself became an important element in the tribal economy.

After endless legal battles, and a lobbying campaign to persuade environmentalist groups that Native Americans could look after wilderness lands every bit as well as the Park Service, the Havasupai finally won their battle in 1975. Almost 200,000 acres were added to the reservation, the largest tract of land ever returned to Native Americans. It came only just in time; almost immediately, the Grand Canyon region experienced a boom in **uranium** mining, with over 3500 claims filed in the Arizona Strip during the ensuing decade.

In 1988, *Energy Fuels Nuclear*, a Denver-based corporation, was granted rights to develop a uranium mine at a sacred Havasupai site in the Kaibab National Forest, known as *Mat Taav Tijundva*. Despite fears that it could contaminate the stream, Havasu Canyon, and ultimately the Colorado itself, federal courts denied Havasupai attempts to stop the mine. Although *Energy Fuels* only offered to pull out in return for $50 million, the worldwide glut of uranium has forced an indefinite postponement of their plans. As that threat recedes, another grows; there are fears that the construction of Canyon Forest Village (see p.296) will deplete the water table for hundreds of miles around, and that Havasu Stream may finally run dry.

– down into the canyon have always been rejected, to minimize the impact on the traditional way of life. Instead the five hundred or so Havasupai earn their keep by ferrying non-hikers up and down the trail on horses and pack mules, and operating a thriving **campground** beside the stream as well as a comfortable lodge in the village of **Supai**. While visitors should not expect sweeping views of the Grand Canyon itself – or to have much interaction with the tribal members – for spectacular desert scenery, and sheer romance, the Havasupai Reservation is beyond compare.

Getting to the reservation

Seligman and Kingman are described on p.285.

The only way to reach the Havasupai Reservation by road is from I-40, turning off at **Seligman** if you're coming from Flagstaff or Grand Canyon Village, or at **Kingman** from Las Vegas or California. Stock up with food, water and gas when you leave the interstate, then follow AZ Hwy-66 to the poorly marked intersection with **Arrowhead Hwy-18**, six miles east of **Peach Springs**.

AZ Hwy-66 is the only surviving segment of Route 66 not to have been superseded by newer roads.

Hwy-18 runs for sixty miles with barely a building in sight, across bare sagebrush desert interrupted by patches of thick ponderosa forest. Despite maps to the contrary, it's paved throughout, and there's no possibility of losing your way. Eventually it starts to wind down through burgeoning canyonlands, coming to an end at the large plateau known as **Hualapai Hilltop**. Although there is no more than a small cluster of dilapidated shacks, there are usually far more vehicles parked here than you might anticipate for such a remote spot.

Do not set off from Hualapai Hilltop unless you have already reserved accommodation; see p.318.

Hualapai Hilltop commands a long view of the white-walled **Hualapai Canyon**, cutting into the tablelands as it stretches off to the north. The trail from the end of the parking lot zigzags steeply down the hillside to the right, and can then be seen threading its way across the valley floor below. **Hikers** are free to set off whenever they choose. If you prefer to **ride** down – which costs $50 per person one-way, $80 round-trip – enquire either at the trailhead, or in the temporary cabins near the entrance to the parking lot. Riders' baggage weighing over ten pounds has to be carried separately – one animal can carry up to four packs, again for $50 one-way, $80 round-trip – while many hikers also arrange to have their bags carried. There's a $15 surcharge for leaving the hilltop after noon, or Supai after 10am.

Helicopter flights between Hualapai Hilltop and Supai village, run by *Action Helicopter of Arizona* (☎520/282-7884) cost $55 each way. As a rule they're only available on Fridays and Sundays, but there's no harm in calling at other times.

Finally, it is also possible to take a helicopter to Havasupai from **Grand Canyon Village**. *Papillon Grand Canyon Helicopters* (☎520/638-2419; see also p.299) operate day excursions, including a horse ride to Havasu Falls but not meals, for $440 per person, and one-night trips, staying at the lodge, for $482.

The trail to Supai

Apart from its initial switchbacks, the **Hualapai Trail** is not especially difficult. It is however a long eight-mile walk, with no shade for the first three miles and no reliable water source until very near the end. Allow around three hours to reach the village (and four or more to come back up again), and be sure to carry all the food and water you will need for a day in the desert.

The route is very obvious, and kept busy throughout the day with small supply trains of mules and horses. Once on the valley floor, it follows the bed of a dry wash between red-rock walls that slowly but inexorably climb to form a deep, narrow canyon. The sand underfoot is so thick that it splashes at every step, but the potential for flash floods is clear from the much-scoured rocks to either side. Mighty boulders occasionally all but block the path, while solitary cottonwoods reach up towards the thin strip of sky overhead.

After almost seven miles, the trail reaches the intersection where Havasu Canyon comes in from the right; until 1910, this was the site of Supai village (see p.315). Do not continue straight ahead into Cataract Canyon at this point – it took three weeks to find a dehydrated camper who did so in 1975. Bear left instead, at a dense cluster of small trees. The sound of rushing water soon signals the emergence of Havasu Stream from hidden crevices in the rock, and before long it's flowing through the parched landscape in all its blue-green splendour.

Not far beyond, you cross a low rise to be confronted by the meadow that holds the modern village, and the two red-rock pillars that watch over Supai from the high canyon wall on the far side. Known as the **Wigleeva**, these twin sentinels are regarded as the guardian spirits of the Havasupai.

Supai

Though located in a superb natural setting, a wide flat clearing surrounded on all sides by forbidding walls of red sandstone, the village of SUPAI is not in itself attractive. The Havasupai were only obliged to build a year-round settlement down in the canyon by the loss of their lands on the plateau above (see p.314) and this site was their second choice after the first proved prone to flooding. It too was seriously damaged by floods in both January 1990 and February 1993, and consists of just a scattering of basic timber-frame houses and prefabricated cabins. The name itself is also a flimsy fabrication; "Supai" is a meaningless abbreviation of "Havasupai", invented by the US Post Office.

Once the Hualapai Trail, running alongside a line of irrigation ditches, has shepherded you into the village, the first building you come to holds the tribal **registration office**. Only campers need to pay the reservation **entrance fee** here (April–Oct $15; Nov–March $12); for lodge guests, it's added to their bill. A back room holds a

*No one visits
Havasu
Canyon as a
day-trip; quite
apart from the
drive to the
hilltop, the
twenty-mile
hike to the falls
and back takes
well over ten
hours.*

*The finest old
Havasupai
baskets to be
seen in
Arizona are in
the Heard
Museum in
Phoenix; see
p.206.*

small **museum** (daily 7am–7pm; $1), with a random but reasonably interesting assortment of turn-of-the-century photographs and newspaper cuttings. Although the Havasupai are famous for crafts such as basket-making, ancient artefacts have become too expensive for the museum to afford.

Fifty yards further on, beyond the only post office in the US still to receive its mail by pack mule, lies Supai's dusty, fly-blown **plaza**. Benches outside the village's one **grocery store** on the right form its main social centre, where the older Havasupai gather each evening. The younger set, together with a vast population of dogs, are more likely to be found on the terrace of the **cafe**, opposite. Once past that the trail skirts the edge of the village school, then branches off left down towards the campground. Visitors are forbidden to wander away from the main trail into the farmlands around the village.

Practicalities

All visitors, whether planning to camp or stay in the lodge, should make advance reservations by calling either *Havasupai Tourist Enterprises* (☎520/448-2141) or the lodge. Space is at a premium in summer, and is often fully reserved several months in advance.

*All prices on
the Havasupai
Reservation
are subject to
an additional
five percent
tribal sales
tax.*

Havasupai Lodge (☎520/448-2111; April–Oct ⑤, Nov–March ③), is located slightly apart from things on the edge of the village, close to the canyon wall behind the school. It's a simple two-storey structure, much like a typical national park lodge, where the reasonable motel-style rooms are without phones or TVs. All sleep four people, with an $8 surcharge per additional guest.

The *Lodge* has a pleasant little garden, but the only place to get a **meal** in Supai is at the *Tribal Cafe* (daily 7am–7pm; ☎520/448-2981). Here the food is far from exciting, with fried breakfasts, and a lunch or dinner of beef stew, Indian fry-bread or burritos; pretty much everything seems to cost $5, or more if you want grated cheese on top. The grocery store has a limited selection of processed items, all carried in by mule and priced accordingly.

Spending a night at the **campground** – see opposite – costs $10 per person in summer, and $9 in winter.

Below Supai

All the **waterfalls** for which the Havasupai Reservation is famous lie further down the canyon beyond Supai. Much of the riverbed immediately below the village remains cluttered with fallen trees and undergrowth deposited by the floods of 1990 and 1993, but after a mile and a half a thundering from the left betrays the presence of **Navajo Falls**. Plummeting down the far wall of the canyon, intervening trees make it hard to spot from the main trail, but hardy hikers can reach it by picking their way down below the path. Once there, clamber across a minor fork of the stream and you'll come to the foot of the falls, which tumble through a series of pools. The falls were named for Chief Navajo, who led the Havasupai at the time the reservation was first established, and died in 1900.

Havasu Falls

The trail beyond Navajo Falls – which was washed away completely in 1993, and has been reconstructed to follow a course higher up the canyon wall – soon reaches the stupendous double cascade of **Havasu Falls**. First seen from an overlook more or less level with the top, this is an absolutely breathtaking sight. The stream foams white as it hurtles over a 150-foot cliff, to crash into shallow terraces filled with limpid turquoise water. The rock formations all around are formed from water-deposited limestone known as **travertine** – the same stuff that creates the stalactites of Carlsbad Caverns, and clogs the inside of domestic kettles. It's the light travertine coating on the riverbed that gives the water its astonishing blue-green glow.

Havasu Falls used to be a long broad expanse of water, which explains the solidified sheets and curtains of travertine that run right across its wide brim. Then a flash flood punched out a notch right in the centre, through which the falls now gush to either side of a small outcrop that's knitted together by a frail cottonwood sapling. Side trails off the main path lead down to an idyllic shaded "beach" beside the largest, deepest pool, where the ceaseless roar makes conversation difficult, but swimming is all but irresistible. On the far side of the natural travertine dams that divide the various terraces – partially reconstructed after the 1993 flood, using artificial groynes that are now buried beneath new deposits – picnic tables stand in a cottonwood grove at the mouth of a side canyon.

A short horseback tour from Supai village down to Havasu Falls costs $45; contact Havasupai Tourist Enterprises - see opposite.

Walking barefoot on the sharp travertine is not recommended.

The campground

A short distance beyond Havasu Falls, two miles down from Supai village, you finally reach the Havasu **campground**, set in an especially narrow and high-walled segment of the canyon. Although this site was once a tribal burial ground, it was only added to the reservation in 1975, having originally been considered to be too rich in mineral deposits to be left to the Indians.

The campground stretches for almost a mile, with tents pitched in clearings in the woods to either side of the stream. Facilities are primitive in the extreme, but it's a wonderful spot, with safe drinking water provided by fresh springs in the canyon wall. Villagers are barred from the area in summer, but groups of horses stand tethered at the entrance, waiting to carry campers back up the hill.

Mooney Falls and the Colorado River

Havasu campground is brought to an abrupt end by the 200-foot **Mooney Falls**. This natural barrier was long regarded as virtually impassable; it was named for an unfortunate prospector who dangled here for three days in the 1890s, after a rope snagged as he was being lowered to the bottom. As rescuers frantically tunnelled through the travertine to reach him, the rope frayed and broke, and he fell to his death.

The trail to the bottom is little better today. Having scrambled down the travertine ledges to reach two successive tunnels that drop through the cliff face, you come to a sheer section that was blasted away in the flood of 1993, and now consists of a vertical series of footholds aided by an iron chain fixed into the rock.

A further set of swimming holes leads down from the bottom of the falls, while a good day-hike from the campground continues on for three miles to **Beaver Falls**. Negotiating a route beyond this quick-fire set of rapids involves climbing up to and along a high ledge, but keep going for four more miles and you'll eventually reach the Colorado itself. Quite possibly, you'll be greeted by river-runners who preferred to get here the easy way, shooting 157 miles of white water from Lees Ferry (see p.322).

The road between the rims

In the absence of a road across the Grand Canyon, the shortest possible driving route between the South and North rims takes 215 miles, or at least four hours. From Grand Canyon Village, follow AZ-64 – the East Rim Drive – to meet US-89 at **Cameron**, head north to cross **Marble Canyon** on Navajo Bridge, and then double back east to **Jacob Lake** to join the 44-mile summer-only AZ-67 south to the North Rim.

Although there are very few towns along the way, the scenery is seldom less than spectacular. Beyond Desert View, AZ-64 runs close to the gorge of the **Little Colorado**; Navajo trinket stalls are dotted along the roadside and at a couple of overlooks, around ten miles west of Cameron.

Cameron

The junction of AZ-64 and US-89 is marked by the small **Cameron Visitor Center**, offering information on the Navajo Nation (June–Sept daily 8am–5pm; Oct–May Mon–Fri 8am–5pm). **CAMERON** itself, which amounts to little more than a handful of buildings, lies a mile or so north, on the south side of the suspension bridge spanning the Little Colorado River.

The **Cameron Trading Post** here, established in 1911, stocks a huge array of Southwest arts and crafts, from mass-produced trinkets and jeans to genuine Hopi *katsinas* and museum-quality Navajo rugs. While busy with tourists in summer, it remains at heart a trading centre for the Navajo Nation, with some of its business still conducted by barter. Part of the main building houses a **cafeteria** serving reasonable food (daily 6am–10pm); accommodation is in the two large **motel** buildings alongside, which look out across the Little Colorado to the open desert (PO Box 339, Cameron AZ 86020; ☎520/679-2231 or 1-800/338-7385; ④).

There's further accommodation at **GRAY MOUNTAIN**, ten miles south of Cameron, in the shape of the *Anasazi Inn* (PO Box 29100, Gray Mountain AZ 86020; ☎520/679-2214; ④).

Marble Canyon and Navajo Bridge

Fifteen miles north of Cameron, US-160 branches off northeast via **Tuba City** (which also has motels; see p.39) towards Monument Valley and Colorado. Continuing north, after another forty miles of emptiness US-89 climbs away up the mesa to the right, heading for Page and Glen Canyon Dam (see p.393). US-89A however presses on at the foot of the **Echo Cliffs**, to reach **Navajo Bridge** after a further fifteen miles.

There are in fact two Navajo Bridges. The original, which opened in 1929, is now reserved for pedestrians only; a wider facsimile opened 150ft downstream in 1995. The Colorado at this point cuts through the chasm of **Marble Canyon**, such a narrow interruption in the vast flat plains that you can't tell it's there until you're right on top of it.

On the west bank of the river, *Marble Canyon Lodge* (☎520/355-2225 or 1-800/726-1789; ③) has over fifty conventional motel-style rooms, and can arrange river and fishing trips. In the atmospheric *Lodge* itself, there's a reasonable **restaurant** that's open for all meals daily, with a 6am start to meet the needs of the crowds of river-runners.

Lees Ferry

Before the construction of Navajo Bridge, ferries struggled across the river at **LEES FERRY**, six miles north. Mormon elder Jacob Hamblin was guided to this remote spot – the only place within hundreds of miles to offer easy land access to both banks of the Colorado – by Naraguts, a Paiute, in 1858.

Thanks to an Act of Congress, there is no apostrophe in Lees Ferry.

Thirteen years later, **John Doyle Lee** was sent here to set up a ferry service to help Mormon missionaries en route south into Arizona. Lee was on the run after the **Mountain Meadows Massacre** in Utah in 1857, when a wagon train of would-be settlers was slaughtered by an armed white band clumsily disguised as Indians (see p.338). He remains a hero to some Mormons (a local plaque calls him "a man of good faith, sound judgment and indomitable courage"); those who have read Mark Twain's account of the massacre in *Roughing It* may disagree. He was finally arrested in 1874, and executed in 1877, but his (seventeenth) wife Emma remained here, at the place they knew as **Lonely Dell**.

The ferry service was always perilous, with the boats in constant danger of being swept downstream, and was finally abandoned after a fatal accident in June 1928. A crucial piece of equipment needed to finish the bridge on the left bank was stranded on the right bank; the only way to get it across was to take it eight hundred miles by road, via Las Vegas.

The reason you can get down to the water at Lees Ferry is because it marks the confluence of the Paria River with the Colorado; **Paria River Beach**, at the foot of the gently sloping road from Marble Canyon, is the official start of the Grand Canyon. To the south, the broad Colorado picks up speed as it squeezes into Marble Canyon. A few hundred yards north, across the Paria, you come to a large parking lot and launching ramp. This is where **whitewater rafting** expeditions set off into the Grand Canyon – the first point where boats can get out again is at Diamond Creek, twelve days away by muscle power – and *Fred Harvey*'s smooth-water trips from Glen Canyon Dam (see p.298) come to an end. A fairly basic **campground** (☎520/355-2334) is located nearby.

From the far end of the lot, a trail leads within a couple of hundred yards to the well-preserved remains of buildings from the ferry era, built not surprisingly with slabs of red sandstone. They're interspersed with lumps of mangled machinery from a steamboat that was hauled here from San Francisco in 1911, and abandoned as a failed experiment after only five trips. It's possible to walk along the tranquil riverside for another mile or so upstream.

Lee's *Lonely Dell Ranch* was located on the fertile banks of the Paria, away to the west, an area that now forms part of the **Paria Canyon-Vermilion Cliffs Wilderness**. It can be explored along an extensive network of trails, including one four- to six-day epic that traces the full length of the Paria Canyon.

The Vermilion Cliffs

*Watch out for
the awesome
wingspan of
the mighty
Californian
condor, which
has recently
been re-
introduced to
the Vermilion
Cliffs.*

West of Marble Canyon, US-89A curves beneath the southernmost section of the **Vermilion Cliffs**. These soaring sandstone walls glow a magnificent red at sunrise and sunset, but the road itself is all but featureless. Only a couple of small **motels** offer any incentive to get out of your car. Both *Lee's Ferry Lodge* (☎520/355-2231; ③) – three miles west of Marble Canyon, and smaller and slightly lower-priced than the *Marble Canyon Lodge* (see p.321) – and the mock-Anasazi *Cliff Dweller's Lodge* (☎520/355-2228; ④), half a dozen miles beyond, have their own stores and restaurants.

Once past the southernmost promontory of the cliffs, the highway is free to run as straight as an arrow across the broad sagebrush desert. Forty miles from the river, it hits the Kaibab Mountains, and climbs through thick forest for the final eleven miles to Jacob Lake.

Jacob Lake and DeMotte Park

The crossroads community of **JACOB LAKE**, deep in the pine forest 44 miles north of the North Rim, looks more like a Canadian logging camp than anything you'd expect to find in Arizona. In winter, when

AZ-67 down to the Grand Canyon is closed by up to 140 inches of snow, Jacob Lake goes into hibernation; in summer, however, it makes a good living from the constant stream of tourists.

As well as a gas station and general store, the *Jacob Lake Inn* (☎520/643-7232) offers simple **motel** rooms (⑤) and log cabins (April–Nov; ④); there are also **campgrounds** for tenters (mid-May to mid-Oct; ☎520/643-7395) and RVs (May to mid-Oct; ☎520/643-7804). The **Kaibab Plateau Visitor Center** (daily 8am–5.30pm; ☎520/643-7298) provides information on the surrounding area.

Jacob Lake is named for Jacob Hamblin, a Mormon missionary to the Paiutes and Navajo. The Mormons made little use of the forests to the south, however, apart from grazing their cattle in the large meadow-like clearings that punctuate the road to the canyon. One of these, **DEMOTTE PARK**, 27 miles from Jacob Lake, is now the site of the *Kaibab Lodge* (☎520/638-2389 or 526-0924 or 1-800/525-0924; ④), whose rudimentary cabins remain open in winter for the use of cross-country skiers. The **gas station** nearby is the last before the canyon; the park entrance is another five miles down the road, with visitor facilities nine miles beyond that.

The North Rim

Higher, bleaker, and far less accessible, the **North Rim** of the Grand Canyon receives less than a tenth as many visitors as the South Rim. While that doesn't mean you'll have the place to yourself, it can still make you feel as though you're venturing into unexplored wilderness. The basic principle however is the same as at the South Rim, with a cluster of venerable park-service buildings where the main highway reaches the canyon, and a handful of rim-edge roads where drivers can take their pick from additional lookouts. Only one **hiking trail** sees much use; the North Kaibab Trail, which follows Bright Angel Creek down to Phantom Ranch.

*The exact **closure dates** of the road to the North Rim depend on the weather; as a rule, it's open mid-May to late October.*

Tourist facilities on the North Rim, concentrated at **Bright Angel Point**, open for the season on May 15 and close on October 15. The park itself remains open for day-use only after October 15, but no food, lodging or gas is available, and visitors must be prepared to leave at a moment's notice. It's shut down altogether by the first major snowfall of winter, which usually comes towards the end of October.

North Rim practicalities

Visitor activity on the North Rim focuses on the glorified log cabin known as *Grand Canyon Lodge*, perched above the canyon at **Bright Angel Point**. As you enter the main lobby, the park **information desk** (daily 8am–5pm; ☎520/638-7864) is on the left, together with a small **bookstore** that stocks detailed trail guides. To the right

The North Rim

is the main **Dining Room**, open daily for all meals (☎520/638-2612 ext 160; dinner reservations required); the prices aren't bad, and the food is better than in the **snack bar**, entered separately from the driveway. The *Lodge* also holds a **saloon** and **espresso bar**, but its best feature is the **viewing lounge** downstairs, with an array of comfortable armchairs facing vast picture windows.

Accommodation at the *Lodge* (④–⑤) is in the cabins that spread back along the ridge from the entrance, very few of which have canyon views. The cheapest deal is a *Pioneer Cabin*, holding four or

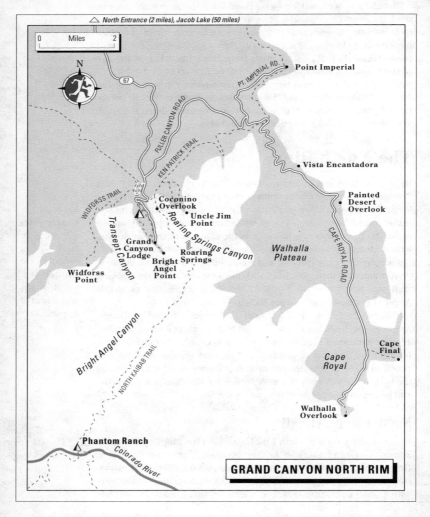

△ *North Entrance (2 miles), Jacob Lake (50 miles)*

0 ___ Miles ___ 2

N

67

PT. IMPERIAL RD. • Point Imperial

FULLER CANYON ROAD

KEN PATRICK TRAIL

• Vista Encantadora

WIDFORSS TRAIL

Coconino Overlook

• Uncle Jim Point

Painted Desert Overlook

Roaring Springs Canyon

Transept Canyon

Grand Canyon Lodge

Roaring Springs

Bright Angel Point

Walhalla Plateau

CAPE ROYAL ROAD

• Widforss Point

Bright Angel Canyon

NORTH KAIBAB TRAIL

Cape Final •

Cape Royal

Walhalla Overlook •

△ Phantom Ranch

Colorado River

GRAND CANYON NORTH RIM

five people. Advance reservations are essential, and are handled by the same agents as for the South Rim; *Amfac Parks & Resorts*, 14001 East Iliff, #600, Aurora CO 80014 (same-day ☎520/638-2631; advance ☎303/297-2757, fax 297-3175). Just over a mile north is the *North Rim Campground*, where spaces can be reserved – though it's not necessary for backpackers – through *DESTINET* (☎1-800/365-2267).

Ask at the information desk for details of **mule rides** (1hr $12, half-day $35, full-day canyon expeditions $85; ☎520/638-9875), and **van tours** along the rim. **Buses** between the North and South rims, run by *Trans Canyon Shuttle* (☎520/638-2820) leave the North Rim daily at 7am and the South Rim at 1.30pm; the fare is $60 one-way, $100 round-trip.

Other North Rim facilities

Camping Equipment Can be bought or rented at the *General Store*, opposite *North Rim Campground*.

Gas Near *North Rim Campground*. Daily 7am–7pm.

Laundromat Near *North Rim Campground*. Daily 7am–9pm.

Medical Help Call ☎911 for emergencies or ☎520/638-2611 ext 222 for the village clinic.

Post Office In *Grand Canyon Lodge*. Mon–Fri 8am–11am & 11.30am–4pm, Sat 8am–2pm.

As this book went to press, the park service was considering introducing a reservation system for access to the North Rim; see p.295.

Bright Angel Point

A short paved trail leads off left of *Grand Canyon Lodge* to the very tip of **Bright Angel Point**. In places, the trail fills the full width of the slender spit of land, with sheer drops to either side. After four hundred level yards, you reach the sanctuary of a railed viewing area, looking out across the canyon. Because the North Rim is a thousand feet higher than the South, the views stretch far beyond the South Rim to the plateaus of Arizona and the San Francisco peaks, but it's hard to spot a sign of life at Grand Canyon Village, eleven miles distant. As usual, the Colorado is too deeply buried in the canyon to be seen; if you hear the sound of rushing water, it's coming from **Roaring Springs**, much closer to hand, which supplies all the water used by the park on both rims (see p.311).

To either side, trees somehow cling to the near-vertical red ridges, while high buttes in the canyon proper reach almost to the level of the rims; most prominent of all is the neat-capped **Brahma Temple** straight ahead, framed between two lesser specimens.

Cape Royal Scenic Drive

Apart from Bright Angel Point, all the **canyon overlooks** along the North Rim are ranged along the eastern edge of the **Walhalla Plateau**, a considerable drive from *Grand Canyon Lodge*. This long

high headland, to the east of Bright Angel Point, is reached by turning east onto **Fuller Canyon Road**, three miles north of the *Lodge*.
Five miles along, you come to a junction where **Point Imperial Road**
branches off to the left, while **Cape Royal Road** winds off into the
cool dense woods to the right.

Even if your time is limited, it's well worth making your way right
to the end of Cape Royal Road – fifteen miles from the junction – to
Cape Royal. From the unremarkable parking lot at the end of the
highway, an even, paved footpath leads first of all to the **Angels
Window**, a natural archway just below the top of a rocky spur. As
you approach, you can look down through it all the way to the
Colorado River. An extremely narrow railed pathway that detours off
the main trail a little further along leads onto the top of the "window",
for views across to the flatlands of the Navajo reservation. Two broad
green-trimmed stretches of the river are visible from this point,
including the foaming Unkar Creek rapids.

Views from **Cape Royal** itself, a couple of hundred yards further
along the main trail, extend much farther west, though the intervening ridge immediately west obscures Bright Angel Point. The canyon
is much narrower here, so flat-topped **Cedar Mountain** is very conspicuous, standing out just above the South Rim.

Other possible halts along Cape Royal Road include the **Walhalla
Overlook**, a mile or so back from the end of the road, where a very
short forest trail ends at the foundation walls of a small **Anasazi
dwelling place**, and the **Painted Desert Overlook**, which looks
across Marble Canyon towards the Echo Cliffs.

Point Imperial

Turning left at the intersection of Fuller Canyon and Cape Royal
roads (see above) brings you after a gradual three-mile climb to
Point Imperial. Although at 8803 feet this is the highest spot along
either rim of the entire canyon, to reach the actual overlook you have
to descend a short distance from the parking lot. A long red sandy
ridge pokes out just below the viewing area, with a stark butte at the
end, while to the right is the thickly wooded ridge that ends at Cape
Royal. Looking down, the landscape is as dry as dust, a labyrinth of
spurs and buttes in which it's virtually impossible to guess which is
the main gorge of the Colorado.

The plateau of the Navajo reservation on the far side is almost three
thousand feet lower, so it spreads for miles at your feet, pierced by further chasms and gorges. To the southeast, the Little Colorado emerges
from its own canyon to join the main onward rush of the Colorado.

North Rim hikes

Hikers on the North Rim of the Grand Canyon should take the
same precautions, and be as aware of their physical capabilities, as
their counterparts on the South Rim (see p.307). There tends how-

ever to be less scope for getting into difficulties, as almost all the North Rim trails suitable for day-hiking stay on top of the plateau. On the only route that descends into the canyon itself, the **North Kaibab Trail**, hiking to the river and back in a single day is completely out of the question – it's a 28-mile round trip with a 6000-foot change in elevation.

As on the South Rim, **permits** are required for all overnight hiking expeditions (see p.308). The same office handles advance requests, but you can also turn up at the North Rim Backcountry Office, in the Ranger Station (daily 8am–noon).

The North Kaibab Trail

Some version of the **North Kaibab Trail**, following Bright Angel Creek down to the Colorado, has been in use for over a thousand years. Its current route, which starts by descending through Roaring Springs Canyon from a roadside trailhead two miles north of *Grand Canyon Lodge*, was established in the late 1920s. Parking at the trailhead is limited, but a **hiker shuttle** runs here on request from *Grand Canyon Lodge* (daily 6am–8pm; $5 for one person, $2 each additional passenger).

When planning a day-hike on the North Kaibab, it's easy to be over-ambitious; the mileages may not seem that great, but the gradient is steep from the word go. Many people go no further than the **Coconino Overlook**, just 1.4 miles down through the fir forests, a high rocky vantage point from which you can see the junction of Roaring Springs and Bright Angel canyons. The **Roaring Springs** themselves come after another 3.6 miles, during which the trail burrows through the **Supai Tunnel** and then crosses the precarious **Redwall Bridge**. Water from this open cascade is pumped up to the *Lodge*, and also piped over to the South Rim, but there's enough left over to keep alive the "gardens" just downstream that were originally planted by the Anasazi.

The well-shaded **Cottonwood Campground**, 2.5 miles beyond the springs, is a major way-station for trans-canyon hikers. The highlight of the final seven mile segment to **Phantom Ranch** (see p.311) is the lacy **Ribbon Falls**, reached via a short spur trail a mile past the campground.

Rim-edge trails

The best canyon-edge trail near Bright Angel Point, the ten-mile **Ken Patrick Trail**, alternates dramatic views with stretches of dense forest as it leads from the North Kaibab Trailhead all the way to Point Imperial. The five-mile **Uncle Jim Trail** branches off it to reach a viewpoint that overlooks the North Kaibab Trail, while the **Widforss Trail** heads the other way, west from the inland end of Bright Angel Point out to the tip of the next headland along.

The Arizona Strip

By any logic, you'd expect the **Arizona Strip** – the anomalous area
that's sandwiched between the North Rim of the Grand Canyon and
the Utah state line – to belong to Utah rather than Arizona. In 1864,
Mormon leader Brigham Young called on Congress to grant the
Mormons all territory that lay within two degrees of latitude of either
side of the Colorado; the boundary was drawn instead along the 37th
parallel, and that remains the Utah–Arizona border. Repeated
attempts to incorporate the Strip into Utah failed, largely because
this remote region became a stronghold of renegade Mormons who
didn't accept their church's reversal of doctrine on multiple marriage
(see p.480). Effective isolation from the state authorities of both
Utah and Arizona suited these die-hard polygamists just fine.

The Arizona Strip is not at all a tourist destination. Virtually no
roads cross it, and those that do hold just a few semi-derelict hamlets. The only visitors who pass through tend to be making their way
as fast as possible between the national parks of southern Utah – particularly Zion, a dozen miles north of the state line (see p.345) – and
the Grand Canyon.

Fredonia

The largest town on the Arizona Strip, **FREDONIA**, stands thirty
miles northwest of Jacob Lake. With the bigger and much more interesting community of **Kanab** a mere seven miles north, across the
Utah border (see p.360), it's hard to see why anyone would choose
to spend the night here, but Fredonia does hold a few small **motels**.
Options include the very plain but reasonably new *Crazy Jug*, 465 S
Main St (☎520/643-7752; ③), and the cheaper but somewhat run-
down *Blue Sage*, 330 S Main St (☎520/643-7125; ②), which also
has space for RVs.

Jacob Lake is 3000 feet higher than Fredonia, and as the highway climbs up into the forests of the Kaibab Plateau, roughly
halfway between the two, you get some tremendous views across
southern Utah. Tier upon tier of cliffs rise one behind the other into
the distance, making it abundantly clear why the entire region is
known to geologists as the **Grand Staircase**. First comes the red
sandstone of the Vermilion Cliffs, the formation pierced by Zion
Canyon (see p.331); next are the White Cliffs, which form the Kolob
Canyons district of Zion National Park; and beyond them, forty
miles away, stand the softer Pink Cliffs, sculpted into the hoodoos
of Bryce Canyon (see p.365).

Pipe Spring National Monument

Thirteen miles west of Fredonia, just off AZ-389, **PIPE SPRING
NATIONAL MONUMENT** (daily 8am–4pm; ☎520/643-7105; $2)
marks the site of one of the very few water sources on the Arizona

Strip. Not surprisingly, ownership of this precious spring has been much contested; a Mormon rancher, Dr James Whitmore, appropriated it from the Paiutes in 1863, and was killed three years later by a party of Paiute and Navajo raiders. The Mormons subsequently enclosed the spring in a fort, known as **Winsor Castle** after its first superintendent, and retained control until it was declared a national monument in the 1920s.

Pipe Spring now stands adjacent to the Kaibab Paiute Indian Reservation, and is largely staffed by Paiute rangers. The buildings remain in good condition, and serve as a not desperately enthralling museum of early ranching life, of most appeal to students of Mormon history.

A couple of miles further off the highway, on reservation land, the Paiute run a small **casino** stuffed with low-stake slot machines.

Colorado City

AZ-389 continues northwest from Pipe Spring, and serves as the most direct connection from the North Rim to the I-15 interstate, between Las Vegas and Salt Lake City. A mile or so before it reaches Utah, a spur road to the right runs up to the staunchly traditional Mormon community of **COLORADO CITY**. Set beneath the towering bluffs of the Vermilion Cliffs, this is a surreal-looking place, laid out with a small grid of extremely broad streets that see very few cars but plenty of gingham pinafores. Everyone will assume you're a magazine journalist hoping to write a sensational article about polygamy, and there's no encouragement to linger.

Chapter 7

Southern Utah

For a full account of the Mormons, and the history of Utah, see Contexts, *on p.465 onwards.*

The time in Utah is one hour later than Nevada all year round, and one hour later than Arizona from April to October; from November to March, it's the same as Arizona.

Southern Utah represents a peculiar combination of the mind-boggling and the mundane. Its **scenery** is stupendous, a stunning geological freakshow where the earth is ripped bare to expose cliffs and canyons of every imaginable colour, unseen rivers gouge mighty furrows into endless desert plateaus, and strange sandstone towers thrust from the sagebrush. The tiny **Mormon towns** scattered across this epic landscape, on the other hand, are almost without exception boring in the extreme. Each has its cluster of characterless motels and dull-as-ditchwater diners; they're not unfriendly places, but finding ways to while away your evenings can be a supreme test of the imagination.

Most visitors therefore spend as much time as possible **outdoors**. Southern Utah has the greatest concentration of **national parks** in the US; in fact there have been serious proposals for the entire area to become one vast national park. The five parks that currently exist are not necessarily the most beautiful or spectacular spots in the state – their boundaries are the result of devious behind-the-scenes wrangling, and exclude lands prized by the ranching and mining conglomerates. Taken together, however, they make an ideal focus for a first tour of Utah, each with its own well-maintained infrastructure of hiking trails and scenic overlooks.

In southwest Utah, **Zion National Park** centres on an awe-inspiring and richly fertile canyon, backed by barren highlands of sun-scorched white sandstone, while **Bryce Canyon** is a roaring inferno of flame-like orange pinnacles. Over to the east, **Arches** holds an eroded desertscape of graceful red-rock fins and spurs, all on a more manageable scale than the astonishing hundred-mile vistas of neighbouring **Canyonlands**. Both lie within easy reach of **Moab**, the dishevelled former mining town that has suddenly become Utah's hippest destination. The fifth park, **Capitol Reef**, stretches down the massive rainbow-tinted Waterpocket Fold in the middle of the region, pierced by slender, ravishing canyons.

Lesser-known but equally dramatic wildernesses include **Dead Horse Point** and **Muley Point** east of the Colorado, and the vast new

Grand Staircase-Escalante National Monument to the west. The most spellbinding wonder of them all, **Glen Canyon**, has been drowned since the 1960s beneath **Lake Powell**, an elongated reservoir whose turquoise waters, lapping desultorily against the red desert rocks, are a playground for houseboaters and jet-skiers.

The defining topographical feature of southwest Utah is the **Grand Staircase**. Named by pioneer river-runner John Wesley Powell, it consists of a series of plateaus, stacked tier upon tier, climbing from the North Rim of the Grand Canyon. The **Chocolate Cliffs**, near the border with Arizona, are followed by the dazzling **Vermilion Cliffs**, then the **White Cliffs** – a 2000-foot wall of Navajo Sandstone, best seen at Zion Canyon – the **Grey Cliffs**, and finally the **Pink Cliffs** of Bryce Canyon. Although it took a billion years of sedimentation for these rocks to form, the staircase itself has only been created in the last dozen million years, by the general upthrust of the **Colorado Plateau**, which stretches away to the east.

The southwest corridor

That the far southwestern corner is now the most accessible and densely populated area of southern Utah makes it easy to forget how forbidding it seemed to early explorers. In October 1776, close to modern Cedar City, fathers Domínguez and Escalante despaired of finding their

way to California, and headed back towards Santa Fe (see p.476). Not until 1830 did the **Old Spanish Trail** establish a permanent route west, and it was another twenty years before Brigham Young ordered Mormon settlers to establish a string of towns at the foot of the **Hurricane Cliffs**.

The largest of those towns, **St George** and **Cedar City**, stand fifty miles apart on I-15, the busy interstate that links Las Vegas with Salt Lake City. Both now depend on tourism for their livelihood – catering especially for visitors to Zion National Park – despite lacking any great appeal themselves. Only devotees of Mormon history bother to tour their humdrum array of museums and pioneer sites before heading into the wilderness that lies to the east.

St George

Spreading beneath a long sandstone escarpment, nine miles north of the Arizona state line, the venerable Mormon town of **ST GEORGE** is southern Utah's major population centre. Its broad thoroughfares and sturdy well-spaced homes may still hold fewer than forty thousand inhabitants, but that's four times the 1970 figure. Most of the newcomers are retirees from elsewhere in the Southwest, attracted by the mildness of the winters at this low elevation of just 2880 feet. They've done little to change the essential character of St George, however, which may be cosmopolitan by Utah standards but anywhere else would seem like a conservative country backwater, albeit with a surprising number of motels.

St George was named not for England's dragon-slaying patron but for a Latter-Day Saint. Apostle George A Smith hand-picked the 309 families who were sent to establish a colony here in 1861. The plan was to make Utah self-sufficient in **cotton**, supplies of which were threatened by the Civil War; thus this appropriately southern region became known as "**Utah's Dixie**".

The cotton-growing era ended when cotton from the Deep South reappeared after the war, made cheaper than ever by the coming of the railroads. St George, however, quietly prospered growing other crops, and became the winter refuge of Brigham Young and other ageing Mormon elders. Young's much-restored adobe **Winter Home** still stands at 200 North 100 West, complete with contemporary furnishings and artefacts (daily 9am–dusk; free).

The gleaming white **Mormon Temple**, 440 South 300 East, was the only LDS temple to be completed during Brigham Young's lifetime. Half fortress, half cathedral, it was a defiant statement that the settlers were here to stay. Young presided over its dedication shortly before his death in 1877, and it remains a powerful symbol to all Mormons. As usual, Gentiles can't go inside; there is a visitor center, however, where the problem is getting out rather than getting in. If you're sufficiently captivated, ask about guided tours of the smaller red-brick **Mormon Tabernacle** on Main Street, of similar vintage and modelled on the meeting houses of New England.

THE GUIDE: CHAPTER 7

Arrival and information

Travellers driving up I-15 can call in at the **Utah Visitor Center**, just inside the state line (summer daily 8am–9pm; winter daily 8am–5pm; ☎801/673-4542). Information on St George is also available from the **visitor center** in the old County Courthouse at 97 E St George Blvd (Mon–Fri 9am–5pm, Sat 9am–1pm; ☎801/628-1658).

Greyhound **buses** between Las Vegas and Salt Lake City stop outside *McDonald's* at 1235 S Bluff St, while the *St George Shuttle* (☎801/628-8320) connects with Las Vegas on request. *Skywest Airlines* (☎1-800/453-9417) and *Pacific Air West Airlines* (☎1-800/729-7229) operate daily **flights** to Salt Lake City and Las Vegas from an airport perched on the mesa high above town to the west, which is also used by *Scenic Airlines* (☎801/628-0481) as a base for aerial tours of the national parks.

The zip code for St George is UT 84770.

R&R Tours (☎801/628-7710) run **bus tours**, including a $60 day-trip to Zion; *Dixie Jeep Tours* (☎801/674-7155) do 4WD trips into the backcountry. **Mountain bikes** can be rented from *Swen's Cyclery*, 1060 E Tabernacle St (☎801/673-0878).

Accommodation

In principle, finding a **room** in St George should be no problem. At the last count, the town had 34 motels, most of them along the main drag, St George Boulevard, as well as several B&Bs tucked away on the back streets. On busy summer weekends, however, everywhere fills up early, and there's enough traffic on the interstate year-round for room rates to remain pretty constant. Watch out too for the sudden influx of students for Spring Break, in late March.

*The best place to **camp** near St George is Snow Canyon; see p.336.*

Reservation **agencies** include *Accommodation Referral* (☎801/673-1546 or 1-800/259-3342) and *Southern Utah Tourist Information & Services* (☎801/628-7710 or 1-800/765-7710).

*As explained on p.15, **accommodation prices**, excluding taxes, are indicated throughout this book by the following symbols:*

Claridge Inn, 1187 S Bluff St; ☎801/673-7222 or 1-800/367-3790, fax 634-0773. Modern, inexpensive motel southwest of the centre; all rooms are non-smoking, most have two queen beds. Sun–Thurs ②, Fri & Sat ③.

Coral Hills, 125 E St George Blvd; ☎801/673-4844 or 1-800/542-7733, fax 673-5352. Very central *Best Western* property, quite large but still characterful, and boasting two pools. ③.

Dixie Palm, 185 E St George Blvd; ☎801/673-3531. The cheapest motel in town, but not the worst. Some rooms have showers not baths, and there's no pool, but the price and central location may make up for that. ①.

Greene Gate Village, 76 W Tabernacle St; ☎801/628-6999 or 1-800/350-6999. Seven century-old structures, most brought by the current owners to this site, facing the Tabernacle. Individual rooms and entire houses for rent; one sleeps 22. All rooms are en-suite with TVs and phones, some have Jacuzzis and/or fireplaces. ③–⑥.

Seven Wives Inn, 217 North 100 West; ☎801/628-3737 or 1-800/600-3737. Two neighbouring historic houses in central St George, one built for a seven-fold polygamist, run jointly as a comfortable, period-furnished B&B inn. All rooms are en-suite, with TVs and phones. ③–⑥.

① up to $30
② $30–45
③ $45–60
④ $60–80
⑤ $80–100
⑥ $100–130
⑦ $130–175
⑧ $175–250
⑨ $250+

Weston's Econolodge, 460 E St George Blvd; ☎801/673-4861 or 1-800/424-4777. Standard motel rooms in all sizes at reasonable rates, with a good big pool. ③.

Eating

Dining out in St George is a question of which highway steakhouse or fast-food outlet catches your eye; there's plenty of choice, but not much excitement. The only area you might stroll around looking for a restaurant is right in the centre, where the small, slightly faded **Ancestor Square** mall holds a handful of lively options.

Basila's, Ancestor Square, 2 W St George Blvd; ☎801/673-7671. Classy restaurant in the heart of town, a bit dimly lit for lunch but romantic in the evening, and serving a welcome menu of Greek specialities with a few Italian items for the less adventurous. Open Tues–Sat only, with a liquor licence.

Dick's Cafe, 114 E St George Blvd; ☎801/673-3841. St George's longest-standing diner has an enjoyable small-town ambience, and you'd be pushed to spend $10 before you burst. Open for all meals daily.

Pizza Factory, Ancestor Square, 1 W St George Blvd; ☎801/628-1234. This friendly pizza-and-pasta joint seems to be inexorably taking over its neighbours in Ancestor Square; its terrace makes a nice spot for a light lunch, and things get lively later on. Closed Sun.

Sullivan's Rococo, 511 Airport Rd; ☎801/628-3671. Upmarket steakhouse, poised on the bluff west of town, where half the customers have come for the panoramic views of town and the other half for the liquor licence. Steak, ribs and seafood entrees cost up to $25 in the evening, but the lunchtime sandwiches are well under $10.

From St George to Cedar City

Much the most direct route between St George and Cedar City is to follow the interstate northeast, but taking Hwy-18 due north leads you through an interesting stretch of mountainous high country. If you're heading for Zion National Park (see p.345), turn right onto Hwy-9 seven miles out of St George on I-15.

Snow Canyon State Park

One of Utah's most attractive state parks, focused on a classic red-rock canyon, lies within ten minutes' drive of downtown St George. **SNOW CANYON STATE PARK** was named for two of St George's leading pioneers, Lorenzo and Erastus Snow, so don't expect to see snow. Instead its most distinctive feature is the layer of jet-black lava that flakes off the tops of its sun-baked sandstone pinnacles, left by a ten-thousand-year-old volcanic eruption.

The road through Snow Canyon remains open day and night; there are no fixed hours.

The park's six-mile **scenic drive** drops left from Hwy-18 seven miles north of St George, shortly beyond a viewpoint that looks out across most of the canyon. Winding down past a succession of overlooks and rounded monoliths, it reaches the **park headquarters** after a couple of miles. There's no visitor center, but this is the place to pay the $4-per-vehicle entrance fee and pick up hiking details. It's also the site of the pleasant, shaded 36-space *Shivwits Campground* (☎801/628-2255 or 1-800/322-3770; Mon–Fri $11, Sat & Sun $12). Reservations are recommended in spring and fall, but things get quieter during the hottest months.

The **Hidden Pinyon Trail**, an excellent hour-long (1.5-mile) round-trip hike, starts a hundred yards further on. After cutting between the craggy outcrops into a peaceful meadow, it zigzags up and over a ridge to enter a heavily eroded landscape reminiscent of Canyonlands' Needles District (see p.411). Vegetation en route includes Utah junipers, creosote bushes and assorted cactuses.

If it's too hot to hike, pull off another two miles on instead, where a cluster of lurid **red sand dunes** threatens to drift across the road. Kids especially will enjoy sliding down the slopes, which had a bit part in *Butch Cassidy and the Sundance Kid*. The dunes also doubled for central Asia in Howard Hughes' movie *The Conqueror*, which starred John Wayne as Genghis Khan; it was filmed in 1954, when the Nevada Test Site, just ninety miles west, was at its busiest; Wayne, Hughes and three quarters of the cast probably died from cancers caused by fall-out from the explosions.

Leaving the park at its southern end enables you to complete a 24-mile loop back to St George, but if you want to press on north, double back when you've had enough of the scenic drive.

Pine Valley

Sixteen miles north of Snow Canyon, a dead-end right turning off Hwy-18 leads for ten miles into **PINE VALLEY**. By the time you reach the valley's eponymous village, you're at 6500 feet, so Pine Valley serves as a summer retreat for the sweltering citizens of St George. Travellers from further afield may well feel that this gentle Alpine landscape is not what they came to Utah to see, but it's undeniably pretty. There's basic **accommodation** in the *Pine Valley Lodge* (☎801/574-2544; ②), and a steakhouse nearby, plus a handful of small forest-service **campgrounds** – and plentiful hiking trails – in the Dixie National Forest beyond.

Along the interstate: Silver Reef and Fort Harmony

In the course of the fifty-mile drive from St George to Cedar City, I-15 climbs three thousand feet, passing between the Pine Valley Mountains to the west and the Hurricane Cliffs to the east.

Fifteen miles northeast of St George, a spur road to the left leads to the ghost town of **SILVER REEF**. Silver mining never came any easier than here, the only spot in the West where silver was found mixed in with ordinary sandstone. It took two decades, the 1880s and 1890s, to scour the hills bare of metal, during which time Silver Reef revelled in a reputation for very un-Mormon hell-raising. Relics of the era, together with a scale model of town, can be admired in the **Silver Reef Museum**, at 3200 Wells Fargo Rd (Mon–Sat 9am–5pm;

Horse rides in the park, ranging from one hour to overnight trips, are offered by Snow Canyon Stables (☎801/628-6677).

The Mountain Meadows Massacre

The lonely high-mountain valley known as **Mountain Meadows**, five miles beyond the turn-off into Pine Valley on Hwy-18, was the scene of one of the most infamous incidents in Western history.

In the summer of 1857, tensions between the ten-year-old Mormon kingdom of Deseret and the rest of the United States were at their peak. With a large detachment of US soldiers known to be advancing on Utah, the long-expected "Mormon War" was seen as inevitable. When the **Fancher Company**, a California-bound wagon train of settlers from Arkansas and Missouri, reached Salt Lake City in early August 1857, the locals refused to sell any of the supplies they were stockpiling for the winter. In retaliation, the migrants raided Mormon farms, taunting that they'd soon return in force. One claimed to be carrying the very gun with which Joseph Smith had been killed in Missouri.

The Fancher party then headed south to Mountain Meadows, a fertile, well-watered halt on the Old Spanish Trail where travellers often stopped to gather strength for the final haul across the desert. Within days, the wagon train was **ambushed** by warriors dressed as Indians. Several of its members were killed before the rest barricaded themselves behind earthwork defences. Whether the attackers were genuine Utes, or white Mormons in disguise – as Mark Twain reported in *Roughing It* – remains controversial to this day. Clearly, however, the Mormon militia responsible for protecting southern Utah saw the hostile wagon train as a threat to be eliminated. Their commander, **John D Lee**, rode up to the beleaguered Gentiles on September 11, claiming to have negotiated a truce with the "Indians", and stated that if they laid down their guns they would be allowed to proceed west in peace.

Desperately short of ammunition, the migrants agreed. Each was assigned a Mormon escort, and together they set off west. Within a mile, Lee called the order "**Halt! Do your duty!**", whereupon the Mormon militiamen killed the entire group, amounting to 120 unarmed men, women and children. Some sources allege that Utes also took part in the slaughter. The only survivors were seventeen infants, who were at first adopted by local Mormons but eventually returned to relatives.

When reports of the massacre reached the rest of the country, it was widely believed to have been carried out on Brigham Young's orders. No serious legal investigation ever took place, however, with the authorities in southern Utah almost certainly complicit in a cover-up, and the federal government too preoccupied with the Civil War to intervene. Most of the perpetrators laid low in remote desert outposts; most famously, John D Lee established a ferry service across the Colorado (see p.321). In time, Young bowed to national pressure and first excommunicated Lee from the church in 1870, and then delivered him for trial. Lee was executed by firing squad in Mountain Meadows on March 23, 1877, bitterly claiming that "Young has sacrificed me through his lust for power". He remains a hero to some Mormons; one plaque calls him "a man of good faith, sound judgment and indomitable courage".

A monument to the massacre was erected in 1990 near the highest point on Hwy-18, a bleak windswept spot overlooking the entire valley. Each of the victims is listed by name, but the inscription simply states that the party "was attacked", without mentioning Mormon involvement. More explicit graffiti is scrubbed away as soon as it appears.

$2.50). Only stunted walls remain of the town itself, however, and few visitors can summon up the energy on a red-hot Utah summer's day to find them of any interest.

There's even less to see at the site of **FORT HARMONY**, another eighteen miles north, just beyond the Kolob Canyons turn-off and fifteen miles south of Cedar City. **John D Lee**, of Mountain Meadows fame, established a fortified outpost to guard this high pass in 1852. It was finally abandoned ten years later, after torrential rain caused its earthen walls to cave in, killing two of Lee's children.

Cedar City

CEDAR CITY, 53 miles northeast of St George and now half its size, has a similar history to its upstart rival. It too was founded in Mormon Utah's precarious early years, as part of the church's bid for self-sufficency. The Mormons urgently needed **iron**, so when scouting parties discovered iron ore in southern Utah, the *Deseret News* published an appeal in July 1850 for "fifty or so good effective men, with teams and waggons" to establish an **Iron Mission**.

Cedar City was established in November 1851, between the iron in the hills to the west and the coal deposits of Coal Creek Canyon to the east. Most of its first inhabitants were British miners; they succeeded in smelting iron within a year, but the venture ultimately failed, and was abandoned in October 1858. Since then, ore mined in the area has been shipped out for processing.

The Cedar City story is told in full at **Iron Mission State Park**, on the main highway a mile or so north of downtown (June to Labor Day daily 9am–7pm; Labor Day to May daily 9am–5pm; $3). Apart from rusty nuggets, the warehouse-like museum is filled with nineteenth-century horse-drawn vehicles, including wagons, sleighs, and hearses (one of which bears the slogan "Why walk around half dead when we can bury you for just $22?"). There's also a small and somewhat dull display of Native American artefacts, plus some homespun craft items – mostly carved vertebrae and crocheted doilies – and 380 individually tagged samples of barbed wire. Several more wagons are parked in sheds at the back, if you feel up to braving the heat.

Otherwise, there's little to see in Cedar City. It's not a place you're likely to want to tour on foot, despite the lure of historical markers detailing the former locations of the town's social hall, hospital, brick yard and flour mill.

Tourists do however arrive in droves during the summer, drawn by the annual **Utah Shakespeare Festival**, a semi-professional event organized by Southern Utah State University since 1962. Running from around June 20 to the end of August, it usually features six productions, with three or four Shakespeares and a couple of other classics. Three theatres are used, the most prestigious being the *Adams Memorial Shakespearian Theater*, a replica of the original *Globe*,

A full account of the Kolob Canyons district of Zion National Park appears on p.358.

and tickets range from $19 to $27 (reservations on ☎801/586-7878 or 1-800/752-9849). Peripheral activities include a regular mock-Elizabethan Medieval Feaste, costing $27.

Arrival and information
Cedar City's **visitor center** is housed in a small roadside cottage at 286 N Main St (summer Mon–Fri 8am–7pm, Sat 9am–1pm; winter Mon–Fri 8am–5pm; ☎801/586-5124 or 1-800/354-4849).

*The zip code
for Cedar City
is UT 84720.*

    Greyhound **buses** (☎801/586-9465) call at 1355 S Main St, while the airport on the northwest fringes of town is used by *Skywest Airlines* (☎1-800/453-9417) for **flights** to Salt Lake City.

Accommodation
While Cedar City doesn't have quite the range of **accommodation** to match St George, around twenty motels and hotels line up along Main Street, including several right in the heart of town. Rooms are liable to be booked well in advance for the Shakespeare festival. The **All Utah Free Reservation Center** (☎1-800/776-4685) handles room bookings for Cedar City and the rest of the state.

    There's a large *KOA* **campground** at 1121 N Main St (☎801/586-9872); for more seclusion head for the public sites that start around a dozen miles east of town, along Hwy-14 towards Cedar Breaks (see opposite). For full details, call in at the **Dixie National Forest Ranger Station**, 82 North 100 East (☎801/865-3200).

*The price
codes used
here are
explained on
p.15.*

Bard's Inn B&B, 150 South 100 West; ☎801/586-6612. Central B&B, open for the Shakespeare Festival and at other times by arrangement, with five en-suite rooms in the main house and two more in the adjoining cottage. ④.

El Rey Inn, 80 S Main St; ☎801/586-6518 or 1-800/528-1234. Very central *Best Western* hotel – one of the first ever – an easy walk away from the Festival events, with rooms of all sizes, plus pool, sauna and spa. ③–⑤.

Raycap Motel, 2555 N Main St; ☎801/586-7435. Inexpensive motel, north of town near exit 62 off I-15, with pool, Jacuzzi and *Ed & Deb's* reasonable diner next door. Winter ②, summer ③.

Super 8, 145 North 1550 West; ☎801/586-8880. Reliable budget motel, with little seasonal variation in price. Well out of town, west of I-15 at exit 59. ③.

Willow Glen Inn, 3308 N Bulldog Rd; ☎801/586-3275. Farm-set B&B, five miles northwest of downtown, near exit 62 off I-15. Rooms with and without baths in main house, and some luxurious suites in garden cottages. ③–⑥.

Eating
A quick-fire succession of chain diners and fast-food outlets punctuates the main highway through Cedar City. For more characterful alternatives, head for the student-oriented places near the university, in the blocks immediately southwest of downtown.

Adriana's, 164 South 100 West; ☎801/865-1234. Wide-ranging menu, from soup and salad to steak, served amid pseudo-English decor. Open daily all year for lunch and dinner, and very busy in summer. Most entrees cost $14–18, and they also serve good-value buffets and have a liquor licence.

Dog and Duck Coffee House, 50 W Center St; ☎801/586-0355. Sandwiches, salads, pastries and espressos, in sociable cafe just off Main Street; popular with students and Shakespearians. Live music and poetry most evenings.

Godfather's Pizza, 241 N Main St; ☎801/586-1111. Fills the spruced-up former railroad station opposite the visitor center, serving good pizzas in all sizes ($7–19) plus all-you-can-eat lunch and dinner buffets.

Pancho & Lefty's Cafe, 2107 N Main St; ☎801/586-7501. Lively dinner-only Mexican option, with a sideline in chunky steaks, and an open-air verandah that's a midsummer night's dream of a spot for a margarita.

Sullivan's Cafe, 86 S Main St; ☎801/586-6761. Popular breakfast place, a cornucopia of eggs and pancakes, that also has a fully-fledged (and licensed) steak and seafood restaurant upstairs.

Cedar Breaks National Monument

Cedar City stands at an elevation of 5800 feet, but the densely-wooded plateau to the east rises a further five thousand feet. **Hwy-14**, the most direct route to Bryce Canyon, climbs steadily onto the plateau from the narrow gorge east of town. The scenery along the way is rarely short of spectacular, with views that stretch south to encompass all of Zion National Park.

For a full account of **Bryce Canyon**, *see p.365.*

Around fifteen miles along, shortly after the highway enters the **Dixie National Forest**, you can't fail to spot the pink, white and orange rocks of **CEDAR BREAKS NATIONAL MONUMENT**, immediately below the forest that tops the high ridge to your left. Cedar Breaks is a sort of pocket version of Bryce, where erosive forces have scooped a natural amphitheatre into the hillside and filled it with brilliantly coloured limestone formations. While it lacks Bryce's opportunities for hiking, it's well worth seeing if you're in the area.

The road through the monument – **Hwy-148**, which branches north from Hwy-14 19 miles out of Cedar City – is snowbound between late October and mid-May. When it's clear, you can choose between four similar cliff-edge viewpoints. The southernmost, **Point Supreme**, is the best, with pinnacles rising from the orange canyon floor at your feet and sweeping views to the south and west. The small **visitor center** just behind is only staffed in summer (summer daily 8am–6pm; ☎801/586-0787); if you make it here in spring or fall, you can visit without paying the usual $4 fee. Overnight temperatures only rise high enough to make the adjoining **campground** an appealing proposition between July and September.

You can hike for short distances along the rim at both Point Supreme and **Chessmen Ridge**, a mile or so north, but no trails descend into the formations.

Panguitch Lake and Brian Head

Near the northern end of Cedar Breaks, Hwy–148 meets Hwy-143 where it turns sharply east towards Panguitch (see p.363). If you're heading for Bryce, it makes little difference whether you continue this way or return to Hwy-14. **Panguitch Lake**, in the heart of the forest halfway to US-89, appeals mainly to local trout fishermen, though the **campground** at *Panguitch Lake Resort* (☎801/676-2657) is nice enough.

Alternatively, keep going north on Hwy-143 and you'll come to tiny **BRIAN HEAD** within a couple of miles. Utah's highest town, at 9700ft, this remains accessible year-round from the north, via a steep fifteen-mile climb from Parowan. It's the site of southern Utah's only **downhill ski resort** (mid-Nov to May; lift tickets around $33 per day; information on ☎801/677-2035 or 1-800/272-7426). Despite offering slopes to suit all levels of competence – and the closest skiing to Las Vegas – Brian Head is not exactly thriving, so don't expect a heady whirl of post-piste partying. In summer, it verges on being a ghost town, but makes a peaceful overnight stop.

In the largest **hotel**, the year-round 200-room *Brian Head Hotel*, at 223 Hunter Ridge Drive (☎801/677-3000; summer ④, winter ⑤), the *Columbine Cafe* serves good-value breakfasts and lunches, while dinner at the swisher, health-conscious *Summit Dining Room* costs around $20. Most of the smaller condo complexes nearby, a few of which have their own restaurants, only open in ski season. The *Bump and Grind* at 259 S Hwy-143 (☎801/677-2864) is a convenient spot for coffee and a sandwich.

The road to Zion

The main road **east** to Zion National Park – **Hwy-9**, which leaves the interstate seven miles northeast of St George – makes a lovely thirty-mile drive. None of the pioneer villages along the way is especially exciting, but the scenery is great, with the cottonwood-fringed Virgin River to the south and gigantic sandstone cliffs to the north.

Hurricane

The westernmost town along Hwy-9 is **HURRICANE**, ten miles off the interstate at the junction with Hwy-59. While not actually on the Virgin River, it's connected to it by a seven-mile canal, conceived in 1863 but not completed until 1906. Only then was the townsite settled, and it's still much the same agricultural community today.

Hurricane's early timber-frame homes have been joined by a handful of **motels**, such as the *Super 8*, at 65 South 700 West (☎801/635-0808 or 1-800/800-8000, fax 635-0909; ③), as well as a **youth hostel**. Known as *HI-Hurricane, the Dixie Hostel*, and located at 73 S Main St (☎801/635-8202; ①/②), it offers $15 dorm beds and a few private rooms, with rates including continental breakfast. The *New Garden Café*, 138 S Main St (☎801/635-9825) is a welcome **vegetarian cafe**.

Southeast from Hurricane, incidentally, Hwy-59 takes twenty miles to reach the Arizona border, marked by the traditional Mormon community of **Colorado City** (see p.329). The **North Rim** of the Grand Canyon is another hundred miles beyond (see p.323).

Virgin, Rockville and Grafton

You'll probably barely notice either **VIRGIN**, seven miles east of Hurricane, or **ROCKVILLE**, ten miles beyond that; in fact it's hard to keep your eyes on the road at all as you come closer to the wonders of Zion.

If you can spare the time, however, follow Bridge Road south across the river from Rockville, turn right onto an unpaved track, and in five minutes you'll reach the photogenic little **ghost town** of **GRAFTON**. Mormon farmers abandoned the struggle against floods and Indians around 1900, but residents of Rockville have kept an eye on it ever since. It's also been touched up by Hollywood crews shooting movies like *Butch Cassidy and the Sundance Kid*; this is where Robert Redford rode a bicycle and sang *Raindrops Keep Falling On My Head* at one and the same time.

Just beyond Rockville, Hwy-9 veers north at the confluence of the North and East forks of the Virgin River, and heads for the maw of Zion Canyon.

Springdale

SPRINGDALE, the last town before Zion, spreads along a leafy three-mile stretch of the Virgin River just south of the park entrance. Settled at the same time as Zion Canyon, in the early 1860s (see p.347), it's now devoted almost exclusively to pampering tourists. By the time you've driven up and down the only road, **Zion Park Boulevard**, a couple of times, you'll have seen everything Springdale has to offer, but spending three or four nights in this lively, friendly community is no hardship whatsoever.

Arrival and information

Springdale has its own **visitor center**, in the Old Church at 868 Zion Park Blvd (summer only, Mon–Fri 9am–5pm; ☎801/772-3072), but for information on Zion you'd do better to go straight to the park (see p.345). You can also learn more about Zion by whiling away an evening at **The Grand Circle**, a multimedia show held in the open-air Obert C Tanner Amphitheater just outside the park (late May to early Sept, nightly at dusk; $4; ☎801/673-4811) or watching **Treasure of the Gods** at the *Cinemax Theater*, at 145 Zion Park Blvd (April–Oct daily 9am–9pm; Nov–March daily 11am–7pm; $6.50; ☎801/772-2400).

Bike Zion, at 445 Zion Park Blvd (☎801/772-3929), offers **bike rental** and guided bike tours, while *Forrest Camping and Hiking World*, also at 445 Zion Park Blvd (☎801/772-3061) can supply basic equipment for hiking and backpacking.

Accommodation

As Zion Park Boulevard runs straight between the burgeoning canyon walls towards the park, all the **motels** and **B&Bs** along the way offer the same attractive views. A couple of new properties

Kolob Terrace Road, which heads north into the Zion backcountry from Virgin, is described on p.357 onwards.

*The **zip code** for Springdale is UT 84767.*

*For details of
staying at the
in-park* Zion
Lodge, *and of*
camping *in*
Zion, *see
p.348.*

appear each year, so except at the height of summer you should have
no difficulty finding a room to suit your budget.

The shaded **Zion Canyon Campground**, half a mile outside the
park at 479 Zion Park Blvd (☎801/772-3237), offers year-round
tent camping and RV hookups, with its own laundry and pizzeria.

Motels

Bumbleberry Inn, 897 Zion Park Blvd; ☎801/772-3224 or 1-800/828-1534,
fax 772-3947. Central but very peaceful motel, set well back from the highway,
with large rooms and a pool. ③.

Cliffrose Lodge & Gardens, 281 Zion Park Blvd; ☎801/772-3293 or 1-
800/243-8824, fax 772-3900. The closest motel to the park is also
Springdale's prettiest, set in the cottonwoods alongside the Virgin River within a few hundred yards of the park entrance, with its own pool. Winter ⑤,
summer ⑥.

El Rio Lodge, 995 Zion Park Blvd; ☎801/772-3205. Small, very friendly and
good value motel, in walking distance of several restaurants. ③.

Zion Park Inn, 1215 Zion Park Blvd; ☎801/772-3200 or 1-800/934-7275.
Modern convention-style hotel at Springdale's southern end, offering spacious
rooms with panoramic windows, and a heated swimming pool. ⑤.

B&Bs

The **price**
codes *used
here are
explained on
p.15.*

Harvest House, 29 Canyon View Drive; ☎801/772-3880, fax 772-3327.
Classy, non-smoking B&B in modern home, tucked beneath the sandstone
cliffs. Four en-suite rooms, an outdoor hot tub, and gourmet breakfasts. ⑤.

Morning Glory Inn, 26 Big Springs Rd; ☎801/772-3301. Large, quirky family home converted to hold three spacious en-suite rooms, with a luxurious self-
contained cottage in the grounds. ④–⑤.

Under The Eaves, 980 Zion Park Blvd; ☎801/772-3457. Homely B&B cottage
in central Springdale; chintzy guest rooms with and without bath, plus two en-
suite rooms in the garden cabin. Rooms ④, suite ⑥.

Zion House, 801 Zion Park Blvd; ☎801/772-3281. Rambling, cosy home run
as a friendly well-maintained B&B inn. Three guest rooms – one has a private
bath, the other share – plus a plusher suite. Rooms ③, suite ⑤.

Eating

Springdale lacks the national chains, offering instead a refreshing
choice of individually-styled **restaurants**. If you prefer a light breakfast, *Oscar's*, at 61 Zion Park Blvd (☎801/772-3232), is one of two
espresso cafes just before the park entrance.

Bit & Spur Saloon, 1212 Zion Park Blvd; ☎801/772-3498. Hectic, evening-
only Mexican restaurant and bar, across from *Zion Park Inn* at the south end
of town, with a predictable Mexican menu and top-notch margaritas.

Flanigan's Inn Restaurant, 428 Zion Park Blvd; ☎801/772-3244. Traditional,
relatively formal steak-and-seafood place not far from the park.

The Shonesburg, *Bumbleberry Inn*, 897 Zion Park Blvd; ☎801/772-3224.
Smart, high-ceilinged, but unatmospheric restaurant. Standard meat and fish
entrees for $15, excellent salads, and tasty *Bumbleberry* (mixed-berry) pie.

Stakeout Grille, 1149 Zion Park Blvd; ☎801/772-3777. Clean, bright, upmarket restaurant at the south end of town beside the *Zion Park Inn*, with a panoramic dining room and patio seating. Wood-fired pizzas, well prepared meat and fish dishes like smoked ribs and spit-roasted chickens, at above average but not extortionate prices, plus delicious fresh-berry smoothies.

Zion Pizza & Noodle Co, 868 Zion Park Blvd; ☎801/772-3815. Intimate and inexpensive restaurant in a pleasant former church, with an outdoor terrace. Simple noodle and pasta dishes, plus pizzas and calzones, mostly under $10.

Zion National Park

With its soaring cliffs, riverine forests and cascading waterfalls, **ZION NATIONAL PARK** is the most conventionally beautiful of Utah's parks. On first glance, it's also the least "Southwestern"; its centrepiece, **Zion Canyon**, is a lush oasis that feels far removed from the other-worldly desolation of Canyonlands or the downright weirdness of Bryce. Like California's Yosemite Canyon, it's a spectacular gorge, squeezed between mighty walls of rock and echoing to the sound of running water; and also like Yosemite, it can get claustrophobic in summer, its one road clogged with traffic and its limited facilities crammed with sweltering tourists.

Too many visitors see Zion Canyon as a quick half-day detour off the interstate, as they race between Las Vegas (158 miles southwest) and Salt Lake City (320 miles northeast). Beautiful though the **Scenic Drive** through the canyon may be, Zion deserves much more of your time than that. Even the shortest **hiking trail** within the canyon can help you escape the crowds, while a day-hike will take you away from the deceptive verdure of the valley and up onto the high-desert table-lands beyond. In addition, two less-used roads – **Kolob Canyons Road** and the **Kolob Terrace Road** – lead into remoter sections of the park.

With elevations varying from under 4000 feet at the visitor center to almost 9000 feet at Kolob Peak, Zion is home to a bewildering array of **flora and fauna**. Its vegetation ranges from the cottonwoods and box elders along the Virgin River to the ponderosa pines and stunted piñons that cling to the high sandstone mesas. Desert flowers and cactuses provide unexpected flashes of colour in the uplands, as do darting hummingbirds. Animals include the bank beaver (so named because it doesn't build dams) and the generally retiring Western rattlesnake. Mountain lions have been re-introduced since a disastrous experiment of the 1930s, when their extermination allowed the deer population first to explode and then all but perish in a terrible famine brought on by overgrazing.

Summer is by far the busiest **season**. That's despite temperatures in excess of 100°F, and the violent thunderstorms, concentrated in August and a week or so to either side, that bring most of Zion's scant fifteen inches of annual rainfall. If you can, come in April or May, to see the spring flowers bloom – though the mosquitoes are also at their peak – or in September and October, to enjoy the fall colours along the river. The park remains open throughout the winter, but daytime highs drop below 40°F in January, while the nights tend to be freezing from November to March.

Zion Canyon

It has taken thirteen million years for the North Fork of the **Virgin River** to carve **Zion Canyon** into the southern edge of the Markagunt Plateau. For most of the year, the Virgin meanders placidly along the valley floor, en route to the Colorado. After summer thunderstorms, however, run-off from the mesa-tops is channelled down into the canyon, turning it into a torrent that carries as much as 600,000 cubic yards of rock and sand – a good-sized city block – in a single day. Each winter, the canyon walls grow further apart, as water that seeps through the porous sandstone turns to ice, and shears mighty chunks off the cliffs.

In Paiute, Markagunt means "highland of trees".

As you approach from the south, the **Markagunt Plateau** – one of the seven high plateaus that make up the Colorado Plateau in southern Utah – is clearly the next rung of the **Grand Staircase** (see p.331).

Zion Canyon serves as a handy cross-section to display the different layers of rock. At the lowest level, around the South Entrance, the thick red **Vermilion Cliffs** rise from a barely discernible bed of the even older and darker Moenave and Kayenta formations. These strata were deposited at the bottom of swampy seas around 200 million years ago, while the 2000-foot walls of the canyon itself are composed of rusty **Navajo Sandstone**, once a mass of drifting sand dunes.

The first of the colossal peaks that crown the chasm look down from either side of the South Entrance. The **West Temple** is one

Zion
National
Park

A History of Zion Canyon

Zion Canyon may seem like an oasis in the Utah wilderness, but it has never held much of a **human** population. Its earliest inhabitants were probably semi-nomadic hunter-gatherers, who from 500 AD onwards grew rudimentary crops beside the Virgin River. Known to archeologists as the **Virgin Anasazi**, they are regarded as less sophisticated cousins of the Anasazi groups to the east (see p.468); living in small bands, they never built the "cliff palaces" or pueblos for which their neighbours are renowned. By 1250 AD, drought had driven them out of Zion, leaving isolated pictographs on the canyon walls to serve as their only monument.

During the centuries that followed, **Paiute Indians** migrated seasonally throughout southern Utah, harvesting the few resources the desert could offer. They saw Zion, however, as the abode of Wai-no-Pits, the evil one, who cursed them with disease, and Kainesava, the God of Fire, whose lightning blazed from its high peaks. When the young **Mormon missionary** Nephi Johnson arrived in 1858 to explore the Upper Virgin River, the Paiute would lead him no further than Oak Creek, at the entrance to the canyon.

Isaac Behunin, who set up a log cabin in 1862 where *Zion Lodge* now stands, dubbed the canyon "**Little Zion**", in the hope that it would be a place of refuge for beleaguered Mormons. Some of his fellow farmers were soon taking things too easy; Brigham Young thundered that their indulgence in tobacco and wine made the name "**Not Zion**" more appropriate. In the long run, Zion Canyon proved too narrow to support efficient farming, and its main commercial role was simply as a route through which timber sawn on the high mesas could be shipped out to the plains. Between 1900 and 1930, logs lowered from "Cable Mountain" built the fine homes of such towns as St George.

Meanwhile, **John Wesley Powell**'s second Colorado expedition in 1872 (see p.401) had brought the scenery of Zion to national attention, under the Paiute name of "Mukuntuweap Canyon". The canyon itself was set aside in 1909 as Mukuntuweap National Monument; a larger area became Zion National Park in 1919, and the Kolob Canyons district was added in 1956.

In its first full year, 1920, the park attracted fewer than four thousand visitors. With numbers now approaching three million per year, and trails and campgrounds little changed since their construction during the 1930s, Zion is currently showing the strain. Five million dollars of federal money was allocated in 1996 to develop a new system of shuttle buses, and it's expected that private vehicles will soon be barred from the Scenic Drive altogether, either all year or in summer only.

SOUTHERN UTAH

3 4 7

of two similar mountains here whose summits consist of neat little box-shaped mesas crowned with pine trees, while the
Watchman stands guard to the east. At this point, the walls are
well over a mile apart; officially the canyon doesn't begin for
another few miles, but within just ten miles north it dwindles to a
mere twenty feet wide.

Most visitors assume Mormon settlers gave Zion's pinnacles and
promontories their portentous names – the **Court of the Patriarchs**,
the **Great White Throne**, **Angel's Landing**, and so on – but in fact
they were coined by a Methodist minister who visited in 1916.

Getting to Zion Canyon

Zion Canyon is 43 miles northeast of St George and sixty miles south
of Cedar City, reached by following **Hwy-9** beside the Virgin River
for thirty miles east of I-15. Not far beyond the park's South
Entrance, just north of Springdale (see p.343), Hwy-9 finally aban-
dons the river, tunnelling its way out of the canyon and continuing
east to meet US-89. Bryce Canyon, often seen in conjunction with
Zion, is a total of 86 miles northeast.

Both Hwy-9 and the **Scenic Drive** within the canyon are open
all year. Vehicles measuring over 7ft 10in wide or 11ft 4in high –
which includes virtually all RVs – pay $10 on top of the usual park
fees to use the Zion–Mount Carmel tunnel on Hwy-9, and in summer can only do so between 8am and 8pm. Cyclists are forbidden
to ride through the tunnel altogether, but park rangers can
arrange rides.

Arrival and information

The **admission charge** for Zion National Park, valid in all sections of
the park for seven days, is $5 per vehicle, or $3 for motorcyclists,
cyclists, and pedestrians. All nationwide passes, including the
Golden Eagle pass (see p.21), are both sold and accepted.

The park's main **visitor center** is just beyond the South
Entrance (late March to early Nov daily 8am–8pm; early Nov to
late March daily 8am–5pm; phone enquiries ☎801//772-3256,
Mon–Fri 8am–4.30pm). Free handouts include park maps and the
useful *Sentinel* newspaper, while the bookstore stocks detailed
guides, and permanent displays explain the park's geology and
history. As well as a full timetable of talks and slide shows, the
park service runs Junior Ranger programmes for 6–12 year olds
in summer.

Zion Canyon practicalities

The only **food** and **lodging** available within the canyon is at *Zion
Lodge*, an appealing if often overcrowded complex of low-slung
wooden buildings set amid well-shaded lawns a couple of miles up
the Scenic Drive. **Reservations** for its motel-style rooms and more

*To receive
information by
mail, write to
Zion National
Park,
Springdale UT
84767.*

*You can also
pay your fee
and pick up
the basic
brochures at
the kiosk that
marks the
park's East
Entrance,
while a sepa-
rate, smaller
visitor center
serves the
Kolob Canyons
district (see
p.358).*

characterful cabins (both ④), and larger studios (⑥), are handled by *Amfac Parks & Resorts*, 14001 East Iliff Ave, #600, Aurora CO 80014 (☎303/297-2757, fax 338-2694). The lodge remains open all year, but to get a room in summer you need to call several months in advance.

Whether or not you stay at the lodge, it's well worth stopping to eat in its bright, cool, upstairs **dining room**. The river views will probably linger longer in your mind than its standard breakfasts

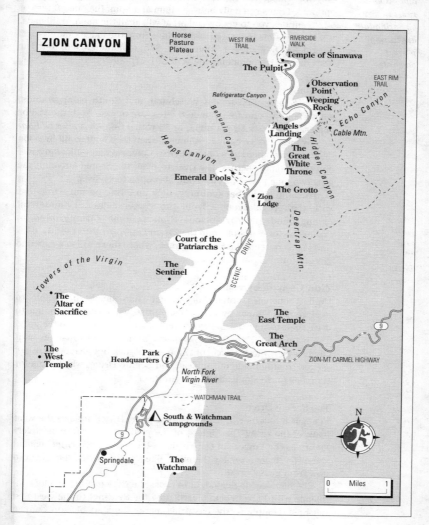

Motels, B&Bs,
campgrounds
and restau-
rants in near-
by **Springdale**
are listed on
p.342
onwards.

(daily 6.30–10am) and lunches (daily 11.30am–3pm), both costing from $5 to $7. Dinners are slightly more sophisticated (daily 5.30–9pm), featuring entrees such as steak or trout for around $12. A snackshop near the main entrance (daily 7am–9pm) serves burgers, sodas and ice creams.

Zion Lodge is the base for guided **tram rides** along the Scenic Drive. As explained on p.347, this will probably soon become the only way to see the canyon, but at the time of writing it remained optional. Trams run daily between 9am and 4pm; the one-off fare of $2.95 entitles you to get on and off at will at all the major trailheads. It's also possible to arrange **horse rides** from the lodge (March–Oct; 3hr rides at 8.30am & 1.30pm daily, $35, minimum age 8; four 1hr rides daily, $12, minimum age 5; ☎801/772-3967).

Camping

The first-come, first-served **Watchman** and **South campgrounds**, which hold around four hundred sites, are across from the visitor center. Each costs $8 per night, or $4 with a *Golden Age* or *Golden Access* pass. Arrive early in summer, when they tend to fill by noon daily; one or other stays open all year. Campers can walk alongside, and occasionally across, the river to meet the Scenic Drive on the easy two-mile paved **Pa'rus Trail**, also open to cyclists.

To camp in the **backcountry**, pick up a free permit – together with park regulations – from the visitor center. **Commercial campgrounds** nearby include *Zion Canyon Campground* in Springdale (see p.344), and the *Zican Campground* (☎801/648-2154) just outside the East Entrance, where there's also a cafe and gas station.

Zion Canyon by road

Until it becomes compulsory rather than simply preferable to explore Zion Canyon by tram, most tourists will no doubt continue to drive their own vehicles beyond the visitor center and into the park. The main road, **Hwy-9**, passes plenty of dramatic formations as it climbs east towards Bryce, but Zion's most memorable monoliths are ranged to either side of the dead-end **Scenic Drive**, which runs for six miles north alongside the Virgin River.

The Scenic Drive

For half a mile north of the visitor center, Hwy-9 follows the west bank of the river. The highest of the peaks to the left, collectively known as the **Towers of the Virgin**, is the **Altar of Sacrifice**, named somewhat macabrely for the blood-like streaks of rust that seem to flow from its flat crest.

The highway doglegs right to cross the river just beyond its confluence with **Pine Creek**. Guarded by the **Sentinel** to the west and the **East Temple** to the east, this marks the start of Zion Canyon proper. The **Scenic Drive** branches left on the far side of the bridge, while Hwy-9 heads on east (see below).

From here on north the canyon is so narrow, and the walls so steep, that there's barely room to squeeze in a road. Erosion is continuing as fast as ever, and a 200-yard segment of the Scenic Drive had to be rebuilt after a landslide in April 1995. The first major roadside pull-out comes after 1.7 miles, facing the **Court of the Patriarchs**, where peaks named for Abraham, Isaac and Joseph stand arrayed around a small canyon west of the river. A mile further on you reach the meadows of *Zion Lodge*. In the height of summer the crowds here can be overwhelming, but for most of the year it's a pleasant, shady place to break the day, and it's also the trailhead for the popular **Emerald Pools Trail** (see p.353).

Full details of
Zion Lodge
appear on
p.348.

Zion Canyon's one designated picnic spot is the **Grotto**, less than a mile beyond the lodge near the foot of the **West Rim Trail** (see p.354). To one side stands **Red Arch Mountain**, named for a natural archway created in 1880 when a vast chunk of the mountain suddenly collapsed and obliterated a newly planted cornfield. To the other is the long western flank of the **Great White Throne**, which from this angle looks neither white nor especially dramatic.

During the next mile the road passes the trailhead for **Weeping Rock** (see p.356) and the **East Rim Trail** (see p.356), as well as a number of unnamed pull-outs where paths lead down to the river. The best views of all come just under five miles from the start of the Drive, as it completes its long curve around the "Big Bend" in the river. The lookout here faces the northern face of the **Great White Throne**, framed between the slender neck of **Angels' Landing** (see p.354) to the right and the pipe-like formations of the lesser **Organ** to the left. Glowing at sunset, the throne is utterly majestic.

A mile or so on, the Scenic Drive comes to an end at a large parking lot that's rarely able to cope with the hordes of frustrated drivers hoping to leave their vehicles and hike the final mile towards the Narrows along the **Riverside Walk** (see p.355). This general area is known as the **Temple of Sinawava**, after a wolfish deity of the Paiute Indians; the most prominent single rock is the **Pulpit**, standing alone near the west bank of the river.

The Zion–Mount Carmel Highway

The side canyon formed by Pine Creek, half a mile north of the visitor center (see p.348), makes it possible for Hwy-9 to continue east, a route known as the **Zion–Mount Carmel Highway**. At first it heads straight for the **East Temple** – like its larger twin, topped by a forested mesa – but it's soon forced to start tacking its way up the hillside. At the eastern end of each extravagant switchback comes a better view of the enormous **Great Arch** at the head of the canyon. Measuring 720 feet wide by 580 feet high, this is not in fact an arch at all, but simply a deep alcove, or what's known as a "blind arch".

Zion National Park

Traffic regulations for the tunnels on Hwy-9 are summarized on p.348.

For accounts of Mount Carmel, Kanab and points east, see p.359 onwards.

For more detailed advice on desert hiking, see p.23.

*No **pets** are allowed on any of Zion's trails.*

Finally the highway burrows into the rock, entering the first and longer of two remarkable tunnels blasted through the canyon walls in the late 1920s. Five "windows" punctuate its one-mile length to allow air and light into the passageway, but you can't stop to admire the views. All the rubble from the excavation was allowed to tumble into Pine Creek far below; the river may seem innocuous, but it cleared the whole lot away in the space of a single year.

Easily seen on the enjoyable **Canyon Overlook Trail** (see opposite), the hot dry plateau beyond the eastern end of the main tunnel feels far removed from the lushness of Zion. These pale, smoothly undulating rocks, capped here and there by strange beehives and hoodoos, are the lithified remains of ancient sand dunes. One huge specimen, crisscrossed with stress lines from eons of erosion and resembling some long-abandoned pyramid, is known as the **Checkerboard Mesa**. It looms south of the highway a couple of miles past the second tunnel, just a quarter of a mile short of the park's East Entrance.

Hiking in Zion Canyon

Every visitor to Zion Canyon should **hike** at least one of its many trails; that's the only way to see the canyon in anything approaching its natural state. However, all trails except the short Riverside Walk require a stiff climb away from the canyon floor, and with summer temperatures in excess of 100°F and elevations of well over 6000 feet, it's all too easy to overdo things. Carry plenty of food and drink, and don't imagine that because you have no trouble walking five miles at home you can do it here, straight up a cliff. Water is available on most trails – although not until around five miles along the West or East rim trails – but must be purified before use.

As for specific **routes**, it makes sense to avoid the sun by hiking the east side of the canyon in the morning and the west in the afternoon. If you're reasonably fit and have just one day, the best combination is probably an hour or two along the **Riverside Walk** and a longer climb either to **Angels Landing** on the West Rim Trail or **Hidden Canyon** on the East Rim Trail.

All the trails detailed below start from parking lots along either Hwy-9 or the Scenic Drive, but some of the longer ones leave the canyon altogether and end up on backcountry dirt roads. If you're planning a one-way hike, look at the **shuttle board** in the visitor center, to see if you can swap vehicles with hikers coming in the opposite direction; *Zion Lodge* also operates a commercial **hiker shuttle service**.

Watchman Trail

Just inside the South Entrance, a right turning leads across the river to the *Watchman* campground (see p.350) and the start of the **Watchman Trail**. This steep mile-long climb switchbacks up a side canyon below Bridge Mountain, then heads back south to loop around a flat promontory below the Watchman itself. Thankfully, it doesn't go right to the top, but its views up the canyon, as well as across to the West Temple and back down to Springdale, tucked among the trees, are a good way to get your bearings when you first arrive. Until around 10am, the canyon walls keep most of the route in shade; later on, it's liable to be baking hot.

Canyon Overlook Trail

Opposite the ranger station at the eastern end of the long tunnel on the Zion–Mount Carmel highway (see opposite), steps cut into the rock mark the start of the **Canyon Overlook Trail**. So long as you don't mind edging along the brink of a precipice – at one point the trail consists of wooden planks braced against the cliff-face – this offers a fascinating variety of terrain in the space of just half a mile. The scenery along the way ranges from fern-filled grottoes fed by seeping water to a bare slickrock mesa topped by tiny hoodoos. An informative booklet, usually available at the trailhead, explains the flora and fauna you may spot.

The trail ends at a railed viewing area at the head of Pine Creek Canyon; you can't see it, but you're directly above the Great Arch. Only one of the tunnel's five "windows" is visible in the rock wall to your left, but the road emerges below to zigzag into the valley. Straight ahead of you is the west wall of Zion Canyon; a helpful sign labels the peaks ranged along the far side of the river, from the ruddy tree-capped West Temple to the paler Sentinel.

Emerald Pools Trail

The **Emerald Pools Trail**, which starts conveniently from *Zion Lodge*, is every bit as pretty as the name implies. It's also suitable for walkers of all levels, as the lowest of the three pools can be seen on a gentle round-trip stroll of little more than a mile, while the highest makes a good objective for a more energetic hike.

On the far side of the footbridge that crosses the Virgin River from the lodge, the pink-paved trail to the right is the direct route to the **lower pool**. After an easy climb through the forest, with views straight up the main canyon, it cuts left into Heaps Canyon, and soon reaches a huge overhang of red rock, streaked black by deposits from a broad cascade of water. The almost constant flow collects in pools that tend be a muddy red rather than an emerald green; the overhang is deep enough for the trail to circle inside them, running behind the waterfall.

From this point, the trail becomes confusing, with several alternative routes and countless "trails of use" made by lost or blundering hikers. If you're pressed for time, head back the way you came; alternatively, continue straight ahead, along the shelf on the canyon wall, and in just over half a mile you'll drop back to cross the river at the Grotto picnic area, half a mile north of *Zion Lodge*.

Allow around two hours to complete the two-mile round-trip hike on the Watchman Trail.

If you can grab one of the few parking spots, it takes around an hour to walk the Canyon Overlook Trail.

*The complete
loop to the
uppermost
pool and back
takes between
two and three
hours.*

*To hike the
West Rim
Trail, it can be
easier to park
at Zion Lodge
and walk or
take a shuttle
from there.*

Most hikers head instead for the **higher pools**, by following a narrow path through the cleft in the gigantic split boulder to the left. Having first doubled back to the top of the waterfall, where the stream bubbles out of the woods to spill across a lip of slickrock, take the spur trail to the right on the far side.

A hot hard climb of not much more than five minutes is rewarded by a delightfully cool seep-fed pool, at the foot of the monumental outer walls of the canyon. Climbing any higher is out of the question, but this is a good place to linger, with a small sandy "beach" and plenty of shade. Once back on the main trail, head right while still above the main falls to complete a loop back to the lodge.

Angel's Landing and the West Rim Trail

Serious hikers and backpackers rate the **West Rim Trail** as Zion's most compelling challenge. Even if you have nothing to prove, its views and variety make it well worth attempting, but it's not to be undertaken lightly. The first couple of miles involve a gruelling 1500-foot climb out of Zion Canyon, while to reach the obvious day-hike destination, **Angel's Landing** – a five-mile round trip from the valley floor – you have to brave a terrifying knife-edge ridge.

The trail starts across the river from the Grotto picnic area, half a mile north of the lodge. As it winds ever more steeply towards the sheer canyon wall, it seems impossible that there's any way on, but in the end it switchbacks several times and cuts back into a crack in the rock. Unless you've made a very early start, you'll have been out in the sun for a long time by now, and the cool shade of this narrow crevice – **Refrigerator Canyon** – comes as a merciful relief.

Soon however things get worse; beyond the brief flat stretch of the canyon you're confronted by a severe set of switchbacks known as **Walter's Wiggles**. Constructed during the 1920s and named for the park's then superintendant, these serve as a ladder up what would otherwise be an impassable cliff. At the top lies **Scout Lookout**, a tranquil patch of sand with views up and down Zion Canyon and a population of scavenging chipmunks that feast on the remains of countless well-earned picnics.

*The round-trip
hike to Angel's
Landing takes
a good four
hours.*

Daredevil day-hikers are invariably drawn to the spur trail from Scout Lookout to **Angels' Landing**. What you're letting yourself in for is obvious from the outset; the trail sets off along the top of the steep promontory straight ahead, with awesome drop-offs to either side, and only token stretches of metal chain to offer the illusion of security. The end is a hideous half-mile on, with a quarter-mile drop to the canyon floor at your feet and the Great White Throne towering a further thousand feet above you on the far side of the river.

Beyond Scout Lookout, the West Rim Trail climbs steadily out of the canyon. After crossing an expanse of slickrock, marked by small cairns and perilously close to the rim, it descends into a spectacular high-country valley. This is another side of Zion altogether,

rimmed with white cliffs, "checkerboarded" by the erosive formation known as cross-bed hatching, and scattered with rounded outcrops of layered sandstone. For a couple of miles, the trail picks its
way gingerly across the valley and up the far side, twice crossing
streambeds that even when not visibly flowing nurture forest
glades. Finally it runs into the monumental wall of red sandstone
that marks the head of **Behunin Canyon**, a huge side canyon off
Zion Canyon (itself way out of view). Doubling back, it clings to the
cliff face on a long exposed switchback that comes out on top of
Horse Pasture Plateau.

Just to set foot on Horse Pasture Plateau is a stiff target for a day-
hike from the floor of Zion Canyon, a total round-trip of something
over eleven miles. In the full heat of summer even that would be too
much to take on, but the trail continues north for another ten miles,
to **Lava Point** off the Kolob Terrace Road (see p.357), with plenty of
optional scenic detours en route. This is Zion's most popular backpacking trip, usually done as a two-day expedition, starting from
Lava Point and working down, and camping near the southern edge
of Horse Pasture Plateau.

*Backcountry
camping in
Zion requires
a permit; see
p.350.*

Riverside Walk

Not least because it involves no climbing, the mile-long **Riverside
Walk** at the end of the Scenic Drive is Zion's best-loved trail. Having
watched the canyon walls converge ever closer, the urge to find out
what happens beyond the end of the road is all but irresistible. You
may well have more company than you'd prefer, but the views from
the gentle paved footpath are too beautiful for that to matter.

*It's easy
enough to
complete the
Riverside Walk
in under an
hour, but
you'll enjoy it
more if you
allow much
longer.*

Walls of deep red sandstone soar to either side of the river, which
is flanked by shimmering cottonwoods that turn a rich gold in the
fall. There are even patches of low-lying "desert swamp", where bull-
frogs bellow in the rushes, and willows thrust from the mud.

Until recently, Riverside Walk was known as the "Gateway to the
Narrows Trail", as it ends where the Virgin emerges from **the
Narrows**, overlooked by the mighty **Mountain of Mystery**. For
eight miles upstream from this sandy little beach, the river fills the
entire gorge, often less than twenty feet wide and channelled
between vertical cliffs almost a thousand feet high. Conditions are
so treacherous that it's now illegal to hike any distance upstream
into the Narrows, against the current – hence the change of name.
However, assuming you'll want to cool your feet, you're free to
wade out from the beach, helped by one of the discarded walking
sticks usually to be found nearby.

*The trail
through the
Narrows is
usually pass-
able during
June, July,
September and
October only;
all hikers must
register at the
visitor center.*

When the danger of flash floods is considered minimal, hikers are
allowed to wade *downstream* through the Narrows from the far end.
The trailhead is at **Chamberlain's Ranch**, a thirty-mile drive from
Zion Canyon, reached by turning left 1.7 miles east of the East
Entrance (just east of milepost 46 on Hwy-9), and then following

North Fork Road, which in due course becomes a rough dirt track, for around seventeen miles north. Permits for the next day are issued from 5pm onwards at the visitor center; eighty people per day are allowed to make the ten-hour trip as a day-hike, while 68 are permitted to camp for one night only en route. It's no easy jaunt, with the water often icy cold and thigh- or even neck-deep, but at least you may be lucky enough to spot the unique Zion Snail, the size of a pinhead and found only in the Narrows.

Weeping Rock

One of the easiest short walks in Zion Canyon – and thus prone to be overcrowded in summer – is the half-mile round-trip hike to **Weeping Rock**. Eaten from the canyon wall by a perennial spring, this damp alcove is filled with ferns and tiny flowers; while it comes as a surprise in the desert, however, it's not as beautiful as you may be led to expect. The paved trail up starts from the parking lot at the mouth of Echo Canyon, halfway between *Zion Lodge* and the end of the road.

Hidden Canyon and the East Rim Trail

Rewarding hikes of almost any length can be enjoyed by taking the **East Rim Trail**, which sets off from the Weeping Rock trailhead but branches right rather than left on the far side of Echo Canyon Creek. Only backpackers who camp overnight on the mesa-top attempt its full 10.5-mile length, and they normally prefer to start from the far end, near the park's East Entrance. However, the strenuous two-mile climb out of Zion Canyon is its most exhilarating segment, and offers several spur trails for day-hikers.

Hidden Canyon is a three-mile, three-hour round-trip hike from the Scenic Drive.

The best goal for a half-day hike is **Hidden Canyon**, a "hanging canyon" that has yet to cut its way down to the floor of Zion. By the time the relevant spur trail leaves the East Rim Trail, you've switchbacked about half a mile up the face of Cable Mountain, but are still only half-way to the top. Hidden Canyon itself is a further half-mile on, beyond a brief stretch of forest and a hair-raising segment where the trail clings to a wall of rock. The broad "lip" of the canyon, perched 700 feet above Zion, turns into a waterfall after heavy rain, while the rounded holes scoured into the slickrock fill with water and life. Strictly speaking, the trail ends here; it's possible to press on into the canyon, but only expert rock climbers have any hope of approaching its head.

Allow six hours for the seven-mile round-trip hike to Observation Point.

The East Rim Trail keeps right on switchbacking beyond the Hidden Canyon turn-off. A mile or so further on, deep in wafer-thin Echo Canyon, the **East Mesa Trail** climbs steeply off to the left. A two-mile walk through the woods on top of the plateau brings you to **Observation Point**, which commands views all the way down Zion Canyon. The massive cliffs of Cable Mountain and the Great White Throne stare you full in the face, while Angels Landing towers proudly on the far side.

If you stick instead to the East Rim Trail, it takes a good mile or more to drag yourself up out of Echo Canyon, and there may be streams to negotiate en route. Atop the mesa, walking becomes much easier, as the trails simply follow former logging roads. **Stave Spring**, the only perennial water source on the East Rim Trail, is roughly halfway between Zion Canyon, five miles west, and the East Entrance, slightly further southeast. Overnight campers can at this point head southwest, along a trail that soon forks to the summits of **Cable Mountain** – where you can take a closer look at the century-old workings that hauled timber down into Zion (see p.347) – or Deertrap Mountain. Either hike is a six-mile detour from Stave Spring.

Zion
National
Park

Kolob Terrace Road

The only road access to the central uplands of Zion National Park is along **Kolob Terrace Road**, which branches inconspicuously north from Hwy-9 at the hamlet of **Virgin**, fifteen miles west of the park's South Entrance (see p.343). Especially in its earlier stages, it's a dramatic drive, deservedly proclaimed a Scenic Byway, but unless you have a high-clearance 4WD vehicle, you won't manage the full 43 miles to meet I-15 just south of Cedar City. Ordinary cars have to turn back after just over twenty miles, so only long-distance hikers or tourists with a spare afternoon to kill tend to come this way.

The Kolob Terrace Road is closed to all traffic in winter.

The road starts by climbing through a dry desert valley, dotted with pine trees, heading for two pyramidal mountains that dwarf the cliffs on the horizon. It dips repeatedly in and out of the park boundaries, reaching Zion after just over seven miles, only to exit almost immediately. As it next re-enters the park, you get superb views north across **Hop Valley** to the russet and white pinnacle of **Burnt Mountain**. Keen backpackers can hike to Kolob Arch from here along the **Hop Valley Trail**, but it's not as easy as it looks; you have to plough through thick sand for most of the way, so the fifteen-mile hike is even more difficult than the route described on p.358.

Soon after you leave the park yet again, twenty miles up from the highway, a dirt road to the right leads 1.7 miles to **Lava Point**, back within the park. As well as being the trailhead for the West Rim Trail, which takes fourteen miles to drop down into Zion Canyon (see p.354), this is a superb vantage point in its own right. Park rangers use the cabin at **Fire Lookout**, a short walk from the end of the road, to keep a vigilant eye on the forests of the Markagunt Plateau. Poised four thousand feet higher than the visitor center, it overlooks a panorama that stretches north to Cedar Breaks and southeast to the Kaibab Mountains, with the monoliths of Zion Canyon mere incidental details in the foreground. There's a **picnic area** and a free six-site primitive **campground** (with no water) nearby.

Kolob Terrace Road is paved for just under two miles beyond the Lava Point turnoff, passing a village of pastel cabins before it turns to dirt for the last mile to **Kolob Reservoir**. Locals flock to this drab little lake to cool off and play with their boats, but it holds no great interest for tourists.

Kolob Canyons

Located just off I-15, twenty miles south of Cedar City, the **Kolob Canyons** have formed part of Zion National Park since 1956. Although easier to reach than Zion Canyon, they remain far less famous and receive far fewer visitors. In all honesty, neither are they as immediately impressive as Zion Canyon, and you'll only get the most out of the area if you can spare the time and energy to **hike**. If you stay in your car, you can drive to the end of the five-mile road, admire the view of the red-rock canyons, and be back on the interstate within the hour, wondering what the fuss is about.

Information on the Kolob Canyons can be picked up from the small **visitor center** at exit 40 off I-15 (May–Sept daily 9am–5pm; Oct–April daily 9am–4.30pm; ☎801/586-9548). As well as providing free hiking advice, rangers also allot 24 numbered backcountry **campsites**. No gas or food is available.

Beyond the visitor center, **Kolob Canyons Road** twists alongside Taylor Creek and then up through Lee Pass. It ends at a parking lot that faces across the riverbed to a succession of narrow, red-walled **"finger" canyons** cut into the west rim of the Markagunt Plateau. Each was carved by a separate tiny stream; one, Hanging Valley, is interrupted by a sheer 1500-foot cliff, stranding an isolated patch of thick forest far above the valley floor. In the distance, you may just be able to make out the West Temple, above Zion Canyon.

Footpaths on the far side of the lot lead to a picnic spot in the woods. From here, the half-mile **Timber Creek Overlook** trail runs through low trees along the top of the ridge, to end at a rocky promontory with views over the endless rolling forests.

Hiking the Kolob Canyons

The two main **hiking trails** in the Kolob Canyons leave from earlier along Kolob Canyons Road. Starting two miles from the visitor center, **Taylor Creek Trail** follows the Middle Fork of Taylor Creek on a five-mile round-trip to **Double Arch Alcove**, passing cabins built by early homesteaders en route. The trail grows progressively less and less distinct before it culminates by climbing into the lush hollow in the canyon wall that lies beneath the Double Arch itself.

It takes around four hours to hike to Double Arch Alcove and back.

The **Kolob Arch Trail**, which ranks among Zion's very finest trails, leads down from Lees Pass along the drainage of Timber Creek. It can be muddy going at times, but at least there's usually plenty of water en route (purify before drinking). The first couple of miles, heading south, feature superb close-up views of the finger canyons; you then veer east to meet **La Verkin Creek** just above a waterfall. The goal for most hikers is **Kolob Arch**, seven miles along, which may or may not be the world's longest natural rock span. Like Landscape Arch, in Arches National Park (see p.420), it's in the region of 300 feet across; no one agrees how to measure arches any more precisely, so they're generally considered equals. Camping somewhere nearby (by prior arrangement at the visitor center) makes for a less gruelling hike, and gives you the option of exploring the remote regions that lie farther along La Verkin Creek.

East from Zion: US-89

Eleven miles east of the eastern entrance to Zion National Park (see p.352), Hwy-9 meets **US-89** at Mount Carmel Junction. Turn **north** from here, and once across a mountainous ridge you'll find yourself driving up the broad **Long Valley**, where the **Sevier River** cuts between the Markagunt and Paunsaugunt plateaus. After just over forty pretty but uneventful miles, punctuated by the occasional tiny Mormon settlement, you can choose between keeping straight on towards Salt Lake City, or veering east towards Bryce Canyon and the other national parks.

The only real point in heading **south** on US-89 is to reach Arizona, with the North Rim of the Grand Canyon (see p.323) almost exactly a hundred miles away. A century ago, when Mormons from Arizona would come this way to be married in the temple at St George, this route was known as the **Honeymoon Trail**. The largest town along the highway, **Kanab**, retains a strong Mormon identity, but it also has a genuine back-of-beyond frontier feel to it, and makes the best overnight stop in the vicinity.

Mount Carmel and Mount Carmel Junction

The eastward progress of Hwy-9 stops when a north–south wall of red cliffs rears up on the far side of the Virgin River. It's a bucolic spot, with cottonwoods lining the river and horses grazing in the meadows to the north. Unless you're ready to stop for the night, however, there's precious little reason to get out of the car.

MOUNT CARMEL JUNCTION, where Hwy-9 intersects with US-89, consists of a couple of fairly upscale and reliable **motels**, both with licensed **restaurants**. The *Best Western Thunderbird* (☎801/648-2203, fax 648-2239; winter ③, summer ④), which boasts a pool, spa and even half a golf course, has a slight edge over the *Golden Hills* (☎801/648-2268; winter ②, summer ③).

In the parent community of **MOUNT CARMEL**, a mile or two north, the summer-only *Mount Carmel Motel* (☎801/648-2323; ①) offers half a dozen rudimentary rooms and an unappealing RV site.

At fourteen miles, the day-hike to Kolob Arch and back is only for confident, experienced desert hikers.

Hwy-14 from Cedar City and Cedar Breaks (see p.341) joins US-89 halfway between Mount Carmel and the Bryce turn-off.

South from Mount Carmel: Coral Pink Sand Dunes State Park

*The park
remains open
24 hours, with
a $4 day-use
fee; informa-
tion is on
☎ 801/874-
2408.*

Few areas in the Southwest conform so exactly to the popular notion of a desert – graceful dunes of fine sand, their parallel crests sweeping towards the horizon – as **Coral Pink Sand Dunes State Park**. This pseudo-Saharan landscape, a dozen miles south of Mount Carmel Junction, is reached by two separate paved roads that leave US-89 four and nine miles southeast of town respectively.

The only dune field in the Colorado Plateau lies at the foot of a seven-mile bluff of the Vermilion Cliffs, which here unusually face the northwest. Its sand grains are so uniformly small because they've already been sifted at least twice by the winds that still keep them swirling; the Navajo sandstone from which they've eroded was itself originally deposited in the form of dunes.

Hikers who launch themselves from the boardwalk near the entrance station usually find that a few minutes of wading knee-deep in sand sates their *Lawrence of Arabia* fantasies. However, in marked contrast to Utah's federal parks, **off-road vehicles** are positively encouraged. The park was created in response to campaigns by local off-road enthusiasts, and plays host to countless formal and informal **dune buggy races**, most notably each July 4.

The well-shaded **campground** (Sun–Thurs $9, Fri & Sat $10; for $5 summer-only reservations, call ☎ 1-800/322-3770) remains open all year, though it only has water in summer. Spending a night here offers the enticing prospect of seeing not only kangaroo rats but, more to the point, the snakes that prey on them.

Kanab

Until new roads were pushed through the region in the 1950s, **KANAB**, seventeen miles southeast of Mount Carmel Junction and just two miles from the Arizona state line, was renowned as perhaps the most inaccessible town in the US. Now it's a significant tourist halt, thanks to a position halfway between the Grand Canyon, eighty miles southeast, and Bryce Canyon, 83 miles northeast.

Kanab started life as **Fort Kanab**, a frontier outpost so prone to Indian attacks that it only survived from 1864 until 1866. The town itself was founded by Jacob Hamblin in 1870, as a God-fearing ranching community with a sideline in harbouring Mormons who fell foul of the federal government, such as the perpetrators of the Mountain Meadows Massacre (see p.338). That lawless image was later cultivated by pulp novelist Zane Grey, while Kanab's rugged surroundings made it a focus for Western movie-makers from Tom Mix, who filmed *Deadwood Coach* here in 1924, to Clint Eastwood.

Ranching in southern Utah has long been in decline, but the citizens of Kanab would still much prefer to wrest their living from the earth. Their biggest payday came in the late 1950s, when this was the original base for the construction of Glen Canyon Dam (see p.393). During the eighteen months it took to upgrade the 72-mile dirt road to the dam site, and build the new town of Page, locals scurried to grab their share of the 200 million federal dollars that were pumped into the project. In November 1958, the workers decamped for Page, and the boom was over.

East from Zion: US-89

Since then, Kanab has pinned its hopes on the prospect of large-scale coal-mining on the **Kaiparowits Plateau** to the northeast. The environmentalists and national politicians who thwarted such plans in the 1970s were burned in effigy on the streets of Kanab, while the town closed down in protest for an hour in October 1996 when President Clinton's declaration of Grand Staircase–Escalante National Monument (see p.374) precluded that possibility forever.

"Green" actor Robert Redford was among those burned in effigy in Kanab in 1976, which may explain why fewer movies are filmed here these days.

Kanab has thus been left to survive by catering for tourists, which it does with reasonably good grace. US-89 is lined with an above-par assortment of motels and restaurants, with the greatest concentration where it briefly doglegs to run east–west along **Center Street**. A few blocks south, US-89 proper branches off east towards Page, while US-89A continues south into Arizona.

Apart from some large Western-themed souvenir stores, such as *Denny's Wigwam*, opposite *Parry Lodge* at 78 E Center (☎801/644-2452 or 1-800/854-8549), there's almost nothing to do in Kanab. Hikers may enjoy the views from the **Squaw Trail**, which leads up the cliffs a few blocks north of downtown, but if you're looking to fill the southern Utah equivalent of a rainy afternoon your best bet is to drive fifteen miles east on US-89 to **Johnson Canyon**. A bizarre local legend says this red-rock canyon conceals a fortune in Aztec gold, smuggled out of Mexico as their empire fell. More prosaically, it's home to a mock-Western township built for the TV series *Gunsmoke*, and also featured in movies such as *How The West Was Won* (daily dawn–dusk; $3, under-18s free).

For an account of Fredonia AZ, seven miles south of Kanab, and the route to the Grand Canyon, see p.328 onwards.

Information

Kanab's **visitor center** – slogan, "The Greatest Earth on Show" – is just south of Center Street at 78 S 100 E (Nov–Feb Mon–Fri 9am–5pm; March, April & Oct Mon–Sat 8am–6pm; May–Sept daily 8am–6pm; ☎801/644-5033 or 1-800/733-5263).

The zip code for Kanab is UT 84741.

Accommodation

Kanab holds a number of good-value budget **motels**, so don't feel compelled to pay extra for a fancier name. All are within easy walking distance of downtown, but since you probably won't want to walk anywhere that makes little difference.

Best Western Red Hills, 125 W Center St; ☎801/644-2675 or 1-800/528-1234, fax 644-5915. Strangely ugly, somewhat over-priced, but very central motel. Large modern rooms plus a pool and whirlpool. Winter ③, summer ④.

Canyonlands International Hostel, 143 East 100 South; ☎801/644-5554. Friendly private hostel, a block east of the highway near the visitor center, that offers $10 dorm beds plus kitchen, library and laundry. ①.

National 9 Aiken's Lodge, 74 W Center St; ☎801/644-2625 or 1-800/524-9999. The ideal budget motel: crisp and clean, right in the heart of town, and with its own pool. ②.

*The price
codes used
here are
explained on
p.15.*

Parry Lodge, 89 E Center St; ☎801/644-2601 or 1-800/748-4104, fax 644-2605. Opened in 1931, Kanab's oldest motel has an undeniable air of romance, with its lobby and restaurant festooned with photos of movie-star guests and name-plates to tell you which rooms they (officially) slept in. You can even bathe in John Wayne's extra-large bathtub. *Parry's* isn't *that* great, though, and some of the newer rooms are both dingy and noisy, even if you can get room service from the restaurant. Winter ③, summer ④.

Shilo Inn, 296 West 100 North; ☎801/644-2562 or 1-800/222-2244, fax 644-5333. Large but very presentable motel, at the north end of town. Some rooms have kitchens, and there's a pool and spa. Winter ③, summer ④.

Super 8, 70 South 200 West; ☎801/644-5500 or 1-800/800-8000, fax 644-5576. Dependable budget motel, with large pool and hot tub, in a quiet location a block south of Center Street. Winter ②, summer ③.

Eating

Around twenty formulaic **restaurants** cling to the edge of the highway as it passes through Kanab, safe in the knowledge that however bad they may be, there's not a better place to eat for a hundred miles in any direction.

Four Seasons Fifties-Style Restaurant, 36 North 300 West; ☎801/644-2635. Fun mock-Fifties diner, with a 10¢ jukebox and a menu of burgers, sandwiches and fried meats, to be washed down with (nothing stronger than) copious malts and shakes. Closes 7pm in winter.

Houston's Trails End, 32 E Center St; ☎801/644-2488. Western-themed family diner, with chicken-fried steaks, fish and fried breakfasts.

Nedra's Too, 310 South 100 East; ☎801/644-5030. Informal local place on the south side of town at the junction of US-89 and US-89A. The unifying factor of the Mexican/American menu is the frier; even the ice cream comes deep-fried, while if you're a newcomer to this neck of the woods you might want to sample the first Navajo taco of your life (see p.26).

Parry Lodge, 89 E Center St; ☎801/644-2601. This atmospheric dining room is as close as Kanab comes to having a gourmet restaurant, with a menu that occasionally hints at the healthy, in the form of dishes like poached salmon, and a licence to sell alcohol. Open all day in summer, dinner only in winter.

North from Mount Carmel: Orderville

*Orderville has
a couple of
shabby motels,
but neither is
worth recom-
mending.*

If you turn north on US-89 at Mount Carmel (see p.359), you'll arrive within four miles at **ORDERVILLE**. From 1875 onwards, this now-negligible settlement was the scene of the longest-lasting of several experiments in communitarian living organized by the **United Order**, a Mormon group that believed all property should be held in common. Each family had its own cabin inside a stockade, but meals were eaten en masse, and each member received the same pay. A man earned $1.50 per day and a woman 75¢, as credit at the village store; money left unspent returned to the pool. In 1886, when Orderville's children were drifting away in search of better-paid work, their parents gave up and shared out their assets.

Glendale

Five miles beyond Orderville, the almost equally insignificant hamlet of **GLENDALE** nestles amid a cluster of apple orchards. A white clapboard house that looks much like the rest – complete with a large upstairs verandah – is grandly designated the *Smith Hotel*, and holds seven pleasant en-suite B&B rooms (☎ & fax 801/648-2156; April–Oct only; ③). The *Home Place*, 200 S Main St (☎801/648-2194; ③), is similar, smaller but slightly more upscale.

Hatch

Long Valley steadily dries out north of Glendale, so travellers from Cedar City who pick up US-89 at the east end of Hwy-14 – see p.341 – encounter further upland forests rather than farmland.

At 7000ft up, little **HATCH**, 25 miles on, makes a cool overnight stop in summer, but that's the only time its handful of motels are at all busy. Both the central *Mountain Ridge Motel* (☎801/735-4258; ②), and the *Riverside Motel*, a mile north (☎801/735-4223, fax 735-4220; ③), have half a dozen basic but reasonable rooms, plus **camping** facilities.

Red Canyon and the road to Bryce

The only road in a hundred miles that manages to climb through the wild country east of US-89 is **Hwy-12**, which was blasted into the rocks ten miles north of Hatch to provide a route to **Bryce Canyon** and beyond. Another seven miles' drive from here brings you to the town of Panguitch, but there's a modern, comfortable motel right at the intersection, in the shape of *Bryce Junction Inn* (☎801/676-2221 or 1-800/437-4361, fax 676-2291; winter ②, summer ③).

Hwy-12 climbs away from US-89 by way of **Red Canyon**. For information on this small precursor of the joys ahead, call in at the Dixie National Forest **visitor center** (☎801/676-8815), a few miles along on the left. This parking lot marks the start of the short Pink Ledges **hiking trail**; longer trails leave from the forest service's *Red Canyon* **campground** ($7, no showers; ☎801/865-3700), half a mile further on. Immediately beyond that, the highway tunnels through two artificial red-rock arches, before topping out on top of the Paunsaugunt Plateau, with another ten miles to go before Bryce.

Panguitch

The squeaky-clean Mormon town of **PANGUITCH** – 24 miles from Bryce, and fifty from Mount Carmel Junction – was established in 1864, and named for no good reason after the Paiute for "Big Fish". After an uncertain start, when like so many of its neighbours it was abandoned in the face of Indian attacks, Panguitch prospered. It became, and remains, the largest town along the Upper Sevier Valley. That was originally due in part to the brick factory responsible for the distinguished brick homes that still adorn its streets, but Panguitch today depends heavily on tourism for its bread and butter. It's a bit too chilly to linger in the off-season, but in summer the pumps at the eight local gas stations rarely stop spinning (one, *Todd's Truck Stop*, stays open 24hr), and twenty-odd budget motels and restaurants are kept busy.

Panguitch's **visitor center**, a roadside cabin at 800 N Main St (May–Oct daily 9am–5pm; ☎801/676-2311), doles out details of a **walking tour** of the town's historic homes. You'd have to be more than a little weird, however, to spend your morning doing that rather than setting off into the wondrous deserts on your doorstep.

The zip code for Panguitch is UT 84759.

Accommodation

An invisible network seems to connect Panguitch's many **motels**, meaning their rates can vary minute by minute according to demand. Broadly speaking, however, peak season runs from late spring to early fall, and you should be able to find a seriously inexpensive room at most other times, although a few winter skiers choose to stay here rather than in Brian Head (see p.341)

The price codes used here are explained on p.15.

Bryce Canyon International Hostel, 190 N Main St; ☎801/676-2300. Dorm beds for $12 in a small, fairly scruffy but very central brick house.

Color Country Motel, 526 N Main St; ☎801/676-2386 or 1-800/225-6518, fax 676-8484. Recently refurbished motel, with around twenty traditional rooms on two stories and a large pool. Winter ②, summer ③.

Historic Panguitch Inn, 50 N Main St; ☎801/676-8871 or 1-800/331-7407, fax 676-8340. Restored inn in the very heart of town, open May–Oct only and offering good clean rooms at low rates and a huge covered parking area. Spring and fall ②, summer ④.

Marianna Inn, 699 N Main St; ☎801/676-8844 or 1-800/331-7407, fax 676-8340. Scrupulously clean, well-run motel on the northern edge of town, near several restaurants, with units ranging from one to four beds. Operated by the same management as the *Panguitch Inn*. Winter ②, summer ⑤.

Sands Motel, 390 N Main St; ☎801/676-8874 or 1-800/497-9261, fax 676-8445. Traditional low motel units with a pastel-blue trim, plus a tiny pool. ②.

Eating

The number of **restaurants** in Panguitch must run into double figures, though it feels more like there's just one restaurant that's repeated at fifty-yard intervals along the highway. You could always pig out on *Pringles* in your motel room instead.

Buffalo Java, 47 N Main St; ☎801/676-8900. Summer-only student hangout, serving espresso coffees plus soups and snacks.

Country Corner Cafe, 80 N Main St; ☎801/676-8851. Predictable family diner, right in the heart of town, and open from 6am daily.

Cowboy's Smokehouse Bar-B-Q, 95 N Main St; ☎801/676-8030. Feast on barbecued meats and huge fruit pies under the impassive gaze of generations of stuffed elk heads. Open for lunch Mon–Sat and dinner nightly, with Western music at weekends.

Flying M, 580 N Main St; ☎801/676-8008. Stacks of breakfast pancakes, and the usual diner-style meals later in the day. Up at the north end of town, and the only place in Panguitch licensed to sell beer.

North of Panguitch: Fremont Indian State Park

US-89 keeps going **north of Panguitch**, following the course of the Old Spanish Trail beside the Sevier River. Travellers heading for **Salt Lake City**, a total of 230 miles distant, can join **I-15** by cutting northwest after ten miles, or stay on US-89 until it meets **I-70** around sixty miles north.

There's no room in this book to cover the myriad small towns along the way, and Utah's mountainous heartland is in any case a far cry from the deserts to the south. However, if you're interested in native cultures of the Southwest, you may want to visit **Fremont Indian State Park**, just off I-70 eight miles east of US-89 (summer daily 9am–6pm; winter daily 9am–5pm; $5 per vehicle). Although the park preserves the site of a large Fremont village, occupied around 1100 AD and discovered during the construction of the interstate, you soon find out that the village has in fact been completely destroyed. However, easy short trails lead through canyons filled with rock art, and the artefacts and arrowheads in the excellent little museum bring the Fremont peoples to life.

The most convenient overnight base nearby is **RICHFIELD**, twenty miles northeast, where budget **motels** include a good *Super 8*, 1575 N Main St (☎801/896-9204, fax 896-9614; winter ②, summer ③), and the *Little Wonder Cafe*, 101 N Main St (☎801/896-8960) is an appealing local diner.

Bryce Canyon National Park

Few more freakish landscapes can exist than those confined within **BRYCE CANYON NATIONAL PARK**. From the safety of the park's rim road, visitors gaze down upon a throng of red, yellow and orange pinnacles of rock, eating like the flames of a forest fire into the thickly wooded plateau. Braver souls can hike down into the inferno and thread their way between the top-heavy towers, to explore a barren desert that's aglow with almost psychedelic colours.

Paiute Indians, who hunted in the vicinity for many generations, had an elegantly precise word for it: *Unkatimpe-wa-Wince-Pockich*, "red rocks standing like men in a bowl-shaped recess". The current name comes from the Mormon settler **Ebenezer Bryce**, who established a short-lived homestead nearby in 1874, and memorably declared that it was "a helluva place to lose a cow". "Bryce's Canyon"

BRYCE CANYON NATIONAL PARK

Dixie
National
Forest

Paunsaugunt Plateau

Park
Headquarters

Fairyland
Point

Pink Cliffs

Fairyland Canyon

Rim Trail

Sunrise
Point

Sunset
Point

Ski Trail

Bryce Canyon

Inspiration
Point

Bryce
Point

Paria
View

Tropic Valley

Swamp
Canyon

Swamp Canyon
Connecting Trail

Whiteman
Connecting Trail

Under-the-Rim-Trail
(Bryce Point to Rainbow Point)

Piracy
Point

Fairview
Point

Natural
Bridge

Agua
Canyon

Ponderosa
Point

Rainbow
Point

Yovimpa
Point

Bristlecone
Loop Trail

Riggs Spring
Loop Trail

0   Miles   3

N

▷ Escalante (33 miles)

▷ Tropic (1 mile)

Park
Headquarters

FAIRLAND LOOP TRAIL

QUEEN'S GARDEN
TRAIL

Queen's
Garden

North

Sunrise
Point

Lodge

Thor's
Hammer

Sunset
Point

Sunset

Silent City

Wall St.

NAVAJO
LOOP TRAIL

PEEKABOO
LOOP TRAIL

Inspiration
Point

Bryce
Point

RIM TRAIL

0   Miles   1

N

is not however a canyon at all, but a row of crescent-shaped amphitheatres, hollowed into a twenty-mile stretch along the eastern edge of the **Paunsaugunt Plateau**. At up to 9000ft above sea level, this marks the final and most spectacular rung of the Grand Staircase's ascent of southern Utah (see p.331). Between sixty and forty million years ago, the **Pink Cliffs** were deposited in layers of varying thickness and strength on the beds of shallow lakes. Some are limestone, some siltstone; all were dyed and stained with combinations of red, white, orange, blue or yellow by different concentrations of minerals, especially iron.

Conditions at Bryce are perfect for rapid erosion, with ice forming overnight and thawing in the morning over 200 times per year. Water seeps into cracks in the ground, then expands as it freezes, to wedge the cracks ever wider. Spurs emerge from the cliff-face as it recedes, then dwindle to slender fins and eventually break into separate standing columns. When the topmost rock of a column is hard enough, lower levels erode away beneath it at a much faster rate. A mighty boulder left precariously perched on a tall, narrow pillar is known as a **hoodoo**. At Bryce, thousands upon thousands of hoodoos are crammed into each successive amphitheatre, to form a menagerie of multihued and contorted stone shapes. The best known, and most precarious, is **Thor's Hammer**, near Sunset Point.

Since it became a national park in the 1920s – with its irregular boundaries designed to minimize the impact on local ranchers – Bryce Canyon has deservedly ranked as a must-see attraction for any visitor to Utah. If you're at all stretched for time, however, this is one park that you can realistically hope to see in the space of a single day, or even an afternoon. Just be sure that you do at least get out of your car, and hike into the technicolour ravines – far more vivid than the Grand Canyon, as well as much more human in scale. Most visitors pass through between June and August, but the park is if anything even more inspiring in the stillness of winter, when the hoodoos rear their heads from a blanket of snow.

Getting to Bryce

Bryce Canyon is around two hours' drive from Zion Canyon, 86 miles southwest, and something over three hours from Capitol Reef, 120 miles northeast. The only approach is along **Hwy-12**, which runs within the northern boundaries of the park on its way across southwest Utah. However, you won't see the rock formations – or be liable for the entrance fee – unless you turn south off the main highway thirteen miles east of US-89 (a total of 20 miles southeast of Panguitch), or eight miles northwest of Tropic (see p.372). **Hwy-63** reaches the park entrance station after a further three miles, then traces the rim of the Paunsaugunt Plateau for eighteen miles before coming to a dead end at Rainbow Point.

*Oddly enough,
Bryce Canyon
Airport is
among the old-
est in the US,
with pine-log
hangars built
by the WPA in
the 1930s.*

*All the nation-
al park passes
detailed on
p.21 are valid
in Bryce.*

*To receive
information by
mail, write to
Bryce Canyon
National Park,
Bryce Canyon
UT 84717.*

No public **buses** serve Bryce, but both *Scenic Airlines* (☎801/702/739-1900 or 1-800/634-6801) and *Air Vegas* (☎801/702/795-7144) fly from Las Vegas to **Bryce Canyon Airport** on Hwy-12. Once on the ground, rent a car from, or join a tour with, *Bryce Canyon Scenic Tours* (see below).

Finally, keen **hikers** should note that it's possible to avoid the crowds by walking into the park from **Tropic** (see p.372).

Arrival and information

After you've paid Bryce's $5-per-vehicle-per-week **entrance fee** at the ranger station, the logical first stop is the **visitor center**, a short way beyond (mid-June to mid-Sept daily 8am–5pm; mid-Sept to mid-June daily 8am–4.30 pm; ☎801/834-5322). A valuable source of information on current weather and hiking conditions, this is also the place to pick up backcountry permits (see opposite).

For information on **guided tours**, call at either *Bryce Canyon Lodge*, inside the park, or *Ruby's Inn*, outside it to the north; see below. The *Lodge* is the base for *Bryce Tours*, which operates a busy schedule of **driving tours** in summer (☎801/834-5361; adults $4.95, under-13s $2), and also *Canyon Trail Rides* (☎801/679-8665), which arranges **horseback expeditions** (2hr $25, half-day $35). *Bryce Canyon Scenic Tours* (☎801/834-5200 or 1-800/432-5383), at *Ruby's Inn*, runs a **shuttle service** in summer between the visitor center, campgrounds and the major stops on the rim road ($5 for an all-day pass), as well as two-hour driving tours ($18), while *Ruby's Outlaw Trail Rides* (☎801/679-8761), has a similar programme of **horse** rides.

Flight-seeing companies based at Bryce Canyon Airport include *Aladdin Air* (☎801/834-5555 or 1-800/914-3215) and *Bryce Canyon Helicopters* (contact via *Ruby's Inn*; ☎801/834-5341)

Bryce Canyon practicalities

Accommodation within the park itself is restricted to the venerable *Bryce Canyon Lodge*, located one hundred yards from the rim between Sunrise and Sunset points, and open between April and November only. This atmospheric stone-and-timber affair offers a handful of luxurious suites (⑥), a row or two of rough-hewn but very comfortable individual cabins (⑤), and about fifty rather ordinary motel rooms (④). All tend to be reserved several months in advance, through *Amfac Parks & Resorts*, 14001 East Iliff Ave, #600, Aurora CO 80014 (☎303/297-2757, fax 338-2694).

The main lobby of the *Lodge* holds a fascinating large-scale relief model of the park, and leads to a good-quality **dining room**, open for all meals, plus several souvenir stores.

A few minutes' walk away, slightly north of Sunrise Point, the *General Store* stocks basic groceries, snacks and camping equipment, and holds a laundromat and public showers.

*The closest
towns offering
a range of
motels are
Panguitch
(see p.363)
and **Tropic**
(p.372).*

Motels near the park

Bryce Canyon Lodge can only hold a tiny proportion of Bryce's summer influx, and is closed altogther in winter. However, half a dozen alternative options loiter just outside the park along highways 12 and 63; the cluster at the intersection is loosely known as **Pink Cliffs Village**, though there's no village to speak of. All remain open year-round, with considerably reduced rates in winter, and have their own unenthralling restaurants.

Best Western Ruby's Inn, PO Box 1, Bryce UT 84764; ☎801/834-5341 or 1-800/528-1234, fax 834-5265. Large motel complex a mile or so outside the park on Hwy-63. Fifty of the 350 rooms feature whirlpool baths, and there's a full programme of tours. Nov–March ②, April, May & Oct ③, June–Sept ⑤.

Bryce Canyon Hostel, PO Box 640006, 13500 E Hwy-12, Bryce UT 84764; ☎801/834-5351 or 1-800/834-0043, fax 834-5256. Simple budget hostel at the intersection in Pink Cliffs Village, three miles from the park entrance, offering dorm beds from $12, and bike rental. ①.

Bryce Canyon Pines, PO Box 43, Bryce UT 84764; ☎801/834-5441 or 1-800/892-7923, fax 834-5330. Reasonable, modern, anonymous motel, three miles west on Hwy-12, with a strangely shallow swimming pool.

Foster's Motel, Star Route, Panguitch UT 84759; ☎801/834-5227 or 1-800/475-4318, fax 834-5304. Cheap if somewhat shabby motel, just under two miles west of the park turn-off on Hwy-12. Winter ②, summer ③.

Camping

Both of the in-park **campgrounds** are first-come, first-served, and cost $7 per night. The **North Campground** stretches alongside the Rim Trail a short walk from the visitor center, while **Sunset Campground** is a mile or so south, across the highway from the lodge near Sunset Point. They're usually open, weather permitting, from early May until late October; in summer, all 218 sites tend to be filled by early afternoon. Neither campground offers RV hookups, and the closest showers are by the *General Store*.

Backcountry campers can choose from several designated sites, all south of Bryce Point below the rim and well away from the main trails. Pick up a permit at the visitor center, and take lots of water.

The nearest **commercial campground** to the park is the slightly more deluxe area adjoining *Ruby's Inn*, a mile north (see above; $12 per site), which also caters for RVs. If your heart is set on a night in the woods, head instead for the roadside campground at **Red Canyon**, ten miles west on Hwy-12 (see p.363).

Seeing the park

Most visitor activity at Bryce is concentrated around **Bryce Amphitheater**, the largest and most accessible of the indentations in the Pink Cliffs. Park off the loop road that leaves Hwy-63 half a mile south of the visitor center, and a brief walk will bring you to the brink of the crescent-shaped depression.

Bryce Canyon National Park

Dawn and dusk are the prime times to take photos at Bryce.

Fairyland Point, reached via a separate turn-off north of the visitor center, is one of Bryce's quietest yet most scenic viewpoints.

Quite where along the Rim Trail you get your first blast of the incandescent rocks makes little difference. Of the two official overlooks, around five hundred yards apart, **Sunrise Point** to the north gets slightly less of the tour-bus crowds than **Sunset Point** to the south. Neither name is particularly appropriate; both face east, so you won't see the sun set, while the best place to catch the dawn is **Bryce Point**, a mile or more further south. Here at the southernmost tip of the amphitheatre, you can look back west as the first rays of the sun strike the toy soldiers below. At any time of day, the views to the east and north are astonishing, ranging as much as a hundred miles to encompass the Aquarius Plateau and the Henry Mountains.

Beyond Bryce Amphitheater, Hwy-63 – also known as the **Scenic Drive** – meanders south for another fifteen miles. It's a slow drive, passing a succession of substantially similar viewpoints; no one stops at them all, though each has its merits. Look out in particular for the **Natural Bridge**, which spans a steep gully around halfway along. Suspended far above the forest, it doesn't cross running water, so technically it's not a bridge but an 85-foot arch.

Hwy-63 climbs steadily as it continues south, until finally the ridge it's following narrows to a slender neck, and it's forced to end at the highest viewpoint of all, **Rainbow Point**. Both this and nearby **Yovimpa Point** command sweeping views south, to Navajo Mountain and the Kaibab forest that fringes the Grand Canyon.

Hiking

The **Rim Trail** follows the lip of the plateau for just over five miles, skirting Bryce Amphitheater between Sunrise and Sunset points, and die-hard backpackers can continue beyond its ending at Bryce Point all the way to Rainbow Point, 22.6 miles on, along the **Under-the-Rim Trail**. By far the most popular trails in the park, however, are those that drop into **Bryce Amphitheater** itself. With several alternative routes to the bottom, and a choice of connections once you're there, you can tailor a hike to suit whatever time you have, from a couple of hours to a full day.

The basic experience is much the same whichever trail you take. The rock stratum that has eroded to form the hoodoos, just below the rim, averages from 300 to 500ft thick, so hiking consists of descending between them until you reach the flatter pine forest beyond, walking through the woods, and then climbing back up again. At an elevation of almost two miles, even a brief hike involves considerable effort; you'll need good footwear and plenty of water.

Allow two hours to enjoy the Navajo Loop Trail without exhausting yourself in the process.

For a concentrated burst of Bryce at its best, the **Navajo Loop Trail** is ideal. The shortest and busiest trail of all, it plummets abruptly from Sunset Point into a group of formations known as the **Silent City**, then circles back up to complete a hike of 1.4 miles. Taking its steeper right-hand branch as you set off makes for an easier hike, and also brings you by way of a precipitous set of switchbacks straight into the cool crevice of **Wall Street**. In places this awe-inspiring gulf of orange rock is less than twenty feet wide, but it's too deep for the 800-year-old Douglas firs that grow from its sandy floor to poke their heads above the cliffs.

Beyond Wall Street, you swiftly reach a small sandy wash. The return leg of the Navajo Loop Trail starts a short way to the left, and follows a slightly gentler incline back to Sunset Point, passing **Thor's Hammer** and other humungous hoodoos en route. Alternatively, continue northwards on the level footpath just above the wash, pausing perhaps to rest in the shade of the pines and junipers. The basin known as the **Queen's Garden** is something over a mile along. Named for an almost translucent fin that's topped by a rocky pile bearing a vague resemblance to Queen Victoria, it's connected by a mile-long trail up the hillside to **Sunrise Point**. During its climb, the path cuts repeatedly through limestone fins and spurs, with each tunnel framing another irresistible photograph. Most of the horseback expeditions in the park – see p.368 – pass this way. Dwarfed beneath the ludicrous, multi-coloured spires and turrets, the horses make an especially surreal spectacle.

As described on p.368, it's possible to hike straight into the most spectacular parts of Bryce Canyon from Tropic.

From Bryce to Capitol Reef: Scenic Hwy-12

Indisputably the most scenic of southern Utah's fifteen or so designated "Scenic Byways" has to be the hundred-mile stretch of **Hwy-12** that connects Bryce Canyon with Capitol Reef. Only completed in 1980, thanks to the difficulty of the terrain and the lack of towns en route, it skirts the southeastern edge of the **Aquarius Plateau**, the highest segment of the Colorado Plateau.

No driver could fail to be awed by Hwy-12's ever-changing panoply of red-rock canyons, crystal-clear rivers and unexpected oases. Most of the visitors who scurry between the national parks in summer remain firmly in their cars, however. The **Escalante River**, which drains this whole region, was the last river to be named, let alone explored, in the continental US, and to this day most maps show the area as a vast blank. Towns such as **Escalante** and **Boulder** make a fairly token effort to accommodate tourists, but you could easily pass through without noticing those few hiking trails and back-country roads that do exist.

All that may be on the point of changing. Over the years, the Mormon inhabitants of this wonderland have made it clear that they'd rather be farming, logging and mining than running motels, but the debate finally seems to be over. In September 1996, faced with renewed proposals to open large coal mines south of Escalante, President Clinton declared the entire region, from the Aquarius Plateau south to Lake Powell, to be under federal protection as the **Grand Staircase–Escalante National Monument** (see p.374).

Tropic

The first community east of Bryce is **TROPIC**, eight miles from the park turn-off. Among the migrants from Panguitch who settled this tiny hamlet in the 1880s – naming it for its allegedly superior climate – was Ebenezer Bryce himself (see p.365). His restored log cabin is now the centrepiece of the *Pioneer Village* motel.

*The **zip code** for Tropic is UT 84776.*

Tropic may turn its back on the flamboyance of Bryce Canyon, ranged along the ridge above it, but it has little appeal of its own; the main street consists of a row of motels and drive-ins, and strolling around the centre is unrewarding. However, the unmarked road that leads west from Bryce's cabin reaches the park boundary in a couple of miles, from where it's a further two-mile hike up to the main formations.

Accommodation

*As explained on p.15, **accommodation prices**, excluding taxes, are indicated throughout this book by the following symbols:*

① *up to $30*
② *$30–45*
③ *$45–60*
④ *$60–80*
⑤ *$80–100*
⑥ *$100–130*
⑦ *$130–175*
⑧ *$175–250*
⑨ *$250+*

You don't gain much by staying in Tropic rather than the motels closer to the park, but it does have quite a reasonable range of **accommodation**. None of the motels expects you to hang around during the day; they don't have pools, for example.

Bryce Pioneer Village, 80 S Main St; ☎801/679-8546 or 1-800/222-0381, fax 679-8607. Complex of dull but adequate motel rooms, with showers not baths, and more atmospheric individual cabins, transplanted from the park and equipped with two double beds as well as either baths or showers. Cabins ②–④, rooms ④.

Bryce Point B&B, 61 North 400 West; ☎801/679-8629. Cheerful family-run B&B attached to private house; all the five large rooms have picture windows facing Bryce Canyon, plus their own baths and TVs, and there's also a shared deck with hot tub. ③.

Bryce Valley Inn, 200 N Main St; ☎801/679-8811or 1-800/442-1890, fax 679-8846. Plain, large motel, with on-site restaurant and souvenir shop. Nov–March ②, April–Oct ④.

Country Inn Motel, 141 N Main St; ☎801/679-8632 or 679-8633, fax 679-8605. Conspicuous modern motel, beside a gas station in the heart of town, with its own store and diner. Nov–March ③, April–Oct ④.

Francisco's B&B, 52 Francisco Lane; ☎801/679-8721 or 1-800/842-4136. Three not especially fancy en-suite B&B rooms in a log-built home, located a block off the main street half a mile south of the centre, and offering all you-can-eat breakfasts. ④.

Eating

No one would make a special trip to eat in Tropic's limited array of restaurants, but once you're here it's not worth driving anywhere else either.

Doug's Place, *Country Inn Motel*, 141 N Main St; ☎801/679-8632. Bustling diner attached to large convenience store, which gets really busy at breakfast time and doesn't make all that romantic a rendezvous for dinner.

Hungry Coyote, *Bryce Valley Inn*, 200 N Main St; ☎801/679-8811. Fully licensed Western-themed restaurant, open for all meals but specializing in giant evening steaks.

The Pizza Place, Hwy-12; ☎801/679-8888. Quick, functional pizza joint, which also does take-outs and deliveries.

Kodachrome Basin State Park

At the village of **CANNONVILLE**, five miles south of Tropic, Hwy-12 veers east across the Paria River. Continue south along Paria Valley instead, on Cottonwood Canyon Road, and the pavement runs out after eight more miles at **Kodachrome Basin State Park**. This assortment of contorted rocky columns, tucked beneath the cliffs that climb to Kaiparowits Peak, was named in honour of the latest *Kodak* film by a *National Geographic* photographer in 1948, who felt that the area's existing name of Thorny Pasture was too prosaic.

The main focus of the park is a geological phenomenon unique to this spot on earth, its 67 **sand pipes**. Each of these misshapen pillars was formed as an underground geyser, created by an earthquake and then blocked with tough calcite sediment. When the softer rock that surrounded them eroded away, they were left towering as much as 150ft above the scrubby plain.

Having paid the $4 day-use **fee** at the entrance station, follow the road for a couple of miles to the left to reach the park's attractive **campground** (Sun–Thurs $9, Fri & Sat $10; ☎801/679-8562). Various trailheads along the way mark the start of short hikes among the formations. Alternatively, the unpaved road that forks right from the entrance station ends after a little over a mile at the trailhead for **Shakespeare Arch**. A pleasant quarter-mile walk brings you to a small high natural arch, named for the park manager who first noticed its existence in 1976, from where you can get good views across the valley to the Pink Cliffs of Bryce Canyon.

To arrange a **horse ride** *through Kodachrome Basin, contact Scenic Safaris in Cannonville (☎801/679-8536).*

When the weather is good enough – check with the park rangers – ordinary vehicles can drive beyond Kodachrome Basin into the new Grand Staircase–Escalante National Monument, along the unpaved section of Cottonwood Canyon Road. Ten miles east, a spur road leads north to the intricate double **Grosvenor Arch**, while the main road turns south, and meets **US-89** thirty miles on, roughly halfway between Kanab and Page.

Henrieville and the Upper Valley

Hwy-12 climbs northeast from Cannonville, passing through the speck that is **HENRIEVILLE** and then ascending the clay cliffs known as "The Blues". On the far side lies the unexpected sight of the high but fertile **Upper Valley**, kept well watered by snowmelt from the Aquarius Plateau.

Escalante

A group of Mormon militiamen who pursued Indian raiders through the Upper Valley in 1866 noted the potential of the meadowland beyond, and dubbed the region "Potato Valley" in honour of its abundant wild sweet potatoes. Within ten years, acting on their own initiative rather than Church pressure, several returned to

**From Bryce
to Capitol
Reef: Scenic
Hwy-12**

*The story of
John Wesley
Powell's two
Colorado-River
expeditions is
told on p.401.*

establish a ranching and farming community. They called it **ESCALANTE**, on the suggestion of a passing member of John Wesley Powell's second expedition, despite the fact that the Spanish explorer-priest Fray Silvestre de Escalante (see p.476) never came within a hundred miles of here.

Life was harsh during Escalante's early years; the pioneers spent their first winter, 1875–76, huddled in primitive dugouts. Then came a period of deceptive ease, as their sheep and cattle multiplied on the open range. By 1910, however, it was becoming apparent that the native grasses on which they grazed were not growing back. The land has never recovered, and Escalante has remained frozen at much the same size and appearance ever since.

Escalante is a neat enough little town, with its main street gently sloping down from west to east and a couple of blocks of four-square brick and timber homes to either side. It's also a screamingly dull place to spend the night, though the wilderness that stretches away in every direction more than makes up for that.

Grand Staircase–Escanlate National Monument

The first proposal to create **Escalante National Monument** was submitted to Franklin Roosevelt by Secretary of the Interior Harold Ickes in 1940. Its boundaries would have enclosed 4.5 million acres, stretching from Lees Ferry as far as Moab and Green River, and taken in 280 miles of the Colorado River, 150 miles of the Green River, and 70 miles of the San Juan. That vast area was then crossed by just one road, and no bridge spanned the Colorado.

In principle, Roosevelt saw himself as an environmentalist, but the greenery of the Hudson River Valley was far more to his taste than the red rocks of the West. In the face of vociferous Mormon opposition in Utah, not to mention the coming of war, the idea was quietly dropped.

When Canyonlands National Park was created in the early 1960s (see p.403), it included only a small proportion of Ickes' suggested tract. Glen Canyon on the Colorado River was by now submerged beneath Lake Powell (see p.390), while the **Kaiparowits Plateau**, which stretches south of Escalante all the way to the lake, remained outside federal protection. That was thanks to pressure from economic interests in southern Utah, acutely aware that what they call Fifty-Mile Mountain stands on top of the world's largest known deposits of coal.

Plans to mine the Kaiparowits Plateau have been the focus of repeated rumours and campaigns for well over fifty years. The closest any came to fruition was in the 1970s, when *Southern California Edison* announced its intention to open a 6000-acre mine, complete with a network of new roads and an on-site electricity generating plant. Controversy over the scheme pitted the so-called **Sagebrush Rebels** – an informal but powerful grouping of Utah's Mormon-dominated business elite, plus the workers whose livelihoods were at stake – against environmentalists from across the nation. Although the abandonment of the project in 1976 was largely due to a slackening of demand for electricity in California, communities

If you do find yourself here in the daytime, the most interesting spot in the immediate vicinity is **Escalante State Park** ($4 day-use fee; information on ☎801/826-4466). Located beside an artificial lake a mile up Wide Hollow Road, which turns north off Hwy-12 just west of town, this holds Utah's largest concentration of **petrified wood**. Two short trails lead through a miniature "forest" of lithified logs, and there's a fully equipped **campground** (Sun–Thurs $9, Fri & Sat $10; for reservations, $5 extra, call ☎1-800/322-3770).

Information

A summer-only kiosk at 100 E Main St (mid-May to mid-Sept daily 10am–6pm; ☎801/826-4810), next to the *Padre Motel*, handles enquiries about Escalante itself. For information on hiking and camping in the surrounding region, head for the **visitor center** of the Grand Staircase-Escalante National Monument, at 755 W Main St (Nov–March Mon–Fri 8am–5pm; April–Oct daily 7am–6pm; ☎801/826-5499), next to City Park at the west end of town.

From Bryce
to Capitol
Reef: Scenic
Hwy-12

For more about petrified wood, see the account of Arizona's **Petrified Forest National Park** *on p.249.*

---

such as Kanab, desperate for jobs, took out their anger by burning effigies of green activists in the streets.

In 1980, a study commissioned by Congress showed that almost 400,000 acres on the Kaiparowits Plateau had already been logged to clear the way for mines. Much of that timber was processed at a mill in Escalante, and when green opposition resulted in a moratorium on tree-felling, Escalante too witnessed its own share of public "hangings". During those years, any stranger with licence plates from the notoriously tree-hugging state of California could expect a frosty welcome in the diners of Hwy-12.

Hopes that mining money might revitalize the economy of Escalante rose once more in the mid-1990s, with the news that a Dutch conglomerate was considering strip-mining the Kaiparowits. By now, however, many observers felt that the pro-mining lobby had become merely a vociferous minority, and President Clinton decided that a grand gesture designed to appeal to environmentalists in every state was more important than appeasing the business community in Utah. On September 18, 1996 – little more than a month before his re-election – he therefore took the stage at the Grand Canyon to declare the creation of the **Grand Staircase–Escalante National Monument**.

Promptly condemned by Utah legislators as "the mother of all land grabs" and "a monumental blunder – pun intended", the new monument is like the final piece in a jigsaw puzzle, placing the left-over lands between Bryce, Capitol Reef, the Dixie National Forest and the Glen Canyon NRA under federal control. Only the farming valleys around towns such as Tropic, Escalante and Boulder remain in private ownership. In the short term at least, the plan is to preserve this huge area as wilderness, rather than "develop" it for tourism; to that end, uniquely, it's being administered not by the National Park Service but by the Bureau of Land Management. Locals can fish, and continue to graze their animals here, until usage is finalized, but no new mining claims can be filed.

From the municipal airport, a couple of miles east of town, *Jaggar Aviation* (☎801/826-4461) runs **scenic flights**, costing from $65 for a half-hour loop over Waterpocket Fold to $190 for an all-day air-and-ground tour of the Grand Canyon.

Accommodation

Escalante's half-dozen tiny **motels** have recently been joined by the more sizeable *Prospector Inn*. Public **campgrounds** nearby include those at Escalante State Park (see p.375) and Calf Creek (see p.378).

*The price
codes used
here are
explained on
p.15.*

Bunkhouse Motel, *Escalante Outfitters*, 310 W Main St; ☎801/826-4266, fax 826-4388. Hikers' and campers' supply store that has seven rudimentary cabins out back, for backpackers who don't mind roughing it, with joint use of a bathhouse. ①.

Circle D Motel, 475 W Main St; ☎801/826-4297, fax 826-4402. Basic old-style motel, perched at the west end of town, where the identikit units share a long wooden verandah. ②.

*The zip code
for Escalante
is UT 84726.*

Moqui Motel, 480 W Main St; ☎801/826-4210. Mundane motel and RV park on the edge of town, as the highway sweeps away westwards. ②.

Prospector Inn, 380 W Main St; ☎801/826-4653, fax 826-4285. Escalante's newest and largest motel, the first to boast a second storey, offers large twin-bedded rooms. ③.

Rainbow Country B&B, 585 East 300 South; ☎801/826-4567, or 1-800/252-8824. Small, friendly B&B; comfortable en-suite rooms share use of a hot tub, large common room and a mountain-view verandah. Local tours available. ③.

Eating

Restaurants seem to struggle to survive in Escalante, and with only so many nondescript diners to choose from it's hard to stretch a night on the town much beyond twelve and a half minutes.

Cowboy Blues Diner & Bakery, 530 W Main St; ☎801/826-4251. Diner/steakhouse, with a Mexican flavour and a few vegetarian alternatives.

Golden Loop Cafe, 39 W Main St; ☎801/826-4433. Typical small-town diner, smack in the middle of downtown Escalante.

Prospector Inn, 380 W Main St; ☎801/826-4653. Conventional motel restaurant, with an emphasis on pancakes by day and steaks by night.

Hell's Backbone

While Hwy-12 is by far the quickest route between Escalante and Boulder, summer thrill-seekers can choose instead to take a forty-mile trip across the top of the Aquarius Plateau, along the old "Upper Road". Turn north on the 300 East block in Escalante, and the paved **Forest Road 153** heads up Pine Creek Canyon, to reach the appealing mountain-set **Posey Lake** fourteen miles on.

Turn east at the lake, onto Hell's Backbone Road, and the fun begins. Having crawled up the flanks of the 10,000-foot Roger Peak, this dirt track teeters along the slender ridge known as **Hell's Backbone**, with sheer drops down to Sand Creek on one side and

Death Hollow on the other. The best views come at the hair-raising bridge halfway along; the bizarrely named **Box-Death Hollow Wilderness Area** far below can only be penetrated on foot. For the last ten miles, as it descends through the woods to Boulder, Hell's Backbone Road is paved, but the backcountry section is usually closed by snow between October and late May.

Hole-in-the-Rock Road

These days, **Hole-in-the-Rock Road**, which turns south from Hwy-12 five miles east of Escalante, is emphatically a dead end. More than fifty slow, hard miles from the highway, its progress is halted by a landslide of tumbled boulders, high above the waters of Lake Powell. When it was created, however, over a century ago, it was intended to become the most direct route across southern Utah.

In November 1879, the 230 Mormon pioneers of the **San Juan Mission** gathered outside Escalante. Intent on reaching their new home, almost 200 miles east, they were convinced they'd find a short cut along the uncharted east flank of the Kaiparowits Plateau and across the Colorado. Even when confronted with the abyss of Glen Canyon, their faith saw them through. In the space of six weeks, they dynamited a narrow slit in a fifty-foot cliff – the **Hole in the Rock** – until it was wide enough to squeeze through. Despite snow and ice they then used ropes to lower 83 wagons down a precipitous "road" that descended 1800ft to the river in less than three quarters of a mile. Once there, they ferried the whole lot across the Colorado on makeshift rafts, and then repeated the entire process to escape the canyon on the far side. A mere hundred more miles of desert brought them to the townsite of **Bluff** – see p.440 – which they established on April 6, 1880. All 230 members of the party had lived through the trek, and they'd been joined by three babies born en route.

Hole-in-the-Rock Road has never been paved, but its first forty miles are passable for ordinary vehicles for most of the year. Staff at the National Monument visitor center in Escalante (see p.375) can provide details of the many opportunities for hikers wishing to set off into the wilderness. The most accessible area is **Devil's Garden**, thirteen miles along, which features an assortment of rock arches and hoodoos.

By the time you reach the trailhead at **Hurricane Wash**, another twenty miles on, the road parallels the soaring Straight Cliffs to the southwest, which form the eastern edge of the Kaiparowits Plateau. A five-mile hike from here leads between the swelling walls of a side canyon to **Coyote Gulch**. In the five miles before this spellbinding creek drains into the Escalante River, you'll pass several gorgeous sandstone bridges and arches. The potential for multi-day hikes up or down the Escalante itself – which for most of its length lies inside the boundaries of the Glen Canyon National Recreational Area (see p.389) – is almost limitless.

The return drive along Hole-in-the-Rock Road takes roughly six hours; be sure to carry water and emergency supplies.

Shortly after Hurricane Wash, Hole-in-the-Rock Road reaches **Dance Hall Rock**, a natural amphitheatre where the 1879 party staged dances to keep its spirits high. Beyond it, the gravel surface gives way to bare slickrock, only negotiable in high-clearance vehicles. The original **Hole in the Rock** lies just past the last parking lot, fifteen miles on. Keen hikers can scramble over the rocks that block it and pick their way down to the lake, which has obliterated the final thousand feet of the pioneers' primitive pathway.

Calf Creek Falls

At an extravagant curve in the road, five miles on from the Hole-in-the-Rock turn-off, a viewpoint beside Hwy-12 looks out over the main channel of the Escalante River. It takes five more miles for the highway to drop down to the river, which it crosses on a low bridge that's designed to allow floodwaters to flow harmlessly over.

Look out for the parking lot at **Calf Creek**, a short distance further on and a total of sixteen miles east of Escalante. There's a nice little **campground** right here, with minimal facilities ($5 per night), but most visitors simply come for the day, to make the six-mile round-trip hike to **Calf Creek Falls**. This beautiful upstream stroll, along a clearly-marked trail, passes ancient petroglyphs and soaring sandstone walls before culminating in a lushly fertile dell. The water cascading 126 feet down the cliff ahead is invariably freezing, but that's no reason not to take a dip in the pool below.

Allow 4 to 6 hours to hike to Calf Creek Falls and back.

If the Calf Creek trail gives you a taste for exploring the Escalante, enquire in Escalante for details of down-river hikes. Backpacking any distance involves wading along the riverbed; the rewards are immense, but don't underestimate the difficulties.

Boulder

BOULDER, thirty miles beyond Escalante, is not so much a town as a group of farms scattered across a pleasant high-mountain valley. Cattle ranching in this remote spot started in 1889, but it was another fifty years before it was connected by road with the outside world, and in that time it acquired a reputation as Utah's own little Shangri-La. Now that it's just another stop on the highway, what magic it may once have had has largely gone.

For more about the Anasazi, see p.468.

As the western terminus of the controversial **Burr Trail** (see p.386), Boulder is an ideal launching point for explorations of the backcountry of Capitol Reef, but few visitors spend much time in the valley itself. On a shallow knoll beside Hwy-12 in the heart of town, **Anasazi Indian Village State Park** holds the excavated and partly reconstructed remains of an ancient Indian pueblo (mid-May to mid-Sept daily 8am–6pm; mid-Sept to mid-May daily 9am–5pm; $1.50). Its 83 rooms were occupied by the Kayenta Anasazi between 1129 AD and 1169 AD, when the whole complex was destroyed by fire. A six-room replica at the end of the ruins trail illustrates their daily life, which revolved around farming along Boulder Creek.

Practicalities

Boulder offers only minimal facilities for visitors. *Pole's Place*, opposite the state park at 465 N Hwy-12 (☎801/335-7422; ③), is a summer-only **motel** with its own cafe and store, while the *Circle Cliffs Motel* nearby (☎801/335-7353; ①–②) is in fact a pink-painted family house that offers three far-from-fancy guest rooms. There's an information kiosk, open erratic hours in season, outside the *Burr Trail Cafe* (☎801/335-7432), a summer-only diner at the junction of Hwy-12 and the Burr Trail.

Boulder Mountain

Hwy-12 is at its most sublime in its newest segment, the 35-mile link between Boulder and Torrey, an hour's drive north. This eastern segment of the Aquarius Plateau is also known as **Boulder Mountain** or Boulder Top. Once the highway has climbed out of Boulder Valley, a succession of roadside lookouts survey fabulous vistas to the east, across a sea of gold and red sandstone outcrops to the Waterpocket Fold and beyond.

Primitive Forest Service **campgrounds** en route include those at **Oak Creek**, fifteen miles along, and **Pleasant Creek** a little further on, where a ranger station can provide full details.

Torrey

Poised at the intersection of highways 12 and 24, eleven miles west of Capitol Reef National Park, **TORREY** has thrown its lot in firmly with the tourist trade. As a result, it has quietly prospered while so many of its neighbours have faltered. It still consists of little more than one pretty tree-lined street plus a handful of slightly stark brick motels on a ridge to the west. However, for visitors who see their evenings as opportunities to meet other travellers, Torrey is the most exciting prospect for at least a hundred miles.

In summer, you can pick up local **information** from a hut (open irregular hours) in the forecourt of the gas station that faces the highway intersection.

Accommodation

Torrey holds well over a hundred **motel** rooms, with rates that range across the full spectrum. If you'd rather **camp**, there are a few private campgrounds in town, such as at the *Torrey Trading Post*, 75 W Main St (☎801/425-3716), but the public sites along Hwy-12, or in the national park, are far more attractive.

*The **zip code** for Torrey is UT 84775.*

Best Western Capitol Reef Resort, 2600 E Hwy-24; ☎801/425-3761 or 1-800/528-1234, fax 425-3300. New, well-equipped motel, three miles east of

Torrey, with great views and a good pool. The closest option to the national park, and the base for trail rides into it. Nov–March ③, April–Oct ④.

Capitol Reef Inn & Cafe, 360 W Main St; ☎801/425-3271. Plain, older motel, just off the highway in the heart of town, looking south to Boulder Mountain. On-site restaurant (see below) and bookstore. Winter ②, summer ③.

Chuckwagon Motel, PO Box 750180; ☎801/425-3335 or 1-800/863-3288, fax 425-3434. Well-kept two-storey "log cabin" motel, beside a tiny church in the town centre, with a couple of cheaper rooms. Winter ②–③, summer ③–⑤.

Days Inn, PO Box 750080; ☎801/425-3111. Clean, modern, friendly chain motel, facing the intersection at the east end of town. Winter ③, summer ④.

The price codes used here are explained on p.15.

Sky Ridge B&B, PO Box 750220; ☎801/425-3222. Five nonsmoking en-suite B&B rooms in tasteful, imaginatively furnished modern home, on the way towards central Torrey from the intersection. ④.

Super 8, 600 E Hwy-24; ☎801/425-3497 or 1-800/800-8000, fax 425-3496. Brand-new chain motel, with indoor pool and all facilities. ③.

Wonderland Inn, PO Box 750067; ☎801/425-3775 or 1-800/458-0216, fax 425-3212. Attractive property, consisting of several spruce new buildings and a separate covered pool, all perched on a bluff just above the highway intersection. Winter ②, summer ③.

Eating

Whether it's the pressure of competition or just a little local pride, the **restaurants** and **diners** of Torrey make considerably more effort to please than you may have come to expect of southern Utah.

Brink's Burgers Drive-In, 165 E Main St; ☎801/425-3710. Summer-only burger bar; a slap-up feed that's a notch or two above the usual standard.

Cafe Diablo, 599 W Main St; ☎801/425-3070. Surprisingly inventive restaurant, offering a slight Southwestern twist to the usual meats and fish. Closed for breakfast, and open mid-April to Oct only.

Capitol Reef Inn & Cafe, 360 W Main St; ☎801/425-3271. Long-established cafe that serves Torrey's best food, using fresh ingredients like just-caught local trout. The amazing ten-vegetable salad can form part of a real vegetarian feast, and there are sumptuous banana pies and espresso coffees to follow.

Wonderland Restaurant, PO Box 750067; ☎801/425-3775. Large, efficient diner at the *Wonderland Inn*; the best item on the menu is the halibut.

Capitol Reef National Park

Capitol Reef National Park, the second largest of Utah's five national-al parks, is also the least visited. Life might be different if it bore the name originally proposed by locals – **Wayne Wonderland**, this being Wayne County. As it is, that word "reef" seems to confuse visitors. It refers to the fact that the hundred-mile rock wall thrust up by the **Waterpocket Fold** presented an almost impenetrable obstacle to nineteenth-century travellers, who therefore likened it to a reef on the ocean. Add the resemblance of the rounded "knobs" of white sandstone that top its central section to the dome of the US Capitol in Washington, and you have "Capitol Reef".

CAPITOL REEF NATIONAL PARK

Capitol Reef National Park

Apart from the unusual name, Capitol Reef is very much of a piece with the Southwest's other national parks. Within its 378 square miles lie hidden canyons, verdant valleys and strange rock formations whose colours are drawn from an extravagant palette of golds and greens, reds and whites. Despite stretching for over a hundred miles north to south, the park is often less than ten miles wide. The one east–west highway, **Hwy-24**, crosses it in under twenty miles, following the gorge of the Fremont River. It's an impressive drive, but that's nothing rare in southern Utah, and you could easily pass straight through Capitol Reef without feeling any great urge to stop. Only if you take the time to explore will you get a sense of the magic of the place, and why it fully deserves its national-park status.

Even a couple of hours is enough to admire the western cliffs from the dead-end **Scenic Drive**, south of the park headquarters at **Fruita**. Given half a day or more, you could venture all the way south to Lake Powell on the unpaved **Notom–Bullfrog Road**, tracing the eastern flank of the Waterpocket Fold, or loop back westward via the **Burr Trail**, halfway along. With **hiking trails** of all lengths and levels setting off into the wilderness, it would be easy to spend a week in this one park.

The best **seasons** to visit Capitol Reef are spring, when the fruit trees blossom and the wildflowers bloom, or fall, when the crowds have gone, the cottonwoods change colour, and hiking conditions are at their peak. Midsummer temperatures can reach 100°F, and August in particular is prone to flash-flooding, but so long as you set your sights appropriately low – say, to lazing on your back in the orchards, eating fresh fruit – a summer visit is not such a bad idea.

The Geology of Capitol Reef

The **Waterpocket Fold**, which slopes from north to south for the full hundred-mile length of Capitol Reef National Park, is what geologists call a **monocline**, created when layers of sedimentary rock buckled under pressure roughly sixty million years ago. Within the last ten million years, it has in turn been lifted a mile or so above sea level by the general raising of the Colorado Plateau. Most of the original fold has long since eroded away; the reef itself is just the rump. Its western face consists of a long, jagged cliff of hard rock; it rises more gently from the east, in multi-coloured waves of sandstone that the Navajo called the "Land of the Sleeping Rainbow".

Here and there, the Fold is pierced right through by deeply incized canyons. Often hundreds of feet deep but less than twenty feet wide, these slender gorges were mostly blocked by fallen rocks until Mormon pioneers cleared a way through. After summer thunderstorms, rainwater can cascade through the canyons in fearsome flash floods. At other times, it collects in depressions worn into the rock – the "**waterpockets**" for which the whole mighty edifice is named.

A history of Capitol Reef

Although traces of human occupation date back ten thousand years, the first known inhabitants of the Capitol Reef region were the **Fremont Anasazi**. This subgroup of the Anasazi farmed along the valley of the Fremont River between 700 AD and 1300 AD, when changes in the climate forced them to move on. Archeologists distinguish them from their more sophisticated cousins to the southeast by the fact that they lived in pithouses dug into the hillsides, rather than in brick houses, and the lack of domesticated dogs or turkeys. The most enduring signs of their presence are the intriguing **petroglyphs** still to be seen on the canyon walls.

After many centuries when only the occasional Paiute hunter passed this way, a small group of Mormons established a permanent settlement beside the Fremont in 1878. The orchards they planted transformed the landscape, and when the post office insisted they gave their community a proper name, a few years later, **Fruita** seemed the perfect choice. The population of the fledgeling town never rose above fifty, however, and it was soon suggested that the region had more future as a park than a home. The immediate vicinity of Fruita became Capitol Reef National Monument in 1937, and that was upgraded to national park status when it was enlarged to include the entire Waterpocket Fold in 1971. Former Fruita townspeople and their heirs are still entitled to graze cattle within the park, but ranching is slowly being phased out.

Arrival and information

The defunct village of **Fruita**, at the heart of the park, ranges for a mile or so around the intersection of Hwy-24 and the Scenic Drive, eleven miles east of Torrey. Bryce Canyon is 120 miles southwest, the I-70 town of Green River a hundred miles northeast; no **public transport** passes this way.

The **visitor center**, right at the road junction, has the usual exhibits and handouts (summer daily 8am–7pm; winter daily 8am–4.30pm; ☎801/425-3791). In addition to the free *Cliffline* newspaper, pick up the dated but detailed 50¢ driving guides to *The Waterpocket Fold* and *The Valley Of Cathedrals*.

Only visitors who embark on the Scenic Drive, beyond the visitor center and campground, become liable for the **admission fee** of $4 per vehicle, $2 for motorcyclists, cyclists and pedestrians. All the nationwide passes detailed on p.21 are both sold and accepted.

There are no motels or lodges inside the park; the closest **accommodation** is in Torrey (see p.379). Torrey is also the place to rent a **bike** (*Pedal Pusher*; ☎801/425-3378 or 1-800/896-5773) or to arrange a **4WD** tour of the park (*Hoodoo Rivers & Trails*; ☎801/425-3519 or 1-800/332-2696); both cost around $60 per day. **Horse** rides, through *Pleasant Creek Trail Rides* of Bicknell (☎801/425-3315 or 1-800/892-5497), are closer to $100 per day.

Capitol Reef
National
Park

For more about the Anasazi of the Colorado Plateau, see p.68.

*The closest **gas station** to Capitol Reef is at the junction of hwys 12 and 24 in Torrey.*

To receive information by mail, write to Capitol Reef National Park, HC 70 Box 15, Torrey UT 84775.

Camping

All three **campgrounds** in Capitol Reef are first-come, first-served and do not take reservations. By far the largest and most popular is the **Fruita Campground** ($8), which makes a good overnight stop even if you never see the rest of the park. Set amid the orchards, a mile south of the visitor center, it remains open all year, but has no showers and in winter can be without water altogether.

Both the **backcountry** campgrounds – much smaller and more primitive, and free – are 35 miles from the visitor center. **Cedar Mesa** is 22.5 miles south of Hwy-24 along the Notom–Bullfrog Road, while **Cathedral Valley** is 25 miles north of Hwy-24 along either the Hartnet Road (which requires you to ford the Fremont River) or the **Caineville Wash Road**. To camp elsewhere in the backcountry, you must have a free permit from the visitor center.

Driving through the park

At its simplest, driving through Capitol Reef on **Hwy-24** takes well under half an hour. However much of a hurry you may be in, it's worth pausing once or twice en route. Rather than a token pit stop at the visitor center, try taking a five-minute hike from one of the clearly-marked trailheads.

The first of these lies a short distance south of the highway, roughly three quarters of the way from Torrey to the visitor center. The brief climb to **Gooseneck Point** is rewarded with a 500-foot view down into the canyon of Sulphur Creek, an "entrenched meander" that once curved across a flat floodplain but has been etched deep into solid rock by the uplifting of the Colorado Plateau.

An even more stupendously sinuous gorge can be seen in Goosenecks State Park, in southeast Utah; see p.439.

Hwy-24 passes the visitor center on the right a couple of miles further along, though the huge, fluted red-rock butte known as the **Castle** to the left is bound to catch your eye first. Whether you fork right to join the Scenic Drive, or continue on the main highway, you'll reach the heart of the village of **FRUITA** within a few hundred yards, where Sulphur Creek meets the **Fremont River**. You may want to peep into its former **schoolhouse**, just north of the highway. Built in 1896, it hasn't had a pupil for over fifty years; park rangers, not a Mormon schoolmarm, keep it spick and span.

The village's old **orchards**, however, are Capitol Reef's crowning glory. A waxy, luxuriant green against the steepling red cliffs, they hold almost three thousand trees planted by the pioneers. The cherries and peaches **blossom** in the first half of April, the apples slightly later, while the **harvest** lasts from the second half of June until well into October. So long as you stay in the orchards, you can eat as much fruit as you like; you only pay for what you take away.

Not far beyond the schoolhouse along the highway, the **Fremont Culture Walk** is an easy amble beside a canyon wall that's crammed with ancient **petroglyphs**. As well as stylized representations of goats and Bighorn sheep, some show how the Fremont people (see p.365) may have seen themselves – unless of course these strange helmeted figures, with triangular bodies and massive shields, really did come from other planets.

Hwy-24 crosses the Fremont two miles east of the visitor center, near the start of the longer **Hickman Bridge Trail** (see p388). Only beyond this point does **Capitol Dome**, high above the north bank another half-mile ahead, resolve itself into a dome; so far you've seen it from the side, as a slender fin. By now Fremont Canyon is at its deepest, and it's joined within the next couple of miles by **Chimney Rock Canyon** from the north and **Grand Wash** from the south (see p.387). A mile past Grand Wash stands the sandstone cabin of one of Fruita's earliest settlers, **Elijah Behunin**, with the eastern boundary of the park another 2.5 miles down the road.

The Scenic Drive

Other than Hwy-24, the only paved road in Capitol Reef is the **Scenic Drive**, which parallels the golden cliffs of the Waterpocket Fold for twelve miles south from the visitor center. The first couple of miles lead through Fruita, where a cluster of restored barns and houses serve as homes for park employees, while overnight visitors camp out in the orchards.

Beyond the village, and the park's fee station, the road undulates through the desert, dipping into dry sandy washes and then climbing scrubby rolling hillocks. Successive individual pinnacles, such as **Fern's Nipple** and the **Egyptian Temple**, line the crest of the red-rock battlements to the east. Until Hwy-24 was pushed through the Fremont Canyon in 1962, this unlikely route was southern Utah's main east–west thoroughfare. For a century, traffic squeezed its way between the narrow walls of **Capitol Gorge**, at the far end. The gravel Capitol Gorge Road now peters out after a mile or two, but hikers can continue on foot, to see the Pioneer Register where early wagon-drivers carved their names (see p.388).

The Notom–Bullfrog Road

If you'd rather survey the Waterpocket Fold from the comfort of your car than sweat it out on foot, the long drive south along the **Notom–Bullfrog Road** is Capitol Reef's best option. Just be sure to stock up on gas and water; you'll have to drive at least seventy miles to find any facilities.

The road leaves Hwy-24 nine miles east of the visitor center, not far outside the park. Only its first four miles are paved, as far as the tiny but well-irrigated settlement of **NOTOM**, now home to perhaps half a dozen ranchers. Thereafter, its rough surface repeatedly rip-

Other rock art sites in Utah are described on p.410 and p.412.

ples into a "washboard" as it follows a dry-as-dust bench above Sandy Creek, with the eerie badlands of the Waterpocket Fold to the west and the volcanic **Henry Mountains** to the east.

Ordinary vehicles should have no problem negotiating the full length of the Notom–Bullfrog Road, which re-enters the park twenty miles along, and then leaves it again in the southeast corner fifteen miles on. Seventy miles from the highway, after a final 25-mile segment where you find yourself constantly stopping to swoon at the turquoise expanse of Lake Powell on the southern horizon, you come to the modern marina at **Bullfrog** (see p.396).

The Burr Trail

These days, most drivers who set off south on the Notom–Bullfrog Road don't make it to Bullfrog, but complete a loop around the Waterpocket Fold by branching onto the **Burr Trail**. This is the only road actually to cross the fold, rather than slice through it, and it does so by means of a fearsome set of switchbacks that climb west from the Notom–Bullfrog Road, roughly halfway down.

The Burr Trail began life as a rutted wagon trail, which was upgraded by uranium prospectors in the 1940s and 1950s. The four miles within the national park remain unpaved, but the remaining thirty, running west to Boulder on Hwy-24, were paved during the late 1980s. Wilderness advocates argued that increased road use would irreparably damage one of Utah's least-spoiled regions; Garfield County authorities, keen to grab a piece of the Capitol-Reef action from their neighbours in Wayne County, went ahead anyway. From their point of view, they were just in time; the area has since been incorporated into the Grand Staircase–Escalante National Monument, which will probably preclude further road construction.

If all that leaves you feeling too guilty to take the Burr Trail, you're missing out. The panorama that unfolds as you ascend the switchbacks and head west is out of this world. Looking back across the Notom–Bullfrog Road, you see the top of Swap Mesa – whose coal deposits may well be the next target of the mining companies – and the stark Henry Mountains. Just past the topmost ridge, the Upper and Lower sections of **Muley Twist Canyon** stretch to north and south through the heart of the Fold. Both provide excellent opportunities for multi-day backpacking expeditions, starting from near the highway. Where the pavement begins, as you leave the park, an extraordinary procession of reefs marches south, with the white canyons of the Waterpocket Fold in the foreground and four or five craggy red cliff-faces beyond, leading on to Lake Powell.

The oval plain just west of the park, ringed by the Circle Cliffs, was described by the nineteenth-century geologist Clarence Dutton as "a spot which is about as desolate as any on earth". The Burr Trail leaves it by way of the deep **Long Canyon**, then struggles on to reach Hwy-24 immediately south of Boulder (see p.378).

Cathedral Valley

Capitol Reef's least accessible section is **Cathedral Valley**, north of the highway. Like the Notom–Bullfrog Road, it parallels the eastern side of the Waterpocket Fold, but the territory here is much more forbidding than the sagebrush plain to the south. In among the heavily eroded red, blue and grey hills lie deep canyons and primeval gardens, populated by strange stone monoliths. Unless you have your own 4WD or high-clearance vehicle, however, you'll only see it by joining one of the 4WD tours detailed on p.383.

Two roads run north into the backcountry from Hwy-24, 11.5 and 18.6 miles east of the visitor center. The first, **River Ford Road**, traverses the Fremont River by means of a crude ford a few hundred yards along. If you're planning a loop drive, come this way first – it's not safe to cross when the water's more than a couple of feet deep, and you wouldn't want to find that out at the end of a sixty-mile drive. The second route, the **Caineville Wash Road**, meets the first – by now Hartnet Road – at the far end of Cathedral Valley. Several more dirt roads leave the park at this northern extremity, connecting with I-70 to the north or joining Hwy-72 above Loa to the west.

Hiking in Capitol Reef

You probably won't drive far in Capitol Reef before the backcountry starts to beckon. Choosing which of the many, mostly short **trails** to hike is largely a matter of whether you feel up to climbing; only a few, such as the walks through the Capitol Gorge or Grand Wash, remain on level ground, while the rest demand mountain-goat-style scrambling up the slickrock.

If you do choose to stick to the canyon floors, bear in mind the danger of **flash floods** after rain, and try not to pause anywhere where there's no clear escape route.

Grand Wash

The busiest Capitol Reef trail connects the Scenic Drive with Hwy-24, by way of the gravelly bed of the **Grand Wash**. Both trailheads are roughly four miles from the visitor center, one at the end of the unpaved Grand Wash Road, which leaves the Scenic Drive a mile past Fruita, and the other on the south bank of the highway a mile or two beyond Capitol Dome.

As a one-way walk, the Grand Wash trail is just over two miles long, though unless you arrange a pick-up at the far end you'll have to double back. In the half-mile stretch known as **The Narrows**, the vertiginous 800-foot canyon walls close in to a mere sixteen feet apart. **Butch Cassidy** and his gang are said to have used the tangle of side canyons that lead off Grand Wash as hideouts, but there's no evidence that Butch ever saw **Cassidy Arch**, reached by a short steep climb from near the southeast end of the trail.

Capitol Gorge

The **Capitol Gorge** trail at the end of the Scenic Drive is every bit as claustrophobic as the Grand Wash. In the space of a mile, it inches all the way through a crack in the Waterpocket Fold, though hikers have to turn back when they reach the private land on the far side. From 1871 onwards, this "**Blue Dugway**" was a major trans-Utah thoroughfare, as the painstaking inscriptions on the **Pioneer Register**, carved into the canyon wall halfway along, will testify.

A couple of twists of the canyon past the Register, side canyons open up to both left and right. The one on the left looks more promising, but is blocked a short way along; to the right, you have to start climbing almost immediately, but within a few hundred yards you'll come to some typical **waterpockets**. Early travellers would break off from the laborious haul through the gorge, in the hope of finding fresh water in these clifftop "tanks".

A separate two-mile trail from the Capitol Gorge trailhead launches itself straight up the hillside to the north. The slickrock flatlands that cap the Waterpocket Fold enjoy huge views to Boulder Mountain in the east and the Henry Mountains in the west. The dominant feature up here, however, is the glowing Navajo-sandstone butte of the **Golden Throne**, at the foot of which the trail ends.

Hickman Bridge

The **Hickman Bridge Trail** may not be the easiest of Hwy-24's roadside trails – the Fremont Culture Walk, detailed on p.365, is far less demanding – but it makes a supremely rewarding two-mile, two-hour hike. Setting off along the north bank of the Fremont River, two miles east of the visitor center, it meanders briefly through the cottonwoods before a brisk climb out of the canyon to the shadeless heights up top.

Once you've marvelled at Capitol Dome, off to the east, fork left at the junction ahead. Three quarters of a mile along, the path loops around and through **Hickman Bridge**. A hundred feet high, a hundred feet wide, it's a genuine natural bridge, worn through the rock by a side channel eager to reach the Fremont below. The rocky chaos beneath somehow complements the grace of the bridge itself.

Taking the right rather than the left fork at the junction lets you in for a nine-mile round trip on the **Rim Overlook Trail**. Highlights include a towering overview of the orchards of Fruita, and the **Navajo Knobs** at its furthermost point.

Lake Powell

Until the early 1960s, it was all but impossible to travel between southwest and southeast Utah. In the unseen heart of the endless desert, the mighty Colorado River churned its way towards the Pacific through a succession of yawning canyons. Here and there boatmen might ferry the occasional passenger across, and a few adventurous souls even rafted down the river itself, but there was no highway for two hundred miles north of Arizona.

Now the Colorado has gone, submerged beneath the huge, docile **Lake Powell**. For many people – especially those who knew the sublime **Glen Canyon** that it destroyed – the new lake is a loathsome abomination. Many more see it as a thing of beauty, and Lake Powell has become Utah's number-one tourist attraction, drawing around four million visitors per year and matched in popularity in the Southwest only by the Grand Canyon. It is, undeniably, an extraordinary spectacle, its lurid turquoise waters rippling against its stark red-rock rim, and cradling islands that once were buttes and mesas. No one could ever mistake this for a natural landscape, however, and you don't have to be an out-and-out green to be disturbed by the transformation of America's last great wilderness into a playground. The concessionaires of the **Glen Canyon National Recreational Area** invite you to "think of Lake Powell as a 160,000-acre bathtub and consider our boats, floats, boards and tubes as your toys".

Lake Powell's success as a wet'n'wild theme park has been a surprise spin-off from its real purpose. Glen Canyon Dam was constructed to regulate the flow of water along the Colorado River. Half is kept back to irrigate the deserts of the plateau, while the rest gushes through its turbines, generating electricity as it goes, and makes for Arizona and California. Demand is so precisely monitored that the level of the lake fluctuates according to whether it's dinnertime in Phoenix. Hence its closest resemblance to a bathtub – the scummy dirty-bath tidemark, up to thirty feet above the water, which sullies the sandstone around its edge.

The whole vast engine cost $300 million to build. Lake Powell is 550 feet deep at the dam, and holds enough water to cover all Arizona five inches deep. It stretches back up 186 miles of the Colorado River and 72 miles of the San Juan River, as well as inundating 96 side canyons formed by rivers such as the Escalante and the Dirty Devil. The total shoreline of 1960 miles is longer than the entire US Pacific coast.

Four of the five **marinas** so far built around Lake Powell are accessible by road. Three of those – **Bullfrog**, **Hall's Crossing** and **Hite** – are in Utah, while the largest, **Wahweap**, lies just across the border in Arizona, not far from the dam itself and the purpose-built town of **Page**. There's surprisingly little accommodation on land; it's assumed you'll want to join the armada out on the water, either in your own vessel or in a rented **houseboat**. For a quick taste, you can join a **guided tour** at either Wahweap or Bullfrog – the half-day trips to **Rainbow Bridge** are by far the most popular – or take the **ferry** service that plies between Bullfrog and Hall's Crossing.

Over half a million visitors flock to Lake Powell on Labor Day alone.

Despite the searing sun, Lake Powell is officially claimed to lose a mere 2.5 percent of its volume each year to evaporation.

Lake Powell's fifth marina, Dangling Rope, is a refuelling station that can only be reached by boat.

Lake Powell: Controversy and Compromise

The western half of the United States would sustain a population greater than that of our whole country today if the waters that now run to waste were saved and used for irrigation.

President Theodore Roosevelt,
State of the Union address, 1901.

The twentieth-century growth of the American West is largely the story of the "taming" of the **Colorado River**. If the Colorado ran dry, Los Angeles, Las Vegas and Phoenix would die, and the exodus from the Southwest would dwarf anything from the Dustbowl era.

In terms of volume, the Colorado does not rank among the top 25 rivers in the US. However, the sheer aggression with which it hurtles from 13,000ft up in the Rockies makes it the fastest and fiercest of them all. That's why it's responsible for so many magnificent canyons; and that's also why civil engineers can't bear to leave it alone. They yearn to harness its energy with hydroelectric dams, and divert its flow to irrigate the desert instead of rushing uselessly to the sea.

Early in the twentieth century, the sparsely populated southwestern states began to fear that southern California's ever-increasing thirst might one day drain them dry. The **Colorado River Compact**, signed in 1922, divided the river between an **Upper Basin**, consisting of Utah, Wyoming, Colorado and New Mexico, and a **Lower Basin** – Arizona, Nevada, and California. Each was to receive 7.5 million acre-feet of the estimated annual flow of 16.8 million, with the dregs left over for Mexico. This was the first of fifteen such agreements in fifty years, largely because the estimates were wrong; the correct figure was more like 13.9 million acre-feet.

The task of distributing the water fell to a new federal agency, the **Bureau of Reclamation**, and the main tool at its disposal was the **dam**. Its engineers saw their mission as being to reshape the West, to "reclaim" it to the way it ought to be. They began in 1935, by damming Black Canyon, on the doorstep of California, with what came to be known as the **Hoover Dam** (see p.453). That project inspired a spree of dam-building, in the US and all over world. Though critics argued the American dams were supplying far more hydro-electric power than the nation could possibly need, it was all absorbed soon enough into feeding the war effort, and fuelling the economic boom of the 1950s. According to the Bureau of Reclamation, yet more dams were needed; its plans for the Colorado Plateau were clear from the subtitle of one report, *A Natural Menace Becomes A Natural Resource*. Proposals included damming the Green River in northwest Colorado, the San Juan in New Mexico, and the Colorado itself in both Bridge Canyon in Arizona and Utah's Glen Canyon.

Almost a century earlier, in 1869, John Wesley Powell had been entranced by the idyllic canyon that lay below the confluence of the Green and Colorado rivers: "A curious ensemble of wonderful features – carved walls, royal arches, glens, alcove gulches, mounds and monuments . . . We decide to call it **Glen Canyon**". Those few river-runners who had seen it since knew it as a cool, tranquil haven, bursting with luxuriant vegetation and desert wildlife, and a far cry from the cataract-filled canyons both up- and downstream. Theirs were lone voices in the wilderness, however; too little known to have been granted federal protection, Glen Canyon's remoteness was to work against it.

As a campaigning force, the environmental movement was in its infancy in the 1950s, and its strategy concentrated on defending national parks at all costs. The Green River dam-site being within Dinosaur National Monument, **David Brower**, the executive director of the *Sierra Club*, argued before a Congressional committee that damming Glen Canyon was a far better idea – in fact he originally endorsed the construction of a dam in the Grand Canyon *on condition* that a dam was built at Glen Canyon as well. Conservationists prided themselves on a job well done when it was eventually decided to dam the Green River outside Dinosaur, at Flaming Gorge to the northwest, and to go ahead with damming Glen Canyon. The one concession to "the abominable nature lovers", as one Utah senator termed them, was that water would not be allowed to encroach upon Rainbow Bridge National Monument.

The first blast at the dam-site was detonated on a signal from President Eisenhower in September 1956. Meanwhile, with Glen Canyon doomed but not yet drowned, archeologists, artists, and photographers set out to chronicle its disappearing treasures. These included the glowing, fern-dripping alcove known as the **Cathedral-in-the-Desert** – described in Eliot Porter's best-selling *The Place No One Knew* as "the single most spectacular place I ever visited" – and the **Crossing of the Fathers**, where the Spanish priests Domínguez and Escalante forded the river in 1776, which now lie far beneath buoys no. 68 and no. 21 respectively. Floyd Dominy, the gung-ho head of the Bureau of Reclamation, preferred to dwell on the future, writing in the glossy coffee-table volume *Lake Powell, Jewel of the Colorado* that "like a string of pearls, ten modern recreation areas will line Lake Powell's shores".

The Colorado River was stopped for the first time in its history on January 21, 1963. That same day, President Kennedy's Secretary of the Interior, Stewart Udall – the great-grandson of John D Lee, of Lees Ferry (see p.321) – announced plans to build two further dams within the Grand Canyon. By now, the *Sierra Club* had realized its mistake; and it promptly made another. This time it argued for building coal-burning power stations instead of hydroelectric dams. The Navajo Nation, imagining that nuclear power might soon render its mineral resources worthless, decided to cash in by permitting the strip-mining of Black Mesa (see p.42), and the hideously polluting Navajo Generating Station was constructed outside Page.

It took seventeen more years – and a Supreme Court decision that Congress could ignore its own previous rulings and allow the lake to lap against Rainbow Bridge – before Lake Powell was filled to the brim, on June 22, 1980. David Brower, who left the *Sierra Club* to found *Friends of the Earth* in 1969, was by now calling his support for Glen Canyon Dam "the greatest sin I have ever committed". As recently as November 1996, the 84-year-old "Archdruid" was back in the headlines with a call for Lake Powell to be drained so the canyon could regenerate. One of the original arguments for the dam had been that the Colorado's phenomenal load of silt would otherwise fill Lake Mead, behind the Hoover Dam, within a few years; Brower now says that the floodgates at Glen Canyon should remain open until that really does happen, perhaps two hundred years from now. Other activists would go much further. The central fantasy of Edward Abbey's *The Monkey-Wrench Gang* involved dynamiting the dam, and Abbey was among the demonstrators who in 1981 signalled the birth of the **Earth First!** movement by suspending a 300-foot strip of plastic down its face to simulate an almighty crack. To some extent, the argument has been won; no major dam has been built since the 1960s, and the general consensus is that Glen Canyon Dam will be the last.

Page

Home to over seven thousand people, **PAGE**, Arizona, is now the largest community in a 720-mile stretch of the Colorado River. Before Glen Canyon Dam was constructed four miles west, this all but barren mesa belonged to the Navajo Nation. Thanks to a small spring, however, it made the best site to house the dam's workforce. The Navajo agreed to swap it for a similar-sized chunk of desert between Bluff and Hatch in Utah, a new road was blasted through the Echo Cliffs, and the town was born on Thanksgiving Day 1958.

At first, Page seemed destined to wither away once the dam was completed. Ironically, it gained a new lease of life when Congress decided that instead of building more dams, the Southwest could meet its power needs by burning coal instead. The **Navajo Generating Station**, which creates electricity using coal from Black Mesa, and pumps water from Lake Powell to Phoenix, went up four miles southeast of town. It may have had a catastrophic effect on the air quality at the Grand Canyon, but it's kept Page in work.

The view as you drop down towards Page, whether from Utah or Arizona, is utterly surreal. The five power-station chimneys stand silhouetted amid the sandstone outcrops, with lines of pylons marching off across the desert and the misty hump of Navajo Mountain rising in the distance. As you get lower, the waters of Lake Powell emerge from the haze, with drowned buttes poking their heads here and there above the surface.

The story of John Wesley Powell's Colorado expeditions is told on p.401.

Page itself, on the other hand, resembles a dull suburban mall writ large. Most of its original trailer homes have been replaced by more permanent structures, but the only sight of any interest is the **John Wesley Powell Memorial Museum**, 6 N Lake Powell Blvd (Oct–April Mon–Sat 9am–5pm; May–Sept Mon–Sat 8am–6pm, Sun 10am–6pm; donations). As well as charting the exploits of the first man to raft down the Colorado, this celebrates later river-runners and also recounts Page's own brief history.

A couple of miles southeast of Page, milepost 299 on Hwy-98 marks the trailhead for **Antelope Canyon**. A seven-mile round-trip hike takes you deep into the most famous "**slot canyon**" in Arizona, a swirling, sinuous gorge whose orange and red walls are often just a few feet wide.

Arrival and information

*On the first weekend of October each year, Page hosts a spectacular air show known as the **Air Affaire**.*

Page's **visitor center** is in the Page Plaza mall at 106 S Lake Powell Blvd (summer Mon–Sat 8am–7pm, Sun 10am–6pm; winter Mon–Fri 8.30am–5pm; ☎801/645-2741). Brochures on local attractions can also be picked up at the Powell Museum (see above).

No **buses** pass through Page, but the local hostel runs a shuttle service up from Flagstaff (see opposite), and the **airport**, a mile east on Hwy-98, is connected daily with Phoenix on *Skywest* (☎520/645-2494 or 1-800/453-9417).

Companies running **tours** include *Grand Circle Adventures* (☎801/645-5088), who do hour-long 4WD trips to Antelope Canyon, including late-evening tours, for $25, plus excursions further afield.

Accommodation

While no one would choose to spend much time in Page itself, Lake Powell is enough of an attraction to keep its **motels** busy for most of the year, and to hike their rates higher than you might expect.

Best Western Arizona Inn, 716 Rim Drive; ☎520/645-2466 or 1-800/528-1234, fax 645-2053. Standard upmarket motel on the outskirts of Page, commanding a massive desert panorama from the poolside. Mid-Oct to March ③, April to mid-Oct ④.

Best Western at Lake Powell, 208 N Lake Powell Blvd; ☎520/645-5988 or 1-800/528-1234, fax 645-2578. Large, good-value motel perched above downtown Page, with pool. Mid-Oct to mid-May ②, mid-May to mid-Oct ④.

Courtyard by Marriott, 600 Country Club Drive; ☎520/645-5000 or 1-800/321-2211, fax 645-5004. Page's most incongruous splash of luxury – complete with golf course – is located down below the mesa in view of the dam. Nov–Feb ④, March–Oct ⑤.

HI-Lake Powell International Hostel, 141 Eighth Ave; ☎520/645-3898 or 1-800/545-5405. Budget hostel near the visitor center, offering dorm beds (with bedlinen) from $12, plus basic private rooms. There's a $10 shuttle service from Flagstaff, and boat tours can be arranged. ①–②.

Navajo Trail Motel, 800 Bureau St; ☎520/645-9508. Reasonable mid-range motel, near the museum. Nov–Feb ②, March–Oct ③.

Eating

Page offers the usual range of **diners** and **fast-food** outlets. If you're just racing through, the *Coffee Gallery* at 105 Page Plaza, next to the visitor center, serves espressos and light snacks.

Bella Napoli, 810 N Navajo Drive; ☎520/645-2706. Classy, dinner-only Italian cuisine, with lots of shrimp and seafood entrees – even Alaskan lobster – plus less expensive pastas and pizza. Closed mid-Nov to Feb.

Pepper's Restaurant, *Courtyard by Marriott*, 600 Country Club Drive; ☎520/645-5000. Upscale hotel restaurant as you approach town from the dam, with a varied if not wildly exciting menu that ranges through salads, pasta, sandwiches and dinner specials.

Porter's Sunset Grille, 125 S Lake Powell Blvd; ☎520/645-3039. Mexican and Southwestern specialities, from *fajitas* and tacos to T-bone steaks. They also do big breakfasts and lunchtime sandwiches.

Glen Canyon Dam

Glen Canyon Dam plugs **Marble Canyon** (see p.321) not at its narrowest point, but at its northern end, just downstream from Wahweap Creek. As US-89 crosses Glen Canyon Bridge four miles outside Page, the vast curve of the dam is to the north, while

Lake Powell

Boat trips from Wahweap Marina are detailed on p.394.

The zip code for Page is AZ 86040.

For further accommodation options near Page, see Wahweap, p.394.

Marble Canyon drops 700ft below you. An east-bank spur road tunnels through the cliffs to reach the river; it's used mainly by river-rafters setting off on the gloriously lazy fifteen-mile float down to Lees Ferry (see p.298).

There's no stopping on the bridge, so if you want a better look call in at the ultra-modern **Carl Hayden Visitor Center** on the west bank, which doubles as the main source of information on the **Glen Canyon National Recreational Area** (winter daily 8am–5pm; summer daily 7am–7pm; ☎520/608-6404). With half an hour to spare, you can take a **self-guided tour** of the actual dam, dropping via two elevators first to the walkway along the top, and then a further 500ft to the generating station at the bottom. Beneath the roar of the 1.3 million kilowatt turbines, a digital counter steadily ticks off the billions of dollars so far earned by the sale of power.

Wahweap

Unlike Page, **WAHWEAP**, a couple of miles west of Glen Canyon Dam, has never become a town. Lake Powell's principal **marina** has however grown steadily since it was established in 1963, co-ordinating most of the boat rental and tour business and also offering several hundred motel rooms.

To the fury of the federal authorities, the first man to appreciate Wahweap's potential did so long before the dam was ever built. Art Greene, the owner of the *Marble Canyon Lodge* (see p.321), ran boat trips upriver to Rainbow Bridge from the 1940s onwards; when he got wind of plans to dam Glen Canyon, he shrewdly leased the land at the mouth of Wahweap Creek at a knockdown rate. Knowing it made the perfect site for a marina, Greene refused to budge, and wound up making a killing as official concessionaire.

Accommodation

Only half the rooms in the plush *Wahweap Lodge* (☎520/645-2433 or 1-800/528-6154, fax 331-5258; Nov–March ⑤, April–Oct ⑦) overlook Lake Powell. Its *Rainbow Room* restaurant, however, has huge lakeside windows, and serves good food daily for all meals.

The same management also operates the summer-only *Lake Powell Motel*, three miles west on US-89 (mid-May to mid-Oct; ☎520/645-2477; ④), and a first-come, first-served **campground**.

Boat tours from Wahweap

Lake Powell Resorts and Marinas (see box opposite) run tours to **Rainbow Bridge** from Wahweap all year round, with a **full-day** rate of $76 for adults, $43 for under-12s, and **half-day** rates of $56 and $33 respectively. Other tours from Wahweap range from a one-hour paddlewheeler trip (adults $10, under-12s $7) up to a dinner cruise ($44.50, no reductions).

Renting a Houseboat

To rent a **houseboat** on Lake Powell, contact *Lake Powell Resorts and Marinas*, PO Box 56909, Phoenix AZ 85079 (☎520/645-2433, 602/278-8888 or 1-800/528-6154, fax 602/331-5258). Between mid-May and mid-October, the smallest houseboat, a *Commander* capable of sleeping six, costs $723 for three days or $1376 for a week. From April until mid-May and in the second half of October, the price goes down to $542/1032, and for the rest of the year there's a further drop to $434/826. Throughout the year, rates for the luxury ten-berth *Admiral* class are more than double.

Any number of **package deals**, offering different combinations of time spent on houseboats, in the marina lodges, and on guided tours, are also available.

Many houseboat users like to **camp** overnight on-shore; NRA regulations insists that anyone who camps within a mile of the lake must carry and use portable toilets.

In addition, Wahweap is the base for **float trips** down Marble Canyon to Lees Ferry. Half-day trips, available all year, cost $42 for adults, $35 for under-12s, while the full-day version (April–Oct only) costs $62 for adults, $55 for under-12s.

These same Marble Canyon float trips are offered by the Fred Harvey Company at the Grand Canyon; see p.298

Rainbow Bridge National Monument

Millions of tourists have Lake Powell to thank for providing effortless access to the world's largest natural bridge, the magnificent **RAINBOW BRIDGE NATIONAL MONUMENT**. The Navajo, seeing this formerly sacred site swarming with visitors, are far less enthusiastic, though at least the height of Glen Canyon Dam, and thus the level of the lake, was mandated to ensure that Rainbow Bridge was not drowned – unlike the nearby and equally revered confluence of the Colorado and San Juan rivers.

Boat tours to Rainbow Bridge from Wahweap and Bullfrog are detailed on opposite and p.396.

Both the Navajo and the Paiute knew of Rainbow Bridge before the first university-sponsored expedition reached it in 1909. Within a year, it was declared a national monument, but it remained far off any beaten track until the coming of Lake Powell. The bridge now lies a mile or two down Forbidding Canyon, a side canyon located just under forty miles by water from either Wahweap or Bullfrog.

Forbidding Canyon twists away from the lake until it peters out at a jetty that floats in a morass of pond scum. A ten-minute walk from there leads to the astonishing sandstone gateway, which springs up nearly 300 feet from just above the waterline. It's also almost 300 feet wide, with Navajo Mountain visible through its superbly smooth curve. The upper section, including the forty-foot-thick span, is composed of Navajo sandstone, while the base belongs to the harder Kayenta formation, not as easily cut by flowing water.

With a great deal more difficulty, Rainbow Bridge can also be reached on **foot**. Two fourteen-mile trails start respectively 38 and

42 miles up Arrowhead Hwy-16, which runs north from Hwy-98 from a junction 57 miles southeast of Page. They loop to either side of Navajo Mountain, before joining for the last half-mile. This hike should only be attempted by experienced canyoneers, all of whom must obtain **permits** from the Navajo Nation (Parks & Recreation Dept, Box 308, Window Rock AZ 86515; ☎602/871-6647).

Bullfrog

The marina at **BULLFROG** is slapped atop the slickrock on the west side of Lake Powell seventy miles upstream from Wahweap, or seventy miles southeast of Capitol Reef National Park on the Notom–Bullfrog Road (see p.385). It's the focus of a small community that now proudly boasts its own high school, as well as a spanking new Glen Canyon NRA **visitor center**, so far open in summer only (April–Oct daily 8am–5pm; ☎801/684-7400).

A houseboat on stilts above the road serves as a sign for the *Defiance House Lodge* (☎801/684-2233, 602/278-8888 or 1-800/528-6154; Nov–March ④, April–Oct ⑥). The best place to enjoy the big lake views from this pricey mesa-top **motel** is its *Anasazi* restaurant, but the food is indifferent. The park concessionaires also have some fully furnished but deeply unatmospheric **housekeeping units** for rent (☎ as above; Nov–March ⑤, April to mid-May and second half of Oct ⑥, mid-May to mid-Oct ⑦).

Boat tours from Bullfrog and Hall's Crossing

All-day tours from Bullfrog and Hall's Crossing to **Rainbow Bridge** run between April and October only, and cost $76 for adults, $43 for under-12s. The only other tour to leave from Bullfrog is aboard the *Canyon Explorer* (April–Oct only; adults $26, under-12s $18). Destinations on its 2hr 30min evening cruises include the Anasazi site known as **Defiance**

The Lake Powell Ferry

The *John Atlantic Burr* takes 25 minutes to cross between **Bullfrog** and **Hall's Crossing**, and leaves at the following times daily:

	Leaves Hall's Crossing	Leaves Bullfrog
mid-April to mid-May	8am, 10am, noon, 2pm & 4pm	9am, 11am, 1pm, 3.30pm & 5pm
mid-May to Sept	8am, 10am, noon, 2pm, 4pm & 6pm	9am, 11am, 1pm, 3pm, 5pm & 7pm.
Oct	8am, 10am, noon, 2pm & 4pm	9am, 11am, 1pm, 3.30pm & 5pm
Nov to mid-April	8am, 10am, noon & 2pm	9am, 11am, 1pm & 3.30pm

Fares: Foot passengers $2, age 5–11 $1, under-5s and over-65s free; bike $2, motorbike $3, ordinary car $9. Increased rates for larger vehicles.

House Ruin, now stranded just above the water level in Forgotten
Canyon, a few miles north of Hall's Crossing, and accessible only by boat.

Hall's Crossing

HALL'S CROSSING, on the east shore of Lake Powell, now plays
second fiddle to its larger neighbour of Bullfrog to the west. As the
name suggests, it was the base of a ferry operator long before the lake
existed. Charles Hall started out by building his own boat at Hole-In-
The-Rock, 35 miles downstream (see p.378), in 1870. Business there
was so bad that he moved here instead in 1881, only to give up altogether when the transcontinental railroad rendered his service redun-
dant. Hall charged $5 per wagon, and 75¢ per passenger; the going
rate these days for a family car is $9 (see box opposite).

The NRA Ranger Station above Hall's Crossing marina is rarely
staffed; call ☎1-800/582-4351 in emergencies. Accommodation
possibilities are limited to housekeeping units in a glorified trailer
park (phone number and rates as for Bullfrog), while if you're looking for a meal you can either take your pick from a small assortment
of *Twinkie* bars at the local gas station, or a marginally wider range
of groceries at the marina store. There's nothing at all at the ferry
ramp, just over a mile beyond the marina.

When they finally get round to colonizing Mars, the first settlement should look much like the airstrip on top of the bare red mesa
that rises above Hall's Crossing. Hwy-276 to the east makes an exhilarating drive, dropping down the Clay Cliffs with views across the
red plains to Monument Valley, and running for forty empty miles to
meet Hwy-95 near Natural Bridges (see p.437).

Ticaboo

Hwy-276 sets off bravely into the desert northwest of Bullfrog, passing a series of unlikely-looking warehouses used to store boats during the winter. Twelve miles up, well past the turning to Notom and
only a few miles short of the red-tinged peak that marks the southernmost point of the Henry Mountains, the grandiose resort development of TICABOO stands to the left of the highway.

An optimistic venture that still hasn't quite paid off, Ticaboo consists of the comfortable *Ticaboo Lodge* (☎801/788-2110 or 1-
800/987-5253, fax 788-2118; Oct–April ④, May–Sept ⑤), plus the
Ticaboo Cafe, which is in theory open all day, serving steak and
pasta, the *Wild Hare* bar and a *Conoco* gas station.

Hite

The fourth and northernmost of the road-accessible marinas on Lake
Powell, at HITE, is reached via Hwy-95, which branches off Hwy-24
halfway between Capitol Reef and I-70 to run for 122 miles southeast
to Blanding. The only highway to cross the Colorado between the

Lake Powell   Glen Canyon Dam and Moab, Hwy-95's most dramatic segment is the twenty-mile stretch as it approaches the river from the west, rattling along beside the North Wash.

Soon after Lake Powell first laps at the canyon walls, the road climbs to **Hite Overlook**. Signboards on this windswept hilltop point out the patch of water that covers the short-lived gold-mining town of **Hite** itself, which flourished for thirty years from 1883. It takes a while before your eyes stop scouring the buttes on the horizon and pick out the ramshackle **Hite Marina** that has replaced it.

Once past the overlook, Hwy-95 loops north to cross first the Dirty Devil River and then the Colorado. Reaching Hite Marina involves a detour of a couple of miles on the far side; unless you need gas or groceries, or are boating, there's no point going out of your way. Renting a **housekeeping unit** here (phone number and rates as for Bullfrog) would be a seriously bad idea.

From Capitol Reef to Canyonlands

No direct route crosses the tract of craggy sandstone and eroded clay that stretches for a hundred miles east of Capitol Reef. Travellers making the circuit of Utah's parks are obliged to make a giant detour to the north or south, either crossing Lake Powell at Hite, or taking **Hwy-24** up to meet I-70 and then looping back down to Moab – a total drive of around 150 miles.

The scenery along Hwy-24 is consistently awesome, beginning with the **badlands** twenty miles beyond Capitol Reef, where the 1500-foot **Factory Butte** rises above corrugated humps of grayish-blue clay reminiscent of Arizona's Painted Desert (see p.250). Only small sections of the backcountry are at all accessible, however, and there's only one town of any size en route, **Green River**.

Hanksville

Forty miles from the Capitol Reef visitor center, Hwy-24 turns sharply north towards the interstate, while Hwy-95 runs south towards Lake Powell. The tiny farming community of **HANKSVILLE** stands at the intersection, a few miles south of the confluence where the Fremont and Muddy rivers join to form the Dirty Devil.

Hanksville is only a spot on the map, but with the next spot a good fifty miles away in any direction, its handful of little **motels** draw in enough weary drivers to keep it ticking over. Dependable options include the *Desert Inn*, 197 East 100 North, (☎801/542-3231 or 1-800/894-3242, fax 542-3231; ②), and the *Whispering Sands*, 140 S Hwy-95 (☎801/542-3238, fax 542-3456; ③). There's also a friendly, good-value, three-room **B&B**, *Joy's*, 296 S Center St (☎801/542-3252; ③), and a **campground**, the *Redrock* (☎801/542-3235 or 1-800/452-4971), which has a reasonable restaurant.

Goblin Valley State Park

Utah's quirkiest park, **Goblin Valley State Park**, nestles at the foot of the San Rafael Reef, a short distance west of Hwy-24 just over twenty miles north of Hanksville. This small patch of barren desert became a park for the simple reason that its rock formations are *funny*. The man who first noticed them, in the 1940s, called it Mushroom Valley, but "goblin" is as good a name as any.

To reach the park, branch west from Hwy-24 near mile post 137 and drive for five miles along Temple Mountain Road, then turn south onto a seven-mile dirt track which, as a sign warns, "May be Washboard". Past the entrance kiosk ($3 day-use fee, open 24 hours; ☎801/564-3633), the road ends beside a sheltered overlook, poised above a slim valley whose sandy floor is completely devoid of vegetation. It's filled instead with parallel fins of pale Entrada sandstone, each topped by a ridge that's indented with weird eroded figures. Some hoodoos also stand alone, while larger buttes and columns loom around the periphery.

A couple of formal trails lead down into the valley, but no one bothers to follow them, preferring to slither at random from one misshapen masterpiece to the next. Once you're on the valley floor, a typical monster in the maze will rise a few feet over your head; some really do look like goblins, complete with eyes and ears.

Away from the main valley, but still engulfed by stunted sandstone sprites, the park has a well-equipped **campground**, open year-round ($9; reservations on ☎1-800/322-3770).

Temple Mountain Road continues beyond Goblin Valley to climb up and over the **San Rafael Swell**. It turns to dirt within another mile, but remains passable for ordinary vehicles for the twenty high-desert miles it takes to loop up to I-70.

Green River

Hwy-24 joins I-70 44 miles north of Hanksville just as the interstate completes a dramatic descent from the uplands of the San Rafael Swell to slope gently east through a landscape of soaring buttes. Within a few miles, a ribbon of green vegetation becomes visible ahead, cutting through the desert at the bottom of a long broad valley – the line of the **Green River**. To the north stand the forbidding **Uintah Mountains**, to the south the stream burrows into a labyrinth of twisting canyons, so this is the best place to ford the river for hundreds of miles.

The town of **GREEN RIVER** has long straddled crucial cross-country routes. For east–west travellers, it remains the major way-station between Colorado and Utah, while river-runners from John Wesley Powell onwards have launched themselves south from here towards the Colorado. The first bridge was built to serve the *Denver & Rio Grande Railroad* in 1883.

*The Goblin Valley turn-off is half a mile north of the dirt road that leads to the **Horseshoe Canyon** sub-section of Canyonlands National Park;* *see p.409.*

While Green River is a welcome oasis, however – fertile enough to be considered the "melon-growing capital of east Utah" – it still amounts to little more than a strip of motels, gas stations and fast-food outlets. Given a sensible reluctance to erect permanent structures too close to the river, there's a gap where you might expect downtown to be; most of the built-up strip lies to the west.

The east bank of the river, however, is noteworthy as the site of the **John Wesley Powell River History Museum**, at 885 E Main St (summer daily 8am–8pm; winter daily 9am–5pm; $1). This recounts the epic journeys of the Canyonlands region's first true explorer, whose second voyage started at Green River on May 22, 1871. Powell made that trip partly because he lost the notes from his first, so the second time around he ensured that his every movement was fully recorded, in photos that now make marvellously evocative viewing. A twenty-minute multimedia show and several rooms of exhibits cover developments in river navigation since then, ranging through several turn-of-the-century steamers – none managed more than a handful of voyages – up to the army-surplus rubber inflatables that triggered the postwar boom in white-water rafting. Spare a moment to glance out of the panoramic windows, and you'll see that the river here is not green at all, but a dark muddy brown.

South of Main Street, sandwiched between the river's west bank, the railroad tracks, and Green River Boulevard, a cluster of fine old cottonwoods marks the attractive waterfront **Green River State Park**. This makes a good spot to break your journey with a picnic, and also holds the area's nicest **campground** (day use $3, camping $10 on weekdays or $11 on weekends; ☎801/564-3633; for summer reservations, costing $5 extra, call ☎1-800/322-3770).

Arrival and information

The Powell museum at 885 E Main St doubles as Green River's **visitor center** (hours as above; ☎801/564-3526), which can advise you on driving local backcountry roads. *Greyhound* **buses** between Denver and points west call at the *Rodeway Inn*, 525 E Main St, while *Amtrak* **trains** pass through daily in both directions en route between Denver and Salt Lake City.

Companies running **rafting trips** from Green River include *Adventure River Expeditions* (☎801/564-3648 or 1-800/331-3324) and *Holiday River Expeditions* (☎801/564-3273, 266-2087, or 1-800/624-6323). Every Memorial Day, hundreds of boats set out on weekend-long convoy trips that cruise down to the Colorado confluence, and then chug back upriver to Moab.

The zip code for Green River is UT 84525.

Accommodation

Although Green River is not much of a destination in its own right, it has almost four hundred **motel** rooms. They tend to fill by early evening in summer, partly with the overspill from Moab and partly

John Wesley Powell

Until **John Wesley Powell** led the first expedition to float down the full length of the Green and Colorado rivers, the Colorado Plateau was a vast blank at the heart of maps of the American West. No one knew how the mountains and waterways of the region fitted together, or whether falls larger than Niagara might prevent river traffic completely.

Powell was born in Ohio in 1834, the son of a travelling preacher, and spent his youth making solo forays along the Ohio, Mississippi and Illinois rivers. He lost his right arm fighting for the Union at Shiloh, where he formed a lasting friendship with the future president Ulysses Grant. Once the Civil War was over, the veteran major headed west, and decided to explore the Colorado Plateau at his own expense.

Powell, his brother Walter, and eight frontier types who volunteered to serve as an unpaid crew, set off from Green River, Wyoming, on **May 24, 1869**. They had four flat-bottomed wooden boats, purpose-built in Chicago; Powell was lashed to an upright wooden chair in the leading vessel. Not long after entering the Uintah Mountains, by way of **Flaming Gorge**, they were reduced to three boats, when one was smashed to smithereens in Lodore Canyon. They then whisked through Green River, Utah, and plunged into the desert, encountering their biggest challenge so far in the shape of **Cataract Canyon**, soon after the Green met the Grand to form the Colorado. Wherever possible, they carried their boats around the fiercest rapids, and with prodigious energy Powell repeatedly climbed out of the canyon to get his bearings. After several terrifying days, they burst out of the gorge, for an idyllic period of respite in **Glen Canyon**.

Three members of the party became demoralized in the depths of the **Grand Canyon**, when the blackness of the walls to either side seemed to presage further ferocious rapids ahead. They decided to hike their way out, only to be murdered by Shivwits Indians who mistook them for a group of trappers who had recently attacked an Indian woman. Powell, however, made it through the remainder of the canyon with unexpected ease. He arrived at the **Grand Wash Cliffs**, at the confluence of the Colorado and Virgin rivers (now beneath Lake Mead) on August 30. Two of his crew continued all the way to the Pacific, but Powell and his brother left the river, after almost a hundred days afloat.

Now a national celebrity, Powell returned for a better funded and much more leisurely trip two years later. Starting this time from Green River, Utah, he documented his experiences in much greater detail, and used them as the basis of a bestselling book. During the voyage, he left the canyon at every opportunity, and even returned to Washington DC for the winter, while his crew holed up in Kanab.

In later years, Powell became director of the Smithsonian Institution's **Bureau of Ethnology** in Washington, and of the **US Geologic Survey**. His forceful opinions as to how the federal government should administer the limited resources of the West – and especially its water – are now regarded as prophetic. Refusing to accept the then current adage that "rain follows the plow", he argued that state boundaries should be drawn along natural watersheds, to prevent water issues from bedevilling the region's political future. It was his advocacy of federally funded water projects that led the bureaucrats to name **Lake Powell** in his honour, but one can't help imagining that Powell himself preferred Glen Canyon as it was in the beginning.

The Green River

But for political shenanigans in the 1920s, the **Green River** might rank among the most famous rivers in the world. It starts by flowing north to loop around the Wind River Mountains of central Wyoming, then heads south into Utah, briefly ducks into the northwest corner of Colorado, and then crosses Utah to meet the Colorado after a 730-mile journey. The only thing is, the "Colorado" at that point – originally known as the **Grand River** – has come a mere 430 miles from the central Colorado Rockies. By geographical convention, the Green River should be regarded as the main course of the Colorado River, and thus renamed.

Until 1859, when Captain J N Mancomb discovered the confluence deep in the heart of the canyonlands, no one knew that the Green and Grand rivers met to form the Colorado. The Colorado had been named by the Spanish founder of New Mexico, Juan de Oñate, in 1606, while the Green River was identified by Fray Alonso de Posada in 1686 as the boundary between the territories of the Ute and the Comanche. French trappers stumbled across the Grand perhaps a century later.

Colorado's legislators were mortified to learn that the "Colorado River" did not after all flow through Colorado, as had always been assumed. When apportioning its waters became a major issue in the 1920s (see p.390), they therefore renamed the Grand the Colorado, which fortunately dovetailed with a vote in conservative Utah against changing the name of the Green River.

with long-distance interstate travellers. The best camping in town is at Green River State Park (see p.400).

*The **price** codes used here are explained on p.15.*

Bankurz Hatt, 214 Farrer St; ☎801/564-3382. Smart B&B in century-old clapboard riverside house. One en-suite room, three share a bathroom. ④/⑤.

Best Western River Terrace, 880 E Main St; ☎801/564-3401 or 1-800/528-1234. Green River's top option, with a pool, river views and adjacent restaurant. Winter ③, summer ⑤.

Budget Host Book Cliff Lodge, 395 E Main St; ☎801/564-3406 or 1-800/493-4699. Low, sprawling complex holding standard motel rooms, a diner, souvenir stores and a gas station, set back from the highway west of the river. Winter ②, summer ④.

Super 8, 1248 E Main St; ☎801/564-8888 or 1-800/800-8000, fax 564-8890. Reliable, reasonably new budget motel, perched on a hill at the east end of town. Winter ②, summer ④.

Eating

As well as the usual fast-food places and a couple of local cafes, several of Green River's motels have their own restaurants.

Book Cliff Restaurant, 395 E Main St; ☎801/564-3650. Pick from a large menu of diner food – mostly under $10, from chicken fried steak to fish and chips – as you gaze across a gas station forecourt. Open daily for all meals.

Tamarisk Restaurant, 870 E Main St; ☎801/564-8109. Brisk, busy restaurant, overlooking the river opposite the museum and open daily for breakfast, lunch and dinner. The food isn't bad, and the evening buffets (adults $8, kids $5) are pretty good value.

West Winds Restaurant, 545 E Main St; ☎801/564-8240. A 24-hour licensed diner, near the river's west bank, where breakfast is available non-stop and burgers, sandwiches, steaks and Mexican dishes are served until 2am.

Canyonlands National Park

CANYONLANDS NATIONAL PARK, the largest and most magnificent of Utah's national parks, is as hard to define as it is to map. Its closest equivalent, the Grand Canyon, is simply an almighty crack in an otherwise relatively flat plain; the Canyonlands area is a bewildering tangle of canyons, plateaus, fissures and faults, scattered with buttes and monoliths, pierced by arches and caverns, and penetrated only by a paltry handful of dead-end roads.

It was Canyonlands that Thelma and Louise mistook for the Grand Canyon at the climax of their road-trip adventure.

The 527 square miles of the park are just the core of a much larger wilderness that stretches to the horizon in every direction. To nineteenth-century explorers, this was the epitome of useless desolation; only since uranium prospectors blazed crude trails across the trackless wastes in the 1950s has it become at all widely known. Even after Canyonlands park was created in 1964, it took a couple of decades before tourists arrived in appreciable numbers.

Canyonlands Fees and Permits

The **entry fee** for Canyonlands National Park, levied between March and October only, is $4 per vehicle, $2 for cyclists or hikers, and is valid for seven days in all sections of the park. All the usual passes (see p.21) are sold and accepted.

Only limited numbers of visitors are allowed to spend a night or more in the backcountry, and all such groups are required to have **permits**. **Backpacking** permits, covering a maximum party of seven persons in the Needles and Island In The Sky districts, or five persons in the Maze, cost $10. **Vehicle campsite permits**, issued for groups of up to three vehicles (carrying fifteen people in the Island In The Sky, ten in the Needles or nine in the Maze), are $25. **Day-use** permits, costing $5, are also required for bikes and 4WD vehicles that enter Salt Creek, Horse or Lavender canyons in the Needles district.

Reservations are essential for the most popular areas, especially in the peak seasons of spring and fall. They have to be purchased at least three days in advance, and are issued for dates throughout each calendar year from the first Monday of August in the previous year. Permits must be picked up in person – with every member of the group present – from the appropriate park visitor center, at least one hour before it closes.

For application forms, and full details of the park's complex regulations, write to the **National Park Service Reservations Office**, 2282 S West Resource Blvd, Moab UT 84532-8000; call ☎801/259-4351 (Mon–Fri 8am–4pm); or contact a park visitor center.

Canyonlands National Park

*A full list of operators who run **tours** into the Canyonlands backcountry appears on p.426.*

Canyonlands focuses upon the Y-shaped confluence of the Green and Colorado rivers, buried deep in the desert forty miles southwest of Moab. There's only one spot from which you can see the rivers meet, however, and that's a five-mile hike from the nearest road. With no way to get down to the rivers, let alone cross them, the park therefore splits into three major sections. The **Needles**, east of the Colorado, is a red-rock wonderland of sandstone pinnacles and hidden meadows that's a favourite with hardy hikers and 4WD enthusiasts, while the **Maze**, west of both the Colorado and the Green, is a virtually inaccessible labyrinth of tortuous, waterless canyons that presents a stiff challenge even to expert climbers and backpackers. In the wedge of the "Y" between the two, the high, dry mesa of the **Island In The Sky** commands astonishing views across the whole park and beyond, with several overlooks that can easily be toured by car. Getting from any one of these sections to the others involves a drive of at least a hundred miles. Both the Needles and the Island In The Sky are reached via long approach roads that leave US-191 north and south of Moab respectively; the Maze is an endless jolting ride on dirt tracks from either Hwy-24 or the town of Green River.

The Geology of Canyonlands

In a land with so little water, the sheer *effort* that went into creating the splendour of Canyonlands is almost impossible to conceive. As you look out from the park's highest point, atop of the Island In the Sky, the cliffs drop away a thousand feet, with the rivers a thousand feet below that. For a hundred miles to the south, successive plateaus, benches and tablelands diminish into the distance, studded with the occasional butte. And yet twelve million years ago, this entire landscape was one vast plain, level with where you're standing. Bit by bit, at the rate of two inches every thousand years, the topsoil has crumbled to silt and been carried away by the rivers. Most of it was deposited at the edge of the Pacific, but these days it's gradually filling up Lake Powell instead.

Canyonlands was not literally carved by the rivers, however. Both the Green and the Colorado began life as gentle streams that ran across the plains. In the last twelve million years, as the Colorado Plateau pushed its way up, they have remained in their original courses, ever more deeply entrenched into the earth. Meanwhile, ice produced in a ceaseless cycle of freezes and thaws has chiselled away at the rocks that surround them, tumbling boulders into the water to be swept away.

Canyonlands is unique in resting on a mile-thick bed of **salt**, which was deposited on the bottom of an ancient sea three hundred million years ago and now fills the **Paradox Basin**. That salt was covered by later layers of sediment, themselves interspersed with further deposits of salt. Under the pressure of thousands of feet of harder rock, the salt layers are squeezed like toothpaste until they flow far underground, then bubble up towards the surface. As they do so, they push up fins and spurs of rock that crack and split to create phenomena such as the Needles, or they may hit ground water and dissolve, leaving gaping caverns behind.

The **rivers** themselves count as Canyonlands' fourth major component. A **rafting** expedition from Moab, with the operators detailed on p.426, is the best way to experience the eerie stillness of the deep canyons, at once exhilarating and supremely restful. However, since there's no way out before Lake Powell, you'll need to set aside several days, and several hundred dollars – and be prepared to face the awesome power of **Cataract Canyon**, just beyond the confluence, which contains some of the most intense whitewater rapids in the US.

Finally, there's one last subsection of the park: **Horseshoe Canyon** in the west, which was added in 1971 to preserve the Southwest's finest collection of ancient **rock art**.

Canyonlands is not a place that lends itself to a short visit. With no lodging, and little camping, in the park, and no loop road to whisk you through it, it takes a full day to have even a cursory look at a single segment. If you're among the many visitors who find the conditions too gruelling to spend much time out of your car – summer temperatures regularly exceed 100°F, and most trails have no water and little shade – then the Island In The Sky is the most immediately rewarding option. On the other hand, if you fancy a long day-hike you'd do better to set off into the Needles.

The largest selection of **motels** *near Canyonlands is in Moab (see p.425); park* **campgrounds** *are detailed on p.406 and p.413.*

The Island In The Sky

It's not obvious from most maps, but like the Colorado River confluence over which it looms, the mesa known as the **Island In The Sky** is itself shaped like a "Y". After a steady climb of around 25 miles, **Hwy-313**, which heads southwest from US-191 eight miles north of Moab, enters the park across the slender **Neck** that forms the right-hand fork of the Y. It then branches to the northwest, to run as far as the crater of **Upheaval Dome**, and to the south, where it ends at the overwhelming **Grand View Point**.

Most visitors to the Island In The Sky content themselves with driving from one overlook to the next. Some also walk one or two of the short, easy trails that cross its thin capping of Kayenta sandstone, to gaze over the brink of the sheer Wingate cliffs that hold it up. It is also possible, however – either in a sturdy 4WD vehicle, or by some very strenuous hiking – to make your way down to the pale plateau of the **White Rim**, prominent a thousand feet below.

Contrary to the official Utah state map, ordinary vehicles **cannot** *reach the Island In The Sky from Moab by way of Hwy-279, the Potash Road.*

Dead Horse Point State Park

Just before you reach the national-park boundary, twenty miles in from US-191, a turning to the east leads in four miles to the smaller but equally breathtaking **Dead Horse Point State Park**. This miniature version of the Island In The Sky stands at the tip of another narrow mesa, poised two thousand feet above a stupendous "gooseneck" loop in the Colorado. Off to the east, the turquoise evaporation ponds of Moab's potash plant (see p.430) make a garish contrast with the red rocks, while the Anticline Overlook (see p.432) stands guard above the far side of Meander Canyon.

Dead Horse Point's **visitor center**, two miles short of the main overlook, is a real period piece, with displays straight out of the 1960s (summer daily 8am–6pm; winter daily 8am–5pm; ☎801/259-2614). It does explain the name, however: nineteenth-century cowboys used the mesa as a natural corral, herding wild horses behind the piñon fence that blocked its ninety-foot neck. One band of horses is said to have been too scared to cross the gap even when the gate was left open, and perished of thirst.

Day-use of the park costs $4, and its *Kayenta Campground* makes an excellent (and much better equipped) alternative if there's no room in Canyonlands ($9 on weekdays, $10 weekends; reservations mid-March to mid-Oct only, $5 extra, on ☎1-800/322-3770).

Island In The Sky Visitor Center

The modern **visitor center** for the Island In The Sky, a mile or so in from the entrance, has full details on road and trail conditions as well as campsite availability (daily 8am–5pm; ☎801/259-4712).

Mesa Arch Trail

Four miles past the visitor center, just short of the fork in the road, the **Mesa Arch Trail** is the Island In The Sky's best short hike. During a mile-long loop around the mesa-top hillocks, it runs right to the rim of the abyss, where long, shallow **Mesa Arch** frames an extraordinary view of the La Sal Mountains, 35 miles northeast. Admiring Washer Woman Arch and Monster Tower, closer at hand, it would be easy to stumble right through the gap – there's no barrier.

Grand View Point Overlook

Grand View Point Overlook, at the southern end of the road, is the Island In The Sky's definitive vantage point, and a real agoraphobic's nightmare. It commands a hundred-mile prospect of layer upon layer of naked sandstone, here stacked thousands of feet high, there fractured into bottomless canyons.

The most conspicuous feature is the plateau formed by the **White Rim** layer, a thousand feet below, whose faint smattering of grass is crisscrossed by abandoned mining trails and ends at the White Rim itself. That peters out in the mass of white-capped red-rock pillars known as **Monument Basin**, where the **Totem Pole** may be 305ft tall but looks the size of a pencil. Neither river can be seen; the Colorado River is tucked out of sight another thousand feet down, while the equivalent canyon of the Green River is hidden by the twin buttes to the west. Everything is however mirrored by an identical chaos on the far side, rising towards the snow-capped peaks of the **Abajo Mountains**, forty miles south.

A stroll along the two-mile **Grand View Trail**, starting from the overlook, enables you to contemplate the whole jigsaw puzzle from countless additional angles.

Green River Overlook and Willow Flat campground

A couple of hundred yards north of the fork in the park road, a reasonable 1.2-mile dirt road leads to the **Green River Overlook**. The clearer, flatter expanse of the White Rim that spreads below is pierced by the green-trimmed meandering course of the river itself, as it flows through placid **Stillwater Canyon**. At this very spot, in the Biblical epic *The Greatest Story Ever Told*, Max von Sydow (aka Jesus) delivered the Sermon on the Mount to an audience of Moab Rotarians bedecked in false beards and tea towels.

The Island In The Sky's only developed **campground**, the free, first-come first-served, and waterless *Willow Flat*, is just back from the overlook. Contact the visitor center for current availability.

Upheaval Dome

The northern end of the park road, five miles up from the fork, comes at the geological oddity of **Upheaval Dome**. This jagged 1500-foot-deep crater is a highlight of park air tours (see p.427), but from close up, at the end of the steep ten-minute climb from the parking lot, it's something of a disappointment. Elaborate theories that explained the prongs of pale stone bursting from its darkest depths as the product of undulating subterranean salt have recently been abandoned in favour of the simpler notion of a sixty-million-year-old **meteor strike**.

Over the Edge: the White Rim Road

The reason the Island In The Sky is accessible at all, and that crude dirt tracks strike off into the wilderness almost everywhere you look, is that this region was a prime target for the freelance **uranium prospectors** of the 1950s (see p.423). They knew that uranium is often found in the grey-green rocks of the **Chinle formation**, which here forms the talus slopes found at the bottom of the Wingate cliffs, not far above the White Rim.

The rough-and-ready hundred-mile **White Rim Road**, scraped out by would-be miners at the base of the cliffs, is now most often explored on three- or four-day **4WD expeditions**, with overnight stops at various primitive campgrounds en route (by permit only; see p.403). Only the hair-raising **Shafer Trail Road**, which drops from just south of the visitor center, connects the mesa-top with the White Rim; otherwise drivers join the White Rim Road by means of the **Potash Road** from Moab (see p.429), or along **Mineral Bottom Road**, which runs west from Hwy-313 a couple of miles north of the Dead Horse Point turn-off.

No sections of the White Rim, Shafer Trail or Mineral Bottom roads should be attempted in ordinary vehicles.

Hikers can however clamber between the Island In The Sky and the White Rim along various trails. All are too demanding for a round-trip day-hike down to the White Rim – let alone to either river – to be a good idea. Register with the park service before you set off on a multi-day trip. Options include the **Lathrop Trail**, an utterly exhausting nine-mile route that makes it all the way to the Colorado, passing close to abandoned but potentially toxic uranium mines; the **Upheaval Canyon Trail**, which drops down to the Green River from the far side of Upheaval Dome; and the **Shafer Trail Road** itself.

Horseshoe Canyon

*In summer, rangers lead six-hour **guided hikes** into Horseshoe Canyon, starting at 9am on Sat & Sun; call ☎ 801/259-2652 to check.*

Remote **Horseshoe Canyon**, a detached chunk of Canyonlands National Park located well northwest of its main body, is home to the most extraordinary **rock art** to be found anywhere in North America. No one now knows the meaning of the mysterious, haunting figures that line the sandstone walls of the **Great Gallery**; although to the modern eye they suggest an astonishing sophistication, they are amazingly enough the **oldest** such images to survive.

Even if you're not a rock-art enthusiast, the six-mile round-trip **hike** down to the gallery – there's no road access – is one of Utah's most beautiful. With either forty miles of dirt road to negotiate south of Green River, or 34 miles east from Hwy-24, before the trail even starts, few visitors come this way, so you may well get the gorgeous red-rock canyon, rustling with wildlife, to yourself.

The San Rafael Desert: the road to Horseshoe Canyon and the Maze

Unless the weather has been dreadful – check at the Green River visitor center (see p.400) for current conditions – ordinary vehicles should have no problem driving to Horseshoe Canyon. From the centre of Green River, follow signs for the airport until you cross the railroad tracks. Once the surface has turned to gravel, fork left at a BLM sign pointing towards the San Rafael River.

After an initial flat section, the road pushes through painted-desert badlands formed by the fossil-rich Morrison Formation, and then winds down to a glorious panorama of Monument-Valley-style buttes. It crosses the **San Rafael River** on a rickety wooden bridge after nineteen miles, then climbs again to offer views that stretch to the Henry Mountains in the west and the La Sals in the east.

Just over forty miles south of Green River, beyond **Antelope Valley** – home to one of Utah's few surviving herds of pronghorn antelope – an easily-missed spur road branches off to the east. The **Horseshoe Canyon trailhead** is at its far end, at the edge of the plateau two miles along.

As the road veers west, a junction 5.5 miles past the Horseshoe Canyon turn-off marks the start of the 21-mile drive south to **Hans Flat Ranger Station**, the main point of access for the Maze (see p.410). Keep going west, and a total of thirty miles from Horseshoe Canyon you'll finally meet **Hwy-24**, just south of Goblin Valley (see p.399). This last stretch crosses Sweetwater Reef before dropping into the **San Rafael Desert**, where it insinuates itself between two impressive buttes known as Little Flat Top and Big Flat Top.

The hike to the canyon

The only route into **Horseshoe Canyon** picks its way down from the trailhead described above, marked by cairns as it crosses patches of deep sand alternating with slickrock. Once you reach the bottom, follow the dry sandy wash to your right, and in ten minutes you'll come to the **Horseshoe Shelter**, nestled beneath an overhanging cliff. When Harvard archeologists excavated this site in 1930, it held several rooms; all that remains is a vivid band of **pictographs** in the palest stratum of the rock, which was above the roofs of the shelters and is thus now out of reach. The animals, squiggles and triangular figures – many with strange protuberances on their heads – date from the Fremont era, but the scattering of ghostly footless figures are in the earlier Barrier Canyon style.

The **Great Gallery** is a good forty minutes' walk on, beyond several twists and turns in the canyon walls, and another small collection of pictographs in a massive sandy alcove. As you round the final bend, suddenly apparent beneath a lesser overhang, the Gallery takes your breath away. Framed between the cottonwoods, a long row of dark, hollow-eyed, other-worldly entities stands stark against

If you're heading east from Capitol Reef, it's much quicker to reverse the route described here; just be sure you have enough gas.

The round-trip hike to the Great Gallery takes at least five hours; start early, or sit out the midday sun down in the canyon.

The Rock Art of Horseshoe Canyon

At the time it was first studied, Horseshoe Canyon was **Barrier Canyon**, and that name still defines the style of art for which it's famous. It's characterized by anthropomorphic figures, roughly life-sized but tending to be weirdly elongated, and often lacking both arms and legs. Those that have eyes have large round ones, or simply empty sockets, and many seem draped in stylized robes; for most visitors to this lonely desert backwater, the cumulative effect is to suggest ghosts or spirits from another, different time.

While spearpoints found in Horseshoe Canyon date back as much as twelve thousand years, archeologists believe that the pictographs were produced by people of the **Archaic** culture, which flourished between 7500 BC and 500 AD. At the start of that period, the climate was much wetter, and the canyon held lakes, ponds and plentiful game. When conditions dried out, it was briefly abandoned, but then re-occupied.

Life was now far more difficult, and **shamanastic rituals** were increasingly used in the attempt to ensure successful hunting. These involved the creation first of clay statuettes, from 5000 BC onwards, and later of figurines made out of split willow-twigs, which have been found here and in the Grand Canyon (see p.293). Many represent what seem to be deities or shamans as well as animals; and the pictographs of the Great Gallery are thought to depict those same entities.

As for **technique**, the Great Gallery is very literally rock art. To produce the paint, different coloured rocks were ground up, dissolved in water and bonded with saliva produced by chewing seeds. The red is hematite, heavy with rust; the white is gypsum or chalk; even the blue comes from a local stratum. Some figures were produced with brushes, others by blowing or flicking paint at a stencil.

Experts estimate the gallery to be anything from 1600 to 6000 years old. Earlier dates are suggested by the inaccessibility of certain sites, due to rock falls, and the carbon-dating of a hearth beneath one panel to 1000 BC. None dates from later than 400 AD, when the Archaic people acquired the bow and arrow – not shown in any of the images – and began to transform into the **Fremont** culture. Fremont art, as seen elsewhere in Utah (see p.385) as well as here in Horseshoe Canyon, has its own very distinct style.

*No **camping** is permitted in Horseshoe Canyon itself, but there's a basic site beside the parking lot at the trailhead.*

the pale rock. Though the details grow clearer the closer you get, somehow a sense of vast, alien distance remains.

Apart from a couple of well-shaded stone benches, there are no facilities for visitors. Look out, however, for two army-issue metal boxes, marked PLEASE OPEN ME: one holds a set of powerful NPS binoculars, the other photostats of relevant academic papers.

The Maze

The name of Canyonland's **Maze** district is no exaggeration. This brain-teaser of convoluted canyons and barren desert washes, west of the Green and Colorado rivers, must be the least-explored region of the United States. If you're determined to get away from it all, the Maze is the place for you; getting back to it all when you've finished is more of a problem.

Somewhere in the heart of the Maze is the legendary **Robbers Roost**, a canyon fastness used as a hideout by nineteenth-century cattle rustlers and bandits such as **Butch Cassidy** and his Wild Bunch. They'd escape the long arm of the law by riding the Outlaw Trail up from the Green River near Mineral Bottom; lacking their familiarity with the terrain, pursuing posses had no choice but to turn back defeated. No roads entered the region until uranium prospectors bulldozed their way in during the 1950s.

Even today, you'll need a high-clearance 4WD vehicle to get any further than **Hans Flat Ranger Station**, which stands 21 miles south of the road through the San Rafael Desert to Horseshoe Canyon, described on p.409. That makes it 46 miles east of Hwy-24, and 66 miles south of Green River. An even worse sixty-mile dirt track also runs south, to connect it with Hite on Lake Powell. Technically the ranger station is in Glen Canyon National Recreation Area, but it's the main source of information for hikers and drivers setting off into the Maze (daily 8am–4.30pm; ☎801/259-2652)

The **jeep roads** beyond Hans Flat take another twenty or thirty miles to jostle and switchback into the actual Maze. There are two main routes in, one ending at the **Maze Overlook**, and the other at **Doll House Butte**, which marks the far end of the **Land Of Standing Rocks**, above the west bank of Cataract Canyon and straight across from the Needles.

Having come this far, most backpackers launch themselves into the wilderness for days or weeks at a time. There are few formal trails, but favoured destinations include **Pictograph Canyon**, not far beneath the Maze Overlook, where Barrier-Canyon-style pictographs (see box opposite) seem to record the moment when the Archaic people first acquired the skills of agriculture. However, unless you're extremely self-sufficient, a workhorse when it comes to carrying vast quantities of water, and a fearless, fully-equipped rock-climber, you're never going to see them.

The Needles

Thanks to its intricate tracery of backcountry trails, which offer the chance to engage with the landscape as opposed to merely marvelling from a distance, the **Needles** district is Canyonlands National Park's most satisfying segment for hikers, bikers and 4WD drivers. While it has its share of long-range vistas – including the park's only **Confluence Overlook** – the Needles is noted primarily for its namesake thickets of candy-striped **sandstone pillars**. Clustered on scrubby rock outcrops, concealing pockets of incongruous grassland, these intriguing formations can be explored on brief forays or multi-day backpacking expeditions.

The **Needles** area is a very long way from civilization, at the far end of the stunning **Hwy-211**, a total of 75 miles from Moab and fifty from Monticello. If you're planning a number of successive day-

*Confusingly, the **Needles Overlook** is not in the national park at all, but in the BLM's Canyon Rims area; see p.431.*

*More detailed
advice on
desert hiking
appears on
p.23.*

hikes, it makes sense to camp overnight in the park, so reserve a spot at *Squaw Flat* or in one of the backcountry sites as soon as you know you're coming (see p.403).

Ordinary mortals, as opposed to obsessive canyoneers, should also be warned that even casual **hiking** in the Needles area may well be the hardest thing you've ever done. Carry a good map and a *lot* of water, stick to the trails, and above all be very careful how far you climb – it's much easier to go up than it is to come down, and you run the risk of getting "rim-rocked".

The road to the Needles: Squaw Flats Scenic Byway

The 35-mile **Hwy-211** – also known as the **Squaw Flats Scenic Byway** – heads west of US-191 forty miles south of Moab, and then follows **Indian Creek** into the park. Winding lazily between the cottonwood-lined stream and canyon walls of rich red sandstone, overlooked by the twin castellated **Sixshooter Peaks**, it seems to carry you back a century, into the unspoiled Wild West. Much of the route lies through open grazing country, making this one of the few spots in the Southwest where you're still likely to see genuine **cowboys** riding the range. The *Dugout Ranch*, halfway along, was established in 1885, and later amalgamated with its neighbours to form the *Indian Creek Cattle Company*, Utah's largest cattle outfit.

*The mountain
road from
Monticello,
described on
p.433, meets
Hwy-211 just
west of
Newspaper
Rock.*

Newspaper Rock

Newspaper Rock Recreation Site, next to Hwy-211 twelve miles west of US-191, preserves a panel of black desert varnish that's inscribed, like some prehistoric newspaper, with literally hundreds of **petroglyphs**. Ancient peoples clearly recognized this as a perfect site, sheltered by a protective rock lintel beneath a hillock at a narrow bend in the valley immediately north of the Abajo Mountains. As well as abstract designs, the images include helmeted human figures, buffalo and bighorn sheep, plus lots of six-toed footprints and what look like bear pawprints. Some are probably symbols left by clans who performed particular ceremonies here, or simply passed by. With the obvious exception of recent graffiti, it's hard to say when they were executed, but you have to suspect that most are not in fact all that old; nineteenth-century Ute are thought to be responsible for the mounted riders, shown hunting with bows and arrows.

*The much-
photographed
Angel Arch
can only be
reached by
hiking from
the 4WD road
through Salt
Creek Canyon.*

The riverside woods across the road from the rock hold a lovely if basic **campground**, free but waterless.

The Needles Outpost

Up a short spur road just outside the park boundary, the privately owned **Needles Outpost** (mid-March to Oct, daily 8am–7pm; ☎ 801/979-4007 or 259-8545) is a summer-only grocery store and gas station that has its own small **campground**, and also arranges **4WD rentals** and **tours**, plus **scenic flights** over the park.

Driving into the Needles

Rangers at the **Needles visitor center**, a mile inside the park, can provide up-to-date hiking information, with a handy model of the whole park to make things clearer (daily 8am–5pm; ☎801/259-4711). They issue 34 **backpacking permits** per night, each for a group of up to seven people; in high season, if you don't have a reservation – see p.403 – the chances are none will be available. Day-hikers don't need permits.

Roughly three miles along from the visitor center, a left turning leads to the first-come first-served *Squaw Flat Campground*, where space is at an absolute premium in spring and fall ($6 mid-March to Oct, when water is available; otherwise free). Ordinary vehicles can continue beyond the campground, on an uneven dirt road, for three more miles to **Elephant Hill**.

The main park road presses on past the Squaw Flat turn-off for another four miles, ending where the **Big Spring Canyon Overlook** confronts an array of mushroom-shaped hoodoos. Of the short hik-

Canyonlands
National
Park

*4WD users
venturing into
the remote Salt
Creek, Horse
and Lavender
canyons –
which there
isn't room to
describe in this
book – require
$5 day-use
permits.*

ing trails along the way, the half-mile **Pothole Point Trail** is an easy stroll to the top of the roadside ridge, while the longer 2.5-mile **Slickrock Trail** provides an enjoyable orientation to the region, following a cairned footpath from one sandstone knoll to the next, each with its own long-distance mountain-and-mesa views.

The Chesler Park Loop Trail

Chesler Park, the high grassy meadow whose stubby sandstone pinnacles gave the Needles its name, makes a great destination for a long day-hike. Simply to reach it requires a six-mile round-trip trek from Elephant Hill, or a ten-mile one from Squaw Flat campground, while looping around the "park" itself adds another five miles.

As you climb across the cairned stretches of slickrock that rise from both Elephant Hill and Squaw Flat, look north for sweeping views to the Island In The Sky, with the White Rim neatly etched beneath it. The two trails meet half an hour up from Elephant Hill, then dip west to cross the wash that runs through **Elephant Canyon** – it may look dry, but there's usually water flowing far beneath the sand – before the final ascent to Chesler Park.

Allow seven hours for the complete hike from Elephant Hill, even longer if you start from Squaw Flat.

For the most part, the **Chesler Park Loop Trail** undulates around the edge of the 600-acre clearing, on the slopes below the red-and-white barber-pole Needles. On the eastern flank, however, it runs straight across the lavender-tinted grassland, while in the far southwestern corner it disappears into an extraordinary mini-canyon whose blackened walls are seldom as much as three feet apart. This claustrophobic segment, almost a mile long and known as the **Joint Trail**, is the highlight of the trip. A ledge perched above its eastern end, a 500-foot detour off the main trail, provides a superb overview of Chesler Park. Through a gap to the west, the gigantic Doll House Butte (see p.411), across the Colorado River, can also be glimpsed.

With a 4WD vehicle, you can join the Chesler Park Loop near the Joint Trail, and walk the loop alone as a five-mile hike.

As an alternative to circling Chesler Park, consider following the spur trail that branches south along Elephant Canyon. It takes just over three miles of steady climbing to reach **Druid Arch**, named for its resemblance to the rough-hewn monuments of Stonehenge.

Several more trails can be used to connect Chesler Park and Elephant Canyon with Squaw Flat, including routes through **Squaw Canyon** and the upper reaches of **Big Spring Canyon**. Backcountry **camping** is however only allowed at specific sites along the jeep road that runs west and north of Chesler Park, of which the closest to the main trails is at Devils Kitchen Camp – and you'd be lucky to get one of the necessary permits (see p.403).

The Confluence Overlook Trail

According to writer Edward Abbey, the local business community only agreed to the creation of Canyonlands park in 1964 on the understanding that its different parts would be linked by a loop drive, of which the focus would be the **Confluence Overlook**. In the absence of such a road, the demanding eleven-mile round-trip hike from **Big Spring Canyon Overlook** remains the only way to see the spot where the Green River meets the Colorado.

The trail starts by descending into Big Spring Canyon, then laboriously climbs out again, with a ladder to help you up one short stretch, only to drop once more into **Elephant Canyon**, at this point several miles north of, and considerably broader than, the segment near Chesler Park (see opposite). Each time you emerge onto the slickrock mesa-top, new views open up, either south to the Needles, or north to Junction Butte beneath the Island in the Sky.

Clambering from rock to rock beyond Elephant Canyon, you pass through several lifeless valleys known as **grabens**, from the German for "ditches". Thought to be a mere 55,000 years old, these were created when shifting underground salt beds caused landslides. Next comes a short section of jeep road – 4WD drivers can get this far via a nine-mile drive from Elephant Hill – before you finally teeter out to the edge of the plateau and see the confluence for the first time.

A thousand feet below the **Confluence Overlook**, the Green River flows in from the west, and the Colorado from the northeast. They're never the same colour. Sometimes the Green really is a pale green, and the Colorado almost red, tinted with dissolved red sandstone; at other times the Green is more of a yellow, and the Colorado a muddy chocolate. In any case, the two hues remain distinct for the first mile or two after the rivers combine, flowing parallel but separate towards the fearsome Cataract Canyon.

Arches National Park

ARCHES NATIONAL PARK seems to have become the national park for people who aren't quite sure whether they like national parks. It's not too hard to get to, just five miles out of Moab; it's not too big, with just twenty miles of paved roads; and it has a catchy name, to tell you what to expect. Well over a million visitors a year drive in, tick off however many arches they feel they have time for, and drive on to their next destination.

Thanks to *Desert Solitaire*, **Edward Abbey**'s lyrical evocation of his year as an Arches ranger, the park is also dear to the hearts of environmentalists and wilderness enthusiasts. The irony is that when Abbey was here, during the 1950s, there was no road into the body of the park, and the only way to explore it was to blaze your own trails. Now you can cruise round in a couple of hours, and barely step out of your vehicle.

For all that, Arches remains well worth visiting. The **Colorado River** here is literally peripheral, running unseen along the park's southern boundary. The emphasis instead is on the stark, strangely disjointed **sandstone scenery** of the higher ground to the north. As at Canyonlands, these rocks rest on an unstable layer of salt. **Salt Valley**, which slopes down across the park towards the Colorado,

Contact the Pack Creek Ranch (☎801/259-5505; see p.425), for horseback trips through Arches; other Moab-based tour operators are listed on p.426.

was formed by the collapse of an underground salt dome. That massive subsidence left high ridges to either side, which cracked along vertical fault lines to create long parallel "fins" of orange-pink Entrada sandstone.

Over the eons, water collects in pores in the fins, and scours them into potholes; piece by piece, the stone flakes away, until a hole is worn right through. Estimates of how many such **arches** the park holds vary from the eighty or so named on maps to the official count of over two thousand. No one has bothered to define whether a "window" is a type of arch or just another word for one, but it's agreed that an arch or window has to be at least three feet wide. Both are distinct from "bridges", which span running water.

As far as Edward Abbey was concerned, the arches themselves were a "small and inessential" feature of the park's landscape. Unless you're a real obsessive – in which case, you can buy specialist arch-and-bridge magazines – the appeal of hunting down arch after arch soon palls. The park's short, straightforward **hiking trails** are enjoyable enough in their own right, however, so you're bound to see a good number of them. **Delicate Arch** is by far the most impressive, because it's a free-standing crescent of rock. Most of the rest are just holes, though **Landscape Arch** is such a big one it would be a shame to miss it.

Apart from one solitary cabin, testament to a failed attempt at cattle ranching, very few traces remain of any human occupation of this forbidding desert. It became a national monument after the Klondike Bluffs area was found by a wandering prospector in the 1920s, and was enlarged into a national park in 1971.

Most visitors now arrive in **mid-summer**, despite blazing temperatures than can reach 110°F. Hiking conditions are much more bearable in spring – when the wildflowers blossom – or fall.

Arrival and information

Arches National Park has just one **entrance**, located east of US-191 five miles north of Moab. The **admission charge**, valid for seven days, is $4 per vehicle, or $2 for motorcyclists, cyclists and pedestrians. All the passes detailed on p.21 are sold and accepted.

The **visitor center** stands at the base of a long, tall escarpment, formed by the Moab Fault, that conceals the bulk of the park from the highway (mid-April to Sept daily 8am–6pm; Oct to mid-April daily 8am–4.30pm; ☎801/259-8161). Its displays help to make the geology of the place a bit clearer, while rangers provide advice on hiking conditions and issue backcountry permits (see below).

Of **park regulations** you'll need to know, the most important is that each **parking lot** along the road is designed to hold a specific number of vehicles, to limit the number of hikers on any one trail. Park illegally, and there's a $25 on-the-spot fine. No vehicles, or bikes, are allowed on the trails, but there are a few **4WD** roads.

To receive information by mail, write to Arches National Park, PO Box 907 Moab UT 84532.

Camping

Rangers at the visitor center will know if there's room at Arches' only **campground**, at the far end of the road across from the **Devil's Garden** trailhead ($8 mid-March to mid-Oct, when water is available; $5 otherwise; no showers). Throughout most of the summer, all its 51 first-come first-served sites are taken by early morning.

*The nearest **motels** to Arches are in Moab; see p.425.*

So long as you pick up a free **permit** at the visitor center, you can camp anywhere in the **backcountry** that's out of sight of roads, trails and named arches. In fact, Arches sees little overnight backpacking, as most people do all the hiking they want within a day.

Park Avenue and Courthouse Towers

Beyond the visitor center, the park road begins its 18-mile journey north to Devil's Garden with a steep climb up the cliffs, offering views across to Moab. A parking lot at the top, a mile along, marks the start of the simple one-mile walk down **Park Avenue**. The trail follows the rocky bed of a dry wash, named for the "skyscrapers" that top the high ridges to either side. It ends amid a group of chunky monoliths known as the **Courthouse Towers**; any arches there may once have been have long since fallen.

Unless you arrange to be met at the northern of its two trailheads, you'll have to walk Park Avenue as a two-mile round-trip. The road in between the two passes the **La Sal Mountains Viewpoint**, which offers the first glimpse of the peaks to the east.

The Windows Section

In the heart of the park, almost ten miles up from the visitor center, the fifty-foot **Balanced Rock** rests precariously on its slanted pedestal. Immediately beyond, a spur road to the right leads in three miles to the **Windows Section**. Several fine arches can be admired from the parking lot at the end, the largest in the park, which is also the starting point for a couple of very popular short trails.

North and South Windows

The busy one-mile loop trail to the North and South Windows ambles gently upwards for a couple of hundred yards towards **North Window**, the only one of the pair that's visible from the road. Take the steeper spur trail that leads right up to it, gaze through, and you'll appreciate why the word "window" is so appropriate. So far the gaping aperture has framed only blue sky, but now a magnificent desert panorama comes into view.

South Window is just a few yards away, though you have to rejoin the main trail and round one last pinnacle to see it properly. This one you can't climb up to, though a much rougher trail continues around the back and leads eventually back to the parking lot. Alternatively, you'll have noticed by now that the lone fin across the main trail is pierced by **Turret Arch**. Wander over there, then look back for a shot of the two windows side by side – a pair of dazzling blue eyes, separated by a bulbous snub nose.

Double Arch

A shorter, half-mile, trail leads from further around the Windows parking lot to **Double Arch**, where the roof of a wedge-shaped

Zion National Park, UT

Bryce Canyon National Park, UT

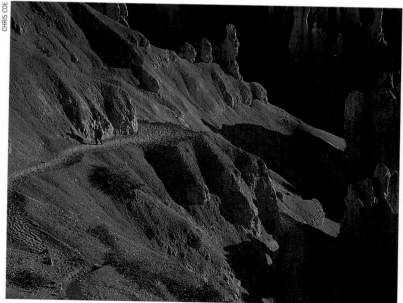

Bryce Canyon National Park, UT

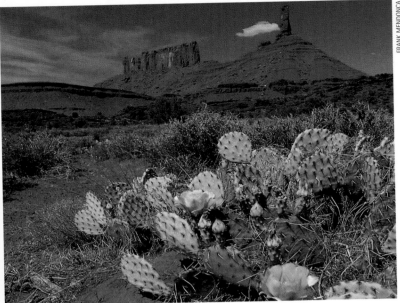

Prickly pears, Valley of the Gods, UT

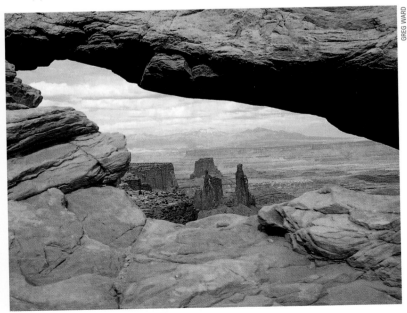

Mesa Arch Trail, Canyonlands, UT

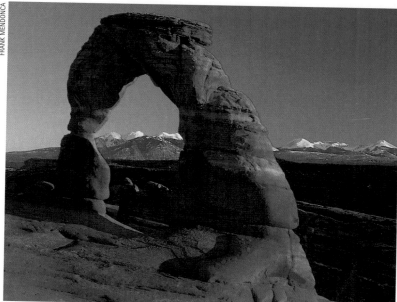

FRANK MENDONCA

Delicate Arch, Arches National Park, UT

GREG WARD

Goblin Valley State Park, UT

Las Vegas, NV

Las Vegas, NV

Bryce Canyon National Park, UT

arch has fallen in to create either a skylight, or two separate arches, depending on your point of view. On the far side, the **Cove of Caves** is packed with incipient future arches, burrowing into the cliffs.

Delicate Arch

As befits the state's single most remarkable natural phenomenon, **Delicate Arch** has become a symbol of Utah. Oddly enough, its sturdy bow-legged form, familiar from automobile licence plates and millions of tourist brochures, is not in fact all that delicate. It was originally called "Landscape Arch", for the view of the La Sal Mountains it so neatly frames, and only swapped names with what's now Landscape Arch (see p.420) due to a map-maker's mistake.

A side road towards Delicate Arch leaves the park road shortly beyond **Panorama Point**. The arch itself can only be reached via the gruelling **Delicate Arch Trail**, which leads up from Wolfe Ranch 1.2 miles along. If you lack the time or energy for that, you can see it from afar from the **Delicate Arch Viewpoint**, at the end of a level hundred-yard trail that begins a mile further on.

For photographs, Delicate Arch Viewpoint is best in early morning, while the Delicate Arch Trail is better in the afternoon.

The Delicate Arch Trail

The **Delicate Arch Trail** may be just 1.5 miles long, but the three-mile round-trip to the arch and back involves a steep climb across bare slickrock that can take the wind out of the hardiest hiker's sails. It starts just short of **Wolfe Ranch**, where Civil War veteran John Wolfe built a cabin in 1906, using cedar and cottonwood logs hauled seven miles from the Colorado. His cattle had by then been denuding the nearby slopes for almost twenty years; when sheep-farmers began to graze their animals on this impoverished soil as well, Wolfe gave up and moved back to Ohio.

Hikers in Arches should take especial care to avoid walking on the cryptobiotic crust; see p.23.

Beyond the cabin, a swaying suspension footbridge crosses the shallow perennial **Salt Wash**, and the trail begins its determined ascent. Considering that fewer than ten inches of rain fall here each year, the terrain is surprisingly varied, from the scrubby river-banks, choked with tamarisk, by way of a small-scale piñon-juniper forest, up to the naked rock three quarters of a mile up. An alcove off to the left, just below the hill top, cherishes "**hanging gardens**" of rushes and even orchids, fed by a spring that stains the rocks.

It's easy to lose the sparsely-cairned trail at the top of the mesa; the trick is to follow a narrow ledge in the rock that leads around the back of a high fin. Suddenly, from a viewing area neatly fenced off by a natural rock parapet, you're confronted by the full glory of **Delicate Arch**. Standing in superb isolation on the high lip of a canyon, it looks taller than its 45 feet.

Allow at least two hours for the round-trip hike to Delicate Arch.

The Fiery Furnace

An uninspiring overlook three miles on from the Wolfe Ranch turn-off gives little idea of the labyrinthine complexity of the **Fiery Furnace**. This warren of high-walled dead-end gullies and parallel fins is so disorientating that you have to have a permit to enter it. Rangers are reluctant to hand them out to inexperienced hikers, but they do lead daily **guided hikes** between spring and fall; register at the visitor center when you arrive.

No backcountry camping is permitted in the Fiery Furnace.

The Devil's Garden

The park's largest concentration of arches is found in the **Devil's Garden**, beyond the far end of the road eighteen miles up from the visitor center. The prime target here is the 300-foot **Landscape Arch**, reached by a gravelled, reasonably level one-mile trail. This slender span is so frail that hikers are not allowed up to or through the arch itself; a sixty-foot-long slab dropped off it in 1991, and lesser rock falls happen all the time. Arch aficionados will probably still be debating whether this or Kolob Arch in Zion National Park (see p.359) is the world's longest arch when it finally disintegrates.

What's now Landscape Arch was originally Delicate Arch, and vice versa; see p.419.

If your appetite for high-desert hiking has been whetted, press on beyond Landscape Arch on a trail that immediately becomes far cruder. After another mile – during which a one hundred-yard section obliges you to totter along the top of a narrow sandstone fin – you round a corner to see **Double O Arch** on the skyline. At first only its large upper oval is visible; as you approach, you'll see the much smaller ring beneath it as well. The pallid alkali wastelands that stretch away to the east were once prime uranium territory, and one heavily polluted section is still known as the "**Poison Strip**".

The four-mile round-trip hike to Double O Arch also leads past half a dozen other named arches, and assorted minor pin-pricks and peepholes. Real gluttons for punishment can turn it into a seven-mile loop, by circling back on the Primitive Loop Trail, but that route is every bit as demanding as its name implies.

Moab

Boom-and-bust cycles are a recurring theme in Western history, but few communities can have experienced quite such a rollercoaster ride as **MOAB**. Within the last fifty years, it has gone from an insignificant backwater in the 1940s to being celebrated as "The Richest Town in the USA" by *McCalls* magazine in the 1950s, only to become what one journalist called "one of the most economically depressed towns in Utah" by 1986, and then find itself transformed, almost against its will, into the Southwest's number-one adventure-vacation destination.

Through it all, Moab has never been a large town – the population still hasn't reached ten thousand – and neither is it an attractive one.

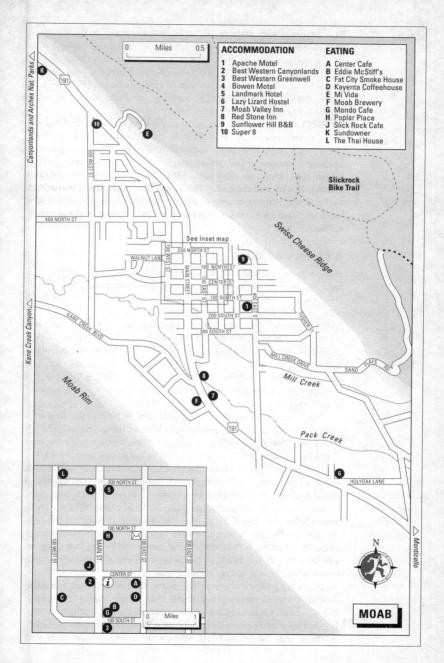

ACCOMMODATION
1 Apache Motel
2 Best Western Canyonlands
3 Best Western Greenwell
4 Bowen Motel
5 Landmark Hotel
6 Lazy Lizard Hostel
7 Moab Valley Inn
8 Red Stone Inn
9 Sunflower Hill B&B
10 Super 8

EATING
A Center Cafe
B Eddie McStiff's
C Fat City Smoke House
D Kayenta Coffeehouse
E Mi Vida
F Moab Brewery
G Mondo Cafe
H Poplar Place
J Slick Rock Cafe
K Sundowner
L The Thai House

Slickrock
Bike Trail

MOAB

Moab

The **setting** is what matters. With two national parks on its doorstep, plus millions more acres of public land, Moab is an ideal base for **outdoors enthusiasts**. At first, it was a mecca for **mountain-bikers**, lured by the legendary Slickrock Bike Trail. Then the **jeep drivers** began to turn up, and the **whitewater rafting** companies moved in. These days it's almost literally bursting, all year, with legions of lycra-clad holiday-makers from all over the world.

Perhaps the main reason Moab has grown so fast is that out-of-state visitors tend to find Utah's rural communities so irredeemably boring. As soon as Moab emerged from the pack, it became a beacon in the desert, attracting tourists ecstatic to find a town that stayed up after dark. Moab amounts to little more than a few miles of motels, restaurants and bars, but that's enough to make it the only southern-Utah town where you can stay for a week and still feel that you haven't seen everything, and everyone, a dozen times.

A history of Moab

Moab stands just south of the Colorado River, at the north end of a long valley created by the collapse of an underground salt dome. Because a similar valley slopes down to the river on its northern side, it's the best place to cross the Colorado in all Utah. Ute Indians passed this way for generations, but the site was first recorded by Juan de Rivera in 1765, and a ferry service later helped travellers on the **Old Spanish Trail**. The **Elk Mountain Mission**, set up in 1855, had to be abandoned after Indian attacks, but Mormon pioneers returned in the 1870s to establish a farming settlement. They named it for the Biblical wilderness of Moab, located at the edge of Zion.

Until Charlie Steen discovered **uranium** in 1952 – the first of a series of major finds in the region – the biggest thing ever to hit Moab was when **Butch Cassidy** hijacked the Colorado ferry on his way home from a bank job. The uranium boom lasted well into the 1970s, but as it petered out the local political scene turned very sour. Moab was a major focus of the **Sagebrush Rebellion** (see p.374), which pitted mine-owners and Utah businessmen, together with their fearful workforce, against the burgeoning national coalition of **environmentalists**, and the federal government that seemed to support them. Grand County commissioners repeatedly defied federal legislation by smashing bulldozers into neighbouring **Negro Bill Canyon**, administered by the BLM, in the hope of opening it and other protected wilderness areas for mineral exploitation.

While they may have won the bitter **Bulldozer Wars** – Ronald Reagan came to power proclaiming that he too was a "Sagebrush Rebel" – Utah's conservatives were no match for the world economy. The uranium market crashed in 1980, thanks partly to the accident at Three Mile Island in 1979, and partly to the discovery of vast deposits of high-grade uranium in Canada in 1980. At the same time, the bottom also fell out of oil, coal and potash. Unemployment in Moab rocketed, and the population dwindled.

The wilderness devotees who saw the region's future as resting with **tourism** now seized the chance to prove their case. They succeeded beyond their wildest dreams; out of nowhere, Moab became the West's hottest new destination, the desert equivalent of chic mountain hideaways like Aspen and Telluride in Colorado.

Sadly, almost everyone agrees that things have gone too far. Most of the old-timers have left, driven out by rising real-estate prices and none too keen to swap mining for motel clerking at a third of the

---

Charlie Steen: The Uranium King

In the early 1950s, as the Cold War gathered steam, and nuclear power stations seemed to hold infinite promise, the US government was desperate to locate a reliable domestic source of **uranium**. The Atomic Energy Commission therefore offered a $10,000 reward to anyone who discovered a mineable uranium deposit – even on public land – and guaranteed to buy whatever it produced for the next ten years.

Freelance prospectors converged on the Colorado Plateau, where uranium had been found and mined as early as 1912. Their war-surplus jeeps piled with provisions, they set off into Utah's uncharted backcountry, waving their Geiger counters at whatever likely-looking rocks might catch their eyes. Most knew which strata offered the best odds, and searched for places along the cliffs and canyon walls where they might be exposed.

Charlie Steen, a geologist from Texas, was mocked for insisting that he could find uranium by **drilling**. He would project the angle of the canyonlands' crazily tilted slopes deep underground, and calculate where the precious mineral might have accumulated atop layers of harder rock. Concentrating his efforts on the **Lisbon Valley**, thirty miles southeast of Moab, he staked out countless claims, and gave each a Spanish name.

In July 1952, the 31-year-old Steen broke his last drill bit in a 200-foot bore on the **Mi Vida** ("my life") claim. Driving back to his trailer home in despair, he pulled into a gas station in Cisco, Utah. The attendant offered to test the final plug of rock on the bed of Steen's pick-up; his Geiger counter went straight off the scale.

Following his $60-million strike, Steen opened a processing mill in Moab that became Grand County's largest employer. As the "**Uranium King**", he built himself a hilltop mansion above town, and threw a lavish annual party for all its citizens. He had his own plane, in which he'd circle above Moab at night to improve the reception on his TV, and was even a celebrity guest on *I Love Lucy*. In quick succession, he was elected to the Utah senate, then resigned after failing to change the state's liquor laws. Selling *Mi Vida*, he moved to Nevada, only to fritter his entire fortune away, losing $250,000 for example on a pickle factory.

By the early 1970s, Steen was back in Utah, this time under a false name and in disguise, once more searching the canyon country as a penniless prospector. Success eluded him however, and he eventually conceded defeat and moved to Colorado, where he still lives.

wages. Low-impact eco-tourism seemed a real possibility when only the select few had even heard of Moab, but the canyonlands now seem to be taking as hard a battering from the fat-tyre brigade as they ever did from the mining conglomerates.

Getting to Moab

No scheduled **buses** connect Moab with the outside world, but *Bighorn Express* (☎801/587-3061 or 1-888/655-RIDE) offers a daily **shuttle service** between Salt Lake City airport and Green River, Moab, Monticello and Blanding. *Alpine Air* (☎801/575-2839) offers daily commuter **flights** between **Canyonlands Airport**, twenty miles north of Moab on US-91, and Salt Lake City, for a round-trip fare of $138 and up. Arriving passengers can rent a car through *Redtail Aviation* (☎801/259-7421 or 1-800/842-9251), or call the two local **taxi** firms, *West Tracks* (☎801/259-2294) and *Arrowhead Shuttle Service* (☎801/259-7356), both of which also provide shuttle services for bikers, rafters, and hikers.

Information

The superb new **visitor center** for Moab and Grand County stands right in the heart of town at Center and Main (summer daily 8am–9pm; winter daily 8am–5pm; ☎801/259-8825 or 1-800/635-6622). As well as stacks of information on Moab itself – look out for the free *Moab Happenings* newsletter – it carries brochures and maps for the nearby parks and public lands, and is the venue for the *Canyon's Edge* **multimedia show**, held twice nightly in summer.

    Other good sources for news and information include Moab's **coffee shops** (see p.428) and the excellent *Back of Beyond* **bookstore**, 83 N Main St (☎801/259-5154). Detailed topographical **maps** can be picked up from *TI Maps*, across from the visitor center at 29 E Center St (☎801/259-5529), while the free *Canyon Country Zephyr* keeps a critical eye on local goings-on.

*The **zip code** for Moab is UT 84352.*

Accommodation

If you've already been in Utah for a while when you reach Moab, the glittering neon signs of **motels** like the *Greenwell* and the *Landmark* will come as a big surprise. At the last count, there were 27 motels in town, but every one of the thousand-plus rooms is taken on many nights between mid-March and October, so **reservations** are strongly recommended. Organizations such as *Moab/Canyonlands Central Reservations* (☎801/259-5125 or 1-800/748-4386) or *Moab Property Management* (☎801/259-5955) can help. In winter, **room rates** can drop as low as $25 per night, but you'd be lucky to find anything much below $50 in season.

Campgrounds

Moab's dozen commercial **campgrounds** can be a godsend, considering the dearth of sites in the national parks, but they do tend to be dominated by family parties.

Canyonlands Campark, 555 S Main St; ☎801/259-6848 or 1-800/522-6468. Large, year-round site in the heart of town, catering mainly to RVs but equipped with tent sites.

Sand Flats Recreation Area, 1924 S Roadrunner Hill; ☎801/259-2444. Barely developed sites, intended primarily for mountain bikers, along the top of the mesa to the east of town, near the Slickrock Bike Trail.

Slickrock Campground, 1301 N-Hwy 191; ☎801/259-7660 or 1-800/448-8873. Moab's biggest site, a mile north of town, but it's a pleasant enough and well-shaded spot, and comes with all mod cons.

*Campgrounds in **Canyonlands** are described on p.406 and p.413, and in **Arches** on p.417.*

Hostels, motels and B&Bs

Apache Motel, 166 South 400 East; ☎801/259-5727 or 1-800/228-6882, fax 259-8989. Long-established two-storey traditional motel, on a quiet backstreet east of the centre. John Wayne stayed here while filming *Rio Bravo* in the nearby canyons. Winter ②, summer ③.

Best Western Canyonlands, 16 S Main St; ☎801/259-2300 or 1-800/528-1234, fax 259-2301. Standard, dependable *Best Western*, across from the visitor center. Winter ③, summer ⑤.

Best Western Greenwell, 105 S Main St; ☎801/259-6151 or 1-800/528-1234, fax 259-4397. Central, modern and very comfortable motel. Winter ③, summer ⑤.

Bowen Motel, 169 N Main St; ☎801/259-7132 or 1-800/874-5439. Renovated 1940s motel, offering good value for such a central location. Winter ②, summer ④.

Castle Valley Inn, 424 Amber Lane, Castle Valley; ☎801/259-6012. Large, tasteful, beautifully furnished B&B, set in spacious grounds in magnificent Castle Valley, twenty miles east of town (see p.430). Five en-suite rooms and three separate bungalows, dinner served five nights weekly. ⑤–⑦.

Landmark Motel, 168 N Main St; ☎801/259-6147 or 1-800/441-6147, fax 259-5556. Upmarket central motel, with two pools and a spa. Winter ③, summer ④.

Lazy Lizard International Hostel, 1213 S Hwy-191; ☎801/259-6057. Amiable, very laid-back private hostel, well south of the centre (just beyond a bowling alley), with $7 beds in six-person dorms and private rooms for $20–25, plus a hot tub, and kitchen facilities. No membership necessary. ①.

Moab Valley Inn, 711 S Main St; ☎801/259-4419 or 1-800/831-6622, fax 259-4332. New, large, and well-equipped motel at the south end of downtown, with indoor and outdoor pools, hot tub, and on-site car and 4WD rental. Winter ③, summer ④.

Pack Creek Ranch, PO Box 1270; ☎801/259-5505, fax 259-8879. Large guest ranch, with individual cabins plus assorted pools and tubs, twenty miles southeast of town, just off the lower reaches of the La Sal Mountain Loop Road (see p.430). Summer rates of around $125 per person include all meals and trail rides on horseback. Winter ⑥, summer ⑧.

Red Stone Inn, 535 S Main St; ☎801/259-3500 or 1-800/772-1972, fax 259-2717. New, bargain-rate motel, a few blocks south of the centre. Winter ②, summer ④.

*As explained on p.15, **accommodation prices**, excluding taxes, are indicated throughout this book by the following symbols:*

① up to $30
② $30–45
③ $45–60
④ $60–80
⑤ $80–100
⑥ $100–130
⑦ $130–175
⑧ $175–250
⑨ $250+

Adventure Travel Outfits in Moab

As southern Utah's main centre for wilderness activities, Moab is filled with companies that specialize in guiding and equipping adventurous travellers. The visitor center can provide full lists of tour operators and rental outlets, plus free maps and route suggestions for bikers and 4WD drivers.

Colorado River Trips

Virtually everyone who goes **rafting** on the Colorado River does so with one of Moab's **river-running operators**. All those listed opposite offer motorized one-day trips for around $40, plus half-day tasters for perhaps $30; most also offer multi-day expeditions, and day-trip combinations such as jeep-and-raft or horse-and-raft.

Shorter trips start northwest of Moab, near Fisher Towers, and arrive near town in the afternoon; many companies give passengers the chance to float quieter stretches in two-person kayaks. While there are enough stretches of small-scale whitewater to whet the appetites of first-timers, a little romance is lost by the fact that the road runs alongside the river for much of the way. **Longer** (2–7-day) trips head through Cataract Canyon and other wild Canyonlands spots. **Oar-powered rafts** are slower but much quieter, and less expensive than motorboat trips.

Mountain Biking

While the Moab area is ideally suited to mountain-bike touring, only experienced riders should attempt its most famous route, the **Slickrock Bike Trail**. Originally laid out as a motorbike trail in 1969, this challenging ten-mile loop explores the sandstone knobs east of Moab, skirting the rim of

---

Adrift Adventures 378 N Main St; ☎801/259-8594 or 1-800/874-4483

Canyon Voyages 690 S Main St; ☎801/259-6007 or 1-800/733-6007

Canyonlands 4x4 Rental 2895 S Hwy-191; ☎801/259-4567

Chile Pepper Bike Shop 702 S Main St, ☎801/259-5223 or 1-800/626-7335

Coyote Expeditions Mile 8, Entrada Bluffs Rd; ☎801/259-6821 or 1-800/COYOTE3

Farabee 4x4 Rentals 83 S Main St; ☎801/259-7494

Kaibab Mountain Bikes 391 S Main St; ☎801/259-7423

Lin Ottinger's Tours 600 N Main St; ☎801/259-7312

Navtec Expeditions 321 N Main St; ☎801/259-7983 or 1-800/833-1278

Nichols Bike Stop 497 N Main St; ☎801/259-3999 or 1-800/648-8488

North American River Expeditions 543 N Main St; ☎801/259-5865 or 1-800/342-593?

Pack Creek Ranch PO Box 1270, La Sal Mountain Rd; ☎801/259-5505

Poison Spider Bicycles 497 N Main St; ☎801/259-7882 or 1-800/635-1792

Rim Cyclery 94 West 100 North; ☎801/259-5333

Slickrock Jeep Rentals 284 N Main St; ☎801/259-5678 or 1-800/792-0165

Tag-a-Long Expeditions 452 N Main St; ☎801/259-8946 or 1-800/453-3292

Western Spirit Cycling 38 South 100 West; ☎801/259-8732 or 1-800/845-BIKE

Western River Expeditions 1371 N Hwy-191; ☎801/259-7019 or 1-800/453-7450

Negro Bill Canyon with views to the La Sal mountains and the Colorado River. Following the white dotted line around this exposed expanse of lithified red dunes, up steep inclines and along narrow ledges, takes at least four hours. Be sure to allow enough daylight, and carry two gallons of water – far more than you can take in bike bottles alone.

To reach the trail, which lies within the **Sand Flats Recreation Area**, climb Salt Flats Road up from Millcreek Drive, which branches off 400 East Street four blocks south of Center Street. There's a fee of $1 per cycle and $3 per vehicle for trail users, but spectators can go in for free.

If you're simply cycling for pleasure, you may prefer to try the red-rock side canyons east and west of Moab, such as **Kane Creek**.

Jeep Tours and Rentals

The dirt roads that crisscross the backcountry to all sides of Moab – most created by 1950s uranium prospectors – make perfect goals for **4WD** explorations. The roads described on p.429 onwards are good for half-day trips, while obvious destinations further afield include the Island in the Sky and Needles districts of Canyonlands. Jeep **rental** rates are in the region of $80 per day; full-day guided tours cost $50–75 per person.

Scenic Flights

From Canyonlands Airport (see p.424), *Redtail Aviation* (☎801/259-7421 or 1-800/842-9251), run unforgettable flights over Canyonlands and beyond. A one-hour reconnaissance costs $60 per person, two-hour trips are $130. *Slickrock Air Guides* (☎801/259-6216 or 1-800/332-2439) have similar rates, while *Geo-Seis Helicopters* (☎801/259-3966) are rather more expensive.

River Tours	River Rentals	Jeep Tours	Jeep Rentals	Bike Tours	Bike Rentals	Horses
•						•
•						
	•					
		•	•			
				•		
•			•	•	•	•
		•				
		•				
•		•				
•		•			•	
•		•				
				•	•	
•	•					
			•		•	
•						

Moab

Sunflower Hill B&B, 185 North 300 East; ☎801/259-2974, fax 259-2470. Antique- furnished former farmhouse, now an 11-room B&B, away from the bustle on a dead-end side street. All units are en-suite, some are in separate cottages. Winter ③, summer ④.

Super 8, 889 N Main St; ☎801/259-8868 or 1-800/800-8000, fax 259-8968. Moab's largest motel, kitted out in *Super 8*'s normal drab colours but offering good value for money, at the north end of town not far from the Colorado. Winter ②, summer ④.

The Town

Main Street, the broad five-mile section of US-191 that sweeps through the centre of Moab, is lined with all the gas stations, diners, motels and other businesses that you'd expect. For two blocks north and south of Center Street, which crosses it at the visitor center in the middle, window-shopping pedestrians stroll the sidewalk and browse the menus. Elsewhere, everybody drives or cycles. Squeezed between Swiss Cheese Ridge to the east and the Moab Rim to the west, the town has little room to expand, but you can still see a few pioneer homes, and the occasional apple orchard, if you venture down the side streets.

The highspots of Moab's calendar are the Jeep Safari at Easter, and the Fat Tire mountain-bike festival in late October.

Local history is enjoyably recalled at the Dan O'Laurie Museum, also known as the Canyon Country Museum, at 118 E Center St (summer Mon–Sat 1–8pm; winter Mon–Thurs 3–7pm, Fri & Sat 1–7pm; donations). Displays start with a mammoth tusk dredged from the Colorado, and the replica of an ancient petroglyph claimed to show the "Moab mastodon". Then follows the usual small-town assortment, ranging from an Anasazi basket to Moab's first telephone switchboard, plus plenty of souvenirs from the uranium days. A gallery upstairs holds separate exhibitions of contemporary art.

On a hot summer's day, you might prefer a quick wallow at Butch Cassidy's King World Waterpark (mid-April to mid-Sept daily 10am–10pm; adults $7.50, under-13s $6.50). This complex of water slides and swimming pools is tucked rather incongruously into a side canyon at the north end of town, said to have been used as a hideout by the Wild Bunch.

Eating

While Moab has yet to acquire the range of restaurants you might find in a major resort, it offers by far the greatest choice in southern Utah, and for once most places make a serious effort to cater for vegetarians. Full menus appear in the *Moab Menu Guide*, available free at local motels. There's also no problem getting a drink – Moab even has two pubs and its own winery – while coffee bars are springing up all over town. Several bike shops have espresso counters for early-morning customers.

Center Cafe, 92 E Center St; ☎801/259-4295. Expensive but exquisite restaurant, offering gourmet dining with a Pacific twist. Appetizers for around $8 include Thai shrimp satay and grilled eggplant pizza; entrees, at more like

$20, range through Asian barbecue salmon and rack of lamb. Open for dinner nightly, plus brunch on Sun, 9am–1pm; closed Dec–Feb.

Eddie McStiff's, 57 S Main St; ☎801/259-2337. Central pub, next to the visitor center, which has some interesting beers, including raspberry and blueberry. The restaurant serves a varied but consistently tasty menu, with inexpensive salads, fancy Southwestern pizzas (with toppings like sundried tomatoes and jalapeño peppers) from $8, plus pasta and steak dinners.

Fat City Smoke House, 36 South 100 West; ☎801/259-4302. Informal Texas-style open-pit barbecue, serving tangy chicken, pork and ribs, and vegetarian sandwiches. Open Mon–Sat 11am until late, Sun 5–9pm.

Kayenta Coffee House, 90 E Center St; ☎801/259-2553. Small cafe-bakery behind the visitor center, aimed at a slightly more sedate crowd.

Mi Vida, 900 N Hwy-191; ☎801/259-7146. Charlie Steen's luxury hilltop home (see p.423) is now one of Moab's finest restaurants, with tasty meat and seafood entrees for $11–22, great desserts, and stunning views across the valley. The tortuous if short approach road from the north end of town (lit at night) means it's no place to drink and drive.

Moab Brewery, 686 S Main St; ☎801/259-6333. Moab's newest microbrewery, a cavernous place a good way south of the centre. The beers aren't bad, but the food is. Open from 11.30 am daily.

Mondo Cafe, 59 S Main St; ☎801/259-5911. Groovy all-day hangout next to *Eddie McStiff's*, serving espresso coffees and the odd pastry or sandwich. Open daily 7.30am–10pm.

The Poplar Place, First North and Main St; ☎801/259-6018. Friendly, classy adobe bar with Anasazi-themed ironwork, serving draft beers and good pizzas. Open daily 11.30am–11pm.

Slick Rock Cafe, Center and Main; ☎801/259-8004. Modern central cafe, which gives every meal of the day a Southwestern flavour. Omelettes, burritos, burgers and sandwiches earlier on, and some good chicken and pasta entrees, for $10–15, in the evening.

Sundowner, 1393 N Hwy-191; ☎801/259-5201. Dinner-only restaurant, not far short of the Colorado, where the German owner serves up heavily Germanic dishes such as *wiener schnitzel* as well as lighter salads and sandwiches. Open daily from 5pm.

The Thai House, 84 West 200 North; ☎801/259-4545. Not the most authentic Thai cuisine you'll ever eat, but a welcome change in Utah nonetheless. Open daily for lunch and dinner.

Around Moab

Although most visitors head straight for the national parks, several lesser-known areas in the Moab region are well worth exploring. Both upstream and downstream, minor roads run alongside the **Colorado River**, while the **La Sal Mountains** to the east make a snowy contrast to the aridity of the desert.

The Potash Road

The dead-end **Potash Road**, Hwy-279, which doubles back south-west along the Colorado's west bank from just north of the bridge on US-191, passes a number of intriguing **rock art** sites, and provides a

Moab

The Potash Road cliffs are often busy with rock climbers; if you fancy a lesson, contact Moab Adventure Outfitters ☎801/259-2725).

great close-up view of the river. In this stretch the Colorado is broad and lazy, tinted the same reddish brown as the Navajo sandstone cliffs that tower above it.

Seven miles down the road, you reach a group of **petroglyphs** a dozen feet up on the canyon wall to the right. Scraped into the dark "desert varnish" by Fremont Indians, some time between 700 and 1300 AD, they depict animals and anthropomorphic figures, including a chain of linked humans resembling paper dolls.

A mile further on, two mounted metal tubes tucked among the roadside bushes point to a group of barely discernable **dinosaur tracks**. More petroglyphs can also be seen, this time higher on the cliffs. The signposted **Jug Handle Arch**, seven miles on, is not all that spectacular, while a smaller and even less enthralling arch is located on the western flank of the same side canyon.

Just past the arches, seventeen miles from US-191, the valley floor widens. The road officially ends here, at the ugly green plant where *Moab Salt* produces salt and **potash**, accompanied by billowing clouds of white smoke. It is possible to drive on, but how much further you go probably depends on whether you own the vehicle you're driving. The surface is paved for another 1.3 miles, while 1.7 bumpy miles beyond that you get your first glimpse of the 23 vinyl-lined **evaporation ponds** where the potash is prepared. Dyed a lurid bluey turquoise to speed evaporation, they're a real eyesore, clearly visible from Dead Horse Point far above (see p.405).

Only **4WD** vehicles can continue past the ponds, and the nearby boat-launch ramp. *Thelma and Louise* freeze-framed their way into the final credits from the mesa-top a few miles further up, and in due course the Potash Road meets up with the White Rim Road in Canyonlands (see p.408).

Castle Valley and the La Sal Mountains

Turning northeast off US-191 just south of the bridge takes you onto **Hwy-128**, which follows the Colorado's east bank for 35 miles, then crosses the river to meet I-70 ten miles further up. In summer, this superbly scenic section of the river is busy with one-day rafting trips, which can be watched from several roadside lookouts. Roughly twenty miles along, the three-pronged red butte of **Fisher Towers** rises to the right of the road.

For an excellent sixty-mile **loop trip** back to Moab, turn right, southeast, fifteen miles along the river road, onto Castle Valley Road. **Castle Valley** is a verdant cleft that boasts some quintessentially Western scenery, with red sandstone walls and buttes such as the **Priest and Nuns** to the east, and high dark hills to the west. At its far southern end, eleven miles along, another right turn sets you climbing up the volcanic 10,000-feet **La Sal Mountains**. A couple of narrow single-file gravel stretches and some hair-raising hairpins

Fisher Towers were originally "Fissure Towers"; there was no "Fisher".

later, you reach a vantage point commanding views across the Colorado to Arches and Canyonlands. Beyond that, the road runs through the high mountain landscape of the **Manti–La Sal National Forest**. A few campgrounds are tucked into the woods, but you won't see another building before the road eventually drops back towards Moab Valley.

Hole N" The Rock (sic)

The peculiarly punctuated **Hole N" The Rock**, 15 miles south of Moab on US-191 (daily 9am–5pm; $2.50), is a classic piece of 1950s' Americana. Having started out with a roadside diner at the foot of a cliff, Albert Christensen and his wife Gladys ended up hollowing an entire home deep into the red sandstone. Albert was a dreadful taxidermist – his unfortunate donkey Henry has to be seen to be believed – and painter – cross-eyed Christs a speciality – but his cool, well-lit house is a masterpiece. He died in 1957, without completing the spiral staircase that was planned to lead 65ft up to a roof-top patio. In the fine tradition of the "jewellery" Gladys made from broken beer bottles, the gift store is stocked with tacky souvenirs.

Canyon Rims Recreation Area

The vast and almost completely empty mesa west of US-191, which separates Moab from the Needles district of Canyonlands National Park (see p.411), is largely taken up by the BLM-run **Canyon Rims Recreation Area**. Not much recreation goes on up here, although it has the usual Jeep roads and a scattering of hiking trails; there are also two basic, waterless **campgrounds**, *Hatch Point* and *Windwhistle* (both April–Oct only; $6; ☎801/259-6111).

Only consider visiting the two main overlooks if you have a lot of time to spare – it involves a two-and-a-half-hour detour from the highway – or if you're not going to get to the Needles district, in which case the **Needles Overlook** provides a (relatively) quick overview that's as dramatic as any in Canyonlands itself.

The Needles Overlook

The paved road into the Canyon Rims Recreation Area leaves US-191 32 miles south of Moab. Its dreary 22-mile course westwards comes to an abrupt halt at the windswept **Needles Overlook**, where a short railed footpath gives eagle's-eye views across the canyonlands. Specific landmarks are hard to pick out amid the orange sandstone ledges that spread below, but looking south you should spot the twin **Sixshooter Peaks**, and Hwy-211 winding alongside Indian Creek towards the Needles district (see p.412). Further west the Needles themselves poke from the hillocks, while the Colorado loops its way from the north towards the confluence.

Snow usually closes the La Sal Mountain Loop Road from November until April. In summer, it takes four hours to complete the loop.

Don't confuse the Hole N" The Rock with the Hole In The Rock pioneer river crossing near Escalante; see p.378.

The Anticline Overlook

Fifteen miles in from US-191, or seven miles short of the Needles Overlook, forking right onto an even, broad gravel road commits you to the 25-minute drive across the tumbleweed-strewn sagebrush desert to the **Anticline Overlook**. You probably won't pass another vehicle before the final parking lot, from which a five-minute walk leads to a high promontory that faces the potash evaporation beds (see p.430) and **Dead Horse Point** across the Colorado.

Some people call this the AntiClimax Overlook, disappointed to realize that they've driven almost all the way back to Moab. As you'll see if you follow the fence around the headland, only **Kane Creek Canyon** – where the creek is the tiniest of green slivers in the red wasteland – intervenes. You'll almost certainly hear motorbikes scrambling across the slickrock of the Moab Rim on the far side. To the northeast, silhouetted above a brief stretch of the Colorado, you also get a remarkable view of the fins of **Arches** National Park, with the line of sight passing straight through the South Window.

Southeast Utah

It may lack big-name national parks, but Utah's **southeast corner** is every bit as scenic as the neighbouring regions. The desert here is so unforgiving that only a handful of widely separated settlements cling to life, and large tracts remain entirely without roads.

Culturally as well as geographically, southeast Utah has much in common with the Four Corners area, covered in Chapter One. The **Anasazi** were here in force, as countless abandoned pueblos can testify. They're thought to have moved off to the south and east around 1250 AD, but even now almost half the population of **San Juan County**, which covers the bulk of the region and is larger than several states, is Native American. A few are Utes, but most are **Navajo**, many of them descended from families who hid here during the 1860s to escape the Long Walk (see p.487).

The first **Mormons** to reach this far-flung corner were the Hole-in-the-Rock pioneers (see p.377), who established **Bluff** in 1880 and went on to found **Blanding** and **Monticello** as well. All those towns make viable bases, but the real attraction, as ever, is the landscape, with hikers heading for **Natural Bridges National Monument**, more ambitious backpackers for **Grand Gulch**, and drivers rattling across the desert to the unbelievable **Muley Point**, **Goosenecks State Park**, and the **Valley of the Gods**.

Monticello

The first fifty miles of US-191 south of Moab are so desolate that it comes as a major shock, on climbing some straggling foothills, to find yourself confronted by ploughed green fields. To Mormon pioneers, this terrain resembled Thomas Jefferson's country home in Virginia – hence the name of **MONTICELLO**, six miles further on. Farming has never been all that easy here, however, and the economy has only recently been put on a steadier footing by the growth of tourism.

The normal route to the Needles District of Canyonlands, fifty miles northwest, is to take Hwy-211 west from US-191, roughly 22 miles north of town. In summer, it's also possible to take a very different approach, through the volcanic **Abajo Mountains**, which rise west of town to over 11,000ft. The road up, from the west end of 200 South, is pretty straightforward, and passes through some lovely quasi-Alpine meadows where you may spot browsing deer. You then veer north and drop down a much rougher track, to meet Hwy-211 near Newspaper Rock (see p.412)

To the east of Monticello, US-666 heads off to Colorado through what looks like a segment of the Great Plains that has wandered astray, complete with grain silos and fields of wheat and beans.

The local pronunciation of Monticello is "Monti-sello".

Southeast Utah

Arrival and information

Information on Monticello, and on the parks and public lands in the vicinity, can be picked up from the multi-agency **visitor center** in San Juan County Courthouse at 117 S Main St (April–Oct Mon–Fri 8am–5pm, Sat & Sun 10am–5pm; Nov–March Mon–Fri 8am–5pm; ☎801/587-3235 or 1-800/574-4386).

From the airstrip three miles north, *Midway Aviation* (☎801/587-2774) run $59 one-hour scenic flights over Canyonlands.

Accommodation

Monticello is not nearly as lively a place to spend the night as Moab, but it does have a reasonable set of **motels** to choose from.

Best Western Wayside Inn, 197 E Central Ave; ☎801/587-2261 or 1-800/633-9700, fax 587-2920. Comfortable upscale motel, with pool and spa, a few yards down US-666 towards Colorado. Winter ③, summer ④.

Canyonlands Motor Inn, 197 N Main St; ☎801/587-2266 or 1-800/952-6212, fax 587-2883. Roadside motel, on the north side of town, that's seen better days; fairly decrepid rooms at reasonable rates. Winter ②, summer ③.

Edge of the Canyon, PO Box 128; ☎801/979-4010. En-suite rooms in rural lodge a 15-minute drive southeast of town, intended in part as a writers' and artists' retreat. ④.

Grist Mill Inn, 64 South 300 East; ☎801/587-2597 or 1-800/645-3762, fax 587-2579. Restored 1930s flour mill with six en-suite B&B rooms. There are three more in an adjoining building, plus a converted railroad caboose. ③–⑤.

Super 8, 649 N Main St; ☎801/587-2489 or 1-800/800-8000. Monticello's newest and northernmost motel, with a pool, clean rooms and friendly managers. Winter ③, summer ④.

Triangle H Motel, 164 E Central Ave; ☎801/587-2274 or 1-800/657-6622, fax 587-2175. Neat, inexpensive single-storey motel, with some two-bedroom units. Winter ②, summer ③.

*The **zip code** for Monticello is UT 84535.*

*The **price codes** used here are explained on p.15.*

Eating

Like any self-respecting farming town, Monticello abounds in wholesome if unexciting **diners**, plus a few fast-food outlets.

Houston's of Monticello, 296 N Main St; ☎801/587-2531. Breakfasts and lunches, with a stress on fresh organic produce; daily except Tues 6am–3pm.

Lamplight Restaurant, 655 E Central St; ☎801/587-2170. Diner-only joint on the eastern edge of town, offering steaks, burgers and meat in general, with plenty of options below $10, and a salad bar. Mon–Sat 4–11pm.

MD Ranch Cookhouse, 380 S Main St; ☎801/587-3299. New, attractive wood-themed restaurant, with attached gift store. Grilled breakfasts and sandwich lunches, but the real *raison d'etre* is to serve big steak dinners, including T-bones for $15 and buffalo for $17, all in; they also have fish, shrimp, ribs and veggie burgers. Live music Fri & Sat.

Mesa Java, 518 N Main St; ☎801/587-2601. Espresso coffees and fresh pastries from 7am, on open-air terrace of a gift store. Closed Wed Oct–April.

Wagon Wheel Pizza, 164 S Main St; ☎801/587-2766. Homemade pizzas of all sizes and one shape, plus deli sandwiches.

Blanding

BLANDING, just over twenty miles southwest of Monticello, was established as "Grayson" in 1905, when a new irrigation channel brought water to this site from the Abajo Mountains. In 1915, **Thomas Bicknell**, an East-Coast millionaire, offered to give a library to any Utah town that would change its name to his own. Two jumped in; Thurber, near Torrey, became Bicknell, while Grayson took his wife's maiden name, Blanding. Each got a new library, though it's said they didn't get as many books as they'd expected.

Having skirted the Abajos, US-191 is running due west as it enters Blanding, and makes a sharp dogleg turn south at the four-way stop in the centre of town. That brief pause is as much time as most travellers give Blanding, but if you head north at this junction, and then west, you'll come to the interesting **Edge of the Cedars State Park**, 660 West 400 North (mid-May to mid-Sept daily 9am–6pm; mid-Sept to mid-May daily 9am–5pm; $1.50; ☎801/678-2238). An excellent museum here, primarily intended as an educational resource for local kids, holds displays that range from the Anasazi to the Anglos. In a town with a notorious reputation for illegal pot-hunting by profit-seeking amateurs – known locally as "Moki poachers" – it emphasizes the role and techniques of proper archeology. Some of the Anasazi artefacts are truly remarkable, including pots and pendants, stylish wooden plates, and a complete loom dated to around 1150 AD. Outside, a footpath leads around an Anasazi pueblo occupied between 700 and 1220 AD. In the one section to have been excavated, visitors can climb down a ladder into a musty, haunting *kiva*. Signs point out that all the buildings face south, probably to maximize sunlight, whereas Navajo dwellings always face east.

*For more about the **Anasazi**, including explanations of the terms used here, see p.468.*

Several blocks further south, the **Nations of the Four Corners Cultural Center**, 707 West 500 South (open 24hr; free) is a small park holding reconstructions of a Navajo hogan, a Ute teepee, a Mormon cabin and an Hispanic hacienda. It occasionally hosts cultural events on summer evenings.

Accommodation

Traffic between Lake Powell to the west and Moab to the north keeps Blanding's **motels** busy enough in summer, but they're not a very inspiring bunch.

Blanding Sunset Inn, 88 W Center St; ☎801/678-3323. Cheap, basic motel on the quieter section of Center St, west of the four-way stop. Winter ②, summer ③.

Cliff Palace, 132 S Main St; ☎801/678-2264 or 1-800/553-8093. Small, slightly rundown 1960s motel that advertises itself with the slogan "Watching Your Pennies? Stay At The Cliff Palace". ②.

Comfort Inn, 711 S Main St; ☎801/678-3271 or 1-800/622-3250, fax 678-3219. Characterless chain motel well south of the centre, with an indoor pool and complimentary continental breakfasts. Winter ③, summer ④.

Four Corners Inn, 131 E Center St; ☎801/678-3257 or 1-800/574-3150, fax 678-3219. Large, modern, two-storey motel, just after the highway doglegs to the right, with free continental breakfasts. Winter ③, summer ④.

Eating

Eating in Blanding is indeed bland eating.

Elk Ridge Restaurant, 120 E Center; ☎801/678-3390. Blanding's busiest diner, open for all meals with a standard menu of chicken, liver, steak and a few Mexican dishes. Daily 6am–10pm.

Kenny's Restaurant, US-191; ☎801/678-3604. The full gamut of Utah cuisine – full breakfasts, lunch sandwiches, dinner meats and Mexican specialities, and loads of pies – at low prices.

Old Tymer, 735 S Main St; ☎801/678-3271. Conventional tourist diner, next to the *Comfort Inn* at the south end of town.

West of Blanding

A mile or so south of Blanding, **Hwy-95** heads west from US-191, to embark on a magnificent 120-mile trans-Utah journey to Hanksville. Until it was completed in 1976 – which is why it's also known as the **Bicentennial Highway** – east–west travel was effectively barred by the massive monocline of **Comb Ridge**, ten miles west of Blanding. To the Navajo, this thousand-foot wall of red rock, which stretches over eighty miles from north to south, was the backbone of the earth, as well as one of four "arrowheads" protecting their homeland. To Mormon pioneers, it was a definitive "reef" (see p.380).

No towns interrupt Hwy-95 apart from the speck that is **Hite**, 87 miles along at Lake Powell (see p.397). Humans have at times occupied the region, however. Several side canyons off Hwy-95 bear

*The **zip code** for Blanding is UT 84511.*

*The **price codes** used here are explained on p.15.*

traces of an Anasazi presence, while the cattle ranchers who tried their hands here a century ago were later succeeded by uranium miners in the 1950s.

The Butler Wash Ruins

Ten miles west of the highway intersection, a short spur road climbs west of Hwy-95 to the parking lot for the **Butler Wash Ruins**, a stimulating Anasazi site that's located on BLM land (24hr; free). A ten-minute hike, much of it up steep bare rock, leads to an overlook into a side canyon just short of the crest of Comb Ridge. The ruins are located in the topmost of three natural rock alcoves; a long stone ledge to the left leads down to the fertile wash where the inhabitants farmed. Archeologists see them as combining elements from what are usually regarded as distinct sub-groups of the Anasazi, in that the complex includes one Kayenta-style square *kiva* and three Mesa Verde-style round *kivas*.

Mule Canyon

Immediately beyond Butler Wash, Hwy-95 picks its way down the lurid red wall of Comb Ridge to a cottonwood-rich valley, then laboriously climbs the far side. Ten miles along, a dirt road to the north, signed for Texas Flat, leads to a trailhead for **Mule Canyon**. The northern sides of each of this shallow canyon's two forks hold several small but well-preserved Anasazi cliff dwellings. Both forks are around six miles long, but the most interesting ruins are roughly one mile and three miles along the South Fork, so a six-mile day-hike is enough for most visitors.

A separate paved turn-off, half a mile along from the Texas Flat road, leads in a few yards to **Mule Canyon Ruin**, a partly restored Anasazi pueblo that dates from around 1000 AD. This small site, a bit too near the highway to be very evocative, is similar to Boulder's Anasazi State Park (see p.378). Its most conspicuous features – a round *kiva* that has been roofed over for preservation, and a two-storey masonry tower – are connected by an underground tunnel, perhaps used for surprise appearances during religious ceremonies.

Through the Bear's Ears

Before Hwy-95 was constructed, the main road west of Blanding – and the principal access to Natural Bridges (see opposite) – was a dirt track that climbed across the southern fringes of the Abajo Mountains. In reasonable weather, ordinary vehicles can still follow this attractive route, by turning north from Hwy-95 seven miles from the intersection. The 32-mile detour takes well over an hour.

After a cool, pleasant drive through the mountain-top woodlands, the road crosses a razorback ridge above Arch Canyon and then descends between two rounded outcrops known as the **Bear's Ears**. This prominent landmark is regarded by the Navajo as the embodiment of a bear, guarding the northern limits of their territory. The road eventually switchbacks down a sheer red cliff to join the approach road that leads into Natural Bridges.

Natural Bridges National Monument

Three of the world's largest natural bridges span the streambeds of the small, unspectacular White and Armstrong canyons, which cut through the white sandstone of **Cedar Mesa** southwest of the Abajo Mountains. NATURAL BRIDGES NATIONAL MONUMENT was the loneliest of spots when prospector Cass Hite stumbled across it in the 1880s, and when it was made Utah's first federal park in 1908. Now, however, it can be easily accessed by a four-mile spur road off Hwy-95, forty miles west of Blanding.

Originally dubbed Edwin, Augusta and Caroline, the bridges were given Hopi names when it was realized that much of the rock art found on the canyon walls represented Hopi clan symbols. It's thought this was one of the many places that the Anasazi ancestors of the Hopi passed through during their migrations, departing around 1270 AD after a stay of perhaps six hundred years.

Each bridge can be seen from overlooks along the one-way, nine-mile **Bridge View Drive** that loops through the monument. With considerably more effort, you can clamber down into the canyons for closer inspection, and also follow the stream from one to the next for a potential hike of up to nine miles.

Practicalities

Admission to Natural Bridges costs $4 per vehicle or $2 per person; the gates to the loop drive are open from dawn until dusk daily. The **visitor center** – which is solar-powered, being so far from any other source of energy – stocks free trail guides and other background material (March–Oct daily 8am–5pm; Nov–Feb daily 9am–4.30pm; ☎801/692-1234). Excellent displays show how the bridges were formed, pointing out that natural bridges occur throughout the US, from West Virginia to Illinois. The visitor center is the only source of water for the first-come first-served **campground** nearby ($5).

The closest **motel** to the monument is the basic but romantically isolated *Fry Canyon Lodge & Cafe* (PO Box 200, Fry Canyon UT 84533; ☎801/259-5334; Dec–Feb ②, March–Nov ③), twenty miles west at mile marker 71 on Hwy-95, which has its own **campground**.

Bridge View Drive

The first and largest bridge, **Sipapu Bridge**, was named for the "hole" through which the Hopi emerged into this world. It stands 220 feet high by 268 feet wide, surpassed only by Rainbow Bridge (see p.395). Although the roadside overlook provides a good straight-on view as it thrusts from a tangle of rocks, you'll only really appreciate its size if you hike down from the trailhead half a mile further on. This is the most difficult trail in the monument, involving three short ladders, two metal staircases, and a couple of stretches of slickrock with steep drop-offs. The best photos come from a ledge halfway down; by the time you're amid the trees directly beneath it, it's too big to fit in the viewfinder.

The next parking lot on the road is the start of a half-mile mesa-top trail that leads to a vantage point above **Horsecollar Ruin**. This small Anasazi site, tucked into an alcove low on the canyon walls, is not visible from below.

Even after a 4000-ton rock fall in 1992, **Kachina Bridge**, the next stop, is much thicker than Sipapu, being more of a tunnel beneath a broad span of desert-varnish-stained sandstone. Seen from the over-look, it's far less distinct, with rocks rather than sunlight visible through the gap. On the trail down, railings guide you across the slickrock, and there's a crude staircase made from sandstone slabs. The stream at the bottom is lined by spledid cottonwoods, while pictographs near the base of the bridge resemble the *kachinas* of Hopi religion (see p.58).

Natural bridges are short-lived phenomena. Even the oldest in the monument – **Owachomo**, two miles beyond Kachina by road – is a mere 5000 years old, and it's unlikely to last much longer. Though 180ft across, it tapers to just nine feet thick. It now stands slightly to one side of the streambed of Armstrong Canyon, reached by an easy half-mile round-trip hike. *Owachomo* means "flat-rock mound", a reference to the hummock at the left end of the span.

Allow five hours for the full 8.6-mile hike from Sipapu Bridge to the two others and back across the mesa.

The **streambed trail** that connects the three bridges makes a delightful walk, meandering along the sandy wash beneath the trees. However, unless you double back, returning to your starting point involves a long hike across the mesa top, which is not as flat as you'd imagine and offers very little shade. One idea would be to start from Owachomo or Kachina and hike back towards Sipapu, hoping you'll meet up with someone who can give you a ride back to your vehicle.

Grand Gulch Primitive Area

If you share a passion for archeology with the stamina for long-distance hiking, an expedition into the **GRAND GULCH PRIMITIVE AREA**, south of Natural Bridges, can make you feel like a real-life Indiana Jones. Every twist and turn of this deep, dramatic gorge seems to be filled with relics of its thousand-year occupation by the Anasazi, although they abandoned the canyon six centuries before it was named by the Hole-in-the-Rock pioneers.

Typical Grand Gulch back-packing expeditions last as long as a week. For more details, call the BLM in Monticello; ☎ 801/587-2141.

Grand Gulch gouges across Cedar Mesa for just over fifty miles, dropping 2700ft to meet the San Juan River. There's no access for vehicles; the only path in starts from **Kane Gulch Ranger Station** (March to mid-Nov; no phone), five miles south of the point where Hwy-261 leaves Hwy-95, two miles east of the Natural Bridges turn-off. All would-be hikers should register here, but only those planning to camp overnight are liable for the $5 fee.

The trail begins by dropping steadily down Kane Gulch, a side canyon that deepens as it goes, and joins Grand Gulch proper four miles along. **Junction Ruin** here, the largest ruin in the canyon system, makes a popular day-hike destination, though **Turkey Pen Ruin**, at 4.7 miles, and **Stimper Arch** just beyond, are also within round-trip reach. If you're making a longer trip, it's possible to leave Grand Gulch via **Bullet Canyon** to the east – in which case a total hike of 23 miles brings you back to Hwy-261 roughly seven miles south of the ranger station – or **Collins Canyon** to the west further along – a 38-mile hike that ends at a dirt road south of Hwy-276. For either of those routes, you'll need a car shuttle to get back to your vehicle, but that's probably easier to arrange than fixing for someone to meet you by boat on the San Juan, which is the only way out if you hike all the way to the end of Grand Gulch. Most visitors find it simpler just to double back at some point en route.

Muley Point

South of Kane Gulch, Hwy-261 crosses Cedar Mesa for its remaining seventeen miles. Before you take the plunge on the **Moki Dugway**, **MULEY POINT**, exactly five miles west of its top along an unmarked red-dirt road, is an absolute must-see.

When they finally get around to declaring all of southern Utah to be one vast national park, Muley Point will surely be the centrepiece. Quite simply, these are among the most stupendous views in the world. You're now at the southernmost tip of Cedar Mesa and the eastern extremity of Glen Canyon National Recreational Area. Far below, the San Juan River goosenecks its way west, while the Navajo Nation stretches off on the far side. Features on the horizon include Monument Valley in all its glory, the Sleeping Ute in Colorado, Navajo Mountain, and the cliffs above the west shore of Lake Powell.

*The views from Muley Point are reminiscent of those from **Dead Horse Point**, poised at a similar elevation ninety miles north; see p.405.*

The Moki Dugway

Hwy-261 doesn't stand on ceremony when it needs to get down off Cedar Mesa; it just plummets over the edge. The unpaved **MOKI DUGWAY**, which drops 1100ft in little more than two miles, is a terrifying but exhilarating ride, switchbacking through repeated hairpin bends on a "washboard" strip of gravel. This ancient trail was improved by mining companies during the 1950s; you'll just have to hope you don't meet a truck-load of uranium coming the other way. If you have the nerve, the pull-outs for vehicles to pass make great viewpoints, but it's best to do all your sightseeing at the top.

*Soon after the pavement resumes at the bottom of the Moki Dugway, another dirt road marks the western end of the **Valley of the Gods**; see p.441.*

Goosenecks State Park

Just before Hwy-261 meets US-163, six miles from the foot of the Moki Dugway and five miles north of Mexican Hat, the inconspicu-

*Goosenecks
State Park has
no visitor
center and no
opening hours,
and charges
no fee.*

ous **Hwy-316** branches off to the west, to end 3.5 miles along at the extraordinary **GOOSENECKS STATE PARK**. Although the railed viewing area here stands a thousand feet below Cedar Mesa, the **San Juan River** is still another thousand feet down.

The river is an amazing sight, looping between huge pyramidal buttes in a textbook example of what geologists call an "entrenched meander". Its serpentine coils – once meanders on a muddy plain, later fixed in stone by the uplifting of the Colorado Plateau – are so extravagant that it flows six miles while advancing little more than one mile west. Above the distant sliver of riverbank greenery, alternate layers of grey limestone and red sandstone stripe the cliffs, while Monument Valley once again stands out on the skyline.

Bluff

*The full story
of the Hole-in-
the-Rock expe-
dition is told
on p.377.*

BLUFF, 23 miles south of Blanding on US-191, is a pretty little riverside settlement whose somewhat humdrum present belies the extraordinary efforts its founders made to get here. The 230 **Hole-in-the-Rock** pioneers who reached this site on April 6, 1880 had trekked right across the heart of Utah, literally blasting their way through the canyons of the Colorado.

*In late
October, Bluff
plays host to
the three-day
**Utah Navajo
Fair**.*

Once they arrived, they settled down to a life of ranching and agriculture, made difficult by the San Juan River's propensity to flood. The back streets still hold a dozen or so of their original sturdy homes, making Bluff the least spoiled, most authentic town in the region. Its setting is consistently stunning, from the red-rock pinnacles known as the **Navajo Twins**, which mark the mouth of the narrow **Cow Canyon** gorge through which US-191 drops in from the north, to the cottonwoods that line the San Juan River, glinting against the sheer red bluff that rises on the far side. **Anasazi** remains abound, including petroglyphs along Hwy-163 to the east, and the unexcavated mound, thought to conceal a buried pueblo, beside the town cemetery on a hillock just north of the centre.

*Bluff makes a
handy
overnight stop
for **Hovenweep
National
Monument**,
forty miles
northwest; see
p.63.*

Bluff is also a centre for **river-running** on the San Juan, with rafts putting in at **Sand Island Recreation Area**, three miles west. The chief local operator, *Wild Rivers Expeditions* (☎801/672-2244 or 1-800/422-7654), runs one-day float trips to Mexican Hat (adults $75, under-13s $55), plus a range of longer voyages.

*The **zip code**
for Bluff is UT
84512.*

Accommodation

There's nothing very fancy in Bluff, but its genuine small-town feel makes it a nicer prospect than any of its neighbours.

Bluff B&B, PO Box 158; ☎801/672-2220. Homely two-room B&B in a 1960s brick house, on the edge of the desert northeast of town. ④.

Kokopelli Inn, PO Box 27, US-191; ☎801/672-2322 or 1-800/541-8854, fax 672-2385. Friendly, quiet roadside motel, adjoining a gas station and grocery with a deli counter. Winter ②, summer ③.

Recapture Lodge, PO Box 309; ☎801/672-2281, fax 672-2284. Pleasantly rural wooden motel, reaching back towards the river, plus a few rooms in two old pioneer homes. For groups, the owners can arrange area tours, including Monument Valley expeditions and llama treks. Winter ②, summer ③.

River House Inn, 500 West & US-191; ☎801/672-2217. Ramshackle six-room motel at the west end of town, beyond the Cottonwood Wash. Winter ②, summer ③.

Eating

Despite its size, Bluff has a good range of **restaurants**, but they're a bit too spread out to walk from one to the next comparing menus.

Cottonwood Steakhouse, US-191; ☎801/672-2282. Open-air barbecue at the west end of town, with wooden tables arranged around a giant cottonwood. A great place to enjoy beer and steaks beneath the stars, though the menu's a bit short if you're not a beef-eater. One corner of the pseudo-Western stockade serves as Fort Crapper.

Cow Canyon Trading Post, Hwy-163; ☎801/672-2208. Former trading post, where Hwy-163 leaves US-161 and heads for Colorado, that's now an imaginative local restaurant. If you've had enough of Navajo tacos, this is the place to try a Navajo quiche. Usually open in summer only, Thurs–Mon.

K&C Trading Post Deli, US-191; ☎801/672-2221. Grocery deli that sells pizzas, sandwiches and fried chicken until 11pm in summer, 9pm in winter.

Sunbonnet Cafe, Bluff Historic Loop; ☎801/672-2201. Small, friendly cafe a block off the highway. Big fried breakfasts, plus Navajo tacos and full meaty dinners for well under $10. Open Mon–Sat 7am–9pm.

Thai House, 100 North 200 West; ☎801/672-2355. Strange but true; genuine Thai restaurant in a brick, backstreet pioneer home. Open daily for dinner only, 4–10pm, with plenty of vegetarian choices.

Twin Rocks Cafe, Navajo Twins Drive; ☎801/672-2341. Glass-fronted diner, set against the rocks north of town, just west of US-191. Breakfast espressos, bagels and muffins, then salads and sandwiches. Open daily 9am–10pm.

The Valley of the Gods

Bluff is very much at the edge of the desert; driving west you soon descend **Comb Ridge** (see p.435) into vintage red-rock badlands, with the buttes of Monument Valley silhouetted above the horizon.

Similar, smaller-scale monoliths can be toured closer at hand, with no restrictions or admission fees, in the **VALLEY OF THE GODS**. This "garden" of isolated sandstone columns – said by the Navajo to be petrified warriors – holds no fixed hiking trails. Drivers can see it all from a winding **seventeen-mile dirt road**, which leaves US-163 on the far side of Lime Creek, roughly eighteen miles west of Bluff, and meets Hwy-261 near the foot of the Moki Dugway (see p.439), 10.6 miles northwest of Mexican Hat.

It's a rough road, which gets impassable when wet, but so long as you don't mind a few bangs on the bottom as you cross dry stony washes you should be able to make it in a rental. The east side holds the best of the "monuments", and the most difficult terrain, but there's something to be said for driving in from the west, which offers great views all the way along.

The only building en route is the *Valley of the Gods B&B* (PO Box 310307, Mexican Hat UT 84531; ☎970/749-1164, fax 801/638-2292; ⑤), which squats in superb isolation half a mile in from the west. All its four rooms have baths, dinner is served by prior arrangement, and the owners can also fix backcountry **tours**.

Mexican Hat

MEXICAN HAT, the last halt in southeastern Utah before the start of the Navajo Indian Reservation across the San Juan River, is an appealingly fly-blown outpost that has never amounted to the status of a town. It first sprang into being in 1901, following false reports that gold had been discovered nearby, and was kept going by a genuine oil strike in 1908, and the uranium boom of the 1950s. For tourists, it now makes a convenient base for **Monument Valley**, twenty miles south (see p.43).

Mexican Hat Rock, the sandstone sombrero for which the settlement was named, looks down on the San Juan a mile north. The highway passes a few hundred yards west, but a gravel road permits closer inspection. It's at its best in the afternoon, when the sun strikes the amazing zigzag striations of the grey and white cliffs across the river. This pattern, known as the **Navajo Blanket**, is said to show the skin markings of a giant bullsnake that lives in the river below, and carved out the "goosenecks" to the west (see p.439).

*The zip code
for Mexican
Hat is UT
84531.*

Accommodation and eating

All Mexican Hat's four **motels** except the budget *Canyonlands* have their own restaurants and stores, and are substantially the same. There are virtually no other buildings around.

Canyonlands Motel, PO Box 310187, US-163; ☎801/683-2230. Very basic ten-room motel, on the higher side of the highway next to the *Texaco* gas station, and open in summer only. ②.

Mexican Hat Lodge, PO Box 310175, US-163; ☎801/683-2222 or 1-800/447-2022, fax 683-2203. Mexican Hat's northernmost motel, with pool and the nondescript *El Sombrero* restaurant. Winter ②, summer ④.

San Juan Inn & Trading Post, PO Box 310276, US-163; ☎801/683-2220 or 1-800/447-2022, fax 683-2210. The number one choice; solid, long-established motel perched fifty feet above the north bank of the San Juan, beside the highway bridge. The *Olde Bridge Bar and Grill* serves a full menu, from Navajo tacos to steaks, plus cold beers. Winter ②, summer ④.

*Don't confuse
the* Valley of
the Gods Inn
*with the Valley
of the Gods
B&B; see
above.*

Valley of the Gods Inn, PO Box 310337, US-163; ☎801/683-2221, fax 683-2246. Modern, timber-built motel, 100 yards up from the river, with an atmospheric cafe, *Burch's*. There's also a separate campground, plus a grocery and a *Conoco* gas station. Winter ②, summer ④.

Chapter 8

Las Vegas and Salt Lake City

Together with Phoenix and Albuquerque, **Las Vegas** and **Salt Lake City** hold the most convenient major **airports** for travellers who plan to explore the Southwest. Las Vegas is just a couple of hours' drive from Zion National Park in southwest Utah, and a quick flight from the Grand Canyon; Salt Lake City is half a day by car from Moab and Canyonlands. Apart from being handy places to rent a car and set off into the wilderness, however, it's hard to imagine two cities with less in common. Which one suits you best depends whether you rank yourself among the Saints – in which case you can have a good night's sleep in straight-laced Salt Lake City before you hit the road – or the sinners, and fancy a lost weekend in loose-living Las Vegas.

Las Vegas

Little emphasis is placed on the gambling clubs and divorce facilities – though they are attractions to many visitors – and much is being done to build up the cultural attractions. No cheap and easily parodied slogans have been adopted to publicize the city, no attempt has been made to introduce pseudo-romantic architectural themes or to give artificial glamor or gaiety. Las Vegas is itself – natural and therefore very appealing to people with a wide variety of interests.

WPA Guidebook to Nevada, 1940

Shimmering from the desert haze of Nevada like a latter-day El Dorado, **LAS VEGAS** is the most dynamic, spectacular city on earth. At the start of the twentieth century, it didn't even exist; now it's home to over one million people, with enough newcomers arriving all the time to need a new school every month. Boasting nine of the world's ten largest hotels, it's a monument to architectural exuberance, whose flamboyant, no-expense-spared **casinos** lure in

Las Vegas

thirty million tourists each year. Las Vegas has been stockpiling superlatives since the 1950s, but never rests on its laurels for a moment. Long before they lose their sparkle, yesterday's showpieces are blasted into rubble, to make way for ever more extravagant replacements. A few years ago, when the fashion was for fantasy, Arthurian castles and Egyptian pyramids mushroomed along the legendary Strip; now Vegas demands nothing less than entire cities, and has already acquired pocket versions of New York, Paris, Monte Carlo and Venice.

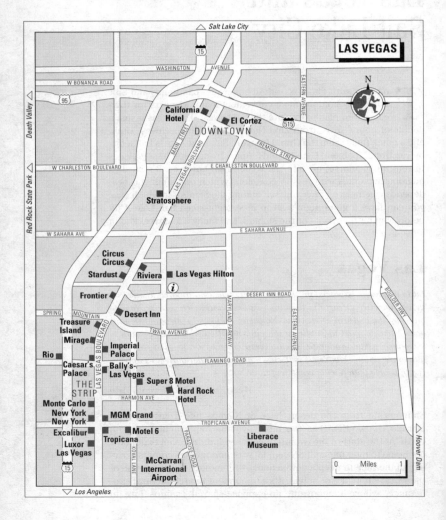

While Las Vegas has certainly cleaned up its act since the early days of Mob domination, there's little truth in the notion that it's become a **family** destination. In fact, for kids, it's not a patch on Orlando. Several casinos have added theme parks or fun rides to fill those odd non-gambling moments, but only five percent of visitors bring children, and the crowds that cluster around the exploding volcanoes and pirate battles along the Strip remain almost exclusively adult. Neither is Vegas as consistently **cheap** as it used to be. It's still possible to find good, inexpensive rooms, and the all-you-can-eat buffets offer unbeatable value, but the casino owners have finally discovered that high-rollers happy to lose hundreds of dollars per night don't mind paying premium prices to eat at top-quality restaurants, and some of the latest developments are budgeting on room rates of more like $300 than $30 per night.

Your first hours in Las Vegas are like entering another world, where the religion is luck, the language is money, and time is measured by revolutions of a roulette wheel. Once you're acclimatized, the whole spectacle can be absolutely exhilarating – assuming you haven't pinned your hopes, and your savings, on the pursuit of a fortune. Las Vegas is an unmissable destination, but one that palls for most visitors after a couple of (hectic) days.

If you've come solely to gamble, there's not much to say beyond the fact that all the casinos are free, and open 24 hours per day, with acres of floor space packed with ways to lose money: **million-dollar slots**, video **poker**, **blackjack**, **craps**, **roulette** wheels, and much much more. The casinos will just love it if you try to play a **system**; with the odds stacked against you, your best hope of a large win is to bet your entire stake on one single play, and then stop, win or lose.

A history of Las Vegas

The name *Las Vegas* – Spanish for "the meadows" – was originally applied to a group of natural springs that from 1829 onwards served as a way-station for travellers on the Old Spanish Trail. For the rest of the nineteenth century, the Paiute Indians shared the region with a handful of Mormon ranchers, and the valley had a population of just thirty in 1900. Things changed in 1905, with the completion of the now-defunct rail link between Salt Lake City and Los Angeles. Las Vegas itself was founded on May 15 that year, when the railroads auctioned off lots around what's now Fremont Street.

Ironically, Nevada was the first state to outlaw gambling, in 1909, but it was made legal once more in 1931, and the workers who built the nearby Hoover Dam flocked to Vegas to bet away their pay packets. Providing abundant cheap electricity and water, the dam amounted to a massive federal subsidy for the infant city. Hotel-casinos such as the daring 65-room *El Rancho* began to appear in the early 1940s, but the Midwest Mafia were the first to appreciate the potential for profit. Mobster Bugsy Siegel raised $7 million to open the *Flamingo* on the Strip in December 1946; early losses forced him to close again in January, and although he swiftly managed to re-open in March his erstwhile partners were dissatisfied enough with their returns to have him murdered in LA in June.

By the 1950s, Las Vegas was booming. The military had arrived – mushroom clouds from **A-bomb tests** in the deserts were visible from the city, and visitors would drive out with picnics to get a better view – and so too had big guns like **Frank Sinatra**, who debuted at the *Desert Inn* in 1951, and **Liberace**, who received $50,000 to open the *Riviera* in 1955. As the stars gravitated towards the Vegas honeypot, nightclubs across America went out of business, and the city became the nation's undisputed live-entertainment capital.

Getting Married in Las Vegas

Second only to making your fortune as a reason to visit Las Vegas is the prospect of **getting married**. Over a hundred thousand weddings are performed here each year, many so informal that bride and groom just wind down the window of their car during the ceremony, and a Vegas wedding has become a byword for tongue-in-cheek chic.

Elvis married Priscilla at the Aladdin on May 1, 1967, nine months to the day before the birth of Lisa Marie, and eight years before Michael Jackson met Lisa Marie at a Jackson Five gig in Vegas.

You don't have to be a resident to get wed here, and you don't need a blood test, either. However, you must be at least eighteen years old and not already married, and purchase a $35 licence from the *Clark County Marriage License Bureau* at 200 S Third St (Mon–Thurs 8am–midnight, & from 8am on Fri to midnight on Sun; ☎702/455-3156) any time before the ceremony.

The city phone book lists fourteen pages of **wedding chapels**, with an inconceivable range of trappings, and most casinos also have their own facilities. Prices start at around $100 for the basic service, and the sky is literally the limit – you can get spliced while floating in a hot-air balloon, or parachuting out of a plane. *Las Vegas Weddings and Rooms* (☎1-800/488-6283) offer all-inclusive wedding packages, or contact the chapels direct.

Graceland Wedding Chapel, 619 S Las Vegas Blvd; ☎702/474-6655 or 1-800/824-5732. Home of the King – an Elvis impersonator will act as best man, give the bride away or serenade you, but unfortunately he can't perform the service.

Little Church of the West, 3960 S Las Vegas Blvd; ☎702/739-7971 or 1-800/821-2452. On the National Register of Historic Places, this fifty-year-old chapel is among the more peaceful and quiet places to exchange your Vegas vows – if that's really what you want.

Little White Chapel, 1301 S Las Vegas Blvd; ☎702/382-5943 or 1-800/545-8111. Where Bruce Willis and Demi Moore married each other, and Michael Jordan and Joan Collins married other people. Open all day every day, with the "The One & Only 24hr Drive-Up Wedding Window", if you're in a major hurry.

Stratosphere, 2000 S Las Vegas Blvd; ☎702/380-7777 or 1-800/789-9IDO. The three highest wedding chapels in the world, 700 feet up.

The beginning of the end for Mob rule in Vegas came in 1966, after reclusive airline tycoon **Howard Hughes** sold *TWA* for $500 million and moved into the *Desert Inn*. When the owners tired of his stingy – specifically non-gambling – ways, he simply bought the hotel, and his clean-cut image encouraged other entrepreneurs to follow his example. **Elvis** arrived a little later; the young rock'n'roller had bombed at the *New Frontier* in 1956, but started a triumphant five-year stint as a karate-kicking lounge lizard at the *International* (now the *Las Vegas Hilton*) in 1969.

Endless federal swoops and stings drove the Mob out of sight by the 1980s, in time for Vegas to re-invent itself on a surge of junk-bond megadollars. The success of Steve Wynn's *Mirage* in enticing a new generation of visitors, from 1989 onwards, spawned a host of imitators. The long-established *Circus Circus* crew swiftly erected the *Excalibur* and the amazing *Luxor*, the *Hard Rock* arrived and *Planet Hollywood*'s on its way, the *Stratosphere* appeared from nowhere to tower over the city, and Wynn himself built *Treasure Island* and will soon open the $1.2 billion *Bellagio*. Beneath the glitz, however, **gambling** remains the bedrock, and Las Vegas' pre-eminence seems little dented by the spread of casinos elsewhere in the US. City boosters point out that only fifteen percent of Americans have so far seen Vegas, and they're confidently expecting the rest to turn up any day now.

Arrival, information and getting around

Las Vegas' busy **McCarran International Airport** is a mile southeast of the Strip, and four miles from downtown (☎702/261-5743). Some hotels run free shuttle buses for guests, while *Bell Trans* (☎702/739-7990) run a **minibus** service to the Strip ($3.50) and downtown ($5), and a **cab** to the Strip costs around $12.

If you plan to see more of Vegas than the Strip – and even there, it's too hot to walk more than a couple of blocks in the daytime – a **car** is invaluable. All the **rental** companies listed on p.19 have out-lets at the airport; *Allstate* (☎1-800/634-6186) is an inexpensive local alternative. **Public transport** does exist, however. The oak-veneered **streetcars** of the *Las Vegas Strip Trolley* (☎702/382-1404) ply the Strip between Hacienda Avenue (south of the *Luxor*) and Sahara Avenue, for a flat fare of $1.30, but don't go downtown. *CAT* **buses** (☎702/228-7433; $1.50) serve the whole city; #301 connects the Strip to downtown. *Greyhound*'s **long-distance buses** use a terminal at 200 S Main St downtown, though arriving buses also stop on the Strip, outside the *Stardust*, 3000 N Las Vegas Blvd.

Any number of local freesheets and magazines – usually bursting with discount vouchers, plus details of accommodation, buffets and the latest shows – provide local **information**. There are also **visitor centers** at 3150 Paradise Rd (daily 8am–5pm; ☎702/892-0711),

*National and international **flights** to Las Vegas are detailed on p.3 onwards.*

*Though Amtrak **trains** no longer serve Las Vegas, Amtrak run connecting buses to Vegas from LA and Bakersfield in California.*

*For details of flights and tours from Las Vegas to the **Grand Canyon**, see p.297.*

near the Strip and next to the vast Convention Center, and 711 E Desert Inn Rd (Mon–Fri 8am–5pm; ☎702/735-1616). There can be no easier city in which to **change money**: the casinos gladly convert almost any currency, and their walls are festooned with every conceivable ATM machine.

Accommodation

*Unless otherwise noted, the **zip code** for all properties listed here is NV 89109.*

Although Las Vegas has well over 100,000 motel and hotel rooms (most of them hitched to casinos), it's best to book **accommodation** ahead if you're on a tight budget, or arriving on Friday or Saturday; upwards of 200,000 people descend upon the city every weekend. Rooms can be very inexpensive, but be sure to get the rate confirmed for the duration of your stay – that $25 room you found on Thursday may cost $100 on Friday, and if a championship fight or other special event is on, room rates hit the roof. The CVB runs a **reservation** service on ☎1-800/332-5333.

Room rates shown here rise during major events.

If you're planning a trip from elsewhere in North America, check local newspaper advertisements for the latest Vegas bargains – virtually all hotels and motels offer discounts and food vouchers.

Caesar's Palace, 3570 S Las Vegas Blvd; ☎702/731-7110 or 1-800/634-6661, fax 731-6636. Right in the heart of the Strip, the epitome of 1960s luxury has recently trebled in size, and offers the last word in pseudo-Roman splendour, with top-class restaurants and shops. ⑥.

Most of the casino-hotels reviewed here are described in detail on p.450 onwards.

California Hotel, 12 Ogden Ave at First St, Las Vegas NV 89101; ☎702/385-1222 or 1-800/634-6255, fax 388-2660. Mid-range downtown casino, with a mere 800 rooms, where the guests are mostly Hawaiian, and Hawaiian food and drink dominates the bars and restaurants. Sun–Thurs ②, Fri & Sat ③.

Circus Circus, 2880 S Las Vegas Blvd; ☎702/734-0410 or 1-800/634-3450, fax 734-2268. Venerable Strip hotel that's a big hit with kids, with circus acts performing live above the casino floor. Sun–Thurs ②, Fri & Sat ③.

Desert Inn, 3145 Las Vegas Blvd; ☎702/733-4444 or 1-800/634-6906, fax 733-4676. The classiest and most expensive of the Strip hotels, with its own golf course and spa, and big-name entertainment. ⑦.

El Cortez Hotel, 600 E Fremont St, Las Vegas NV 89101; ☎702/385-5200 or 1-800/634-6703, fax 385-1554. Long-standing downtown hotel, charging bargain rates for reasonable rooms; suites cost just a little extra. ①.

*For information on **gay** accommodations, nightlife, and events in Las Vegas, access the Gay Las Vegas Website at www. gayvegas.com.*

Excalibur, 3850 S Las Vegas Blvd; ☎702/597-7777 or 1-800/937-7777, fax 597-7040. Arthurian legend built larger than life, with plenty to amuse the kids while the adults gamble away their college funds. Four thousand rooms plus assorted drawbridges, turrets and nightly jousting matches; staff have to call guests *M'Lord* and *M'Lady*. Sun–Thurs ③, Fri & Sat ④.

Hard Rock Hotel, 4455 Paradise Rd; ☎702/693-5000 or 1-800/473-7625, fax 693-5010. "The world's only rock'n'roll casino", over a mile east of the Strip, is a pale imitation of Las Vegas' showcase giants, but the guest rooms are above average, and there's a great pool. Sun–Thurs ⑤, Fri & Sat ⑦.

Las Vegas International Hostel, 1208 S Las Vegas Blvd, Las Vegas NV 89104; ☎702/385-9955. Friendly, bare-bones *AAIH* hostel north of the Strip, which arranges tours to state and national parks. Dorm beds cost $14, rooms with shared baths under $30 – little cheaper than some Strip hotels. ①.

Luxor, 3900 S Las Vegas Blvd; ☎702/262-4000 or 1-800/288-1000, fax 262-4452. Vast smoked-glass pyramid, where guests sail Nile barges to the elevators up to their desert-view rooms. All that plus seven restaurants, virtual reality experiences, and the obligatory casino. Sun–Thurs ③, Fri & Sat ⑤.

MGM Grand, 3799 S Las Vegas Blvd; ☎702/891-1111 or 1-800/929-1111, fax 891-1030. The world's largest hotel, with 5005 rooms, is home to the world's largest casino, as well as several of Las Vegas' finest restaurants, a vast events arena, an amusement park and a model of Oz's Emerald City. ④.

Mirage, 3400 S Las Vegas Blvd; ☎702/791-7111 or 1-800/627-6667, fax 791-7446. Glitzy casino, with its own volcano, rainforest, and coral reef, some good restaurants and surprisingly tranquil rooms. Sun–Thurs ⑤, Fri & Sat ⑦.

Motel 6 – Tropicana, 195 E Tropicana Ave; ☎702/798-0728, fax 798-5657. At 880 rooms, the largest *Motel 6* in the country; a ten-minute walk off the Strip from the *MGM Grand*. Sun–Thurs ②, Fri & Sat ③.

New York New York, 3790 S Las Vegas Blvd; ☎702/740-6969 or 1-800/NYFORME, fax 740-6520. Mock Manhattan, looped by a high-speed roller-coaster and a riot of neon at night; the 2000 rooms are plush by usual Strip standards. Sun–Thurs ⑤, Fri & Sat ⑦.

Sam's Town, 5111 Boulder Hwy, Las Vegas NV 89122; ☎702/456-7777 or 1-800/634-6371, fax 454-8014. Old-style Western-themed casino over six miles east of the Strip that's popular with older visitors. Sun–Thurs ③, Fri & Sat ④.

Stratosphere, 2000 S Las Vegas Blvd, Las Vegas NV 89104; ☎702/380-7777 or 1-800/99-TOWER, fax 380-7700. Hundred-storey tower just north of the Strip, with amazing views, nauseating thrill-rides, good restaurants, and the world's three highest wedding chapels. Sun–Thurs ②, Fri & Sat ④.

Super 8, 4250 Koval Lane; ☎702/794-0888 or 1-800/800-8000, fax 794-3504. The closest of Vegas' three *Super 8*s to the Strip has its own little casino and a reasonable restaurant. Sun–Thurs ②, Fri & Sat ③.

Treasure Island, 3300 S Las Vegas Blvd; ☎702/894-7111 or 1-800/944-7444, fax 894-7446. Sister hotel to the neighbouring *Mirage*, where an endless pirate battle plays to the passing crowds on the Strip, the restaurants within are swathed with rigging, and one TV channel shows the movie *Treasure Island* non-stop. Sun–Thurs ④, Fri & Sat ⑦.

Tropicana, 3801 S Las Vegas Blvd; ☎702/739-2222 or 1-800/634-4000, fax 739-2469. Jungle-themed casino, recently spruced up to compete with its giant neighbours, but still offering swim-up gaming tables around the world's largest indoor–outdoor swimming pool. ④.

The City

Though the Las Vegas sprawl measures fifteen miles wide by fifteen miles long, most tourists stick to the six-mile stretch of **Las Vegas Boulevard** that includes the **downtown** area, slightly southeast of the intersection of I-15 and US-95, and the **Strip**, home to the major casinos. In between lie two somewhat seedy miles of gas stations, fast-food drive-ins and wedding chapels, while the rest of town is largely residential, and need barely concern you at all.

*As explained on p.15, **accommodation prices**, excluding taxes, are indicated throughout this book by the following symbols:*

① *up to $30*
② *$30–45*
③ *$45–60*
④ *$60–80*
⑤ *$80–100*
⑥ *$100–130*
⑦ *$130–175*
⑧ *$175–250*
⑨ *$250+*

The Strip

For its razor-edge finesse in harnessing sheer, magnificent excess to the deadly serious business of making money, there's no place like the Las Vegas **Strip**. It's hard to imagine a time when Las Vegas was an ordinary city, and Las Vegas Boulevard a dusty thoroughfare scattered with the usual edge-of-town motels. After five decades of capitalism run riot, with every new casino-hotel setting out to surpass anything its neighbours ever dreamed of, the Strip seems to be locked into a hyperactive craving for thrills and glamour, forever discarding its latest toy in its frenzy for the next jackpot.

Each casino is a self-contained fantasyland of high camp and genuine excitement. Almost against your will, huge moving walkways sweep you in from the sidewalk; once inside, it can be almost impossible to find your way out. The action keeps going day and night, and in this sealed and windowless environment you rapidly lose track of which is which. Even if you do manage to get back onto the streets during the day, the scorching heat is liable to drive you straight back in again; night is the best time to venture out, when the neon's blazing at its brightest.

As the Strip pushes deeper into the desert, the newest casinos tend to rise at its **southern** end, not far west of the airport. The procession kicks off with the 36-storey bronze and glass pyramid of the **Luxor**, which opened in 1993. From the palm-fringed avenue of sphinxes guarding the entrance, to the reconstruction of Tutankhamun's tomb inside, the whole building plays endless variations upon the theme of Egyptian archeology. In Las Vegas' closest approximation to Disneyland, three separate simulator rides and 3-D movies combine to reveal the *Secrets of the Luxor Pyramid*, a confusing saga of derring-do that's overpriced at $13. Meanwhile, the most powerful artificial light beam ever created shines up from the pyramid's apex; visible from planes circling over LA, 250 miles west, it supposedly pays tribute to the ancient Egyptian belief that the soul of a dead Pharaoh would rise directly into the skies.

The Luxor's architect, Veldon Simpson, had previously designed the **Excalibur**, immediately north. A less-sophisticated mock-up of a medieval castle, complete with drawbridge, crenellated towers, and a basement stuffed with fairground-style sideshows for the kids, it's usually packed out with low-budget tour groups. Its brief reign as the world's largest hotel, from 1990 to 1993, ended when the five-thousand-room **MGM Grand Hotel and Theme Park** – another Simpson creation – opened across the street. Entered beneath the gaping jaws of MGM's trademark lion, it has become the most prestigious **big-fight venue** in town, and offers the Strip's finest selection of **restaurants**. Turnover in its casino is so phenomenal that when the crowds after the Holyfield–Tyson debacle in June 1997 mistook the popping of champagne corks for gunfire, and the resulting panic forced the tables to close down for two hours, the loss was estimated in millions

*The **hotels** in the Luxor and the other major casinos are reviewed on pp.448–449, while selected **restaurants** are described on p.453 onwards.*

The current MGM replaced a previous version, further up the Strip, which was destroyed by a 1980 fire in which 74 people died.

of dollars. **MGM Grand Adventures**, a 33-acre theme park behind the hotel, is however disappointingly thrill-free for adults, though they plan to add more high-speed rides in due course (daily 10am–6pm, unlimited rides $17).

Excalibur and the MGM Grand are not the only giants facing off across the intersection of Las Vegas Boulevard and Tropicana Avenue. The northwest corner, diagonally opposite the veteran **Tropicana**, is now occupied by a brash newcomer, **New York New York**. Fronted of course by the Statue of Liberty, and approached across a 300-foot Brooklyn Bridge, this miniature Manhattan boasts a skyline featuring twelve separate skyscrapers, while the interior depicts Central Park at dusk (not perhaps somewhere you'd choose to be in real life). The one respect in which it surpasses New York itself is that for $5 you can swoop around the whole thing at 65mph on the hair-raising *Manhattan Express* **roller coaster**.

A couple of blocks north – which in Vegas terms means almost a mile – and just beyond the intersection where rapper Tupac Shakur was gunned down in 1996, the long-established **Caesar's Palace** still encapsulates Las Vegas at its best. Here the walkway delivers you past grand marble staircases that lead nowhere, and full-sized replicas of Michaelangelo's *David*, into a vast labyrinth of slots and green baize, peopled by strutting half-naked Roman centurions and Cleopatra-cropped waitresses. Above the stores and restaurants of the extraordinary **Forum**, the blue-domed ceiling dims and glows as it endlessly cycles from dawn to dusk and back again. Caesar's also has its own giant-screen **OMNIMAX** movie theatre ($7), and has recently added the elaborate **Magical Empire**, a dinner-cum-magic-show for which tickets cost up $70.

Night-time crowds jostle for space on the sidewalk outside the glittering **Mirage**, beyond Caesar's Palace, to watch the somewhat half-hearted volcano that erupts every fifteen minutes, spewing water and fire into the lagoon below. Next door, a pirate galleon and a British frigate, crewed by actors, do noisy battle outside **Treasure Island** (every ninety minutes, daily 4–11pm). The family-oriented **Circus Circus**, another mile north, uses live circus acts to pull in the punters – a trapeze artist here, a fire-eater there – and also has an indoor water-oriented theme park, **Grand Slam Canyon**, vaguely modelled on the Grand Canyon, where you pay separately for each roller coaster or river-ride. If you really want to cool off, you'd do better to head on to the flumes and chutes of Vegas' one purpose-built water park, **Wet'n'Wild**, 2601 S Las Vegas Blvd (summer daily 10am–8pm; $22). Alternatively, as this book went to press the **Las Vegas Hilton** – off the Strip at 3000 Paradise Rd, half a mile east of Circus Circus – was due to open the **Star Trek Experience**. For around $10, visitors will get to dress up as their favourite *Star Trek* character and take a virtual-reality trip aboard the *Enterprise*.

Circus Circus has traditionally marked the northern limit of the Strip, but the 1996 opening of the **Stratosphere Tower**, half a mile towards downtown, may change that. At 1149 feet, the Stratosphere is the tallest building west of the Mississippi, and the outdoor deck and indoor viewing chamber in the sphere near the summit offer amazing panoramas across the city ($5). Two utterly demented thrill rides can take you even closer to heaven; the world's highest roller coaster swirls around the outside of the sphere, while the ludicrous Big Shot shunts you to the very top of an additional 160-foot spire, from which you free-fall back down again ($5 each). Financial difficulties are said to have delayed plans to build a King-Kong-shaped elevator that would climb the exterior of the tower.

Downtown and the Liberace Museum

As the Strip has gone from strength to strength, **downtown Las Vegas**, the city's original core, has by comparison been neglected. Long known as "Glitter Gulch", and consisting of a few compact blocks of lower-key casinos, it has recently embarked upon a revival. Between Main Street and Las Vegas Boulevard, five entire blocks of Fremont Street, its principal thoroughfare, have been roofed with an open-air mesh to create the **Fremont Street Experience**. This "Celestial Vault" is studded with neon, choreographed in dazzling nightly displays of colour, and shelters a mall of bars, restaurants and souvenir stores as well as several rapidly expanding casinos. However, there's still a long way to go before it can really compete with the Strip.

Almost all Las Vegas' handful of **museums** are eminently missable, with one unarguable exception: the **Liberace Museum**, two miles east of the Strip at 1775 E Tropicana Ave (Mon–Sat 10am–5pm, Sun 1–5pm; $6.50). Popularly remembered as a beaming buffoon who knocked out torpid toe-tappers, Liberace, who died in 1987, started out playing piano in the rough bars of Milwaukee during the 1940s. A decade later, he was being mobbed by screaming adolescents and ruthlessly hounded by the scandal-hungry press. All this is recalled by a yellowing collection of cuttings and family photos, along with electric candelabra, bejewelled quail eggs with inlaid pianos, rhinestone-covered fur coats, glittering cars and more. The music, piped into the scented toilets, may not have improved with age, but the museum is a satisfying attempt to answer the seminal question "how does a great performer top himself on stage?".

Red Rock Canyon

For a blast of sunlight and fresh air away from the casinos, and a sample of some classic Southwestern canyon scenery, head twenty miles west of the Strip along Charleston Boulevard to the **Red**

Rock Canyon National Conservation Area. This BLM-run park consists of a cactus-strewn desert basin surrounded by stark red cliffs that are pierced repeatedly by narrow canyons accessible only on foot.

Red Rock Canyon's **visitor center**, which has displays about the canyon and a viewing window overlooking its main features (daily 8am–5pm; free; ☎702/363-1921), stands just before the start of the **Scenic Drive** (daily 7am–dusk). As this thirteen-mile loop road meanders around the edge of the basin, it passes trailheads like the one for the cool, slender **Ice Box Canyon** (a 2.5-mile round-trip hike), and the three-mile **Pine Creek Trail**, which follows a flower-lined creek beyond a ruined homesite towards a towering red-capped monolith.

Lake Mead and the Hoover Dam

Almost as many people as go to Las Vegas visit **LAKE MEAD**, the vast reservoir thirty miles southeast of the city that was created by the construction of the Hoover Dam. As with the similarly incongruous Lake Powell (see p.388) it makes a bizarre spectacle, the blue waters a vivid counterpoint to the surrounding desert, but it gets excruciatingly crowded all year round.

Though the **Lake Mead National Recreation Area** straddles the border between Nevada and Arizona, the best views come from the Nevada side. Even if you don't need details of how to sail, scuba-dive, water-ski or fish from the marinas along the five-hundred-mile shoreline, call in at the **Alan Bible visitor center** (daily 8.30am–4.30pm; ☎702/293-8990), four miles northeast of Boulder City on US-93, to enjoy a sweeping prospect of the whole thing.

Eight miles on, beyond the rocky ridges of the Black Mountains, US-93 reaches the **Hoover Dam** itself. Designed to block the Colorado River and provide low-cost electricity for the cities of the Southwest, it's among the tallest dams ever built (760ft high), and used enough concrete to build a two-lane highway from the West Coast to New York. It was completed in 1935, as the first step in the Bureau of Reclamation programme that culminated with the Glen Canyon Dam (see p.393). Informative half-hour **guided tours** of the dam leave from the new **Hoover Dam Visitor Center** on the Nevada side of the river (daily 8.30am–5.45pm; $5; ☎702/293-1824).

Bus tours to the dam from Las Vegas, with Gray Line (☎702/384-1234) or other operators, cost around $23 for a five-hour trip.

Eating and drinking

Eating is one of the real treats of Las Vegas. All the casinos are so keen to entice visitors onto their premises – and keep them there – that they offer good-value round-the-clock **buffets**. Even when the food isn't that great – the buffets at the *MGM Grand* and the *Excalibur* spring to mind – you're bound to find something you can keep down. As a rule, the process starts off with breakfast, typically costing between $3 and $6 – or even free with a voucher – followed by lunch, served until

3 or 4pm, for perhaps $4 to $7, and then dinner for anything from $5 up to $15. If possible, try to avoid eating between 6pm and 9pm, when the lines at the bigger casinos can be endless.

Each casino has in addition at least one top-quality conventional **restaurant**, and though there are plenty of dining places away from the Strip, only a small proportion of eccentric tourists bother to venture off in search of them. **Drinks** – beer, wine, spirits and cocktails – are freely available in all the casinos to anyone gambling, and very cheap for anyone else.

Buffets

Bally's Big Kitchen Buffet, *Bally's Casino*, 3645 S Las Vegas Blvd; ☎702/739-4930. The best of the Strip buffets; a quite phenomenal spread of fresh seafood, meats and salads, for $9 between 7.30am and 2pm, and $13 from 4.30–10pm. *Bally's Champagne Sterling Brunch*, served in a separate room Sun 9.30am–2.30pm, is magnificent – as it should be, for $50.

Golden Nugget Buffet, *Golden Nugget*, 129 E Fremont St; ☎702/385-7111. Downtown's classiest buffet, with full carvery and a fine spread of salads; ranges from $6 for breakfast up to $10.50 for dinner.

Rio's Carnival World Buffet, *Rio Hotel*, 3700 W Flamingo Rd; ☎702/252-7777. Superb, albeit meat-heavy buffet, with a lush array of desserts; $4 breakfasts and $6 lunches Mon–Fri, $8 dinner nightly and all day Sat & Sun.

Sam's Town – The Great Buffet, *Sam's Town*, 5111 Boulder Hwy; ☎702/456-7777. Unassuming, inexpensive but top-quality buffet, a few miles east of the Strip. Prices only exceed $8 for the $12 Friday-night seafood extravaganza, and there's live country music and dancing with no cover charge.

Restaurants

The original Coyote Cafe, in Santa Fe, is reviewed on p.108.

Coyote Cafe, *MGM Grand*, 3799 S Las Vegas Blvd; ☎702/891-7349. Outpost of Mark Miller's definitive "Modern Southwestern" restaurant, with entrees priced at up to $30 in the dinner-only *Grill Room* and under $20 in the adjoining *Cafe*, open from 9am daily.

Emeril's New Orleans Fish House, *MGM Grand*, 3799 S Las Vegas Blvd; ☎702/891-7374. Excellent seafood, most but not all with spicy Cajun flavourings. Crispy baby calamari, steamed bass, crabmeat fishcakes and lobster at $20 and up per entree, plus an oyster bar. Open daily for lunch and dinner.

The Noodle Kitchen, *Mirage*, 3400 S Las Vegas Blvd; ☎702/791-6362. Inexpensive noodles and dim sum, served daily 11am–4am.

Spago's, *Caesar's Palace*, 3570 S Las Vegas Blvd; ☎702/369-6300. Utterly surreal Californian restaurant that's become Vegas' premier site for star-spotting, with a space-age decor to complement the weirdness of *Caesar's* blue-domed Forum. Entrees at up to $30 in the dinner-only *Dining Room*, half that in the all-day *Cafe*.

Top of the World, *Stratosphere*, 2000 S Las Vegas Blvd; ☎702/380-7711. The food at this 106th-floor revolving restaurant is little more than ordinary – though the Asian-influenced dinners, at up to $30, are a cut above the $12 lunch-time salads and sandwiches – but the amazing views make it well worth paying the premium prices.

Nightlife and entertainment

The days of the big-budget Vegas "spectacular" are far from over, though as the great names of the past fade from view few individual stars are now considered capable of carrying an extended-run show. These days the tendency is to rely on lavish stunts and special effects, with the illusionist-magicians **Siegfried and Roy** ruling the roost at the *Mirage* (Fri–Tues 7.30pm & 11pm; $84), and the *MGM Grand* featuring a show called **EFX**, in which David Cassidy has recently replaced Michael Crawford (Mon, Fri & Sat 7.30pm & 10.30pm, Tues, Wed & Sun 7.30pm; $70). There's a more contemporary feel at *Treasure Island*, where the postmodern **Cirque du Soleil** have signed up for a long-term residency (Wed–Sun 7.30pm & 10.30pm; $60, under-12s $30). If only **Elvis** will do, he's one of several performers impersonated in the *Legends in Concert* show at the *Imperial Palace*, 3535 S Las Vegas Blvd (Mon–Sat 7.30pm & 10.30pm; $30, under-13s $15).

Entertainment schedules are of course subject to change without notice; for full details of what's coming up, consult papers like the *Las Vegas New Times*, or call casinos such as the *Hard Rock* – the best bet for big-name touring acts – ahead of time.

Salt Lake City

Disarmingly pleasant and easy-going, **SALT LAKE CITY** is well worth a stopover of a couple of days. It may not be a particularly thrilling destination in itself, but its setting is superb, towered over by the mountains of the **Wasatch Front**, which mark the dividing line between the comparatively lush eastern and the bone-dry western halves of northern Utah.

That Salt Lake City today seems so quietly prosperous, even complacent, is a remarkable tribute to the energy and dedication of its **Mormon** founders. When established, in 1847, it lay beyond the boundaries of the United States. Brigham Young, who had led his persecuted flock westwards in search of a land that "nobody else wanted", emerged from the western flank of the Rockies and declared "This is the place". The city was thereupon laid out according to plans prepared for the "City of Zion" by the church's original Prophet, Joseph Smith, in 1833, with **Temple Square** at its heart. Within ten years, thanks to an extensive missionary programme back East, its population had grown to fifty thousand, while the economy had been kick-started by its role in provisioning the Gold Rush wagon-trains that struggled through en route to California.

For a detailed account of Mormon history, see p.478.

Salt Lake City is now home to around 160,000 citizens, though thanks to the proximity of the further 600,000 who live in suburban areas ranged along the Wasatch Front it feels a whole lot larger. Around seventy percent are Mormons, and it remains the worldwide headquarters of the Mormon church. As a result, people elsewhere in the US tend to imagine Salt Lake City as one step away from *The*

For a note on
the easy system
of grid-refer-
ence **addresses**
prevalent in
Utah, see p.331.

Stepford Wives in terms of spontaneous public fun; and they're not
far wrong. There is a fundamental lack of things to do, in the way of
museums or other cultural diversions, but if you're willing to switch
gears and slow down, its unhurried pace, and the lack of pretence
and positive energy of its people, can make for a surprisingly enjoyable experience. In addition, the proximity of the mountains means
that the region offers great hiking or cycling in summer and fall, and
some of the world's best skiing in winter.

Arrival, information and getting around

Salt Lake City International Airport (☎801/575-2400) is a mere
four miles west of downtown. A cab into town costs around $10,

while *Super Express* shuttle vans (☎801/566-6400) charge $10
for the first passenger to any downtown destination, and $5 for
each additional one. On the whole, *Utah Transit Authority*'s
buses are not wildly useful, but #50 serves the airport hourly
(75¢), and there's a fairly restricted free-fare zone downtown
(☎801/287-4636). Long-distance *Greyhound-Trailways* **buses**,
160 W South Temple Blvd (☎801/355-4684), and *Amtrak* **trains**,
320 S Rio Grande Ave, also arrive downtown.

Gray Line (☎801/521-7060) and *Scenic West Tours*
(☎801/572-2717) both offer **bus tours** ranging from half- and full-
day city jaunts to multi-day trips to the various national parks. To
reach the best parts of the surrounding mountains, however, you'll
need a car – all the rental companies are represented at the airport –
or a cycle and strong legs. **Bikes** can be rented from *Utah Ski
Rental*, 134 W 100 South St (☎801/355-9088).

Visitor centers supplying information on the city itself can be
found downtown at 180 S West Temple Blvd (Mon–Fri 8am–5pm,
Sat 9am–4pm; ☎801/521-2868), or in Terminal 2 of the airport
(Mon–Fri 9am–9pm). For details on the rest of Utah, stop by the
Utah Travel Council, across from the capitol at 300 N State St
(Mon–Fri 8am–5pm, Sat & Sun 10am–5pm; ☎801/538-1030). The
main downtown **post office** is at 230 W 200 South St (Mon–Fri
8am–5.30pm, Sat 8am–1.30pm; ☎801/978-3001)

Accommodation

Salt Lake City is well equipped with accommodation, with downtown
options that range via budget **motels** and **B&B** inns up to rather
more luxurious **hotels**, and the usual mid-range places near the airport and along the interstates.

Avenues Youth Hostel, 107 F St, UT 84103; ☎801/359-3855 or 1-800/881-
4785, fax 532-0182. This central hostel, five blocks east of Temple Square,
offers dorm beds for $14 and a couple of cheap private rooms, but since our
last visit *Rough Guides* have received serious complaints about its cleanliness
and security. ①.

Best Western Olympus, 161 W 600 South St; ☎801/521-7373 or 1-800/426-
0722, fax 524-0354. Good-value mountain-view rooms downtown, convenient
for *Amtrak*, airport and interstates. ⑤.

Brigham Street Inn, 1135 E South Temple Blvd, UT 84102; ☎801/364-4461
or 1-800/417-4461. Luxurious, peaceful – and rather inconspicuous – B&B a
few blocks east of downtown towards the mountains. ⑤.

Colonial Village Motel, 1530 S Main St, UT 84111; ☎801/486-8171, fax 486-
8180. Basic motel, well out from the centre. ②.

Doubletree Hotel, 215 W South Temple Blvd; ☎801/531-7500 or 1-800/222-
TREE, fax 328-1289. Plush modern high-rise, with indoor pool, in the Salt Palace
complex downtown, offering good views of both the Temple and the mountains. ⑤.

Holiday Inn Airport, 1659 W North Temple Blvd, UT 84116; ☎801/533-9000
or 1-800/HOLIDAY, fax 364-0614. Well-equipped top-end hotel with reason-

*Unless other-
wise stated,
the **zip code**
for all these
properties is
UT 84101.*

As explained on p.15, **accommodation prices**, excluding taxes, are indicated throughout this book by the following symbols:

① up to $30
② $30–45
③ $45–60
④ $60–80
⑤ $80–100
⑥ $100–130
⑦ $130–175
⑧ $175–250
⑨ $250+

able rates, connected with the airport by free airport shuttle buses and not too far from downtown. ④.

Motel 6, 176 W 600 South St; ☎801/531-1252. Budget downtown motel, handy for the *Amtrak* station. ②.

Peery Hotel, 110 W 300 South St; ☎801/521-4300 or 1-800/331-0073, fax 575-5014. Refurbished 1910 downtown landmark, with small but characterful rooms. ④.

Pinecrest Bed and Breakfast Inn, 6211 Emigration Canyon Rd, UT 84108; ☎801/583-6663 or 1-800/359-6663. Top-quality accommodation in six-acre pine forest, high above the city, with massive breakfasts. ④.

Saltair Bed and Breakfast Inn, 164 S 900 East St, UT 84102; ☎801/533-8184 or 1-800/733-8184. Attractive B&B in historic downtown building, not quite as old as it looks but enjoyably modelled on the nineteenth-century Saltair resort beside the Great Salt Lake. ④.

Shilo Inn, 206 S West Temple Blvd; ☎801/521-9500 or 1-800/222-2244, fax 359-6527. Clean rooms in a downtown tower, with pool, sauna and gym. ⑤.

Travelodge-Temple Square, 144 W North Temple Blvd; ☎801/533-8200 or 1-800/578-7878, fax 596-0332. Most central and least expensive of three local *Travelodges*. ③.

Quality Inn-City Center, 154 W 600 South St; ☎801/521-2930 or 1-800/521-9997. Spacious downtown motel, with pool and free airport shuttle. ④.

Ute Hostel, 21 E Kelsey Ave, UT 84111; ☎801/595-1645. Much the better of Salt Lake City's two hostels, this small private establishment, a few miles south of downtown, offers $14 dorm beds and a couple of private rooms, plus bike rental, a hot tub, and free airport pickup. ①/②.

The City

Thanks to its straightforward grid of streets, it's so easy to get to grips with the layout of Salt Lake City that you start to feel like an expert after a couple of hours. It's also especially easy to negotiate by car; the sweeping one-way principal boulevards were designed to be "wide enough for a team of four oxen and a covered wagon to turn around", traffic is generally light, and parking spaces plentiful.

The snag is, there's not a hell of a lot to **do**. For Mormons worldwide, of course, Salt Lake City is something of a place of pilgrimage, and most Gentiles too enjoy at least a short visit to the main complex of church buildings, Temple Square. Apart from that, however, the city's crop of museums are unusually disappointing, and once you get behind the wheel you'll soon find yourself tempted to head out of town, and up into the mountains to the east.

Temple Square

The geographical – and spiritual – heart of Salt Lake City is **Temple Square**, the world headquarters of the **Mormon Church** (or Church of Christ of Latter Day Saints – LDS) and the only real public space in the city. Its focus is the monumental **Temple** itself, completed in

1893 after forty years of intensive labour. The multispired granite edifice rises to 210 feet above the city – it's not the tallest building on the mainly flat skyline but, thanks to its crisply angular silhouette, it's just about the only interesting one. Only confirmed Mormons may enter the Temple, and even they do so only for the most sacred LDS rituals – marriage, baptisms and "sealing", the joining of a family unit for eternity.

Salt Lake City

For more about the Mormons, see p.478.

Wander through the gates of Temple Square, however, and you'll swiftly be snapped up by one of the many waiting Mormons, and shepherded to join a free 45-minute **tour** of the various sites within. As well as monuments to Mormon pioneers, and the seagulls who fortuitously saved them by consuming a plague of locusts that threatened their first harvest, you'll be ushered into the odd oblong shell of the **Mormon Tabernacle**. No images of any kind adorn its interior, which is home to the world-renowned **Mormon Tabernacle Choir**; a helper at the lectern laconically displays its remarkable acoustic properties by tearing up a newspaper and dropping a nail.

There's free admission to the Mormon choir's 9.30am Sunday broadcast, and its rehearsals on Thursday evenings at 8pm.

The primary aim of the tours is to awaken your interest in the Mormon faith; differences from Christianity are played down in favour of a soft-focus video of Old Testament scenes. The tour ends in the northern of the Square's two visitor centers, where an array of touch-screen computers provide woolly answers to questions like "What is the purpose of life?" and "Who was Joseph Smith?". In the southern visitor center, a surprisingly good free movie tells the story of the arrival of Salt Lake City's first Mormon settlers.

Capitol Hill

Quite why the Mormons chose not to put their Temple on the gentle hill that stands above today's Temple Square is anyone's guess. As a result, when Utah was finally granted statehood in 1896, it was free to become the site of the imposing, domed **Utah State Capitol** (summer Mon–Sat 6am–8pm; winter Mon–Sat 6am–6pm; free). Along with all the plaques and monuments you might expect, the corridors of power are packed full of earnest and rather diverting exhibits of great Utah moments. The basement area in particular holds a fine assortment of historical what-nots, ranging from mining dioramas to the 18-cylinder, 750-horsepower Mormon Meteor, raced by Ab Jenkins across the Bonneville Salt Flats in the 1950s.

Now called **Capitol Hill**, the neighbourhood around the Capitol holds some of Salt Lake City's grandest turn-of-the-century homes, with dozens of ornate Victorian houses lining Main Street and Quince Street to the northwest; walking tour maps of the district are available from the *Utah Heritage Foundation*, 355 Quince St. Directly opposite the Capitol stands another architectural landmark, **Council Hall**, the old Territorial Legislature building that was dismantled and rebuilt here in the 1960s. The main chamber off the entrance has been restored to its period appearance, while the rest of the building houses the *Utah Travel Council* (see p.475).

Downtown Salt Lake City

A block east of Temple Square along South Temple Boulevard, the **Beehive House** (Mon–Sat 9.30am–4.30pm, Sun 10am–1pm; free) is a plain white New England-style house, with wraparound verandahs and green shutters. Erected in 1854 by church leader **Brigham Young**, it's now a small museum of Young's life, restored to the style of the period. Free twenty-minute tours, which you have to join to see much of the house, are given at least every half-hour.

The **Family History Library**, across West Temple Boulevard from Temple Square (Mon 7.30am–6pm, Tues–Fri 7.30am–10pm, Sat 7.30am–5pm; free), is intended to enable Mormons to trace their ancestors, and then baptize them into the faith by proxy, but it's open to everyone. The world's most exhaustive genealogical library is surprisingly user-friendly, giving immediate access, through CD-ROMs and banks of computers, to birth and death records from over fifty countries, some dating back as much as five hundred years. All you need is a person's place of birth, a few approximate dates, and you're away; out of respect for the privacy of those still living, most of the information pertains to centuries prior to our own. Volunteers provide help if you need it, but leave you alone until you ask. Next door to the library, the **Museum of Church History and Art** (Mon–Fri 9am–9pm, Sat & Sun 10am–7pm; free) charts the rise of the Mormon faith in art and artefact.

The area southwest of Temple Square, now the site of the massive **Salt Palace** convention centre and sports arena (home of the Utah Jazz basketball team), has undergone a rapid transformation. The surrounding district of brick warehouses around the Union Pacific railroad tracks is quickly filling up with designer shops and art galleries, signs that even Mormons can be yuppies.

Further west, the "other side of the tracks" around the interstate, remains one of the city's most run-down and forgotten areas, the last resort of transient winos and Utah's growing homeless population. The museum run by the **Utah Historical Society** in the *Amtrak* station, 300 S Rio Grande Ave (Mon–Fri 8am–5pm, Sat 10am–2pm; free), is too mediocre to make it worth passing this way.

Bingham Canyon Copper Mine

Roughly 25 miles south of downtown Salt Lake City on I-15, what looks at first like just another bizarre bit of Southwestern badlands, off to the west, is in fact the largest man-made hole in the world. Since 1906, the vast open-pit **Bingham Canyon Copper Mine** has yielded copper, gold, silver and molybdenum to a value greater than the entire Californian and Klondike gold rushes combined; two thirds of all Utah's mineral production has come from this one mine. In doing so, it has replaced a mountain with a terraced hole that's 2.5 miles across and twice the depth of the world's tallest building. Briefly shut down in the 1980s, it is now owned by *Rio Tinto Zinc*, and hard at work again. Visitors drive to the very top of the astonishing abyss, where a **visitor center** does its best to stress the positive aspects of what in most eyes is an ecological hellhole, while the occasional disconcerting boom tells of ongoing blasting in its bowels (April–Oct daily 8am–8pm; $3 per vehicle).

Great Salt Lake

The **GREAT SALT LAKE**, in the barren desert west of Salt Lake City, is the last remnant of a 20,000-square-mile inland sea that once stretched into Idaho and Nevada. In the late nineteenth century, the lake's shores were lined with extravagant resorts, and steamboats and pleasure cruisers plied across its surface. After years of mysterious decline, when enough of its contents evaporated to make it the world's second-saltiest body of water, it has since the 1980s started equally mysteriously to re-fill. Its level today is far higher than state planners ever bargained for, and has forced the raising of the adjacent I-80 interstate by several feet.

On the plus side, the lake's formerly abundant **wildlife**, and especially its migratory **birds**, have begun to re-appear, but it's still not especially attractive to humans. **Great Salt Lake State Park**, sixteen miles west of town on I-80, is the dingiest affair imaginable (daily 8am–sunset). It marks the site of the flamboyant 1890s *Saltair* pavilion, which closed down in 1968 when the waters receded, and was promptly destroyed by fire. A smaller version re-opened in 1983, just in time to be flooded out; it's now pretty decrepit and threadbare, but still gamely showing videos of the lake, while gaudy railroad cars and a lake boat outside act as gift shops.

Eating

Though Salt Lake City has a perfectly good selection of **restaurants**, it lacks an atmospheric – let alone hip – dining district. If you like to compare menus, the only downtown area with much potential is the block or two to either side of West Temple Street, south and east of the Salt Palace; otherwise, for good food in scenic surroundings, head for *Ruth's Diner* or the *Santa Fe Restaurant*, in Emigration Canyon at the edge of the mountains, three miles east of downtown.

Bill and Nada's Cafe, 479 S 600 East; ☎801/359-6984. All-American 1940s diner, open 24hr. Great for breakfast, but worth a visit anytime for its ace jukebox, the best west of Memphis – packed with Hank Williams, Patsy Cline, blues and bebop tracks.

E.I.B.O.'s Mesquite Broiler, 300 Trolley Square; ☎801/531-7788. Open-air dining in popular upmarket mall, not far southeast of downtown, and serving tasty wood-grilled meats and seafood at $10–15 for a full meal.

Einstein Brothers Bagel Bakery, 147 S Main St; ☎801/537-5033. Downtown outlet of a local institution, serving a wide range of espressos along with bagels and salads.

Lamb's Restaurant, 169 S Main St; ☎801/364-7166. Great breakfasts, best eaten at the long shiny counter, and excellent-value set meals throughout the day in one of Utah's oldest restaurants. Open Mon–Sat 7am–9pm.

Le Parisien, 417 S 300 East; ☎801/364-5223. Large, long-established downtown French restaurant, where the menu also features a few Italian specialities. Open for lunch Mon–Sat, when entrees such as *coq au vin* cost $6–10, and dinner nightly, at more like $10–15.

Market Street Grill, 48 Market St; ☎801/322-4668. As close as Salt Lake City comes to a New York City bar and grill, open for all meals daily. Fresh seafood is the prime attraction, but you can also get steaks in all shapes and sizes. Full meals $12–30.

Oasis Cafe, 151 S 500 East; ☎801/322-0404. New, inexpensive cafe with plenty of appealing vegetarian options. Live acoustic or jazz in the evening.

Pierpoint Cantina, 122 W Pierpoint Ave; ☎801/364-1222. Large downtown Mexican restaurant, open for lunch Mon–Fri and dinner daily, with top-quality *ceviche* and gourmet dishes plus the usual standards, all competitively priced.

Rio Grande Cafe, 270 S Rio Grande; ☎801/364-3302. Spirited and stylish Mexican *cantina* housed in the old *Denver and Rio Grande* railroad station, still used by *Amtrak*, three blocks west of downtown.

Ruth's Diner, 2100 Emigration Canyon Rd; ☎801/582-5807. Good-value indoor and patio dining, often accompanied by live music, set in and around old railroad carriages in a narrow canyon just three miles east of town. Wide selection of fresh dishes, great salads and Utah's best breakfasts.

Santa Fe Restaurant, 2100 Emigration Canyon Rd; ☎801/582-5888. Sophisticated upmarket sister restaurant to *Ruth's* (above). Eclectic menu of the best of Southwest cuisine; brilliantly presented grilled meats and fish, and an excellent $9.95 Sunday brunch.

Shogun Sushi, 321 S Main St; ☎801/364-7142. Central Japanese dining, tasty if rather upmarket, with American and Japanese-style formal seating and a sushi bar.

Drinking and nightlife

Salt Lake City doesn't roll up the sidewalks when the sun goes down. As explained on p.331, many drinking venues are technically private clubs, in which a nominal membership fee entitles the cardholder and up to five guests to two weeks' use of the facilities. However, Salt Lake City now has a handful of **brewpubs**, for which membership is not required; they're distinguishable from their counterparts in other states only by the requirement that that they can't sell beer with an alcoholic content of greater than 3.2 percent.

To find out about the city's broad range of fringe art, music and clubland happenings, pick up free papers such as the fortnightly *Event* or the monthly *Catalyst*, or tune to radio station *KRCL* 91FM.

The Bar and Grill, 60 E 800 South St; ☎801/533-0341. Prime venue for alternative and local bands.

Club Zephyr, 301 S West Temple Blvd; ☎801/355-5646. Salt Lake's premier live jazz and blues venue – technically a private club – with semi-famous names most nights. Upmarket clientele, elegant decor, cover $5–15.

Dead Goat Saloon, 165 S West Temple Blvd; ☎801/328-4628. Raucous semi-subterranean saloon, with loud live music most nights.

Red Rock Brewing Company, 254 S 200 West St; ☎801/521-7446. Two dozen micro-brewed beers and a varied food menu, served until at least midnight daily.

Squatters Pub, 147 W 300 South St; ☎801/363-2739. Casual, friendly brewpub with a range of beers available until midnight every day.

Contexts

A History of the Southwest

What is now the Southwest USA has been home to Native Americans for around twelve thousand years. Around four hundred years ago, they were joined by a small group of Hispanic colonists, who claimed the region for Spain as **New Mexico**. After over two hundred years of Spanish rule, it passed briefly into the hands of the newly independent nation of Mexico, before being taken over by the United States, which has now held it for just over 150 years.

Throughout that long history, the Southwest has been either controlled, or at least heavily influenced, by distant powers. Its best-known ancient peoples, the Anasazi and the Hohokam, drew their cultural inspiration from the civilizations of Mexico; the settlers of Santa Fe looked to Madrid and Mexico City for financial and spiritual support; and even the twentieth-century status of the region owes much to federal funding from Washington.

What makes the history of the Southwest so fascinating is that so many of the different peoples who have migrated into the region are still there, and still inter-reacting with each other. In the words of an anthropologist from Zuni Pueblo, "the Anasazi are alive and well and living in the Rio Grande valley". The Navajo, relative latecomers, form the majority population in the Four Corners region, though they've never displaced the Hopi. Santa Fe remains a visibly Hispanic, Catholic city, while Utah is still seventy percent Mormon, and Phoenix and Las Vegas typify the Anglo impact.

The Paleo-Indians

No one knows when humans reached the American continent. While ancient campfires have been tentatively dated back as far as 30,000 BC, there's no firm evidence to suggest that the Southwest, or anywhere else in the modern United States, held a significant population until 10,000 BC.

These **Paleo-Indians** were originally Siberian nomads, who worked their way into Alaska along a "**land-bridge**", exposed when the level of the ocean dropped, which followed the approximate line of what's now the Bering Strait. Though that entire region was treeless tundra, no

more appealing than it is today, it supported sufficient quantities of large mammals to make hunting worthwhile. Quite possibly, a band of no more than fifty individuals completed the journey. Their descendants then spread so quickly across the new continent that they reached the southernmost tip of South America within a couple of thousand years.

Between 10,000 BC and 8000 BC, the Southwest was dominated by what archeologists call the **Clovis** culture, whose distinctive flaked-stone spear-points were first identified at Clovis, New Mexico. Living in small groups, constantly on the move, Clovis hunters pursued their prey across large distances. Their weapons have been found poking from the ribs of dead mammoths, and they seem to have been such successful killers that they drove the indigenous fauna – which also included giant sloths, camels and even horses – to extinction.

The Archaic culture

As the large animals died out, early Southwesterners had to adapt, and became **hunter-gatherers**. The people of the **Archaic** or **Desert** culture learned where and when particular plants would ripen, and migrated seasonally within much smaller areas – often between canyons or valleys and nearby hillsides – in search of fresh food. Hunting for small mammals such as rabbit and deer was still important, however, and they began to develop shamanastic rituals, as evidenced by the clay statuettes and split-twig figurines, depicting what appear to be deities as well as animals, that have been found in remote locations in the Grand Canyon and elsewhere. Few substantial remains of their dwellings survive, however; it's thought they lived in caves wherever possible. The most remarkable manifestation of Archaic culture was the haunting, mysterious rock art of the **Great Gallery** in Canyonlands National Park (see p.411); they also constructed "intaglios", giant earthworks in the shape of enigmatic figures or snakes, in the deserts of southwest Arizona.

The Archaic era was brought to an end by the gradual infiltration of Mexican influences from the south. The first and most crucial was agriculture. **Corn** – in the shape of tiny fingers of maize, much smaller than today's strains – may have been cultivated in the highlands of southern Mexico as early as 5000 BC. The skill of growing it was then passed northwards from group to group, accompanied no doubt by the prayers and rituals necessary to ensure a good harvest, and may have reached southern New Mexico around 1200 BC. However, anthropologists have noted a common reluctance among hunter-gatherers to give up what they regard as a pleasant lifestyle, which offers individuals food in return for comparatively little effort, and lots of free time. The Southwest followed that pattern, in that a low level of farming – more like gardening – served at first to supplement the traditional diet, and communities only made the transition to intensive agriculture when forced to by increasing population levels.

The Basketmakers

The first society to embark on the large-scale cultivation of crops – corn, together with a more recent arrival, **squash** – from around 100 BC onwards, was confusingly named **Basketmaker II** by early archeologists, who assumed that more primitive "Basketmaker I" sites would subsequently be found. The basketmakers lived in extended family groups, in shallow **pithouses** – rectangular pits dug two to six feet into the ground, with earth-covered roofs that rose above ground level. They hunted using the *atlatl* – a lever-like spear-throwing device used throughout the Americas – and cooked by dropping hot rocks into yucca-leaf baskets that had a waterproof lining of pitch. By now they had also domesticated **dogs**, for hunting, and **turkeys**, used mainly for feathers rather than food.

Pottery is thought to have spread from Mexico, by way of the Mimbres region of southwest New Mexico (see p.193), in the first few centuries AD. All pots were made by women, using the technique of hand-coiling, which involves layering successive strips of rolled clay on top of each other and then smoothing them together. The use of fragile ceramic vessels presupposes a relatively sedentary society, but brings great benefits; it's much easier to boil **beans** in a pot than a basket, so the Southwest acquired its third great staple food, and basket-making declined.

By around 500 AD, the so-called **Basketmaker III** culture had emerged. As well as corn, squash and beans, they grew another Mexican import, **cotton** – originally cultivated mainly for its oil-rich edible seeds – and used **bows and arrows** for the first time. Sizeable **villages** (what the Spanish later called **pueblos**) started to grow up.

Each village soon focused around one specific pithouse that was larger than the rest, and was probably set aside for public or ritual use. Such buildings are recognizable as the first *kivas* – the ceremonial underground chambers that remain at the heart of Pueblo religion to this day. Each *kiva* was entered from above, via an opening that also served as the smokehole for the central firepit. A bench ran around its circumference, and there were also niches set into the walls for ritual objects may have been placed. A small depression in the floor in front of the firepit, known as the *sipapu*, symbolized the hole through which human beings emerged onto this earth.

The Anasazi

By 700 AD, much of the Southwest was populated by the forerunners of the modern Pueblo Indians. This book follows popular usage in calling these people the **Anasazi**. However, Pueblo Indians object to that name, which comes from a Navajo word meaning "enemy ancestors", and it's gradually being phased out in favour of either "ancestral Pueblo peoples" or the Hopi word for "ancestors", **Hisatsinom**.

Over the course of six centuries, from 700 AD to 1300 AD, Anasazi civilization spread beyond the **Four Corners** region to cover most of what's now northern Arizona and New Mexico, as well as southern Utah and Colorado, reaching as far as the depths of the Grand Canyon and into southern Nevada. At the start of that period, there was a steady increase in the size and sophistication of their villages, and also a crucial change. Individuals stopped living in pithouses, and instead built surface structures of mud plastered onto a framework of brushwood – a style known as wattle-and-daub. However, they continued to dig large subterranean *kivas*, which kept the pithouse form but were exclusively designed for communal or ceremonial use. Many such *kivas* could now be accessed not only through the roof, but also via concealed underground tunnels, which may have enabled costumed priests or dancers to make surprise appearances during rituals.

The Anasazi were the first North Americans to use looms to weave cotton. In addition to cotton clothes, they made blankets and even socks from yucca leaves interwoven with turkey feathers, and wore yucca sandals. For a time, they seem to have deliberately flattened and broadened their skulls by binding the heads of babies against cradleboards. As you might imagine from their tiny doorways and cramped living quarters, they were on the small side, with women averaging five feet in height and men a few inches more. Life expectancy was thirty or less, although perhaps one in ten reached the age of fifty. Adults were plagued by the twin problems of arthritis, often exacerbated by years of carrying heavy loads, and loss of teeth. Their teeth were worn away by the grit in their food, the result of grinding corn between a hand-tool or *mano* and a flat slab known as a *metate*, both made from sandstone; in the words of a modern Hopi saying, "a person eats a rock in a lifetime". They also had some medical expertise, using cottonwood bark, which contains the main active ingredient of aspirin, as a painkiller, and the sap from piñon pines as an all-purpose antiseptic.

The Four Corners Anasazi reached a cultural peak during the eleventh century. By that time, three main sub-groups had emerged – centred on Chaco Canyon in what's now northwest New Mexico, Mesa Verde in southwest Colorado, and the Kayenta region of northeast Arizona – and there were also lesser concentrations such as the Virgin Anasazi of southern Utah.

The **Chacoans** seem to have been the most sophisticated of all, as witnessed not only by the architectural complexity of the multi-storey pueblos of Chaco Canyon, but by the fact that the canyon was so unsuited for large-scale occupation that they must have survived by extracting tribute from surrounding regions. A detailed account of the "Chaco Phenomenon" appears on p.80.

The wealth of Chaco demonstrates that by 1050 AD the Southwest was criss-crossed by extensive **trading routes**. In the absence of pack animals, most of the trade was in ritual or ornamental artefacts rather than the necessities of life. In exchange for **turquoise** from the mines of Cerrillos (see p.114), which passed from group to group all the way down to the Aztecs in central Mexico, the Anasazi received silver and copper artefacts from Mexico, sea-shells from the Pacific Coast, and the most prized ceremonial objects of all – live **macaws**.

The decline of Chaco, during the first half of the twelfth century, was mirrored by a general decline in the Anasazi population. Following a period of instability, and mass migrations, however, Anasazi civilization had a majestic final flourish in the Four Corners. The thirteenth century, when they constructed the "**cliff dwellings**", squeezed dramatically into narrow alcoves high on canyon walls, for which they're now celebrated, was also characterized by the widespread growth of major towns. Colorado's Montezuma Valley was typical in holding around eight large pueblo complexes, ranged across the valley floor and along neighbouring ridges, each home to over a thousand people. The nearby cliff dwellings preserved in **Mesa Verde** National Park (see p.65) were home to a smaller, probably peripheral group; though compellingly beautiful to modern eyes, they represent a relatively minor aspect of Anasazi life.

The disappearance of the Anasazi

Between 1275 AD and 1300 AD, the Anasazi vanished from the entire Four Corners region. Their "**disappearance**" is still widely presented as a great mystery, although modern Pueblo peoples are so self-evidently descended from the Anasazi that it's clear they migrated away rather than simply dying out. Why they did so is harder to explain. Traditional accounts say that a sustained **drought** forced them to leave, but it has now been demonstrated that such droughts were not uncommon, and that the region remained capable of producing enough food to support them.

It seems more likely that the drought coincided with a period of cultural upheaval. While archeologists argue as to whether individual Anasazi cliff dwellings were intended for defence, there's no disputing the fact that the region as a whole was prone to violent conflict at this time. Recent proof of cannibalism in the Montezuma Valley has shattered notions of Anasazi society as being utterly peaceful, and isolated groups appear to have banded together in larger settlements for mutual defence.

The influence of the blood-drenched civilizations of ancient Mexico was also at its highest. As described on p.58, the *kachina* religion, which centred on supernatural entities that at this formative stage closely paralleled the warring deities of the Aztecs, spread rapidly across the Southwest. In time, the emphasis of the *kachina* cult shifted away from blood and sacrifice towards ceremonies designed to bring rain, and thus corn. The drought of the late thirteenth century may have seemed like the first crucial test of, or judgement upon, those rain-making powers, and it may be that charismatic religious leaders persuaded their followers that the failure of the harvest was a signal to move on.

In addition, the Anasazi had severely depleted their **environment**. The need for fuel and building materials meant that the landscape for many miles around their settlements had been stripped bare; the pueblos of Chaco Canyon, for example, used over 200,000 large wooden beams. Cutting down trees not only made the search for firewood increasingly arduous, but led to the process known as *arroyo*-cutting, whereby, once the trees that held their banks together were removed, previously placid streams became savage torrents that destroyed prime riverside farmland. It may be no coincidence that the Four Corners remained all but deserted until the arrival of the Navajo during the sixteenth century (see p.486); it may have taken that long to recover from over-exploitation

The Hohokam

While the Basketmakers and the Anasazi held sway further north, the deserts of southern Arizona and northern Mexico were home to the equally sophisticated **Hohokam** civilization. This region was not then so barren as it appears today – much of it was covered with grass until the Spanish allowed their cattle to over-graze – and the Hohokam were primarily **farmers**. They lived not in compact pueblos but in what the Spanish later called *rancherías* – sprawling farming communities, where each separate homestead consisted of a framework of timber and brush coated with mud. Thousands of such villages, most of which were occupied for many generations, were scattered across the desert, interspersed with larger "towns" that were probably ceremonial and trading centres rather than residential districts. The population was most heavily concentrated in the **Phoenix Basin**, where they compensated for the lack of rainfall by digging over three hundred miles of irrigation **canals**. Constructed without the use of

metal tools, and requiring constant maintenance, these enabled the Hohokam to grow two crops each year – corn, beans and squash, and also cotton for trade.

Whether the Hohokam migrated into the region from central Mexico around 300 BC, as some archeologists believe, or simply evolved from indigenous desert peoples, they were clearly heavily influenced by Mexican culture. Each major town had at least one Mexican-style **ballcourt**, where a ritual game with similarities to modern basketball was played with a rubber ball, and a raised-earth **platform mound** – a primitive pyramid – used for religious ceremonies. Like the Anasazi, with whom they had little direct contact, the Hohokam traded commodities like cotton and salt for treasured ritual items from the south, such as copper bells, onyx, parrots and macaws.

During the eleventh century, the Hohokam trading complex known as **Snaketown**, at the confluence of the Gila and Salt rivers, rivalled Chaco as the largest settlement in the Southwest. Though Snaketown then declined, the Phoenix Basin became one of the most densely populated areas in North America, with perhaps eighty thousand inhabitants in the thirteenth century. However, the Hohokam **disappeared** from history at much the same time as the Anasazi, around 1350 AD. It's thought that they damaged the region's delicate ecological balance so extensively that their descendants were reduced to an impoverished subsistence lifestyle. In addition, the arrival of European **diseases** such as smallpox, measles and typhus reduced the population of the Phoenix Basin to less than five thousand by the end of the seventeenth century.

While no modern Native American group claims direct physical descent from the Hohokam, it's possible to trace certain cultural continuities. The *rancheria* style of dwelling endured until recent times among tribes such as the Yavapai, the Havasupai, and the **'O'odham** people of southern Arizona (known to the Spanish as the Pima and the Papago). Those peoples also follow an individualistic system of belief, without *kachinas* or *kivas*, and depending on shamans rather than priests, that seems to be in line with what little is known about Hohokam religion.

The Mogollon

Archeologists distinguish a third significant group among the pre-Columbian peoples of the

Southwest – the **Mogollon**. Contemporaneous with the Anasazi and the Hohokam, and sharing elements of both cultures, the Mogollon occupied an extensive area in what's now west-central New Mexico and east-central Arizona. The main geographical feature of the region is the **Mogollon Rim**, a 200-mile long, 2000-foot high escarpment that marks the southern limit of the Colorado Plateau. The Mogollon people lived on the cool plateau above the rim, farming the upland meadows and hunting in the adjacent mountains.

Being so close to Mexico, the Mogollon heartland, which focused on the valleys of the **Gila** and **Mimbres** rivers, was probably the first area of the Southwest to acquire the techniques of agriculture and pottery. The Basketmaker phase lasted longer here than in the Four Corners; the Mogollon only stopped building pithouses around the eleventh century, and the few pueblos they constructed, such as the one now preserved as Gila Cliff Dwellings National Monument (see p.194), were on a smaller scale than their Anasazi counterparts. In one respect, however, Mogollon culture was unsurpassed – the extraordinary **pottery** produced by the **Classic Mimbres** people, a Mogollon offshoot described in detail on p.193.

Much like the Four Corners, the entire Mogollon region became **depopulated** during the fourteenth century. As the Mogollon peoples had probably been instrumental in introducing the *kachina* religion to the Southwest, it makes sense to suppose that their descendants helped to create modern Pueblo culture. Specific Mogollon-descended pueblos may well have been the hardest hit by the arrival of both the Spaniards and the Apache, however, and if their inhabitants survived at all they probably fled north as refugees.

The Pueblo world and the Spanish invasion

Although the Anasazi era ended with their departure from the Four Corners, their immediate descendants created the Southwest's largest pre-Hispanic communities of all. In particular, the city of **Casas Grandes**, which flourished in what's now the northern Mexican state of Chihuahua between 1300 AD and 1400 AD, consisted of over two thousand rooms, and served as a major macaw-breeding centre.

However, the most enduring legacy of the Anasazi was the emergence of **Pueblo** communities throughout what had until the fourteenth century been relatively uninhabited areas of northern New Mexico. Most of the people of Mesa Verde migrated to the northern reaches of the **Rio Grande** valley, where they founded pueblos such as Taos and Santa Clara; their language, known as Tanoan, evolved into the Tiwa and Tewa languages spoken today. The Chacoans, on the other hand, who spoke the language that became Keresan, moved further south to establish pueblos like Cochiti and Santo Domingo, as well as Ácoma and Zuni to the west.

Other population centres – not so well known today, as they failed to survive the impact of the Spanish – included the **Galisteo Valley**, not far southeast of Santa Fe, which held around a dozen large pueblos, the **Chama Valley**, and the **Tigüex** region near modern Albuquerque.

By the time the Spanish arrived, the Southwest may have held as many as a hundred separate pueblos, with a total population approaching one hundred thousand. New forms of social organization had emerged, and individual pueblos consisted of alliances of either **clans** – each with its own religious or military responsibilities – or **moieties** – the technical term for a society divided into two halves, in which half the pueblo might belong to a *kiva* associated with winter ceremonies, and the other half to one connected with summer. However, pueblos did not have chiefs or leaders in the European sense, and neither was there any tradition of alliances between pueblos. That lack of political unity seriously weakened their ability to resist the Spanish invaders, who turned their attention northwards after completing the conquest of Mexico.

The coming of the Spaniards

The first Spanish expedition to reach what's now the USA, led by **Ponce de Leon**, sailed up the Atlantic Coast in 1513 and named **Florida**. The next Spanish voyage, in 1528, ended in shipwreck in Tampa Bay, but a junior officer, **Alvar Núñez Cabeza de Vaca**, survived. Together with three shipmates, he spent eight years on an extraordinary trans-continental odyssey. Living with various Native American groups – sometimes held as slaves, sometimes revered as seers – they made their way across Texas, following the Pecos River and the Rio Grande. Whether they reached modern New Mexico or Arizona is uncertain, but while staying in the pueblo of the Jumano tribe, somewhere on the Rio Grande, they heard tales of larger pueblos further north, and in northern Mexico they were given emeralds that had been purchased with parrot feathers from a people who lived to the north.

Cabeza de Vaca's eventual arrival in Mexico City in 1536 created a sensation, and the Viceroy of New Spain resolved to investigate his tales of golden cities deep in the desert. One of Cabeza de Vaca's companions had been a black African from Azamor in Morocco, called **Esteban de Dorantes**. Rather than return to a life of slavery, he volunteered to map the route for a new expedition led by **Fray Marcos de Niza**. In 1539, Esteban set off ahead of Fray Marcos, and followed a long-established Indian trading route north across the Rio San Pedro into what's now Arizona.

A giant of a man, dressed like a shaman in jewellery and feathers, and accompanied by two colossal greyhounds, he amazed the native peoples he encountered, and soon acquired a large entourage. Having arranged to send a signal back to Fray Marcos if he discovered anything to rival the marvels of Mexico, he duly did so as he approached the pueblo of **Zuni** (see p.83). Zuni at this time was a major trading centre, where the trail from the south met others from the Pacific Coast to the west and the Rio Grande pueblos to the east. The Zuni villages were nonetheless simply clusters of adobe houses, not cities on the Mexican scale. According to the Zuni, Esteban's demands for tribute were incompatible with his claims to be a medicine man, and they punished his sacrilegious behaviour by killing him, cutting him into strips, and distributing his flesh among their neighbours.

Fray Marcos reported that he was in sight of Zuni when he heard of Esteban's death and fled back to Mexico; it seems more likely that he never reached Arizona. Even so, he announced "this land . . . is the greatest and best of all that have been discovered". Rendering the Zuni name Shi:wona as Cíbola, he called the six Zuni villages the **Seven Cities of Cíbola**, and identified them with the legendary Seven Cities of Antilla, long sought by Spanish explorers.

On February 22, 1540, therefore, a further expedition, led by **Francisco Vásquez de Coronado**, set off into the Southwest from Compostela in northern Mexico. Consisting of over three hundred Spanish soldiers plus hundreds more Indian "allies" and servants, and accompanied by several thousand horses and cattle, they marched up through Arizona and reached Zuni on July 7. In front of the town of Hawikku, the Zuni drew a line of sacred cornmeal along the ground, which they forbade the Spaniards to cross. During the pitched **battle** that ensued – the first ever fought between Europeans and Native Americans – Coronado himself was knocked unconscious, but Spanish weapons prevailed. The town was taken, its storehouses revealing not gold, but something that by now seemed equally precious – food.

Within two weeks, news of the fall of Zuni spread throughout the Southwest. Coronado made his headquarters in the conquered pueblo, and despatched exploratory parties in all directions. One such, under Pedro de Tovar, forced the "warlike" Hopi pueblos to surrender (see p.483), and reached as far as the **Grand Canyon**; another, commanded by Melchor Díaz, crossed the Colorado further south, and thus penetrated modern **California**. A detachment led by Hernando de Alvarado headed east, passing Ácoma Pueblo – the "greatest stronghold ever seen in the world" – and reaching the pueblos of the Rio Grande.

Meanwhile, emissaries from the Pueblo world were travelling to Zuni. Peaceful overtures from two men from **Cicuyé** (now Pecos National Historical Park; see p.130), known to the Spaniards as **Cacique** (meaning Governor) and **Bigotes** (Whiskers), persuaded Coronado to move his expedition east. They camped for the winter beside the Rio Grande, in a region they called **Tigüex**, and commandeered an entire pueblo as their new base. This may have been Kuaua, now preserved as Coronado State Monument (see p.112) – it's hard to say, because relations with the Tigüex soon degenerated into full-scale war, and in a bloody succession of sieges and massacres all the Tigüex pueblos were destroyed.

Coronado remained convinced that gold was somewhere to be found. In the spring of 1541, he decamped northeast to Cicuyé, which was a prosperous community where Pueblo peoples traded with nomads from the Plains. In what may well have been a deliberate plot, Cacique and Bigotes introduced him to **"The Turk"**, a Pawnee captive, who knew of a city far to the east, **Quivira**, that was rich in gold. Details of the Turk's story suggest that he was familiar with the culture of the Mississippi Indians, but he was probably released by the leaders of Cicuyé in the hope that he'd lead the Spaniards into oblivion on the endless Plains.

In the event, the expedition wandered for three fruitless months across what they called "the domain of the cows", in honour of its vast buffalo herds. From the Llano Estacado or "Staked Plains" of **Texas**, where they drove wooden stakes into the ground to avoid losing their way, they veered northeast into **Kansas**, following the Arkansas River along the route of what later became the Santa Fe Trail. There they did indeed reach a land known as Quivira, but its inhabitants were nomadic and utterly gold-free buffalo-hunters. At that point, Coronado lost patience; the Turk was garrotted, and the Spaniards returned to the Rio Grande. After another beleaguered winter in Tigüex, they embarked on the long journey back to Mexico, leaving behind a handful of (swiftly martyred) missionaries and many of their Mexican-Indian allies. Popular myth has it that Coronado was disgraced on his return home, but while his expedition was certainly seen as a failure, the man himself held important offices in Mexico City for the rest of his life.

The colony of New Mexico

During the fifty years after Coronado's departure, unauthorized Spanish adventurers made occasional forays into the Southwest. Not until 1598, however, was **Don Juan de Oñate** granted royal permission to establish a permanent **colony** in the region. His expedition, consisting of 130 families and two hundred single men, crossed the Rio Grande near modern El Paso on May 1, and took possession of the land under the name of **New Mexico**. The geography of the region remaining unknown, the precise boundaries of the colony were not specified, but broadly speaking it extended from the Colorado River in the west to the Pecos River in the east, and included not only what's now New Mexico, but all of Arizona, plus parts of Utah, Colorado, Nevada and California. At that time, the name "Mexico" referred only to what we call Mexico City – the modern country was known as "New Spain" until 1821 – so "New Mexico" was named in the hope that it would match the riches of the Aztecs.

As Oñate's party travelled north along the river, each pueblo they came to turned out to have been hurriedly deserted by its inhabitants, fearful of being captured as slaves. Eventually, at the confluence of the Rio Grande and the Chama River near what's now Española, the settlers took over the pueblo of O'ke, renamed it San Juan, and made it their **capital**. Like Coronado before him, Oñate sent soldiers to all quarters of his new realm in search of gold; and like Coronado he soon found himself at war. After a group commanded by Oñate's nephew was all but wiped out, he launched a full-scale artillery onslaught on Ácoma Pueblo. Over eight hundred Acomans were killed, and eighty male prisoners had their feet chopped off in public ceremonies in the pueblos of the Rio Grande.

By the time Oñate returned to his capital, most of the colonists had given up and returned to Mexico, and Oñate himself was recalled to Mexico City in disgrace once Franciscan missionaries reported his cruelty to their superiors. Meanwhile, however, Captain Pérez de Villagrá had trumpeted Oñate's "achievements" in an epic poem, *Historia de Nueva México*. In the face of all the evidence, Villagrá still insisted that New Mexico had the potential to become the greatest kingdom in the Spanish empire, and he was sufficiently believed in Madrid for another attempt at colonization to be launched. **Don Pedro de Peralta** was therefore sent to New Mexico with orders to found a new capital, and the city of **Santa Fe** was duly laid out in 1610.

The early Spanish colonists of New Mexico dreamed of emulating their predecessors in Mexico, who had accumulated both land and wealth in prodigious quantities. However, it soon became clear that New Mexico was the end of the road, with no access to the ocean and no rich neighbours for the Spaniards either to trade with or plunder. Santa Fe never grew into a mighty city, but remained a remote military outpost of crude adobe buildings. Enterprising colonists therefore dispersed up and down the valley of the Rio Grande, appropriating Pueblo farmlands – and often enslaving Pueblo peoples – to create **ranches** on which they raised sheep and corn, and planted orchards of peaches, plums and cherries. **Wheat** was the most significant of the new crops. Unlike the traditional triumvirate of corn, beans and squash, which have to be grown entirely in spring and summer, it can be planted in December for harvest in June.

At the same time, **Franciscan missionaries** set out to convert the Pueblo Indians to Catholicism. One or two friars would attach themselves to a specific pueblo, recruit Indian labour to build adobe mission churches, and set about persuading the Pueblos that their *kachina* cults and corn ceremonies were wicked.

Throughout the seventeenth century, the Spanish civil and religious authorities in New Mexico were at loggerheads. The church deplored violence against the Pueblos and yet demanded the eradication of their beliefs; the military governors preferred not to antagonize the Indians unnecessarily, but felt their authority ultimately rested on the sword.

Quite apart from any specific actions, the very presence of the Spaniards utterly disrupted the region. Settled communities like the villages of the Rio Grande were especially vulnerable to **epidemic diseases** such as smallpox, measles and typhus, which were unknown before the arrival of the Europeans. By 1640, the Pueblo population had dropped from a hundred thousand down to around thirty thousand, and more than half of all pueblos had been abandoned. Existing patterns of **trade** across the Southwest had also been shattered, and the Rio Grande valley became a prime target for Native American raiders who coveted Spanish arms and, above all, **horses**. Tribes such as the Navajo and the Apache – see p.486 – turned from wandering nomads into fearsome mounted warriors, and all too often it was the Pueblo peoples who bore the brunt of their attacks.

The Pueblo Revolt

In 1675, as it became ever more obvious that traditional Pueblo beliefs still endured beneath a veneer of Catholicism, the Spanish arrested 47 Pueblo religious leaders. Three were condemned as "witchdoctors" and hanged at Santa Fe; the rest were publicly horsewhipped. One of these, a man called **Popé** from San Juan Pueblo, made his way to Taos Pueblo, and turned one of its *kivas* into the centre of a campaign of resistance. A date was set for a concerted uprising against the Spanish, and knotted strings were sent out to all the pueblos, with the instruction to untie one knot each night until the last signalled the arrival of the great day. Somehow, the plot was

betrayed, so the **Pueblo Revolt** began a day early, on August 9, 1680.

For the first and only time in their history, the Pueblos of the northern Rio Grande, plus their cousins in Ácoma, Zuni and the Hopi mesas, combined in unison; they were even joined by the Navajo and the Apache. Their anger fell especially upon the missionaries; 21 out of New Mexico's 33 priests were murdered, as were 375 men, women and children out of a total of 2350 Spanish colonists.

After a ten-day **siege of Santa Fe**, the Governor, the garrison and around one thousand citizens were allowed to retreat south. They were joined en route by the Christianized majority from Isleta Pueblo – the only modern pueblo not to join the attack – and all the Pueblo peoples who lived south of Albuquerque. For the next thirteen years, the refugees remained together at what's now Ciudad Juarez, across the Rio Grande from El Paso. Those Indians who had joined the exodus founded Ysleta and other pueblos in the neighbourhood, while the former colonists, refused permission to continue any further south, awaited an opportunity to return north.

Back in Santa Fe, the doors and windows of the Palace of the Governors had been sealed up, and the building turned into a typical multi-storey pueblo. Popé was nominally in control, but the concept of a central political administration was alien to the Pueblos, and the alliance soon fragmented.

Not until 1692 did the Spanish crown appoint a new Governor of New Mexico, **Don Diego de Vargas**, but his exploratory expedition encountered no opposition when it returned to the city that September. As a result, he set off again with a party of colonists the following year; this time they had to fight before they could re-enter Santa Fe, in December 1693. The return of the Spanish triggered mass migrations throughout the region – as described on p.487, modern Navajo culture originated with the inter-mingling of the ancestral Navajo with Pueblo refugees during this period – and there were further minor insurrections in the years ahead, but the **Reconquest** was completed by 1696.

The eighteenth century

Although Hispanic settlers continued to dominate the region for 150 years after the Pueblo Revolt,

New Mexico was always a peripheral part of the Spanish empire. Separated from the rest of Mexico by vast tracts of empty desert, the colonists were obliged to be self-sufficient, and found themselves thrown into alliance with the Pueblo peoples to resist the threat of Ute and Comanche attack. The Spaniards and the Pueblos had much in common; the New Mexican landscape was similar to that of Andalucia in Spain, as indeed were its adobe hamlets or *pueblos*. The Pueblos had long been subsistence farmers who traded for rare luxuries with far-off civilizations to the south, and the Hispanic ranchers slotted into the same pattern. There was little inter-marriage, although Pueblo communities came to acquire sizeable populations of *genízaros*, the bastard offspring of captured Plains Indians and their Spanish masters.

In the first half of the eighteenth century, the **French** established their own colony to the east, **Louisiana**. The immediate Spanish response was to set up missions among the Indians of what now became a separate province of New Spain, **Texas**. As the French and Spanish zones of influence expanded, there were armed clashes; thus a combined force of Spaniards and Pueblos was defeated by a French-Pawnee alliance near North Platte, Nebraska, in 1720.

In general, the French co-existed more amicably with Native Americans than did the Spanish; they were predominantly traders, eager to acquire beaver and other furs and not interested in converting Indians to Christianity. Unlike the Spanish, they were also prepared to supply Indians with **guns**. As a result, the Comanche, Ute and Apache, equipped with the latest European firearms, consistently raided along the Rio Grande at harvest time, seizing crops and livestock, while the Hispanic villagers, inadequately supplied from Mexico, could only offer minimal resistance with their bows and arrows. The colonists financed the occasional retaliatory expedition by selling Indian captives to work as slaves in the silver mines of Mexico, thereby incurring ever greater Indian hostility.

Louisiana having proved no more profitable to France than was New Mexico to Spain, Louis XV of France simply gave it to Spain in 1762. The Spanish frontier in North America was now the Mississippi river. Determined to resist encroachment by the infant United States, King Carlos III placed the entire region under his direct control from Spain in 1776. However, far too few Hispanic settlers moved in to make any difference, and in 1802, as the Spanish empire weakened, he handed Louisiana back to Napoleon. Carlos' hope that the French would serve as a buffer against the Yankees was misplaced; Napoleon sold his American territories to the US in the following year, in the **Louisiana Purchase**.

At the end of the century, Santa Fe was home to around two thousand Hispanic citizens, while the Pueblo population had dwindled to perhaps nine thousand, in a mere nineteen pueblos.

The settlement of Arizona

Before the Pueblo Revolt, the Spanish presence in New Mexico was confined to the valley of the Rio Grande and the scattered pueblos to the west. Under the names of **Pimería Alta** and **Papaguería**, what's now southern Arizona was left to peoples the Spaniards called the **Pima** and the **Papago**, known today as the **'O'odham**.

Around 1700, however, **Jesuit** missionaries conceived the notion of constructing a chain of missions all the way from New Spain to California, and built churches in a couple of 'O'odham villages. Hispanic ranchers and prospectors also drifted in. In 1736, a Yaqui Indian created a silver mining camp, a few miles southwest of modern Nogales, called **Arizonac**. The name either came from the 'O'odham *ali shonak*, meaning "small springs", or from the Basque language of Spain, in which *arritza onac* means "valuable rocky places", and *aritz onac* means "good oaks".

After an 'O'odham rebellion killed several Jesuits, the Spanish installed a military garrison at **Tubac** (see p.230) in 1752. This *presidio* (fort) was relocated forty miles north to San Agustín de **Tucson** in 1776. Another Indian revolt in 1781, in which 150 settlers were wiped out during mass at **Yuma**, dashed Spanish hopes of establishing a permanent trail to California, and Tucson, like Santa Fe, came to be seen as a remote and insignificant dead-end town. In 1804, by which time there were around a thousand Spanish colonists in the vicinity, its commander reported "we have no gold, silver, lead, tin, quicksilver, copper mines, or marble quarries . . . the only public work here that is truly worthy of this report is the church at **San Xavier del Bac**" (see p.230).

The end of the Hispanic era

The decline in New Mexico's importance to its Spanish rulers was mirrored by increasing contacts with the rest of North America. In the closing years of the eighteenth century, permanent trails were established both west to California – in the form of the **Old Spanish Trail**, painstakingly mapped across Utah by the Franciscan friars **Domínguez and Escalante** in 1776 – and east to St Louis, along the **Santa Fe Trail** blazed by French explorer Pedro Vial in 1792. After the Louisiana Purchase, expeditions sponsored by the US government also crossed the Plains, such as **Lewis and Clark**'s trek to the Northwest in 1804, and **Lt Zebulon Pike**'s incursion into New Mexico in 1807.

Within a few years, the Spanish grip on the New World was finally loosened; following a **revolution** led by General Agustín Iturbide, Mexico became an independent nation in 1821. Although their governors swiftly transferred allegiance to Mexico City, neither New Mexico nor California perceived any advantage in their new status as Mexican territories. As the flow of resources from the south – including the handouts that had started to keep the Apache relatively docile – dwindled to rock-bottom levels, the effect on the New Mexican economy was crippling.

For the authorities in Santa Fe, the only answer seemed to be to increase trade with the US. Traffic along the Santa Fe Trail swiftly turned New Mexico into an entrepôt through which American goods were shipped south into Mexico. No Americans were permitted to live in New Mexico, but freebooting Anglos began to make their way across the Plains to seek their fortunes in the West. Among them were fur-trapping **"mountain men"** such as **Bill Williams** and **Kit Carson**, who made extended forays along the region's rivers in pursuit of beavers (known as "hairy banknotes"). **Taos** became renowned for its annual rendezvous, gatherings of Anglo, Hispanic and Native American traders far from the authority of any government. Northern New Mexico was now also beyond the reach of the Catholic Church; devout Hispanics kept their faith alive by forming sects such as the **Penitentes** (see p.129), and established a tradition of religious folk art that endures to this day.

Meanwhile, enough Yankee newcomers had flocked into **Texas** to outnumber its loyal Mexican subjects. In 1836, after Texas fought to gain independence from Mexico and then voted for annexation by the US, the president of Mexico attempted to hold onto New Mexico by closing down the Santa Fe Trail. It was too late. The doctrine that it was the United States' **"Manifest Destiny"** to extend across the whole continent led the US government first to attempt to **buy** New Mexico and California, and then, when negotiations failed, to declare **war** on Mexico in 1846. American economic might was neatly illustrated when the US Army of the West took Santa Fe without a fight, in August 1846; the Mexican governor was simply paid $50,000 to leave, together with his garrison.

Territorial days: New Mexico and Arizona

Under the **Treaty of Guadalupe-Hidalgo**, signed in September 1847 after US soldiers had captured Mexico City, the United States took formal possession of New Mexico, Texas and California – seen as the real prize – in return for a payment of $18.25 million. New Mexico, which consisted of all those parts of modern New Mexico and Arizona that lie north of the Gila River, plus areas of Nevada and Utah, was generally regarded as an arid, worthless wasteland. General Sherman is said to have jibed that "We had one war with Mexico to take Arizona, and we should have another to make her take it back".

Ironically, only the discovery of **gold** in California in 1847 gave New Mexico any great value to the US – as a route west. Surveyors mapping possible courses for a southern transcontinental railroad soon realized that the best routes lay on the Mexican side of the border. The Mexican government accepted the least extensive of five suggested land deals, and in June 1854, the $10 million **Gadsden Purchase** gave the US what's now southern Arizona, including Tucson, Tubac and Tumacacori.

Another 25 years were to pass before the railroad reached the Southwest – during that time, **Yuma** on the lower Colorado River burgeoned as a major port – but prospectors trekking to and from California soon began to investigate the region more thoroughly. After gold was found near the confluence of the Gila and Colorado rivers, **miners** fanned out across central Arizona, and reports of rich silver and copper lodes lured ever more migrants in.

Feeling that they had little in common with the Hispanic farming communities of the Rio Grande, the new arrivals argued that the territory was too large to govern as a single unit, and should be split in two. Many came originally from the South, and they seized upon the start of the **Civil War** in 1861 to declare the formation of the Confederate Territory of **Arizona**, which consisted of all the Gadsden Purchase lands. Its capital was Mesilla, in what's now New Mexico. The Confederate cause in the Southwest was short-lived; a Confederate army sent to establish a military presence was turned back by Union forces at **Glorieta Pass** – outside Santa Fe, near modern Pecos – in March 1862. The federal government recognized the existence of Arizona in 1863, but to avoid giving it a built-in Confederate majority drew a north–south boundary rather than an east–west one, and thereby delineated the two modern states.

The Indian wars

In the early years of the Civil War, US Army outposts throughout the Southwest were abandoned when the troops were sent east. That spurred a new era of raiding by the **Apache** and **Navajo**, and the Anglo and Hispanic settlements of southern Arizona in particular became depopulated. By late 1861, there were only two significant white settlements left in Arizona; two hundred citizens remained in Tucson, and a band of miners held out at Patagonia.

However, the Army soon returned in greater strength than ever, resolved to eradicate the Indian "menace" once and for all. As detailed on p.487 onwards, Brigadier General James Carleton and Kit Carson drove the **Navajo** into exile in New Mexico in 1865 – they were soon back in Arizona, but never again posed a military threat – while a long cycle of treaties, betrayals and guerrilla campaigns wore down **Apache** resistance by 1886.

Towards statehood

The way was open for a large-scale influx of Anglo settlers. During the 1860s, ancient Hohokam canals in the Salt River Valley were cleared to irrigate the new city of **Phoenix**, which swiftly became the capital of Arizona. Mining camps in the mountains, such as **Silver City** in New Mexico, and **Tombstone** and **Jerome** in Arizona, turned into fully-fledged towns, while

massive cattle ranches began to spread across the open desert.

At first, the Anglo newcomers were almost exclusively male, and married into Hispanic families. Spanish remained the lingua franca, Catholicism the dominant religion, and silver Mexican pesos the common currency. With the coming of the **railroad**, however, around 1880, things began to change, and the pattern of north–south links were replaced by commerce oriented towards the east and west. The Southwestern economy became increasingly **extractive**, digging up minerals and depleting natural resources for shipment to distant cities. Where Native Americans and Hispanics had farmed for self-sufficiency, the Anglos sought profit. During the 1880s, huge herds of sheep and cattle were introduced to marginal grasslands that swiftly proved incapable of supporting them; well over half a million cattle died in southern Arizona when drought hit in 1893.

Towards the end of the nineteenth century, the tensions that pitted the large-scale mining or cattle-raising concerns, backed by wealthy eastern corporations and the federal government, against individual prospectors and cowboys, were so acute, and so recurrent, that some historians speak of a **Western Civil War of Incorporation**. Many legendary Wild-West incidents, like the **Gunfight at the OK Corral** in Tombstone, Arizona (see p.237), and the **Lincoln County War** in New Mexico, which brought Billy the Kid into the public eye (see p.174), stemmed more from behind-the-scenes political manoeuvring than from the whims of trigger-happy outlaws.

As well as bringing an influx of cowboys, miners and other adventurers to the Southwest, the railroads also created new industries. Communities such as Flagstaff and Williams sprang up to exploit the vast ponderosa forests of northern Arizona – not least to build the railroads themselves – and the increased accessibility of the Grand Canyon, recently publicized by the voyages of John Wesley Powell (see p.401), meant that the first **tourists** began to arrive.

Meanwhile, in New Mexico, Hispanic villagers looked on helplessly as huge tracts of their lands were parcelled out to newly arrived Anglo ranchers. New Mexicans had traditionally owned small plots for individual use, and shared all grazing lands in common, but American courts refused to recognize communal land rights. Families who had been farmers, ranchers and skilled labourers found themselves increasingly obliged to work as unskilled labourers.

To a considerable degree, it was anti-Hispanic Anglo racism that delayed **statehood** for both Arizona and New Mexico. For many years, Republicans in Washington clung to the idea that they should be re-united and admitted as a single state, in the hope that Arizona's larger Anglo population would help to "temper" the Hispanic majority in New Mexico. Arizonans overwhelmingly defeated that proposal in a referendum in 1906 (which passed in New Mexico), and both were finally admitted in 1912 – **New Mexico** in January as the **47th** state, **Arizona** in February as the **48th**, the last of what are now known as the "Lower 48".

Utah in the nineteenth century

Until the nineteenth century, the history of what's now the state of **Utah** forms a minor adjunct to the story of the Southwest as a whole. Its main Anasazi groups, the **Virgin** and the more nomadic **Fremont** peoples, abandoned southern Utah at much the same time as their Four Corners brethren moved away. By the time Spanish explorers such as Domínguez and Escalante (see p.476) began to pass through, in search of a route to California, it had become the domain of **Ute** and **Paiute** Indians. An estimated twelve to thirty thousand of them were present in 1850; most had traditionally been farmers, but they had recently acquired horses and were starting to raid travellers on the newly created **Old Spanish Trail**, which linked Santa Fe to Los Angeles.

The reports of men such as the fur trapper **Jedediah Smith**, who named the Virgin River, and **John C Frémont**, who mapped much of southwest Utah in the early 1840s, attracted the first permanent white settlers to the region. By far the most important of these were the massed ranks of the Church of Jesus Christ of Latter-Day Saints, known to the world as the **Mormons**.

The Mormons

The Mormon church was founded by **Joseph Smith**, who was born to a family of itinerant farmers in Sharon, Vermont, on December 23, 1805. Smith was a farmhand in Palmyra, western New York, in 1823, when he had his first vision of the **Angel Moroni**. On his third annual visit, Moroni led him to a set of golden plates hidden in a nearby hillside. Only Smith was ever to see them; concealed behind a curtain in his house, he translated them from the "reformed Egyptian" with the aid of two mysterious devices he called the Urim and the Thummim, and thus dictated the *Book of Mormon*. Harshly described by Mark Twain as "chloroform in print", this revealed that two Israelite families fled Jerusalem around 600 BC, and sailed east from the Red Sea to the "Promised Land", led by a man named Lehi. His sons later quarrelled; Nephi remained loyal, and was rewarded by a visit from the risen Christ, while Laman and Lemuel led the dissident, cursed Lamanites, the ancestors of the Native Americans. After a thousand years of conflict, the Lamanites finally defeated the Nephites in a great battle at the hill of Cumorah. The one Nephite survivor – Moroni, son of Mormon – buried the plates close by.

Smith proclaimed his new church on April 6, 1830. He was not unique among contemporary frontier prophets in attracting thousands of followers. His vision of an ordered, communalistic society was clearly rooted in the economic uncertainty of his own life, and struck a deep chord with his peers. To their unconverted "**Gentile**" neighbours, on the other hand, leadership by divine revelation smacked of Catholicism, and like the Catholics the Mormons were suspected of owing their first loyalty to their church and not their country. Their most controversial trait was the practice of **polygamy**, or "celestial marriage". Smith denied this to outsiders, pointing to a passage in the *Book Of Mormon* that called polygamy "abominable". In private, however, he declared his disciples to have a sacred duty to marry and produce children, thereby freeing disembodied spirits from limbo by giving them bodily form. Preaching the salvation of the dead, which said that the dead could be baptized by proxy, he argued that Mormon marriage was different to the "until death do us part" Christian sacrament. Church elders had a duty to establish polygamous, patriarchal families that would endure into the afterlife. Smith also became a Mason, and many of his church's rituals were inspired by Masonic practices.

In the face of constant harassment, Smith moved his family to Kirtland, **Ohio** – where they built their first temple – and then on to **Missouri** in 1838. After bloody clashes between slave-holding Gentiles and the Mormon militia, the sons of Dan, he was captured and sentenced to death, then allowed to escape by sympathetic guards. The Mormons were next given sanctuary by the governor of **Illinois**, who saw them as hard-working potential citizens, and their new settlement of **Nauvoo** swiftly became the largest city in that state, with a population of 25,000.

In 1844, when Joseph Smith announced that he was running for President, the Latter-Day Saints were being attacked not only by their neighbours, but also from within. When a group of anti-polygamy dissenters attempted to establish a rival church in Nauvoo, and set up their own newspaper, Smith ordered that its presses be destroyed. Together with his brother Hyrum, he was arrested and imprisoned in nearby Carthage. A "blackface" mob attacked the jail, and both men were shot.

It was widely assumed that the Mormon church would disintegrate after Smith's death. However, although one of his sons decamped to Missouri with his own monogamous splinter group, Smith's successor, **Brigham Young**, held the flock together. Young, who was also of Puritan Vermont stock, promised the governor of Illinois in 1845 that the Mormons would abandon Nauvoo the following year, and set about organizing a mass **westward migration**. In the winter of 1846, ten thousand Saints camped near modern Omaha, Nebraska, while Young scouted ahead. Descending the western flank of the Rockies, he declared "This is the place", and in 1847 his followers founded **Salt Lake City**, as detailed on p.455.

At that time, the all but empty wilderness claimed by the Mormons as **Deseret** (a Mormon word meaning "honeybee", to denote industry), or the **Great Basin Kingdom**, still belonged to Mexico. As well as what's now Utah, its putative boundaries included almost all of modern Nevada, most of Arizona and southern California, and sizeable chunks of four other present-day states. Mormon dreams of establishing an independent theocracy, outside the United States, were dashed within a year, when the US government annexed the entire region and the Gold-Rush wagon trains began to roll west. The Saints therefore petitioned Congress for Deseret to be granted statehood. Suspicious of its religious underpinnings, Congress instead recognized a smaller area as the **Territory of Utah** in 1850, and appointed Brigham Young as its first governor.

Recognizing that individual farmers could make little impact on the uncompromising terrain of the West, the Mormons embarked on a massive communal effort to irrigate the desert. They were joined over the next decade by thousands more converts recruited by missionaries throughout America and Europe, to reach a total by 1860 of over fifty thousand. Fifteen thousand arrived from England alone, of whom three thousand literally walked across America, pushing their belongings in handcarts ahead of them.

During the 1850s, and especially after Young, who felt no further need for diplomacy, publicly acknowledged the existence of polygamy in 1852, the federal government came to see the Mormons as a significant threat to the Union. The newly formed Republican party – whose presidential candidate in 1856 was John C Frémont, the veteran Western explorer – railed against slavery and polygamy in equal measure, as "twin relics of barbarism". Congress decided to appoint a new non-Mormon Governor of Utah, and sent him west with a detachment of 2500 soldiers, representing one-sixth of the US army. Salt Lake City was temporarily abandoned, but thanks in large part to the secession of the Confederacy, the Mormon War never quite happened.

When the **Civil War** in the East cut off supplies of commodities such as cotton, Brigham Young redoubled his commitment to making the Mormons **self-sufficient**. Pioneer parties were despatched to create "missions" throughout the Southwest, but while many of the small farming communities they established still survive – especially in southern Utah, where examples include **Cedar City** and **St George** – they did little to diminish Utah's economic interdependence with the rest of the US. The arrival of the railroads, and the arrival in Utah of ever-increasing numbers of non-Mormons – especially miners – exacerbated the situation.

As the Mormons set out to "tame" the wilderness, the **Ute** fought back. Reciprocal raids by Utes and whites escalated into the **Black Hawk War**, waged between 1865 and 1867, in which the Utes were eventually worn down and finally confined to reservations in the territory that by now bore their name. In an eerie postscript, the dying Ute leader, Black Hawk, insisted on making a personal tour of all the towns affected by the war, to apologize in person. With Indian resistance broken, the Mormons spread throughout southern Utah. The "**Hole in the Rock**" party (see p.377), for example, made the gruelling trek across the central deserts in the winter of 1879–80 to establish the community of **Bluff** in the east. Little now survives from simultaneous Mormon attempts to settle in **northern Arizona**, apart from a few tiny settlements along the Arizona Strip (see p.328).

Meanwhile the federal authorities renewed their attacks on polygamy. The **Morrill Anti-Bigamy Act** of 1862, which was upheld by the Supreme Court in 1878, subjected polygamists to disenfranchisement and the confiscation of their property; as one federal judge put it "we want you to throw off the yoke of the Priesthood, to do as we do, and be Americans in deed as well as name". Utah retaliated by giving women the vote, so Mormon women could consolidate the Church's hold on State power; the **Edmonds-Tucker Act** of 1887 hit back, dissolving the Church and confiscating its assets, and once more disenfranchising women.

Brigham Young had died in 1877, and the new Mormon leaders now sensed that they would do better to drop polygamy on their own terms before they were forced to do so. Polygamy was therefore formally renounced in 1890 – although a few dissidents still practise it to this day – and the way was cleared for Utah to become a **state** in **1896**. Mormons were now encouraged to participate in national politics; church authorities even suggested that half should become Democrats, and half Republicans.

The Southwest in the twentieth century

Arizona, New Mexico and Utah spent most of their first century of statehood battling to secure ever greater quantities of **water**. In the early years, the main objective was to prevent California – already undergoing rapid development – from grabbing the lion's share of the flow of the Colorado River. Later on, cities such as Phoenix fought for federal funds to build grandiose water-diversion schemes. The political machinations behind the construction of the **Hoover Dam** in the 1930s, and the controversial damming of **Glen Canyon** in the 1960s, are chronicled on p.390. Suffice it here to say that with the completion of the **Central Arizona Project** in 1991, John Wesley Powell's nineteenth-century prediction that "All the waters of all the arid lands will eventually be taken from their natural channels" has now all but come true.

While New Mexico at the start of the century remained much what it had always been – a cluster of farming towns along the Rio Grande Valley – Arizona was prospering on the large-scale exploitation of its mineral wealth. **World War I** saw a leap in copper prices, and in alliance with state politicians the mine-owners easily quashed labour disputes such as the one that led to the **Bisbee Deportation** in 1917 (see p.238). Arizonan employers could also take cynical advantage of the vast pool of potential workers just across the border. After the Wall Street Crash of 1929, for example – by which time the state was responsible for half of all US copper production – over 500,000 Mexican labourers, now surplus to requirements, were deported.

Though the **Depression** hit hard across the Southwest, the region also benefited from a massive injection of federal cash, in the form of make-work public projects such as dam- and road-building. **World War II** not only renewed demand for copper and other metals, but kick-started the phenomenon of **urbanization** throughout the Southwest. Partly to make them less vulnerable to attack, defence installations were relocated away from the coasts, presenting **Albuquerque** and **Phoenix** in particular with their first major industrial plants, as well as greatly increased numbers of consumers. A former school in **Los Alamos**, New Mexico, was transformed into the laboratory that developed the atomic bomb – hence, some say, the alien crash-landing at **Roswell** in 1947 (see p.180).

After the war, the defence and other industries stayed on, and the ensuing period of mass migration to the Southwest resulted in an extraordinary population boom. Arizona and New Mexico were home to around 500,000 people each in 1940; Arizona has now reached almost four million, with half that number in the metropolitan Phoenix area alone, while New Mexico has around 1.6 million. Even more striking is the fact that whereas at the start of the century, Arizona was 84 percent rural, around ninety percent of the population are now city-dwellers. **Las Vegas**, Nevada, did not even exist until 1905; it now boasts over a million inhabitants.

Meanwhile, though **Salt Lake City** has grown at a steady pace throughout the twentieth century, **southern Utah** has remained sparsely inhabited. Attempts at large-scale ranching in the late 1800s resulted in destructive over-grazing, and the region relied on subsistence farming until the discovery of **uranium** in 1952 (see p.422) triggered a **mining bonanza** that sent prospectors scurrying into every nook and cranny of the wilderness. Local Mormon businessmen of southern Utah lobbied hard for mine and dam projects in the face of growing environmental opposition. Calling themselves the "**Sagebrush Rebels**", they attracted support from President Reagan, but were ultimately defeated as much by the realities of world commodity markets as by the "tree-huggers" they despised. Since the collapse of mining in the early 1980s, **tourism** has finally been appreciated as a major industry, and towns like **Moab**, which formerly revelled in their isolation, have begun to develop facilities for travellers smitten by the lure of the desert.

Individual histories of cities such as **Phoenix** (p.199), **Albuquerque** (p.156), and **Las Vegas** (p.445) are scattered throughout the text of this book.

The Hopi

Nowhere in the Southwest is the continuity between the pre-Hispanic past and the present day more apparent than on the three **Hopi mesas**, on the southern edge of Arizona's Black Mesa. The Hopi have lived here for at least one thousand years, preserving their culture despite repeated incursions from outsiders, and their history is sufficiently distinct to be worth relating as a separate narrative.

For a guide to visiting the Hopi mesas today, and an account of the *kachina religion*, see the section that starts on p.57.

The origin of the Hopi

According to Hopi mythology, this, the **Fourth World**, is inhabited by the righteous people who escaped the destruction of the Third World by climbing a reed through the dome of the sky. They emerged in the depths of the Grand Canyon, through a hole beside the Little Colorado River known as the *sipapu*. There they were greeted by the terrifying but nonetheless kindly disposed deity **Maasaw**, who explained the rules of life in this world and despatched them on migratory journeys to the four points of the compass. Their wanderings ended with a return to the **Sacred Circle**, and the establishment of the villages on what are now the Hopi mesas.

Myth and history agree on a picture of the Hopi as a peripatetic people who became ever more sedentary as they learned the techniques of agriculture, pottery and so on. Archeologists and Hopi alike recognize the cultural continuity between the Hopi and the ancient peoples of the Southwest, although the Hopi refer to their ancestors as the **Hisatsinom**, and object to the more familiar Navajo term **Anasazi**, which means "ancient enemies". There's no doubt that the earliest occupants of the Hopi mesas migrated here from nearby Kayenta Anasazi and Sinagua settlements, but whether they had previously wandered further afield – most obviously, into central America, where the language and beliefs of the **Aztecs** show clear parallels to the Hopi – remains unproven.

The Hopi mesas were probably inhabited from around 700 AD onwards, but the process the Hopi describe as the "**gathering of the clans**" was at its peak between 1100 AD and 1300 AD, and thus coincided with the abandonment of the most famous Anasazi sites. One by one, small groups of refugees arrived at the mesas and petitioned those who were already there for land and the right to settle. Each was required to demonstrate what it could offer the rest, with the crucial factor being the ceremonial power to produce rain. After being allowed to stay, each group – in reality, most were probably no more than individual families – was regarded as a separate **clan**.

The Bear clan, said to have come from Mesa Verde, was the first to arrive – which is why it retains precedence to this day – and established the Second Mesa's "mother village", at the foot of the mesa. Originally called Maaseeba, this village changed its name to **Shungopavi** when it relocated to the mesa-top several centuries later. Similarly, **Walpi** on First Mesa, when founded by the Snake clan from Hovenweep, stood several hundred yards below its present, highly defensible mesa-top site. **Oraibi**, the "mother village" of Third Mesa, is generally regarded as the oldest of the Hopi villages because it has occupied the same spot since its foundation; beams used in its construction have been dated to 1260 AD, but earlier dwellings may be a century or more older.

By 1275 AD, the three mesas held 35 villages. The Fire, Water and Coyote clans had come from the cliff dwellings of Keet Seel and Betatakin, now in Navajo National Monument; the Flute clan from Canyon de Chelly; the Rabbit clan from the south, perhaps Casas Grandes in Mexico; and others had streamed in from Chaco Canyon, and the Sinagua sites of Wupatki and Walnut Canyon. While each village remained autonomous, this disparate community forged a common culture, adopting its own variation of the *kachina* religion as it spread throughout the pueblos of the Southwest (see p.58).

The coming of the Spaniards

Hopi prophecies have long predicted the return of *Pahaana*, the "True White Brother" who was separated from the Hopi at an early stage of their migrations. Assuming that he finds the Hopi living lives of purity and righteousness, he will help solve whatever problems they may be facing, and lead them in due course into the Fifth World. If the Hopi saw *Pahaana* in the first **Spanish** explorers to reach the mesas, in 1540 – a detachment of Coronado's expedition led by Lieutenant Pedro de Tovar (see p.472) – their illusions were soon shattered.

Exactly what happened is uncertain. Warned by the Zuni, the Hopi greeted the party in the fields, signalling that they should not cross a line of sacred cornmeal sprinkled on the earth. According to the official Spanish report, a Franciscan friar, exasperated by the rigmarole, commented "To tell the truth, I do not know why we came here" – and that was enough to trigger a Spanish onslaught. By the next sentence, the two sides are at peace, and Hopi guides went on to lead a group of Spaniards to the Grand Canyon (see p.293). Some sources suggest that this encounter took place at a village called Kawaika-a, which was completely destroyed by the Spanish.

During that and subsequent sixteenth-century Spanish incursions the Hopi seem to have taken care to make their lands – which the Spanish called **Tusayan** – appear as valueless as possible. As a result, the Spanish never bothered to leave either a garrison or any settlers in the vicinity. Franciscan **missionaries** did however return in 1629, and set about building churches in Awatovi, Shungopavi and Oraibi. The one at Awatovi was on a similar scale to the San Esteban del Rey mission that still survives at Ácoma (see p.88), and required a similar amount of forced Indian labour; others involved the filling-in and "re-dedication" of existing *kivas*. The missionaries also brought sheep and cattle to the mesas, so the Hopi were the first people to raise livestock in Arizona.

The Hopi were enthusiastic participants in the **Pueblo Revolt** of 1680, sacking the churches and killing four priests. Fearing a Spanish return, they welcomed Tewa-speaking Pueblo refugees from the Rio Grande, who founded the First-Mesa village of Hano. By now, the **Navajo** – whom the Hopi called *Tasavuh* or "head pounders", as they were said to bash in their captives' skulls with a rock – had entered the picture. They too joined the Pueblo Revolt, but were also starting to crowd the Hopi away from their summer farming and grazing lands, and to raid for animals. It was during this unsettled period that the villages of Walpi, Shungopavi and Mishongnovi moved to occupy fortified positions up on the mesa tops.

After the Spanish did reconquer New Mexico, those Hopi who still regarded themselves as Christians gathered in **Awatovi**. When the other Hopi villages realized their willingness to invite the missionaries back to stay, they determined to eradicate the Christian menace once and for all. At the end of 1700, the men of Awatovi were betrayed by their headman, who called a pre-dawn meeting in the *kiva*. Warriors from all the other villages pulled up the ladder, rained arrows down on the trapped men, and then set light to the *kiva*; surviving women and children were shared out as booty.

That act of savagery probably spared the Hopi both from internal dissent and missionary interference for the remainder of the Spanish and Mexican era. The mesas were however increasingly beleaguered by mounted Navajo and Ute war parties, and slave raiders from the south.

The Hopi under the United States

By the time the Southwest was acquired by the United States, during the 1840s (see p.476), the Hopi were desperate for protection from the marauding Navajo. Hopi scouts eagerly participated in General Carleton's 1864 round-up which despatched the Navajo on the Long Walk to Bosque Redondo (see p.487).

Within a few years, the Navajo were back, re-asserting their control over their former territory and raiding extensively to replenish their herds. Called upon to define who "owned" what land, the US government was inadequate to the task. The very concept of a "tribe" was a federal invention; neither Navajo nor Hopi recognized any overall authority above clan or village level. Moreover, the idea of a reservation only worked if one group or other had exclusive use of an area. Only villages and fields counted as the "possession" of land; hunting grounds were regarded as unoccupied. Because the San Francisco Peaks are sacred to, and used by, both the Navajo and the Hopi, they belong to neither.

The **Moqui Indian Reservation**, established in 1882, was a rectangle measuring seventy miles by 55 miles. It did not even include all the Hopi villages; the hundred Hopi at Moenkopi were excluded, while an estimated three hundred Navajo lived within the boundaries. As was standard, the decree creating the reservation states that it was intended not only for the Hopi but for "such other Indians as the Secretary of the Interior shall settle thereon". The resultant disputes have simmered ever since.

Outsiders now appeared on the mesas in ever-increasing numbers. Mormon and Mennonite **missionaries** came and went, and **anthropologists** stuck their oars in; Jesse Walter Fewkes called the Hopi "the most primitive aborigines of the United States" in 1891. **Tourists** too came by bus and railroad, with two thousand or more turning up for the annual Snake Dances. Turn-of-the-century images of Hopi ceremonies make it clear why photography was soon barred altogether; the crowds and cumbersome equipment made it all but impossible to move. Above all, the federal agents of the **Bureau of Indian Affairs** caused the most grief, by such actions as ordering haircuts for all Hopi men, for whom long hair is a sign of initiation, and kidnapping Hopi children to attend distant boarding schools, from 1887 onwards. Nineteen elders who protested against compulsory Christian education were imprisoned on Alacatraz in 1894.

The twentieth century

At the start of the twentieth century, the Hopi were divided between what outsiders perceived as the "**Friendlies**", who if not well disposed towards the government at least felt resistance was futile, and the "**Hostiles**", who sought to defend and preserve the old ways. Their differences in fact had as much to do with tensions between clans, and a breakdown in the allocation of resources and land now that Hopi territories were so circumscribed. The split became explicit at **Oraibi**, where the two factions declared themselves unable to co-exist any longer. On September 8, 1906, each lined up behind its leader, with each man's hands on the shoulders of the next, for a "pushing contest". The "Hostiles" were literally pushed out, and established their own village of **Hotevilla** nearby.

The dispute at Oraibi politicized the role of the ceremonial priest at each village, known as the *kikmongwi*. When the Hopi were obliged to adopt a Tribal Constitution in 1936, under the provisions of the New-Deal Indian Reorganization Act, the *kikmongwis* were automatically appointed as governors of their village. Part of their function was to endorse members elected to the new **Hopi Tribal Council**. Ever since then, however, many *kikmongwis* have refused to recognize the authority of the tribal council, and aligned themselves instead with the **Traditionalists**, the heirs of the "Hostiles".

Paradoxically, the Traditionalists, who regard themselves as the guardians of all that is truly Hopi (and speak of their opponents as the *pensilhoyam*, or "little pencil people"), have raised awareness of the Hopi throughout the world. Rather than waiting for a saviour to come to them, they have embarked on a "search for *Pahaana*". The movement started immediately after World War II, when certain Hopi elders announced that following the use of the atomic bomb it was time to reveal teachings and prophecies that were supposed to remain secret until "a gourd of ashes fell from the sky". Since 1948, the Traditionalists have written to every US President, and addressed the United Nations, with a message stressing Hopi sovereignty and religious integrity, and the importance of respecting the environment. Among their successes was the recognition of Hopi religion as a "peace religion", which excluded Hopi from military service.

In practical terms, the Traditionalist movement has been a focus for opposition to **mineral leasing**. Since the Hopi Constitution's definition of the role of the tribal council as being to *prevent* leasing was illegally over-ruled by the Secretary of the Interior in 1961, strip mining by the *Peabody Company* has devastated much of Black Mesa (see p.42). Almost all the income brought by the leases during the 1960s was invested by the tribal council in an unsuccessful bra factory near Winslow. Traditionalist lawsuits have however failed to put a stop to the mining, which has become more acceptable to most Hopi since the leases were renegotiated on much more favourable terms, including environmental stipulations, in the 1980s. Mineral leasing is now responsible for around seventy percent of the tribal budget, and four hundred Hopi work as miners. To some extent, Traditionalist resistance to modernization is based on a refusal to become dependent on external agencies. Thus while Hotevilla forcibly rejected the installation of public utilities, there is little objection to individual use of solar energy.

Meanwhile, the **Navajo-Hopi land dispute** has raged on. By 1958, the ranks of the Navajo living on Hopi lands had swollen to outnumber the Hopi by more than two to one, while the Navajo reservation had completely surrounded the Hopi mesas. Much of the impetus to resolve the problem came from the federal authorities and the mineral companies, who could not commence mining operations until definite title to the land was established. Public sympathies, and court rulings, swayed back and forth for decades. A **Joint Use Area** was established in 1958, to be shared equally between the Hopi and the Navajo, but it soon became evident that 98 percent of it was being used by the Navajo alone. In the 1970s, therefore, separate Hopi and Navajo

Partitioned Lands were defined, with Hopi living on the Navajo side of the line, and vice versa, being expected to relocate. More Navajo than Hopi were affected, and the plight of the **Big Mountain** Navajo in particular, who were given five years to move in 1981, made them a national *cause célèbre*.

The latest solution, the **Navajo-Hopi Land Dispute Settlement Act**, was signed by President Clinton in October 1996. It allows Navajo residents of Hopi land to sign 75-year leases, after which ownership will revert to the Hopi. If enough Navajo sign, the Hopi will receive $50 million to buy land elsewhere in northern Arizona (though their water rights will be restricted, which goes against more than a century of Indian policy). Dissident Navajo argue that the problem has simply been postponed for another generation.

The Navajo and the Apache

The best known Native American peoples in the Southwest – mainly on account of the fierce resistance they put up against the US Army in the nineteenth century – are the **Navajo** and the **Apache**. Both are now largely concentrated in Arizona, though both also occupy parts of New Mexico, and the Navajo Nation also extends into southern Utah. They are also relative newcomers to the region, having moved into their current territories at much the same time as the first Spaniards were arriving, and their impact was every bit as devastating as that of the European colonists.

Although the Navajo and the Apache are now distinct peoples, their languages are, with patience, mutually comprehensible, and their paths have only diverted within the last five hundred years. Both are descended from **Athabascan** peoples, whose Asian ancestors crossed into Alaska seven or eight thousand years ago, long after the New World's first migrants. Other Athabascans remained in the north, becoming the **Dene** peoples of Alaska and northwest Canada, and the **Na** of what's now the northwest USA, who included the Haid and Tlingit. At some point, however, the ancestral Navajo and Apache migrated south, hauling their possessions on dog-sleds as they pursued bison down the eastern flanks of the Rockies.

Estimates of when they reached their first base in the Southwest – probably on the edge of the Plains, somewhere east of the Rio Grande, range from 575 to 1525 AD – with the most likely date being 1250 to 1300 AD. Like nomads the world over, they traded the fruits of their hunting and gathering, especially buffalo hides, for the agricultural produce of more settled communities like the Rio Grande pueblos. Chroniclers with the earliest Spanish venture into the Southwest, Coronado's expedition of 1540 (see p.472), drew no distinction between the Navajo and the Apache, referring to both as **Querecho**. However, by the time the Spanish returned at the end of the century, the Navajo who called themselves the **Diné**, had separated off from the Apache, the **Ndee**.

The Navajo

It used to be thought that it was the arrival of the warlike Navajo in the Four Corners region that forced the Anasazi to leave, at the end of the thirteenth century (see p.469). In fact, however, the Navajo only moved west to occupy the now-empty San Juan Basin well after the Anasazi had gone. It's even suggested that it was the Anasazi who ejected the Navajo, when the Chaco Canyon and Mesa Verde communities fragmented, and the Anasazi headed east to establish pueblos along the Rio Grande.

During the late sixteenth century, a region centred on Largo Canyon, east of modern Farmington – still the core of Navajo territory – became known as the **Dinétah**, meaning "Among the People". The *Diné* defined their new realm as lying between four **sacred mountains**: Blanca Peak, or *Sis Naajini*, away to the east in Colorado; Hesperus Peak (*Dibé Nitsaa*), also in Colorado but to the north, near modern Durango; Mount Taylor (*Tsoodzil*), further south in New Mexico; and the San Francisco Peaks (*Dook'o'ooslíid*), near what's now Flagstaff, Arizona. Legends began to grow up that detailed how First Man and First Woman lived near **Huerfano Mountain**. They found a baby on **Gobernador Knob** who they named Changing Woman, and she in turn gave birth to the Navajo Twins, Monster Slayer and Child Born for Water.

The Lords of the World

By the 1580s, the Navajo had started to impinge upon the pueblos of Ácoma, Zuni and Hopi. Their expansion was soon given a huge boost when the establishment of a permanent Spanish presence enabled them to start acquiring **horses**. From 1606 onwards, the Navajo embarked on a cycle of raiding Hispanic and Pueblo settlements along the Rio Grande, seizing livestock, new crops, and metal artefacts. In the Tewa language, spoken in many pueblos, *apache* means "strangers" or "enemies", and *nabajú* means "big planted fields". The first Spanish mention of the "*Apaches de Nabajú*" appeared in 1626, and the name was soon truncated to "Navajo".

The Navajo and the Pueblos were not always at war, however, and some Navajo participated in the **Pueblo Revolt** of 1680 (see p.474), which briefly succeeded in expelling the Spanish from the Southwest. When the Spanish returned to reconquer the region a dozen years later, many Pueblo peoples escaped their revenge by retreating to join the Navajo. The culture of the modern Navajo, which anthropologists regard as a hybrid of Athabascan and Pueblo elements, was forged in the remote fortresses known as the "**Pueblitos of Dinétah**", in Largo and Gobernador canyons.

While any explicit Pueblo-Navajo alliance soon foundered, the Navajo had by the eighteenth century acquired Pueblo skills such as pottery and weaving, as well as Pueblo-influenced social and religious structures. Their horses gave them a vastly increased mobility, while their large flocks of **sheep** enabled them to live well on what had previously been considered marginal lands. They therefore expanded westwards to cover a much greater area, occupying most of northeast Arizona and encircling the Hopi.

To the Spanish, the Navajo at this time were *Los Dueños del Mundo*, the "Lords of the World" – feared horsemen with a solid economic base in their own lands who nonetheless continued to plunder the pueblos at will. For most of the eighteenth century, however, the Navajo and the Hispanic settlers of New Mexico were nominally at peace, united in resisting incursions by the allied **Utes** and **Comanches** of the north. Then the Navajo began to realize that in fact the Spanish were tacitly encouraging Ute and Comanche raiders, and buying their Navajo captives as slaves. After 1786, when the Spanish signed a formal treaty with the Comanche, they were at constant war with the Navajo.

With conversion to Christianity for an excuse, Navajo women and children were shipped into slavery in Mexico; the Navajo replenished their numbers by carrying off Pueblo villagers. Certain mission settlements had to be abandoned in the face of Navajo attacks. By and large, the Navajo heartlands remained impregnable, although **Lieutenant Narbona**'s party of 1805 penetrated the Canyon de Chelly and massacred over a hundred Navajo (see p.50).

War with the United States

Mexican independence in 1822 did nothing to diminish the conflict, and the Navajo and the Hispanic settlers of New Mexico were still at loggerheads when the US Army marched in and took control of the Southwest in 1846. The Navajo were amazed to find that the American invaders expected them to make peace with their old enemies, on the basis that the New Mexicans were now themselves considered to be Americans.

A major factor in the American failure to sign and keep treaties with the Navajo was the fact that the Navajo were not a single homogenous group. They did not have "chiefs" as the Americans understood the term, let alone a single paramount chief. No Navajo could speak for much more than his immediate family, or felt bound by a pact signed by another without his knowledge or consent. Even so, the Navajo remained broadly at peace with the Americans until a widely respected elder – who, confusingly, had taken the name **Narbona** – was murdered and scalped by US soldiers, under a flag of truce, in 1849. For the next fifteen years, Narbona's son-in-law, **Manuelito**, fought a running war with the US cavalry, based at **Fort Defiance**, near Window Rock. New Mexican slave raiders, meanwhile, continued to steal Navajo children.

In 1863, **General James Carleton** resolved that the Navajo should be removed from their lands altogether, partly so that they might "become an agricultural people and cease to be nomads" and partly to allow New Mexicans to expand beyond the Rio Grande valley and seize whatever agricultural and mineral wealth the *Dinétah* might hold. Aided by veteran scout **Kit Carson**, he launched a scorched-earth campaign that culminated early in 1864 with the destruction of the Canyon de Chelly's *hogans*, fields and peach orchards. As the starving Navajo surrendered, they were despatched to "Fair Carletonia", the **Bosque Redondo** reservation at Fort Sumner in eastern New Mexico (see p.168).

A total of nine thousand Navajo made the **Long Walk** of 370 miles to Bosque Redondo, where three thousand of them were to die. The reservation was utterly unsuitable for agriculture; far from being self-supporting, it became a burden on the federal government. Carleton was dismissed, and in 1868, after four years, twelve Navajo leaders – including **Barboncito**, who pleaded "I hope to God you will not ask me to go to any other country except my own" – signed a treaty that allowed them to return home.

The Navajo Nation

By treating the Navajo as an independent people, the **"Old Paper"** formed the basis of the Navajo Indian Reservation – which the Navajo prefer to call the **Navajo Nation** – as it endures to this day. The original reservation of 1868 was, however, just a small rectangle of northeast Arizona and northwest New Mexico, which included Canyon de Chelly and Shiprock but not Window Rock. Here the survivors of Fort Sumner rejoined those Navajo who had evaded capture in the backcountry; some had hidden near **Navajo Mountain**, and now regarded it too as a sacred peak.

In the past century, the Navajo **population** has grown at a phenomenal rate, from 20,000 in 1900 to around 250,000 now. In over a dozen different transactions, the boundaries of the reservation have expanded from 6000 to 27,000 square miles. A formal Navajo **government** was only established in 1923, when the major oil companies needed to find someone who could sign leases allowing them to exploit the reservation's newly discovered oil reserves. The **chapter** system of local administration was set up soon afterwards, and Window Rock became tribal headquarters in 1927.

The most traumatic event of the twentieth century was the 1933 **stock reduction**, when the federal authorities killed off a million sheep and goats and reduced the total Navajo herd to half a million animals. They argued that over-grazing was washing silt into the Colorado that threatened the new Hoover Dam; the effect was to force a change away from pastoralism towards wage labour.

Since World War II, the Navajo Nation has continued to modernize, acquiring its first paved road in 1947, and the first college ever built on an Indian reservation, Tsaile's Navajo Community College, which opened in 1969. While many families still manage to live a traditional Navajo lifestyle, the greatest change has been the increasing exploitation of **mineral** resources. Mines and generating stations have appeared all across the region, often just outside the reservation but dependent on Indian labour. Many projects have been deeply controversial. The **Four Corners** plant near Farmington has been described as the single worst source of pollution in the United States, while the *Peabody Company*'s strip-mining of **Black Mesa** to feed the **Navajo Generating Station** at Page is widely regarded as an environmental tragedy. In 1979, **Church Rock**, northeast of Gallup, was the scene of the worst contamination in the history of the nuclear industry, when a dam burst at the *United Nuclear Corporation* mill released almost a hundred million gallons of radioactive water, and a thousand tons of radioactive mud.

In 1975, Tribal Chairman **Peter MacDonald** helped set up the Council of Energy Resource Tribes, which he described as a "domestic OPEC". While the mineral leases of the 1950s and 1960s paid pitifully low returns, more lucrative agreements have now strengthened the Navajo economy. Navajo opposition to the principle of mineral exploitation has however also

---

Navajo Clans

The basis of Navajo society and family life is the **clan** system. Each Navajo child is said to be born "to" its mother's clan, and born "for" its father's clan. Navajo identify themselves to each other by the clans of their parents, and no one is supposed to marry a member of either their mother's or father's clan. Traditionally, all members of a clan were responsible for each other's crimes or debts.

Originally, there were just four clans, each descended from one of the four pairs of men and women said to have been created in the west by Changing Woman. There are now more like sixty clans, with each new clan having arisen when a woman from another tribe, or another place, has married into the Navajo. While certain clan names identify the descendants of Zuni, Mescalero, Mexican, Ute and Jemez newcomers, most hark back to specific locations on the reservation, mythical incidents or other attributes – the Turning Mountain Clan, Salt Clan, the People That Have Fits Clan, the Rock-Extends-into-Water clan, and so on.

For a detailed guide to travelling in the Navajo Nation, see Chapter One.

grown, as its long-term effects become apparent. Many feel that the long-running **Navajo–Hopi land dispute** (see p.485) has been manipulated by federal politicians and mineral companies for their own ends.

Peter MacDonald's efforts to diversify the economic base ranged from computer software companies to *shiitake* mushroom farms, but suspicion that he was feathering his own nest in the process was confirmed by a fourteen-year jail sentence in 1989. Although found guilty by a federal court of bribery, corruption and conspiracy, MacDonald remains popular on the reservation; tribal elections since then have alternated between his opponents, and pro-MacDonald factions who have granted him "pardons" not recognized under federal law.

The Apache

Around 1600 AD, as the Navajo began to incorporate Pueblo elements and become an entirely distinct people, the Apache fragmented into several separate groups. The **Western** Apache occupied the mountains of central Arizona; the **Jicarilla**, regions of northwest New Mexico between the Chama Valley and the Four Corners, and the **Lipan** moved east onto the plains of west Texas. At the same time, in southern New Mexico, the **Mescalero** started to range east of the Rio Grande while the **Chiricahua** spread west as far as what's now southern Arizona.

Even these groups were not really "tribes" in the way outsiders like to imagine. Apache lived in nomadic, clan-based societies of between thirty and two hundred people, each of which would elect its own "chief". A chief's primary responsibility was to ensure his band got enough food; his authority soon collapsed in the event of failure. Most groups raised a few seasonal crops, but they supported themselves above all by **raiding**, not only against settled Pueblo communities, but against the Navajo, and even each other.

The coming of the Spaniards gave the Apache **horses** for the first time. At first, they stole them solely to eat, but once they learned to ride they swiftly adapted to a regular calendar of raiding the villages of the Rio Grande at harvest time, while allowing them to continue largely unmo-

lested for the rest of the year. It was beneath Apache dignity even to breed their own horses, let alone sheep like the Navajo; they simply stole livestock as they required it.

The colonists of New Mexico, who remained confined for the whole period of Spanish and Mexican rule to a fragile ribbon of riverside land, knew the huge Apache-dominated territories that surrounded them as **Apacheria**. As the Apache never united to engage in formal warfare – no Apache war party in history exceeded two hundred warriors – it was impossible to take concerted action against them. In the first half of the eighteenth century, the Apache were nonetheless forced to consolidate into smaller and more mountainous areas, as the even more aggressive mounted **Comanche** warriors swept in across the Plains with ever-increasing regularity.

Later in the eighteenth century, the Spaniards managed to pacify the Apache to some extent by establishing *presidios* or forts that supplied them with food, alcohol, and even guns that were adequate for hunting but not war. When Mexico became independent, however, in 1821, the new administration could no longer afford such subsidies. Instead it placed a bounty of $100 on each Apache scalp – male or female, young or old – that was brought into the *presidios*.

The Apache Wars

To the federal government of the United States, which took over New Mexico in the 1840s, the Apache way of life was utter anathema. As a group of Mescalero Apache acknowledged to a US Army quartermaster in 1850, "We must steal from somebody . . . if you will not permit us to rob the Mexicans, we must steal from you or fight you". In total, the Southwest held between six and eight thousand Apache. By far the strongest resistance came from a group of just over a thousand, the **Chiricahua**, led by a chief known as **Cochise**, meaning "Oak".

Conflict between the US Army and the Apache flared into war in 1861, when Cochise agreed to meet Lt George Bascom in southeast Arizona, and found himself falsely accused of kidnapping a child. Although Cochise managed to escape into the Dragoon mountains, his brother and two nephews were hanged. Cochise then rampaged across Arizona, killing miners, prospectors, stagecoach passengers and soldiers wherever he might find them. As Anglos packed up and fled the territory, he imagined he had driven them out forever. What he didn't realize was that his campaign coincided with the start of the **Civil War**, which meant that all US forces were withdrawn east.

Within a year, the Union army was back, under the leadership of General James Carleton (see p.487). His Apache policy was simple, though directed at first against the Mescalero rather than the Chiricahua: "All Indian men of that tribe are to be killed whenever and wherever you can find them". During the winter of 1862–63, the Mescaleros were rounded onto the **Bosque Redondo** reservation at Fort Sumner in eastern New Mexico, where they were later joined by the Navajo (see p.487).

In 1862, Cochise's group had been joined by another Chiricahua band, the **Warm Springs** Apache of New Mexico, under the veteran **Mangas Coloradas**. The treacherous murder of Mangas Coloradas the following year, by US soldiers at Pinos Altos, where he had been invited for peace negotiations, hardened Chiricahua resolve even further. Over the next ten years, the US Army spent an estimated $38 million on campaigns that killed a total of a hundred Apache; the Apache meanwhile accounted for over a thousand Americans.

It was during this period that the name of **Geronimo** became widely feared. He was born into the Bedonkohe sub-group of the Chiricahua Apache, near the Gila cliff dwellings in New Mexico (see p.194), around 1823. Named Goyahkla, meaning "One Who Yawns", he reached adulthood without seeing a white American. After his mother, wife and three children were killed by Mexican soldiers at Janos in northern Mexico, in March 1851, he sought revenge in repeated raids on Mexico for years to come. Somehow, the Mexican battle-cry to St Jerome, "Geronimo", became the name he used for the rest of his life. Although he became a respected healer and medicine man, he was never strictly speaking a "chief".

In the **Camp Grant Massacre** of 1871, a Tucson-based alliance of Tohono 'O'odham Indians, Hispanics, and Anglos massacred 144 Apache – of whom no more than eight were men – supposedly under the protection of the US Army in Aravaipa Canyon, Arizona (see p.214). A public outcry back East led President Grant to

adopt a new policy towards the Apache, under which the **White Mountain** (also known as the Fort Apache Indian Reservation; see p.254) and **San Carlos** (see p.213) **reservations** were established in 1872.

Any Apache who failed to present themselves at the reservations, however, were deemed to be renegades. The task of hunting them down was given to **General George Crook**, who adopted the new scorched-earth strategy of "total war", developed during the Civil War. Employing White Mountain Apache scouts, on the basis that the best person to track an Apache was another Apache, he "overhauled" the Tonto Basin during the winter of 1872–73, killing around five hundred Indians.

Following an uneasy truce, the Chiricahua were granted their own reservation, a small square measuring roughly fifty miles in each direction that centred on what's now Chiricahua National Monument (see p.239). Within three years, however, renewed cross-border raiding after the 1874 death of Cochise caused the reservation to be disbanded. The Chiricahua were moved onto the San Carlos reservation, despite the fact that they traditionally regarded the San Carlos Apache as "Bi-ni-e-Dine", or "brainless people".

In 1877, another Chiricahua leader, **Victorio**, assembled a five-hundred-strong band of Apache from the many different groups who hated life at San Carlos. A lengthy guerrilla campaign across New Mexico and West Texas resulted in another thousand Anglo deaths before they were driven into Mexico and killed in Chihuahua in October 1880. The few survivors were sold into slavery.

Geronimo, who had not joined Victorio, now became the focus for dissident Apache. During the 1880s, he repeatedly burst out of the reservation and went on the warpath, with a dwindling band of followers each time. The first time was in 1881, when he passed within a few miles of Tombstone, and was pursued by Wyatt Earp and his brothers. In 1883, General Crook tracked him down in the Sierra Madre in northern Mexico, and was briefly captured by the Apache before Geronimo chose instead to surrender to him.

Geronimo fled the reservation again in May 1885, and surrendered to Crook once more in Mexico in 1886, on the understanding that he'd be exiled to the eastern United States for not more than two years. Before Crook could get him back to San Carlos, Geronimo got drunk and escaped yet again. Crook resigned his command, to be replaced by **General Nelson Miles**.

The Chiricahua's final five-month guerrilla campaign, in the summer of 1886, pitted a band of 37 Apache, of whom eighteen were warriors, against five thousand soldiers, a quarter of the entire US Army. General Miles eventually managed to contact Geronimo in Mexico, and falsely told him that all the Chiricahua who remained on the reservation had been shipped to Florida. In despair, Geronimo **surrendered** for the fourth and final time in Skeleton Canyon, Arizona on September 3, 1886. The general's lie now became the truth; Geronimo and five hundred Chiricahua – along with the Apache scouts that had fought on the side of the US army – were indeed despatched to **Florida** by rail. Men and women were segregated in separate camps. In time, the Chiricahua were re-united on reservations in first Alabama, and then Oklahoma, but Geronimo never returned to the Southwest. Among many public appearances in his later years, he rode at the head of Teddy Roosevelt's inaugural procession in 1905; he died in 1909.

In 1913, the 261 surviving Chiricahua were allowed to choose between remaining in Oklahoma or joining the Mescalero Apache in New Mexico; around two thirds made the trip. In addition, it's thought that around ten Chiricahua never were rounded up by the Army, and stayed hidden in Mexico; free Apache were reported still to be fighting in the Sierra Madre as late as the 1930s.

The Apache today

A total of around twenty thousand Apache now live in the Southwest. Both their largest reservations are in Arizona: the **Fort Apache** reservation (see p.254), which has the third highest population of all Native American reservations in the US, and the neighbouring **San Carlos** reservation (see p.213). The **Jicarilla** still live in northwest New Mexico, concentrated around the settlement of Dulce (see p.149).

Visitors are however most likely to come into contact with the **Mescalero** Apache, who share their lands with the descendants of the last Chiricahua in the mountains of southeast New Mexico. Among unlikely ventures here that have brought them a rare degree of economic security are the Ski Apache **ski resort** (see p.176), which the tribe bought for $1.5 million in 1962, and features the luxurious *Inn of the Mountain Gods* hotel/casino. More controversially, the Mescalero have also signed an agreement permitting the storage of high-level nuclear waste adjacent to the reservation.

Books

The following list is a personal selection of books that proved most useful, interesting or entertaining during the research for this guide. A large proportion are only available in the US, and most of those you'd be lucky to find anywhere outside the Southwest.

History and archeology

Fray Angélico Chávez, *My Penitente Land* (Museum of New Mexico Press, US only). An inspirational history of Hispanic New Mexico, written by a Franciscan friar, which stresses the parallels between the New Mexican landscape and pastoral lifestyle – and soul – and both Spain and ancient Palestine.

William Cronin, George Miles and Jay Gitlin (eds), *Under An Open Sky – Rethinking America's Western Past* (W W Norton). Enjoyable essays on different aspects of Western history.

Robert Gottlieb and Peter Wiley, *America's Saints* (HBJ). When it appeared in the 1980s, this study of the growth of Mormon economic and political power was considered controversial in Utah; if anything, it's surprisingly tame.

Paul Horgan, *Great River: The Rio Grande in North American History* (Gulf Publishing Company, US o/p; University Press of New England, UK). Horgan's monumental study of New Mexican history makes

Unless otherwise specified, all books are published by the same publisher in the US and the UK.

weighty reading; his more accessible *The Centuries of Santa Fe* (University of New Mexico Press, US only) is a lightly fictionalized set of biographies drawn from different periods of history.

J Donald Hughes, *In The House of Stone and Light* (Grand Canyon Natural History Association, US only). The human history of the Grand Canyon in words and pictures.

Clyde A Milner II, Carol A O'Connor, Martha A Sandweiss, *The Oxford History of the American West* (Oxford University Press). Fascinating collection of essays on Western history, covering topics ranging from myths and movies to art and religion.

David Grant Noble, *New Light on Chaco Canyon* (SAR Press, US only). Accessible and informative overview of the latest research into New Mexico's most important Anasazi site.

Donald G Pike, *Anasazi* (Crown Publishing Group, US only). Beautiful celebration of the Anasazi achievement, with photographs by David Muench.

Stephen Plog, *Ancient Peoples of the Southwest* (Thames and Hudson). Much the best single-volume history of the pre-Hispanic Southwest, packed with diagrams and colour photographs.

Caroll L Riley, *Rio del Norte* (University of Utah Press, US only). Fascinating history of the upper Rio Grande valley from prehistoric times up to the Pueblo Revolt.

Thomas E Sheridan, *Arizona – A History* (University of Arizona Press). Stimulating reassessment of 11,000 years of Arizona history.

Stewart L Udall, *Majestic Journey* (Museum of New Mexico Press, US only). Lively, well illustrated chronicle of Francisco Coronado's 1540–42 entrada into the Southwest, written by a former US Secretary of the Interior, plus an attempt to reconstruct the Spaniard's route.

Richard White, *It's Your Misfortune and None of My Own* (University of Oklahoma Press). Dense, authoritative and all-embracing history of the American West, that debunks the notion of the rugged pioneer by stressing the role of the federal government.

Native Americans

Between Sacred Mountains (Sun Tracks & University of Arizona Press). Superb overview of Navajo history, culture and politics, written by Navajo teachers and parents as a sourcebook for Navajo students.

Richard O Clemmer, *Roads In The Sky* (Westview). A history of the Hopi, with an emphasis on the twentieth century and the role of prophecy.

Angie Debo, *Geronimo* (University of Oklahoma Press, US; Pimlico, UK). Gripping full-length biography of the Apache medicine man who led the last Native American uprising against the US Army.

Paula Richardson Fleming & Judith Lynn Luskey, *The Shadow Catchers* (Laurence King, UK only). A history of nineteenth-century photographers of Native Americans, with some stunning images of the Hopi and Navajo.

Basil C Hedrick, J Charles Kelley and Carroll C Riley (eds), *The Meso-American Southwest* (Southern Illinois University Press, US o/p). Intriguing essays exploring possible trade, cultural and religious links between the ancient Southwest and the "high cultures" of Mexico.

Raymond Friday Locke, *The Book of the Navajo* (Mankind, US only). Comprehensive history of the Navajo, from their mythic origins to the present day.

Jerry Mander, *In The Absence of the Sacred* (Sierra Club, US only). Intriguing diatribe that pits the endurance of Native American values – with much discussion of the Hopi and Navajo – against the shortcomings of modern technology.

Peter Matthiesen, *Indian Country* (Viking Penguin, US; Flamingo, UK o/p). Contemporary state-of-the-nation review of the situation facing the Native Americans of the West.

Robert S McPherson, *Sacred Land Sacred View* (Signature Books, US only). Intriguing anthropological account of how the Navajo perceive the Four Corners region.

David Roberts, *Once They Moved Like The Wind* (Simon & Schuster). Excellent, fast-moving history of the Apache.

Polly Schaafsma (ed), *Kachinas in the Pueblo World* (University of New Mexico Press, US only). Well-illustrated survey of the *kachina* cult in the Southwest (see p.58).

Stephen Trimble, *The People* (SAR Press, US only). Excellent introduction to all the Native American groups of the Southwest, bringing the history up to date with contemporary interviews.

Frank Waters, *The Book of the Hopi* (Viking Penguin, US; Penguin, UK). As authoritative an account of Hopi religion as it's possible to find, though it's said that Waters' informants were not themselves initiated into all the secrets of the *kiva*.

Travel

Kenneth A Brown, *The Four Corners* (Harper Perennial, US only). Slightly dry but very comprehensive journalist's account of his wanderings in search of the geology and history of the Four Corners region.

Pedro de Castañeda, *The Journey of Coronado* (Dover). An invaluable historic document; the eyewitness journals of a Spaniard who accompanied Coronado into the Southwest in 1540.

Colin Fletcher, *The Man Who Walked Through Time* (Random House, US only). Enjoyable account by the first man to hike the full length of the Grand Canyon.

Thomas Keneally, *The Place Where Souls are Born* (Touchstone, US o/p; Sceptre UK). Disappointingly superficial travel narrative, though Keneally is too good a writer not to make some interesting observations.

Susan Shelby Magoffin, *Down the Santa Fe Trail and into Mexico* (University of Nebraska Press, US only). Absorbing first-person account by a trader's wife who reached Santa Fe in August 1846 in time to witness the Yankee takeover of New Mexico.

Melanie McGrath, *Motel Nirvana* (St Martin's Press, US; Flamingo, UK). Entertaining account of a British traveller's experiences in the Southwest, with some enjoyable swipes at various New-Age nonsenses.

John Wesley Powell, *The Exploration of the Colorado River and Its Canyons* (Dover). Powell is said to have adapted the details of his first epic journey down the Colorado – see p.401 – for public consumption, but his journals still make exhilarating reading.

Mark Twain, *Roughing It* (Penguin). This rollicking account of Twain's peregrinations across the nineteenth-century West may well be the greatest story ever told, though only his account of the Mormons is of much relevance here.

Ted J Warner (ed), *The Domínguez-Escalante Journal* (University of Utah Press, US only). The extraordinary diary of two Franciscan friars who crossed Utah in 1776 in search of a new route to California.

The contemporary Southwest

Rodney Barker, *The Broken Circle* (Ivy Books, US only). True-crime tale of the beating to death of a Navajo by White youths in Farmington, New Mexico, and its long-term consequences.

Scott Norris (ed), *Discovered Country* (Stone Ladder Press, US only). Anthology of essays focusing on the impact of tourism in the Southwest, with some interesting material on the repackaging of Native American culture for Anglo consumption.

Debra Rosenthal, *At the Heart of the Bomb* (Addison Wesley, US only). Intriguing reportage of what really goes on in New Mexico's vast defence laboratories.

Hunter S Thompson, *Fear and Loathing in Las Vegas* (Random, US; Paladin, UK). Classic account of a drug-crazed journalist's lost weekend in early-1970s Vegas; what's really striking is how much further over-the-top Las Vegas has gone since then.

Mike Tronnes (ed), *Literary Las Vegas* (Mainstream Publishing, UK only). Sin City, Nevada, as seen by Tom Wolfe, Joan Didion, Noel Coward and others.

Environment and natural history

Edward Abbey, *Desert Solitaire* (Simon and Schuster Trade, US; Robin Clark Ltd, UK). Abbey's classic evocation of his year as a ranger at Arches National Park was the first of his many volumes championing the wildernesses of the Southwest.

Donald L Baars, *The Colorado Plateau: A Geologic History* (University of New Mexico Press, US only). Among the more readily comprehensible explanations of the geology of the Four Corners.

Philip L Fradkin, *A River No More* (University of California Press). The story of the Colorado River, from John Wesley Powell to the water-management issues of today.

Edward A Geary, *The Proper Edge of the Sky* (University of Utah Press, US only). Loving evoca-

tion of the history and topography of southern Utah.

Ed Marston (ed), *Reopening the Western Frontier* (Island Press, US only). In-depth articles on the changing Southwestern environment from the *High Country News* newspaper; particularly good on southern Utah.

Russel Martin, *A Story That Stands Like A Dam* (Henry Holt, US only). Meticulously chronicled indictment of the West's last great dam, which inundated Glen Canyon in the 1960s.

Barbara J Morehouse, *A Place Called Grand Canyon* (University of Arizona Press, US only). Fascinating academic analysis of how the Grand Canyon has been defined and exploited.

Marc Reisner, *Cadillac Desert* (Viking Penguin, US; Secker & Warburg, UK). The damning saga of the twentieth-century damming of the West.

Raye C Ringholz, *Uranium Frenzy* (University of New Mexico Press, US only). Lively account of the 1950s uranium boom on the Colorado Plateau, with plenty of hard-hitting material on the health consequences for the miners.

Bette L Stanton, *Where God Put The West* (Four Corners Publications, US only). Photo-packed history of movie-making in Monument Valley and Moab.

Ann Zwinger, *Wind in the Rock* (University of Arizona Press). An inveterate canyoneer's account of the natural history of southeast Utah.

The Southwest in fiction

Edward Abbey, *The Monkey Wrench Gang* (Ballantine Books, US only). Classic wishful thinking from the wilderness advocate, this fast-paced novel centres on plans by environmental saboteurs to destroy the Glen Canyon dam.

Willa Cather, *Death Comes For The Archbishop* (Random, US; Virago, UK). Not as sensational as the title implies, but a magnificent evocation of the landscapes and cultures of nineteenth-century New Mexico. Cather's *The Professor's House* (Vintage) features an extended account of the discovery of Anasazi remains on a remote New Mexican mesa.

Clyde Edgerton, *Redeye* (Viking Penguin, US; Penguin, UK). Brief, bumptious, Western, focusing on the discovery of Anasazi cliff dwellings and the aftermath of the Mountain Meadows Massacre.

Natalie Goldberg, *Banana Rose* (Bantam, US only). Taos-based creative-writing guru – her *Wild Mind* (Bantam, US; Century, UK) and *Writing Down the Bones* (Shambhala Publications) have inspired countless would-be writers – practices what she preaches in this evocative novel, set partly in New Mexico.

Zane Grey, *Riders of the Purple Sage* (Penguin). Gloriously purple prose, first published in 1912, from the doyen of Western writers.

Tony Hillerman, *A Thief of Time* (HarperCollins, US; Penguin, UK), *The Dark Wind* (HarperCollins, US; Sphere, UK o/p), and several others. Hillerman has written about a dozen entertaining, intricately-plotted detective novels set on and around the Navajo Nation, all packed with fascinating detail about Navajo, Hopi and Zuni culture and beliefs.

Barbara Kingsolver, *Pigs in Heaven Time* (HarperCollins, US; Faber, UK). Enjoyable romp through modern Arizona, by Tucson-based writer.

Cormac McCarthy, *Blood Meridian* (Random, US; Picador, UK). A disturbing portrayal of the West in all its bloody reality – the scenes at Yuma Crossing are horrendous – if a tad macho for some tastes.

N Scott Momaday, *House Made of Dawn Time* (HarperCollins, US; Penguin, UK o/p). Pulitzer Prize-winning novel, written by a Kiowa Indian, about the spiritual crisis of a young Pueblo Indian.

John Nichols, *The Milagro Beanfield War* (Ballantine Books, US; Deutsch, UK o/p). Thanks to the Robert Redford movie, this entertaining saga of a water-rights rebellion by dispossessed Hispanic villagers in northern New Mexico is the best-known of Nichol's *New Mexico* trilogy (the others are *The Magic Journey* and *The Nirvana Blues*).

Michael Ondaatje, *The Collected Works of Billy the Kid* (Random, US; Picador, UK). Slim volume of poetry and contemporary accounts which add up to an evocative picture of New Mexico's most famous tearaway.

Leslie Marmon Silko, *Almanac of the Dead* (Simon & Schuster, US o/p; Penguin, UK). Epic novel, by a Laguna Pueblo Indian, of a Native American mother searching for her lost child on the fringes of the Tucson underworld; look out also for Silko's *Ceremony*.

Glossary

Adobe Construction material, consisting of bricks of mud, sand, and grass or straw, and by extension a building itself; see p.90.

Anasazi Ancient people of the Four Corners region; see p.468.

Anticline Geological term for a dome or ridge shoved upwards by subterranean bulging.

Arroyo Flat, often dry desert stream-bed.

Backcountry Term used particularly in national parks to signify wilderness areas that cannot be reached by road (as opposed, occasionally, to frontcountry).

Atlatl Spear-throwing device – a sort of detachable, lever-like handle that gave extra power and accuracy – used by ancient Native Americans.

Bulto or *santo bulto* Carved wooden statue of a saint, characteristic of Hispanic New Mexico.

Butte Geological term for a flat-topped outcrop of rock that's taller than it is wide, usually formed by the erosion of a larger mesa.

Casita Cottage, now applied mainly to individual guest accommodations in upmarket B&Bs.

Cuesta Long sloping mesa terminated by an abrupt bluff.

Genízaros In colonial New Mexico, the mixed-race offspring of captured Plains Indians and their Spanish masters.

Graben Geological term, from the German for "ditches", applied to narrow valleys created by the erosion of underground salt beds.

Grand Staircase Topographical feature of southwest Utah, stretching from the Grand Canyon to Bryce Canyon; see p.331.

Great House Archeological term for a defensively oriented, multi-storey Anasazi pueblo with hundreds of rooms, as seen at Chaco Canyon; see p.78.

Great Kiva Archeological term for a *kiva* that was used by an entire community rather than an individual clan or family.

Heishi Necklace of threaded disks, usually cut from seashells, as made originally by the Anasazi and now by Santo Domingo Pueblo.

Hisatsinom The preferred Hopi term for the Anasazi.

Hogan Navajo dwelling; see p.54.

Hohokam Ancient people of southern Arizona; see p.470.

Hoodoo Natural sandstone formation in which a boulder is left balanced on a slender pillar, as at Bryce Canyon; see p.367.

Kachina (also spelled *katsina*) "Spirit messengers", central to the religions of the Hopi and other Pueblo Indians; see p.58.

Kiva Underground chamber used for religious ceremonies by Pueblo Indians, usually located underground; see p.468.

Latilla Light pole used in the roof construction of adobe buildings.

LDS Abbreviation to denote the Latter-Day Saints, or Mormons.

Mano Hand-held stone traditionally used to grind and crush seeds.

Mesa From the Spanish for "table"; geological term for a large, broad flat-topped outcrop of rock.

Metate Stone slab or trough, used with a *mano* for grinding seeds.

Mimbres Ancient people of southern New Mexico, renowned for their pottery; see p.193.

Moki or **Moqui** The former name for the Hopi people of northern Arizona.

Monocline Geological term for an abrupt irregularity in the usual stratification of rocks, often resulting in a dramatic cliff.

Penitentes Catholic sect in nineteenth-century New Mexico; see p.129.

Petroglyph Ancient rock-art image carved or pecked into stone.

Pictograph Ancient rock-art image painted into stone.

Presidio Spanish term for a fortress built during the colonial period.

Pueblo Spanish word meaning "village"; applied to ancient Native American dwellings and also to modern Indian communities and peoples.

Reef Word applied by early white settlers to such natural barriers to their progress across the desert as Utah's Capitol Reef; see p.380.

Reredos Painted altarpiece, as seen in Hispanic churches at Chimayó (see p.127) and elsewhere.

Retablo Kind of Hispanic religious folk art, painted on tin or wood.

Ristra garland of chile peppers, sold as souvenirs in New Mexico.

Santo In Hispanic folk art, an image or holy object.

Sipapu In Pueblo religion, the hole through which humans reached this earth; see p.468.

Sinagua Ancient people of central Arizona.

Slickrock Pioneer term for smooth, undulating stretches of sandstone, as a rule only slick after rain.

Syncline The opposite of an anticline, a rock formation created by an underground collapse.

Viga A broad beam of ponderosa or fir, as used by the Anasazi in roof construction, and prominent in adobe architecture today.

Index

H

Top Ten Drives

I

Top Ten Ancient Native American sites

Top Ten Small Towns

---

the perfect getaway vehicle

low-price holiday car rental.

rent a car from holiday autos and you'll give yourself real freedom to explore your holiday destination. with great-value, fully-inclusive rates in over 4,000 locations worldwide, wherever you're escaping to, we're there to make sure you get excellent prices and superb service.

what's more, you can book now with complete confidence. our £5 undercut* ensures that you are guaranteed the best value for money in holiday destinations right around the globe.

drive away with a great deal, call holiday autos now on **0990 300 400** and quote ref RG.

holiday autos miles ahead